S-8252

BLUE & GRAY
AT SEA

ALSO EDITED BY BRIAN M. THOMSEN

Shadows of Blue & Gray: The Civil War Writings of Ambrose Bierce

The American Fantasy Tradition

Commanding Voices of Blue & Gray

The Man in the Arena: Selected Writings of Theodore Roosevelt

BLUE & GRAY
AT SEA

Naval Memoirs of the Civil War

EDITED BY

BRIAN M. THOMSEN

A TOM DOHERTY ASSOCIATES BOOK

New York

A Forge Book
Published by Tom Doherty Associates, LLC
175 Fifth Avenue
New York, NY 10010

www.tor.com

Forge® is a registered trademark of Tom Doherty Associates, LLC.

Library of Congress Cataloging-in-Publication Data

Blue & gray at sea : naval memoirs of the Civil War / edited by Brian M. Thomsen.—1st ed.
     p.   cm.
  "A Tom Doherty Associates book."
  ISBN 0-765-30895-9 (acid-free paper)
    1. United States—History—Civil War, 1861–1865—Naval operations.   2. United
States—History—Civil War, 1861–1865—Personal narratives.   3. United States.
Navy—Biography.   4. Confederate States of America. Navy—Biography.   I. Title: Blue and
gray at sea.   II. Thomsen, Brian.

E591.B59   2003
973.7'5—dc21   2003054960

First Edition: December 2003

Printed in the United States of America

0   9   8   7   6   5   4   3   2   1

Contents

Contents

Editor's Note

After finishing the compilation of *Commanding Voices of Blue & Gray*, a colleague of mine pointed out that I had given short shrift to the naval war. True, there were no seminal classics of the military memoir milieu to rank with those of Sherman or Longstreet (let alone the masterwork memoir of U.S. Grant), but surely there had to be material on par with that of Doubleday and Early.

Thus *Blue & Gray at Sea*.

The contents herewith are a curious amalgam and as a result have been divided into two sections.

The first section is a direct complement to *Commanding Voices*, with excerpts from five memoirs that included coverage of the Civil War years—though it must be noted that three of the books cover careers that ranged much further than just the Civil War years.

The second section incorporates memoirlike material along with letters, journals, and articles that flesh out the collection, though because not intended for publication, they were written in a less self-conscious manner. In many ways the Waddell and Farragut materials are even more honest a depiction of the experience, as neither was written with the intention of eventual publication.

A final observation, or shall I say distinction that separates this volume from its companion, is that with the exception of Farragut and his "Damn the Torpedoes," we tend to forget that the Civil War had a naval component, but in reality it was a watershed for modern naval warfare, filled with the same sort of innovation that was taking place on the battlefields themselves. Indeed, the ironclad and the submarine came into play, and names like the *Monitor* and the *Hunley* have taken their place in the annals of military history with more prominence than that given to those who actually served on them. For this reason I have included documentary materials that might serve as their memoirs as well.

—BRIAN M. THOMSEN

Memoirs

During the Civil War, George Dewey (before he was either a commodore or an admiral) was a junior officer on a Union wooden side-wheeler as part of a battle flotilla under the command of the legendary Admiral Farragut. His baptism under fire forged and tempered his naval acumen, laying the groundwork for an illustrious career in naval command.

The Autobiography of George Dewey was published by Charles Scribner and Sons in 1913, and the following excerpt deals with his Civil War years.

Excerpt from *The Autobiography of George Dewey, Admiral of the Navy*

BY ADMIRAL GEORGE DEWEY

Chapter IV.

BEGINNING OF THE CIVIL WAR.

After the Napoleonic wars an exhausted world knew a long period of peace, which, until the beginning of the Civil War, had been broken only by our war with Mexico in 1846, the Crimean War in 1854, and the Franco-Austrian War in 1859. This period had seen the development of steam. It had ushered in the great age of inventive genius and industrial organization in which we now live.

As Mexico had no navy our war with her had given us no naval experience of value except that of the mobility of the steam-vessels on a blockade and in co-operation with the landing of troops. In place of sails, dependent on the variability of the winds, had come a motive power equally dependable in a ten-knot breeze or a calm. Our older officers had to admit that for expeditiousness in carrying messages, in getting in and out of harbors and landing troops, steam did have the advantage over sail, and that it was a valuable auxiliary, but they still maintained that the talk about iron-clads as fighting-ships belonged to the realm of theorists and dreamers.

Later came the action at Sinope in the Crimea, of which I have already spoken, when the progressives saw their prophecies fulfilled by the success of the French floating batteries which led to the construction of the first ironclads in Europe. The naval lessons of the Franco-Austrian War were as insignificant as those of the Mexican; but at the decisive land battle of Solferino rifles in place of smoothbore cannon were used for the first time in battle. This innovation, as vital in arms as that of iron ship-building, was the first step toward the enormous range of modern guns. It remained for the Civil War to test ironclads in action, as well as the rifled gun, and also the ram. In the case of the ram the innovation was only the renewal of a form of attack of the days of the Roman galleys when the mobility of the vessel had been dependent upon the sweat of slaves. But the ram was soon to become again obsolete. It is inconceivable that with the long-range guns of later days opposing ships can ever survive long enough to come to close quarters, except when one or the other has already surrendered.

There was a saying in the sixties that the men of 1840 in our navy would have been more at home in the ships of Drake's fleet or in those of Spain's Invincible Armada than in the ironclads of the Civil War; and I think that it is also safe to say that the men brought up to service in such a vessel as the *Mississippi,* in which I saw my first service in the Civil War, would be more at home in the Armada than in a ship of the Dreadnought class. The inauguration of steam made naval science one of continual change and development, which it still remains.

It was borne home to the students of Annapolis in my day, as I have already indicated, that the officers of the navy, in its senior grades, should be men of progressive minds and of energetic and rapid action. Otherwise they would be quite unequal to the prompt adaptation of everything which the progress of science and industry offered for their use. At the outbreak of the Civil War our navy had no staff, and nothing like an adequate organization.

Mr. Lincoln had chosen Mr. Gideon Welles as his secretary of the navy. We are familiar with Mr. Welles's character through his very voluminous diary, which has lately been published. It has always been amazing to me how Mr. Welles was able to do so much writing and conduct the Navy Department in the midst of a great war.

He was certainly a man of prodigious industry. His lack of technical knowledge would have been a great handicap, if it had not been for the selection of an assistant secretary of the navy whose training made him an excellent substitute for a chief of staff. Gustavus V. Fox had served in the navy, but had resigned and become a most successful man of business. We cannot overestimate the value of his intelligent service to the country on meagre pay in sacrifice of private interests, for which he received hardly his fair due of honor. To him we owe the conception of the New Orleans campaign and, in part, the building of the *Monitor,* which took the mastery of Hampton Roads away from the *Merrimac.*

Upon taking up the reins of office he found a naval personnel with no retiring age limit; and a state of demoralization. Under President Buchanan, the most ordinary preparations had been neglected in face of an inevitable conflict. Our ships were scattered over the seas. Some were on the coast of Africa, some in the Far East, and some in South American waters. The excuse for this was the prevailing naval custom of the time which made the navy a disseminated force to protect our citizens in case of trouble in distant lands, and also to protect our foreign commerce, which then was wide-spread and now, unfortunately, has become almost obsolete. Now the battle-ship fleets of all nations are concentrated in home waters, and the cable keeps governments in touch with any danger-spots, which may be reached promptly with fast cruisers.

At the head of the officers' list at the beginning of 1861, were seventy-eight captains. A few of them, including Farragut, then quite unknown to the public, were men of energy who were in touch with the tendency of their time. But the great majority were unfitted for active service afloat. According to the existing law there was no supplanting them with younger men. The commanders, who were next in rank to the captains, were themselves fifty-eight or sixty years of age. Upper lieutenants were usually past forty, some being as old as fifty. David D. Porter, who was later to become an admiral, was only a lieutenant. Thornton, the executive officer of the *Hartford,* the flag-ship of the East India Squadron at that time, later to become the famous flag-ship of Farragut in the Gulf, had been in the service thirty-four years.

Such a system was killing to ambition and enterprise. It made mere routine men to face a crisis in which energy and initiative were needed. No subordinate was expected to undertake any responsibility on his own account. So used were the junior officers—these "boys" of forty and fifty to the old captains—to being subordinate machines that their one care was to escape official censure by any action on their own account. Promotion had become so clogged that, as the secretary of the navy had already put it in 1855, the system was "neither more nor less than elevating the incompetent and then ordering the unpromoted competent to do their work."

If the men of forty and fifty were boys to those fine old veterans of the War of 1812, who had been rendered by age incapable of active command, then we young men out of Annapolis ranked as children. The first requirement, as Mr. Fox so well knew, was a complete and drastic reorganization of personnel, but not until

December, 1861, was a law passed retiring all officers at the age of sixty-two, or after forty-five years of service. By this law, disregarding seniority, the President might put any captain or commander he chose in charge of a squadron with the rank of flag-officer.

The next year the grades of rear-admiral and commodore were established and the President had his authority for selection of the fit further strengthened. In this way the younger men, by virtue of their progressive training and ideas and the inevitable initiative, which youth develops in time of war, came to accept readily responsibilities which would have frightened men of fifty a few years previously. With many new ships going into commission, we were very short-handed, which accounts for the fact that I was to become executive of the *Mississippi* at the age of twenty-four.

Aside from the loss in numbers by retirement at the very beginning of the struggle, there was the loss due to the resignations of the officers who saw fit to follow the flags of their States and enter the Confederate service. One can only say that the latter responded to the call of duty in a period when the constitutional right to secession was sincerely held; and that many brilliant men, who must have risen to high place had they remained loyal, knew defeat and the deprivation of honor and pleasure of service in their profession in after years. They took the risk and they lost.

But not all Southern officers held the secession view. Loyalty was stronger relatively in the navy than in the army, for the reason that the naval officer felt an affection for the flag born of the sentiment of our splendid record in the War of 1812, and a realization born of his foreign cruises, that our strength before the other nations of the world, who selfishly wished to see our growing power divided, was in unity. Besides, naval life separates one from State and political associations.

It was inevitable, however, that Southern officers should feel that they would be held under suspicion by the National Government at a period when feeling ran so high. This was a contributing factor in the decision of many who hesitated long before they went over to the Confederacy. Flag-Officer Stribling, commander of the East India Squadron, was relieved simply because he was a South Carolina man, though he did not enter the service of the Confederacy after he returned home. Farragut, born in Tennessee, was one of the Southern officers who not only remained loyal, but of whose loyalty from the first there was never any question by the authorities. In his outright fashion in speaking to his Southern comrades, he left no doubt of his position, and he also warned them that they were going to have a "devil of a time" of it before they were through with their secession enterprise. It is only fair to add that they also gave us a "devil of a time."

Quite different factors entered into the war afloat and the war on shore. The

South had soldiers, and it could find rifles for them. But it had few ships, and it lacked the resources with which to build more. Such a thing as offensive tactics at sea, except by the commerce-destroyers of the *Alabama* class, and in its harbors, except by river iron-clads, was out of the question. The offensive must be entirely on our side; the defensive was the enemy's, and splendidly and desperately he conducted it.

Our first duty was the blockade of all that immense coast-line from Hampton Roads southward to Key West and westward to the boundaries of Mexico. As the South was not a manufacturing country, it was dependent for funds on the export of cotton and on Europe for manufactured material. We had to close its ports and we had to prevent the running of the blockade wherever possible. Moreover, a blockade which was not effective did not hold in international law. Never before had any navy, and never since has any navy, attempted anything like such an immense task. That of the Japanese off Port Arthur was comparatively insignificant in the extent of coast-line which had to be guarded. At the close of the war the United States, in carrying on the war and blockade, had six hundred ships in commission.

In the strategy of the campaign on land the navy played an important offensive part which is unique in naval history. President Lincoln wished the Mississippi to flow "unvexed" to the sea. Once the great river was in the possession of the federal Government, we had cut the Confederacy in two and separated its armies from the rich sources of supplies to the westward. In order to accomplish this feat, which was not finished until Vicksburg and Port Hudson were taken, a number of gun-boats built for the purpose were to work their way down the river, while we of the main fighting force of the Gulf Squadron were to begin our part in working up the river, running Forts Jackson and St. Philip and laying New Orleans under our guns. After my pleasant midshipman cruise, seeing the sights of the Mediter-ranean, I was to witness a style of warfare as picturesque as it was hazardous and exacting in its hardships.

Cruising in the open sea on the lookout for an enemy whom you are to meet in a decisive battle is simple, indeed, compared to the experience that was to try our nerves on the Mississippi. Here was a sufficient outlet for the abundant spir-its of any young lieutenant or midshipman. It was war for us for four years, a war which brought us so frequently under fire, and required such constant vigilance, that war appeared to be almost a normal state of affairs to us.

The leaders on the other side were men bred to the same traditions as we were. Officers fought officers with whom they had gone to school, and with whom they had served and had messed. The recollection of old comradeship, while soft-ening the amenities of a civil conflict, also touched us the more deeply with the sense of its horrors and waste, and brought to its conduct something of the spirit of professional rivalry. Unlike the officers of volunteer infantry who marched South to meet strangers against whom a strong sectional feeling had been aroused, we knew our adversaries well. We were very fond of them personally. To us they had neither horns nor tails. We felt that they were fine fellows who were in the wrong, and we knew that they entertained the same feeling toward us. We did not mean that they should beat us. They did not mean that we should beat them. This accounted for the fearful stubbornness with which we fought; and future generations, who may wish that all the energy spent had not been against brothers but in a common cause against a foreign foe, can at least rejoice in the heritage of the skill and courage displayed in a struggle which has no equal in magnitude or determination, unless in the Napoleonic wars.

On May 10, 1861, I reported for duty on board the old side-wheeler *Mississippi* (known as a steam-frigate), on which I served until she was set on fire by the batteries of Port Hudson in March, 1863, when she perished on the river for which she was christened. It was the wonder of her funnels, spouting smoke to make her wheels move, and the sight of her guns that so impressed the Japanese, when Commodore Perry appeared off Tokio with her as his flag-ship, that they concluded the treaty which opened up Japan to Western progress. From her, Mississippi Bay, in the neighborhood of Yokohama, takes its name.

She was now assigned to the blockade of the Gulf, and her captain was T. O. Selfridge, who was in command of a steam man-of-war for the first time. As yet the blockade was hardly maintained in a rigid fashion. The old captains were so fearful of the loss of their ships that they were inclined to take few risks. A quasi-engagement near the mouths of the Mississippi took place, which was hardly more gratifying to the navy than Bull Run was to the army. The steam sloop *Richmond,* two sailing sloops, and a small side-wheel steamer, having entered the river, were surprised at anchor at the head of the passage just before daybreak by a ram, later known as the *Manassas,* which had been originally a Boston tug-boat. She rammed the *Richmond* and drove the Federal ships into retreat. This incident, known as "Pope's Run," from the name of the Federal commander, was pretty exasperating to the pride of service of the more energetic-minded officers of the navy.

The *Mississippi* saw only the dreary monotony of blockading without any fighting until Flag-Officer David G. Farragut arrived off Ship Island in February, 1862, to begin the campaign which was to lay New Orleans under our guns. From the day that he took command the atmosphere in the neighborhood of Ship Island, which was our important naval base for the Gulf, seemed to be surcharged with his energy. When Mr. Fox had proposed the attack on New Orleans, the most wealthy and populous city of the Confederacy, Mr. Lincoln had said: "Go ahead, but avoid a disaster"; by which he meant, no doubt, that in case of failure he did not want to see a loss which would be a serious blow to Northern prestige.

After a canvass of all the captains in the navy, Farragut, on the recommendation of Mr. Fox and of Porter, had been chosen for this enterprise, which was to make his reputation. Though there is truth in the saying, "Young men for war, and old men for counsel," it does not always hold. Farragut was not one of the captains whose initiative had been weakened by age. The only criticism ever offered of him was that possibly he had too much of it. But that proved a very winning fault for him. He was sixty; which I, at least, ought not to consider too old, as I myself was sixty, or within two years of statutory retiring age, at the outbreak of the Spanish War.

In the late seventies, when there seemed no hope of our ever having a modern navy, and many officers were talking of voluntary retirement, I always answered:

"Not until the law makes me. While you are on the active list there is a chance for action."

Farragut has always been my ideal of the naval officer, urbane, decisive, indomitable. Whenever I have been in a difficult situation, or in the midst of such a confusion of details that the simple and right thing to do seemed hazy, I have often asked myself, "What would Farragut do?" In the course of the preparations for Manila Bay I often asked myself this question, and I confess that I was thinking of him the night that we entered the Bay, and with the conviction that I was doing precisely what he would have done. Valuable as the training of Annapolis was, it was poor schooling beside that of serving under Farragut in time of war.

Commander Melancthon Smith succeeded Captain Selfridge in command of the *Mississippi*, before the advance on New Orleans. By this time the six officers who were senior to me had all gone to other ships. With their departure I ranked next to the captain and became executive officer.

I was very young for the post, but fortunately looked rather old for my years. Indeed, I remember being asked one day, when there was a question about seniority for a court-martial, whether or not I was older than another lieutenant, who was in fact my senior by ten years. When Farragut explained to Captain Smith that there was complaint on the part of some officers on the navy list about my holding a position higher than theirs, the captain said:

"Dewey is doing all right. I don't want a stranger here."

Farragut, who was fond of the captain, answered:

"Then we will let him stay."

For many trying months I was about as close to Smith officially as it is possible for one man to be to another, and I learned to know and enjoy all his qualities. His was a pronounced character, absolutely fearless, with something of Farragut's grim determination in the midst of battle. He smoked continually, lighting one cigar with the butt of another, whether shells were bursting around him or he was lounging on deck.

In action he became most energetic; but in the periods between action he was inclined to leave all detail to his executive. His hobby, except in the matter of cigars, was temperance. I recollect that he saw me take a glass of champagne that was offered to me when I was in the house of a Union officer after the troops had taken New Orleans. He was puffing at a cigar as usual.

"Dewey, do you drink champagne?" he asked.

I had not tasted any for months, and very hard months they had been.

"Yes, I do when it is as good as this. I don't very often get a chance, these days," I answered.

"If I had known that," he said, very soberly, "I do not think that I should have had so much confidence in you."

However, he made a report after the loss of our ship that indicated that he still thought pretty well of me; and on his death after the war, when he had reached the rank of rear-admiral, he left me his epaulets and cocked hat.

He was also quite as religious as Farragut, who had unswerving belief in Providence as he had faith in the righteousness of the Union cause. One of the stories that went the rounds about Farragut was that once after he had said grace at dinner in his cabin he followed his amen with an outburst of "It's hot as hell here!" The time was midsummer on the Mississippi.

In the course of the preparations for taking New Orleans, when every man Jack of us was hard at it from sunrise to sunset, there was, naturally, some profanity. The men swore over their exasperating task, and I have no doubt that, as the director of their efforts, I may have sworn. One day, when we had a particularly trying job on hand, the captain appeared on deck from his cabin, where he had been overhearing the flow of sailor language. He looked as if he had borne about all he could. He told me to have all the crew lay aft. I ordered them aft. Then he said:

"Hereafter, any officer caught swearing will be put under suspension, and any man caught swearing will be put in double irons."

Having delivered this ultimatum he returned to his cabin. There was an end of swearing on the *Mississippi* from that minute. Profanity in the navy, particularly on the part of officers, was a relic of the days of rations of grog and boarding with the cutlass. An oath by an officer in giving a command, however exasperated he is, has ceased to be a means of expressing emphasis. The crew of the *Mississippi* found that they could work just as well without swearing.

And how we did work! Many of the junior officers were volunteers from the mercantile marine, not yet familiar with naval customs, and many of the men were practically raw recruits yet untrained. In fact, a leavening of experienced naval officers had more or less to act as teachers for the greatly increased personnel in the midst of active war conditions.

The *Pensacola* and our ship, the *Mississippi*, were the heaviest draught vessels that had attempted to go up the river. On account of our heavy gun-power it was most important that we should take part in the forthcoming battle of New Orleans. Farragut already had the rest of the fleet in the river waiting for us to get over the bar of the Southwest Pass when we came in from the blockade. We lightened ship by removing most of our spars and rigging and by emptying our bunkers. With our boats we took a day's supply of coal from the collier each day. Under a full head of steam, and assisted by the use of anchors and by tow-lines from the steamers of the mortar flotilla, both the *Mississippi* and the *Pensacola* worked their way through a foot of mud over the bar.

But the forty-gun frigate *Colorado* had to remain outside. Her crew was largely distributed among other ships. Her captain, Theodorus Bailey, a most gallant old officer, did not want to miss being in the forthcoming engagement. Farragut told him that he might go on board any ship he chose and such ship should lead in the attack, a suggestion which, of course, had to reckon with a welcome from the commanding officer of the ship chosen. No naval captain wants another man who ranks him on board, particularly during an action.

Captain Smith expressed himself very candidly to this effect when Captain Bailey concluded that he should like to go on board the *Mississippi*, and Farragut decided to put Captain Bailey as a divisional commander on board the *Cayuga*, one of the gunboats which was to lead the first division. Thus Captain Bailey had a better assignment than he anticipated, while all the captains of the larger vessels were equally pleased at the arrangement.

Between us and New Orleans were the two strong forts, St. Philip and Jackson, facing each other at a strategic point across a bend in the river where the channel was narrow; and above them was an obstruction of chain-booms and anchored hulks, which we must pass through. Once we had cleared a way through the obstruction we had to face the Confederate River Defense Squadron.

David D. Porter, now advanced to the rank of commander, had brought from the North a mortar flotilla of which great things were expected. It was thought that the mortars might reduce the forts by their heavy bombardment, or a least silence their guns while the fleet made its passage. There were twenty of the mortar schooners, each mounting a thirteen-inch mortar. Porter put them in position close to the wooded bank of the river, quite hidden from the forts, and disguised them by securing tree branches to their masts.

On the 18th, the day after we were over the bar, he opened fire. By carefully weighing the powder and measuring the angle excellent practice was made. All night long, at regular intervals of about ten minutes, a mortar shell would rise, its loop in the air outlined by the burning fuse, and drop into the forts. It must have been pretty hard for the gunners of the forts to get any sleep. We, with the fleet, were too busy to sleep much, but we were soon so accustomed to the noise, and so dog-tired when we had a chance to rest, that we could have slept in an inferno.

Every day gained was vital to Farragut. One day might make the difference of having to face either one or both of the new Confederate ironclads being rushed to completion with feverish haste. As so frequently happened, his celerity served him well.

After crossing the bar the vessels had to be prepared for the river work before them. They were trimmed by the head, so that if they grounded it would be forward. In the swift current of the river, if we grounded aft the ship would at once turn with her head downstream. Where feasible, guns were mounted on the poops and forecastle, and howitzers in the tops, with iron bulwarks to protect the gun crews. Farragut believed in plenty of armament. From him we have that *multum in parvo* of tactics: "The best protection against an enemy's fire is a well-directed fire of your own." But heavy gun-power in relation to tonnage was a principle with our navy from its inception.

It was an oddly assorted fleet that had been mobilized for the battle of New Orleans. A year had now elapsed since Sumter had been fired upon, and most of that time had been spent in getting ready for war, rather than in making war. As both sides were equally unprepared, the nation scarcely realized the effect of unpreparedness. How bitterly we would have realized it against a foe ready in all respects for conflict! It was not a matter of building a navy according to any deliberate and well-conceived plan, but of providing such material as we could in haste with the resources of the times, having in mind that we were in the midst of a revolution in naval warfare, when any enterprising development like the *Monitor* or the ram might upset all calculations.

First, Farragut had the big screw sloops *Hartford, Pensacola, Richmond,* and *Brooklyn;* then the side-wheeler *Mississippi;* the screw corvettes *Oneida, Varuna,* and *Iroquois;* nine screw gunboats of five hundred tons, which were known as the "ninety-day gunboats," because, with characteristic American enterprise in a crisis, they had been turned out by our ship-yards in ninety days. In addition was the mortar flotilla, not to mention ferry-boats and many other craft that did service of one sort or another. Farragut was always on the move, overseeing everything in person, breathing an air of confidence and imparting a spirit of efficiency. In those days he went from ship to ship, rowed by sailors, but later he had a steam tender.

There was hardly a night that the flag-ship did not signal to send boats to tow fire-rafts. These fire-rafts were one of the pleasantries of the enemy to try our nerves. In connection with the luminous flight of the mortar shells, they offered us quite all the spectacular display that we were able to appreciate. A fire-raft floating down with the current at five knots an hour, flaming high with its tar and resin, would illuminate the river from bank to bank; and if it could have rested alongside a ship for even a few minutes it must inevitably have set the ship on fire. Launches used to throw grapnels into the rafts, and other boats, forming line, would tow them to the shore, where they would burn themselves out.

On the night of the 20th of April occurred one of those brilliant exploits of daring courage so common in the Civil War that they became merely incidents of its progress. Any one of them in a smaller war, when public attention is not diverted over a vast scene of activity, would have won permanent fame. Lieutenant Caldwell, commanding one of the ninety-day gunboats, the *Itasca,* and Lieutenant Crosby, commanding another, the *Pinola,* undertook the duty of cutting the obstruction across the river above the forts. Until there was a way through this, the whole fleet would be held helpless under the fire of the forts; while turning for retreat in the swift current would have meant confusion.

During a heavy bombardment from the mortars they slipped upstream under cover of the bank. At times so rapid were Porter's gunners in their work that there were nine shells in the air at once. His object, of course, was to keep down the fire of the forts as much as possible in case the *Itasca* and the *Pinola* were discovered. They were discovered, but not until they had reached the obstruction.

As they had taken out their masts it was difficult for the gunners in the uncertain light to distinguish the gunboats from the anchored hulks that had been used in making the obstruction complete. Laboring under fire, the gunboats succeeded in a task which took them hours, and which would have been suicidal had the forts possessed a modern searchlight. It was concluded in dramatic fashion. After Caldwell, in the course of his and Crosby's manoeuvring, had got above the obstruction, with a full head of steam and the current to assist him, he rammed a stretch of chain, which snapped and left a space broad enough for any vessel of the fleet to pass through.

Chapter V.

THE BATTLE OF NEW ORLEANS.

About midnight on April 23 came the signal for which we were all waiting, two red lights at the peak of the flag-ship. It meant that the fleet was to get under way. We were ready and eager for the test after the long strain of preparation, in which all manner of ingenious suggestions had been applied in order that the fleet might get by the forts with as little damage as possible. Our hulls had been daubed with river mud in order to make them less visible in the darkness. Captain Alden, of the *Richmond,* had the idea, which worked out excellently, of having the decks around the guns whitewashed so that the implements required in the working of the guns could be easily identified by the gunners as they picked them up for use.

And with what insistent care we had drilled the guns' crews in order to insure rapidity of loading and firing! To protect vital parts of the ships from the impact of projectiles, chain cables were secured to the ship's sides. As the *Mississippi* was a side-wheeler we stowed our cables in the coal bunkers, between the wheels and the boilers and machinery. Though we hoped that the fire of the mortars might keep down the fire of the forts, it was evident from all these precautions that Farragut was not over-sanguine on this score. Before the fleet started, Lieutenant Caldwell, early in the evening, made another trip up the river to make sure that the way was clear, and this time a cutter actually rowed through the opening and sounded with a lead line.

The *Mississippi's* position in the advance was directly astern of the *Pensacola* in the first division under Captain Bailey, while Farragut with the *Hartford* led the second division. Our orders were to keep in column, maintaining distance from the ship ahead. It was evident that the ship in the lead would have the advantage, perhaps, of getting well by the forts before she was discovered, while the ships following would be subject to any delays caused by her. Captain Smith, of the *Mississippi,* had opposed trying to make the passage in the night. His idea was to go ahead full speed by day, fighting our way. Thus there would be no danger of running aground and we would know just what we were doing.

"I cannot see in the night," he declared, with characteristic brevity. "I am going to leave that to you, Dewey. You have younger eyes."

He took charge of the battery, while I took up my post on the hurricane deck from which we handled the ship. For a man of twenty-four I was having my share of responsibility. I was also to have my baptism of fire. But I had little time to consider the psychology of an experience which is the source of much wonder and speculation to the uninitiated. When it comes, you are utterly preoccupied with your work; you are doing what you have been taught is your duty to do as a trained unit on a man-of-war. Only after the danger is over is it time to reflect. The wait before action is the period of self-consciousness, which ends with the coming of the first shot from the enemy or the command to "Fire!" from your own side.

Adapting our speed to that of the *Pensacola,* which was without lights, as all the vessels were, we steamed ahead, while the booming of the howitzers and the swish of their shells through the air made music for our progress.

Just as the *Pensacola* drew abreast of the forts the enemy discovered her and opened fire. We were so near the forts that we could hear the commands of the officers. The *Pensacola* stopped and fired both broadsides which at first seemed to demoralize the enemy.

A second time the *Pensacola* stopped and discharged broadsides; and it was soon evident from the fact that the forts kept on firing that, although the mortars might reduce the fire from the forts, they could by no means silence them; nor could the *Pensacola,* which had the heaviest armament of any of our ships, silence them except for a brief interval during the effect of her broadsides. Therefore, all the ships, in order to get by, must run the gauntlet of a heavy fire.

It was most puzzling to me why the *Pensacola* had stopped, in view of the orders to steam past without delay. Either she could not resist pausing to engage the forts, or else there was something wrong with her engines. The latter, I believe, was the real reason. At all events, she did stop twice, which meant that we also had to stop. The *Mississippi* herself was already under fire and returning it, and while my attention was centred in trying to keep astern of the *Pensacola,* I received warning of an attack from another quarter.

Farragut had assigned to us Mr. Waud, an artist for an illustrated weekly. When he had asked for the best position from which to witness the spectacle Captain Smith advised the foretop, where we had a twenty-four-pound howitzer. Waud was an observant as well as a gallant man, and from the foretop he could see everything that was taking place even better than we could from the hurricane deck.

"Here is a queer-looking customer on our post bow," he called to me.

Looking in the direction which he indicated I saw what appeared like the back of an enormous turtle painted lead color, which I identified as the ram *Manassas,* which had driven the Federal ships from the mouth of the river the previous autumn, in the action called "Pope's Run." She was rebuilt entirely for the purpose of ramming, and if she were able to deliver a full blow in a vital spot she was capable of disabling any ship in the fleet.

The darkness and the confusion perfectly favored the rôle for which she was designed. By prompt action we might put a dangerous opponent out of commission before she had done any damage. There was no time in which to ask the advice of the captain, who was busy with the battery below. I called to starboard the helm and turned the *Mississippi's* bow toward the *Manassas,* with the intention of running her down, being confident that our superior tonnage must sink her if we struck her fairly.

But A. F. Warley, her commander, a former officer of our navy, was too quick for us. His last service had been in the *Mississippi* in a round-the-world cruise. He appreciated her immobility in comparison with the mobility of his own little craft and sheered off to avoid us. But, then, sheering in, he managed to strike us a glancing blow just abaft the port paddle-wheel.

The effect of the shock was that of running aground. The *Mississippi* trembled and listed and then righted herself. When I saw the big hole that the ram had left in our side I called, "Sound the pumps!" to the carpenter, an experienced old seaman, who was on the main deck near me.

"I have already, sir," he answered, "and there is no water in the wells."

He had acted promptly and instinctively in his line of duty. If there were no water I knew that there was nothing to worry about. It was the sturdy construction of the *Mississippi* that had saved us from serious damage. As she was one of our earliest steam men-of-war, her builders had taken extreme care lest the fear expressed in some quarters that her engines, making about ten revolutions a minute, would shake her to pieces, should be justified. She was filled in solid between the frames. The impact of the ram, which would have sunk any other ship in the fleet, had taken out a section of solid timber seven feet long, four feet broad, and four inches deep. About fifty copper bolts had been cut as clean as if they were hair under a razor's edge. I remember seeing their bright, gleaming ends when I looked down from the hurricane deck in my first glimpse of that hole in our side.

If Warley, who knew just where the *Mississippi* was vulnerable, had been able to strike forward of the paddle-wheel, as he evidently was planning to do when we caught sight of the *Manassas* and went for her, he would have disabled one of our leading ships. This would have been a feather in his cap. But he gave a very lively account of himself, however, before the night was over, and the *Mississippi* had another chance at him.

The formation of the ships in our rear was pretty well broken up. Every ship was making its own way in the mêlée out of danger. Particularly was this true of the second division, under the lead of the *Hartford* with Farragut on board. When she came abreast of the forts the enemy had steadied down. The prefatory period of bombardment by Porter's flotilla had hardened them to mortar fire; and now they were hardened to broadsides and had the range of the passing ships. So they stuck to their guns calmly and made the most of their own fire. The *Hartford* and *Brooklyn* received a terrific cannonade.

Meanwhile the *Manassas*, like some assassin in the night, had proceeded down through the fleet, greeted by fire from our ships whenever she was recognized, and watching a chance for a murderous thrust. She succeeded in putting a hole in the *Brooklyn*, which might have been most serious were it not for the anchor chains on the *Brooklyn's* side which resisted the blow.

Throughout the passage of the forts fire-rafts were coming down-stream to add to the picturesqueness of the lurid scene and the difficulty of keeping our course. One of these rafts nearly brought the career of Farragut's flag-ship to a close. It was pushed by a little thirty-five-ton tug called the *Mosher,* manned by a dozen men under the command of a man named Sherman. To him belongs the credit of one of the most desperate strokes of heroism I have ever known. It is an example of how the South, with its limited resources, was able to maintain its gallant struggle for four years against great odds.

His tug had no guns and no armor. In the face of certain destruction from the guns of the *Hartford,* he pushed the raft against the *Hartford's* side. The *Mosher's* captain and crew all lost their lives, as far as is known, but they had the satisfaction of seeing flames darting up the *Hartford's* rigging and bursting through the ports, which, thanks to the discipline of her crew, were quenched. But though he had lost his flag-ship, Farragut would have gone past the forts with what remained of his fleet. We may be sure of that.

In passing the forts the *Mississippi* had fired grape and five-second shell from alternate guns. I was surprised to see how well the forts stood our own pounding and also how well we stood theirs. Though the *Mississippi* had been hit a number of times, our loss had been trifling—two killed and a few wounded. To judge by the noise, and the flashes of the mortars in air, and the guns from the forts, and the busy fleet, it seemed as if the destruction done must be far worse than it was.

I remember, however, as we passed out of range of the forts, thinking that some of the ships certainly would not get by. Three failed, these being in the rear of the second division. Of course we were all new to war. Neither our aim nor the Confederates' was as accurate as it was later; for example, at Port Hudson. In time we learned to pay attention less to the quantity of fire and more to the extent of its effect.

From all we had heard we were expecting a hard fight once we were beyond the obstructions above the forts. The Confederates had taken pains not to minimize the reports of the formidability of their River Defence Squadron. But, as so often happens, the enemy in reality was not anything like so powerful as rumor had made him. The big iron-clad *Mississippi* had not been completed in time to leave her dock in New Orleans, while her sister ship, the *Louisiana,* unable to move under her own steam, had been anchored above the obstructions to play the part of a floating battery.

The business of taking care of the other vessels of the Confederate River Defence Squadron fell to the other vessels of our fleet. The *Mississippi* had an individual score to settle. Dawn was breaking and we were just making out the ships around us, off the quarantine station, when we sighted that persistent ram *Manassas* coming up astern in her effort to attack the fleet a second time. The work of the battery being over, Captain Smith was on the hurricane deck with me. So deeply was he imbued with the spirit of ante-bellum days, when officers might be censured for acting on their own initiative without waiting for an order from a superior, that he felt that he must first ask permission before attacking the ram. He steamed alongside a gunboat which he had mistaken at first sight for the *Cayuga*, the flag-ship of the flag-officer of our division, Captain Bailey.

"I want permission to run down the ram!" he called to the gunboat.

Just as we saw our error, while every minute was valuable, the *Hartford*, smoke-blackened from the fire which the firecraft had caused, and looking a veritable battle-stained and triumphant veteran of war, came steaming by. Farragut was in her rigging, his face eager with victory in the morning light and his eyes snapping.

"Run down the ram!" he called.

I shall never forget that glimpse of him. He was a very urbane man. But it was plain that if we did not run the *Manassas* down, and promptly, he would not think well of us. I never saw Captain Smith happier than he was over this opportunity. He was a born fighter.

"Can you turn the ship?" he asked me.

"Yes sir," I answered.

I did not know whether I could turn her or not, but I knew that either I was going to do so or else run her aground. Indeed, the *Mississippi* had not yet made a turn in the narrow part of the river, and it was a question if she could turn under her own steam without assistance. But with so strong an incentive at the first trial we succeeded beautifully.

When Warley saw us coming he did not attempt to ram. He realized that the momentum of his three hundred and eighty-four tons was no match for our sixteen hundred and ninety-two tons when we were coming straight for him. As the *Mississippi* bore down on him, he dodged our blow and drove the nose of the *Manassas* into the bank. We fired two broadsides that wrecked her. Her crew began crawling ashore over her bows, and Captain Smith immediately sent a boat in charge of an officer to board and report her condition. He returned with Warley's signal-book and diary, to say that the outboard delivery pipes had been cut, and that the *Manassas* was sinking by the stern.

Captain Smith disliked to give up the idea of saving her. But, meanwhile, the gunners in the forts had found that the *Mississippi* was in range, and they began to pour in an increasingly heavy fire. As one weary gun's crew after another was called to their stations, and their welcome of our return to the scene of the night's activities grew hotter, it was out of the question for the *Mississippi* to remain a stationary target. There was nothing to do but to send the boat back in a hurry to set the *Manassas* on fire, and for the *Mississippi* to join the fleet at the quarantine station.

A little later the weight of the water flowing into the *Manassas's* stern raised her bow so that she floated free and drifted down the stream. As she appeared around the bend the mortar flotilla, which was not yet entirely certain of the result of the night's work, had a few moments akin to panic, and some of the unprotected auxiliaries of the fleet made ready for flight. When her condition was recognized an effort was made to secure her, but before anything could be accomplished she exploded and sank.

The *Mississippi,* proceeding upstream, found the fleet anchored seven miles above the forts at quarantine, and, as we steamed among the vessels, all the crews broke into hearty cheers for us over the news that we had brought. It was then that we saw our *Varuna,* a screw corvette of thirteen hundred tons, sunk to her top-gallant forecastle. But she was the fleet's only loss. She had been the second ship in line astern of the *Mississippi* in the first division. Being very speedy she had gone ahead of us, passing the forts in less than fifteen minutes, and found herself in the van of the whole fleet, engaging the Confederate River Defence Squadron. For a while she was without support. She fought with a gallantry worthy of her impetu-osity, until she was finally rammed by the *Stonewall Jackson,* while the *Cayuga* and the *Oneida* coming up finished the work which she had begun by utterly rout-ing the enemy. We saw its results in the burning wrecks of the Defence Squadron along the banks of the river. A broadside of canister had decided part of a Confed-erate regiment in camp along the levee to surrender. From the time that the two red lights had given the signal from the flag-ship to get under way until we were at quarantine only five hours had elapsed.

The fleet steamed from the quarantine station to a point about fifteen miles below New Orleans, where it anchored for the night. Weary as we were, there was very little sleep for any one, as fire-rafts and burning ships were drifting past us all night.

So far as we knew, the rest of the journey up to New Orleans would be with-out obstacles and in the nature of a parade. The next morning we were under way early, with everybody eager for a first sight of the city whose location we knew by the smoke rising from the Confederate storehouses and shipping which had been set on fire. Our purser, an elderly man whose place in battle was below looking after the wounded, was standing beside me on the hurricane deck, when suddenly batteries opened fire from both banks of the river at the ships ahead.

"Oh, that rash man Farragut!" he exclaimed. "Here we are at it again!"

But the opposition from the batteries *Chalmette* and *McGehee* was not formi-dable. Breaches for fourteen guns had been made in the levee walls, which was to become a favorite method of expeditiously emplacing a battery for a few salvos at a passing ship in the Mississippi River campaign. We suffered little damage our-selves, while we smothered *Chalmette* and *McGehee* with our broadsides. Soon we were abreast of the panic-stricken city, where we found that the Confederates had destroyed everything which they thought would be of military assistance to us, including the formidable iron-clad *Mississippi,* which was on the ways. Our guns not only commanded the streets, but also the narrow strip of land which was the city's only outlet except through the swamps.

The taking of New Orleans was the sensational achievement of the war thus far. With the flash of the splendid news through the North, Farragut became the hero of the hour. Succeeding victories could only brighten the fame that he had won. If he had not been a conspicuous captain before the war, probably it was because he had not the gift of self-advertisement which often wins attention in time of peace.

How many bubble reputations of that sort were burst in the first stages of the Civil War! But happily Mr. Fox knew Farragut professionally, and therefore his merits, and he was given important work to do immediately. Under another commander the story of New Orleans might have been different. Success always makes success seem easy. Many a commander could have found excuses for not trying to run the forts or for delay, which would have meant that both of the new Confederate iron-clads would have been ready for battle when the passage was finally made. Like Grant, Farragut always went ahead. Instead of worrying about the strength of the enemy, he made the enemy worry about his own strength.

The Confederates had felt that New Orleans was secure. It did not seem to them that Yankee enterprise would be equal to a stroke over-sea at such a distance from our Northern ports. Surrounded by low land, the most populous city of the Confederacy was protected from land attack; but not from occupation by troops under escort of a naval force making a dash up the river.

As soon as it was evident that New Orleans was ours for the occupation, Farragut sent the *Mississippi* and the *Iroquois* back down the river to reinforce the force which he had left at quarantine. Neither the forts nor the iron-clad *Louisiana* had yet surrendered. But the position of both was untenable. We were in their rear and they were effectually cut off from the rest of the Confederacy. Indeed, a part of the weary garrison of the forts practically mutinied against holding out any further.

On the 28th the final terms of surrender were made, through Porter, in command of the mortar flotilla below the forts, which had not, of course, followed the fleet. I had the pleasure of stretching my legs ashore and of inspecting the results of the mortar fire on the forts. I was not deeply impressed by the damage that had been done. The shells had cut the levee bank in places and seepage had filled the bottom of the forts with mud. When a shell sank in this it made a great splutter without much destructive effect. Yet there is no doubt of the moral value of the mortar fire in assisting the passage of the fleet.

Among the Confederate ships was the *McRae*, which had been mercilessly engaged by the *Iroquois*. Her casualties in the exchange of broadsides at close quarters had been very heavy. Among the mortally wounded was her commander, Thomas B. Huger, whose case parallels that of Warley, of the *Manassas*. His last service in the United States Navy had been in the ship which he unsuccessfully engaged. Charles W. Read succeeded to the command of the *McRae*.

Read had been appointed to Annapolis from Mississippi, and was at the Naval Academy part of the time that I was, being in the class of 1860. Now, I met him under circumstances that could appeal only to the chivalry of the victorious side.

"Savey" Read, as he was known to his fellow-midshipmen, came on board the *Mississippi* to get permission to take his dying captain and the other wounded of the *McRae* to New Orleans. Later during the war he captured one of our vessels, and set forth on a career up and down our coast worthy of the days of Drake. Whenever he took a vessel that he liked better than the one with which he made the capture, he would transfer his flag to her. Appearing suddenly in the harbor of Portland, Maine, which was about the last place in which any one would have expected to see him, he was able to cut out one of our revenue-cutters, but was taken before he could get away with his prize.

As a prisoner of war he had to be quiet for a while; but eventually he was exchanged. Just before the close of the war he reappeared on the Red River. There he loaded the ram *Webb* with cotton and succeeded in passing our ships at New Orleans; but about fifty miles below the city he met the *Richmond*. Though it seems possible that he might have got by her, he ran the *Webb* ashore and set her on fire. He was on his way to Havana, and if he had arrived there with his cargo, such was the high price of cotton at the time, he would have made a small fortune with which to make a fresh start in life. I understand that he closed his career as a pilot of the Southwest Pass in the Mississippi delta.

Chapter VI.

IN NEW ORLEANS.

We were invaders and in our own land. I was to have plenty of time in which to appreciate the bitterness toward the Northerner on the part of the people of a Southern city which was noted for its hospitality to strangers. For the *Mississippi* was stationed off New Orleans as a guard-ship for nearly a year. She was thought to be of too heavy draught to proceed up the river with the other ships in the spring of 1862, when Farragut made his first run past Vicksburg. Remaining behind with her was the *Pensacola*.

Moreover, it was important that some naval force should keep the streets under its guns and be ready to assist the army. General Benjamin F. Butler's army of occupation was none too numerous to look after a population that was doing everything possible to hamper it, while no doubt the adult males who were still at home—most of them were up the river with the Confederate army—would have risen at the first opportunity. In fact, they often declared that they would yet drive the Yankees into the river.

One of the forgings of the *Mississippi's* paddle-wheel had been broken. We could not repair it and must have a new one to take its place. When we sought to have this made we found that the only place with facilities was the foundry and ship-works that had been constructing the Confederate iron-clads *Louisiana* and *Mississippi*. The owner positively refused to serve a Yankee ship in this fashion. We had to admire his loyalty to his cause; but war is war and we needed the forging. So General Butler was informed of the refusal. He acted with customary promptness by putting the recalcitrant foundryman under arrest, and was about to send him to Fort Jackson, when his wife came on board the *Mississippi* to see Captain Smith. She said that her husband's health was very poor, and confinement in Fort Jackson, which was in an insalubrious location, must mean his death. He had changed his mind and would make the forging now if he were released. She had been timid about going to General Butler—whom New Orleans regarded as a veritable monster—but wouldn't Captain Smith intercede with the general?

Captain Smith said that he had no interest in having her husband imprisoned, and he would much rather have him making the forging than on his way to Fort Jackson. He sent me to see the general, an eccentric, resourceful, determined character, hardly inclined to suavity, who had about the most thankless task that could fall to a general officer. He was in no danger of allowing sentiment to interfere with his rigorous sense of duty. He meant to make sure that there was no uprising against him and that his soldiers were respected.

I found him in full uniform at a desk, with his sword on and two loaded revolvers lying in front of him as a precaution against assassination, of which he was in some danger from the rougher elements of the population. He agreed with the view of Captain Smith; and while he was having a note written for the prisoner's release I remember that he pointed to a chest in the room and said:

"That contains all of Judah P. Benjamin's private papers."

Benjamin was then secretary of state of the Confederacy. He afterward became a queen's counsel, with an immense practice as a barrister, in England.

I was able to deliver the note for the foundryman's release just as the boat with him on board, bound for Fort Jackson, was casting off from the wharf.

On occasion the general could manifest a good deal of acerbity of temper.

Some hitches occurred between the land and the sea forces, as usually happens when the two sister but distinct services, reporting to separate commands, are aiming to work in harmony.

One of the general's cares was sanitation. He was guarding against an epidemic of yellow-fever with a rigid quarantine. The *Tennessee,* one of the men-of-war, under command of Captain Philip Johnson, came up the river, and, contrary to the general's regulations, ran past quarantine. In fact, the ship had been off the yellow-fever-infected port of Galveston on the blockade, but had never allowed any of her crew ashore. And her reason for not stopping was a good one. She was leaking badly, and the only way that she could stay afloat was by keeping her circulating pumps at work. If she stopped her engines the pumps would stop. When Butler heard of this infraction of his rules he sent for Captain Johnson, and, despite Johnson's explanation, broke into one of those abusive tirades of which he was known to be a master.

"I have a great mind to put you in the parish prison," Butler announced in the presence of a number of his officers.

"Oh, no, you won't," Johnson answered. "And, besides, you must not talk to me that way. If your own officers will permit it, I won't."

As a lawyer Butler saw the point and waived the argument on this score, but sent word to Commodore Henry W. Morris, of the *Pensacola,* the senior naval officer present, that the regulations must be obeyed and the *Tennessee* must return and ride out her quarantine. Commodore Morris could be as urbane as Farragut. He was agreeable to the general's ultimatum, but he said that inasmuch as there had been exchanges of visits between the *Tennessee* and the other vessels of the navy lying in the river their crews must also have been infected, and therefore they would all go to quarantine. This would leave the general's force of occupation without the moral support of the guns of the navy commanding the streets. Though he affected controversially not to have a very high opinion of the navy, he had not so poor an opinion of it that he wanted to see us depart. So he allowed the crippled *Tennessee* to remain. She did not develop any cases of yellow-fever.

Butler was so extraordinary a character that perhaps another anecdote which refers to him may be worth repeating. When the *Mississippi* returned down the river after Farragut had anchored his fleet off New Orleans, we found a French gunboat at quarantine. She had been cruising along the coast, as many foreign gunboats were doing, looking after the interests of their nations and gaining professional points about naval warfare which would be of service to their naval staffs at home. The French commander asked Captain Smith if there were any objection to his going to New Orleans, where, of course, there were a great many French subjects living. It was quite within his international rights that he should go, and

Captain Smith consented. When Butler, who was disembarking his troops and preparing to occupy the city, heard of this, he took a contrary view.

"We don't want the Frenchman around. He might make trouble," he said.

Captain Smith sent me aboard the gunboat to say that General Butler would rather that she waited a few days before proceeding up the river.

"General Butler? General Butler?" said the French commander. "Oh, yes! He is *l'avocat-général*. He says I shall stay? *Voilà*, I will go!" So he went, leaving the "lawyer-general" pretty angry but helpless.

Our social life ashore while we were off New Orleans was limited mostly to the scowls of the people we passed. But there were a few Union families where we were welcome. The courage of their loyalty in the midst of what seemed to us universal disloyalty was very appealing. In most instances they were families who had recently come from the North and had not yet imbibed the sentiments of their surroundings. But the true Southern woman would as soon have invited Satan himself as a Union officer to her house. To the creoles we were loathsome Yankees, and, in turn, we thought of them as "rebels." Confederate was a little-used word on the Federal side in those days.

As an example of our own feeling I recall an occurrence during the visit of a British gunboat, the *Rinaldo*. She was commanded by Commander, later Vice-Admiral, Hewett. His sympathies, as were the sympathies of so many Englishmen, were with the Confederacy. As New Orleans was now again in the control of the United States, there was nothing to prevent his presence there. It was merely a visit to the port of a country with which England was at peace. He was popular with the New Orleans people, and went about a great deal in creole society, and, in return, gave entertainments on board the *Rinaldo,* at which the Confederate cause was acclaimed, and to which none of the Federal officers were invited. This was somewhat exasperating to the Federals. One day when there was a party on board the *Rinaldo* the band began to play the "Bonnie Blue Flag," which was a Confederate air. Captain Smith sent for me at once and told me to go on board the *Rinaldo* and tell Hewett that that air was not permitted in New Orleans. Hewett was pretty angry when he received the captain's message, but he had to recognize that this time we were in the right. The air was not played on board the *Rinaldo* again.

Later Hewett put his sympathy for the Confederate cause into action. Though an officer of the British navy, he became commander of one of the blockade-runners which were fitted out in England. When our government privately sent word, as I understand that it did, that any British naval officers who were taken serving on a blockade-runner would be returned to the British government in double irons Hewett resigned his command. Many years afterward, in 1886, I happened to meet him in the United Service Club, in London. We had a pleasant conversation without once alluding to the time when I had told him that he must revise his musical programme.

Being on board a man-of-war off New Orleans through the summer was like being in a floating oven. It was out of the question to sleep in our cabins. We slept on deck. I do not suppose that the character of the mosquitoes on the Mississippi has changed with the passage of time. There was a big kind popularly called "gallinippers," which seemed to find shoe-leather an effective means of sharpening their proboscides before they reached the vulnerable part of your ankle.

Our existence was pretty monotonous for naval officers in the midst of the great war. We envied the men on the other ships on the blockade or up the river with Farragut. They were at least on the move, though they saw little fighting. But we had one compensation. While the health of the officers and crews up the river had been bad, we had extemporized a distilling-plant on board the *Mississippi* which gave us pure water to drink, and our health had been excellent.

Chapter VII.

THE BATTLE OF PORT HUDSON.

The passage of Forts Jackson and St. Philip had been lively enough for the fleet, but that of running the batteries of Port Hudson was to prove a far more serious undertaking. I have often said that in this action I lived about five years in one hour.

At the beginning of the spring of 1863 Grant's and Sherman's armies were pressing toward Vicksburg. The farther that the Confederates fell back the more concentrated became their forces and the more desperate their resistance. After Farragut had returned down the river in the fall they had become awakened to the weakness of the river's defences and the necessity of keeping open communications with the rich granary to the west of the Mississippi in northern Louisiana, Arkansas, and Texas.

Their natural strongholds were Vicksburg and Port Hudson, and these they fortified with all the guns that could possibly be spared from other points. They had not the facilities that the North had for making artillery. Otherwise, by the plentiful distribution of batteries on the banks of the river where it was narrow and the current swift, the problem for the Union fleet would have been much worse than it was. Efforts at blockade with single detached vessels had failed, owing to the activity of improvised rams and gunboats which the Confederates kept up the tributaries. Farragut's object in trying to take the fleet above Port Hudson was to shut Vicksburg off from supplies on the river side, while the army was shutting it off on the land side.

He needed every available ship for his purpose; and he now concluded that the *Mississippi* was not of too heavy draught to navigate in the river above New Orleans. She was never meant for such work, but we were delighted over the opportunity for any kind of action after the dreary monotony of surveying from our deck the wharves of New Orleans. As executive officer in charge of the general details of the ship, I had aimed to make the best of the recess and overcome the handicap of my youth by my zeal in training the crew of three hundred men, for whom I was responsible to the captain in the same way that the manager of a corporation is responsible to its president and board of directors. We had developed the discipline of a regular force, and certainly, if drill of the guns' crews counted for anything, we should be correspondingly efficient in battle.

On March 14, 1863, we had anchored off Profit's Island, which is seven miles below Port Hudson, a little town that went into history because it happened to mark a sharp bend in the river running west-southwest for a distance of a mile or more. Beginning at the bend was a line of bluffs on the east bank, varying from eighty to a hundred feet in height. On the opposite bank there was a dangerous shoal-point. On the bluffs were heavy guns that could bear the length of the bend and cover this point. They had a plunging fire on us, while we had to fire upward at them. There were also guns at the base of the bluffs. The time chosen for the passage was night, again much against the predilections of Captain Smith.

First and last, the old *Mississippi*, on account of her side-wheels, had been in a class by herself in Farragut's fleet. Now the other big ships, the *Hartford*, the *Monongahela*, and the *Richmond*, each were to have a gunboat made fast to the port side, which was the opposite side from the batteries. The object of this pairing was the assistance of the gunboat in helping her heavy-draught companion off the bottom if she ran aground around. Thus Farragut applied the principle of the twin screws' facility in making a short turn by backing with one screw and going ahead with the other. But the *Mississippi*, being a side-wheeler, had to make the passage without a consort. We had an experienced pilot at our service, as had every ship. He was in one of the cutters under the guns on the port side, where he would at the same time be safe—for his safety was most important—and near enough to call his directions to the man at the wheel. Thus a river pilot had become a factor in fighting a ship which had been built to fight in the open sea with plenty of room for manoeuvring.

Starting at 10 P.M., after the *Hartford*, which led, came the *Monongahela* and then the *Richmond*, with the *Mississippi* bringing up the rear. Possibly Farragut realized that the *Mississippi* would be the most likely of the four to run aground, and therefore assigned her to a position where she would not get in the way of any following ship if she did run aground. The *Hartford* was already past the first of the batteries before the enemy threw up a rocket as a signal that she was seen, and the whole crest of the bluff broke into flashes. Piles of cordwood soaked with pitch were lighted on the shore opposite the batteries in order to outline the ships to the Confederate gunners. One of my Washington friends, Chief-Justice White, was a boyish aide to the commanding general of the Port Hudson defences. He tells me that the Confederates got the better of us that night, and I must say that I have to agree with him.

The air was heavy and misty. Almost immediately after we were engaged, a pall of smoke settled over the river and hung there, thickening with the progress of the cannonading. This was more dangerous than the enemy's fire, which was pounding us with good effect, while we could see nothing but the flashes of their guns as a target. The *Hartford,* however, had good luck as well as advantage of position. She was at least pushing ahead of her own smoke, while every other ship was taking the smoke of those in front of her. The *Mississippi* had the smoke of all three.

At the bend, the current caught the *Hartford* and swept her around with her head toward the batteries, her stem touching ground. But the *Albatross,* her gun-boat consort, helped her off. Then, applying the twin-screw method, with the *Hartford* going ahead strong with her engines while the *Albatross* backed, the *Hartford* got her head pointed upstream again and steamed out of the range of the batteries with a loss of only one killed and two wounded. The Confederate gunners had not depressed their guns enough for the *Hartford,* but they did not make this error as the other ships came in range.

When the *Richmond,* the second ship in line, was in front of the last battery, a shot tore into her engine-room. Such was its chance effect that it twisted the safety-valve lever, displacing the weight and quickly filling the engine-room, fire-room, and berth deck with steam. In short order the steam pressure fell so low that she could not go ahead under her own motive power. The *Genesee,* her gunboat, was not able with her own power to make any headway for the two vessels against the strong current. There was nothing to do but for the pair to make an expeditious retreat downstream to safety.

The *Richmond's* gunners, working in furious haste, intent on delivering the heaviest possible fire, did not know that their ship had turned around. Therefore they were firing toward the bank opposite that from the batteries. Mistaking the flashes of the *Mississippi's* guns for the flashes of the enemy's, they fired at her. On our part we did not know in the obscurity of the smoke and darkness that our ships had been disabled. The *Richmond's* casualties included her executive officer, Lieutenant A. Boyd Cummings, who was mortally wounded.

As the *Monongahela* came along she found herself in the range of musketry from the low bank on the port side, which was silenced by her gunboat, the *Kineo*. But the *Kineo* received a shot which jammed her rudder-post and rendered the rudder useless. As a result the *Monongahela* had to do all the steering. She ran aground, and the *Kineo,* carried on by her momentum as the *Monongahela* suddenly stopped, tore away all of her fasts by which she was bound to the *Monongahela* except one. Then the *Kineo* got a hawser to the *Monongahela,* and, laboring desperately, under fire, succeeded after twenty-five minutes' effort in getting the *Monongahela* free of the bottom.

Meanwhile, Captain McKinistry, of the *Monongahela,* had had the bridge shot away from under his feet, and had received such a fall in consequence that he was incapacitated. Lieutenant-Commander N. W. Thomas took command in his place. The *Kineo* drifted on downstream, while the *Monongahela* proceeded on her way until a heated crank-pin stopped her engines, when she had to drift back downstream under the fire of the batteries. She sustained a heavy loss in killed and wounded.

I refer to the experiences of the three ships which had preceded the *Mississippi* in order to show the hazardous nature of Farragut's undertaking. His flagship, the *Hartford,* and her consort, the gunboat *Albatross,* were all of his command which he had with him the next morning, and it was many weeks before any of the other ships could join him.

The *Mississippi,* bringing up the rear, was soon enveloped in the pall of smoke. We went by the *Monongahela* when she was aground without, so far as I know, either seeing or being seen by her. Both Captain Smith and myself felt that our destiny that night was in the hands of the pilot. There was nothing to do but to fire back at the flashes on the bluffs and trust to his expert knowledge. It was a new experience for him, guiding a heavy-draught ocean-going ship in the midst of battle smoke, with the shells shrieking in his ears. By the time that the *Mississippi* came within range of the batteries they were making excellent practice. Our mortar flotilla posted below the bend was adding to the uproar. When there was a cry of "Torpedoes!" it might have been alarming had we not seen that bombs striking close to the ship had splashed the water upon the deck. None actually struck us. Some one else shouted, "They're firing chain-shot at us!" an error of observation due to the sight of two bombs which passed by in company, their lighted fuses giving the effect of being part of the same projectile.

We were going very slowly, feeling our way as we approached the shoal-point.

Finally, when the pilot thought that we were past it, he called out: "Starboard the helm! Full speed ahead!" As it turned out, we were anything but past the point. We starboarded the helm straight into it and struck just as we developed a powerful momentum. We were hard aground and listing, and backed with all the capacity of the engines immediately. In order to bring the ship on an even keel, we ran in the port battery, which, as it faced away from the bluffs, was not engaged. Every precaution to meet the emergency was taken promptly; and there was remarkably little confusion, thanks to the long drills which we had had off New Orleans, and to the fact that all but a few of the crew had already been under fire in passing Forts Jackson and St. Philip.

But no amount of training could altogether prepare men for such a situation as we were in. With our own guns barking, and the engines pounding, and the paddle-wheels making more noise than usual, because we were aground, it was difficult to make commands heard. In half an hour the engines never budged us, while steadfastly and even unconcernedly the engine-room force stuck to their duties. We were being more frequently hit; the toll of our dead and wounded was increasing. Naturally, too, gunners of the enemy, who could see the ship outlined by the bonfires on the bank on the opposite side of us from the batteries, had not failed to note that we were aground. The advantages of training on a stationary target allowed them to make the most of our distress, while the flashes of our own guns and the bursting of the enemy's shells only made the intervals of darkness the more baffling to the eyes. I remember hunting about the deck for Captain Smith and finding him lighting another cigar with a flint quite as cooly as if he were doing it when we lay anchored off New Orleans.

"Well, it doesn't look as if we could get her off," he said.

"No, it does not!" I had to tell him.

Then came the report that we were on fire forward in the store-room. Investigation proved that this was true. The store-room was filled with all sorts of inflammable material and was below the water-line, supposedly out of reach of any shot.

It was not until forty years afterward that I learned how the fire had started, and this from a gentleman whom I met at Palm Beach, Florida. He had served in what was called the "hot-shot" battery. This battery had a furnace in which they heated their round shot red-hot before firing them. When I asked him how they kept the shot from igniting the powder, he said: "We put wads of wet hay or hemp between the shot and the powder." Our bow in grounding had risen so that the store-room was above the water-line, and one of these hot shot having a plunging trajectory had entered. While we were fighting the fire in the store-room, Captain Smith had given the order to throw the guns of the port battery overboard in the hope that this would lighten the ship enough to float her. But the order was never carried out. He had to face the heartbreaking fact, to any captain of his indomitable courage, of giving up his ship. He had opposed fighting in the night and in the night he had come to grief.

"Can we save the crew?" he asked me.

"Yes, sir!" I told him.

But there was no time to lose. Delay only meant still more wounded to move, with the danger of the fire in the store-room reaching the magazine before they were away. Not once had our starboard battery ceased firing. The gunners had kept to their work as if they were sure of victory, gaps caused by casualties among the guns' crews being filled in a fashion that was a credit to our *morale;* for it is in such a crisis as this that you may know whether all your labor in organization and drills has had a vital or a superficial effect.

And the battery must continue to fire up to the very minute of abandoning the ship, the gunners being the last of the enlisted men to go. Down on the spar-deck I found everybody full of fight. I remember as I passed along seeing Ensign Barker, now Rear-Admiral Albert S. Barker (retired), sighting a gun. To show what a small detail, even in a time of such tension as that was, may impress itself on the mind, I recollect that Barker was wearing eyeglasses. I had never seen him with them on before.

"What are we leaving her for?" Barker asked. He was thinking only of his part, without knowing that there was a fire forward. When I explained, he comprehended the situation. It was Barker who brought the *Oregon* out to Manila after the Spanish War and who took over the command of the Asiatic station on my departure for home.

The three boats on the starboard side toward the enemy's batteries had all been smashed by shells. The three on the port side were still seaworthy.

We got all of the wounded in the first boat, and started that down the river, with directions to go on board one of our ships. The second and the third, which had some of the slightly wounded, as well as members of the crew who were unhurt, were told to make a landing near by on the bank and to send the boats back immediately. They were slow in returning. As soon as they were against the ship's side the crew began crowding and the officers had difficulty in keeping order. For the moment the bonds of discipline had been broken. The men were just human beings obeying the law of self-preservation.

I apprehended the reason why the boats had been slow in returning. There was disinclination on the part of the oarsmen who had reached safety to make the trip back. What if the next time the boats did not return at all? They were our only hope of safety. To swim in that swift river-current was impossible. To expect rescue in the midst of battle, when no one could be signalled in the darkness and pandemonium, was out of the question. It would be a choice of drowning or of burning for those who were caught on board the *Mississippi.*

I determined to make sure of the boats' return, and in the impulse, just as they were going to push off, I swung myself down by the boat-falls into one of the boats. Not until we were free of the ship did I have a second thought in realization of what I had done. I had left my ship in distress, when it is the rule that the last man to leave her should be the captain, and I as executive officer should be next to the last.

That was the most anxious moment of my career. What if a shot should sink the boat? What if a rifle bullet should get me? All the world would say that I had been guilty of about as craven an act as can be placed at the door of any officer. This would not be pleasant reading for my father up in Vermont. He would no longer think that I had done the "rest" reasonably well. If the ship should blow up while I was away and I should appear on the reports as saved, probably people would smile over my explanation.

We were under fire all the way to the shore, but nobody was hit. As we landed on the beach I said to the men in the boats:

"Now, all of you except four get to cover behind the levee. Those four will stay with me to go off to the ship."

They obeyed one part of my command with great alacrity. That is, all but one scrambled over the levee in a free-for-all rush. The one who remained standing was a big negro, the ship's cook. He evidently understood that I meant him to be one of the four.

"I'm ready to go with you, sir!" he said. And he was perfectly calm about it.

Each of the others had thought that the order was not personal. But when I called out, shaming them, in the name of their race, for allowing a negro to be the only one who was willing to return to save his shipmates, I did not lack volunteers.

Then in the dim light I discerned one man standing by the other boat, which had landed some distance up the beach.

I called:

"Who is that standing by the cutter?"

The answer came: "It is I, sir, Chase" (one of the acting masters).

"Why don't you go off to the ship and get the rest of the officers and men?" I asked.

"I can't get the men to man the boat!" he said.

When I called out asking if they meant to desert their shipmates there was no reply. Then I told Chase to use his revolver and make them go, which he did. It is my firm belief that neither one of the boats would have ever returned to the ship if I had not gone ashore in one of them.

I was certainly as relieved to reach the ship as the men had been to reach shore. When I say that I lived five years in an hour, I should include about four and a half of the years in the few minutes that I was absent with the boats.

As soon as I was on deck Captain Smith came to me and said:

"I have been looking all over for you. I didn't know but that you had been killed."

I explained hastily, and added that we had two empty boats alongside, which we might not have had except for my indiscretion.

"We must make sure that none is left aboard alive," said the captain.

Then we began a search whose harrowing memory will never fade from my mind. We went up and down the decks, examining prostrate figures to make sure that no spark of life remained in them, haste impelling us in the grim task on the one hand, and, on the other, the fear that some poor fellow who was still unconscious might know the horror of seeing the flames creep up on him as he lay powerless to move. Meanwhile, we kept calling aloud in the darkness that this was the last chance to escape. As a result of the thorough search, we found one youngster, little more than a boy, who was so faint that he could scarcely speak. We pulled him out from under the body of a dead man, in the midst of a group of dead who had been killed by the bursting of a shell.

The next step was to make certain that the ship should not fall into the hands of the enemy. Captain Smith gave orders to fire the ship in two places in order to make absolutely sure of her destruction. This was our last service to that old vessel which had known so many cruises, and it was performed while the batteries on the bluff were continuing to improve their practice.

With Ensign O. A. Batcheller I went below to start a blaze in the wardroom, which is both the officers' sitting-room and mess-room and, in a sense, their home afloat, while the rest of the ship is their shop. I had a lantern with me, I remember, and when I got below I looked around at the bare oak table and chairs, wondering what there was that I could ignite. I did not want to delay the boat, and, under the circumstances, as long as we had to go, we did not care to remain in that inferno of shellfire any longer than necessary. I ran into my stateroom, and pulling the mattress off the berth hurried back with it to the wardroom. Then I ripped it open and put it under the dining-table.

When I had piled the chairs and any other combustibles around the table, I took the oil lamp out of the lantern and plunged it into the mattress, with the result that I had a blaze which required immediate evacuation of the wardroom by Batcheller and myself. My mattress was all that I had tried to remove from my stateroom. But just as we were going Batcheller cried: "I'll save that, anyway!" and seized a uniform frock-coat before he ran up the ladder ahead of me.

In the last boat, besides the captain, were one of the engineers, Batcheller, myself, and four men. I waited on my juniors to precede me, and then the captain waited for me, so that he was the last man ever to press his foot on the *Mississippi's* deck. This order of our going was carried out as regularly in keeping with naval custom as if it had been some formal occasion in a peaceful port.

As soon as we were free of the ship's side the powerful current caught us and swung us downstream. At the same time, the fire we had started in the wardroom broke through the skylight in a great burst of flame, illuminating the whole after part of the ship. It must have revealed our boat clearly on the bosom of the river, and it was a signal to those on the bluffs along the banks to break into that rebel yell which I then heard in full chorus of victory for the first and only time in my life. It was not pleasant to the ear. The Confederates were gloating over what was the most triumphant of sights to them and the most distressing of sights to us. I remember thinking: "How they must hate us!"

Meanwhile, there was no cessation in the fire, and our boat was a target for the batteries. Not one of the officers and crew, except Ensign Batcheller, had saved any of his personal belongings. All the clothes we had were those in which we were clad. Captain Smith had on his sword, and also buckled to his belt a pair of fine revolvers. He still had a cigar in his mouth, and was as calm as ever. But suddenly he unbuckled his belt and threw both sword and revolvers overboard.

"Why did you do that?" I asked.

He was a man of few words, who made up his mind decisively, and his answers were always prompt.

"I'm not going to surrender them to any rebel," he said. This illustrated very well the strong feelings of the time, which now, happily, have no interest for us except in the psychology of history.

"We need not land, but go to one of our ships downstream," I answered.

At all events, I concluded to keep my sword. Every one in the boat, except Captain Smith and myself, was at the oars, rowing as energetically as if we were in a race. I had the tiller. We were moving so rapidly that we were not hit, and when we were safe around the bend and in sight of the *Richmond* of our fleet, which we were to board in safety, it was evident that the captain had been a little precipitate. A few days afterward, when he was still without a sword, Captain Smith gave my sword a glance and remarked:

"You would not have had that if you had followed your captain's example."

This was said without a smile, very much in the manner of a bishop. The captain would have made a most dignified bishop and of the church militant.

I recollect, too, Ensign Batcheller holding up the uniform coat he had saved, after we had reached the *Richmond,* as a token of the advantage he had over the rest of us. Ensign E. M. Shepard examined the coat and said:

"Thanks, very much, Batcheller, but that's my coat!"

So it was.

Besides setting her on fire in two places, as an additional precaution before abandoning her, we had cut the *Mississippi's* outboard delivery pipes. Thus she filled with water astern, just as the wreck of the ram *Manassas* had in the battle of New Orleans, and with the same result. Her bow was lifted sufficiently for her to float free of the bottom, and she swung around with the current. Her port guns were loaded, and now, as they faced the Confederate batteries, the heat reached the primers and she came downstream, a dying ship manned by dead men, firing on the enemy; and some of the shots, I am told, took effect.

As she drifted toward us a mass of flame, she had the whole river to herself, lighting its breadth and throwing the banks of the levee in relief. The *Richmond* slipped her chain in order to make sure of not being run down. Captain Smith and his officers were standing on the deck of the *Richmond* watching her, while I, with that rebel yell of triumph still echoing in my ears, was thinking of the splendid defiance of the last shots in her guns being sent at the enemy.

"She goes out magnificently, anyway!" I said to the captain, glad to find some compensating thought for our disaster in a moment when all of us were overwrought by what we had been through.

"I don't think so!" he returned sharply.

I saw that he had misunderstood the idea that led to my remark. I shall never forget the look on his face as he saw his ship of which he had been so proud drifting to her doom. Farther downstream she went aground and soon after exploded. Such was the end of that brave, sturdily built old side-wheeler.

It is hard to say whether or not Port Hudson can be considered as a set-back for the navy. Farragut himself got through. The affair was in keeping with his character. Though the three other ships failed, the navy had appeared before the country as ready to take any risk. We had made amends for the disaster at Galveston some two months previously, when the *Westfield* had been destroyed and the *Harriet Lane* captured, which had been unfortunate in its effect. Considering the state of mind of the country, the need was for some deed of daring aggressiveness. However, the Navy Department determined to hold in its leonine old fighter a little, and he was told not to risk his ships where it could possibly be avoided.

In speaking of the loss of the *Mississippi,* Farragut said that he was sorry to lose a good vessel and so many brave men, but that you could not make an omelet without breaking eggs. When Captain Smith, who was as serious as Cromwell and withal extremely sensitive, heard this remark, he appeared hurt; for he said, in his sober fashion: "He calls us an omelet!" Far from any criticism ever being passed in any quarter on the abandonment of the *Mississippi,* the captain had letters of praise for his conduct from both Mr. Welles and Mr. Fox. "The noble ship has gone," wrote Mr. Fox, "but the navy and the country have gained an example. However, it was to be expected of him who in this war has done all things well."

In that disaster, as in every action, I myself had gained experience in the midst of danger and confusion when I was still young enough to profit by the lesson. No word of commendation I have received is more precious to me than that of Captain Smith's report, in which he said:

"I consider that I should be neglecting a most important duty should I omit to mention the coolness of my executive officer, Mr. George Dewey, and the steady, fearless, and gallant manner in which the officers and men of the *Mississippi* defended her, and the orderly and quiet manner in which she was abandoned."

Chapter VIII.

PRIZE COMMISSIONER.

After the battle of Port Hudson I had a radical change of occupation and scene. My new duties called for the abilities of a judge and a merchant rather than those associated with my profession. As prize commissioner at New Orleans I had to adjudicate controversies concerning cargo captured on the blockade, and, when I had declared it legitimate prize, to sell it for the government. As most of the contraband was cotton, I became quite an expert in the fluctuations of the cotton market.

The auctioneer who acted as salesman for me, though born in Kentucky, was a pronounced Union man. When he first came to New Orleans he had sold a great many negroes as a matter of course in his business. Though this was not exactly agreeable work, he had not developed any keen sensitiveness about it. Slavery was an accepted institution to which everybody had become accustomed. However, a single revolting and illuminating experience made him an abolitionist.

One day he was asked to go to a hotel to look at some human "property" with a view to its sale to the highest bidder. The man who owned the "property" took him into a room where three girls were seated sewing. The girls, being octoroons and having the peculiarly white complexion of many octoroons, were, as the auctioneer declared, whiter than his own daughter.

"I told that fellow that he would have to get somebody else to sell those girls," he said.

He made up his mind that an institution that permitted such a thing ought to be wiped out. He was not against the South, but against slavery.

As I lived on shore rather than on shipboard, I came to see a great deal more of New Orleans than I had while I was serving on a ship alongside the wharves. The life of the city had now adapted itself to the Union occupation. Business went on quite as usual. Except for the absence of many of the men in the Confederate army, you would hardly have realized that a state of war existed.

With the appetite of youth, after navy rations and that stiff fight at Port Hudson, I was able to do justice to New Orleans cookery, which I found was worthy of its reputation. Never before had I known such good food and so cheap. We had not only the pompano and other delicious fish, but also that delectable upland plover, the "papabote."

My service as Prize Commissioner was relatively brief. Summer found me back on the river as executive officer of the sloop *Monongahela*, which was stationed below Port Hudson, under my old captain, Melancthon Smith, for a short time until he was ordered north, when Captain Abner Read took command. As the *Hartford* was above Port Hudson, Farragut made the *Monongahela* his flag-ship when he was looking after operations on the lower reaches of the river. He lived mostly on deck and naturally at such close quarters that I saw a great deal of him.

He was not given to "paper work" or red tape, by which I mean lengthy written detail in his conduct of operations. I remember the simplicity of his methods particularly in contrast with those of another admiral with less responsibility, who could not get along without a force of clerks. There was a saying that his principal place for filing papers was his own coat-pocket. His was the supreme gift of directness and simplicity in great affairs, so valuable in time of war. Generally he wrote his orders himself, perhaps with his knee or the ship's rail as a rest. I recall that one day when he was writing he looked up and said:

"Now, how in the devil do you spell Appalachicola? Some of these educated young fellows from Annapolis must know!"

A man who had such an important command could hardly have been more democratic. One night I had given orders for a thorough cleaning of the ship the next morning. I was awake very early, for it was stiflingly hot. Five o'clock came and I heard no sound of the holy-stones on the deck. So I went above to find out why my orders were not obeyed, and my frame of mind for the moment was entirely that of the disciplinarian. There was no activity at all on deck. I looked around for the officer of the deck. He was an old New England whaler, brown as a buccaneer, who had enlisted for the war from the merchant service. I recollect that he wore small gold rings in his ears, a custom with some of the old-fashioned merchant sailors who had travelled the world over. I found him seated up in the hammock netting where it was cool, with Farragut at his side.

"Why aren't you cleaning ship?" I asked.

"I think I am to blame," said Farragut, with his pleasant smile. "We two veterans have been swapping yarns about sailing-ship days."

The old whaler did not see how he could leave Farragut when Farragut wanted to talk, and inwardly, perhaps, he did not fail to enjoy his position as superior to the young executive officer's reprimands.

As a rule, no captain or executive officer likes having his ship the flag-ship of a commander-in-chief. But Farragut was so simple in his manners and so free from the exactions due to official rank, that he was most welcome, crowded as our quarters were. Being a companionable man, he liked company, even when he was under fire. I recall a certain afternoon when he announced that he was going in his little steam tender to have a look at the Port Hudson batteries. First he asked Captain Thornton A. Jenkins, his chief of staff, if he would not like to come along. The captain begged to be excused. Then he asked Captain Smith, who also begged to be excused. Neither saw any purpose in an interruption of his duties to make a trip in the heat in order to be shot at. But Farragut was not going alone. He clapped me on the shoulder and said: "Come along, youngster!" which was equivalent to a command to one of my rank. As I went over the side Captain Jenkins said to me:

"Did you ever know a man before who always had a bee buzzing in his ear?"

We went up into the range of the batteries and drew their fire. But as we steamed rapidly and in a zigzag course we were not hit. Meanwhile Farragut seemed to be having the best kind of a time. No doubt, he got the information that he wanted.

It was while serving on the *Monongahela* that I had the closest call in my career. We were steaming up the river, escorting a small gunboat with ammunition for Banks's army. As I have previously mentioned, all that a field-battery had to do in order to have a little practice against a Union man-of-war was to cut embrasures for its guns in the levee and let drive. The levee furnished both an excellent screen and excellent protection. In fact, the gunners used these embrasures with much the effect of the modern disappearing gun. They ran the muzzle through the opening when they wanted to fire and then drew it back out of sight for loading, with neither themselves nor the gun at all exposed, while our shots would either be buried in the levee walls or whistle harmlessly overhead. But a man-of-war was a big target, and a single shot striking in a vital part might do great damage.

When a field-battery, hidden in the fashion I have described, unexpectedly opened on the *Monongahela* at close range in the vicinity of Donelsonville, Captain Jenkins, Farragut's chief of staff, who was aboard, thought that the only thing to do was to get out of range at full speed. This did seem the part of wisdom. Certainly our experience proved that it was for poor Read. He paid the penalty for taking a contrary view.

"I have never run from any rebel yet," Read declared, "and I'm not going to run now."

So he slowed the *Monongahela* down to engage the battery. He and Captain Jenkins and myself were standing near each other on the quarter-deck and we had fired only a few shots when there was a blinding flash in my eyes. I felt the stunning effect of the concussion of an exploding shell—which always raises the question of whether you will be alive or dead the next second. However, I realized that I was unhurt, and as the air cleared and I was once more standing solidly on my feet, with full possession of my faculties, I saw Read prostrate on the deck, his clothing badly torn and blood pouring from several places. Captain Jenkins was also down. It was clear that the command of the ship had devolved upon me, so I gave the order, "Full speed ahead!" The *Monongahela*, being very fast for a ship of her time, was soon out of range of the batteries.

Captain Read had been mortally wounded and died the next day, while Captain Jenkins had been wounded slightly, but in a curious way. The shell had exploded at a point in the ship's side where a rack of cutlasses was located and had hurled fragments of cutlass in all directions. Although our station on the quarter-deck was some distance from the point of explosion, a cutlass blade (about half length) had struck Captain Jenkins's leg with such force as to knock him down. That nothing worse than a bruise resulted was due to the fact that the blade struck fairly with its flat surface. Had the edge been turned, serious injury would have been inflicted.

When we examined the spread of the shell by the places where the fragments had struck, it was inexplicable how I had ever escaped without a scratch. It almost made me believe in luck. For that matter, any one who has seen much fighting becomes a sort of fatalist. Evidently my time had not yet come.

With the taking of Vicksburg in July, Port Hudson fell in consequence. At last President Lincoln had his wish. The Mississippi "flowed unvexed to the sea." There was no longer the need of any large naval force on the river. I was transferred to the *Brooklyn*, Captain Emmons, which had been ordered North to report to Rear-Admiral Dahlgren, who was in charge of the blockade off Charleston, South Carolina.

Chapter IX.

ON THE JAMES RIVER.

After eighteen months of service on sea-going ships navigating a river, it was a pleasure to be back in a sea-going ship's natural element; and I thoroughly enjoyed our cruise across the Gulf of Mexico with our sails spread. Captain Emmons, who had his nickname, as every officer of the navy had, was known as "Pop." He would never get my name right, always calling me "Mr. Dewar." We stopped in at Port Royal, and I recall, as we entered the harbor, that I was standing between him and the pilot when we sighted a vessel coming out.

"Starboard the helm!" said the pilot.

"Port the helm!" said Captain Emmons.

"Steady!" I said.

Captain Emmons turned on me.

"What do you mean, Mr. Dewar, by countermanding my orders?" he demanded.

"Well, sir, the pilot said starboard and you said port, so I wanted to avoid having the helmsman try to do both at once," I responded.

"Steady, then!" returned the captain. It transpired that this compromise in authority saved us from any danger of collision.

The prospect of taking part in Dahlgren's operations against Charleston was not altogether inviting to the officers of the *Brooklyn*. Farragut had fought his campaign on the lower Mississippi with wooden ships of the ante-bellum type and small gunboats. There were some ironclads on the upper Mississippi, but those built for use in harbors where they must stand some seaway were all on the Atlantic coast. It was out of the question to add armor to the wooden ships, as they had not the buoyancy to carry it. At Charleston the Confederates had their most powerful batteries. If the *Brooklyn* engaged them it would be pitting wooden sides and smooth-bore guns against the latest type of rifled gun. In fact, ours would be the only fighting-ship in Dahlgren's command that was not armored.

Upon our arrival at Charleston, while Captain Emmons went on board Dahlgren's flag-ship to report, we had time to look over his vessels and to realize how suicidal it would be for us to join in any attack on the defences of the harbor. We had an example in the monitors, which we saw for the first time, of how rapidly both the offensive and the defensive features of men-of-war had improved under the impulse of war conditions. Besides the division of monitors with their revolving turrets—modelled on that first experiment which had driven the Confederate *Merrimac (Virginia)* to cover—there was also the *New Ironsides,* that followed conventional ship construction and had armored sides. The combination of the two principles, an armored ship with revolving turrets, forms the principle of the battleship of to-day.

Having been executive officer of one ship that had been lost, I did not care to repeat the experience. We were all pleased when Captain Emmons came off to report that it was not the *Brooklyn* that Dahlgren wanted, but Captain Emmons to serve on his staff. So the *Brooklyn* proceeded to the New York Navy-Yard to be overhauled before returning to Farragut's command in the Gulf, where she was to participate in the battle of Mobile Bay. Meanwhile, I had my first holiday from duty since the war had begun, which I spent at my home in Vermont.

Captain James Alden succeeded Captain Emmons in command of the *Brooklyn* and he wanted me to go with him as executive officer; so did Farragut. But strong objections on account of my youth were made to the Navy Department on behalf of officers who were my seniors and held less important assignments. As I was now nearer the influence of Washington than when I was directly under Farragut and his great personal prestige, the objections prevailed, and in one sense fortunately for me. It will be recalled that it was the *Brooklyn* that led the wooden ships in past the forts at Mobile, following the monitors. When the monitor *Tecumseh* was sunk by a torpedo and Captain Alden saw torpedoes ahead of the *Brooklyn,* he stopped his ship, throwing the column out of formation. Farragut, with his famous call of "Damn the torpedoes! Go ahead!" signalled to proceed and steamed past the *Brooklyn* in the *Hartford,* taking the lead away from her.

My next ship was hardly of the importance of the *Mississippi,* the *Monongahela,* or the *Brooklyn.* I was to put the *Agawam,* a third-rate, wooden, side-wheel steamer, into commission at Portsmouth. My friends explained to me that I had been given this task in organization and discipline because I had made a reputation as an executive officer equal to any emergency. However that may be, there can be no doubt that both the crew of the *Agawam* and the nature of the vessel and of the service expected of her gave me quite enough to do from the moment that I reported on board her, in November, 1863, until I was detached from her, a year later.

She was built particularly for river service and being a double-ender, with two rudders of the ferry-boat type, she was as difficult in handling as in keeping ship-shape. During the spring and summer of 1864 I saw some pretty active and trying service on the James River, where we were operating in support of General Butler's abortive expedition toward Richmond, while Grant was fighting the Wilderness campaign.

For about a month the *Agawam* was the flag-ship of Rear-Admiral S. P. Lee, commanding the North Atlantic Squadron. Lee was another one of the captains who, at the outbreak of the Civil War, was still in the prime of his powers. He was off the Cape of Good Hope in command of a ship bound for China when he heard that Sumter had been fired on. Without waiting on an order from Washington, he started home on his own responsibility, in the conviction that the services of his ship would be needed. He was a man of prodigious and conscientious industry.

Commander A. C. Rhind, in command of the *Agawam,* had earned a reputation for fearlessness in the war and fearlessness in controversy before the war. While in the Pacific Squadron years before, as I recall, he had been suspended by Boutwell, the commander of his ship. Afterward, when his case was on trial in Washington, he posted a notice outside the Navy Department to this effect: "Boutwell is a liar and a scoundrel." Though the Retiring Board dropped him from the navy, he was able to have himself reinstated, and to prove that, however eccentric he might be in time of peace, he could be of great service in battle.

The *Agawam's* most important action occupied her off and on for six days in pounding the Confederate batteries at Four Mile Creek to aid General Butler's attack. On the first day we engaged one battery of rifled guns which we could locate and two batteries of mortars and heavy guns which we could not locate; and we kept up a continuous fire for four hours, until our ammunition was exhausted. But we had pretty well silenced the enemy before we drew off, and on succeeding days we did not have to endure so heavy a fire. The *Agawam* was little damaged, though hit a number of times, and our only loss was from an exploding shell on the quarterdeck which killed two men and wounded six.

In one sense the fighting was the easiest part of the work. The hard part was the life aboard the stuffy double-ender in the midst of heat and mosquitoes, striving all the while to develop a kind of efficiency suited to the tasks for which such a clumsy craft was adapted.

But if the *Agawam* were not much to look at, Commander Rhind surely fought her as if she were a battle-ship. She exemplified the spirit which our naval force had developed by the summer of 1864. We were hardened and ready for any kind of service; and the survival of the fittest, through the test of the initiative required and the hardships suffered, had brought to the front a type of man who sought responsibilities instead of waiting for them to find him out.

When Rear-Admiral David D. Porter succeeded Rear-Admiral Lee in command of the North Atlantic Squadron in September, 1864, he sent for me to become executive officer of the *Minnesota,* one of the big steam-frigates of the same class as the *Wabash* in which I had made my midshipman cruise on the Mediterranean. But I was on board the *Minnesota* less than one day. Her captain voiced the old complaint about my youth, and Porter not being of the mind to assign him an executive whom he did not want, I returned to the *Agawam.*

But Porter had kept me in mind, and later he wrote to Assistant Secretary of the Navy Fox asking him to assign me to be executive officer of the *Colorado,* of the same class as the *Wabash.* From the outset of the war, Fox had had great confidence in Porter's judgment; and so, in spite of my youth—twenty-seven—I was to have a position which is equivalent in these days to being executive of a first-class battle-ship. Instead of vegetating on the *Agawam* on river blockade duty, I was to be in both actions against Fort Fisher, for which Porter was now making his preparations.

Porter, though only a lieutenant in '61, was most influential by right of his very active mind and energetic personality. He had been partly responsible for having the then unknown Farragut given command of the Gulf Squadron, which Porter himself could not have taken because of insufficiency of rank. It was thought, however, that Porter, on account of his command of the mortar flotilla, which was a new and spectacular addition to our forces, would receive most of the distinction for the battle of New Orleans. Farragut running past the forts in the darkness with his wooden ships became the hero of the operation; though it might be said that the glory was kept in the family, as Porter and Farragut were foster-brothers. It was intended that Farragut should take command at Fort Fisher, but his health, after the wearing campaign in Southern waters which had culminated at Mobile, would not permit. He gladly relinquished the honor in favor of Porter, thus, in a way, reciprocating the favor that Porter had done him three years previously.

Chapter X.

THE BATTLE OF FORT FISHER.

We were now coming to the final act of the terrific drama of civil conflict. With the length of the Mississippi in our possession, with every port on the Gulf of Mexico flying the national flag, our forces were closing in on the last remnants of the Confederacy, which had only two ports remaining that would admit of the approach of a vessel of over twelve feet draught, Charleston in South Carolina and Wilmington in North Carolina.

Charleston was not so difficult to blockade as Wilmington. While we had some twenty vessels on the blockade off Charleston, more than thirty had usually been watching off the two entrances to Wilmington. Even then the runners would frequently slip by under cover of fog or when a gale was blowing. The Confederates fully realized the strategic importance of the position, and commanding New Inlet, at the mouth of the Cape Fear River, was Fort Fisher, which they had sought to make impregnable with all the resources at their command. Once both Charleston and Wilmington were effectually closed, then, with Sherman's army swinging in northward and Grant's approaching Richmond, the enemy was literally sealed up and must face the spring of 1865 without hope of supplies.

The plan was to silence Fort Fisher by the fire of the fleet and then to take it by assault with troops which were brought by sea under General Butler. For the purpose Porter had the largest naval force yet assembled. Including every available fighting-ship, it was even more heterogeneous than that of Farragut at New Orleans. Big frigates of the *Colorado* type, iron-clads and monitors, double-enders, gunboats, and merchant-vessels transformed into ships-of-war, and every one, according to the American custom, bristling with all the armament that it could possibly carry. The *Colorado,* which had an armament of forty smooth-bore guns before the war, now had one rifled 150-pounder, one 11-inch shell gun, and forty-six 9-inch shell guns.

Commodore H. K. Thatcher, in command of the *Colorado,* welcomed me on board heartily, notwithstanding my youth. He said that the ship was in a bad state and gave me full authority in the government of the crew of seven hundred men. My predecessor as executive officer had had a pretty wearing and unhappy time of it and was retired shortly after leaving the ship. There had been as many as a hundred men in irons chained between the guns along the gun-deck at one time. As officers passed along, the men would call out: "Look at the brass bound——," "brass bound" referring to the officer's gold braid. My predecessor was what is known as a rather erratic martinet. He was harsh, yet he did not secure discipline. I was told that one of his favorite questions to a culprit had been: "How would you like to walk through hell barefoot?" One seaman was reported to have answered: "A dozen times to get out of this!"

Most of the junior officers, as they had been on the other ships on which I had served, were volunteers. Some were highly efficient, others, who had secured their commissions through political influence, were inferior in every way to many of the men over whom they were supposed to exercise command. A portion of the crew which had been recently shipped was a motley collection of flotsam of various nationalities. We were in the period of recruiting by draft and of "bounty jumper" substitutes. While too much cannot be said in praise of the heroism and devotion of the men who enlisted for the war out of patriotic motives, there is little danger of exaggerating the toughness and worthlessness of many who came in at the close of the conflict and, in a later time, helped to swell the pension fund. One glance by a recruiting officer of to-day would have been enough to have rejected at least one-third of the crew of the *Colorado,* just on their looks.

In passing, I think that I may say that our lowest types of men to-day are not so depraved, ignorant, and generally intractable as the corresponding type of the sixties. After all, the world does grow better.

I did not mean on a ship where I was responsible for discipline to have a hundred men in chains on the gun-deck or to have them calling out abusive epithets to their superiors. If the state of insubordination on board had been responsible for Porter's desire to have me become executive of the *Colorado,* then I felt myself bound to live up to his expectations. It had been my experience that only a minority of any crew were trouble-makers. A larger proportion was all on the side of discipline and decency. But one professional tough is capable of corrupting at least two other men who are easily led. It was a case of my being master, or the rough element being master.

When I called all hands my first morning on board, not all responded. It was explained that on account of the cold weather a number of the men would not get up. Certain of the junior officers seemed afraid of some members of their own crew. I went among the hammocks, and whenever I found one occupied I tipped the man out of it; and I aimed to do this in a way that left no doubt of the business-like intentions of the new régime. The men saw that I meant to be obeyed, and afterward when I called all hands all appeared on deck.

Gradually I was able to identify the worst characters. They were the ones I had to tame, and then those who were insubordinate out of a spirit of emulation would easily fall into line. The ringleader was a giant, red-headed Englishman by the name of Webster. Many of his mates were in bodily fear of this great brute. The prison being full, I had him put down in the hold in irons.

One day I heard a breaking of glass and the orderly reported to me that Webster had broken free of his irons, had driven the sentry out of the hold, and in a blind rage was breaking up stone bottles of soda and ale which were stored there. I sent the master at arms to arrest him, and the master at arms came back to report that Webster had sworn that he would kill the first man who tried to come down the ladder into the hold.

Such a situation was not to be endured. I took my revolver and started for the hold. When I came to the ladder Webster yelled up the threat which had made the others hesitate in view of his known ferocity. Of course, any one going down the ladder would expose his whole body to an attack before his head was below the deck level and he could see his adversary. But any temporizing with the fellow meant a bad effect on the whole ship's company.

"Webster, this is the executive officer, Mr. Dewey," I called to him. "I am coming down and, Webster, you may be sure of this, if you raise a finger against me I shall kill you."

I stepped down the ladder quickly, to see Webster standing with a stone ale bottle in his hand ready to throw. But he did not throw it and submitted to arrest peaceably.

This incident and a few others, while the junior officers were developing a new spirit under Commodore Thatcher's wise support and firm direction, soon brought a change over the ship. The ruffians were cowed and we were free of the obnoxious spectacle of men in irons on the gun-deck and of abuse in answer to an officer's commands.

The Confederates had counted much on the weather to delay any bombardment on Fort Fisher. December and January are the season of the heaviest blows off the coast. While preparing for the attack the ships must lie exposed to the seas sweeping in from the open ocean. A gale rose just as the fleet was mobilizing. It dragged many anchors and pretty well dispersed the vessels, increasing the discomforts of the soldiers aboard the transports by sea-sickness.

An act of gallantry of the same order as that of Lieutenants Crosby and Caldwell in cutting through the obstructions above Forts Jackson and St. Philip was to prepare the way for the actual bombardment and assault. An old vessel, the *Louisiana,* was filled with powder and disguised as a blockade-runner, with a view to running her in close to Fort Fisher in the night and deserting her after laying time fuses to the powder. It was thought that the force of the explosion of such an enormous amount of powder would damage the fort and dismount the guns. Commander Rhind, my old captain of the *Agawam,* was in charge of the undertaking. He carried it out without being discovered by the enemy.

I recall how we who were on board the fleet at anchor some twenty-five miles from the fort waited through the night of December 23d for the explosion. Shortly before two o'clock on the next morning we saw something like distant lightning on the horizon. After a time came a dull, thundering sound, and a couple of hours later a dense cloud of smoke swept over us, such as might have come from a volcanic eruption.

The effect of the enormous charge, which was necessarily at some distance from the fort, was negligible for our purposes. This experiment was magnificent and spectacular but not helpful, as both Porter and Butler were soon to learn. Many were of the opinion that it might have been effective if the *Louisiana* had been grounded instead of having been blown up while floating free of the bottom. As it was, the shock was lost in the water and the gunners in the fort were so little disturbed that they thought the sound was that of the boiler of some blockade-runner that had blown up.

At daylight our ill-assorted fleet stood in for New Inlet, which the forts commanded. We were attempting something in the way of formation which this fleet had never tried, but which would have been child's play to a fleet of the present time. An officer who may have been with our squadron entering Manila Bay, with the ships keeping their intervals precisely, or who is used to the manoeuvres of the North Atlantic fleet at the time of writing, can hardly realize the difficulties of securing anything like precision with the utterly inharmonious elements that Porter had under his command.

As we approached the Inlet it looked for a while as if our long column would be tied in a knot. However, it straightened out with surprising regularity, thanks to the experienced officers, each of whom knew how to handle the peculiarities of his own ship. Vessel after vessel in order, if not keeping its proper distance, came into the position assigned it, without any break in Porter's plan.

Shortly before 1 P.M., the *New Ironsides,* which was at the head of the first division, opened fire; and at 1.30 the *Colorado,* second in the column of the heavy ships, or the second division, was engaged. Each vessel dropped anchor from bow and stern. Each one practically became a floating battery pouring shells into the fort. For over three hours the cannonade continued, that of the fort gradually weakening. When the flag-ship signalled at 5.30, "Prepare to retire for the night," it seemed to us that we had pretty effectually silenced Fisher. The *Colorado* had been struck a number of times, but not seriously. All the casualties in the fleet that day, with the exception of a boiler explosion on the *Mackinaw,* were due to the bursting of the 100-pounder Parrot rifled guns. These proved to be about as dangerous to us as to the enemy and were not used again.

Meanwhile, the transports had been delayed in getting up. But that night all arrived and the land attack was planned for the following day. Having found that the depth of water permitted, the *Colorado, Minnesota,* and *Wabash,* heavy-draught ships, were the next morning able to approach closer to the fort. We fired at slow intervals, as if we were at target practice, and we could see shell after shell taking effect. It seemed as if our fire must reduce these earthworks to so many sand dunes. With such a long line of ships firing and at such a long face of works; with the air in a continual thunder and screech, there was no time to observe anything except the work of your own ship and the signals from the flag-ship.

At times the *Colorado* would be the target for a number of guns, and again we would seem to have silenced the batteries facing us. But there was never a moment when our men were not doing their work steadily and without a thought on the part of any one but that we had the fire of the forts well under control. We had one rifled gun disabled, and were receiving only desultory attention from the enemy when, under signal from the flag-ship, the other ships began drawing off.

The *Minnesota* and the *Colorado* remained anchored before the forts while the rest of the fleet was passing out of range. Suddenly the batteries concentrated on us.

Our capstan was shot away; a 10-inch solid shot penetrated the starboard side, carrying away the lock and screw of No. 4 gun, killing one man and wounding five men, and carrying away the axle and starboard truck of No. 5 gun on the port side.

It was a time for quick thinking on the bridge. We had been told to discontinue action, but not to withdraw; and it was out of the question to endure that grilling fire in which we were being repeatedly hit. For an instant the alternative of slipping anchors and steaming away was considered by Commodore Thatcher, but that meant retreat without orders and possibly having our decision misconstrued, while we should be heavily pounded in the very act of retiring. We had silenced those guns that were barking at us once and we could do it again, the commodore concluded. As senior officer present he signalled the *Minnesota* to fire for her own protection, and repeated to the flag-ship the reason why we were opening fire contrary to orders. I ran along the gun-deck, where I found the men chafing in their inaction or astounded and apprehensive over the damage that was being wrought, and I kept calling:

"Fire! Fire as fast as you can! That is the way to stop their fire!"

Our gun crews obeyed with the avidity of desperation. Occupation with their work gave them no time to consider the effect of the enemy's shells, to which our guns blazed in answer with telling accuracy. The batteries found out that we were anything but disabled, and they were silent when the signal from the flag ship came, this time not to discontinue but to retire from action. These few minutes of splendid and effective gunnery developed a fine spirit in the whole ship. We steamed out of range with the satisfaction of the victor amid the cheers of the fleet.

All day we had been watching in vain for signs of the approach of the army's assaulting force over the sand dunes. When we received orders that night to proceed to our base at Beaufort we knew that Fort Fisher was not to be ours this time. Butler had decided that the fire of the fleet had not done the fort enough damage to make the assault practicable; and after all the powder we had burned he returned with his troops on board his transports.

It is not for me to go into the details of an old controversy; but the fact remains that three weeks later another assault did succeed after the defences of Fort Fisher had been considerably strengthened. The upshot was not an altogether felicitous ending of Butler's military career, and its lesson would seem to be that the thing to do when your country expects you to attack is to attack.

While Porter was continuing the blockade he sent any vessels not needed for this purpose to Beaufort for ammunition, and asked for further instructions. Their character at that stage of the war was inevitable. Gentle and patient as President Lincoln was, he had indomitable firmness on occasion. Only four days after Butler had withdrawn with his transports, Porter had a message from the secretary of the navy that Lieutenant-General Grant would send immediately "a competent force, properly commanded," to undertake the assault in which Butler had failed.

"Properly commanded" meant the choice of Major-General A. H. Terry. While we mobilized at Beaufort and waited for his coming we labored in heavy weather getting coal and ammunition on board and a second time going through the details of making ready for bombardment. We were practically at anchor in the open sea, with the breakers rolling in from thousands of miles. Some of the heavy transports rode out a gale in the company of the men-of-war. But no accident occurred and no appreciable delay in the preparations.

The fact that the Confederates had boasted of a victory after Butler's withdrawal—though they had not sunk a single vessel and had inflicted but few casualties and little damage, while our troops had not attempted an assault—aroused in both our army and navy the determination to wipe out such an impression promptly. On the 12th of January we sailed from our base at Beaufort, forty-eight-men-of-war in all, escorting the numerous army transports. That night we anchored within twelve miles of the fort. The next day we proceeded to take up our old positions. As the smaller ships were ahead, they received a vigorous fire until the heavier ships came up, when their powerful armament soon drove the Confederate gunners into their bomb-proofs. Meanwhile Terry's troops had been put ashore. This time there was no question of discretion on the part of the army commander. Fort Fisher was to be taken at any cost.

As darkness fell, the fleet was pouring out ammunition without stint. A breeze rising lifted the pall of smoke, revealing the fort clearly, lighted by the flashes of our shells. At 9 A.M. the next morning, the 14th, the signal came from the flag-ship, which meant that all was ready to carry out the plan that had been arranged between Porter and Terry. While the troops assaulted on the land side, a force of sixteen hundred sailors and marines were to assault the sea face of the fort. Every ship sent its quota. As executive officer, I should have been in command of the *Colorado's* force, but, despite my plea, Commodore Thatcher would not let me go. Being the senior officer present after Porter, if anything should happen to Porter the command of the fleet would fall to him and, in consequence, the command of the ship to me. In view of such an eventuality I was ordered to remain on board, much to my disgust.

The *Colorado's* part during the day was the same as that at the previous bombardment. We joined the other ships in pounding the batteries as hard as we could with all our guns. How terrific that bombardment was may be realized when I say that in the two days Porter's fleet discharged against Fort Fisher over eighteen thousand shells.

This time we did not have to watch in vain for signs of the assaulting force. We could see very clearly the naval detachment which had landed under the face of the fort. The seamen were to make the assault, while the marines covered their advance by musketry from the trenches which they had thrown up. For weapons the seamen had only cutlasses and revolvers, which evidently were chosen with the idea that storming the face of the strongest work in the Civil War was the same sort of operation as boarding a frigate in 1812. Such an attempt was sheer, murderous madness. But the seamen had been told to go and they went.

In face of a furious musketry fire which they had no way of answering they rushed to within fifty yards of the parapet. Three times they closed up their shattered ranks and attempted another charge, but could gain little more ground. How Flag-Captain Breeze, who was in command, leading his men and waving his sword, escaped death, is one of those marvels that almost make one accept the superstition that some men do lead a charmed life.

Our losses in the assault in officers alone were four killed and fourteen wounded, which is proof enough of how unhesitatingly they exposed themselves, following Breeze's example. The falling figures of the killed and wounded and the desperate rallies of the living were as clear as stage pantomime to their shipmates on board the fleet, who witnessed a piece of splendid folly of the same order as the charge of the Light Brigade, in which, however, it was not a case of one wild ride but of repeated attempts at the impossible. We may be proud of the heroism, if not of the wisdom, of the naval landing force's assault on Fort Fisher, which, no doubt, did serve some purpose in holding the enemy's attention while the army pressed in from the rear.

We had glimpses of the blue figures of the soldiers as they progressed in taking the outer defences, finally storming the way into the works themselves with a gallantry and precision in the face of heavy losses which would not be gainsaid. Soon after nightfall the last shot in resistance was fired from the fort. The fleet sent up rockets celebrating the victory won by an attack which must stand high in history, both for its skill and its courage. Indeed, the manner in which Major-General Terry had conducted the whole operation was significant of the efficiency of the officers and men of the veteran army which was the instrument with which Grant won peace at last.

What Appomattox was for the Federal army, Fort Fisher was for the Federal navy. Professionally the war had meant nearly four years' training for me as an executive officer. Had I had my choice of experience, it could not have been better in its training for command. I knew the business of being the responsible executive of a large crew on a big ship, with my work subject to the direction of an older head.

Soon after Fort Fisher Commodore Thatcher was relieved from the *Colorado* and promoted to acting rear-admiral to relieve Farragut in command of the Gulf Squadron. He wished me to go with him as his chief of staff, but I was only about to receive my promotion as lieutenant-commander, and the Navy Department again found my youth an obstacle. And my youth in the eyes of Captain R. H. Wyman, who took Thatcher's place, also made me inacceptable to him as executive. In six months after I left the *Colorado,* however, she had lost a hundred men by desertion. A sort of left-handed promotion took me to the *Kearsarge,* the victor over the *Alabama,* as executive, and I was on board her on that happy day for the Union cause when we dressed ship in honor of the surrender of Lee to Grant.

Recollections of a Rebel Reefer (first published in 1917) by James Morris Morgan is a typical wide-ranging old soldier's memoir of his exploits during his younger years in service to the Confederacy and beyond.

Part legitimate navy sailor, part rebel raider, his exploits are retrospectively an odd mix of Hornblower with Gone with the Wind, *prone to the typical old soldier virtues/faults of sentimentality and embellishment.*

Nonetheless, the memoir still conveys a portrait of a young man learning his way at sea against the backdrop of the War Between the States.

Excerpt from
Recollections of a Rebel Reefer

BY JAMES MORRIS MORGAN

Chapter VII.

The summer dragged its slow length into July. My brothers Gibbes and George were by this time in Virginia, one in Blanchard's brigade and the other with General 'Dick' Taylor's brigade, also in 'Stonewall' Jackson's division. Everybody, with the exception of the loud-mouthed orators, seemed to have gone to the war. The spellbinders now had only aged men and cripples for audiences, but they could always invoke a feeble cheer by dramatically exclaiming, 'One Southern man can whip ten Northerners.' This bold statement did not arouse any enthusiasm in my breast, as I doubted its correctness. I had already tackled two Yanks with rather worse than indifferent success. I had eight more coming to me for my share, and as I knew a lot of little fellows from New England, with whom I had skylarked at Annapolis, without showing myself possessed of any marked physical superiority over them individually, I felt justified in my doubts about being able to manhandle the eight combined.

At last there came a great excitement for the town, and the inhabitants, many of whom had never seen an ocean-going steamship, rushed to the riverside and there beheld the bark-rigged Confederate States sloop-of-war *M'Rae,* of seven guns, which had come up the river to receive her ammunition from the arsenal. She was a beautiful sight as she lay at anchor in the stream with her tall, graceful masts and her yards squared in man-of-war fashion, looking so trim and neat.

I went aboard as soon as possible to see the midshipmen, of course, and was most heartily welcomed. As soon as the captain and lieutenants learned that I had been at Annapolis, they too were very kind to me, agreeing with me that it was a shame I was not in the service. Before the week was ended I went on board again, and reported to Captain Thomas B. Huger for duty. How that delightful moment was brought about is best told by a letter from my father to my elder brother, which was given to me by one of my nieces fifty years afterwards:—

BATON ROUGE, L.A., *JULY* 17, 1861.

MY DEAR SON,— The mail has arrived without bringing any letter from Virginia or from you. This has disappointed me much, as Charles La Noue tells me he saw in the *True Delta* of Sunday a letter advertised for you coming from the First Regiment, Louisiana Volunteers. I presume it must have escaped your attention.

It is now nearly a month since I have heard from George and I am becoming anxious.

On yesterday Jimmie's warrant as midshipman arrived, at which he is highly delighted, especially as Captain Huger on yesterday, before the arrival of the mail, requested me to telegraph the Department that there was room for him on the *M'Rae* and that he desired to have him. The little scamp seems to take the fancy of all the officers he falls in with; those on the *M'Rae* seem to be very clever, and the midshipmen are all acquaintances of his. . . . —Ever Yours,

THOMAS GIBBES MORGAN.

HON. P. H. MORGAN,
    NEW ORLEANS, LA.

When that telegram arrived ordering me to report to Captain Huger for duty on the *M'Rae,* my joy knew no bounds, and rushing to my room it took me about ten seconds to remove those velvet covers from the brass buttons on my jacket, and in less than three minutes more I was in that uniform and had torn off the glazed cover of my cap and displayed my silver anchor. In those days all the naval officers wore the blue uniforms of the United States Navy which they had brought South with them, and they kicked like steers when they were afterwards compelled to don the grey, contemptuously demanding to know, 'Who had ever seen a grey sailor, no matter what nationality he served?'

I was in mortal dread that the *M'Rae* would sail before I could get to her (she in fact only lay there for ten days longer), but it took me only about ten minutes to get to the river, where I commenced frantically to signal for a boat. I must have been kept waiting for fifteen minutes: to me it seemed an eternity.

Reporting, I was assigned to my watch and station, and in less than an hour was sent ashore, on duty, in charge of the first cutter, and how my small heart swelled with pride and how my fellow townsmen's eyes opened with amazement as they heard 'little Jimmie Morgan' giving orders to the sailors and their every ready, 'Aye, aye, sir!' in reply.

Having got our ammunition on board, at last we started for New Orleans to fill up with coal, and then steamed for the mouths of the river, or rather to the 'Head of the Passes,' to await an opportunity to run the blockade. Captain Semmes with the *Sumter* had succeeded in doing it—why should not we? But it was not to be. The passes were much better guarded than when the *Sumter* escaped. Several times we got ready to attempt the feat at night, but on each occasion the pilots raised objections, saying that the *M'Rae* drew too much water for them to take the responsibility, or that they were not pilots for the bar of the pass selected. Strange to say, most, if not all, the pilots, were Northern men. So we spent weeks lying at the Head of the Passes, or between there and Forts Jackson and St. Philip, waiting our chance until our coal supply was exhausted and then we returned to New Orleans to refill our bunkers.

The 'Crescent City' was gay in those days, as the people had not yet realised what a serious thing war was, or what it was to live in a captured city, an experience that was to be theirs before many months had passed. There were balls and dinners ashore, and the ship was constantly filled with visitors.

In the olden times little midshipmen were punished by being 'mastheaded,' which consisted in the youngster having to climb up to the cap of the foretopmast and stand there with barely space enough for his two little feet, and he had to hold on to the stays to keep from falling. Unfortunately I was frequently detected in some deviltry, and as a consequence, passed much of my leisure time aloft. I am doubtful if I ever quite forgave our gallant second lieutenant, Mr. Eggleston, for saying to me on one occasion, after I had presented the first lieutenant's compliments and requested him to masthead me, 'Well, sir, you surely ought to know the way up there by this time!'—I always suspected that he meant to be sarcastic.

Captain Huger was a very handsome man; he was also a widower, his late wife having been a sister of General Meade, U.S.A., of Gettysburg fame. The captain was at the time of which I write engaged to one of the most beautiful girls in New Orleans, so it was not strange that when lying off the city he always found it convenient to anchor the *M'Rae* in front of Jackson Square, because the Pontalba buildings faced the park, and in one of them, near the old Cathedral of St. Louis, his sweetheart dwelt. I knew all about the courtship because I carried so many notes from the captain, and the young lady made such a pet of me.

When the month of October arrived, it brought with it some excitement. Three towboats and a river tug, each armed with a smooth-bore thirty-two pounder, had been added to the Confederate fleet on the Mississippi. There was also a tugboat, called the *Enoch Train,* belonging to private parties, who had covered her over with a wooden turtleback, over which they had placed railway iron 'T' rails, dovetailed, for an armour. The patriotic owners wanted to make a contract with the Confederate Government (for a huge sum) for every Federal vessel they would sink.

The United States fleet, consisting of the steam sloop-of-war *Richmond* of twenty-six nine-inch guns, the *Preble* and *Vincennes,* sailing sloops-of-war of twenty-two guns each, and the *Waterwitch,* a steamer carrying five guns, one of which was a rifle, had taken possession of the Head of the Passes of the Mississippi, and put an end to any possible blockade running.

Commodore Hollins had now assumed command of the naval defences of the Mississippi River. He was no longer young, having been a midshipman on the U.S. frigate *President* when she was captured by a British fleet in the War of 1812. He was also the man who had (in the U.S. sloop-of-war *Cyane*) bombarded Greytown in Nicaragua. He now determined to attempt to drive the United States fleet out of the river: and to do this he decided to seize the ram, now called the *Manassas,* which was anchored in the stream. To a polite request that she should be turned over to us came the reply that we 'did not have men enough to take her.' The *M'Rae* was ranged up alongside of her and a boat was lowered. Lieutenant Warley ordered me to accompany him. On arriving alongside of the ram we found her crew lined up on the turtleback, swearing that they would kill the first man who attempted to board her. There was a ladder reaching to the water from the top of her armour to the water-line. Lieutenant Warley, pistol in hand, ordered me to keep the men in the boat until he gave the order for them to join him. Running up the ladder, his face set in grim determination, he caused a sudden panic among the heroic crew of longshoremen, who incontinently took to their heels and like so many prairie dogs disappeared down their hole of a hatchway with Mr. Warley after them. He drove them back on deck and then drove them ashore, some of them jumping overboard and swimming for it. With the addition of two fire-rafts our fleet was now complete and we proceeded to the forts, where we anchored awaiting an opportunity to attack the enemy. This chance arrived on the night of the 12th of October, when we weighed anchor and proceeded down the river, the *Manassas,* under the command of Warley, leading, followed by the fire-rafts in tow of tugs, the *M'Rae* the *Ivy,* the *Tuscarora,* the *Calhoun,* and the *Jackson.* The *Calhoun,* a towboat, with a walking-beam engine, was considered too vulnerable in her boilers and machinery, so she was ordered to keep out of it. The *Jackson,* a high-pressure paddle-wheel towboat of great power, made so much noise from her escape pipes that she could be heard ten miles away, so she was ordered to stay as far behind as possible. It must have been about three o'clock in the morning when we saw a rocket go up, which was the signal agreed upon that the *Manassas* had rammed something. Instantly the heavy broadsides of the United States ships blazed forth as they shot holes through the darkness, or, as we hoped, through one another. Our fire-rafts also burst into flame and were floating down upon them. It was a magnificent spectacle to those of us who were a mile away.

When daylight came, all firing ceased, and to our amazement we saw the Federal fleet fleeing down the Southwest Pass, and the *Manassas* (which we had never expected to see again), lying a helpless wreck in the marsh, against which she had drifted. She had rammed the *Richmond* and torn off of that vessel's bow a couple of planks, but as the *Richmond* had a coaling schooner alongside, the speed of the ram had been checked by the hawser of the collier which was made fast to the bow of the warship. The cable had slipped over the bow of the *Manassas* and mowed off her little smokestacks even with the turtleback, rendering her helpless. The *Richmond* had frantically worked her broadside, but the ram lay so low in the water that all the projectiles passed over her. This was fortunate, as the dense smoke which filled the *Manassas* had forced her crew to take refuge on her deck. The little ram was too light for the work, and too weak in power. She had been a good tug, but the weight of her armour had completely deadened her speed, and while she did very well going downstream she could not make more than one or two knots an hour against the current.

'It is a poor cock that won't chase a fleeing rooster.' Emboldened by the sight of the retreating enemy we gave chase. On arriving at the mouth of the river the *Preble* and *Waterwitch* passed over the shallow bar safely, but the big *Richmond* and the *Vincennes* grounded, the latter with her stern pointing upstream. The *Richmond* when she struck the bottom was swung around by the current, and presented her formidable broadside to us. Outside, in the Gulf, about three miles away, was the fifty-gun sailing frigate *Santee* under a cloud of canvas, sailing back and forth like a caged lion, unable to get into the fray on account of her great draft, but she made as glorious a picture as ever delighted the eye of a sailor.

We opened fire with our nine-inch pivot gun on the *Richmond,* but from a very respectful distance, as otherwise we might have spoiled her pretty paint. She replied at first with single guns, and afterwards with broadsides, many of the projectiles passing over us. The *Waterwitch* from outside used a rifled gun, but her shots also, fortunately for us, went high.

The towboat *Ivy,* commanded by Lieutenant Fry (the man who was some years later captured in the blockade-runner *Virginius,* and so cruelly put to death by the Spaniards at Santiago, Cuba), made a dash for the helpless *Vincennes,* and, taking up a position under her stern, commenced to throw thirty-two-pound shells, from her one little smooth-bore gun, into the sloop-of-war's cabin windows. Suddenly, to our amazement, we witnessed a sight the like of which was never before seen in the United States Navy. The boats of the *Vincennes* were lowered and her crew, after putting a fuse to her magazine, abandoned her, and took refuge on the *Richmond!*

The shots from the *Richmond,* in her efforts to protect the *Vincennes'* boats, almost drowned the little *Ivy* with spray, and she was recalled.

A most extraordinary thing had occurred on the abandoned ship. Her cartridges were in red flannel bags, as was the custom at that time, and they were packed in metal cylinders about the size of barrels. One of these had been emptied and the fuse end was placed at its bottom and the powder cartridges replaced. The fuse led out of the magazine and up the hatchway on to the upper deck for some distance. It burned its way along the deck and down into the magazine, up the side of the cylinder, and down through the spaces between the cartridges to the bottom without exploding a cartridge!

Commodore Hollins, knowing that the *Richmond,* alone, could whip the Gulf of Mexico full of such vessels as he commanded, if she could only get at them, withdrew from action and proceeded up the river, taking possession of three schooners on the way which the Federal fleet had left behind them in their hurry to get away.

Arriving at the forts we anchored and I was sent up to New Orleans as a bearer of despatches. The news of the fight had preceded me, and we found a great crowd on the levee when the steamboat made her landing. For the only time in my life I experienced the delights of having myself made into a hero. When it became known to the crowd that I had been in the fight, they cheered and seemed wild with excitement, but unfortunately for our glory the enthusiasm wore off when a 'newspaper admiral' came out in an editorial denouncing Commodore Hollins, stating that his conduct was most reprehensible in that he had not brought to the city, as prizes, the whole Federal fleet. I suppose the frigate *Santee,* which drew so much water it would have required a rather large truck to have carried her over the bar, ought to have been brought also!

I had the permission of my captain to visit my home in Baton Rouge after mailing the commodore's despatches, and when I arrived there I found my father dying. I went into his room, and he made a sign that he wanted to speak to me. Bending over him, I placed my ear close to his mouth, and he whispered, 'Good-night; God bless you, my son.' Those were his last words.

Chapter VIII.

Here is a coranach for Confederate soldiers evidently written by an 'unreconstructed rebel.' It appears on a headstone in the Methodist Cemetery, St. Louis:—

> *Here lize a stranger braiv,*
> *Who died while fightin' the Suthern Confederacy to save*
> *Piece to his dust.*
> *Braive Suthern friend*
> *From iland 10*
> *You reached a Glory us end.*
> *We plase these flowrs above the stranger's hed,*
> *In honer of the shiverlus ded.*
> *Sweet spirit rest in Heven*
> *Ther'l be know Yankis there.*

When I returned to the *M'Rae,* I found great changes had occurred during my two weeks' absence. All idea of running the blockade and going to sea as a cruiser had been abandoned, and judging from my later experience in a 'commerce destroyer' it was well that the intention had been abandoned, for with her limited coal capacity, and her want of speed owing to the small power and uncertain humour of her gear engines, it is doubtful if she would have lasted a month in that business.

I now found her much changed in outward appearance. The tall and graceful spars, with the exception of the lower masts, had disappeared. With the exception of Captain Huger, Sailing Master Read ('Savez'), and Midshipman Blanc, all of the line officers, whom I loved so dearly, were detached. Lieutenant Warley was to command permanently the *Manassas*; Lieutenant Eggleston and Midshipman Marmaduke were to join the *Merrimac* at Norfolk; Lieutenant Dunnington was to command the gunboat *Ponchartrain*; Midshipman Sardine Graham Stone was to go to the cruiser *Florida*; and Midshipman Comstock was to go to the gunboat *Selma,* on board of which he was cut in two by a shell at the battle of Mobile Bay; and I was appointed aide-de-camp to Commodore Hollins, whose flag-ship the *M'Rae* was to be.

Three river steamboats had been converted into men-of-war by having their luxurious cabins removed and their boilers protected by iron rails. They each carried four guns—three forward and one aft—and there had also been built (from designs by a locomotive round-house architect, I suppose) the most wonderful contraption that ever was seen afloat called the *Livingston*. She carried six guns, three forward and three abaft the paddleboxes, and she was almost circular in shape. She was so slow that her crew facetiously complained that when she was going downstream at full speed they could not sleep on account of the noise made by the drift logs catching up with her and bumping against her stern. These boats, with the *Ivy* and the tug *Tuscarora,* constituted our fleet.

Information reached us that a number of real ironclads which the Federal Government was building at St. Louis and on the Ohio River were completed and were about to come down the river.

The Confederates hastily fortified Island Number 10, a few miles above New Madrid, Missouri, and at the latter place had built two forts (Bankhead and Thompson). Our fleet was ordered to make all haste up the river to assist them in preventing the Federal fleet from coming down.

On the way up the river our first disaster happened, when on a dark and foggy night we rammed the plantation of Mr. Jefferson Davis, President of the Confederacy. For this heroic performance, it is needless to say, none of us were promoted, and we lay ingloriously stuck in the mud until we were pulled off by a towboat. Disaster number two came when we were passing Helena, Arkansas—the *Tuscarora* caught fire and was destroyed.

Day after day, with our insufficient power and great draft, we struggled against the mighty current of the Mississippi, occasionally bumping into a mud bank and lying helpless there until we were pulled off. At the cities of Vicksburg and Memphis we received ovations. The dear people were very enthusiastic, and knowing nothing about naval warfare, they felt sure we could whip the combined fleets of the Universe.

When we finally arrived at Island Number 10, we found a lively bombardment going on. It was, however, decided that we should drop down to New Madrid to assist in the defence of that city.

The winter of 1861–62 was a very cold and bleak one in that part of the country, and for several weeks the monotony of our lives was only broken by the sound of the distant booming of the guns at Island Number 10.

The *M'Rae* had been laid alongside the river-bank at the head of the main street of the town and the muzzles of her guns were just above the levee, thus giving us the whole State of Missouri for a breastwork.

Everything seemed to be very peaceful until one day a solitary horseman made his appearance galloping at full speed. He stopped when he arrived opposite the *M'Rae,* and shouted from the shore that he wanted to see Commodore Hollins. The commodore, who was standing on the deck, asked him what he wanted, and the excited cavalier shouted back: 'I am General Jeff Thompson, the swamp fox of Missouri. There are a hundred thousand Yankees after me and they have captured one of my guns, and if you don't get out of this pretty quick they will be on board of your old steamboat in less than fifteen minutes!' Just then another man, apparently riding in a sulky, between the shafts of which was hitched a moth-eaten mule, appeared on the scene. On closer inspection it was discovered that he was sitting astride of a small brass cannon, which was mounted on a pair of buggy wheels. This piece of ordnance was scarcely three feet long. The general gazed on it admiringly, and for our information said: 'That is a one-pounder—I invented it myself. The Yanks have got its mate, and if you don't get out of this they will hammer you to pieces with it.' By this time there was great commotion in the two forts—seeing which General Jeff Thompson, nodding his head at the commodore, said, 'So long!' and galloped away. That was the last we saw of him in that campaign.

As the gallant 'swamp fox' disappeared in the distance, the gun's crew of his one-gun battery resignedly observed, 'I can't keep up with Jeff'; and brought down his thong on the mule's bony back, and the poor beast leisurely walked away.

Above New Madrid a bayou emptied itself into the river. It meandered through a swamp for miles into the interior and was supposed to be impassable by troops, but General Pope and his thirty thousand men had accomplished the feat and taken New Madrid in the rear. His army was marching boldly up to our lines, and had they kept on they would have taken the place at once; but when the *M'Rae's* big nine-inch Dahlgren gun opened on them at long range, they stopped and proceeded to lay siege to it. It was evidently intended that they would take the place by regular approaches, and the dirt commenced to fly while the artillery kept up a desultory fire.

The Confederate forts were situated at each end of the town and the flotilla of gunboats lay between them. Unfortunately the *M'Rae's* battery was the only one mounted at a sufficient height above the river-bank to fire over it while at the same time using it for a breastwork; the other boats had to lie out in the stream, where they were very much exposed to the enemy's fire.

Some three thousand raw recruits formed the garrisons and manned the trenches which connected the forts. The forts had been built with regard to commanding the river and were very weak on the land side.

Day by day the Union troops drew nearer and the firing increased in fury. Commodore Hollins sent me frequently with communications to General Bankhead, who commanded our land forces. One day, when the firing was particularly furious, I was sent with one of these missives, and found General Bankhead on the firing line. Shells were bursting frequently in unpleasant proximity to where he was standing with his field-glasses pressed to his eyes. Just behind him stood several officers. I saluted the General and handed him the envelope. He told me to wait until he could send back an answer. As I joined the group of officers I distinctly heard a major say, 'What a damned shame to send a child into a place like this!' The other officers must have noticed that my dignity was offended, for they spoke very kindly, but I could not get over the insult—it stuck in my gorge. I was so mad I could hardly speak. Returning to the ship I at once consulted my friend, the first lieutenant, who was now Mr. Read ('Savez'), on the propriety of sending the major a challenge, but 'Savez' soothed my wounded feelings by telling me that 'the commodore would not approve of such action and anyhow I need not mind what the major said, as he was nothing but a damned soldier, and a volunteer at that, and of course did not know any better.'

The enemy got to the river-bank below us and a new danger menaced us. They prevented our transports from coming up the stream. The levees were breastworks ready-made, and day after day our gunboats had to go down to clear them out. We would be drifting down the apparently peaceful river, when suddenly a row of tall cottonwood saplings would make us a graceful bow and fall into the stream as a dozen or more fieldpieces poured a galling broadside into us. Of course, with out heavy guns we would soon chase them away, but only to have them reappear a mile above or below in a little while, and then the same thing had to be gone through again. Later they brought up some heavy guns and then we had some really good tussles with them.

Our troops were forced back until they were under cover of the forts, leaving the space between, which was the abandoned town, to be protected by the guns of the *M'Rae*. I was standing by the commodore on the poop deck watching the firing when we saw a light battery enter the other end of the main street. Our nine-inch gun was trained on them, and when it was fired the shell struck the head of the column and burst in about the middle of the company. To see horses, men, and guns cavorting in the air was a most appalling sight. Flushed with success, the officer in charge of the gun reloaded and tried another shot, when the gun exploded, the muzzle falling between the ship's side and the river-bank, while one half of the great breech fell on the deck beside its carriage. The other half went away up into the air and coming down struck the rail between the commodore and myself, and cut the side of the ship, fortunately glancing out instead of inside. The commodore coolly remarked, 'Youngster, you came near getting your toes mashed!'

We had a rough little steam launch, about twenty-five feet in length, which acted as a tender to the *M'Rae,* and as our gunboats were makeshift ones, they were not provided either with signals or any place to fly them from. I used this launch to convey to them the flag-officer's orders. The commodore suspected that the enemy were fortifying the point above us, so as to cut us off from communication with Island Number 10, which was making a heroic defence and preventing the Union ironclads from coming down and annihilating our little mosquito fleet. So he sent me on a reconnaissance, cautioning me to be careful and not approach too close to the point until I was satisfied there was no battery there.

The launch had no deck and consequently her little boiler and engine were all exposed to the weather. Her crew consisted of a fireman from the *M'Rae* and a sailor to steer her. I proceeded to the point keeping well out in the stream, but saw nothing suspicious. Being of a curious turn of mind I wanted to see what was around the river bend, so kept on. As we turned the point my helmsman exclaimed, 'The *Tom Benton!*' The *Tom Benton* was the largest Union ironclad on the river and all ironclads were *Tom Bentons* to us. Sure enough, across the next bend we saw a column of black smoke, evidently issuing from the funnel of a steamer, and we turned tail and ran for the *M'Rae* with all speed possible. As we passed the point, which I had previously satisfied myself was absolutely harmless, the small cottonwood trees fell into the river and a battery opened on us, one of the shells exploding as it struck the water, drenching us. But our noble craft kept on her way, the engineer by this time having tied down the safety-valve. Arriving within hailing distance of the flag-ship, I sang out, '*Tom Benton* coming down, sir!' Commodore Hollins being on deck shouted back, 'Come aboard, sir!'—My *chief* engineer gasped out, 'For God's sake, don't stop, sir; she will blow up!' We ran around the *M'Rae* while the officer of the deck, and it seemed to me everybody else, was shouting, 'Come aboard!' The safety-valve by this time had been unlashed and she was blowing off steam, while the whirling engine was also using up as much of the surplus as possible as around and around we went, while the commodore was stamping on the deck and fairly frothing at the mouth. At last—it seemed to me an age—the engineer pronounced it safe to stop, and we went alongside the flag-ship. As I stepped on to the quarterdeck, Commodore Hollins demanded to know why I had disobeyed his instructions and gone around the point. Hesitatingly I answered, 'I thought, sir—' But I got no further, as the commodore interrupted me with, 'You thought, sir! You dared to think, sir! I will have you understand I am the only man in this fleet who is allowed to think!' I was so badly scared that probably that awful interview with the commodore was the reason I was never afterwards so thoughtless.

The Federal ironclad, not knowing our weakness, after she had run by the Island Number 10 batteries in the night, was quietly waiting at her anchors for her consorts to do likewise before attacking us.

The houses of New Madrid interfered with our fire. They were just as their owners had left them when they fled in such haste that they had not time to move their furniture or belongings, and it had up to this time seemed a pity to destroy them, but now they had been riddled by shells and were very much in the way. The commodore sent for me one night and ordered me to take a detail of men and go ashore and set fire to the town. I begged him not to send me, and told him the history of the place, and how in 1787 the King of Spain had given my great-grandfather, Colonel George Morgan, formerly of the Revolutionary Army, a grant of land comprising, according to Gayarré, in his history of Louisiana, some seventeen millions of acres, and how my ancestor had founded the city of New Madrid on it, and that it would be dreadful for me to have to destroy it. The old commodore simply remarked that it would be a singular coincidence, and that it was all the more appropriate that I should destroy my ancestor's town.

I went ashore with a number of men all provided with matches and fat-pine torches. The wind was blowing toward the river and we sneaked along in the darkness, until we arrived at the last houses in the suburbs. I then remembered that in my frequent visits to the army headquarters I had noticed a barn that was filled with straw situated some two hundred yards beyond the last house in an open field. I knew that the enemy's pickets were very near and did not like to send one of my men to set it on fire, so I gave them instructions to wait until I myself touched it off or the pickets commenced to shoot and then to set fire to everything within reach as rapidly as possible. I knew little of the effects of lights and shadows. I made my way out to the barn all right and found the straw bulging out of a window well within my reach. I struck a match and applied it to the straw with the result that a mass of flame instantly leaped many feet above the roof, and the Minié bullets commenced to sing like so many big mosquitoes around my ears. I fled toward my comrades. I don't think I ever ran so fast in my life as I did on that occasion. I was fairly flying when I felt a sting in the upper part of my left arm, and I also distinctly remembered that I exclaimed, 'Thank God, it is not in one of my legs!' The only effect of the shot was to increase my speed, if that was possible: the bullet had only grazed my arm. A line of houses was in flames by the time I rejoined my men. The wind fanned the flames and the light exposed us to the fire of the enemy, but we succeeded in reaching the ship without the loss of a man. I had undone the work of my ancestor, and I was not particularly proud of the job.

A few days after this adventure things at New Madrid came to a head. We were cut off from Island Number 10 by the ironclad, and the batteries below cut us off from communication with the lower river. We commanded only the little stretch along which our gunboats lay. Our soldiers were completely demoralised, and it was decided to evacuate New Madrid. At midnight the gunboats were brought alongside the bank, gangplanks were put out, and we had not long to wait before the terrified troops, every man for himself, rushed aboard the smaller gun-boats in the greatest disorder. They at once rushed to the side furthest from the enemy, and in doing so almost capsized the top-heavy and cranky little *Ivy.*

But it was a different thing with the *M'Rae,* where they found a sentry at the gangway who ordered them to halt. They raged and swore and openly threatened to rush the sentry, but at that moment the gentle 'Savez' Read appeared on the scene and told the men that if they came on board it would have to be in an orderly manner as soldiers, and not as a mob. At this the men commenced to threaten him, but he only asked them where their officers were, and was told that they did not care a rap where they were, but that they were coming aboard. By this time Read had gone ashore and was standing amongst them. He quietly asked them to be silent for a moment, and then inquired who was their head man. A big fellow, with much profanity, said he 'had as much to say as any other man.' Instantly Read's sabre flashed out of its scabbard and came down on the head of the mutineer, felling him to the ground, as in a thunderous voice the usually mild 'Savez' roared, 'Fall in!'—and the mob ranged themselves in line like so many lambs and were marched quietly across the gangplank and on to the ship.

We carried the frightened creatures across the river to the Tennessee side, and put them ashore at Point Pleasant, some two or three miles below New Madrid, and near Tiptonville. That was the last we saw of them.

The garrison of Island Number 10 also escaped, but some five hundred of them were afterwards captured. I mention this fact because these men composed the ten thousand prisoners General Pope telegraphed Washington that he had taken in his great victory. All the Northern newspapers published this despatch at the time and made such a hero of Pope that he was shortly afterwards placed in command of the Army of the Potomac, with what result history records. My brother-in-law, the late Brigadier-General R. C. Drum, who was adjutant-general of the United States Army for many years, told me that he had frequently seen that despatch in the archives of his office, but some years after he was retired, General Pope denied that such a paper existed and dared the newspaper reporters to pro-duce it. They were allowed to search the archives, but it was not to be found.

We lay for several days at anchor near Tiptonville, expecting every moment that the Federal ironclads would come down and attack us, but they did not put in an appearance before we left. Nevertheless, we received a very unpleasant surprise one morning while we were at breakfast when the cottonwood trees on the opposite side of the river suddenly tumbled down and a long line of guns opened fire on us. We got up our anchors as quickly as possible and went into action, with the result that our flotilla suffered considerably. The first disaster happened when a shell burst in the pantry of the *Livingston* and smashed all of Commander Pinckney's beautiful chinaware, of which he was very proud. The *General Polk* then received several shells in her hull on the water-line and was run ashore to keep her from sinking, and the other boats were cut up considerably, but running close in to the masked batteries the grape and canister from our big guns caused the enemy to limber up and disappear. Commodore Hollins said 'the campaign had taught him one thing and that was that gunboats were not fitted for chasing cavalry.'

It was at Tiptonville that Commodore Hollins received a message from the senior naval officer at New Orleans begging him to bring his gunboats as quickly as possible, as it was certain that Admiral Farragut would soon try to dash by Forts Jackson and St. Philip. No one knew the danger better than the old commodore did. Ordering his flag-ship to follow, he went on board of the fast *Ivy*, accompanied by his small aide, and we started at full speed for New Orleans.

At Fort Pillow we stopped so that the commodore could send a telegram to the Secretary of the Navy asking him to order all the gunboats to follow him. I also carried a communication to General Villapigue, the commander of Fort Pillow, telling him of the fall of Island Number 10 and New Madrid, and advising him to prepare for an attack by the enemy's ironclads. We also stopped at Baton Rouge, where I took ashore more telegrams for the Navy Department at Richmond, for the capital had been removed to that city by this time. The authorities at Richmond, like swivel-chair naval strategists all over the world, differed entirely from the naval officers as to what was best to be done with the gunboats, and never sent them any instructions at all.

Arriving at New Orleans, Commodore Hollins made his headquarters at the old St. Charles Hotel, and I was immediately sent down to the forts with a communication for General Duncan, who was in command, in which the commodore asked the general where he would like the gunboats placed for the coming fight and suggesting the head of the reach above the forts as the most effective position for them to take up.

I found on my arrival that Fort Jackson was undergoing a most terrific bombardment from Commander Porter's mortar fleet, which was hidden behind the trees around the bend below. The air was full of shells and the fort was full of smoke from their explosions.

Accompanying Commander Kennon, captain of the *Governor Moore,* we crossed the bridge over the moat which was the only means of access to the old-fashioned brick fortress. As we walked a shell fell into the moat and gave us a dirty shower bath, at the same time disturbing several large alligators who lashed the water furiously with their tails. Entering through the sally-port we saw no one but a solitary sentry, as the whole garrison was gathered in the casemates to protect them from the mortar fire. The fort was filled with débris. However, we had a very pleasant dinner with General Duncan, after which I returned to New Orleans.

I found the commodore busy with the preparations of the *Louisiana,* a most marvellous craft shaped like a huge square box. From her midship section aft she divided into two hulls and between them were placed two paddle-wheels, one large and one small, the smaller one being placed in front of the big one, so as to insure the latter's working in a mill-race when both were turning at the same time. On her sides were iron rails for an armour. At her trial trip it was found that it was with difficulty she kept up with the current when going downstream, and when pointed upstream she was carried down at the rate of two or three knots an hour. Towed back to the wharf, two engines from little tugs were placed aboard, one in each of her sterns. This increased power was not perceptible, and as she would not steer, she was towed down the river and moored to the bank where she served as an additional fort.

The other ironclad was a magnificent vessel. She had real plates for her armour and they were of great thickness. She had great power, having triple screws, and her battery was to consist of eighteen of the heaviest guns. Had she been completed in time, she would have been like a bull in a china shop among Admiral Farragut's light wooden sloops-of-war. But the great admiral knew as much about her as we did and had no intention of postponing his attack until she was finished.

Our gunboats from up the river had not arrived—they never did—but instead were run into the various tributaries of the lower Mississippi and destroyed by their own crews. I cannot say that they would have stopped Admiral Farragut's fleet, but their eighteen guns would have made it more interesting for him when he passed the forts.

All was work and hurry preparing for the great fight when one morning I went into the commodore's room, and found the old gentleman seated by his work-table holding a telegram in one hand while his head was bowed in evident distress. When he became aware of my presence he raised his head and proffering the telegram said, 'Read this.' If the message had been sent to a cabin boy it would have been sufficiently curt to have wounded his feelings. It read: 'Report in Richmond in person and give an account of your conduct'—signed, 'S. R. Mallory, Secretary of the Navy.' On arriving at Richmond a court of inquiry on his conduct was held, and as New Orleans had fallen, of course he was acquitted.

Admiral Farragut's victory is a matter of history. The *M'Rae* was in the thick of the fight. Her sides were riddled and the heavy projectiles knocked her guns off the carriages and rolled them along the deck crunching the dead and wounded. Her deck was a perfect shambles. Captain Huger was struck in the groin by a grapeshot and afterwards his temple was laid open by a canister bullet. When taken below he pleaded with Mr. Read, saying, 'Mr. Read, don't surrender my little ship. I have always promised myself that I would fight her until she was under the water!' And right gallantly did 'Savez' Read keep his word to his stricken captain, for when day broke the *M'Rae* was the only thing afloat with the Confederate flag flying. Admiral Farragut, with his flag-ship the *Hartford,* was by this time at the Quarantine Station, about four miles above the forts. Read sent the only boat he had that would float over to the *Hartford* to tell Admiral Farragut the condition of his vessel and the difficulty he was having to keep her afloat—that he did not have a gun left on a carriage, and no one to care for his dying captain or the many other wounded. Admiral Farragut asked why he did not haul his flag down and was told of the promise to the captain. Admiral Farragut then sent word to Read to bring the *M'Rae* alongside the *Hartford,* and then gave him permission to proceed to New Orleans, saying that he would tell him there what disposition he would make of the ship. When she arrived at New Orleans the *M'Rae* was leaking like a sieve; the exhausted remnant of the crew refused to continue at the pumps, and as the last wounded men were taken out of the ship—down she went.

Admiral Dewey, the admiral of the United States Navy, was a shipmate of Read's on board of the frigate *Powhatan* when the war broke out, and at the battle of New Orleans was the executive officer of the frigate *Mississippi,* which was afterwards sunk at Port Hudson. The admiral told me that Read had not acted fairly about the sinking of the *M'Rae* and escaping himself, as he had cut the sea-pipes to hasten her foundering. But the *M'Rae* did not go down with her flag flying, for just as her spanker gaff was about to disappear beneath the muddy waters of the Mississippi, a boat from one of the Federal men-of-war (already arrived opposite the city) dashed up to the sinking ship and removed the flag from its proud position at the peak.

Commodore Hollins I saw once again after the war was over—it was at Charleston, South Carolina, in 1867. This fine old gentleman and able seaman, who had commanded fleets in the United States Navy as well as in the Confederacy, and who had been the honoured guest of royalty, was then in command of a miserable little coaster trading between Baltimore and Charleston. He died a few years afterwards while holding the position of 'crier' of a minor court in Baltimore.

A like fate was the lot of many of the officers who resigned from the old navy to serve the Confederacy.

Chapter IX.

Admiral Farragut's fleet was anchored in line in front of New Orleans. He sent Captain Bailey and his flag lieutenant on shore to demand the surrender of the city. The mayor received them at the Mint, a public building situated on Esplanade Street, near the river. I saw a great crowd gather in front of the place of meeting and heard the threats made that they were going to kill the Federal officers when they came out. The mob little knew that the sailors of the fleet were standing with lanyards in hand, and that the great guns were trained on the city as well as on themselves. They were also ignorant of the fact that Admiral Farragut had sworn, if a hair on the heads of his officers was hurt, he would not leave two stones on top of each other in the city of New Orleans.

The mob, which was composed of men who had funked going to the front, seemed determined to bring destruction on themselves as well as on the innocent women and children of the place. How to get the Federal officers out of the building after the meeting and thus avoid disaster was the question which agitated the city officials when Mr. Soulé, formerly a United States Senator, and also United States Minister to Spain, came to their rescue. He was the possessor of wonderful eloquence and a hypnotic forefinger. He told the Mayor that he believed he could hold the attention of the mob while the naval officers were passed out of a back door. He appeared on the portico and was received with cheers. He raised his arm and that magic forefinger commenced to tremble and there was instant silence. I thought the finger would never stop trembling, but it was evident that as long as it did so it fascinated the crowd. I don't remember what he said, but I do recollect that he commenced his speech with the words, 'Sons of Louisiana,' when at last he broke the silence with his wonderful and sonorous voice, which had a strong French accent. Long before he had finished talking the United States officers were safely back on board of the *Hartford*. New Orleans never paid her debt to Mr. Soulé. It is appalling to think of the havoc a few hundred bushels of grapeshot scattered amongst that mob would have wrought, to say nothing of the destruction of the old city.

Leaving the Mint, Mr. Soulé proceeded to the telegraph office and wired the provost-marshal at Vicksburg to arrest the Tift brothers, the contractors who had built the formidable iron-clad *Mississippi,* charging them with treason for having destroyed that vessel and ordering them to be confined in prison. This order was carried out, although at the time Mr. Soulé occupied no office either civil or military under the Confederacy, and despite the fact that Captain St. Clair was on board of the same steamboat with the Tifts when it arrived at Vicksburg, and assured the provost-marshal that the *Mississippi* had been burned by his, St. Clair's, orders when he found it impossible to tow her up the river on account of her size, as he wished to prevent her falling into the hands of the enemy.

I had neither ambition nor desire to take a trip North or to spend an indefinite time in a Northern prison, so with all speed I hied me unto the country behind the city, where I found a train waiting on a siding, and with neither money nor ticket and without invitation. I boarded it without the least idea of where I was going—and I did not care much so long as my destination was outside of the limits of the city where I was born.

I found the train crowded with a lot of prosperous and ponderous old gentlemen who were members of the 'Home Guard,' clothed in every conceivable garb, except that of a soldier—each one of them being hampered by a musket which he did not know how to handle. They were all swearing by a multitudinous variety of strange gods that death was preferable to existence under the detested Yankee's rule. At the first stop at Manchac Pass it was noticed that their numbers perceptibly decreased, and after passing the second station there was plenty of room in the coaches and some people had even a whole seat to themselves. We arrived at Amite, where I had once been at school, and we detrained. General Lovell, who commanded the troops, had determined to make this place his headquarters and already there was quite a large camp there. The remnant of the 'Home Guard' stood the rigours of camp life for a day or two and then, deciding that the duty of a home guard was to guard his home, silently and singly, without consulting their superiors, they sneaked off to count how many railroad ties there were between Amite and their home comforts. It was afterwards said that the wretched condition of Napoleon's soldiers on the retreat from Moscow was not a circumstance to the plight in which these fat old gentlemen arrived at their comfortable mansions in New Orleans, convinced that the killing of Yankees was work fitted only for butchers.

We spent several days at Amite waiting for transportation farther north, I say 'we,' because on the train I had met Commander Pegram and a number of naval officers who were to have been attached to the ill-fated *Mississippi*. Among these officers was gallant Clarence Cary, who was to become my lifelong friend, and Frank Dawson, who was eventually to become my brother-in-law. These officers had recently made a sensational dash through the blockade in the *Nashville,* and they were now on their way to Norfolk for further orders. A waif myself, I decided to join their party.

The trains in the Confederacy were not allowed to run faster than ten miles an hour, and the particular train on which we travelled to Virginia broke down every few miles, so I doubt if we even averaged that slow speed. There were so many soldiers on the train that it was difficult to get refreshments at the various little stations, and on this journey I had my first experience in going hungry for more than twenty-four hours at a time, but as I was ill and suffering from old-fashioned chills and fever, which I had contracted on the lower Mississippi, I don't remember that I missed the food greatly.

Arriving at Norfolk I parted with my *compagnons de voyage* and went on board of the *Merrimac,* on which I knew two of my old shipmates on the *M'Rae* were serving—Lieutenant Eggleston and Midshipman Marmaduke. It was only recently that the *Merrimac* had been engaged in her great fights in Hampton Roads. I gazed with admiration on the shot-holes in her armour and felt sure that she could whip anything afloat, and I believe her officers and crew thought so too. I little dreamed that before many hours she was to be ingloriously destroyed by her own crew on account of her drawing too much water to go up the James River.

Mr. Eggleston advised me to go at once and report to Captain Sidney Smith Lee, the elder brother of General Robert E. Lee, who was in command of the naval station, and ask him for orders. As I passed through the streets on my way I saw many batteries of artillery and regiments of infantry hurrying in one direction and accompanied by trains of wagons. When I came into the presence of Captain Lee, before I had a chance to say a word, he demanded to know what I was doing there. When I told him that I was a fugitive from New Orleans, his whole manner changed and he said, 'You appear to be ill, sir.' I replied, 'Chills and fever, sir.' And the next moment he said, 'You must leave here at once; this place is being evacuated!' I asked him where I should go, and he replied, 'Any place so that you get out of here.' And then turning to a clerk he told him to make out an order for transportation for me to Richmond.

On my way to and at the station, I saw many queer sights. There were orderly commands marching out of the place, and disorganised mobs of men in uniform who were free from all restraint and discipline. At one place a gang of men were trying to put a heavy piece of artillery on a light spring wagon drawn by one horse! I don't think they succeeded in doing it, but I did not wait to see the result of their labours. At the station there was a crowd of civilians, and piles of household goods; also many pretty and jolly girls, who seemed to regard the matter as a picnic devised to amuse them. Government mules were being driven by in droves, scattering the crowd in every direction. There were crates containing pigs and chickens blocking the way, and everything seemed to be in inconceivable confusion—infantrymen with arms, and infants in arms, jostling each other. One poor old stout woman carrying her baby was anxiously searching for her baggage, and only found somebody else's lost four-year-old boy who clung to her skirts with such a grip that she could not shake him off. Everybody was in a hurry to get to some place, but few seemed to know what the name of the place was.

After a most uncomfortable journey I arrived in Richmond. I had noticed in Norfolk that people looked at me askance, if not with real enmity expressed in their glances in my direction, but that was nothing in comparison to the gruff way I was treated in Richmond if I dared ask a stranger to direct me on my way. It did not take me long to find out the cause—it was my blue uniform with the United States naval buttons. The grey uniform for naval officers had not reached New Orleans before its fall, but the blue was an unusual sight in Richmond except when it was worn by a Union soldier who was a prisoner. I was told that but for my youth and small stature I might have been roughly handled. However, I soon got rid of the hated blue, as I had a little money due me and had the good fortune to meet Paymaster Semple, a son-in-law of ex-President Tyler, with whom I had been shipmates for a time on board of the *M'Rae*. He advanced me on my pay and I was soon arrayed in grey like the rest.

I was a very lonely little boy in Richmond for a few days. Louisiana was farther away in those days than it is in these of fast express trains, and somehow I was made to feel as though I was a foreigner. I suppose that was on account of our accent being different from that of other Southerners. It was only a few years ago in Washington when I was introduced to a Southern lady, my only recommendation being that I was a Confederate veteran, that she looked at me doubtfully and said, 'Mr. Morgan, I can't believe that you are a Southerner; you neither look nor talk like any Southerner I ever met before.' I replied, 'Madam, I can assure you that had I been born any farther south than I was, I would have had to come into this world either as a pompino or a soft-shell crab, for the hard ground stops where I was born in the southern part of Louisiana!'

When I received my orders they were to the naval battery at Drewry's Bluff, seven miles below Richmond on the James River—a place of great natural strength. Pits were dug, wooden platforms were built at the bottom of them, and the guns were mounted on navy carriages with all their blocks and tackle such as were used on board of the men-of-war of that day. It was manned by sailors principally from the gallant crew of the *Merrimac*. The river had been barricaded by sinking in the channel the ocean-going steamship *Jamestown* and several gunboats, besides crates made of logs and filled with stone, leaving only a narrow passageway for our own boats. It was while there that I witnessed a most magnificent exhibition of coolness and nerve—Commander John Rodgers, U.S.N., had been ordered to test the new ironclad under his command to find out whether she was shot-proof or not. Her name was the *Galena*.

It was about eight o'clock on the morning of the 16th of May 1862, that we saw a squadron consisting of the *Galena,* the original *Monitor* (the one that fought the *Merrimac*), the iron-clad *Naugatuck,* and two wooden gunboats coming up the river, and our drums beat to quarters while we rushed to our stations at the guns. Neither Commander Farrand, who commanded at Drewry's Bluff, nor Commander Rodgers, who commanded the Federal squadron, seemed in any hurry to open fire, so we in the battery waited patiently at our silent guns while the *Galena* came up to within four hundred yards of us accompanied by the *Monitor,* the rest of the squadron remaining below the bend seeking its protection from our plunging fire. The *Monitor* also dropped below, as her flat decks made her particularly vulnerable. The *Galena* quietly and peacefully, as though no enemy was within miles of her, let go her anchor. She then got out a hawser, which sailors call a 'spring,' and made it fast to her anchor chain. Paying out her cable she swung across the stream which brought her broadside to bear on us. Down the river-bank, hidden by the bushes, were two or three thousand Confederate infantry men.

Commander Rodgers was most leisurely in his movements. At last he fired a shot to get our range; there were no range-finders in those days, and it could only be found by experiment. That gun was the signal for the fun to commence. It was not necessary for us to find the range, as from our great height we had only to fire down on him; our guns were depressed to such an extent that we had to put grommets of rope over our round projectiles to keep them from rolling out of the muzzles. The shot from the *Galena* was our signal to open fire, and for three hours we were at it hammer and tongs. The *Galena* was perforated twenty-two times without counting the shots which struck her without going through her armour. The riflemen on the river-bank fairly rained bullets at her portholes, one of which became jammed, and when a sailor put his arm outside in an attempt to free it, the limb fell into the river amputated by musket balls. The wooden gunboats around the bend also suffered the loss of several men.

Although we were supposed to be safe in our covered gun-pits perched so high on the bluff, all had not been cakes and ale with us. Several men had been killed and wounded; among them my classmate at Annapolis, Midshipman Carroll, of Maryland, had been literally cut in two by a shell.

When Commander Rodgers had satisfied himself that the *Galena* was not shot-proof, he weighed his anchor as deliberately as though he was about to leave a friendly port, and dropped slowly and in a most dignified way down the river. He had lost many men in killed and wounded. Commander Rodgers, in his report to the Secretary of the Navy, says: 'The result of our experiment with the *Galena* I enclose. We demonstrated that she is not shot-proof; balls came through and many men were killed with fragments of her own iron. . . . The *Galena* should be repaired before sending her to sea.'

Sailors are a generous lot and admire gallantry whether shown by friend or foe, and the men in the gun-pits at Drewry's Bluff gave hearty cheers for the *Galena* as she drew out of action.

Historians seem to be ignorant concerning the importance of this fight. At the time there was nothing between Richmond and the Federal squadron but the guns of Drewry's Bluff. A passage had purposely been left through the obstructions in the river for our own boats, and it was sufficiently wide and deep for the Federal vessels to have passed through. M'Clellan's army was within a few miles of the capital, and if Commander Rodgers's squadron had not been stopped by the naval battery there was nothing else to prevent them from going on to Richmond.

General Joe Johnston's army was now at Richmond, and I obtained a short leave to go to the city to see my brother George, who was now a captain and acting quartermaster in Blanchard's Louisiana brigade. I accompanied him to the front and found many friends among the Louisiana boys. There was with the brigade a light battery, in which there were many young men from Baton Rouge, and one day, while a number of us were sitting at the foot of a large tree, in fancied security, and watching a captive balloon belonging to the enemy, bullets began to rattle against the trunk of the tree, and we got away from there as rapidly as possible. Horses were rapidly hitched to the caissons, the guns were limbered up, and the battery dashed off to another part of the field. The picket firing by that time had increased until it had become a constant rattle, sounding somewhat like the roll of hundreds of snare-drums.

Blanchard's brigade was in Huger's division on the extreme right of our army. I made my way to the camp of the First Louisiana, which I found under arms. Their part in the battle of Seven Pines, or Fair Oaks, as the Federals called it, had begun. The regiment advanced and I followed on behind, until suddenly I saw an officer riding up to where General Blanchard and his staff were seated on their horses. Before he reached them his horse suddenly reared and in that instant I recognised my brother. The horse fell dead, and when I came up I found he was lying on one of George's legs and that George could not extricate himself. It was a big undertaking for me, but I managed to move the fore-shoulder of that horse far enough to free my brother. He was quite severely hurt and had to be removed to the rear. That was all I saw of the battle of Seven Pines. Could I have seen what was going on on the other side, I should have beheld my dear cousin, Colonel

A. S. M. Morgan, being borne off the field—shot through both hips, while gallantly leading his regiment, the Second Pennsylvania.

I accompanied my brother to Richmond, where he was carried to the most fashionable hostelry in the city, the old Spotswood Hotel, and I remained there for several days with him. The doors of the bedrooms on the corridors were mostly kept open, and it seemed to me that a game of poker was going on in every room. The lobby of the hotel was crowded with officers, most of whom carried an arm in a sling. The cause of this was the wearing of the flaring gold chevrons on their sleeves to indicate their rank. They made beautiful targets for the sharpshooters; but not for long, as later in the war even generals only wore three small stars on their coat-collars.

Passing through the lobby one morning I met an old acquaintance, a Louisiana Zouave, dressed in red Turkish trousers with a short blue jacket elaborately trimmed with yellow braid—of course he too had an arm in a sling. He stopped me and asked if I had seen the 'zoozoo' fight—he was very enthusiastic and very excitable. 'Oh!' said he, in broken English, 'you ought to seeze zoozee fight. Colonel Copin he draw his long sabre and say, "Charge!" We charge and we charge right on top ze Yankee breastwork; Yankee drop down and say "Quatta!" "quatta!" I say, "No quatta fer Bootla" [Butler]: I stick he wid de bayonette!' Those Acadians imagined that they were only engaged in a holy crusade against the tyrant of New Orleans.

My brother George thought that a little trip to the hills would benefit my health, and as he had heard that 'Stonewall' Jackson's division was at Gordonsville, he furnished me with the means to go there, where I would be with my brother Gibbes, then a captain in the Seventh Louisiana Regiment. I found him flushed with victory, having just returned from the marvellous Shenandoah Valley campaign in which Jackson had fought so many battles in so few weeks, and he seemed very proud to belong to Jackson's 'foot cavalry.' To my great delight I found my brother's young and beautiful wife with him. It was no uncommon thing at that time for the wives of officers to follow their husbands so as to be near the battlefields. Unfortunately for me, my pleasure at being with my favourite brother and his wife was of short duration, as in a few hours after my arrival in Gordonsville, Jackson's 'foot cavalry' moved on, and I returned to Richmond.

On my arrival in Richmond I saw several thousand Union prisoners, guarded by Confederates, seated on the ground, resting themselves. Few if any of them could speak English, and the most accomplished linguists among them could only say, 'I fights mit Sigel.'

At Drewry's Bluff we lived in tents and were very comfortable. Parties composed of ladies and gentlemen would frequently visit the Bluff and they made it quite gay; besides, by this time, quite a large number of midshipmen were stationed there, and they made it lively for their superior officers as well as for themselves. I had while there an interesting experience in steering the boat from which Commander Matthew F. Maury buoyed the places in the river where he afterwards had placed what were probably the first floating mines used in war. We called them 'spar torpedoes,' as the mines were attached to an anchored and floating spar.

I shall never forget a very unpleasant hour in connection with these mines. Colonel Page, a former officer of the Navy, who looked to be about seven feet high, wanted to go from Drewry's Bluff to Chapin's Bluff, a fortification which he commanded, on the opposite side of the river and about a mile below. I was ordered to take charge of the boat that was to take him to his post, because it was supposed I knew where the mines were. It was a dark night, but we got on all right for some distance. Suddenly the side of the boat grated against something and the boat slightly careened. Colonel Page, whose sobriquet in the navy was 'Ramrod' on account of his erect bearing, and who was well known in the service as a very strict disciplinarian, exclaimed, 'What is that?—I thought you knew where the torpedoes were.' 'Yes, sir,' I replied, 'that is one of them.' There was silence in the boat until we reached the little wharf at Chapin's Bluff, and when Colonel Page disembarked he expressed his opinion of me and my professional accomplishments in language which left nothing for the imagination to work on. Had the boat been a little heavier we should all have gone to heaven by the most direct route.

––––––––––

'Stonewall' Jackson's army came down from the Valley and joined General Lee. I went over to the camp of the Seventh Louisiana to see my brother Gibbes, and while I did not participate in any of the battles of the 'Seven Days,' I saw some of the fighting. One day M'Clellan sent an ammunition train, with a fuse attached to it, down the railroad tracks—of course it was running 'wild.' Jackson's division, thinking that it carried reinforcements, rushed for the railroad intending to fire into it as it passed, but while they were some distance away the train exploded destroying many windows in Richmond, several miles away. For two or three days after the explosion a negro boy who waited on my brother and the officers of his company was not to be found. This boy had always bragged that in action he was to the front, and continually boasted about the number of Yankees he had killed. When he finally turned up and was asked the meaning of his long absence, he replied: 'Mass Gibbes, I stood their shot and shell and bullets, but when it came to shootin' a whole train of cars at one poor nigger I tell you de truf, sah, I done lit out right dar and den!'

At this time I had been detached from Drewry's Bluff and was on board of the gunboat *Beaufort,* a small river tug about forty feet long and carrying one small gun on her forecastle; her complement consisted of two officers and eight men— she was crowded. This little boat had covered herself all over with glory when the *Merrimac* sank the frigates *Congress* and *Cumberland.* The *Beaufort* was then commanded by Lieutenant William H. Parker, and it was to the *Beaufort* that the *Congress* surrendered. She was now commanded by Lieutenant Sharp, who had many other duties to attend to at the ordnance works and elsewhere, so that he was very little on board his ship.

We were lying alongside the river-bank at Rockett's (the lower end of Richmond) one day, when my brother Gibbes made me a visit. We were cozily chatting about home when a quartermaster poked his head in at the little cabin door and, saluting, said, 'Jurgenson has come aboard, sir.' I replied, 'Very good, quartermaster.' The man then said, 'Jurgenson is drunk and noisy, sir.' I said, 'Tell Jurgenson to turn into his bunk and keep quiet.' There was an awful din going on forward and the quartermaster came back and reported that the man would not keep quiet. 'All right,' I said, 'tell the master-at-arms to put him in double irons and gag and buck him unless he stops his racket.' The quartermaster saluted and again withdrew. Gibbes looked at me with amazement and asked me if it was possible that a little boy like myself had authority to order such severe punishment. I told him that I was not a little boy on that boat, but for the moment I was her commanding officer. He then expressed doubts as to whether the master-at-arms would obey the order and wanted me to go outside with him and see. I declined, on the ground that it might look as though I doubted if my orders would be carried out, and Gibbes went forward to see for himself. He came back shortly shaking his head and said that he must return to his command, as he wanted to tell the boys what he had seen that day. I tried to make him understand that I had not indulged in any cruelty on my own part, but that in the navy every misdemeanour had its punishment set forth in the Regulations and that I was liable to punishment myself if I did not carry out the orders. I told him that Jurgenson was an old man-of-warsman, and knew as well if not better than I what was going to happen if he did not obey the order to keep silence and behave himself. I could not make Gibbes believe that I was very fond of old Jurgenson; that he was one of the best men in the ship, and that he would have lost all respect for me if I had not carried out the discipline of the service; that I was going to have the gag taken out of his mouth as soon as he stopped yelling. It was all of no avail, my gallant volunteer brother left, still shaking his head and repeating, 'I must go back and tell my boys what I have seen this day.' That was the last time I ever saw my brother.

Chapter X.

With all my State pride, I must acknowledge that the article of chills and fever handed to me on the James River was superior to the brand on the lower Mississippi, and, complicated by chronic dysentery, so sapped my strength that the doctor ordered me to show myself at the Navy Department and ask for orders to some other station. Commodore French Forrest was chief of the Bureau of 'Orders and Detail,' and I really thought he had some sympathy for my condition when he looked me over. He asked me where I would like to be ordered to, and I quickly said that I would be delighted if I was sent to the naval battery at Port Hudson. The commodore then asked if I had relatives near there, and on my assuring him that my mother and sisters were refugees and were staying at the plantation of General Carter, only a few miles distant, he turned to a clerk and said, 'Make out an order for Midshipman Morgan to report to Commodore Ingraham at Charleston, South Carolina. I don't believe in having young officers tied to their mothers' apron strings.' And so to Charleston I went.

Commodore Ingraham, to whom I reported, was the man who some years previously, when in command of the little sloop-of-war *St. Louis* in the port of Smyrna, had bluffed an Austrian frigate and compelled her to surrender Martin Koszta, a naturalised American citizen, whom they held as a prisoner. This act made Ingraham the idol of the people at that time; if repeated in this day (1916), it would cost an officer his commission. Commodore Ingraham also commanded the Confederate gunboats when they drove the Federal blockading fleet away from Charleston.

I was assigned to the *Chicora,* a little ironclad that was being built between two wharves which served as a navy yard. She was not nearly completed, so I was forced to hunt for quarters on shore. Being directed to a miserable boarding-house which was fourth-rate, and consequently supposed to be cheap, I found that the cheapest board to be had was at the rate of forty-five dollars a month, so I did not see exactly how I could manage it, as my shore pay was only forty. However, the generous hotel proprietor, when the situation was explained, consented to let me stay for that sum on condition that I would make up the other five dollars if my friends at home sent me any money. The man was certainly taking a long chance for that extra five dollars. Where were my friends, and where was my home?

Lieutenant Warley, with whom I had served on the *M'Rae,* was the only living human being I knew in Charleston, and the great difference in our rank, as well as age, precluded the possibility of my making a companion of him; so, a lonely boy, I roamed the streets of the quaint old city. Evidently the war as yet had had no effect on the style kept up by the old blue-bloods, for I was amazed to see handsome equipages, with coachmen in livery on the box, driving through the town. Little did their owners dream that before very long those same fine horses would be hauling artillery and commissary wagons, and those proud liveried servants would be at work with pick and spade throwing up breastworks!

To my great delight, George Hollins, a son of my dearly loved old commodore, a boy of about my own age with whom I had been shipmate on the Mississippi River, arrived in town, and the boarding-house man consented to allow him to share my little room at the same rate charged me. George had been in Charleston only a few days when yellow fever became epidemic. It was the latter part of August and the heat was something fearful. I had no fear of the fever, as I had been accustomed to its frequent visits to my old home, but with Hollins, a native of Baltimore, it was different.

One afternoon he came into our room and complained of a headache and a pain in his back. The symptoms were familiar to me, so I persuaded him to go to bed and covered him with the dirty rag of a blanket. I then went quickly downstairs and asked the wife of the proprietor to let me have some hot water for a footbath and also to give me a little mustard. The woman was shocked at my presumption, but consented to give me the hot water; at parting with the mustard she demurred. As I was about to leave her kitchen she demanded to know what I wanted with hot water, and when I told her that my friend had the yellow fever, there was a scene in which she accused me of trying to ruin the reputation of the house and threatened me with dire punishment from her husband.

I made Hollins put his feet in the hot water and then I went to a near-by druggist, telling him the situation, and asking him if he would credit me for the mustard, explaining that neither Hollins nor myself had any money. The kindly apothecary gave me the mustard and told me I could have any medicines needed, and also advised me to go at once and see Dr. Leby, who, he was sure, would attend to the case without charge. The doctor came and did all that was possible. Poor George grew rapidly worse; he seemed to cling to me as his only friend, and could not bear to have me leave him for an instant. We slept that night huddled up together in the narrow bed.

The next morning a strange negro man, very well dressed, and carrying a bunch of flowers in one hand and a bundle in the other, entered the room and proceeded to make himself very much at home. When asked what his business was, he said he was a yellow-fever nurse. I told him that we had no money and could not pay a nurse, at which he burst into a broad grin and said that he did not want any money; that he belonged to Mr. Trenholm who had sent him there. Throughout the day all sort of delicacies continued to arrive, and to every inquiry as to whom they came from, the reply was, 'Mr. Trenholm.'

The second night of his illness George was taken with the black vomit, which, as I held him in my arms, saturated my clothes. A shiver passed through his frame and without a word he passed away. Leaving my friend's body in charge of the nurse I went in search of Lieutenant Warley, and he told me not to worry about his funeral, as Mr. Trenholm would make all the arrangements. This Mr. Trenholm, unknown to me, seemed to be my providence, as well as being all-powerful. George Hollins was buried in the beautiful Magnolia Cemetery and immediately after the funeral Mr. Warley told me that I was not to go back to the boarding-house, but was for the present to share his room at the Mills House, a fashionable hotel.

A few days after the funeral I was walking down Broad Street with Mr. War-ley, and we saw coming toward us a tall and very handsome man with silvery hair. Mr. Warley told me that he was Mr. Trenholm, and that I must thank him for all his kindness to my friend. Mr. Trenholm said that he was only sorry that he could not have done more for the poor boy, and, turning to the lieutenant, said: 'Warley, can't you let this young gentleman come and stay at my house? There are some young people there, and we will try and make it pleasant for him.'

I thanked Mr. Trenholm and told him that I had recently been sleeping in the same bed with my friend, who had died of the most virulent form of yellow fever, and of course I could not go into anybody's house for some time to come; but the generous gentleman assured me that his family had no fears of the fever and insisted on my accepting his kind invitation. However, I did not think it right to go, and did not accept at that time; a day or two afterwards, however, I again met him with Mr. Warley, and he said, 'Warley, I am sorry this young gentleman won't accept my invitation: we would try to make it pleasant for him.' Mr. Warley turned to me, saying, 'Youngster, you pack your bag and go up to Mr. Trenholm's house.'

That settled it and I went, arriving at the great mansion shortly before the din-ner hour. I did not, however, take a bag with me. If I had owned one, I would not have had anything to put in it.

I will not attempt to describe Mr. Trenholm's beautiful home. For more than half a century now it has been pointed out to tourists as one of the show places of Charleston, and has long since passed into the hands of strangers. I must confess that as I opened the iron gate and walked through the well-kept grounds to the front door I was a little awed by the imposing building, with its great columns supporting the portico. I could not but feel some misgivings as to the reception I would get, stranger as I was, from the family whom I had never met. Still, I did not dare run away, and so I timidly rang the bell. A slave, much better dressed than myself, and with the manners of a Chesterfield, appeared and showed me into the parlour; it was all very grand, but very lonely, as there was no one there to receive me. I took a seat and made myself comfortable; it had been a long time since I had sat on a luxurious sofa. In a few minutes two young ladies entered the room. Of course I had never seen either of them before, but the idea instantly flashed through my mind that I was going to marry the taller of the two, who advanced toward me and introduced herself as 'Miss Trenholm.'

Soon there arrived a Frenchman, a Colonel Le Mat, the inventor of the 'grapeshot revolver,' a horrible contraption, the cylinder of which revolved around a section of a gun barrel. The cylinder contained ten bullets, and the grapeshot barrel was loaded with buckshot which, when fired, would almost tear the arm off a man with its recoil. Le Mat's English vocabulary was limited, and his only subject of conversation was his invention, so he used me to explain to the young ladies how the infernal machine worked. Now that sounds all very easy, but one must remember that Le Mat was a highly imaginative Gaul and insisted on posing me to illustrate his lecture. This was embarrassing—especially as he considered it polite to begin all over again as each new guest entered the room. At last relief came when Mr. Trenholm came in with a beautiful lady, well past middle age, leaning on his arm; and I was introduced to my hostess, whose kind face and gentle manner put me at my ease at once.

Oh, but it was a good dinner I sat down to that day! After all these years the taste of the good things linger in my memory and I can almost smell the 'aurora,' as Boatswain Miller used to call the aroma, of the wonderful old Madeira. It was in the month of September and the weather was intensely hot; I had my heavy cloth uniform coat buttoned closely, and only the rim of my paper collar showed above. Dinner over, we assembled in the drawing-room, where we were enjoying music, when suddenly I found myself in a most embarrassing position. Dear, kind Mrs. Trenholm was the cause of it. Despite my protestations that naval officers were never allowed to open their uniform coats, she insisted, as it was so warm, that I should unbutton mine and be comfortable. Unbutton that coat! Never! I would have died first. I had no shirt under that coat; I did not own one.

When bedtime arrived, Mr. Trenholm escorted me to a handsomely furnished room. What a sleep I had that night between those snow-white sheets, and what a surprise there was in the morning when I opened my eyes and saw a manservant putting studs and cuff-buttons in a clean white shirt. On a chair lay a newly pressed suit of civilian togs. I assured the man that he had made a mistake, but he told me he had orders from his mistress and that all those things and the contents of a trunk he had brought into the room were for me, adding that they had belonged to his young 'Mass' Alfred,' a boy of about my own age, whose health had broken down in the army and who had been sent abroad. I wanted the servant to leave the room so I could rise. I was too modest to get out of bed in his presence and too diffident to ask him to leave; but at last reflected that everybody must know that I had no shirt, so I jumped up and tumbled into a bath, and when the 'body-servant' had arrayed me in those fine clothes I hardly knew myself.

After breakfast two horses were brought to the front of the house, one, with a lady's saddle, was called Gypsy and was one of the most beautiful Arabs I ever saw (and I have seen many); the other, a grand chestnut, called Jonce Hooper, one of the most famous racehorses on the Southern turf when the war commenced. He had been bought by Colonel William Trenholm, my host's eldest son, for a charger, but Colonel Trenholm soon found that the pampered racer was too delicate for rough field work in time of war. Miss Trenholm and I mounted these superb animals, and that morning and many mornings afterwards we went for long rides. In the afternoons I would accompany the young ladies in a landau drawn by a superb pair of bays with two men on the box. Just at that time the life of a Confederate midshipman did not seem to be one of great hardship to me; but my life of ease and luxury was fast drawing to an end.

In the evenings the family and their friends used to sit on the big porch where tea, cakes, and icecream were served, and the gentlemen could smoke if they felt so inclined. One day the distinguished Commodore Matthew F. Maury, who was on his way to Europe to fit out Confederate cruisers, dined at the house and after dinner, with Mr. Trenholm, had joined the gay party on the piazza. Mr. Trenholm was the head of the firm of Fraser, Trenholm and Co., of Liverpool and Charleston, financial agents of the Confederate Government. Suddenly Mr. Trenholm came over to where I was laughing and talking with a group of young people, and asked me if I would like to go abroad and join a cruiser. I told him that nothing would delight me more, but that those details were for officers who had distinguished themselves, or who had influence, and that as I had not done the one thing and did not possess the other requisite, I could stand no possible chance of being ordered to go. Mr. Trenholm said that was not the question; he wanted to know if I really wished to go. On being assured that I would give anything to have the chance, he returned to Commodore Maury and resumed his conversation about the peculiarities of the 'Gulf Stream.'

Imagine my surprise the next morning when, after returning from riding, I was handed a telegram, the contents of which read: 'Report to Commodore M. F.

Maury for duty abroad. Mr. Trenholm will arrange for your passage'; signed, 'S. R. Mallory, Secretary of the Navy.' It fairly took my breath away!

Chapter XI.

Mr. Trenholm owned many blockade-runners—one of them, the little light-craft steamer *Herald,* was lying in Charleston Harbour loaded with cotton and all ready to make an attempt to run through the blockading fleet. Commodore Maury, accompanied by his little son, a boy of twelve years of age, and myself, whom he had designated as his aide-de-camp for the voyage, went on board after bidding good-bye to our kind friends. About ten o'clock at night we got under way and steamed slowly down the harbour, and headed for the sea. The moon was about half full, but heavy clouds coming in from the ocean obscured it. We passed between the great lowering forts of Moultrie and Sumter and were soon on the bar, when suddenly there was a rift in the clouds, through which the moon shone brightly, and there, right ahead of us, we plainly saw a big sloop-of-war!

There was no use trying to hide. She also had seen us, and the order, 'Hard-a-starboard!' which rang out on our boat was nearly drowned by the roar of the war-ship's great guns. The friendly clouds closed again and obscured the moon, and we rushed back to the protecting guns of the forts without having had our paint scratched. Two or three more days were passed delightfully in Charleston; then there came a drizzling rain, and on the night of the 9th of October 1862 we made another attempt to get through the blockade. All lights were out except the one in the covered binnacle protecting the compass. Not a word was spoken save by the pilot, who gave his orders to the man at the wheel in whispers. Captain Coxetter, who commanded the *Herald,* had previously commanded the privateer *Jeff Davis,* and had no desire to be taken prisoner, as he had been proclaimed by the Federal Government to be a pirate and he was doubtful about the treatment he would receive if he fell into the enemy's hands. He was convinced that the great danger in running the blockade was in his own engine-room, so he seated himself on the ladder leading down to it and politely informed the engineer that if the engine stopped before he was clear of the fleet, he, the engineer, would be a dead man. As Coxetter held in his hand a Colt's revolver, this sounded like no idle threat. Presently I heard the whispered word passed along the deck that we were on the bar. This information was immediately followed by a series of bumps as the little ship rose on the seas, which were quite high, and then plunging downward, hit the bottom, causing her to ring like an old tin pan. However, we safely bumped our way across the shallows, and, plunging and tossing in the gale, this little cockleshell, whose rail was scarcely five feet above the sea level, bucked her way toward Bermuda. She was about as much under the water as she was on top of it for most of the voyage.

Bermuda is only six hundred miles from Charleston; a fast ship could do the distance easily in forty-eight hours, but the *Herald* was slow: six or seven knots was her ordinary speed in good weather and eight when she was pushed. She had tumbled about in the sea so much that she had put one of her engines out of commission and it had to be disconnected. We were thus compelled to limp along with one, which of course greatly reduced her speed. On the fifth day the weather moderated and we sighted two schooners. To our surprise Captain Coxetter headed for them and, hailing one, asked for their latitude and longitude. The schooner gave the information, adding that she navigated with a 'blue pigeon' (a deep-sea lead), which of course was very reassuring. We limped away and went on groping for Bermuda. Captain Coxetter had spent his life in the coasting trade between Charleston and the Florida ports, and even when he commanded for a few months the privateer *Jeff Davis,* he had never been far away from the land. Such was the jealousy, however, of merchant sailors toward officers of the navy that, with one of the most celebrated navigators in the world on board his ship, he had not as yet confided to anybody the fact that he was lost.

On the sixth day, however, he told Commodore Maury that something terrible must have happened, as he had sailed his ship directly over the spot where the Bermuda Islands ought to be! Commodore Maury told him that he could do nothing for him before ten o'clock that night, and advised him to slow down. At ten o'clock the great scientist and geographer went on deck and took observations, at times lying flat on his back, sextant in hand, as he made measurements of the stars. When he had finished his calculations he gave the captain a course and told him that by steering it at a certain speed he would sight the light at Port Hamilton by two o'clock in the morning. No one turned into his bunk that night except the commodore and his little son; the rest of us were too anxious. Two o'clock bells struck and no light was in sight. Five minutes more passed and still not a sign of it; then grumbling commenced, and the passengers generally agreed with the man who expressed the opinion that there was too much d——d science on board and that we should all be on our way to Fort Lafayette in New York Harbour as soon as day broke. At ten minutes past two the masthead lookout sang out, 'Light ho!'—and the learned old commodore's reputation as a navigator was saved.

We ran around the islands and entered the picturesque harbour of St. George shortly after daylight. There were eight or ten other blockade-runners lying in the harbour, and their captains and mates lived at the same little white-washed hotel where the commodore and I stopped, which gave us an opportunity of seeing something of their manner of life when on shore. Their business was risky and the penalty of being caught was severe; they were a reckless lot, and believed in eating, drinking, and being merry, for fear that they would die on the morrow and might miss something. Their orgies reminded me of the stories of the way the pirates in the West Indies spent their time when in their secret havens. The men who commanded many of these blockade-runners had probably never before in their lives received more than fifty to seventy-five dollars a month for their services; now they received ten thousand dollars in gold for a round trip, besides being allowed cargo space to take into the Confederacy, for their own account, goods which could be sold at a fabulous price, and also to bring out a limited number of bales of cotton worth a dollar a pound. In Bermuda these men seemed to suffer from a chronic thirst which could only be assuaged by champagne, and one of their amusements was to sit in the windows with bags of shillings and throw handfuls of the coins to a crowd of loafing negroes in the street to see them scramble. It is a singular fact that five years after the war not one of these men had a dollar to bless himself with. Another singular fact was that it was not always the speedier craft that were the most successful. The *Kate* (named after Mrs. William Trenholm) ran through the blockading fleets sixty times, and she could not steam faster than seven or eight knots. That was the record; next to her came the *Herald*, or the *Antonica* as she was afterwards called.

Commodore Maury was a deeply religious man. He had been lame for many years of his life, but no one ever heard him complain. He had been many years in the navy, but had scarcely ever put his foot on board of a ship without being seasick, and through it all he never allowed it to interfere with his duty. He was the only man I ever saw who could be seasick and amiable at the same time; while suffering from nausea he could actually joke! I remember once entering his stateroom where he was seated with a Bible on his lap and a basin alongside of him. I told him that there was a ship in sight, and between paroxysms he said, 'Sometimes we see a ship, and sometimes ship a sea!'

Not knowing of his world-wide celebrity, I was surprised to see the deference paid him by foreigners. We had no sooner settled ourselves at the hotel than the governor sent an aide to tell Lieutenant Maury that he would be pleased to receive him in his private capacity at the Government House. In Europe the commodore was only known as 'the great Lieutenant Maury': they entirely ignored any promotions which might have come to him. The commandant of Fort St. George also called on him, but took pains to explain that it was the great scientist to whom he was paying homage, and not the Confederate naval officer. As the commodore's aide I came in for a little of the reflected glory, and had the pleasure of accompanying him to a dinner given in his honour on board of H.M.S. *Immortality* at Port Hamilton. She was a beautiful frigate and her officers were very kind to me.

We remained in Bermuda for more than two weeks, waiting for the Royal Mail Steamer from St. Thomas, on which we were to take passage for Halifax, Nova Scotia. Simultaneously with her arrival the U.S. sloops-of-war *San Jacinto* and *Mohican* put in an appearance, but did not enter the harbour, cruising instead just outside the three-mile limit and in the track the British ship *Delta* would have to follow. Instantly the rumour spread that they were going to take Commodore Maury out of the ship as soon as she got outside, colour being lent to this rumour by the fact that it was the *San Jacinto* which had only a year before taken the Confederate Commissioners, Mason and Slidell, out of the Royal Mail Steamship *Trent*—and I must say that we felt quite uneasy.

On the day of our departure a Mr. Bourne, a gentleman of whom I had never heard before, asked me to accompany him to his office and there counted out a hundred gold sovereigns, sealed them in a canvas bag, and asked me to sign a receipt for them. I assured him that there must be some mistake, but he insisted that I was the right party and that it was Mr. Trenholm's orders that he should give the money to me. Having had free meals and lodging on the blockade-runner, it was the first intimation I had that money would be necessary on so long a journey as the one I was about to undertake.

We sailed out of the harbour, and the two American warships, as soon as we got outside, followed us. As we rounded the headland we saw the *Immortality* and the British sloop-of-war *Desperate* coming from Port Hamilton under a full head of steam, and we expected every moment to witness a naval fight; the American ships, however, seemed satisfied with having given us a scare, while the British followed us until we lost sight of them in the night.

The governor of the colony of Nova Scotia, the general commanding the troops, and the admiral of the fleet, all treated 'Lieutenant' Maury, as they insisted on calling him, with the most distinguished consideration, inviting him to dinners and receptions, etc., to which, as his aide, I had to accompany the great man. I particularly enjoyed the visit to Admiral Milne's flag-ship, the *Nile,* of seventy-two guns carried on three decks. The old wooden line-of-battle ship with her lofty spars was a splendid sight, and the like of her will never be seen again. What interested me most on board was the eighteen or twenty midshipmen in her complement, many of them younger and smaller than myself. They all made much of me and frankly envied me on account of my having been in battle and having run the blockade.

The officers of the garrison were also very kind to me, and told me a story about their commander, General O'Dougherty, which I have never forgotten. It was about a visit the chief of the O'Dougherty clan paid to the general. Not finding him at home, he left his card on which was simply engraved, 'The O'Dougherty.' The general returned the visit and wrote on a blank card, 'The other O'Dougherty.'

After a few pleasant days spent in Halifax the Cunard steamer *Arabia*, plying between Boston and Liverpool, came into port and we took passage on her for Liverpool. The Americans on board resented our presence and of course had nothing to do with us, but a number of young officers of the Scots Fusilier Guards, who were returning home for the fox hunting, were very friendly. They had been hurriedly sent to Canada when war seemed imminent on account of the *Trent* affair. It was the first time a regiment of the Guards had been out of England since Waterloo, and they were very glad to be returning to their beloved 'Merry' England. Among these young officers was the Earl of Dunmore, who, a few months before, wishing to see something of the war between the States, had obtained a leave of absence, passed through the Federal lines and gone to Richmond and thence to Charleston. He had travelled incog. under his family name of Murray.

At Charleston he had been entertained by Mr. Trenholm, and that gave us something to talk about. Dunmore was of a very venturesome disposition, and instead of returning North on his pass, he decided to enjoy the sensation of running the blockade. The boat he took passage on successfully eluded the Federal fleet off Charleston, but she was captured by an outside cruiser the very next day. The prisoners were, of course, searched, and around the body of 'Mr. Murray,' under his shirt, was found wrapped a Confederate flag—the flag of the C.S.S. *Nashville*, which had been presented to him by Captain Pegram. Despite his protestations that he was a Britisher travelling for pleasure, he was confined, as 'Mr. Murray,' in Fort Lafayette. The British Minister, Lord Lyons, soon heard of his predicament and requested the authorities in Washington to order his release, representing him as being the Earl of Dunmore, a lieutenant in Her Majesty's Life Guards. But the commandant of Fort Lafayette denied that he had any such prisoner, and it required quite a correspondence to persuade him that a man by the name of Murray could at the same time be Lord Dunmore.

Another of the Guardsmen was Captain Richard Cooper, who, at the relief of Lucknow, was the first man through the breach in the wall, on which occasion he received a fearful wound across his forehead from a scimitar in the hands of a Sepoy, which had left a vivid red scar. Several of the young Guardsmen had never yet flirted with death; they envied Captain Cooper and would gladly have been the possessors of his ugly scarlet blemish.

The *Arabia* was a paddle-wheel, full-rigged ship. She appeared to us to be enormous in size, though, as a matter of fact, she was not one tenth as large as the modern Cunard liner. She did not even have a smoking-room, the lovers of the weed, when they wished to indulge in a whiff, having to seek the shelter of the lee-side of the smokestack in all sorts of weather. A part of this pleasant voyage was very smooth, but when we struck the 'roaring forties' the big ship tumbled about considerably, and my commodore was as seasick and amiable as usual.

Excerpts from *Incidents and Anecdotes of the Civil War*

BY ADMIRAL DAVID DIXON PORTER

Chapter I.

REJOICINGS IN WASHINGTON AT THE SECESSION OF SOUTH CAROLINA.

During the Presidency of James Buchanan, and just previous to the inauguration of Mr. Lincoln, I was ordered to the command of the Coast-Survey
steamer Active on the Pacific coast.

I could not conceive why I was thus ordered, except that ships and officers
were at that period being sent out of the way. This, too, at a time when the Southern States were threatening to secede, and it seemed probable the Government
would require the services of all its officers to maintain the integrity of the Union.

At that moment I was in a despondent frame of mind, and troubled with the
most gloomy forebodings. I felt that a crisis was impending that might influence all
my prospects in life and cast me upon the world without resources and with a large
dependent family.

I sought consolation by visiting the houses of Southern members of Congress
in Washington whom I knew, but obtained little satisfaction from the sentiments I
there heard expressed.

One night in December, 1860, on my way home from a visit to Congress, where I had listened to a great deal of incendiary language from Southern members and plenty of vituperation from Northern ones, a gentleman met me in the street and informed me of the secession of South Carolina.

The news, though not unexpected, was startling, and, viewing the matter in the most philosophical light possible, I proceeded homeward to carry the unpleasant intelligence.

On my way I had to pass the house of a distinguished Southern gentleman whom I knew well and for whom I entertained a high regard. I had always heard him discuss the questions at issue between the North and South in the most dispassionate manner, whatever may have been his course in Congress.

There were a dozen carriages standing before the door, and the house was all ablaze with lights, making the interior look cheerful enough, while a drizzling rain rendered everything gloomy without. Those were not the days of well-lighted streets and asphalt pavements. Washington was a city of muddy highways, and corporation moonlight was more frequent than convenient.

As I entered the mansion the lady of the house, in bonnet and shawl, was descending the stairs. She was a magnificent woman, greatly esteemed in Washington society for her genial manner, and admired for her wit and intellect. Had she aspired to do so, this lady might have been the leader of fashion in the Federal capital, but I do not think her ambition ran in that direction. She had a small and select circle of friends, mostly Southern people, and chiefly affected politics.

Her heart was fixed on what she called the emancipation of the South from Northern thralldom, and with her handsome person and dignified bearing she seemed worthy to occupy the loftiest position.

As this lady saw me she exclaimed, "Ah, captain"—for so she always called me—"I am so glad to see you! I want you to escort me to the White House. The horses are sick, and I am going to walk over."

"It is impossible for you to walk," I replied, "through the rain and mud; but there are ten or twelve hacks at the door, and I will press one of them into your service." So saying, I called a carriage, helped the lady in, and got in after her.

"I was under the impression," I said, as we started, "that you were having a party at your house, seeing it so brilliantly lighted up, and I thought I would venture in uninvited."

"No, indeed," she replied, "but we have received glorious news from the South, and my husband's friends are calling to congratulate him. South Carolina has seceded, and, O captain!" she continued, with increasing fervor, "we will have a glorious monarchy, and you must join us!"

"Yes," I said, "and be made Duke of Benedict Arnold."

"Nonsense!" she exclaimed, "but we will make you an admiral."

"Certainly," I replied, "Admiral of the *Blue*, for I should feel blue enough to see everything turned upside down, and our boasted liberty and civilization whistled down the wind."

"What would you have?" she inquired. "Would you have us tamely submit to all the indignities the North have put upon us, and place our necks under their feet? Why, this very day my blood fairly boiled while I was in Congress, and I could scarcely contain myself. That old Black Republican, Mr.——, was berating the Southern people as if they were a pack of naughty children. However, I was indemnified in the end, for Mr. Rhett took the floor and gave the man such a castigation that he slunk away and was no more heard from. We can stand these outrages no longer, and will take refuge in a monarchy—a glorious monarchy!"

"Of course you will be queen," I said. "Well, I should be happy to serve under such a beautiful majesty, but somehow I like this homely republicanism under which I have been brought up, and so I will stick to it; but don't repeat to others what you have said to me, for it might compromise your husband."

"Ah," she exclaimed, "he thinks as I do!"

Just then we reached the White House. I helped the lady from the carriage and escorted her into the great hall. I proposed to take my leave, but she insisted on my remaining, saying, "I want to tell the President the good news."

Heavens and earth! thought I, what will happen next? "No, thank you," I said, "I will take some other opportunity to see the President," and, taking my leave of the lady, I went out and never saw her afterward.

I rode back to the house to return the borrowed carriage, and, when I reached the door, heard sounds of merriment issuing from the mansion, and was induced to step into the parlor.

As I entered I was welcomed with boisterous shouts by a dozen gentlemen, only two of whom I had ever met before. They embraced me, and insisted on my drinking with them, but this I declined, thinking there had been too much drinking already.

I can only compare the scene to Pandemonium.

"The people all acted like the jacks at the Nore,
And ran the Palmetto flag up to the fore,
Where all ranted and raved, and their language, O dear!
Was so full of billingsgate 'twas shocking to hear.
Cooney and lawyer, politician and sage,
And the craziest men of the palmetto age,
    With defiant looks,

> *Full of crotchets and crooks,*
> *Were chafing and swearing and scowling so black*
> *As hosts sometimes do when the dinner's put back.*
> *Yet few of the folks at that chivalric fair*
> *Seemed willing to think—nor a curse did they care—*
> *That a sword hung over them just by a hair.*
> Old Clootie *was there, and said all was right;*
> *'Twas he held the bottle, and urged on the fight,*
> > *And stood up in his place,*
> > *With his stoical face,*
> *His hands meekly folded, as if he'd say grace,*
> *While Rebellion was moving at an awful fast pace."*

The only person who seemed to preserve his equanimity was the master of the house, who sat, calm and smiling, conversing with an uproarious friend who had partaken deeply of the flowing bowl.

When I had an opportunity I asked the host quietly if there was anything in this excitement, and if it could be possible that the Southern States would secede. "What more do they want?" I inquired. "They have a majority in the Senate and in the House, and, with the Supreme Court on their side, they can make laws to suit themselves."

"Yes," he replied, his bright eye almost looking through me, "most people would be satisfied with that.

> " *'Better to suffer from the ills we have,*
> *Than fly to others that we wot not of.'*

"But you will join us," he continued, "and we will make you an admiral."

"Thank you," said I, "but I am going to the California gold-mines, and when the South and the North have done quarreling, and all you seceders have come back and taken your seats in Congress, I will join the navy again."

"You must join *us*," he said, "for we will have a navy to be proud of."

A few weeks later my friends left Washington for the South, regretted by all who knew them. Their house had been the rendezvous of the most brilliant and refined persons at the capital. The clever women of the South met there to discuss the prospects of a Southern confederacy or monarchy, and to urge on their slow-moving husbands in what they considered the path of duty.

These ladies saw in the distance the gleam of the coronets that were to encircle their fair brows, and certainly none were more fitted, by the graces of mind and person, to wear them than the beautiful Southern women who formed the bright galaxy of stars in Washington society.

As to the lady whom I accompanied to the White House, she shone, like Venus, brighter than all the other planets, and her departure cast a gloom over the firesides of the friends she left behind in Washington, soon to be overshadowed by the stirring scenes at the outbreak of the civil war—the tramp of legions of soldiers through quiet streets where, since the rebuilding of the Capitol, had been heard nothing more stirring than

"Sounds of revelry by night,"

or the simple pageants which accompanied the President to and from the Capitol at the quadrennial inauguration.

No wonder the capital and its surroundings seemed stupid to these vivacious Southerners, and that their hearts were not satisfied with our plain republican trappings.

An opera-house or two, half a dozen fine theatres, and a court, or the semblance of one, at the White House—something more in the style of the present day—might have prevented the catastrophe which overwhelmed both North and South.

The Romans understood these things better than we. They omitted nothing to keep the people amused; they even had the street fountains at times run with wine, and the investment was worth the money spent.

But what could one expect at a court presided over by an old bachelor whose heart was dead to poetry and love; who sat at dinner with no flowers to grace the festive board, and never even wore a *boutonnière* on his coat-lapel; who eschewed everything like official state, and was content to live out his term of office in plain republican simplicity?

What was there to attract charming women to an administration like that of Abraham Lincoln, conducted with even more simplicity than that of his predecessor, and only to be appreciated by sturdy republicans that despised all the vanities of a court and took no stock in monarchy?

Barren and dreary as the fair Southerners left the city of Washington—to which they intended to return when a Southern court should be established—it has since risen from its ashes like a Phoenix, and blooms as it never did before.

The angels of heaven smile serenely over the happy meeting of those who did all they could to imbrue their hands in each other's blood, but she who once moved radiant amid the throng is still absent from the Federal capital.

"She was superb—at least so she was thirty summers ago—
As soft and as sallow as autumn, with hair
Neither black nor yet brown, but that tint which the air
Takes at eve in September, when night lingers lone
Through a vineyard, from beams of a slow-setting sun;
Eyes the wistful gazelle's, the fine foot of a fairy,
A voice soft and sweet as a tune that one knows.
Something in her there was set you to thinking of those
Strange backgrounds of Raphael, that hectic and deep
Brief twilight in which Southern suns fall asleep.
Thou abidest and reignest forever, O Queen
Of that better world which thou swayest unseen."

It is not my intention at this late day to reflect upon the motives of those whose acts brought about such desolation. Let them rest in peace, and may the future bring back to us those who once formed the most refined and delightful society at the capital.

They will find the Federal city improved and beautified, ready to receive them with warm hearts and friendly greetings. The capital will smile as of yore when the bright galaxy of Southern ladies which once illumined its halls again take their places in a society they are so well fitted to adorn.

And those clever men of the South—the successors of the great statesmen who played such a prominent part in our early history—may they realize the task before them of reconstructing their several States and making their people feel that we all belong to one country, which, if united, can be made the grandest in the world.

Chapter II.

PLAN TO SAVE FORT PICKENS—
DISLOYALTY IN THE NAVY DEPARTMENT—
STEALING A MARCH ON THE SECRETARY OF THE NAVY.

Mr. Lincoln had been installed in the Presidential office, and the subject of relieving Fort Sumter was under discussion. A small squadron was being fitted out for the supposed purpose of relieving the fort, the final action of which was to be guided by Mr. G. V. Fox, afterward Assistant Secretary of the Navy.

My orders to California were still hanging over me, and I had even engaged my passage in the steamer from New York, and was taking my last meal with my family, when a carriage drove up to the door.

It brought a note from the Secretary of State (Mr. Seward), requesting me to call and see him without delay; so, leaving my dinner unfinished, I jumped into the carriage and drove at once to the Secretary's office.

I found Mr. Seward lying on his back on a sofa, with his knees up, reading a lengthy document.

Without changing his position he said to me, "Can you tell me how we can save Fort Pickens from falling into the hands of the rebels?"

I answered, promptly, "I can, sir."

"Then," said the Secretary, "you are the man I want, if you can do it."

"I can do it," I said, as Mr. Seward rose to his feet.

Those familiar with the history of that period will remember that Lieutenant Slemmer was holding Fort Pickens with a small force and had refused the summons of General Bragg to surrender, and all the naval guns and munitions of war that had fallen into the Confederates' hands were being placed in position behind earthworks, preparatory to opening on the Union lines.

It was to save Slemmer and the Union works that made Mr. Seward so interested in this affair.

"Now, come," said Mr. Seward, "tell me how you will save that place."

I had talked with Captain (now General) Meigs a few days before about this matter. That officer broached the subject to me, and it appears first suggested the matter to Mr. Seward, and the latter, being anxious to show the Southerners that the Government had a right to hold its own forts, and seeing the likelihood of our losing Fort Sumter, listened very kindly to Captain Meigs's suggestions.

Our plan was to get a good-sized steamer and six or seven companies of soldiers, and to carry the latter, with a number of large guns and a quantity of munitions of war, to Fort Pickens, land them on the outside of the fort under the guns of a ship of war, and the fort would soon be made impregnable—that was all.

I repeated this to Mr. Seward, and said to him, "Give me command of the *Powhatan*, now lying at New York ready for sea, and I will guarantee that everything shall be done without a mistake."

Mr. Seward listened attentively, and, when I had finished what I had to say, he invited Captain Meigs—who had come in in the meantime—and myself to accompany him to the President.

When we arrived at the White House, Mr. Lincoln—who seemed to be aware of our errand—opened the conversation.

"Tell me," said he, "how we can prevent Fort Pickens from falling into the hands of the rebels, for if Slemmer is not at once relieved there will be no holding it. Pensacola would be a very important place for the Southerners, and if they once get possession of Pickens, and fortify it, we have no navy to take it from them."

"Mr. President," said I, "there is a queer state of things existing in the Navy Department at this time. Mr. Welles is surrounded by officers and clerks, some of whom are disloyal at heart, and if the orders for this expedition should emanate from the Secretary of the Navy, and pass through all the department red tape, the news would be at once flashed over the wires, and Fort Pickens would be lost for ever. But if you will issue all the orders from the Executive Mansion, and let me proceed to New York with them, I will guarantee their prompt execution to the letter."

"But," said the President, "is not this a most irregular mode of proceeding?"

"Certainly," I replied, "but the necessity of the case justifies it."

"You are commander-in-chief of the army and navy," said Mr. Seward to the President, "and this is a case where it is necessary to issue direct orders without passing them through intermediaries."

"But what will Uncle Gideon say?" inquired the President.

"Oh, I will make it all right with Mr. Welles," said the Secretary of State. "This is the only way, sir, the thing can be done."

At this very time Mr. Welles was—or supposed he was—fitting out an expedition for the relief of Fort Sumter. All the orders were issued in the usual way, and, of course, telegraphed to Charleston, as soon as written, by the persons in the department through whose hands they passed.

Mr. Seward was well aware of this, and he wanted to prevent such a thing happening in this instance.

Mr. Welles, no doubt, had the *Powhatan* on his list of available vessels, and may have relied on her to carry out his plan for the relief of Sumter. Orders had been sent for the several vessels to rendezvous off Charleston on a certain day, but, strange to say, no orders had been issued for the *Powhatan* to join them, for reasons that will appear in the course of my narrative.

I observed one thing during this interview, and that was that the best of feeling did not exist between the heads of the State and Navy Departments. Mr. Seward doubtless thought that he had not been as much consulted as he ought to have been in the fitting out of the expedition for the relief of Sumter. He looked upon himself as Prime Minister, and considered that the Secretary of the Navy should defer to him in all matters concerning movements against those in rebellion, in which opinion Mr. Welles did not concur. Mr. Seward was by nature of an arbitrary disposition, and wanted everything done in his own way—not a bad quality on occasions, but apt to create confusion if persevered in in too many cases.

In this instance it was eminently proper that the Secretary of State should take the initiative.

In the course of the conversation Mr. Lincoln remarked: "This looks to me very much like the case of two fellows I once knew: one was a gambler, the other a preacher. They met in a stage, and the gambler induced the preacher to play poker, and the latter won all the gambler's money. 'It's all because we have mistaken our trades,' said the gambler; 'you ought to have been a gambler and I a preacher, and, by ginger, I intend to turn the tables on you next Sunday and preach in your church,' which he did."

It was finally agreed that my plan should be carried out. I wrote the necessary orders, which were copied by Captain Meigs and signed by the President, who merely said as he did so, "Seward, see that I don't burn my fingers."

The first order was for me to proceed to New York and take command of the steam frigate *Powhatan,* proceed at once to Fort Pickens, run across the bar and anchor at all hazards on the inside, where I could cover the fort and co-operate with Captain Meigs while he was landing the troops, which were to go in a steamer chartered for the occasion.

The second order was for the commandant of the New York navy-yard, directing him to fit out the *Powhatan* with all dispatch and with the greatest secrecy, and under no circumstances to inform the Navy Department until after the ship had sailed.

The third order was to the commanding officer of the *Powhatan,* informing him that circumstances required that the utmost dispatch and secrecy should be observed in fitting out the ship, and that it was necessary for the President to confide the execution of his plans to some one who understood them thoroughly, in order that they might be carried out; that for this reason he was compelled to detach Captain Mercer from the command of the *Powhatan,* but that, having the highest confidence in his abilities and patriotism, the President gave him the option to select any other ship in the navy, etc.

Armed with these documents, I bade the President good-day, and, in company with Captain Meigs, proceeded to the headquarters of the General-in-Chief, General Scott, then the military oracle, without whose authority no troops would have been granted.

Lieutenant-Colonel Keyes was at that time General Scott's Military Secretary, and when we called on the general he showed us into the anteroom, where Meigs unfolded to him our plans and instructions, requesting that the general would grant us an audience as soon as possible.

When Keyes delivered the message, General Scott gruffly inquired what we wanted, and, when informed, said, "Tell Captain Meigs to walk in; I won't see any naval officer; *he* can't come in."

The fact was, the general at that moment was suffering from a severe attack of gout, which made him unwilling to see anybody outside of his military family.

Captain Meigs shortly rejoined me in the anteroom. With the aid of Keyes, he had succeeded in getting the general to give him the desired force of troops for the relief of Pickens, and we therefore departed to carry out the plans.

Next morning at nine o'clock I was at the New York navy-yard, and found that Commodore Breese, the commandant, was absent on a two weeks' leave, and that Captain A. H. Foote was in command. This was a fortunate circumstance, for if I had to deal with Commodore Breese I should have experienced no end of trouble in keeping the expedition secret. Breese was a particularly "cautious man," a by-word in the navy to express a lack of the higher qualities, and he would have eventually let the cat out of the bag, or insisted on telegraphing to the Secretary of the Navy for orders, notwithstanding the President's instructions. It is hard to get an old officer out of a groove in which he has been running for many years, and this way of carrying on operations would have seemed altogether wrong to a man of Commodore Breese's way of thinking.

As it was, I had trouble enough with Foote to bring him to reason, and it was only after three hours' earnest conversation that I convinced him I was not a rebel in disguise plotting with the *Powhatan's* officers to run away with the ship, and deliver her over to the South.

"You see, Porter," he said, "there are so many fellows whom I would have trusted to the death who have deserted the flag that I don't know whom to believe." He read my orders over and over, turned them upside down, examined the water-mark and Executive Mansion stamp, and surveyed me from head to foot. "How do I know *you* are not a traitor? Who ever heard of such orders as these emanating direct from the President? I must telegraph to Mr. Welles before I do anything, and ask further instructions."

"Look at these orders again," I said, "and then telegraph at your peril. Under no circumstances must you inform the Navy Department of this expedition. Now give me a cigar, let me sit here in quiet, and you may take an hour or two to look over those letters if you like; but if you telegraph to Mr. Welles the President will consider it high treason, and you will lose the best chance you ever had in your life. If you must telegraph, send a message to the President or Mr. Seward."

"Yes," replied Foote, "and what would prevent you from having a confederate at the other end of the line to receive the message and answer it—there is so much treason going on?"

I burst out laughing. "What would you say," I inquired, "if I were to tell you that Frank Buchanan, Sam Barron, and Magruder were going to desert to the rebels?"

Foote jumped from his chair. "God in heaven!" he exclaimed, "what next? You don't expect me to trust you after that? How do I know you are not in league with the others? But, man, that can't be, for I saw by the morning papers that President Lincoln was at a wedding last night at Buchanan's, and Buchanan had the house festooned with American flags, and all the loyal men of Washington were there."

"So they were," I replied, "but, nevertheless, they will all desert in a few days, for their hearts are on the other side. Ingraham is going also—his chief clerk has already preceded him, and carried off the signal-book of the navy."

"Good Lord deliver us!" exclaimed Foote, piously. "I must telegraph to Mr. Welles. I can't stand this strain any longer. It will kill me. You sit smoking and smiling as if this was not a very serious matter. Here"—to his chief clerk—"bring me a telegraph blank."

"Before you send that message," said I, "let me call your attention to a paragraph of the President's order: 'Under no circumstances will you make known to the Navy Department or any one else the object of this expedition, or the fact that the *Powhatan* is fitting out.' Just think," I continued to Captain Foote, "of the President taking you into his confidence so early in these troubles; think what a high position you may reach before the trouble with the South is over if we succeed in carrying out this expedition successfully. Then, again, think what a tumble you will get if you disobey a positive order of the President. He will believe rebellion rampant everywhere, and won't know whom to trust. Think of Captain Foote being tried and shot like Admiral Byng for failing to carry out his orders."

"Hush, Porter!" exclaimed Foote, "hush at once! I believe you are a rebel in disguise, for after Frank Buchanan, Barron, and Magruder preparing to desert, and Ingraham, too, with his Kosta record, I won't trust any one. Where are your trunks?"

"At the Irving House," I replied.

"Send the postman here," said Foote. When the man came he said to him, "Go to the Irving House, pay Lieutenant Porter's bill, and take his trunks to my house and tell Mrs. Foote to prepare the best room.—There, my boy, I have you now. You shall stay with me, and I will be ready to arrest you the moment I find there is any treason about you. After all," continued Foote, "you have come on a wild-goose chase. The *Powhatan* is stripped to a girt-line. Her engines are all to pieces, her boilers under an order of survey, her boats are worn out, and the ship wants new planking all over. Her magazines are too damp to keep powder in, and we are pulling them all to pieces. She wants a new fore-yard and painting throughout. In fact, the ship is worn out, and I gave orders to haul her into dock this morning preparatory to thorough repairs."

"So much the better," said I; "she is just the ship I am looking for. Never mind paint, never mind repairing the boilers, never mind new spars, or repairs to magazines. I will take her as she is; only set your people to work and put everything in place, and we can get off in four days. I want a ship that can be sunk without any great loss."

"But," said Foote, "all the *Powhatan's* officers have been granted leave, and her crew transferred to the receiving-ship."

"Telegraph the officers to return at once, and send the crew on board to rig and equip her," I replied.

"I can't do that," he said, "unless I telegraph to Mr. Welles."

I repeated from the order of the President, "Under no circumstances will you make known to the Navy Department the object of this expedition."

Captain Foote was puzzled. At last, after considering the matter, he said, "I will trust you, though I am utterly nonplussed; it's such a doubtful business. I will set to work immediately, and by night we will have the spars up and by noon tomorrow I will have all the officers back. Come home with me now and take lunch, and I will give the sentry at my house orders to keep an eye on you when I return to the office."

"And I will return to the office," I replied, "and watch you to see that you don't telegraph to Mr. Welles. I want to save you, if possible, from the fate of Admiral Byng."

Foote laughed heartily now that the weight was off his mind, and he had determined to carry out the President's instructions. A double set of men were put on board the *Powhatan* with orders to work day and night that the ship might be ready in three days.

Captain Foote and myself sat up nearly all that night talking over this adventure, for Foote had now as much interest in the matter as I had, and was very enthusiastic over the anticipated success of the expedition.

It was cold weather, and a fire was burning in my room. To make things comfortable, I said, "Suppose you send for a kettle of water, some lemons and sugar, and let us have some hot punch."

Foote, although a teetotaler, had every kind of liquor in his house for the use of his friends. "If you ever tell anybody, you bad fellow," said he, "that I sat up with you after midnight brewing punch, I'll never forgive you."

But in ten minutes I had brewed some whisky-punch which I thought admirable. "Let me make you one," I said.

"Well," he replied, "if you will take some hot water, lemon and sugar, and mix them together, and put in a very little whisky 'unbeknownst' to me, I will keep you company."

So there we sat during the long hours of the night, discussing the future prospects of the navy, and before daylight the captain had given up all idea of telegraphing Mr. Welles.

Next morning I accompanied Foote to his office. Captain Mercer was sent for and the President's letter read to him, and he was enjoined to secrecy. Captain Meigs also came over and explained the part he was to bear in the expedition, and informed Foote that he had transcribed all the orders in the President's presence; this settled all Foote's qualms, and the work on the *Powhatan* proceeded rapidly.

The boilers and machinery were put in pretty fair order, and the officers returned in obedience to the telegrams. Captain Mercer took nominal command, and my presence in the navy-yard caused no comment, as I never went near the ship.

On the fourth day the ship was all ready for sea, with steam up and the pilot on board, and Captain Meigs had informed me he would sail in the Atlantic at 3 P.M. with the troops under command of Colonel Harvey Brown.

My luggage had been sent on board the previous night, and I was in Captain Foote's office, having a last talk with him, when a telegram came from the Secretary of the Navy: "Prepare the *Powhatan* for sea with all dispatch."

Foote handed the telegram to me, quite dazed. "There," he said, "you are dished!"

"Not by any means," I replied; "this telegram is all right, only the President has got uneasy about the ship not sailing, since he was under the impression that she was ready for sea at a moment's notice, and has made a confidant of Mr. Welles. Let me get on board and off, and you can telegraph that the *Powhatan* has sailed."

"No," said Foote, calling for pen and ink, "I must telegraph to Mr. Welles."

"Don't make any mistake," I said. "You must obey the Commander-in-Chief of the army and navy in preference to all others," and I quoted the President's order: "Under no circumstances will you make known to the Navy Department the object of this expedition."

Foote threw down his pen. "Porter," he exclaimed, "you will be the death of me; but I will send for Mercer and Captain Meigs to join our conference."

Both these gentlemen were soon at the office, and both urged Foote to obey the President's order, which he concluded to do.

I afterward ascertained that other telegrams had been sent to Captain Foote, while I was staying at his house, by the Secretary of the Navy in relation to the fitting out of the *Powhatan*, but he never mentioned the fact to me—a circumstance for which I can not account.

"Now go right on board, my boy," said Foote to me, "and get off, and as soon as you are under way I will telegraph the Secretary that you have sailed." So, bidding Captain Foote good-by, I slipped on board the *Powhatan*, unnoticed amid the crowd, and locked myself in the captain's stateroom.

Captain Mercer was to remain in command until we got to Staten Island, when he was to go ashore and the ship proceed down the bay in charge of the first lieutenant. After the ship passed the bar and the pilot had left, I was to appear.

The moment the ship turned her head down stream Foote telegraphed her departure to the Secretary of the Navy.

We met with many obstacles in our progress down the East River, and did not have steam fairly up for an hour after leaving the navy-yard. We were an hour and a half in reaching Staten Island, and consumed another hour in landing Captain Mercer, as the old boat nearly filled with water going on shore, and kept half the crew bailing her out.

Just as the boat was hoisted up and the order given to go ahead, the quartermaster reported, "A fast steamer a-chasin' and signalin' of us, sir, and an officer wavin' his cap!"

Perry, the first lieutenant, did not know who was captain or that I was in the cabin, so he stopped until the steamer came up, although she would have caught us anyhow, for Foote had chartered the fastest little steamer out of New York, and kept her with steam up, ready to start after me the moment the expected telegram should arrive.

The steamboat was soon alongside the *Powhatan,* and Lieutenant Roe came on board and delivered a telegram. Perry walked into the cabin, and, to his astonishment, found me there and handed me the dispatch. It read as follows:

"Deliver up the *Powhatan* at once to Captain Mercer.

SEWARD."

I telegraphed back:

"Have received confidential orders from the President, and shall obey them. D. D. PORTER."

I then went on deck and gave orders to go ahead fast. In an hour and a half we were over the bar, discharged the pilot, and steering south for an hour, and then due east, to throw any pursuers off our track (for I was determined to go to Fort Pickens). At sundown I steered my course.

When my answer to the Secretary of State was handed to Captain Foote he was astonished. "He's clean daft!" said he, "or has run off with the ship to join the rebels. They would have tried him by court-martial anyhow. Well, I'll never trust any one again, for I have lost faith in human nature. Porter would have been such a help to our side, whereas if he can get a fast vessel he will be the most destructive pirate that ever roamed the seas."

We often laughed together afterward over this episode, but Foote always ended by saying, "You ought to have been tried and shot; no one but yourself would ever have been so impudent."

Mr. Seward, however, was of a different opinion, and chuckled over the success of his pet scheme and at the idea of circumventing Mr. Welles. The President smiled complacently when he read my telegram, and said, "Seward, if the Southerners get Sumter we will be even with them by securing Pickens." I made a warm friend in each of them, and Mr. Lincoln and Mr. Seward both stood by me during the war whenever Mr. Welles—who was not partial to me—was disposed to be annoying.

When Mr. Welles received Captain Foote's telegram announcing the departure of the *Powhatan,* he hurried over to the White House, where he found Mr. Seward with the President, and forthwith protested against the interference of the Secretary of State in the affairs of the Navy Department, demanding the restitution of what he termed "the stolen ship," and informing the President that on the *Powhatan* depended the success of the relief expedition to Fort Sumter, as she carried the large boats necessary for that occasion—when in fact the *Powhatan* would not have been of a particle of use, as she drew too much water to cross Charleston bar, and the boats in question were good for nothing, as they had been so long exposed to the weather without paint that they filled with water as soon as they were lowered overboard.

If Mr. Welles had reflected a little he would have discovered that the *Powhatan* could not have reached Charleston in time to be of any use, for his order to prepare the ship for sea did not reach New York until the morning of the 1st of April, 1861, and if the vessel had not been taken in hand when she was, she would have been on that date in dry-dock, pulled to pieces, and with half her boilers on shore. As it was, the rebels opened fire on Sumter from their heavy earthworks as soon as the vessels composing Mr. Welles's expedition approached the bar, and they could not have done a particle of good. Had they tried to succor the people in the fort, they would have been sunk in a very few minutes. A more foolish expedition was never dispatched, and Mr. Lincoln remarked, when the news was brought to him, "It's a good rule never to send a mouse to catch a skunk, or a polywog to tackle a whale."

The attempt to relieve Sumter was a curious muddle, and had, from the first inception of the design, no chance of success. Mr. Seward was evidently opposed to it, feeling sure that it would be a failure, and so he got up the expedition to Pickens, certain that it could not fail to be successful. The Secretary of State wished to show that he was a better sailor than Mr. Welles.

We reached Fort Pickens the day after the *Collins* steamship transporting the troops, although she sailed after we did. I ran in for the harbor, crossed the bar, and was standing up to Round Fort, when a tug put out from Pickens and placed herself across my path. Captain Meigs was on board the tug, waving a document, and, hailing, said he had an order from Colonel Brown. It was to the following effect: "Don't permit *Powhatan* to run the batteries or attempt to go inside. It will bring the fire of the enemy on the fort before we are prepared."

I felt like running over Meigs's tug, but obeyed the order. The stars and stripes were hoisted, in hopes the enemy would open fire, but they did not, nor do I believe they had any intention of so doing. The people in this part of the country were not in the same state of excitement as the Charlestonians, and would have been more careful about firing the first gun. Besides, I do not think they were prepared for hostilities, for they had mounted a number of guns all *en barbette,* and did not seem to have any intention of using them.

The *Powhatan* had her ten ports on the port side filled with nine-inch guns, and there was one eleven-inch pivot. All were loaded with grape and canister. Besides, there were twelve howitzers placed in different parts of the ship and loaded with shrapnel. With our trained gunners we could have swept the raw soldiers from the rebel batteries.

It was therefore unfortunate that Captain Meigs interfered by presenting the order. A fine opportunity was lost for the Government to demonstrate its power and determination to maintain its authority at all hazards.

Mr. Welles claimed that this expedition to Pickens was useless, as he "had already instructed the commanding officer of the forces off Pensacola Bar to send re-enforcements to Fort Pickens in case it was attacked." (!) But that prudent officer lay at anchor five miles from the fort, where he could be of no manner of use in case of a surprise.

General Bragg had a large force of troops in and around the navy-yard, and the second day after our arrival a number of tugs and schooners, filled with soldiers, came down from Pensacola and approached Fort Pickens, whether with the intention of attacking it or not I don't know. They no doubt took the *Powhatan* and the *Collins* steamer for store-ships, and thought it a good time to commence operations and secure "loot," but I changed the programme by sending an eleven-inch shrapnel among them, which, bursting at the right time, threw up the water in all directions.

The flotilla scampered off in quick time, and left us to quietly prepare the fort for any emergency, and it remained in our possession during the whole of the civil war.

At that time the news that Sumter had been fired on had not reached us, and we were under the impression that our shot was the first that had been fired.

When I left Washington it had seemed to be the leading idea that nobody should get hurt, and that the sensitive feelings of our Southern brethren should not be ruffled; but when I beheld Bragg's transports approaching, I thought it high time to try the persuasive power of an eleven-inch shell.

My sentiments at that moment were like those of an old fellow they tell of at Bunker Hill, who was much amused at the repeated volleys of musketry poured out by the advancing British until a ball struck him in the fleshy part of the leg, when he roared out to his son, who stood near him, "Dang it, Jim, they're firin' bullets; we must fire back at 'em!" I thought it time to be firing bullets.

The above is the way Fort Pickens and the gallant Slemmer and his men were saved from capture.

If the commanding officer of the naval forces off the bar had been left to his own discretion, Slemmer would have had but a poor show in case he had been attacked, although Mr. Welles no doubt thought everything was being done to guard the fort against surprise. The commander of the squadron, however, assured me that he was so tied down by instructions "*not to commit any overt act*" that he would not dare to undertake anything without specific orders. He thought me very reckless in firing a shell among General Bragg's vessels, as, "after all, they perhaps meant nothing, and were merely going to land stores at the navy-yard!" It seemed to me shameful, with such a force as this officer had under his command, that the rebels should be holding the navy-yard at all.

There was a great want of discretion among some of the leading officers of the squadron. As an example, I will mention that Lieutenant Renshaw, who had deserted his flag, went out from Pensacola in a sail-boat, and, after spending some time in the cabin of the flag-ship, came out with a boy carrying a large bag of ship's biscuit, which was passed into his boat.

The sailors gathered at the gangway to witness this novel proceeding, and many a hearty curse did Renshaw receive as he slid down the man-ropes into his boat. The general expression was, "Double-dyed traitor!" yet the same captain who had entertained Renshaw told me I would probably be tried by court-martial for firing at Bragg's men, who I had every reason to suppose were trying to capture Fort Pickens.

I must leave the reader to judge what were Mr. Seward's motives for making this movement on Fort Pickens, and whether or not it was a good one. Without doubt the Government vindicated its authority, and maintained possession of its own property.

Chapter III.

INCIDENTS AT PENSACOLA—TWO DISTINGUISHED
TRAVELLERS WHO PROVE TO BE OLD ACQUAINTANCES—
A MEMORABLE BREAKFAST.

When one takes a retrospective view of the events which occurred twenty-four years ago, he can not help but admit that this is a progressive age; and when he sees a building burn down he may console himself with the idea that he will live to see a finer one springing up from its ashes, particularly if the old one has been well insured. There may be pleasant recollections associated with the original building, for the loss of which we can never be repaid; but time heals all things, and we learn to do without the old associations and form other and dearer ties.

I have often lamented the wicked waste of life and property caused by our civil war; but I have now learned to look upon all these matters philosophically, and sometimes think it was intended the nation should pass through such an experience, as children go through with their various diseases, by way of preparing them for the greater trials of life.

If we take this view of the matter, we may find some consolation for the events of a fratricidal war which should never have taken place.

It seems difficult, however, to find any compensation for the numerous blunders that were committed by those in authority. Our house has indeed sprung from its ashes more beautiful than ever, but how much better it would have been to have saved it from the fire by using proper precautions!

When I look back to the time when it was considered so important to secure Fort Pickens and the Pensacola navy-yard, I have often wondered why our vessels did not go in and take possession, since it was easy enough to do so, and, in all probability, no one would have been hurt; but our Government was so exceedingly sensitive about wounding the feelings of the seceders that although we had the force at hand no steps were taken to prevent General Bragg from fortifying the navy-yard and the approaches to Pensacola. Fort Pickens after it was re-enforced could have knocked all Bragg's batteries to pieces in half an hour; or a single frigate under cover of the fort could have driven the enemy away and recovered a large amount of valuable public property.

But no; the officers of the army and navy were obliged to look quietly on the unceasing labors of the Confederates, apparently waiting the completion of works that they would then proceed to knock to pieces, at the same time destroying the public property which it was their duty to preserve.

After Fort Pickens was fully manned, the Union squadron hauled in closer and looked placidly on, while the people of Mobile were supplying the rebel army with everything they wanted by means of tugs and schooners.

At first the Confederates were cautious how they sent in supplies; but, finding that they were not molested, or even questioned, they began to send them openly by sea in large quantities.

Vessels loaded with lumber departed daily from Pensacola harbor, and others entered, but not a boat was sent from the flag-ship to inquire what were the cargoes and for whom intended, and Bragg and his officers lived quietly in the navy-yard houses, no doubt wondering why they were permitted to enjoy themselves so pleasantly, and hoping the truce would last an indefinite period.

I went on board the senior naval officer's ship several times to try and get an explanation of this very peculiar method of carrying on war, but the only satisfaction I received was the information that the commanding officer's orders were to "commit no overt act." These orders were the last communication received from the department some thirty days previous.

I asked the senior officer to let me take the responsibility of blockading the port of Pensacola, but he objected to my doing so. There was in all this business an inanity of which I had never conceived. The commanding officer of Fort Pickens had no orders at all that I am aware of, except to hold the fort, and not draw the fire of the Confederates.

One day the commander of the squadron signaled me to meet him at the fort for a conference, and I at once repaired there.

The Confederates had hauled the dry dock out of the basin at the navy-yard and anchored it about two hundred yards from Fort Pickens. There were a number of men on the dock, and four heavy anchors were hanging from its ends.

When I reached the fort the senior naval officer was there in consultation with the commanding officer of the troops. They had written to Bragg to ask what were his intentions with regard to the dry dock. Bragg replied that the dock got adrift and that he would restore it to its place. About four hours afterward it *accidentally* sunk in the middle of the channel! Of course, nobody believed that this was really an accident, but our senior officers thought they had done their duty by inquiring of Bragg what he intended to do, and, after having seen him carry out his intentions, they sat down quietly to dinner. Colonel Brown filled up some more sandbags, and Bragg mounted an extra gun; they were like two boys daring each other to knock off chips from their shoulders and playing a farce of war.

Next day the smoke of two steamers was descried to the westward, and I signaled for "permission to chase," which was granted. In an hour I came up with two large river boats loaded with provisions for General Bragg's army, of which they made no secret. I put each vessel in charge of an officer and prize crew, and escorted them to the flag-ship, where they were anchored.

These vessels had on board some $375,000 worth of stores, and the captains made many silly threats because they were interfered with—enough in fact, to make the senior naval officer think he had committed an "overt act"! So he was willing to compromise, and let the steamers off, provided they would return to Mobile, which they were very glad to do. I was ordered to escort them back to the place where I had captured them, and one of the steamers attempting to run into Pensacola, I sent a nine-inch shell after her, which burst over the vessel, whereupon she turned and preceded me toward Mobile. A nine-inch shot is a terribly effective argument in such a case.

I convoyed the vessels some miles down the coast, and, disgusted with such humiliating duty, I told the steamboat captains to get ready to go on board and take command of their vessels again, saying, as I did so, "Now let me give you a piece of advice. Don't try this again; if you do, and come within reach of my guns, I will sink you. I have a great mind to do it anyhow." They never tried it again.

If permitted, the rebels would have gone on committing infractions of the mutual truce which seemed to have been tacitly established, until finally they would have demanded Fort Pickens, and I am not sure but what it would have been considered "an overt act" to have refused them.

I returned to my anchorage completely disgusted, and went immediately to call on the senior officer and to protest against my officers and ship being employed on such humiliating duty. I demanded permission to blockade the port of Pensacola and stop the supplies that were being constantly taken in to Bragg's army. Much to my surprise my demand was granted, provided everything was done on my own responsibility and that I should commit no "overt act." That seemed to be the stumbling-block in the senior officer's way. The quotation appalled him.

Next day I established a rigid blockade of the harbor with my boats and a small pilot-boat of which I had obtained possession, and Bragg got no more supplies by water, for not even a canoe was allowed to pass in or out. My communications with the senior officer ceased altogether, and for a week I did not see him.

Ever since the re-enforcement of Pickens I had been made to "eat dirt," as the Turks say, and I began to fear there would be no end to our humiliation; but, thank Heaven, it was over at last, and I had the satisfaction of hoping that Bragg and his men would occasionally be short of rations, although he could get provisions by hauling them over the sand from Mobile.

Amid the most serious events there is often something calculated to bring a smile to the face. Much stupidity was practiced by the United States forces at Pensacola, and a good deal of cunning and zeal shown by the Confederates. I changed the aspect of affairs and made things lively for the first few days. When I got hold of the pilot-boat I put Sailing-Master George Brown in charge of her, and with the boats of the *Powhatan* operated very successfully. There was no prize-money made, but we caused a deal of disappointment to the enemy.

On the third day of the blockade a thick fog set in, giving blockade-runners a fine opportunity to get in and out of Pensacola.

Of course everybody in the Southern States knew the condition of affairs at Pensacola, and how easy it was to get away from there or to enter through the unguarded gates of Fort Pickens. A number of people were picked up and sent back in both directions.

On the third morning one of our boats returned alongside the ship, towing a good-sized sail-boat with two persons sitting in the stern dressed like travelers, each with a traveling-bag by his side.

The moment I saw these persons I recognized them and told the officer of the deck not to give them my real name, but to show them to the cabin and say that "the captain would be on board in half an hour and expected them to breakfast, etc." I wanted to have a little amusement out of this incident.

When the travelers mounted the side and found themselves standing on the deck of a large ship bristling with guns, they both looked exceedingly disturbed, and, though muffled in heavy overcoats to keep out the chilling fog, they trembled perceptibly.

One of the men, a bluff Briton, in rather an arrogant manner asked the officer of the deck who was the captain of the ship, and by what right he dared to detain one of her Majesty's subjects while in transit from one country to another. If he was not at once allowed to proceed, and an apology made for his detention, he would lay the whole matter before her Majesty's Government and claim heavy damages.

"You will have to wait," said the officer of the deck. "Captain Jones will be here in half an hour, and he expects you to breakfast with him, as you must feel quite exhausted after your long journey from Montgomery."

The two travelers started, and the one who had not before spoken said, in an agitated voice, "Bless my soul, there must be some mistake; we don't know Captain Jones, in fact never heard of him. We are simply travelers getting out of that nasty place where you can't get a decent cup of coffee or a glass of wine. My name is Wilkins; my friend here is Mr. Blarney."

"*Barney,* if you please," interrupted his companion.

"Yes, bless my soul," said Wilkins, "you're right. I'm a little confused this morning. Here are our cards."

The cards read, "Mr. Barney, British Legation," and "Mr. Wilkins, Commissioner of Agriculture, Berlin."

"Please walk into the cabin, gentlemen," said the officer of the deck, "and wait the captain's coming. I will have your greatcoats dried by the galley fire."

While this conversation was going on I had directed the steward to set the breakfast-table for three persons, and to give us the best breakfast possible, not forgetting claret and Rhine wine, and some hot pickled peppers. The cards had been handed to me through my stateroom window after the gentlemen were shown into the cabin.

Both looked surprised when they saw the table set for breakfast. "Egad!" said Wilkins, "we're in for a lark, old boy; this is better than sailing about in a fog."

I could hear every word they said, and, by moving the slats in the blinds of my stateroom, could see the puzzled faces of two old acquaintances, who had no idea I was within a thousand miles of them.

"By George! old fellow," said Wilkins, "the captain does expect some one to breakfast, sure enough; and just look at this old Lafitte and Rhine wine; why, this Jones must know how to live; and, by George! if he hasn't some *chilé colorado* in that pickle-dish—napkins, glassware, silver; why, Barney, old boy, we are in clover; I hope Jones will invite us to stay a week."

"The chances are," said Barney, in a melancholy voice, "that this is all a mistake, and that we will be turned out in half an hour to mess with the crew, or tarred and feathered and sent back to Dixie, as those blasted fools on shore call it. But if this Captain Jones takes any liberties with me, one of her Majesty's squadrons will come down here and open this port in short order."

"Bosh!" said Wilkins. "Devil take me, old boy, if I am going to quarrel with Captain Jones, Brown, or Smith, or whatever his name is, as long as he sets as good a table as this. Ah! my lips smack at the thought of getting some of that Lafitte. You Britishers are so stupid about your dignity! Why, I don't believe Queen Victoria would care a snap if these fellows were to swing you up at the yard-arm to-morrow. She wouldn't trouble herself to send any squadron to look after you, old boy. Come, get in a good humor—God bless the old lady, rule Britannia if you please, but don't let's lose a good breakfast by your stupid English ways."

At that moment, through the blinds of my stateroom came the sounds, "Pretty Poll! Polly have a pepper?" as natural as life.

The travelers started, then looked around. "D—n that Poll parrot; this don't speak well for Jones. No one but an ass would keep a parrot. However, his Lafitte seems to be all right."

"Polly, put the kettle on! Britannia rules the waves," yelled the parrot, winding up with a demoniac laugh.

"Well," said Barney, "the parrot isn't as big a fool as its owner, for he knows who rules the waves."

"Bosh!" exclaimed Wilkins, "didn't the Yankees thrash you in the year 1812?"

"Ha! ha!" shouted the parrot, "Yankee Doodle came to town and whipped the British nation!"

"I'd wring that parrot's neck if I had him," said the Englishman; "he's a bigger fool than your friend Jones."

"Don't abuse Jones," said Wilkins, "until we find out what kind of a cook he has."

At that moment the supposed parrot sang out, "Fie! fie! fie! Sam, does your mother know you're out? Polly wants a cracker!"

Wilkins jumped from his chair. "Did you hear that?" he said.

"Yes, I heard it," replied Barney. "Don't pay any attention to that infernal bird; you will make as big an ass of yourself as Jones, who must be hard up for amusement to keep a parrot."

"Watch your bag, Sam," sang out the parrot. "Contraband! contraband! Spy! spy!"

Wilkins rushed for the stateroom door; it was locked on the inside. "I'll wring the d—d parrot's neck," he shouted. "What does this mean?"

" 'Conscience makes cowards of us all,' " replied the other. "It's only parrot's nonsense. I knew of one once that could repeat words as fast as he heard them uttered."

"Cowards of us all!" yelled the parrot; "I belong to that ass Jones!"

"That's the devil," said Wilkins; "I wish I could throttle him."

"Ha! ha! ha!" laughed the parrot. "O Sam Ward, Sam Ward, Sam Ward! ha! ha! ha! Polly wants a cracker!"

Wilkins turned pale, seized his traveling-bag and rushed to the cabin-door, but, on opening it, was met by the orderly, who informed him that he could not pass out.

"What!" inquired Wilkins, "am I a prisoner?"

"My orders are, sir," replied the orderly, "that you gentlemen must remain in the cabin until the captain comes on board."

The parrot laughed and sang out, "Sam Ward a prisoner! fie! fie! fie! Sam! fie! fie!"

Wilkins rushed again to the stateroom door, which he tried in vain to open, while the parrot inside sang out, "Sam Ward!"

Wilkins sank exhausted on the sofa. "I'll give this Captain Jones a piece of my mind for teaching his rascally parrot such twaddle. I wonder where he could have heard of me."

Just then the parrot shouted, "Walk in, Captain Jones; Sam Ward says you're an ass!" and I opened the stateroom door and walked into the cabin.

If a thunderbolt had fallen, Sam Ward, *alias* Wilkins, could not have been more astonished.

"In the name of Heaven," he exclaimed, "where did you come from? Do you belong to this ship?" and he seized me by the hand and almost shook my arm from its socket. "Do you know Captain Jones? He owes me an apology for teaching his parrot a lot of infernal nonsense about me."

"Fie! fie! fie! Sam Ward!" exclaimed a small messenger boy, sitting demurely on a camp-stool; said boy having been brought in to personate a parrot—which bird he could imitate to perfection—"Polly wants a pepper."

"Good gracious!" exclaimed Sam Ward, "that was your nonsense, then?—and I might have known it the moment I saw you. I haven't forgotten your tricks and jokes when we went through Magellan Straits in the old Panama; but what are you doing here?"

"I am Captain Jones," I replied. "I suppose I have as much right to an *alias* as you have."

"Well, thank Providence, I am sure of a good breakfast; but let me introduce you to my friend Mr. Barney, who is traveling with me; we won't be sent to Fort Lafayette, will we?"

"How do you do, Mr. R——?" I said, addressing the *soi-disant* Barney. "I knew you through your full whiskers, and congratulate you upon being under a real flag once more. I don't think her Majesty will send a squadron to break up the blockade, but we will get some breakfast and then talk business."

Sam Ward said he had got caught in the South, and he and R—— had to get out of the country the best way they could. Hearing that Pensacola was not blockaded, they came there, and, hiring a boat and a man to manage it, were coming out under cover of a fog when captured. "Thank fortune, I smell the coffee," said Sam, "and know that breakfast is coming."

R—— also became quite communicative, told me he had traveled South to see how things were going, and was glad enough to get out of the country.

That was a pleasant breakfast. Sam Ward, as usual, took charge, called for all the sauces in the pantry, and paid his best respects to the Lafitte and Rhine wine.

Sam Ward talked Union like a man; R—— was evidently bitten with the secession mania. He said we should have a long and bitter war, and could never restore the Union unless we granted the Southern people all they asked for.

That night I sent my guests off in the pilot-boat with their own boat in tow, with directions to take them to the entrance of Mobile Bay and let them go.

The last thing Sam Ward did was to extort from me a promise never to tell that parrot story, and I only do so now that he has gone to his long home, where, if he takes cognizance of what is occurring here below, he will not be displeased at my bringing in an old friend in connection with this little incident of the war.

I had my suspicions about the two travelers, and thought possibly they might have been messengers from the Southern cabinet to friends in the North, but I was not going to raise a question that might have vexed the Secretary of State and burned my own fingers. I took their word as gentlemen, and dismissed them after they had enjoyed my hospitality.

When I knew how loosely the blockade of Pensacola had been maintained, and how the Confederates had been encouraged to mount guns, complete their defences, and bring in provisions and stores for their troops, I thought it would be idle for me to interfere with the movements of two gentlemen who claimed to be running away from the South and trying to reach the flesh-pots of the Yankees. They could not do much harm, I thought, and I have always been glad that I had it in my power to contribute to their comfort in their journey through the lines.

Four days after the above episode Captain McKean arrived in the frigate *Niagara*. I went immediately on board and informed that officer, in as few words as possible, how matters stood, and how badly affairs had been conducted.

He signaled at once for all commanding officers to repair on board the *Niagara,* and, when we were all in the cabin, Captain McKean addressed us as follows:

"Gentlemen, these are ticklish times, and it is necessary for the senior officers of the navy to set an example to the younger ones. What I propose will keep people to their duty; but if the officers present have any conscientious scruples about taking an oath of allegiance, they can state them or for ever after hold their peace. I propose that we all do now take the oath of allegiance to the United States, and sign a paper to the effect that we will serve the Government until death do us part and, forsaking all others, cleave unto her our natural mother."

The old gentleman was deeply religious, and had evidently been reading the marriage ceremony, but his remarks were forcible and to the point.

The officer, whom I have before mentioned, declined point-blank to take the oath—and it was not an "iron-clad" affair either—whereupon I stepped forward and said, "I think every man should be obliged to take that oath, for I have seen more treason in the last ten days than I ever supposed could exist in the United States Navy." So I signed the paper, and Captain McKean administered the oath to me.

Captain McKean looked coolly at the captain who had declined to sign. "Now, captain," he said, "will you sign this paper and take the oath of allegiance or not?"

"I solemnly protest against it," replied the other; "you have no authority to require it of us. We took our oaths when we entered the navy."

"Yes," said the old captain, "so did many others, and they violated them. You must either take the oath or suffer the consequences for not doing so."

"I will sign the paper under protest, and take the oath with a reservation."

"I don't care *how* you do it," said Captain McKean, "but do it you must."

The officer sulkily signed the paper, took the oath, and, turning on his heel, left the cabin without saying "Good-morning" to any one.

"I fear I have made a mistake," said Captain McKean, "in not arresting that officer."

"Yes," replied I, "you never made a greater mistake in your life; but he will keep his oath with a reservation never to fire a shot at the South in anger," and so it turned out.

In a few days Captain McKean scattered all the vessels in different directions, leaving the above-mentioned officer in charge at Pensacola Bar, with orders to maintain a strict blockade and not let even a canoe pass in or out.

Months passed away. Bragg built his fortifications and never molested Fort Pickens. Colonel Brown piled up sand-bags and never troubled Bragg. Neither of them committed an "overt act." A more innocent war was never carried on.

Chapter XIII.

INTERVIEW WITH GENERAL GIANT AT CAIRO—FIRST MEETING WITH GENERAL SHERMAN—OUR FLAG HOISTED OVER ARKANSAS POST—GENERAL GRANT AND THE SIEGE OF VICKSBURG—HOAX ON THE VICKSBURGERS.

I assumed command of the Mississippi Squadron at Cairo, Illinois, in October, 1862. There were the sturdy ironclads that had fought their way from Fort Henry to Donaldson, to Island No. 10, and White River, and destroyed the enemy's navy at Memphis. All had done good service under their gallant commanders, Foote and Davis.

The *Benton, Carondelet, Cairo, Baron de Kalb, Mound City,* and *Cincinnati* were designed and constructed by that universal genius, James B. Eads, in less than three months, and became famous in the annals of the navy. Besides these were the *Tyler, Conestoga,* and *Lexington.*

See the old warriors out in the stream,
Open in many a wood-end and seam!

As soon as I arrived, the ironclads were put in the hands of five hundred loyal mechanics, and in a week were ready for any service.

The rest of the vessels under my command were not very formidable, consisting of some side-wheel river steamboats and three or four "tin-clads," and this was the force with which the navy was expected to batter down Vicksburg.

Soon after my arrival at Cairo I sent a messenger to General Grant informing him that I had taken command of the naval forces, and should be happy to co-operate with him in any enterprise he might think proper to undertake. I also informed him that General McClernand had orders to raise troops at Springfield, Illinois, prior to undertaking the capture of Vicksburg. I thought it my duty to tell him this, as it was not information given to me in confidence.

Several weeks later Captain McAllister, quartermaster at Cairo, gave a supper party to me and the officers on the station on board the quartermaster's steamer, a large, comfortable river boat.

Supper had been served when I saw Captain McAllister usher in a travel-worn person dressed in citizen's clothes. McAllister was a very tall man, and his companion was dwarfed by his superior size. McAllister introduced the gentleman to me as General Grant, and placed us at a table by ourselves and left us to talk matters over.

Grant, though evidently tired and hungry, commenced business at once. "Admiral," he inquired, "what is all this you have been writing me?"

I gave the general an account of my interviews with the President and with General McClernand, and he inquired, "When can you move with your gun-boats, and what force have you?"

"I can move to-morrow with all the old gunboats and five or six other vessels; also the *Tyler, Conestoga,* and *Lexington.*"

"Well, then," said Grant, "I will leave you now and write at once to Sherman to have thirty thousand infantry and artillery embarked in transports ready to start for Vicksburg the moment you get to Memphis. I will return to Holly Springs to-night, and will start with a large force for Grenada as soon as I can get off.

"General Joe Johnston is near Vicksburg with forty thousand men, besides the garrison of the place under General Pemberton. When Johnston hears I am marching on Grenada, he will come from Vicksburg to meet me and check my advance. I will hold him at Grenada while you and Sherman push on down the Mississippi and make a landing somewhere on the Yazoo. The garrison at Vicksburg will be small, and Sherman will have no difficulty in getting inside the works. When that is done I will force Johnston out of Grenada, and, as he falls back on Vicksburg, will follow him up with a superior force. When he finds Vicksburg is occupied, he will retreat via Jackson."

I thought this plan an admirable one. Grant and myself never indulged in long talks together; it was only necessary for him to tell me what he desired, and I carried out his wishes to the best of my ability.

General Grant started that night for Holly Springs, Mississippi, and, I believe, rode on horseback nearly all the way, while I broke up the supper party by ordering every officer to his post of duty, to be ready to start down the river next day at noon.

And this was the preliminary step to the capture of Vicksburg.

Grant, in his plain, dusty coat, was, in my eyes, a greater general than the man who rides around,

All feathers and fuss.

Here in twenty minutes Grant unfolded his plan of campaign, involving the transportation of over one hundred thousand men, and, with a good supper staring him in the face, proposed to ride back again over a road he had just traveled without tasting a mouthful, his cigar serving, doubtless, for food and drink.

Three days after, with all the naval forces, I started down the Mississippi, and at Memphis found General Sherman embarking his troops on a long line of river steamers, and sent word to the general that I would call upon him at his headquarters.

Thinking it probable that Sherman would be dressed in full feather, I put on my uniform coat, the splendor of which rivaled that of a drum-major. Sherman, hearing that I was indifferent to appearances and generally dressed in working-clothes, thought he would not annoy me by fixing up, and so kept on his blue flannel suit; and we met, both a little surprised at the appearance of the other.

"Halloo, Porter," said the general, "I am glad to see you; you got here sooner than I expected, but we'll get off to-night. Devilish cold, isn't it? Sit down and warm up." And he stirred up the coal in the grate. "Here, captain"—to one of his aids—"tell General Blair to get his men on board at once. Tell the quartermaster to report as soon as he has six hundred thousand rations embarked. Here, Dick"—to his servant—"put me up some shirts and under-clothes in a bag, and don't bother me with a trunk and traps enough for a regiment. Here, Captain"—another aid—"tell the steamboat captains to have steam up at six o'clock, and to lay in plenty of fuel, for I'm not going to stop every few hours to cut wood. Tell the officer in charge of embarkation to allow no picking and choosing of boats; the generals in command must take what is given them—there, that will do. Glad to see you, Porter; how's Grant?"

This was the first time I had ever met General Sherman, and my impressions of him were very favorable. I thought myself lucky to have two such generals as Grant and Sherman to co-operate with.

I soon returned to my flag-ship, the *Black Hawk,* and gave Captain Walke orders to proceed with several vessels to the Yazoo River, take possession of the landings in order to prevent the erection of batteries, and drag the river above Chickasaw Bayou for torpedoes. Captain Walke was directed to use all possible expedition, so as to reach the Yazoo at least a day in advance of us.

We departed from Memphis as arranged, and reached the Yazoo in good time. The *Cairo,* one of my best ironclads, had been blown up while grappling for torpedoes; but the landing of Sherman's army had been secured.

The rest is a matter of history, and is registered in the chronicles of the times with many variations and not a few misrepresentations. The reporters who followed the army did not all confine themselves to the truth, and when I asked one of them, on a certain occasion, why he did not state facts as they occurred, he replied:

"If I stated facts I would lose my place, for nothing but sensational articles will satisfy the public."

We reached Chickasaw Bayou in safety, but the army did not get much farther.

Grant's plans were well laid—"man proposes but God disposes"—and the plans were unsuccessful after all.

When Grant started from Holly Springs he left behind him a large depot of stores on which his army depended for supplies, and marched on Grenada with a force (I think) of sixty thousand men.

General Pemberton, as soon as he learned of this movement, saw that he would be locked up in Vicksburg if he let Grant get to the rear of that place, and his plan, therefore, was to check Grant's advance until other troops could be sent by rail to re-enforce Vicksburg.

Grant and Pemberton were marching toward each other as fast as possible, when the ubiquitous General Van Dorn got in Grant's rear and destroyed his supplies at Holly Springs.

I believe, however, that Grant had partly accomplished his object by drawing Pemberton a long way from Vicksburg, with the idea that, in the latter's absence, General Sherman would have comparatively little trouble in getting into the city.

No one, at that time, had any idea of the magnitude of the defenses that had been erected in every quarter to keep a foe out of Vicksburg, as if the Titans had come to the rescue of the rebel stronghold.

Sherman at every point encountered obstacles of which he had never dreamed. Forests had been cut down in the line of Chickasaw Bayou, and through the *chevaux-de-frise* the soldiers, standing up to their waists in water, had to cut their way with axes across the dismal swamps. All this, of course, took time; there seemed to be no other route to Vicksburg. Haines's Bluff had been fortified so that no troops could pass in that direction without it was first reduced by the gunboats. Every available soldier in Vicksburg had been brought to the point where Sherman was making his approaches, and they worked like devils.

> *Old Clootie was there in his vigor and might;*
> *He held the bottle and urged on the fight,*
> *As he dashed with his imps o'er the blood-sprinkled plain,*
> *His horses' hoofs trampling the wounded and slain.*
> *What cared he who died in their vigor and sin,*
> *As long as the devil and imps could but win?*

On the first sight of the gunboats clearing out the Yazoo, the officer in command at Vicksburg saw through the whole plan, and telegraphed at once to General Pemberton, who immediately hurried back to Vicksburg, while Grant returned to Holly Springs.

Had not General Sherman been stopped by unforeseen obstacles, he would have captured the Southern Gibraltar; but the impediments which an energetic adversary threw in the way disconcerted all his plans.

To add to Sherman's difficulties, the rain came on—and such a rain! The heavens seemed trying to drown our army; the naval vessels and transports were the only arks of safety. The level lands were inundated, and there were three feet of water in the swamps where our army was operating.

Notwithstanding this dismal situation of affairs, Sherman ordered an assault on the enemy's works. Part of General Blair's and part of another division reached the interior of the works and held them for a time.

The tables were soon turned, for, just as victory seemed to crown our arms, General Pemberton appeared on the scene with his army, just returned from Grenada, and drove our small body of men out of the works back to the place from which they started.

That ended the second campaign against Vicksburg, and our disheartened troops returned to the transports, where they were free from attack, as the enemy could not follow them through the waste of waters between their fortifications and the gunboats. We picked up all that we had landed, including an old, worthless horse, determined that the enemy should have no more than we could help.

It was still raining, and the current ran so strong in the river that the vessels had to be fastened securely to the trees. The wind howled like a legion of devils, though which side it was howling for I have no idea.

That night General Sherman came on board my flag-ship, drenched to the skin. He looked as if he had been grappling with the mud, and got the worst of it.

He sat down and remained silent for some minutes.

"You are out of sorts," I said, at length. "What is the matter?"

"I have lost seventeen hundred men, and those infernal reporters will publish all over the country their ridiculous stories about Sherman being whipped, etc."

"Only seventeen hundred men!" I said. "Pshaw! that is nothing; simply an episode in the war. You'll lose seventeen thousand before the war is over, and will think nothing of it. We'll have Vicksburg yet before we die.—Steward, bring some punch for the general and myself."

"That's good sense, Porter!" exclaimed the general, "and I am glad to see you are not disheartened; but what shall we do now? I must take my boys somewhere and wipe this out."

I informed the general that I was ready to go anywhere.

"Then," said he, "let's go and thrash out Arkansas Post." And it was arranged that we should start next morning for that place. This attempt on Vicksburg gave occasion for some fine strategy on both sides.

Had General Grant determined in the first instance to advance on Vicksburg, leaving a sufficient force of men at Holly Springs to protect the place, no doubt Vicksburg would have fallen; but he had every reason to believe that, with the plans he had made, Sherman would get in. The appointed time had evidently not arrived, and it was necessary that a final demonstration of the power and determination of the Federal Government should be made, to satisfy the Southern people that none of their strongholds could finally prevail against the Union forces, and that no earthly power could dismember the Union,

For God in his wisdom had devised the best plan
For the union of States and the freedom of man.

Next morning a colonel, dressed in a new suit of uniform, sought an interview with me. I knew he could not belong to Sherman's army, for all his officers had long ago worn the brightness from their accoutrements.

"I come," said he, "from General McClernand, who is at the mouth of the Yazoo River, and wants you to call and see him as soon as possible."

"Well," thinks I to myself, "that's cool!" "You can tell the general," I said, "that my duties at present are so engrossing that I am making no calls, and that it is his place to come and see me. What is the general doing, and how did he get here?"

"He has come," said the officer, "to take command of the army; he took passage down in one of your ram gunboats."

Here was a pretty kettle of fish! I bade the officer good-morning and he took his departure.

Just then I saw General Sherman in a small boat pulled by two soldiers. I hailed him, and when he was near enough I said, "Sherman, McClernand is at the mouth of the Yazoo, waiting to take command of your army!"

Sherman looked serious as he inquired, "Are you going to call on him?"

"No," I replied, "I am not making calls just now."

"But I must," said Sherman, "for he ranks me."

In two hours General Sherman returned with General McClernand, and I received the latter on board the flag-ship with all due courtesy, and inquired if he had brought an army with him and siege-tools to insure the fall of Vicksburg.

"No," replied McClernand, "but I find this army in a most demoralized state, and I must do something to raise their spirits."

"Then, sir," I said, "you take command of this army?"

"Certainly," he replied; "and if you will let me have some of your gunboats, I propose to proceed immediately and capture Arkansas Post."

Sherman made a remark the purport of which I have forgotten, but McClernand made a discourteous reply, whereupon Sherman walked off into the after-cabin. I was angry that any one should dare treat General Sherman with discourtesy in my cabin.

I informed General McClernand that the proposition to capture Arkansas Post had been broached by General Sherman the previous evening, and that I never let my gunboats go on such an important expedition without me. "If," I said, "General Sherman goes in command of this army, I will go along with my whole force and make a sure thing of it; otherwise I will have nothing to do with the affair."

Just then Sherman beckoned to me, and I went in to him. "My God, Porter!" he exclaimed, "you will ruin yourself if you talk that way to McClernand; he is very intimate with the President, and has powerful influence."

"I don't care who or what he is, he shall not be rude to you in my cabin," I replied.

"Did you understand my proposition, General McClernand?" I inquired, on my return to the forward cabin—he was at that moment consulting a map which lay on the table.

"Yes," said McClernand, "I understand it, and agree to it. There is no objection, I suppose, to my going along?"

"None in the world," I answered, "only be it understood that General Sherman is to command this army."

We started as soon as possible and arrived at "the Post," a fort, mounting eleven heavy guns, on the Arkansas River. I attacked it with three ironclads and several smaller vessels, and in three hours disabled all the guns. General Sherman surrounded the place with his troops, and, after heavy losses, it surrendered—the fort, in charge of naval officers, to me, and the Confederate army of six thousand men, under General Churchill, to General Sherman.

Our flag was no sooner hoisted over Arkansas Post—January 11, 1863—than General McClernand assumed command of the army and wrote the report of the capture—a most ungenerous thing for him to do under the circumstances.

The moment the prisoners were secured and the fort rendered untenable General McClernand ordered the army to proceed to Vicksburg, and I went in company, sending a message in advance to General Grant that I anticipated no good results from McClernand's commanding the army, that it was unjust to Sherman, that I was certain McClernand and myself could never co-operate harmoniously, and I hoped he would come and take command himself. I do not know that General Grant ever received my message, but we had hardly landed the troops on the bend opposite Vicksburg when he appeared and assumed command of the army, and the third attack on the rebel stronghold immediately commenced.

The siege was conducted with great perseverance on our side and with great bravery and endurance on the other, and when Pemberton surrendered—July 4, 1863—there was nothing left for the subsistence of the soldiers or the inhabitants.

An elaborate history of the siege of Vicksburg would be a most interesting military work, but to write it would require much time and research, and a consultation not only of official documents but of the experience of the principal officers on both sides who were engaged in this memorable struggle.

General Grant has gained a world-wide reputation for his military achievements, but I think no event conferred more credit on him than the siege of Vicksburg against the most formidable series of earthworks ever erected on this continent.

I saw the celebrated Malakoff and the Redan two days after they fell into the hands of the allied English and French army, and they were nothing in comparison with the defenses of Vicksburg.

Grant's action in turning the flank at Vicksburg with but fifty-six thousand men, and defeating two armies aggregating eighty thousand strong, forms one of the most remarkable chapters in the history of the civil war.

I do not believe that any of the accounts that were written of the events transpiring around Vicksburg during the siege did justice to the subject, and I am sorry that the limit of these pages will prevent my giving even an outline of this remarkable siege.

Having encamped directly opposite to Vicksburg, our army had a good opportunity of contemplating the task before it.

It was evident that the place could not be taken from the front; the rebel army and the inhabitants were receiving all the supplies they wanted, not only *via* Jackson but by steamers from Red River. It was desirable to stop this communication.

I had under my command a semi-naval organization called the "Marine Brigade," which had done good service at Memphis and elsewhere. Several of the vessels in this organization were commanded by members of the Ellet family, the senior member of which, Brigadier-General A. W. Ellet, commanded the brigade.

Colonel Charles Ellet, Jr., a young man of twenty-two, commanded the *Queen of the West,* a ram improvised from a river steamboat.

I ordered young Ellet to pass the batteries of Vicksburg at night, proceed to the mouth of Red River, intercept the supplies for Vicksburg and Port Hudson, and capture everything he could overtake.

I don't know whether it was from love of glory or from want of judgment, but, instead of taking advantage of the darkness to run the batteries, Ellet chose early daylight, got well hammered as he passed the forts, and nearly defeated the object of the expedition. Not being accustomed to strict discipline, Ellet did not realize the necessity of carrying out his orders to the letter.

After Colonel Ellet reached Red River he captured several steamers loaded with provisions for Port Hudson, and having on board a number of Confederate officers; and hearing that other steamers were on their way down Red River, his youthful ardor led him to go on up that stream.

He arrived at Fort De Russy, and there, by the treachery of his pilot, was run on shore near the batteries. The enemy opened fire on the *Queen of the West,* killing and wounding numbers of the crew and cutting the steam-pipe. The vessel was now helpless, and Ellet and all his officers and men who were able jumped overboard and drifted down the river to a point where one of their prizes lay, got on board of her, and made their escape.

In the mean time I had prepared the iron-clad *Indianola* and sent her down to assist the *Queen of the West.* The *Indianola* passed the batteries at night with little damage, and met Colonel Ellet and his men coming up in their prize steamer *New Era.*

The *Indianola,* with two coal-barges in tow, continued down until she reached the mouth of Red River, then turned back and proceeded up river again until near the plantation of Mr. Joseph Davis, the brother of the Confederate President.

At daylight next morning, after the *Queen of the West* had been abandoned, the Confederates took possession and soon repaired damages.

The Confederate ram *Webb* joined the *Queen of the West* from Alexandria, and the two vessels, well manned and armed, proceeded in search of the *Indianola,* came up with her at Davis's plantation, rammed her, and she ran into shoal water and sank, February 24, 1863.

We heard of the disaster a few hours after, and all my calculations for stopping the enemy's supplies were for the time frustrated; but I took a philosophical view of the matter as one of the episodes of the war. However, it was necessary to try and prevent the rebels from raising the *Indianola,* and, as I was not ready to go down the river myself, as it would interfere with an important military movement, I hit upon a cheap expedient, which worked very well.

I set the whole squadron at work and made a raft of logs, three hundred feet long, with sides to it, two huge wheel-houses and a formidable log casemate, from the portholes of which appeared sundry wooden guns. Two old boats hung from davits fitted to the "ironclad," and two smokestacks made of hogsheads completed the illusion; and on her wheel-houses was painted the following: "Deluded Rebels, Cave In!" An American flag was hoisted aft, and a banner emblazoned with skull and crossbones ornamented the bow.

When this craft was completed, she resembled at a little distance the ram *Lafayette,* which had just arrived from St. Louis.

The mock ram was furnished with a big iron pot inside each smokestack, in which was tar and oakum to raise a black smoke, and at midnight she was towed down close to the water-batteries of Vicksburg and sent adrift.

It did not take the Vicksburg sentinels long to discover the formidable monster that was making its way down the river. The batteries opened on her with vigor, and continued the fire until she had passed beyond the range of their guns.

The Vicksburgers had greatly exulted over the capture of the *Queen of the West* and the *Indianola;* the local press teemed with accounts of the daring of the captors, and flattered themselves that, with the *Indianola* and *Queen of the West* in their possession, they would be able to drive the Union navy out of the Mississippi. What was their astonishment to see this huge ironclad pass the batteries, apparently unharmed, and not even taking the trouble to fire a gun!

Some of our soldiers had gone down to the point below Vicksburg to see the fun, and just before reaching Warrenton the mock monitor caught the eddy and turned toward the bank where these men were gathered.

The soldiers spent several hours in trying to shove the dummy off into the stream, when daylight overtook them in the midst of their work, and the *Queen of the West,* with the Confederate flag flying, was seen coming up the river and stopping at Warrenton.

As we afterward learned, she came up for pumps, etc., to raise the *Indianola.*

In the mean while the military authorities in Vicksburg had sent couriers down to Joe Davis's plantation to inform the people on board the *Webb* that a monster ironclad had passed the batteries and would soon be upon them. The crew of the *Webb* were busy in trying to remove the guns from their prize, and, when they heard the news, determined to blow her up.

Just after the *Queen of the West* made the Warrenton landing the soldiers succeeded in towing the mock ironclad into the stream, and she drifted rapidly down upon the rebel prize, whose crew never stopped to deliberate, but cut their fasts and proceeded down the river. Their steam was low, and for a time the mock ironclad drifted almost as fast as the *Queen of the West;* but at length the latter left her formidable pursuer far behind.

The *Queen of the West* arrived at the point where the *Indianola* was sunk just as the people on board the *Webb* were preparing to blow her up, bringing the news that the "great ironclad" was close behind. So the *Webb* cast off and, with her consort, made all speed down the river.

The *Webb* had been so greatly injured in ramming the *Indianola* that she had to go to Shreveport for repairs, and the *Queen of the West* was shortly after recaptured and destroyed.

The results of the capture of the *Indianola* were, however, deplorable. It is wonderful how rapidly news was transmitted along the river, and the *Indianola* had scarcely sunk before Farragut heard of it on board the *Hartford*. He was also informed that the Confederates had raised the vessel and were about to use her against his fleet at Port Hudson.

Farragut had obtained the false impression that the *Indianola* was a very powerful vessel, and so he thought it necessary to pass the batteries at Port Hudson and encounter her before she could get under the protection of the Confederate works at that place.

This induced him to attempt to run past Port Hudson with a portion of his fleet, when he met with considerable loss.

Owing to the smoke from the guns which hung over the river, the pilots could not see their way. The frigate *Mississippi* grounded opposite the forts, and there remained, while the enemy poured shot and shell into her to their hearts' content.

Her commanding officer did everything that was possible to get his vessel off; but, finding all his efforts useless, and that his officers and men were being sacrificed, he set fire to the ship and abandoned her.

As the frigate's upper works were consumed the ship became lightened; she slid off the mud-bank and, drifting down the river, blew up with an awful sound that carried joy to the hearts of the Confederates.

A thousand memories clustered around the dear old ship, and she will be handed down in history with the *Hartford,* whose fortunes up to this time she had shared.

Only two of Farragut's vessels passed Port Hudson—the *Hartford,* his flagship, and another which was lashed to her; so he arrived at the mouth of Red River with but a small portion of his fleet.

So much for the loss of one ironclad of which much was expected and by which little was accomplished. The *Indianola* lay imbedded in the mud until after the fall of Vicksburg, when we raised her.

The Vicksburg people were furious at the trick we played them, and the newspapers reviled their military authorities for not being able to distinguish an old raft from a monster ironclad! They were consoled, however, in a day or two when the news of the destruction of the *Mississippi* reached Vicksburg.

Notwithstanding their gallant defense, the garrison of Vicksburg were daily growing weaker while our strength was all the time increasing. They began to realize that we had come to stay until we could plant the Union flag over their stronghold.

Chapter XIV.

GENERAL GRANT'S PLANS FOR TAKING VICKSBURG— THE YAZOO PASS EXPEDITION—NAVAL EVOLUTIONS IN THE WOODS—PILES OF COTTON BURNED BY THE CONFEDERATES—MR. TUB, THE TELEGRAPH-WIRE MAN— THE PASS AT ROLLING FORK—END OF THE STEELE BAYOU EXPEDITION.

I intended by this time to have departed from before Vicksburg, and to leave it to future scribblers to write about, as no doubt they will do, just as tourists visit the plains of Waterloo to pick up relics and write an oft-told tale; but there is a fascination about the place (Vicksburg) that prevents me from tearing myself away.

Everything about that siege is an anecdote or a reminiscence worthy of being treasured up.

One of the liveliest reminiscences I have of the siege is what is called the Yazoo Pass expedition—one of three attempts we made to get behind Vicksburg with a fleet of ironclads and a detachment of the army—in which I have to say that we failed most egregiously.

At one period of the siege the rains had swollen the Mississippi River so much that it had backed its waters up into its tributaries, which had risen seventeen feet, and, overflowing, had inundated the country for many miles.

Great forests had become channels admitting the passage of large steamers between the trees, and now and then wide lanes were met with where a frigate might have passed.

The ironclads drew only seven feet of water and had no masts or yards to encumber them, and but little about their decks that could be swept away by the bushes or lower branches of the trees. I had thoughts of trying the experiment of getting the vessels back of Vicksburg in that way, and sent Lieutenant Murphy in a tug to examine the woods as far as he could go, and to let me know the results of his cruise as soon as possible.

Murphy soon returned with the most cheering news, and induced me to go with him and take a look for myself. General Grant accompanied me, and, prepared with lead-lines to measure the depth, we started off.

A few miles up the Yazoo, before reaching Haines's Bluff, we came to an opening in the woods. Under the pilotage of Murphy, the tug *Jessie Benton* darted into the bushes, and the man at the lead took the soundings—nothing less than fifteen feet. Presently we reached an opening between the trees sufficiently wide to admit two ironclads abreast. I suppose it was an ancient road in the forest by which to haul cotton to the river.

We followed this for five miles until we reached a forest of large trees without any undergrowth, but with width enough between them to admit the passage of our heaviest ironclad. This forest permitted us to steam along about five miles farther, when we came to a wide opening where there were but few trees. Here we found a bayou leading to the westward with from ten to twelve feet of water—more than enough for our purposes.

We knew this bayou led into the Rolling Fork, Yallabusha, and Sunflower Rivers, though there was not generally enough water in it to float a canoe. We could not ascend it then for fear of alarming the inhabitants, or letting them know the news of our arrival in these woods and having it conveyed to Vicksburg.

We saw all we wanted, and General Grant approved of the plan I proposed of going up with some ironclads, tugs, etc., and trying to get into the Sunflower; that would lead us into the Yazoo again, and we could come down and take Haines's Bluff in the rear.

General Grant also determined to send General Sherman on the expedition with ten thousand troops, and said we could make a reconnaissance if we could do no more, for he saw from the first that there was no use in sitting down before Vicksburg and simply looking at it, or bombarding it to bring about a surrender; we would have lost time, and deposited our shell in the hills, increasing their weight in iron, without getting nearer to our object. General Grant had from the first an idea of turning Vicksburg, but *how* to do it was the question. He was obliged to have transports if he went below the city and desired to cross the river to land on the Vicksburg side, and enough of these transports to carry troops and provisions. How was he to get these frail vessels below Vicksburg without passing the batteries? One shot would disable them. He could depend upon the gun-boats to pass the batteries, but there were not enough of them to convey the necessary number of troops, and they had no accommodations for carrying provisions.

Besides, it would not do to take too many of the gun-boats below Vicksburg, for it would leave the upper Mississippi unguarded, and the enemy would commence at once to erect batteries along the river and stop the transportation of troops and stores. During all Grant's operations before Vicksburg, while I had command of the river force, he never had a transport molested. I so guarded the Mississippi—from Cairo down—with gun-boats (which I was building or altering incessantly) that flying batteries and guerrillas—so called—were never able to make any headway.

General Grant had to think of all these things before he could make a move for below.

He talked with me about it, and I assured him I was ready to go the moment he desired it. He thought he might do something that would enable him to get by Vicksburg without bringing his transports under fire. He tried cutting a ditch across the peninsula, in hopes that the river would burst through there and leave Vicksburg out in the cold. This occurred finally (after the war), but too late for our operations, for, notwithstanding the high stage of the water, it refused to run through the ditch; heavy eddies extended from the shore far out into the river and kept the current away from the bank; there was no cutting power in the eddies.

Grant tried to make a channel through what was called Lake Providence, but some of the vessels that tried this passage got entangled in the woods, and came near remaining there.

Every known expedient had been tried without success, and now it remained to attempt the route through the woods to the west of the Yazoo River.

Sixty or seventy miles above Vicksburg there was, many years ago, an old pass into the Yallabusha and the Sunflower called the Yazoo Pass. This had long since been closed up by a deep levee, and the land, once overflowed through this pass, had become flourishing plantations.

It was proposed by some one to open the pass once more and let the water flow in, making a deep channel by which we could send in an expedition of gun-boats. These might reach the Yazoo River that way back of Vicksburg and clear the way for the troops.

This plan met with approval, and General Grant and myself determined, at the same time we were trying to get up through the woods and the bayou into the Sunflower, that we would send a naval and military expedition through the old Yazoo Pass.

This expedition consisted of two heavy ironclads, three or four light-armed vessels, and about four thousand troops in transports. The force arrived at the point selected, a few men dug a small trench with spades, and in an hour the water was rushing in with the force of a cataract, carrying away a hundred yards of the levee and inundating hundreds of acres of land. It took twenty-four hours for the water to reach a level, and then the gunboats, without more ado, pitched in regardless of consequences, followed by the transports. Then came the tug of war. The vessels were swept along with great velocity until they got beyond the great pressure of the water, or were stopped by the trees with their overhanging branches, which brought them up all standing, bringing their smokestacks on deck and knocking off some of the upper cabins.

The ironclads stood the thumping better than the lighter vessels, for they had no cabins above, and all they had to fear was the loss of their smokestacks and boats, some of which were crushed to pieces.

All the vessels were at the mercy of the strong current. If one of them for a moment grappled a tree to hold on by, she would find another one sweeping down on her from astern, and, for fear of being crushed, she had to let go, and then all floated on together.

During the years in which the old Yazoo Pass had been closed the heavy trees had mingled their branches across the stream, and now often stopped the progress of the fleet. Then a thousand hands would be set to work with axes and saws to clear away overhead for a mile or two in advance.

Sometimes the vessels would come bump against a small "Red River raft," held securely by running vines or wedged in so strongly with a key-log that it would require hours of labor before they could get the raft loose and let it go drifting down with the current; then the fleet would push on again, and this lasted three or four days, while the expedition only progressed forty miles.

Most of the light vessels were perfect wrecks in their upper works. Their machinery and boilers held out, and that was all that was required of them. It was a painful and ever-to-be-remembered expedition to those who took part in it.

To make matters worse, the naval officer commanding the expedition showed symptoms of aberration of mind, and the other officers with him had great difficulty in getting him to pursue proper measures. The officer in charge of the troops got discontented with the hard work his men had to perform in cutting down trees and other obstructions. Still they kept pushing on, and no such word as fail was heard. All wondered how they would get out of that, or back again through that cataract; but then their orders were to push on and to come out behind Vicksburg! Day and night they moved along, taking no rest, though they would not make more than two miles in twelve hours. It was work that tried men's souls, and there are few naval officers left of all that party who can sit down and tell of that adventure. Death's avaricious hand has snatched most of them away, and it shows the effect the toil and excitement of war will have on men of iron, with nerves of steel, who, if they had been left to pursue the peaceful avocations of life, would probably have been here now.

There is an end to all hard work, privation, and exposure. Every one is either killed or used up, or gets to some place where he can lie down and rest.

There is a certain amount of endurance sailors and soldiers possess which is kept up as long as the nerve-power holds out, and it was with a relieved feeling that the people of this expedition could finally lie down and sleep without the disturbing noise of crushing bulwarks, or the fall on the decks of decaying limbs. They did not shun death nor danger, and at last they earned their reward: "they slept."

The expedition reached an opening at last that entered another stream almost wide enough for two vessels abreast, and without overhanging trees, "Red River rafts," or sand-bars—a pleasant, swift-running stream that seemed willing to carry them whithersoever they wished to go, and they thought how their companions who had stayed behind would envy them when they heard their guns booming back of Haines's Bluff, startling the Confederates out of their secure and comfortable sleep.

They were anxious to get on, and the command, owing to the unfortunate condition of the senior officer, fell upon the next in rank, as brave a fellow as ever stepped on a ship's deck. He had the whistles blown for getting under way, and sang out, "On to Vicksburg, boys, and no more trees to saw!" The flotilla moved on about a mile, and, on turning a bend, ran almost into a fort in the middle of the river, with the channel each side blocked by sunken steamers. Heavy rifled guns were mounted in the works, and there was a large body of troops in the fort who jumped to their pieces the moment our vessels appeared in sight.

These works were all new, and the guns just mounted; the sunken steamers had scarcely blown off their steam. They had but a few hours ago brought the guns and carriages, and thrown up breastworks on the sudden bend in the river (or half island), and seeing our forces close at hand, they had sunk the steamers to prevent our gunboats from running past the battery. All this took our people by surprise. They knew from the truthful contrabands that there was no such work on this stream until they should reach Haines's Bluff.

Here was a check with a vengeance. Had the fort been altogether ready it would have given the lighter vessels of the expedition a warm reception as they came so confidingly down the river, and were so mixed up. As to the transports and troops, they would have fared badly. There was no way of turning the steamers around and going up stream again, for the river was too narrow.

The vessels had to get hold of each other and back up against the stream until they could reach a bend where they could not be seen. While they were doing all this they would have been exposed to a raking fire had the enemy had his powder ready. *Laus Deo!* he had not loaded his guns, and was in quite as much excitement over the apparition of two large ironclads and a dozen transports and light gunboats with the pipes all knocked over, and their cabins and light work all gone, as was our party.

They no doubt wondered where they all came from, and how they got there.

The Yazoo Pass expedition was supposed to have been prepared without any one knowing anything about its destination except General Grant and myself and the commanding naval and military officers, and, even until a spade was stuck into the earth to open the pass, it was thought that the destination of the expedition was a profound secret. Yes, pretty much such a secret as a dozen women would keep.

Secret or not, here the expedition was met—almost at its first entrance to those inland waters—by heavy earthworks, three or four rifled cannon, and a body of troops. The question was, What was to be done?

The ironclads, after going backward for a time, tied up to the bank, and, overlapping each other, opened fire on the enemy's work, which turned out to be named Fort Pemberton, after the wily old soldier in command at Vicksburg.

Ours was a pretty piece of strategy for getting into the rear of Vicksburg, but Pemberton's was better, as it checkmated us completely, and this often happened in the siege.

The Confederates were a wide-awake set of adversaries, full of energy and courage, and not lacking in resources. They were working with all their souls to attain an object which they considered conducive to their happiness, and they did not care whom they hurt, so long as they could succeed.

Our people, though quite as energetic as the Southerners, fought with a different sentiment. There was still some kindly feeling left in them for their foes, whose courage and endurance under great privation often called forth applause. We were not fighting with the courage of despair. A man of ordinary intellect could see the end which would be the downfall of the Southern Confederacy. It was as plain as the writing on the wall at the feast of Belshazzar.

The Southerners were fighting with the energy of despair, hoping that some untoward event might spring up to help them. At all events, they were determined to command their enemy's respect for their courage and ability, and I don't think any brave sailor or soldier ever withheld it.

Our troops were flocking to the fields of battle by the hundred thousands at a time, when the Confederate troops began to give out in numbers. We were certain of means, suffered very little of the discomforts by sieges and bombardments experienced by the Confederates, had no rancorous feeling to urge us on, and simply desired to see the laws vindicated and the authority of the Government established over revolting States. There were occasions when we did not seem to count the value of time, and our energies, though well put forth, did not equal those of our enemies.

On our side there was not a sufficient *unity* in command; there was a kind of "stand-off" between the army and the navy when acting together, which prevented them from working in harmony and with one purpose. There should always have been one man in an expedition in command of the whole, and his authority should have been so manifest that there would have been no appeal from his orders.

This was not the case in the Yazoo Pass expedition. Each corps commanded its men independent of the other, and there seemed no disposition to act in concert.

The course of General Grant and myself in all such matters corresponded entirely with what I have suggested. Though he had no control over me whatever, and I was never tied down by any orders from the Navy Department, but left to my own discretion, I always deferred to his wishes in all matters, and went so far as to give orders to those under my command that they should obey the orders of Generals Grant and Sherman the same as if they came from myself. Hence we always acted with the most perfect accord.

In this case the officer commanding the troops should have been subject to the orders of the naval officer. Then, I think, we would have discomfited General Pemberton's strategy by taking possession of his fort.

When the ironclads, the *Chilicothe, Captain Foster*, and the *Baron de Kalb*, under Captain Walker, opened their bow guns (the only ones they could use), the fort responded promptly, and in a short time jammed the port shutters of the *Chilicothe* so that they could not be opened. It was certain death for a man to go out on the bow to work with chisel and hammer, and *Captain Foster* had to withdraw from action until he could remedy the difficulty. In the mean time the *Baron de Kalb* remained and sustained the action alone, and so well was the fire directed that half an hour after the *Chilicothe* returned to her station the fort stopped firing, though the Confederate flag was kept flying.

Now was the time for the troops to operate; they should have been sent out as sharpshooters, should have crawled within fifty yards of the works, and kept up such a fusillade that nothing could have stood it.

The vessels could not get near to the fort without being blown up by torpedoes. One torpedo did explode right in front of the Chilicothe when she took her position the second time, and no doubt they were planted all around the works, and for some distance from them.

There were not sailors enough to undertake to carry the works in boats, and everything was at a stand-still. The army officer in command took no suggestion from any one, and declined to assault the fort (which was a low one) and have his men sacrificed. Pemberton's strategy succeeded, and our party left the place, struggling back again wearily through the Yazoo Pass, which we had taken so much trouble to clean out, having inundated many thousands of acres to no purpose at all.

Great complaints were made by both sides as to whose fault it was that there was a failure, but I told the navy I didn't want to hear anything about it; they did not get through, and didn't get the fort, and the less said about it the better. "It was just one of the episodes of the war" (my consolation when I met with a failure), and I never wanted to hear of the Yazoo Pass expedition again.

I had gone through the mill myself and knew exactly how it was, and didn't feel much like blaming any one. These expeditions don't sound badly on paper, but they were enough to try men's souls.

About the time the Yazoo Pass expedition got off I proposed an expedition to go through the woods by the same route explored by General Grant and myself.

I determined to go myself, and, to make it a success, I omitted nothing that might possibly be wanted on such an expedition. I selected the ironclads *Louisville,* Lieutenant-Commanding Owen; *Cincinnati,* Lieutenant-Commanding Bache; *Carondelet,* Lieutenant-Commanding Murphy; *Mound City,* Lieutenant-Commanding Wilson; *Pittsburgh,* Lieutenant-Commanding Hoel, and four tugs; also two light mortar-boats built for the occasion, to carry each a thirteen-inch mortar and shells enough to bombard a city.

I really do believe I thought I was sure of getting in the rear of Vicksburg, and could send some more shells into the hills that would keep them fastened down to eternity.

At the same time General Sherman prepared his contingent to accompany the expedition.

General Grant was so much interested in this work that he went up to the end of the woods on one of the transports to see Sherman start on his march alongside of the gunboats, and gave his personal attention toward pushing ahead those of Sherman's troops that had not reached us in the transports. These now and then got lost in the thick woods, and sometimes got their pipes knocked down.

This was one of the most remarkable military and naval expeditions that ever set out in any country, and will be so ranked by those who read of it in future times.

Here was a dense forest, deeply inundated, so that large steamers could ply about among the trees with perfect impunity. They were as much at home there as the wild denizens of the forest would be in dry times.

The animals of all kinds had taken to the trees as the only arks of safety. Coons, rats, mice, and wild cats were in the branches, and if they were not a happy family, it was because when they lay down together the smaller animals reposed within the larger ones.

It was a curious sight to see a line of ironclads and mortar-boats, tugs and transports, pushing their way through the long, wide lane in the woods without touching on either side, though sometimes a rude tree would throw Briarean arms around the smokestack of the tin-clad *Forest Rose,* or the transport *Molly Miller,* and knock their bonnets sideways.

It all looked as though the world had suddenly got topsy-turvy, or that there was a great camp-meeting in the woods on board ironclads and transports.

The difficulty was to preserve quiet, so that our presence might not be detected by the enemy's scouts. It could not be possible, I thought, that the besieged in Vicksburg would not have sought an opportunity to reconnoitre our lines by means of canoes, or even communicate with some of those who were always to be found faithless to their trust. Indeed, I would not have been much surprised to see a rebel iron-clad ram lurking somewhere in the bushes, ready to spring out on us. They were building two of them in Yazoo City, where the ram *Arkansas* came from. Why should we not meet them here?

If one had suddenly slid down a tree and attacked us I should not have been much surprised. The only reason why that was not likely to happen was that the Confederates were not lucky "in *Aries,*" and generally managed to lose their rams and ironclads soon after they were built. They would perform some creditable feat with these vessels, and then blow them up, or set fire to them, to keep them from falling into our hands.

Besides, I had little fear of the rams at Yazoo City, as I knew their condition, through a truthful contraband, who informed me, "Dey has no bottom in, no sides to 'em, an' no top on to 'em, sah, an' deir injines is in Richmon'."

We ran on, in line of battle, eight or ten miles through the open way in the trees, carrying fifteen feet of water by the lead-line. Let the nautical reader imagine an old quartermaster in the "chains" of an ironclad steaming through the woods and singing out, "Quarter less three!" Truth is stranger than fiction.

At last we came to a point where the forest was close and composed of very large trees—old monarchs of the woods which had spread their arms for centuries over those silent solitudes: Titans, like those in the old fables, that dominate over all around them.

In the distance, between the trees, would spring into sight gray, sunless glens in which the dim, soft ripple of day seemed to glimmer for a second so fancifully, indeed, that it required but a slight stretch of imagination to see the wood-nymphs disporting in their baths.

The sun seldom reached these woody glades, and, if it did, it was but to linger for a moment and disappear, like the bright star of eve, behind a silver cloud.

It all looked like some infinite world in which we were adrift, where the sky, soft and serene (which we had been accustomed to see), had been furled in anticipation of a squall.

Every turn of the wheels sent an echo through the woods that would frighten the birds of prey from their perches, whence they were looking down upon the waste of waters, wondering (no doubt) what it all might mean, and whom these mighty buzzards, skimming over the waters and carrying everything before them, could possibly be.

Our line of battle was broken on approaching the large trees; then we had to go more cautiously. What, thought I, if the trees should become so dense that we could not pass between them; what would we do then? I solved the difficulty at once. "Ram that large tree there," I said to the captain of the *Cincinnati;* "let us see what effect the old turtle will have on it." It was an unnecessary act of vandalism to injure the old Titan, but it would shorten our road, and we would not be obliged to go meandering about to find a channel. We struck the tree while going at the rate of three knots an hour, and bounded off, but started it about twenty degrees from the perpendicular. The light soil about its roots had become softened by the water, and the tree had not much staying power. I backed again and gave it another ram, and the weight of eight hundred tons, with a three-knot velocity, sent it out of all propriety. I hailed the ironclad astern of me, and ordered her to bend a heavy chain to it and pull it down, which was accomplished in half an hour.

I wanted to see what we could do at ramming and pulling at big trees, and our experience so gained came into play before we got through the expedition.

It was all very pleasant at first, skimming along over summer seas, under the shade of stalwart oaks, but we had no conception of what we had before us.

We had to knock down six or eight of these large trees before we could reach the point where Sherman was disembarking part of his troops. When I came up he was on a piece of high ground, on an old white horse some of his "boys" had captured.

"Halloo, old fellow," he sang out, "what do you call this? This must be traverse sailing. You think it's all very fine just now, don't you; but, before you fellows get through, you won't have a smokestack or a boat among you."

"So much the better," I said; "it will look like business, and we will get new ones. All I want is an engine, guns, and a hull to float them. As to boats, they are very much in the way."

At this point we ran up alongside higher land which looked like a levee.

"Is this the last of it?" I asked Sherman.

"No," he said; "steam on about twenty yards to the west, and you will find a hole through a kind of levee wide enough, I think, for your widest vessel. That is Cypress Bayou; it leads into the Sunflower about seventy-five miles distant, and a devil of a time you'll have of it. Look out those fellows don't catch you. I'll be after you."

Sherman knew every bayou and stream in that part of the country better than the oldest inhabitants knew them.

I pushed on, my fleet following, and soon found myself inside the bayou. It was exactly forty-six feet wide. My vessel was forty-two feet wide, and that was the average width of the others. This place seemed to have been a bayou with high levees bordering, reaching, indeed, above the vessel's guns.

It had been made, I suppose, into a kind of canal to connect the waters of the Sunflower by a short cut with those of the Yazoo, near Haines's Bluff. All on the left of the levee was deep water in the woods. On the other side were cornfields. The levee had stopped the further encroachment of the flood. This bayou had not been used for many years for the purposes of navigation. It had almost closed up, and the middle of it was filled with little willows which promised to be great impediments to us, but, as there was nine feet of water in the ditch, I pushed on.

Sherman told me he would follow me along the left bank of the ditch with his troops, and be up with me before I knew it, as he would make two miles to my one.

It was intended from the first that we should travel along together for mutual support. We to transport him across rivers and marshes, he to keep off sharp-shooters, whom we could not reach with our guns on account of the high banks. We left Sherman at the point where we found him arranging his men, and I pushed into the bayou with my whole force, keeping one tug in the advance with one mortar-boat, the ironclads in the middle, and the other tugs and mortar-boat with the coal-barge bringing up the rear.

We supposed we were doing all this very secretly, and were going to surprise the natives. No doubt we did surprise those who dwelt on and along the Cypress Bayou, but our movement was probably no surprise to the Confederates in Vicksburg. I am quite satisfied in my own mind that, while we were steaming along and performing naval evolutions in the woods, the President of the Southern Confederacy was reading something like the following dispatch to his Cabinet:

"Sherman and Porter pirouetting through the woods in steamers and ironclads. Are keeping a lookout on them. Hope to bag them all before to-morrow."

We had not entered the bayou more than half a mile before we saw the greatest excitement prevailing. Men on horseback were flying in all directions. Cattle, instead of being driven in, were driven off to parts unknown. Pigs were driven by droves to the far woods, and five hundred negroes were engaged in driving into the fields all the chickens, turkeys, ducks, and geese, and what were a few moments before smiling barn-yards, were now as bare of poultry as your hand. I had issued an order against capturing anything on shore, but the difficulty was to find out where the shore was, as apparently the Cypress Bayou ran right through the middle of a stable-yard.

I informed the sailors that loot naturally belonged to the army, but that prize in the shape of cotton marked "C.S.A." belonged to them. A mile from the entrance to the bayou there were two piles of cotton containing six thousand bales, and placed opposite each other on the banks of the stream in which we were then just holding our way against its two-knot current.

Suddenly I saw two men rush up from each side of the bayou and apply a lighted pine-knot to each pile. "What fools these mortals be!" I said to an officer, "but I suppose those men have a right to burn their own cotton, especially as we have no way of preventing them."

"I can send a howitzer-shell at them, sir," he said, "and drive them away."

"No," I replied, "that might kill them, and we don't want to do that except in battle."

So the two men went on with their work of destruction. They applied the torches to every part of the two piles, and in twenty minutes there was a column of smoke ascending to the skies, and the passage between the piles became very much obscured.

"How long will it take that cotton to burn up?" I inquired of a darkey who was asking permission to come on board.

"Two day, Massa," the negro answered; "sometime t'ree."

By this time all the outside of the cotton was blazing. "Ring the bell to go ahead fast," I ordered, "and tell those astern to follow after me." I was on board the *Cincinnati*. "Go ahead fast the tug and mortar-boat," and away we all went, darting through between the burning bales.

All the ports were shut in and the crews called to fire quarters, standing ready with fire-buckets to meet the enemy's *fire*.

It reminded me a little of the fire-raft at Fort Jackson, but we soon got used to them.

The fellows on the tug wet themselves and boat all over very thoroughly, and as they darted through, being below the bank, they did not suffer much; but the paint was blistered on the boat, and the fire scorched the men.

Myself, captain, and wheelman were the only ones on deck when the *Cincinnati* passed through, but the heat was so intense that I had to jump inside a small house on deck covered with iron, the captain following me. The helmsman covered himself up with an old flag that lay in the wheel-house. The hose was pointed up the hatch to the upper deck and everything drenched with water, but it did not render the heat less intolerable.

The boats escaped with some blistering. The smoke was even worse than the heat, and I have often since imagined how a brave fireman feels when he is looking through a burning house in search of helpless people.

Just after we passed through the fire there was a dreadful crash, which some thought was an earthquake. We had run into and quite through a span of bridge about fifty feet long, and demolished the whole fabric, having failed to see it in the smoke.

There was a yell among the negroes on the bank, who looked on with amazement at the doings of "Mas' Linkum's gunboats."

"What dey gwine ter do nex'?" said an old patriarch.

The next we did was to stop and breathe after getting through that smoke, and look back and regret the loss of the cotton. The worst thing to be done with cotton is to burn it, especially when it is not your own.

Here was the Confederate Government complaining of Northern oppression, and yet their own agents were riding around on horseback, setting fire to the people's cotton to keep it from falling into our hands, while, if they had let it alone, it would not have been troubled by us, except by giving a receipt for it, and, when the war was over, the owners would have netted more than the full value of their property.

This was one of the worst cases of vandalism I had yet seen.

When all the vessels had passed through the flame and smoke we hauled up at a small collection of houses, where the negro women were running around screaming and driving in the pigs and poultry.

A burly overseer, weighing over two hundred pounds, sat at the door of a log-hut with a pipe in his mouth. He was a white man, half bull-dog, half blood-hound, and his face expressed everything that was bad in human nature, but he smoked away as if nothing was the matter—as Nero fiddled while Rome was burning.

He looked on us with perfect indifference; our presence didn't seem to disturb him at all. Doubtless he felt quite secure; that we didn't want anything so bad as he was.

I called to him, and he came down in his shirt-sleeves, bare-headed, and looked stolidly at me as if to say, "Well, what do you want?"

"Why did those fools set fire to that cotton?" I inquired.

"Because they didn't want you fools to have it," he replied. "It's ourn, and I guess things ain't come to such a pass that we can't do as we please with our own."

"Tell them we won't trouble it," I said; "it is wicked to see such material going off like smoke."

In five minutes he had a dozen negroes at his side, and they were all sent up the bayou on a full run to stop the burning of cotton. He believed our word, and we did not disappoint him.

"And who are you?" I inquired of the man.

"I am in charge of this plantation," he replied; "this is the mother of my children"—pointing to a fat, thick-lipped negress who stood, with her bosom all bare and arms a-kimbo, about ten yards away—"and these fine fellows are my children," he continued, pointing to some light-colored boys who had followed him down.

"I suppose you are Union, of course? You all are so when it suits you," I said.

"No, by G——, I'm not, and never will be; and as to the others, I know nothing about them. Find out for yourself. I'm for Jeff Davis first, and last, and all the time. Do you want any more of me?" he inquired, "for I am not a loquacious man at any time."

"No, I want nothing more with you," I replied; "but I am going to steam into that bridge of yours across the stream and knock it down. Is it strongly built?"

"You may knock it down and be d—d," he said. "It don't belong to me; and, if you want to find out how strong it is, pitch into it. You'll find a hard nut to crack; it ain't made of candy."

"You are a Yankee by birth, are you not?" I asked.

"Yes, d—n it, I am," he replied; "that's no reason I should like the institution. I cut it long ago," and he turned on his heel and walked off.

"Ring 'Go ahead fast,' " I said to the captain; "we will let that fellow see what bridge-smashers we are."

In three minutes we were going four knots through the water, and in one more we went smashing through the bridge as if it was paper. I looked toward the over-seer to see how he would take it, but he did not even turn his head as he sat at his door smoking.

This man was but one remove from a brute, but there were hundreds more like him.

We came to one more bridge; down it went like nine-pins, and we steamed slowly on, forcing our way through small, lithe willows that seemed to hold us in a grip of iron. This lasted for an hour, during which we made but half a mile.

But that was the last of the willows for a time. Had they continued, we would have been obliged to give it up. The small sprouts, no larger than my little finger, caught in the rough plates of the overhang and held us as the threads of the Lilliputians held Gulliver.

Now we came to extensive woods again on either side, the large trees towering in the air, while underneath they looked as if their lower branches had been trimmed to give them a uniform appearance; but they had only been trimmed by the hand of Nature, whose fair impression fell on all about us. Man only marred the prospect there.

The *banks* of the bayou were high with large, overhanging trees upon them, and the long branches of the latter stretched out into the stream, endangering our pipes and boats. The channel was here exactly the width of the ironclads—forty-two feet—and we had to cut our way with the overhang through the soft soil and the twining roots. It was hard and slow work. The brutal overseer felt quite sure that we would be bagged before night. He didn't know that Sherman was right behind us with an army, and an army, too, that was no respecter of ducks, chickens, pigs, or turkeys, for they used to say of one particular regiment in Sherman's corps that it could catch, scrape, and skin a hog without a soldier leaving the ranks. I was in hopes they would pay the apostate Yankee a visit, if only to teach him good manners.

The gunboats, at this stage of the cruise, were following each other about a quarter of a mile apart. The only idea I can give of Cypress Bayou is to *fake* a string up and down a paper two hundred or more times. We did nothing but turn upon our course about every twenty minutes. At one time the vessels would all be steaming on different courses. One would be standing north, another south, another east, and yet another west through the woods. One minute an ironclad would apparently be leading ahead, and the next minute would as apparently be steering the other way. The tugs and mortar-boats seemed to be mixed up in the most marvelous manner.

There was a fair road on the right of the bayou, along which Sherman's troops would have to march, and all that was required to make the situation look confusing and confounding was to have the soldiers marching beside the gunboats.

I was in the leading vessel, and necessarily had to clear the way for the others. The bayou was full of logs that had been there for years. They had grown soggy and heavy, and sometimes one end, being heavier than the other, would sink to the bottom, while the other end would remain pointing upward, presenting the appearance of *chevaux-de-frise*, over which we could no more pass than we could fly. We had to have working parties in the road with tackles and hook-ropes to haul these logs out on the banks before we could pass on.

Again, we would come to a "Red River raft" that had been imbedded in the mud for ages. All these had to be torn asunder and hauled out with a labor that no one who had not tried it could conceive of.

Then, again, we would get jammed between two large, overhanging trees. We could not ram them down as we did in the woods, with plenty of "sea room" around us. We had to chop away the sides of the trees with axes.

A great many of these large trees had decayed branches, and when the heavy ironclad would touch the trunk of one (though going only at the rate of half a mile an hour, which was the most we could make at any time in the ditch), the shock would be so great, and the resultant vibration of the tree so violent, that the branches would come crashing on deck, smashing the boats and skylights and all the frame-work that they reached.

An hour after entering the very narrow part of the ditch, where we really had not a foot to spare, we had parted with everything like a boat, and cut them away as useless appendages. Indeed, they were of no use to us, and only in the way. When we got rid of them we got along better.

The vessels behind learned a good deal from our experience, and lowered their boats and towed them astern, though that did not relieve them entirely.

Sometimes we would have to pass a dead tree, with its weird-looking branches threatening us with destruction in case we should handle it too roughly. We received quantities of dead branches, and we never knocked a dead *tree* without suffering terrible damages.

No wonder the overseer took our going on so coolly. He expected that we would get jammed before we went a mile.

That day, by sunset, we had made eight miles, which was a large day's work, considering all the impediments, but when night came—which it did early in the deep wood—we had to tie up to the bank, set watches, and wait until daylight, until which time we hoped to give our men to rest.

But, the reader will ask, what was the Confederacy doing all this while? They may imagine that Pemberton didn't know anything about this romantic pirouetting through the woods of "Mas' Linkum's gunboats."

Not a bit of it; he knew all about it. He had sent telegrams, no doubt, to Richmond, announcing the fact that the Union navy was making a cruise through the woods and over the farms in the Yazoo country, and would likely, in course of time, reach Richmond itself in that way. He was not afraid of Vicksburg—that never struck him—and he didn't know (or I thought he didn't) that I had two mortar-boats with which I expected to bombard Vicksburg in the rear!

No doubt the Confederate Cabinet chuckled when they were informed that the authorities at Vicksburg would, in the course of a day or two, bag the whole

American navy in the western waters, though, strange to say, that idea never entered my head.

We stopped that evening about seven o'clock, and about an hour later we heard the chopping of wood in the forest. We had seen no one along the stream since we had left that burly overseer. The truthful and intelligent contrabands, in whom I was wont to repose confidence, were nowhere to be seen, whereat I marveled much, knowing their sociable disposition and the lofty aspirations they felt with regard to the liberty of their race.

They were so faithful in adherence to their protectors that they would come in in crowds with wild inventions of moves on the part of the enemy if they could not find something real to tell.

I missed these ingenious creatures, and wondered what had become of them. It was true we were hard to get at in this swamp, though there was a road on one side and a levee on the other; the southern side was an interminable waste of water and wood.

I was always of an inquiring mind, and determined to find out what the wood-chopping meant. It seemed to me that there were a dozen axes at work.

I put a twelve-pound boat-howitzer on the tug, and sent her ahead to see what was going on. In twenty minutes I heard the report of the howitzer, and then another, and another. Then a steam whistle was blown from the tug, and all was silent. No more axes heard cutting wood.

In a very short time the tug was heard returning, snorting as if carrying a heavy pressure of steam, and every now and then giving some playful screams with the whistle. The forest fairly reverberated with the sound.

The officer in charge reported that he had suddenly come upon a large body of negroes, under the charge of some white men carrying lanterns, cutting trees on the banks of the stream we were in; that they had felled a tree three feet in diameter, and this had fallen right across the bayou, closing the stream completely against our advance.

There was the secret of our not meeting the truthful contraband. He was employed in hemming us in. He was too accustomed to implicit obedience to his master to refuse to do anything imposed upon him. He was too ignorant to have formed any opinions on the subject of doing something to deserve liberty. Oppression was second nature to him, obedience one of Heaven's first laws, and he helped to chop down those trees with as much glee as children would feel at setting fire to a hay-stack.

There was but one thing to do: Move ahead and clear the channel of a tree across it, three feet in diameter, spreading its branches over an area of seventy by one hundred and fifty feet.

We worked ahead slowly with men in advance on the bank, with lanterns to show what dangers there were. We arrived at the fallen tree in less than an hour, and made arrangements while under way for removing it.

It was not a matter of great labor. Two large snatch-blocks were strapped to standing trees as leaders. The largest hawser was passed through the snatch-blocks, one end made fast to the fallen tree, and the other end taken to a steamer. "Back the ironclad hard," and the obstruction began to move slowly over the water. In less than ten minutes it was landed clear across the road, so that Sherman's soldiers wouldn't have to march around it.

A second application of this improvised "power gear," and the route was again free.

The Confederates didn't think of all that when they tried to bag us in that way. They forgot the ingenuity of American seamen.

"Now," I said to the officer in charge of the tug, "go ahead with all the speed you have, and see that no more trees are cut down to-night; and, though I shall be sorry to harm that faithful friend and brother, the contraband, if he continues to chop at any one's dictation you must give him shrapnel," and off the tug started.

We could already hear the faint strokes of the axes in advance of us, and no doubt the managers, having cut one tree down and supposing that they had blocked the game on us for the night, and not knowing our facilities for removing trees, had, as soon as they imagined themselves out of reach of the howitzer, set to work at cutting other trees, with the intention that we should never see the Sunflower, nor get in the rear of Vicksburg. The Confederates were energetic, and it was wonderful how soon they got their machinery to work.

Some twenty minutes after the tug left us we heard the howitzer firing rapidly, and then all was quiet, excepting three steam whistles, which meant *all well*.

At one o'clock that night the tug's small boat returned to us with the report that the choppers had commenced cutting about twenty of the largest trees, but that none had been completely felled; that they had captured two truthful contrabands, who informed them that the parties directing the cutting of trees were officers from Vicksburg; that they had pressed three hundred negroes into the work and made them use their axes with pistols to their heads, and gave them plenty of whisky.

"The officers are from Vicksburg!" I said; "and we thought ourselves so smart! No doubt they started before we did, and got their instructions from Richmond. What next?"

"The officer" (Lieutenant Murphy) "says, sir, he will continue on all night, and thinks no more trees will be cut down at present."

I didn't care about the trees. I was just then thinking how I would feel if they should block up the head of the pass with cotton bales and earth, and leave me and mine sticking in the mud at the bottom of the bayou.

What a time, I thought, Sherman would have digging us out—but I was sure he wouldn't mind doing it.

Nevertheless, we put out guards along the road, and slept as comfortably as if we had been at the Fifth Avenue Hotel. Somehow or other I didn't think the Confederacy could bag me as long as I had Sherman in company with his stalwart fellows—half sailor, half soldier, with a touch of the snapping turtle.

At daylight next morning we moved ahead, and all that day toiled as men never toiled before. Our vessels looked like wrecks, and there was scarcely a whole boat left in the fleet. Evening found us fourteen miles ahead, but where was Sherman? There was only one road, so he couldn't have taken the wrong one.

I had been rather precipitate in rushing ahead with the fleet, though I could not have been of any help to Sherman, but I would have had the services of the army to stop the tree-cutting, which I now had to do myself by sending out a detachment of two hundred men from the vessels. These men were ordered to march all night along the road while the tug covered them with her howitzer.

It were vain to tell all the hardships of the third day. The plot seemed to thicken as we advanced, and old logs, small Red River rafts, and rotten trees overhanging the banks, seemed to accumulate.

The dead trees were full of vermin of all sorts. Insects of every kind and shape, such as are seen only in Southern climes, infested these trees. Rats and mice, driven from the fields by the high water, had taken up their abode in the hollow trunks and rotten branches. Snakes of every kind and description had followed the rats and mice to these old arks of safety. These innocent creatures knew nothing of the insecurity of their adopted homes in presence of the butting ironclads. Small wonder. Who would have dreamed of such things in these regions?

A canoe might have been seen, perhaps, of late years winding its way down these tortuous channels of a moonlight night, manned by a couple of dissipated darkies out on a coon-hunt, but navigation by anything larger in these waters was unknown.

Sometimes, when we would strike against one of these trees, a multitude of vermin would be shaken out on the deck—among them rats, mice, cockroaches, snakes, and lizards, which would be swept overboard by the sailors standing ready with their brooms. Once an old coon landed on deck, with the life half knocked out of him, but he came to in a short time and fought his way on shore. Even the coons were prejudiced against us, and refused to be comforted on board, though I am sorry to say we found more Union feeling among the bugs of all kinds, which took kindly to the ironclads, and would have remained with us indefinitely had they been permitted to do so.

Three days' hard work and no hope of seeing the Sunflower River! We had made one capture. Lieutenant Murphy had gone ahead and taken possession of an Indian mound as old as the deluge; no one remembered its age.

Why had not the Confederates taken possession of the place and fortified it? It must have been because they thought it worthless. They showed themselves to be poor judges in such matters. But Lieutenant Murphy, who had been following engineering for some years before the war, saw some strong point in this mound (which I did not), and urged me to fortify it. At length he persuaded me to let him have four boat guns to place on the top of it. "It would be," he said, "*a point d'appui* for Sherman's troops to assemble about in case they were attacked!"

"Where are the attacking forces to come from?" I inquired.

"Can't tell, sir," said Murphy, "but I think it a strong point."

"Go ahead, then, and fortify it," I replied; "it will keep you employed."

We had arrived nearly at the head of the pass, or bayou, to what was called the Rolling Fork, and, after all our toil and trouble, did hope to see the road clear to Vicksburg in the rear.

There was a small collection of houses at the point where we had stopped, and all the contrabands in the country were assembled there. The tree-cutters had disappeared and liberated from duty all those who had been pressed into service, but took all the axes away with them. The negroes were jubilant over being able to join "Mass' Linkum's gunboats."

We could readily have dispensed with their services. They were only an encumbrance to us. They could give us no information. They had never been taught to think or know anything but to hoe and pick cotton. That's all they were wanted for.

We had steamed, or rather bumped, seventy-five miles, and had only six hundred yards to go before getting into the Rolling Fork, where all would be plain sailing; but I waited for all the vessels to come up to repair damages, and start together.

I noticed right at the head of the pass a large green patch extending all the way across. It looked like the green scum on ponds.

"What is that?" I asked of one of the truthful contrabands.

"It's nuffin but willers, sah," he replied. "When de water's out ob de bayou— which it mos' allers is—den we cuts de willers to make baskits wid. You kin go troo dat like a eel."

I thought I would try it while the vessels were "coming into port." I sent the tug on ahead with the mortar-boat, and followed on after.

The tug went into it about thirty yards, began to go slower and slower, and finally stuck so fast that she could move neither ahead nor astern. I hailed her and told them that I would come along and push them through. We started with a full head of steam, and did not even reach the tug. The little withes caught in the rough iron ends of the overhang and held us as if in a vise. I tried to back out, but 'twas no use. We could not move an inch, no matter how much steam we put on. Ah, I thought, this is only a temporary delay.

We got large hooks out and led the hook-ropes aft, and tried to break off the lithe twigs, but it was no use; we could not move. We got saws, knives, cutlasses, and chisels over the side, with the men handling them sitting on planks, and cut them off, steamed ahead, and only moved three feet. Other withes sprang up from under the water and took a fresher grip on us, so we were worse off than ever.

Just as well, I thought, that Murphy seized upon that mound. It will be three or four days before we can get through here. He can hold it as a lookout, and if any sharpshooters should appear he can fire on them.

Just then a rebel steamer was reported coming up the Rolling Fork and landing about four miles below. We will catch that fellow after dark, I thought. He has come up here after stores.

This was the Vicksburg granary—full of everything in the way of grain, cattle, and poultry. "Hog and hominy" was abundant.

I went at it again, and worked hard for over four hours, but not one foot did I gain with that ironclad. I wished ironclads were in Jericho.

While I was pondering what to do, and the negroes were looking on in admiration upon the ingenious devices we put into play to get rid of those willow fastenings, wondering to myself if the Confederacy had planted these willows on purpose to keep me out of the Sunflower River, I heard the faint reports of two guns, and directly after the shrill shriek of rifle-shot, which came from directions at right angles to each other. The shells burst over the Indian mound where Lieutenant Murphy was studying the strategy of war. They were Whitworth shells. I knew the sound too well to be mistaken. I had heard them before. There were two six-gun batteries with a cross-fire upon us.

"Now's your chance, Murphy," said I to myself, "to show some good practice. You did well in selecting that mound."

I forgot for a moment that we had only four twelve-pounder smooth-bores there, with a range of about twelve hundred yards.

The two field batteries were keeping up a rapid fire, and fifteen shells a minute were coming from the enemy's spitfires and bursting in all directions, throwing the pieces of iron and the bullets of the shrapnel down on the decks of the ironclads, where they rattled like hail.

Here was a dilemma. We could not use our large guns; they were away below the banks, and lying so close to it that we could not get elevation enough to fire over.

Suddenly I saw the sides of the mound crowded with officers and men. They were tumbling down as best they could; the guns were tumbled down ahead of them; there was a regular stampede. Murphy hadn't found the top of the mound a fine strategic point, and that was the reason why the Confederates had not adopted it.

The fire from the enemy's Whitworths was incessant, and every one was running to cover.

As the retreaters passed me I shouted to them to stop. The majority obeyed, but a number kept on. They had left their guns on the road.

I made those who stopped bring the guns alongside my vessel. "You shall have them no more," I said; "you don't know how to take care of them."

The shells from the enemy came so rapidly that it became annoying, so I ordered the mortars manned, measured the distance by the sound—2,800 yards on one range, and 2,600 on the other—and opened fire.

The shells seemed to be well timed; they fell in the midst of the artillerists, and the two batteries ceased by mutual consent, while we not only kept up the fire there, but all through the woods where these parties were located.

This little diversion being over, I set to work again to overcome the willows.

"What a dodge this was of the Confederacy," I said to the captain, "to plant these willows instead of a fort! We can take their forts, but we can't, I fear, take their willows."

I stepped out to the bank (where the negroes had assembled again as soon as the shooting was over) to see if I could learn anything about willows from these innocent people.

All I could find out from them was that "dey was mo' tougher'n ropes."

"Why don't Sherman come on?" I said aloud to myself. "I'd give ten dollars to get a telegram to him."

"I'm a telegram-wire, Massa," said a stubby-looking negro, coming up to me. "I'll take him for half a dollar, sah; I'm de county telegraph, sah. I does all dat bizness."

"Where's your office, Sambo?" I inquired.

"My name ain't Sambo, sah. My name's Tub, an' I run yer line fer yer fer half a dollar."

"Do you know where to find General Sherman?" I said.

"No, sah, I don't know him. Ef he's in Vicksburg, I kin find him."

"Can you carry a note for me without betraying it to the Confederates?"

"I don't understan' one of dem words, sah, but I'll take a note to Kingdom Kum if yer pay me half a dollar."

Then I told him who General Sherman was and where to find him. "Go along the road," I said, "and you can't miss him."

"I know nuff better 'an dat manner when I carry telegraph, sah. I don't go de road; I takes de ditches. It's nuff shorter an' mo' safer. On de lef' han' comin' up dars all marsh an' wata, an' a kenoe kin allers git 'long dar. I'll go de way we nigs takes when we go chicken huntin'."

"Where will you carry the dispatch?" I inquired.

"In my calabash-kiver, Massa," he answered, pointing to his thick, woolly head.

I wrote the dispatch and handed it to him. He stowed it away in a pocket in his hair, where it was as safe as a telegram traveling on a wire. I wrote:

"DEAR SHERMAN: Hurry up, for Heaven's sake. I never knew how helpless an ironclad could be steaming around through the woods without an army to back her."

I had no sooner got off the telegraph (as he called himself) than another steamer was reported as landing at the same place as the one which brought up the artillery.

Upon examining her with the glass, it could be seen that she was full of troops. Those fellows would not have landed there if they had not known that we were blockaded.

The stream, for some reason, began to run rapidly, and large logs began to come in from the Rolling Fork and pile up on the outside of the willows, making an effectual barricade. It was the water rushing down through the cut-off and creeks from the opening into the "Old Yazoo Pass" of the Mississippi River. What was doing good to those fellows was bad for us. I wondered if they had found the Confederacy as smart as we had. I had no doubt of it.

Just then the two rifle batteries of the enemy opened again viciously from other positions, and it was reported to me that two thousand men had landed and were marching to get into our rear. Pleasant, that!

I had sent the rear tug back to see if anything could be heard of General Sherman coming on. It returned with the information that ten miles in our rear the enemy were cutting down the largest trees across the pass, that eight had been felled within a short distance of each other, and the channel behind us was effectually blocked. I did not mind this so much, as I knew that Sherman was not far off.

I found another telegraph man among the negroes, and sent him off to Sherman. He pursued the same method as his predecessor, but was captured by the enemy.

We kept our mortars hard at work, but the artillery shifted position every three minutes, and were sending among us about twenty shells a minute. The men had to keep between decks.

We were in the narrowest part of the pass; it was the same width as the ironclads. We fitted in nicely—too nicely!

The Confederates had completely checkmated us. Every knight and pawn and castle was in check, and my vessel, the *Cincinnati,* was checkmated by the willows!

There was nothing easier than for two thousand men to charge on us from the bank and carry us by boarding. Only the enemy didn't know the fix we were in. They didn't know how it was that we could fire those thirteen-inch shell, that would burst now and then at the root of a great tree and throw it into the air. They didn't know that we had only four smooth-bore howitzers free to work, that our heavy guns were useless, below the bank. So much for their not being properly posted. But I was quite satisfied that they would know all this before Sherman came up.

We drove the artillery away about four o'clock in the afternoon. Then I sent a hawser to the tug, and another to the ironclad astern of me, while the latter made fast to another ironclad. Then we all backed together and, after an hour's hard pull, we slipped off the willows into soft water. *Laus Deo!*

Then went forth the orders to unship the rudders and let the vessels drift down stern foremost, and away we all went together with a four-knot current taking us—bumping badly—down at the rate of two miles an hour—which was twice as fast as we came up. The enemy did not discover our retreat for some minutes, but when they did they made a rush for the Indian mound and took possession of it.

After all, Murphy was right; it was a strategic point! But only with the Whitworth rifles, not with smooth-bores.

I suppose we passed that fort twenty times in following the crooked pass, and the enemy were pouring it into us all the time, but they didn't do much harm.

They were evidently greenhorns, and failed to understand that we were ironclad and didn't mind *bursting* shell. If they had fired solid shot, they might have hurt us.

I cared very much more about that infantry than I did about the artillery. As our bow guns were bearing astern now and *up* the bayou, we could each of us give the enemy now and then, at the turns, a dose of nine-inch shrapnel, giving the same attention to their infantry, which we could see were marching in the direction we were pursuing. But our broadside guns were useless.

The artillery kept up their fire for about two hours, and then I think they began to find out that our bow guns were bearing and doing them some injury.

At dark we tied up at a point where we had about four feet of water between us and the bank, greased the ironsides, and, elevating the lower-deck guns after loading them with grape, we made the best of our position. I landed five hundred men with howitzers after dark, and placed them in position to enfilade any attacking party. Scouts were also thrown out to see if some of the enemy could be picked up, and the remainder of the crews slept on their arms at quarters. So passed the night; but Sherman's whereabouts were a continual source of conjecture to me. I was quite sure the Confederates had not captured *him*.

About ten o'clock my scouts brought in four prisoners—two officers and two sergeants—and conducted them, at my direction, into the cabin.

The commanding officer was quite a youngster, and when brought in was as stiff as a poker.

He walked up to me and, presenting his sword, said, "There, sir, you will likely recognize that; it is the sword of one of your officers who skedaddled off that Indian mound. We picked up two of them, and captured caps and shoes enough to fit out a regiment. Why, your fellows left a lot of ammunition behind them."

"Yes," I said, "but you look tired; won't you sit down and take some supper with me? I have a cold supper and wine on the table."

"I don't care if I do," he answered, "and I have the less compunction in taking it as it belongs to us anyhow. In two hours you will be surrounded and bagged. You can't escape. How in the devil's name you ever got here is a wonder to me."

"I should like nothing better," I said, "than for your friends to try that kind of business; they would learn something. But sit down, gentlemen, and eat."

They did sit down, and ate with an appetite I never saw equaled.

"We have had nothing to eat or drink since noon," said the youngster; "we could eat our grandmothers and drink up Niagara Falls."

"Drink some wine," I said, and I shoved over the sherry to them. Their throats were dry as powder-horns. "Help yourselves," I said; "don't stand on ceremony. You know it will all be yours when you surround us, and you had better get your share before the other fellows arrive."

"Won't you drink with us?" asked the youngster.

"Yes," I said, "with pleasure. Tell me how Colonel Higgins is."

"He's here," replied the youngster, "and came along on purpose to catch you. He says he'd give ten thousand dollars to do that."

"Here's his health," I said, and they all drank bumpers to Higgins.

"I can't drink with you any more now. I have to look out for these vessels; but, as you are prisoners, and have no responsibility, you may empty the bottle if you like, and there are the cigars."

"You're a trump, and no mistake!" said the youngster; "I would like to capture you myself."

"Well, I promise you that if I surrender to any one it will be to you."

The quartette drank until they became very lively and loquacious, and boastful of what they were going to do.

"How far off are your troops?" I inquired.

"About four miles," the leader answered. "They will bag you at daylight."

"That," said I, "is about a good distance. Sherman will be on them about three o'clock, and capture the whole of them."

"Sherman!" he exclaimed; "what has he to do with it?"

"Only," said I, "that he is at this moment surrounding your troops with ten thousand men."

"Holy Moses!" he cried, "we're sold. We didn't know anything about any troops. We thought it was something like that Yazoo River affair—a gunboat excursion, and we liked to have bagged *them*. They're wandering around in the ditches yet."

Having obtained all the information I desired, I went on deck, put a sentry over the cabin-door, had the stern-ports closed, and gave orders to call me at two o'clock.

Then the shore parties were called on board, and we went on the *back track* for three miles. We either threw the enemy off the scent, or the captured officer deceived me about the contemplated attack. We heard nothing of them, and determined to go on down again.

At the first start the leading vessel sunk the coal-barge, and there we were blocked and unable to move. It took hours to remove the coal and spread it out on the bottom.

In the midst of the work we were attacked by the enemy's artillery in the rear.

I was in the rear ironclad—bows up stream; we steamed up after the artillery, got within range, and with the bow guns scattered them like chaff. One of their guns was knocked over, and some of their men and cattle were hurt, but they were getting less timid and were gradually closing around the ironclads.

The stream cleared of the coal, we bumped along, stern foremost, down stream, knocking down dead branches from the trees upon our decks, with the usual accompaniment of vermin, until we thought the limit of ill-luck had been reached by the vessels; but we looked worse before we got through.

Sharpshooters made their appearance in the morning. About sixty of them surrounded us. First it was like an occasional drop of rain. Then it was *pat, pat* against the iron hull all the time. The smokestacks seemed to be favorite marks to fire at. They no doubt took it for the captain, or the great motive power which kept us a-going.

The sharpshooters were not, as a rule, the brightest I have seen, but then they had bomb-shells falling among them, and now and then a tree, behind which they were, would suddenly be lifted out of the ground or canted sideways. The bomb-shells were demoralizing.

I adopted a new plan. I turned *all* the guns into mortars by firing them at the greatest elevation (to clear the banks), and with very low charges. With short time-fuses and a range of about six hundred yards this had a good effect, and the sharpshooters kept a long way off.

The smokestacks still attracted considerable attention from them, though it was true they had wounded some of our people.

Suddenly the *Louisville,* Captain Owen, brought up all standing. There were eight large trees cut down ahead of us—four from either bank, and they seemed to be so interlaced that it was apparently impossible to remove them.

I sent out two hundred riflemen, and found that they were quite equal to the enemy. They drove them to a safe distance with the aid of the mortar fire. We had been firing heavily, great guns and mortars, for two days and nights, and thought Sherman must have heard us and been worried about us, but he had his troubles in getting along as well as others. He was doing his best to come to our assistance. It may seem ridiculous for ironclads to be wanting assistance from an army, but without that army they would likely have been in an ugly scrape. Its proximity alone, without its immediate aid, made us perfectly at ease.

Under fire from the sharpshooters we removed the eight trees in three hours, and started to push on, when we found those devils had sunk two large trees across the bayou under water, and *pinned* them down.

Another hour was spent in getting them up, and under renewed sharpshooting. Every one was kept under cover except those it was absolutely necessary to expose. The captains and myself had to be on deck.

We had no sooner got rid of these obstructions than we saw a large column of gray-uniformed soldiers swooping down on us from the woods.

We opened mortar fire on them. They didn't mind it. On they came. They were no doubt determined to overwhelm us by numbers, and close us in. Their artillery was coming on with them. Now would come the tug of war. We were jammed up against the bank, and the stream was so narrow where we were we could not increase our distance from it. Their sharpshooters had now taken up positions behind trees about one hundred yards from us, and our men were firing rapidly at them as they opened on us.

We had picked up a few cotton-bales along the road to make defenses, and good ones they were.

The sharpshooters were becoming very troublesome about this time, when suddenly I saw the advancing column begin to fall into confusion; then they jumped behind trees, or fell into groups, and kept up a rapid fire of musketry. It looked as if they were fighting among themselves. But no! they were retreating before some one. They had run foul of Sherman's army, which was steadily driving them back.

The enemy were much surprised at encountering such a force. They never dreamed of meeting an army of five or six thousand men. I believe there were more.

I made signal to beat the retreat. We would have no more trouble now. But, just as I had given the order, half a dozen rifle bullets came on board, and one of them struck the first lieutenant, Mr. Wells, in the head while I was talking to him and giving him an order.

He fell, apparently dead, at my feet. I called an officer to remove him, and *he* fell dead, as I supposed, on the other's body.

Then an old quartermaster came, dragging a large quarter-inch iron plate along the deck, and stuck it up against a hog post. "There, sir," he said, "stand behind that; they've fired at you long enough," and I was wise enough to take the old fellow's advice. Poor old man! he was shot in the hand as he turned to get behind his cotton-bale.

But that was about the last of it. In the course of half an hour Colonel Smith, of the 8th Missouri, rode up and told me his troops were in pursuit of the enemy, who were in full retreat, and that we should hear no more of them. Again, *Laus Deo!*

They were a perplexing set of fellows, these rebels, and showed a great amount of courage, considering the prestige of "Mas' Linkum's gunboats"; but then, it must be remembered, they had caught the ironclads in a ditch in the woods. They could hardly be said to be afloat.

The Confederates never dreamed of finding us where they did, or they would have come provided with torpedoes, and left us all imbedded in the mud of Black Bayou, where in future ages mementos of us would be found, and as much be known of us as was known of the Indian mound which we *did not* find such a fine strategic point.

But the rebs missed their opportunity, though they rather had the laugh on us. We had the satisfaction of knowing, however, that none of us had lost our heads, though at one time matters looked rather embarrassing.

I didn't notice a single officer on that expedition who, though exposed almost at all times to an unpleasant fire from sharpshooters, showed the least desire to avoid being shot, except when they hurried down so rapidly from the top of the Indian mound!

I am happy to say that the two officers, who fell at my feet apparently dead, both recovered. Theirs were only scalp wounds, owing to the enemy's bad powder. They were both volunteers, and did good service all through the Rebellion.

"Old Tecumseh" came riding up, about half an hour after the last mishaps, on the old horse he had captured. He had received my county telegraph man, who explained to him pretty well how we were situated, and he had pushed on at night, by the aid of pine torches, through swamps and canebrakes, having undertaken a short cut recommended by the telegraph "operator," Mr. Tub, and found the traveling almost as bad as that experienced by the gunboats.

"Halloo, Porter," said the general when he saw me, "what did you get into such an ugly scrape for? So much for you navy fellows getting out of your element; better send for the soldiers always. My boys will put you through. Here's your little nigger; he came through all right, and I started at once. I had a hard time getting my troops over; some of them marched over from the Mississippi.

"This is the most infernal expedition I was ever on; who in thunder proposed such a mad scheme? But I'm all ready to go on with you again. Your gunboats are enough to scare the crows; they look as if you had got a terrible hammering. However, I'll start at once, and go back with you; my boys will clean those fellows out."

"Thank you, no," I said, "I have had enough of this adventure. It is too late now; the enemy are forewarned, and all the energies of the Confederacy will be put forth to stop us; they will fill all the rivers with torpedoes, and every hill will be turned into a heavy fort. They have the laugh on us this time, but we must put this down in the log-book as 'One of the Episodes of the War.' We will take Vicksburg yet, when it is more worth taking."

"You are satisfied, then," said Sherman, "with what my boys have done for you and can do?"

"Yes, perfectly so," I answered, "and I never knew what helpless things ironclads could become when they got in a ditch and had no soldiers about. Won't you come aboard?"

"No," said he, "I must call in my men; they could not catch those fellows if they chased them a week. Good-morning," and "Old Tecumseh" rode off on his ancient horse, with a rope bridle, accompanied only by one or two aids.

After Sherman had departed I went down into the cabin to see my prisoners. The cabin was dark, and they were sitting there very quiet.

"Well," I said to the young officer, "they have got us at last; we are surrounded."

"I knew they would bag you in the end," he replied; "I felt that I was not going to be a prisoner yet. Well, sir, I will see that you are treated handsomely when you surrender."

"Surrender to whom?" I said. "What are you talking about?"

"Didn't you say you were surrounded?" asked the perplexed youth.

"Yes, I did," I replied, "but by Sherman's boys, and your fellows are skedaddling off as fast as they can go."

"But not faster," he retorted, "than your fellows did down that Indian mound! But I'm sorry not to be able to take you to Vicksburg; they'd treat you kindly there." With that he lay down and went to sleep.

The game was up, and we bumped on homeward. The current was running very rapidly now, and the vessels were so helpless, dropping down stern foremost, that we could not protect them in any way. There was no knowing what part of them would strike the trees, or when huge dead branches would fall upon the decks. Every one remained between decks except those who were absolutely required above. There was still a chance of the enemy playing us a bad trick by blocking the head of the pass at Rolling Fork; there was plenty of cotton along the road to do it with, if they only should think of it. Twelve hundred bales of cotton would turn the water off from our bayou, and in an hour after we would be on the bottom. With these unpleasant possibilities before me, I continued on homeward, and protracted my run until eight o'clock that night, when I came up with the main body of Sherman's army, which was encamped along on the road near the edge of the pass.

Encamped! I say. They had no tents, but a plentiful supply of fence-rails and bonfires of pine-knots. The whole route for miles was all in a blaze.

It was great fun for the soldiers to see our dilapidated condition. "Halloo, Jack," one fellow would sing out, "how do you like playing mud-turtle? Better stick to the briny."

Another would say, "You've been into dry dock, ain't you, and left your boats behind?"

"Don't go bushwhacking again, Jack," said another, "unless you have Sherman's boys close aboard of you; you look as if your mothers didn't know you were out."

"Where's all your sails and masts, Jack?" said a tough-looking fellow who was sailor all over, though he had a soldier's uniform bent.

"By the Widow Perkins," cried another, "if Johnny Reb hasn't taken their rudders away and sent them adrift!"

"Dry up," sang out an old forecastleman, "we wa'n't half as much used up as you was at Chickasaw Bayou!" for which the old tar got three cheers. And so we ran the gauntlet until we reached the middle of the line.

"Where's General Sherman?" I inquired of some of the men.

"He's in his tent, sir, waiting supper for you," answered one of them.

Sherman's tent! As if he would have a tent when his soldiers were lying about on fence-rails.

But I came to his tent at last; and, reader, I wish you could have seen it: it was three fence-rails set up in a triangle, but with only a small fly over the apex. It was raining hard at the time, and Sherman was standing leaning against one of the rails, while a large bonfire was blazing brightly before his "tent"! "You go on," he said; "I'll follow you to-morrow." We passed the compliments, and I ran on down past the lines and tied up, having run the gauntlet of jokes that were showered on us by the soldiers.

As we were getting made fast to the bank a canoe with two soldiers in it tried to squeeze past us, but got stuck between us and the bank. They had a large pile of something in the bottom of the canoe covered over with a tarpaulin.

"What have you got in those bags?" I asked.

"General Sherman's baggage, sir," said one; "we've just brought it up from a transport."

"General Sherman's baggage!" I said; "how long has it been since he took to carrying baggage? Let me see what you've got there."

"Only baggage, Admiral, I assure you," said the speaker, "except some turkeys we picked up for you on the road up here," and he uncovered and displayed a pile of picked turkeys, geese, chickens, and sucking pigs.

"Where's the baggage?" I asked.

"Why, sir," said the man, "there was so much of it, it's coming up on a tug—a large carpet-bag of it, sir," and he handed up one of each.

The steward came, and took a turkey. "Pass General Sherman's baggage," I said to the captain, and the sailors, taking hold of the painter, pulled the canoe through.

Sherman had a hard set of boys on foraging, and they enjoyed this trip up the bayou, where they were in the very midst of the enemy's granary, and the people of Vicksburg no doubt sighed when the Yankees had found their way to the flesh-pots of the South. Most of them went without turkey, chicken, goose, or pig for many a day thereafter.

There is not much more to be said about the Steele Bayou expedition; it didn't amount to much in effecting changes in the condition of Vicksburg, but we gained a lot of experience which would serve us in the future. We might, perhaps, have passed the willows if we had waited for the army, and got the soldiers to pull us through with ropes stretched along the bank; but to have delayed pushing astern would have insured the cutting down of five hundred trees by the enemy, and given them time to send to Vicksburg for torpedoes and have them planted all along that ditch.

I never saw a copy of the telegram Pemberton sent to Richmond, but I imagine it was as follows:

"The enemy made an excursion into our overflowed country and pirouetted around exceedingly. 'They buttered no parsnips.' Nature fought for us, as it always does for the Confederacy. The elements even helped us. The trees fought for us against the invaders of our soil, and the huge limbs fell down upon the enemy's decks and demolished them. The vermin swarmed over them, and they returned looking like picked chickens.

"They will never try it again. Vicksburg is safer than ever, and can never fall while hog and hominy last.

"We spit on their grandfathers' graves."

I am quite satisfied that no one who went on that party desired to try it again. It was the hardest cruise that any Jack Tar ever made, and we all determined to cultivate the army more than we had done, in case we should go on a horse-marine excursion.

It was with the greatest delight that we got out of that ditch and into the open woods again, with plenty of "sea room" and no lee shores. We took our time, went squirrel-hunting in the few boats we had left, and got a fine mess of turkey-buzzards out of the old oaks which surrounded us.

In ten days more we anchored again in the mouth of the Yazoo River and commenced to repair damages.

I always carried a large steamer along with the squadron fitted as a carpenter's shop. She had a good supply of mechanics on board, with all that was necessary to repair a vessel after an action.

In a week we were all built up again, were supplied with new boats from the store-ship, and, with our new coats of paint, no one would have supposed we had ever been away from a dock-yard.

Some of the officers were talking of going again, and of the pleasure of the trip, as people who have gone in search of the North Pole, and have fared dreadfully, wish to try it once more.

This was one of the many expedients adopted to bring about the reduction of Vicksburg, and, of all of them, never one more hazardous or more laborious. The whole siege was a series of patient labors, more wearing than active excitement in the field; and while the enemy, on the one hand, displayed the greatest endurance and determination, we, on the other, exhibited the greatest patience under many disappointments.

As President Lincoln truly remarked, "Vicksburg was the backbone of the Rebellion and the key to the situation." And, as I said, to bring about what we wanted was the best general, a large army and naval force, and—patience.

Yet on no occasion during the war did the Government and people of the North display so much *im*patience as they did about this siege. While General Grant was working with that imperturbable determination which distinguished him to try and get into the rear of the place, and his trusted generals were always ready to forward his views (as were myself and all my officers), some implacable foe, with a corps of reporters "at his beck and call," was inundating the country with false accounts of Grant's actions, which had no foundation whatever. They were the creation of a malignant brain, and were circulated from personal motives.

The worst of it was, the Government was partly influenced by the same spirit, and, had it not been that President Lincoln was governed by feelings of justice, disaster might have befallen the Union.

No ordinary general could have taken Vicksburg at all; it required a man full of military ability and knowledge, and one who knew whom to select from all the able men of the army—those who were best qualified to undertake the many vexatious problems that would arise during so important and difficult a siege.

Some men would have given it up and said that it was not worth the loss of time and the waste of human life which would ensue; some would have demanded half the resources of the Union; but Grant never wavered in his determination, or in his hopes of success.

He had a smaller force than the enemy, who, knowing the importance of the place, kept a garrison of forty thousand or more men inside the walls and forty thousand more just outside, under those they considered their ablest generals.

When General Grant had tried every rational expedient, he resorted to the last and only true one, which not one general in a thousand would have approved, and which he followed in opposition to the opinions of a majority of his commanders.

When I look back, after the lapse of nearly a quarter of a century, and remember the libels I used to read in Republican papers against the men who were doing all they could to take Vicksburg, I lose all patience with them. Fortunately, newspaper writers are not always exponents of public opinion, and the sensational articles, written on the scene of action to please the morbid taste of the public, did not have the anticipated effect, any more than the implacable misrepresentations made by a vindictive foe of all prominent officers had upon the President, when made to him personally.

Nearly all the clever young officers who went on that expedition with me are dead and gone. One I know of is broken down and on the retired list. Such is the insatiable greed of the great maelstrom—war.

All are swallowed up who are not made of iron and steel.

Old Tecumseh and myself hold on, two tough old knots, with a good deal of the steel in us yet, and quite enough vitality to lay out any number of those who pride themselves upon what they can do.

We can sit down and write out our reminiscences for the benefit of the young men who are coming along, and perhaps they may learn something from our experience.

Chapter XV.

A COUNCIL OF WAR—PASSAGE OF THE FLEET BY THE BATTERIES OF VICKSBURG—GENERAL SHERMAN VISITS THE FLEET IN ITS PASSAGE—WOODEN GUNS ON CART-WHEELS—A HANDFUL OF CORN AND A DEAD CONFEDERATE SOLDIER.

I gave General Grant a faithful account of our reconnoissance, and he was satisfied that he could not carry on military operations against Vicksburg in the way we had attempted.

"I will go below Vicksburg," he said, "and cross over if I can depend on you for a sufficient naval force. I will prepare some transports by packing them well with cotton-bales, and we'll start as soon as you are ready."

"I will be ready to-morrow night," I replied, "and in the mean time will lay in a full supply of provisions and ammunition, and prepare coal-barges to take along."

General Grant called a council of war that afternoon on board my flag-ship—the *Black Hawk*—and, after informing the generals what he proposed to do, asked their opinions.

General McClernand did not attend the council, but wrote to Grant approving the plan. I think General Sherman was present, but did not favor the plan, as it would take the army a long distance from its base of supplies, and for other good reasons which Grant considered it necessary to set aside on the present occasion.

All the other generals present at the council strongly objected to Grant's plan. He listened patiently and, when they had finished, remarked, "I have considered your arguments, but continue in the same opinion. You will be ready to move at ten o'clock to-morrow morning. General McClernand will take the advance; General Sherman will remain here with his division and, if possible, make an attack on Haines's Bluff in conjunction with such of the gunboats as the admiral may not want with him below." So ended the council.

Everything connected with this movement of General Grant's had been conducted with as much secrecy as possible, yet I believe the intended change of base was known in Vicksburg almost as soon as it was in the Union army. The Confederates had unknown means of finding out what was going on, though we certainly supposed they would know nothing of the intended movement of the *gunboats*.

As night approached, all on board the gunboats were in a state of pleasurable excitement at the prospect of getting away from the Yazoo River.

At the appointed hour we started down the Mississippi as quietly as possible, drifting with the current. Dogs and crowing hens were left behind, and every precaution taken to prevent the enemy from becoming aware of our design.

We knew they were to have a grand ball that night in Vicksburg, and thought the "sounds of revelry" would favor us in getting the transports past the batteries. All of these vessels had been protected with cotton-bales, and, under the management of their brave and experienced pilots, followed along in line.

I was in advance, in the Benton, and as I looked back at the long line I could compare them only to so many phantom vessels. Not a light was to be seen nor a sound heard throughout the fleet.

We approached the bend in the river where the frowning heights were covered with heavy batteries.

"We will, no doubt, slip by unnoticed," I remarked to the captain of the *Benton;* "the rebels seem to keep a very poor watch."

Just then a bright light along the levee illuminated everything, showing the city and forts as plainly as if it were daylight.

"The town is on fire!" exclaimed the captain. On the opposite side of the river was a large railroad station with outbuildings, and as soon as the first fire broke out, these also burst into flames. The upper fort opened its heavy guns upon the *Benton,* the shot rattling against her sides like hail, but she had four inches of iron plating over forty inches of oak, so that not much impression was made upon her hull. There being no longer any concealment possible, we stood to our guns and returned the enemy's fire.

Every fort and hill-top vomited forth shot and shell, many of the latter bursting in the air and doing no damage, but adding to the grandeur of the scene. As fast as our vessels came within range of the forts they opened their broadsides, and soon put a stop to any revelry that might be going on in Vicksburg.

The enemy's shells set fire to the transport *Henry Clay,* and she was soon in a blaze, adding her light to that of the tar-barrels kept by the enemy in readiness for the occasion, for we had not surprised them in the least by our movement to run the gauntlet.

The courageous pilot of the *Henry Clay* stood at his post and, with his vessel all ablaze, attempted to run past the fleet.

When a man is in trouble the world is generally down on him, and so it was with the *Henry Clay;* the enemy found her a good target, and showered all their attention on her.

The blazing cotton-bales were knocked overboard by the rebel shot, and the river was covered with bits of burning cotton, looking like a thousand lamps.

The men of the *Henry Clay* finally had to jump into the water to save their lives, while the vessel floated until she burned up.

Another transport was sunk by the rebels, but the rest of them passed the batteries, though not without suffering considerable damage.

As to the naval vessels, they had to go slowly and take the enemy's fire. The logs on their sides and the bales of hay with which they were packed saved them in many cases. We had few people killed, and the enemy's artillery fire was not much to boast of, considering that they had over a hundred guns firing at us as we drifted down stream in such close order that it would seem to have been impossible to miss us.

The sight was a grand one, and I stood on deck admiring it, while the captain fought his vessel and the pilot steered her through fire and smoke as coolly as if he was performing an everyday duty.

The Vicksburgers must have been disappointed when they saw us get by their batteries with so little damage. We suffered most from the musketry fire. The soldiers lined the levee and fired into our port-holes, wounding our men, for we were not more than twenty yards from the shore.

Once only the fleet got into a little disorder, owing to the thick smoke which hung over the river, but the commanding officers, adhering to their orders "to *drift* only," got safely out of the difficulty.

I had just passed the last battery in the *Benton,* and the vessels behind were crowding rather closer than I liked, so I gave the order to "Go ahead slow," to let the line straighten up. This soon put us a hundred yards ahead, when I was hailed by some one in a boat, "Benton ahoy!"

"Halloo!" I replied, and presently I recognized the voice of General Sherman.

"Are you all right, old fellow?"

"Come on board and see," I replied, and Sherman came over the side to hear about our fortunes.

"One man's leg cut off by a round-shot, half a dozen shell and musket-ball wounds," I said.

"You are more at home here than you were in the ditches grounding on willow-trees," said Sherman. "Stick to this, old fellow; it suits Jack better. There are a lot of my boys on the point ready to help you if you want anything. They hauled this boat over for me. Good-night! I must go and find out how the other fellows fared," and I believe he visited every vessel in turn. He would have liked to have been in the storm of shot could he have done so with propriety.

When the *Benton* had passed all danger we still continued to drift on. The cannon were yet booming, and fire was apparently issuing from a dozen burning vessels.

It might have answered for a picture of the infernal regions.

We were an hour and a half in passing the batteries, which extended along the river for about four miles. I could not stop to ascertain what damage had been done to the other vessels, as I had to keep moving to make way for those behind me.

The sound of guns gradually decreased as the vessels passed the batteries, and then all was silent. The fires had burned out, and the river had returned to its former obscurity.

I came to anchor around a point, and in ten minutes the gunboats began to come in sight one after another in the same order in which they had started, anchoring in line under the stern of the *Benton*. Bunches of cotton still ablaze, and burning fragments of the wreck of the *Henry Clay*, continued to come down with the current, giving an old rebel, who stood on the shore abreast of our anchorage, an opportunity to call out, "Whar are yer gunboats now? I tole yer dam' soldiers thar wouldn't be mor'n one on 'em left by ther time Vicksburg war done with 'em!"

And this worthy went to sleep, happy in the thought that the floating bits of cotton were the remains of the unfortunate gunboats, only to wake on the morrow to disappointment.

General Grant had turned the enemy's flank with his army, I had turned it with the gunboats; now Grant had to cross the river and trust to his brave soldiers, who were glad to do anything rather than sit down day after day with nothing to do but carry on the ordinary routine of an army. Yet such must be the fate of those who enter upon a siege like that of Vicksburg, where Nature has thrown almost insurmountable obstructions in the way of a hostile army.

Grant ought to have felt happy that night when it was reported to him that the gunboats and transports had arrived at Carthage ready for work, for he knew that he had now a prospect of getting in the rear of the rebel stronghold. As for myself, I felt sure of success, and was certain that Vicksburg would soon be ours.

General Sherman seemed to take much interest in the passage of the fleet by

Vicksburg. Not long ago he employed Mr. Taylor, an artist of New York, to paint a picture of the affair, I furnishing photographs of the vessels and other material in my possession. The picture, which is a very correct representation of the scene, is now in the War Department, while the original study hangs in my library.

When daylight broke, after the passage of the fleet, I was besieged by the commanding officers of the gunboats, who came to tell me of their mishaps; but when I intimated that I intended to leave at Carthage any vessel that could not stand the hammering they would be subject to at Grand Gulf, everybody suddenly discovered that no damage had been done their vessels, which, if anything, were better prepared for action than when they started out!

Opposite where I lay was a body of Union troops, and, supposing it was McClernand's corps, which had the advance, I steamed up to the levee to greet them.

I found they had thrown up intrenchments, and had a log on a pair of cartwheels to represent a field-piece.

General McClernand had pushed ahead with three or four hundred men of Osterhaus's brigade, and, upon arriving at the point where I found them, they discovered themselves confronted by a couple of Confederate regiments, who had thrown up earthworks and armed them with four guns supposed to be thirty-pounder rifles.

Generals McClernand and Osterhaus came on board the *Benton* as soon as she was made fast to the bank. The former seemed pleased to see us, but Osterhaus was beaming all over.

"Now," said he, "dose dampt fellers, dey'll catch it; give dem gunboat soup!"

One of Osterhaus's staff ran up to an ensign—an old friend of his—and, giving him a fraternal hug, exclaimed, "Ah, Pill, mein Gott! how glad I am to see you! De sight of you ish petter ash goot. Effery soldier in der army ought to carry a gun-pote mit his pocket!"

"Ya! ya!" said another, "I knosh someding petter as dot. Effery man shoult pe a gun-pote; dot's what I calls de ticket for soups!"

In the works which the Confederates had thrown up opposite McClernand were two or three flags which I thought we might as well capture. McClernand requested that I would let the gunboats get under way and settle that work.

I signaled for Captain Shirk, of the *Tuscumbia,* and directed him to go down and drive the Confederates out of the fort, keeping up such a rapid fire of grape and shrapnel that the enemy could not carry off a single gun.

The Confederate earthworks were distant about eight hundred yards from us on the bank of the river, and in twenty minutes' time the *Tuscumbia* had opened her batteries at a distance of about three hundred yards, and the enemy soon evacuated their fortifications, carrying their flags with them.

Captain Shirk returned almost immediately, having failed to carry out my orders and bring the guns with him. But when he came on board the *Benton* he held in his hand a canvas knapsack.

"What is that, sir?" I inquired, a little severely; "and where are those guns?"

The guns, he said, were four logs mounted on cart-wheels, and the knapsack contained all the enemy's commissary stores, which he dropped as he was running away.

In the knapsack was an old shoe and an ear of corn. Heavens! what a commentary on the war was this! A soldier fighting for an idea he did not comprehend and against the only form of government which could insure the freedom of the poor white man of the South, and willing to live on an ear of corn a day in order that an oligarchy might be formed to bring him down to the level of a brute.

Just think of the Spartan courage, though combined with ignorance, on the part of those who bore arms for the South! Who could help admiring such men, even though fighting against them?

I witnessed many similar cases when visiting battle-fields, and, led by curiosity, examined the knapsacks of the dead soldiers.

On one occasion I found but a handful of corn; on another, a few ounces of corn-bread; and in both cases the dead men were so emaciated by hard labor and the want of proper food that they were reduced to skin and bones.

In point of endurance they set us an example it would have been hard to follow. I do not know whether we could have endured the hardships as well as they, as we were never called upon to try it. Our Commissary Department was the best in the world, and the waste of our provisions would have supplied a European army.

The presence of the gunboats enabled General McClernand to take a more comfortable position, and he established his headquarters close by the advance of his corps, being about five miles from Grand Gulf, where it was at that time supposed General Grant would cross over if the gunboats could drive the enemy from their batteries at that place.

Chapter XVI.

NAVAL BATTLE AT GRAND GULF—THREE COMMISSIONERS
FROM WASHINGTON TO EXAMINE INTO THE CONDUCT OF
AFFAIRS—ONE OF THE COMMISSIONERS IN A "LONG SHIRT"—
TAR AND FEATHERS—LANDING OF THE ARMY AT
BRUENSBURG—AMUSING STORY OF AN IOWA REGIMENT—FIRST
MEETING WITH GENERAL A. J. SMITH—A CONFEDERATE RAM.

The battle of Grand Gulf was fought April 29, 1863, and won by the navy, and it was as hard a fight as any that occurred during the war.

For more than five hours the gunboats engaged the enemy's batteries at close quarters, the latter having thirteen heavy guns placed on commanding heights from eighty to one hundred and twenty feet above the river. We lost seventy-five men in killed and wounded, and silenced all the enemy's guns. We passed all the transports by the batteries without damage, and General Grant was at liberty to cross the Mississippi and commence operations on the Vicksburg side as soon as he thought proper.

He had marched some thirty-two thousand men to the point opposite Grand Gulf, and gunboats and transports were all assembled there, waiting to go whithersoever they were wanted.

General Grant witnessed the action at Grand Gulf from a tug in the middle of the river.

There had come to visit the army three persons who were reported to be commissioners sent from Washington to examine into the conduct of affairs—Mr. E. B. Washburn, Governor Yates, and Adjutant-General Thomas. These gentlemen were on board the tug with General Grant during the engagement between the forts and the gunboats, and I think were favorably impressed with the result of the conflict. For the official report of the fight I must refer my readers to the Secretary of the Navy's Annual Report for 1863.

When night came I made General Grant and the commissioners very comfortable on board my flag-ship, the *Benton,* for the army, by Grant's order, had brought no tents, and to old General Thomas I gave up my stateroom. On such occasions people will be jolly if the company is at all congenial, and that night formed no exception to the rule.

The commissioners expressed their satisfaction that the army had moved from before Vicksburg, and that we could keep open communications with our base of supplies.

Sherman, with a large army and a considerable naval force, was left near Milliken's Bend to act as might be advisable, and Grant could either get in the rear of Vicksburg *via* Bruensburg or try some other point.

I was particularly interested that night in making General Thomas comfortable, helping him unpack his carpet-bag and get out his *"long shirt,"* in which attire he looked every inch an adjutant-general! To supplement his "long shirt," I furnished him with a "night-cap," under the influence of which the old gentleman grew confidential and told me the whole story of the commission.

"Great complaints," said the general, "have come to the President from some one in the army before Vicksburg in regard to Grant's manner of conducting operations, and Mr. Lincoln therefore determined to find out for himself the true state of affairs; so he sent the present commissioners to examine with full powers." Here the general stopped and swore me to secrecy. Mr. Washburn was sent as the fast friend of General Grant, Governor Yates as a man in whose conscientious opinions the President could depend, and General Thomas "as a military expert, who could explain to his colleagues the exact situation of affairs and the defects in Grant's plans if any existed!"

"We stopped first," said the general, "at McClernand's camp, to ascertain his style of doing things. He gave us a grand review and a good lunch, but had no ice for his champagne; then we called on Grant, and, Admiral, I'll give you a piece of information."

"Wait a moment," I interrupted; "your throat sounds dry; try this glass of toddy; it will make you sleep like a top, and you won't feel the mosquitoes."

The general drank it down without winking. "You would have made a fortune, Admiral, as a barkeeper," he said; "you have such a talent for mixing drinks; but don't mention what I'm going to tell you. I carry in my bag full authority to remove General Grant and place whomsoever I please in command of the army;" and the old general drew himself up and looked at me as much as to say, "What do you think of that?"

I reflected for a moment, and then asked whom it was proposed to put in Grant's place.

"Well," replied General Thomas, "that depends; McClernand is prominent."

"General," I said, "no doubt your plans are well considered, but let an old salt give you a piece of advice. Don't let your plans get out, for if the army and navy should find out what you three gentlemen came for, they would tar and feather you, and neither General Grant nor myself could prevent it."

"Is it possible?" exclaimed the general. "But I don't intend to do anything. We are delighted with all we have seen, so there will be no change. I should have pursued the same course as General Grant had I been in command myself!"

"Stick to that, General," I said, "and don't forget that I am in earnest about the tar and feathers; now go to sleep and dream of being made major-general for the good service you will perform by telling the President that everything has been done that could be done, that the army and the navy are all right, and that Vicksburg will be ours in thirty days, if not sooner."

I never mentioned General Thomas's conversation until some years after the close of the war, when I gave General Badeau, who was then writing the "Military History of General Grant," my journal to look over.

I have read several accounts of the siege of Vicksburg, but none of them convey a good idea of the operations which led to the fall of that stronghold. The true history of the siege of Vicksburg must not be the sensational work of a penny-a-liner. It will be a chronicle of patient labor. There were no "dashing moves" while our army was sitting down before the place or before the city was turned. There was no place to dash into except the Mississippi River.

At daylight, on the morning after the Grand Gulf fight, the troops began to throng on board the gunboats and transports, and, when all were embarked, we headed down stream instead of crossing over, and in an hour and a half hauled up at Bruensburg, on the Vicksburg side.

There some thirty-two thousand men with rations for four days were landed, and then commenced that remarkable series of movements which placed our army in the rear of Vicksburg, our troops forcing their way between two formidable armies of forty thousand men each, posted in commanding positions.

Our troops had to assail the enemy after long and tortuous marches, with a deep river on one side and almost inaccessible hills bristling with bayonets to oppose them.

It was in my opinion the most remarkable and most successful military operation of the civil war, and was the crowning move toward placing the Father of Waters once more under the absolute control of its legitimate rulers.

If any one had heretofore doubted General Grant's ability, it would seem that the latter's arrival on the heights in the rear of Vicksburg, driving Pemberton with forty thousand men into the intrenched city, and causing General Joe Johnston with an equal force to retire beyond Jackson, must have removed his doubts.

I at once opened communication with Grant's army by way of the Yazoo, and the city of Vicksburg was in a day or two sealed up so tight that even the "intelligent contraband" found it impossible to get in or out.

There we will leave the army, for we can not tell the story of the hardships and trials they underwent, the disappointments they suffered, and the fortitude they exhibited.

The entire operations were marked by a happy co-operation on the part of the army and the navy, on which success so much depends on such occasions.

It could not be expected that an army which started out with but four days' rations and cut themselves off from their base of supplies could do otherwise than live upon the country. There were certain regiments in that army which had a reputation as pot-hunters as well as fighters, and one of these was the 13th Iowa, in General A. J. Smith's brigade.

Bruensburg and the surrounding country was the great depot for live-stock, grain, etc., and, in twenty-four hours after the arrival of our army, fresh meat abounded in camp, and the soldiers' lines seemed to have fallen in pleasant places. Foraging was not prohibited; in fact, the soldiers were cautioned to save the Government rations for an emergency; so that the squealing of pigs, and the bleating of calves and sheep, and the cackling of poultry were common sounds in camp, and many a fence-rail was burned to cook provisions for some veteran who had proved himself a good forager.

The day after General Grant's arrival at Bruensburg, so goes the story, as he was sitting in his tent, the flap was pushed aside and an old rebel, who had long passed the time to bear arms, thrust his head through the opening. In his hand he held a rope, which was attached to a large, raw-boned mule with swelled knees and minus an eye. At least twenty summers must have passed over the head of this interesting animal.

The old fellow gazed curiously at the general, as if he had expected to see one of the huge ogres such as figure in the chronicles of Jack the Giant Killer. "Be you the gin'ral of this here army?" he inquired; "ef so, I got a complaint agin one of your rigiments, an' I want you to 'tend to it to onst. I don't come here to ask favors, but to deman' my rights, for, if these ain't granted, dem my picter if yer don't see some tall talkin' w'en this here war's over an' the Confed'rit Gov'ment makes claim for damages to her loyal citizens. I'm Abel Doolittle, that's who I am, an' ef I hadn't the alfiredest nicest farm in all these parts afore your bummers come along, I'll swell up an' sneeze. An' ef you don't see me righted, w'en this blasted war is ended, you'll hear on this, I tell you! Fust comes them Confed'rit fellers an' takes two tenths uv all we got, an' gin us a bar'l uv Confed'rit shin-plasters; then comes along *yer* blasted pot-hunters an' takes the tother eight tenths, and never even said Thank ye! What you think uv that?"

"Didn't they give you a receipt?" inquired the general.

"Receipt! thunder!" said the old man. "Yes, they giv' us receipts enough, but them things ain't wuth nothin'; an', I tell you, I'm goin' ter be paid, or you'll hear on it."

"What is your complaint?" inquired the general.

"Well," replied the old man, "I ain't got no complaint, as I knows on just now, ceptin' the rheumatiz an' fever an' ager, same's all ov us has at this season."

"I mean," said the general, "what charges have you to make against any one? Speak out, and don't take up my time. Here, Rawlins, attend to this man," and the general walked away.

"Now," said General Rawlins, "say quickly what you have to say, and then get out of this."

"Ah, yes!" exclaimed the old man, "that's demed pretty talk. You fellers come along and eat us out of house and home, an', when a man wants his money, you turn up yer nose as if yer owned the Guano Islands."

"What happened to you?" said Rawlins.

"Why," said the old fellow, "I had the finest lot ov chickens, turkeys, pigs, an' sheep as ever you seen, but dam' my buttons ef you fellers ain't gone an' tuk everything except this ole muel an' an ole goose. There was two ov them geese, an' they tried one uv 'em; but ef a hull rigimint didn't break their teeth out after tearin' away at that ole goose, well, I don't know what loosin' teeth is. Why, Gin'ral, ef I hadn't brought the muel away they'd a eatin him."

"But what do you expect me to do?" inquired General Rawlins. "How are you going to find out who did all that you complain of?"

"Well, I know who did it," said the old fellow; "it's one of Gin'ral A. J. Smith's regiments. I know the sargint what led them men on. He belongs to the 13th Iowy, an' he kin skin a hog quicker'n grease lightnin'."

Just then General A. J. Smith walked into the tent. "Here, General," said Rawlins, "this man has a complaint to make against some of your boys."

"What is it?" said General Smith.

"Just what I tole this here gin'ral," replied the old man; "your men come on ter my place an' they stole everythin' they could lay han's on, an' only lef' me an' ole goose an' this ole muel."

The general looked at him with contempt. "Pray what regiment did all this damage?"

"The 13th Iowy," said the man.

"They weren't my men, thir," said General Smith. "Ith's a damned lie; they never were on your farm. I know my boys too well. If it had been the 13th Iowa they'd have taken everything on the place, and wouldn't have left a goose or a mule or anything else. No, thir! my boys don't do things in that way. If you don't keep your eye on that mule they'll get him away from you before sundown."

The old man turned around to gaze upon his beloved mule, then shouted,

"By the great Jehosophat, ef they ain't gone an' tuk him an' leff a darned sojer at the end of the rope!"

General Smith glanced proudly around. "Ah, Rawlins!" he said, "those must have been my boys after all; if I could only hear that they had eaten the old man's goose I should be certain of it."

"They're a hard set, General," said Rawlins.

"Yes," said General Smith, "but they don't cost the Government anything for transportation, and, no matter where they camp, they find a store of provisions half an hour afterward."

General A. J. Smith was one of those glorious old veterans who shared with his men all the dangers and hardships of the campaign. He never permitted any of his command to indulge in luxuries if he could help it; and once, in trying to express his contempt for a certain person, said, "He is one of those fellows who carry a shelter-tent!"

General Smith and myself served together a good deal, and I never knew him to falter. He was as brave a man as Grant had in his army, and, although he allowed his men a great deal of latitude, he was a rigid disciplinarian.

My first meeting with General A. J. Smith was an amusing one. It took place at Fort Hindman, Arkansas. Fort Hindman, formerly called "Arkansas Post," was captured by the navy. About an hour after the surrender, when the prisoners had all been secured, a large number of Union officers on horseback were seen approaching the fort. The marines had been posted as sentinels, and the sailors were taking the prisoners off to the gunboat. An adjadant galloped up, and, jumping from his horse, sang out, "Get out of this; everybody clear the fort. General Smith is coming to take possession. Clear out at once!" The naval officers were watching the approaching cavalcade from the summit of a mound. I was dressed in a blue blouse with nothing but a pair of small shoulder-straps to indicate my rank, and, stepping down, I said to the newcomer, "Who are you, pray, that undertakes to give such orders here? We've whipped the rebels out of this place, and if you don't take care we will clear you out also!" At that moment General Smith rode in with the cavalcade. "Here, General," said the officer, "is a man who says he isn't going out of this for you or anybody else, and that he'll whip us out if we don't take care!" "Will he, be God?" said General Smith; "will he, be God? Let me see him; bring the fellow here!" I stepped forward and said, "Here I am, sir, the admiral commanding this squadron." At this announcement Smith laid his right hand on the holster of his pistol. I thought, of course, that he was about to shoot me, but, instead of that, the general hauled out a bottle and said, "Be God! Admiral, I'm glad to see you; let's take a drink!"

This was the origin of my acquaintance with General A. J. Smith, resulting in a friendship which lasted through the war.

After landing the army at Bruensburg I steamed down the Mississippi to the mouth of Red River, where Farragut was in the *Hartford,* relieved him of the blockade of that stream, and he rejoined his squadron. Fort Hudson had not yet surrendered.

Then I started up Red River, took possession of Fort de Russy, and partly destroyed that work.

Farragut had cautioned me against a ram said to be building up Red River. After finishing with Fort de Russy I began to inquire about the ram, for I did not desire to suddenly encounter such an enemy while turning a bend in the river, and perhaps lose one or more of my vessels.

I entered into conversation with a man whom we met near Fort de Russy, and said to him, "Well, stranger, I hear you have a Confederate ram up here somewhere. Whereabouts is she?"

"Lemme think," said the native, scratching his head while going through the thinking process. "Yes, thar is a ram 'bout eight miles above hyar."

"Is it a powerful one?" I inquired.

"Wall, I reckon you'd think so ef you seen it; it's the allfiredest strong thing ever I seen, an' I guess at buttin' it ud knock them ar bows of yourn into smithereens."

"How large is it?" I asked.

"Wall, it's 'bout the biggest thing I ever seen."

"Tell me all about it," I said, for I was beginning to get interested.

"Wall, Gin'ral," said the man, "that's easier said than done. It's an allfired buster, an' kin beat all creation at buttin'. That's all I knows about it. I seen it on Mr. Whitler's place, as I tole yer, eight miles above hyar; an' one day, w'en I was up thar, whar thar war a bull weighin' twenty-eight hunder, an' as soon as the bull seen the ram he 'gan to paw the airth an' throwed up his tail, an' the ram put down his head an' the bull bellered, an' they went slap dash at each other, an' ef that ram didn't knock daylights out o' that bull, and knock his tail out by the roots, and his horns off, and lay him out as flat as a pancake, I'm a liar!"

"But," said I, "I am asking you about a Confederate ram—a vessel covered with iron."

"Wall, Gin'ral," said the man, "I don't know nothin' 'bout any Confed'rit ram, but I'm sure the one I seen could knock the bows off them ar turtles ov yourn afore you could wink, an' I reckon he mus' be a Confed'rit ram, seein' he war born in these parts."

Any apprehensions I might have had in regard to a Confederate ram were put at rest, and I made no more inquiries.

I was afterward informed that this simple native whom I had questioned was a Confederate officer in disguise, who regaled his friends with the story of how he had beguiled the Yankees. However, he was entirely welcome to his little joke.

Chapter XVII.

SIEGE OF VICKSBURG.

See those hills, with their heads so defiant and bold,
Standing up as if reared by the Titans of old;
The deep rolling river just laving their feet,
And the cool glens and valleys defying the heat.
There are caves in those hills where a ripple of light
Scarce enters within—where the darkness of night
Reigns supreme, like some great and imperial king,
Where the sun not even a shadow can fling;
For darkness is sovereign, the light of the day,
When peeping in there, flies frightened away.
The thick fog in the noon-time almost baffles the sight,
And, obscuring the sun, turns day into night.
On the rugged hill-tops great forests abound,
And the day throws no light in that stillness profound;
In the foreground are gorges, rifted and torn
By fire and wind, and by swift torrents worn,
Where brambles and scrub-oaks, all twisted in one,
Bar the way to invaders or the light of the sun.
High on the plateau, higher than all,
Stands the labor of man—a marvelous wall—
Its guns and its mortars protecting the rear,
Half-moons and counterscarps, where defenders need fear
No assailants who'll come in the gloom of the night.
The ramparts are manned with men who will fight.
Each house is a castle throughout the old town,
And the front with strong works is environed around;
The right wing is protected by a frightful abyss,
On the other side faced by a steep precipice;

Here would be scattered assailants and all,
And they long would remember that o'erhanging wall.
On the left runs a line, showing bright in the sun,
Of earthworks in numbers, mounting many a gun,
With rough-looking rocks crowding round them in piles,
And intrenchments bewildering extending for miles.
This is Vicksburg—the heart of this terrible strife—
Prepared at all points to contend for its life.
Ah! those beautiful valleys, so bright and serene,
The red blood will deluge their grass-plots so green;
The hill-sides and rocks will be soon red and gory,
And in ages to come they'll be famous in story.

We surround the doomed city, the pressure's begun,
And we're throwing in missiles from mortar and gun.
Months pass, and a gloom, like the mantle of death,
Hangs over the scene, where not even a breath
Of hope could be felt. While the brave foemen fell
By the hundreds beneath our merciless shell,
We bombarded in front, we assaulted the rear,
And every attack only cost us more dear.
There's an end to endurance; the long-gnawing fast
Could not be withstood; the fall came at last.

In the trenches, in battle, ah! the days of the past
Rose before the poor soldier breathing his last;
He would turn his dimmed eyes to the light in the west,
And waft a fond sigh to those he loved best.
But how many were wrapped in the garments of Death
Who welcomed Life's ending! War's withering breath
Had wrested from many every joy in this life,
For what joy could one find in this murderous strife?
Many breathed their last sigh on that wide gory plain,
And welcomed the bullet that ended their pain.
And the angels rejoice o'er the soldier's repose,
And drop tears o'er the life just brought to a close;
For no longer he'll battle on the chill, dreary plain
With hunger and thirst, in the cold sleety rain,
Where day's turned to night, and night into day,

And where shrapnel and shell sweep hundreds away.
Thank God! the sweet angel of mercy is by
The brave soldier who dies, and will catch his last sigh;
Soars aloft with his soul, while never again
In hardship or battle will it grapple with pain.

The cold, bitter blasts of winter have come,
And bring back the thoughts of a once-cherished home;
The snow, which is red with the blood of the brave,
Piles up in rifts o'er the poor soldier's grave;
And the cold, piercing wind, in its merciless wrath,
Is howling a requiem of death in its path,
As if searching for something still further to blast,
And dealing destruction all round to the last.
The angel of mercy sits out in the storm,
A halo of light flashes round her pure form,
And she drives off in anger that demon of sin
Who is watching his chance in the storm to get in,
And now flies in dismay, back, back to his shades,
Down, down to the bottomless pit of dark Hades,
For God in his mercy claims as his own
Those fallen in war who great honors have won.
There's that broken-down soldier sitting out in the storm;
Pinched is his face and bent is his form;
His uniform's ragged, his whole look is forlorn,
His breakfast is simply a handful of corn.
Shivering he sits, most sad is his look,
He has no commissariat, no victuals to cook.
Torn from his home—what a terrible fate!—
To fight 'gainst his will and nourish a hate
For the flag he once loved, and that beautiful plan
The Creator designed for the freedom of man.
What can console him? what can repay
For privations he's suffered, his life thrown away?
Who sits by his side in the withering cold,
Looking so sickly, so wretchedly old?
'Tis a comrade he cares for. He can scarce draw a breath;
He is leaving last words, he is fighting with Death.
So passes the night, so passes the day,

Hundreds by Death are oft snatched away.
Shot and shell do their work, but privations do more,
And fill up the grave-yard along the lone shore.

See that bright youth of eighteen, looking afar
At the western horizon, on the bright evening star.
Another is looking at that star in the west,
And, knowing he sees it, thinks herself blest.
They promised, at parting, when the rays of the sun
Were melting in twilight and the day's work was done,
They'd go out in the evening and look at that star,
And their souls be united, though parted so far.
He hears the sweet chimes of the soft vesper bell—
And quickly he knelt as it soothingly fell—
And he sends up a prayer to the Ruler on high,
And falls dead as he kneels, and wafts her a sigh,
For a ball strikes his heart. He will see her no more;
She will watch now alone, his watching is o'er.
A cloud, dark and threatening, obscures all the west,
And that poor maiden feels she no longer is blest.
Her soldier is dead, his marching is done,
An angel stoops o'er him, a triumph is won;
A soul flies to heaven, there's joy in the skies,
There's a whisper of mercy as upward it flies.
Look at those soldiers, how they hobble away!
There's no work for them now, they can no longer stay;
They've been wounded and starved, they go out on parole,
Their limbs are all shattered, naught is left but a soul.
At night, on the road, they'll have no place to lie,
Yet they'll struggle along, for they go home to die.
Already they see the home-fire's bright glare,
And father, and mother, and sister are there.
Though they've suffered with cold and have no place to sleep,
And live on mild charity as onward they creep,
They keep their eyes fixed on that star in the west;
Just beneath it they hope to find welcome and rest.
Yet who pities the pains of the soldiers so poor?
They crawl with crushed limbs past the rich man's closed door;
Still they keep their eyes fixed on that star in the sky,

Which points out the road to their homes where they'll die.
The poor ones would help them, but they barely can live;
They are starving themselves—they have nothing to give.
Move on! they can't help you, they nothing can do;
Go to some richer mansion—they are poorer than you.
And they move on. At night on the wet soil they lie,
And they reach home at last, but to lie down and die.
And the bright star of eve still shines in the west,
And sheds its light on the graves of the soldiers at rest.
Tears are shed on the sod, a wife's last fond claim,
And the poor soldier sleeps—his last sleep—without fame.

Just observe those sweet villas, once with beauty bedecked,
They are shattered and torn, without tenants, and wrecked.
The rose, which in clusters sheds its perfume around,
Is lying all trampled and crushed on the ground.
Gaunt desolation now dwells in those halls,
And the bomb-shells' rude blows have destroyed all the walls;
The owls and the foxes in these rooms make their home.
Those who lived there, and loved there, now have to roam,
Seeking for shelter in damp holes in the hills,
Breathing foulest of air, and air that soon kills.
In vain they seek safety; the deep, piercing shell
Makes their homes in the caves little better than hell;
But, though suffering all evils, and without light of day,
They kneel down at eve and in hopelessness pray.
And the loose, yielding earth only gives them a grave,
For they die, when fast sleeping, with no hand to save.
No one can hear that loud, piercing cry
That ascends to their God (for mercy) on high.
In ages to come, men in digging below
Will find their poor bones, but they never will know
Of the anguish and pain of the inmates who fell
(In the close, pent-up cave) by the deep, piercing shell.

There are the dead in their graves—in long, mournful rows—
What anguish they suffered in dying! Who knows?
Who kept a record? Who is there can tell
Who died of starvation, or whom by the shell?

All we know is, they lie by the deep river shore,
A board at their heads with a number—no more.
Friends may ask for their bones, when the war's at an end;
Who can tell, midst that crowd, who's relation or friend?
What havoc those bomb-shells have made in that ground—
Heads, legs, and arms all scattered around!
No peace for the living, no peace for the dead,
What cared the gunners, so Death could be fed?
Uprooted are coffins, and the grave-yard débris
Is scattered about in confusion, you see.
It were useless to try and regather the dead;
That can not be done till the day when the dread
Trumpet calls us before God's awful throne;
Then the dead will all rise and bone spring to bone.

That street is much torn by the thirteen-inch shell,
Cobble-stone, curb-stone are mixed up pell-mell
With remains of strong horses and dead mules in the roads—
They were all blown to pieces while drawing their loads.

See those stone-houses crushed, those church-steeples knocked down,
And disaster and ruin all over the town;
No pen can describe, no language can tell,
The terrible blow of a thirteen-inch shell.
It bursts in the air, it bursts in the ground,
And scatters its death-dealing fragments around;
It brings sleepless nights when it bursts in the air,
And warns the besieged that the foe is still there.

Mark that company coming from church. A fair bride
Has an officer by her—how she clings to his side!
They have plighted their vows and are now man and wife,
And have promised to cling to each other through life.
Life's uncertain at best, and how little we know
By day or by night when will come the death-blow!
They at least hope to gather some flowers in spring,
And sit hand in hand where the mocking-birds sing,
Or list to the lark as it soars in the sky,
While the swift mountain stream goes murmuring by.

But who, in their wildest conjectures, could tell
These two were to die by a murderous shell?
But grim Death spares neither the young nor the old.
It did not spare them; the story's soon told.
Hand in hand they walked on. A terrible shell
Burst in their midst, and both of them fell.
A Peri from paradise, lingering near by,
Flew quick to the spot and caught their last sigh,
And, springing aloft quicker than thought,
To the closed gates of heaven the welcome gift brought.
Here's a trophy for angels; it is free from all sin;
Wide open the gates, let me bring the gift in.
Harps of seraphs resound through the portals on high,
While God's hosts rejoice o'er the lovers' last sigh.

Hark! hark to the sound of the evening gun!
The night-watch is set and the day's work is done.
The sentry on post walks along on his beat,
And all that is heard is the sound of his feet;
He is thinking of mother and sisters at home,
And the bright joys of life hereafter to come.
He stops on his beat. Say, what does he hear?
'Tis the hoot of the night-owl which strikes on his ear.
He continues his walk with monotonous tramp,
Wraps his thin coat about him, the night-air is damp;
He strides on while he looks at the stars in the west,
Going down, one by one, to seek their night's rest.
They would rise in the morning, and again they would set,
And, like him, make their rounds o'er their pathway—but yet
They were there for eternity: that he plainly could see;
But, by mid-day to-morrow, where would he be?
A breeze blows, a bough breaks, a leaf falls to the ground;
Again he now stops to list to that sound.
Comes a shriek through the air, and a small glittering light;
It descends through a curve and dazzles his sight.
He watches it keenly; it comes from afar;
'Tis a fire-fly surely, or a small falling star.
He has no time to think; it drops at his feet
And explodes, tears up rocks. He falls dead on his beat.

All around know the sound of that bursting too well,
And turn pale o'er the work of that merciless shell.
By starlight they bear him to the deep river's side,
And inter him in silence, where hundreds have died.

Lo! there's an old shattered church, all ready to fall.
See how the green ivy still clings to the wall,
As a woman will cling, from the days of her youth,
To the man whom she's loved, who's lost honor and truth.
But the ivy and tendrils will fall to the ground,
And the wall, unsupported, very soon will come down.
Though holy the church, and so sacred the shrine,
Shells have no respect for walls so divine.
In war, men ne'er think of the ruin they bring
On the sweet, loving homes, or the most sacred thing.
In war, man's a demon. His nature set free,
His soul is a desert, parched as deserts can be.
From its throne Human Reason steps down so debased,
Truth, love, pity, friendship—all soon run to waste.
Man, urged by his passions, without due restraints,
Will desecrate altars and martyrize saints.
There's glory and fame left. Each passion a snare,
War is ruin in all shapes; it brings but despair.
But enough of this subject. Let us close up the theme.—
Of the great horrors there, no one would dream.—
Gaunt famine killed hundreds, and sickness as well,
But worse came from the fall of the merciless shell.
There's a fête *in old Vicksburg. The great and the small*
Are preparing to go to the officers' ball,
Just to throw off their ennui, *gloom, and despair,*
Which, with famine and death, pervade the foul air.
The soldiers, in perfect abandon, *no doubt,*
Determine to have all their friends at a rout,
Where the music would cheer, and sweet converse would flow,
And sound like the echo of joys long ago.
Little dress wants the soldier: he has made his toilet,
He is booted and spurred, has skin gloves on, and yet
He needs to look in the glass to adjust his cravat,
Or admire his curls, ere he sits down to chat.

Pray, why this grand ball? We can only surmise.
Isn't that lovers may bask in beauty's bright eyes?
Or that viands so rare would enliven the sight,
And that scents of sweet flowers would perfume the night?
No, it is none of these. There'll be no viands there,
No sherry nor champagne selected with care;
No tables with ices, fruits, or salads are set,
Where the gay and the witty in laughter are met,
Where lights so resplendent reflect on the wall,
And make each one remember the officers' ball.
Yet they'll bask in the looks of the dark and the fair,
"And bring back the smiles which joy used to wear."
There is nothing there but music full sweet,
Which gives pulse to the heart and life to the feet.
The men come to woo the lovely and fair,
And they all come this eve to beguile away care,
As the moths, that are lost in the gloom of the night,
Will fly on, confiding, to the hot, glaring light,
Heedless, forgetting, the poor foolish things!
That in wooing the light they are burning their wings.
It is but a change in their terrible life—
To get rid, for an hour, of gloom and of strife,
Though they only could hope to go back in the morn
To their caves where they'd cherished their hatred and scorn.
The fair ones wear neither bracelet nor ring;
They've sold all for their cause—Rebellion is king.
They are neither adorned with pearls nor rich laces;
The attractions they have are their forms and their faces,
Which, though marked with strong lines of sorrow and care,
Possess all the grace of their class—which is rare.
They dim with their brightness each planet and star
Which beams on those beautiful dames from afar;
No diamonds can vie with their sparkling black eyes,
Which are brighter by far than those lights in the skies,
And their faces but look more lovely and fair,
Rich framed in full coils of bright golden hair.
Dressed in plain fashion, they came one and all,
Each worthy to be the belle of the ball.
Their rich dresses have gone to the hospital store,

To be used for the wounded; and, such as they wore,
Are the simplest and cheapest chenille to be found,
And their shoes are so worn their feet touch the ground.
This gay night many dance, forgetting their ills,
While others sit leaning on the cool window-sills.
Some round the ball-room gracefully walk
With their lovers, while others sit, flirt, and talk.
The ball-room's a barrack, where the murderous shell,
In the worst of the siege, never yet fell;
And none there ever thought that shrapnel or ball
Could invade this retreat—so thick was the wall.

Silently, slowly the fleet moves away
From the mouth of the Yazoo, where in safety it lay,
And it drifts along quietly, moved on by the stream,
Not turning the wheels or using the steam,
All looking like phantom-ships groping their way
Through the darkness of night to the confines of day.
They move o'er the river with the silence of death;
None whisper a word, or draw a long breath.
The moon has gone down, there's no sound in the camp,
Not even is heard the sentry's loud tramp.
That sentry's neglectful; he must be asleep;
No good soldier in war such poor vigil would keep.
Not so in this instance. The soldier's keen sight
Catches phantom-ships drifting along in the night,
And the fire leaps forth along the broad shore,
And is answered at once by the cannon's loud roar.
The ball is deserted, not a moment is lost,
Each officer rushes at once to his post.
The husband stops not to speak one fond adieu
To the wife of his soul, and the lover so true
Tears away from his idol, with sorrow and pain,
To marshal his men. They ne'er meet again.
From fortress and valleys, from casemates on high,
Rifle-shell, shrapnel, and grape-shot now fly;
And the fleet lends its cannon to add to the din,
And each soul is now nerved this battle to win.
But the shell from the ships sweep o'er the broad plain,

And, bursting in air, is re-echoed again
O'er the hill-tops, in caves, or wherever they fall.
They e'en burst on the scene of the officers' ball.
There is grief in the camp, and loud wailing this night,
For the wounded and dead who fell in that fight.
But the fires burned down, leaving Vicksburg in gloom,
And the phantom-ships floated on—sealing her doom.
The besieged fight boldly 'mid the fire and blaze,
But their efforts are vain; they look on in amaze
At the phantom-ships floating along on the stream,
And passing so swiftly, without using steam.
Who can tell what despair envelops them all
As they fly to the place where the officers' ball
Had been held? It had been swept by the shell,
And dying and dead are now mingled pell-mell.
The eyes that once sparkled, and were wont to beguile,
Are now closed in death. Lips no longer smile.
Their reward is in heaven for the good they have done;
Their misfortunes are over, their battle is won.

Once more are united the blue and the gray—
Rancor and hatred have both passed away.
No longer war's ogres, the defense, and the siege,
Keep up hostile feeling—the Union is liege.
The atmosphere, filled with thick smoke and gloom,
No longer resounds with the cannon's loud boom.
Peace reigns triumphant all over the land,
And the North and the South move on hand in hand.
Death in his avarice has glutted the grave,
War has bathed its foul hands in the blood of the brave;
But the sun shines again, as bright as of yore,
And the gay stars of heaven all twinkle once more,
While the moon, going down in its daily decline,
Sheds a soft mellow light on our tents all in line,
Where our soldiers are resting in honor and glory,
And are eulogized now in ballad and story.
The spirits of good in high heaven all smile
On the brave boys in blue—the rank and the file—
And sailors, God bless them! who in days that are past,

In misfortune or glory, fought on to the last,
And were always so faithful, and pressed on the more,
When memory brought back the hard fighting of yore.
Dear reminiscences: they mellow with time,
And those dread scenes of war seem almost sublime,
Like old wine that's been binned and bottled for years,
Is more tasteful with age, and more precious appears.
Now we look back again on those terrible days,
And would give to each one his due meed of praise.
For those who were killed, tears of sorrow will fall,
And warm hearts in remembrance still beat for them all.

Now our flag waves serene, and its stars brightly shine,
And the sun gilds its stripes with a halo divine,
I will drink to the past in a bumper of wine.
That past which to many seemed doubtful at first
Was hopeful to me e'en when looking its worst.

In the history of the world's sieges nothing will be found where more patience was developed, more endurance under privations, or more courage shown, than by the Union forces at the siege of Vicksburg, while on the part of the besieged it was marked by their great fertility of resource in checking almost every movement of ours, and for the long months of suffering and hardship they underwent.

It belongs of right to General Grant to tell the story of that event, for in no case during the war did he more clearly show his title to be called a great general, nor did he elsewhere more fully exhibit all the qualities which proved him to be a great soldier.

If General Grant had never performed any other military act during the war, the capture of Vicksburg alone, with all the circumstances attending the siege, would have entitled him to the highest renown. He had an enemy to deal with of greater force, and protected by defenses never surpassed in the art of war.

I saw, myself (at Sevastopol), the great strongholds of the Malakoff tower and the Redan the day after they were taken by a combined army of one hundred thousand men; and these strongholds, which have become famous in ballad and story, never in any way compared with the defenses of Vicksburg, which looked as if a thousand Titans had been put to work to make these heights unassailable. I am told that there were fifty miles of intrenchments thrown up one within the other. I don't know how true it is.

The hills above, with their frowning tops standing in defiance, were enough to deter a foe without having intrenchments bristling with cannon and manned by the hardiest troops in the Confederacy.

After it was all over, and General Grant could see the conquered city lying at his feet, he could well afford to laugh at his traducers, who were doing all they could to hamper him by sending telegrams to the seat of Government questioning his fitness for so important a command.

If those who lent themselves to such things could be followed through the war, it would be found that they never made a mark, put them where you would; nor did they achieve any good for the Government.

That was a happy Fourth of July when the Confederate flag came down at Vicksburg and the stars and stripes went up in its place, while Meade's force at Gettysburg was driving Lee's army back to Richmond tattered and torn.

That day, so glorious in the annals of our history, lost nothing by the two brilliant events which were added to our fame, and made it still more dear to the heart of every true American.

When the American flag was hoisted on the ramparts of Vicksburg, my flagship and every vessel of the fleet steamed up or down to the levee before the city. We discerned a dust in the distance, and in a few moments General Grant, at the head of nearly all his generals with their staffs, rode up to the gangway, and, dismounting, came on board. That was a happy meeting—a great hand-shaking and general congratulation.

I opened all my wine-lockers—which contained only Catawba—on this occasion. It disappeared down the parched throats which had tasted nothing for some time but bad water. Yet it exhilarated that crowd as weak wine never did before.

There was one man there who preserved the same quiet demeanor he always bore, whether in adversity or in victory, and that was General Grant. No one, to see him sitting there with that calm exterior amid all the jollity, and without any staff, would ever have taken him for the great general who had accomplished one of the most stupendous military feats on record.

There was a quiet satisfaction in his face that could not be concealed, but he behaved on that occasion as if nothing of importance had occurred.

General Grant was the only one in that assemblage who did not touch the simple wine offered him; he contented himself with a cigar; and let me say here that this was his habit during all the time he commanded before Vicksburg, though the same detractors who made false representations of him in military matters, misrepresented him also in the matter above alluded to.

For my part, I was more than pleased to see Vicksburg fall, for I realized my proudest hopes in beholding the great Father of Waters opened to the sea, and lived to see all my predictions fulfilled. I was one of the first who urged that all the power of the Government should be exerted to get possession of this stronghold, and I gave my whole attention during the siege to bring about this most desirable event.

The Alabama *was the most successful Confederate cruiser of the war.*

Arthur Sinclair IV, author of Two Years on the *Alabama, published in 1895, served as an officer on board from the day she was commissioned to the day she was sunk.*

In addition to the war in the gulf, the Alabama *saw action off the Indies, Cape Town, and eventually went down off Cherbourg, all under the command of Confederate commander extraordinaire Raphael Semmes, the South's answer to David Farragut.*

Excerpt from
Two Years on the Alabama

BY ARTHUR SINCLAIR

Chapter III.

GETTING ACQUAINTED WITH THE NEW SHIP; HER GOOD
QUALITIES; PERSONNEL OF OFFICERS AND CREW; DRILLING;
OUR FIRST PRIZE; THE OLD FLAG LOWERED.

The time has now arrived for good-bys. Look at her, reader, from the deck of the *Bahama;* a long, trim, black hull, elliptic stern, fiddle-head cutwater, long, raking lower masts, and you have the picture of the rover. Bulloch, with a hearty shake of the hand and a God-speed to each of us, steps over the gangway. The *Bahama's* crew give us three cheers, which are answered by our gallant tars, the steamer turns her head for old England, and is soon lost on the horizon. And now for two long, weary, watchful years, in which the motto on our steering-wheel, *"Aide toi, et Dieu t'aidera,"* is to be tested.

"Our march is o'er the ocean wave,
Our home is on the deep."

The representative of the Confederate States is now alone on the ocean, the last friend and companion ship having disappeared from our view.

We have been some days at sea, and have marked the speed and wonderful working qualities of our newly acquired cruiser. It will be fully appreciated by our sailor readers, when we can say that the *Alabama* would go "in stays," and without fail, with a breeze giving her little more than steerage way; and in "working ship," later on, around prizes, the captains of these vessels would be struck with the remarkable quickness and sureness with which she was handled. Frequently has the writer heard them to remark, upon hearing the orders given, "Ready about!" "Why, Lieutenant! You don't tell me this vessel will 'stay' in this light wind?" and have been lost in admiration upon witnessing the manoeuvre successfully accomplished. Indeed, she could be worked around a prize like a pilotboat. There is nothing so excites Jack's pride and interest in his ship as to learn she can be depended upon in emergencies. It not only secures his confidence, but hints at much less brace-hauling of an unnecessary character.

The engine-room fires are banked, screw hoisted, and under easy canvas our head is turned to the north-east. This formidable engine of destruction is fairly launched on its mission, and we may speculate on the outcome of her efforts; but even with the acme of our wishes and expectations fully realized, how very far short shall we find them of results to be accomplished! That we look forward to seriously cripple and demoralize American commerce, unless promptly captured or sunk, goes without saying; but that a state of affairs bordering on total annihilation of it should have been the outcome of the *Alabama's* cruise was more than the most sanguine of us hoped for, and many times surpassed our fondest daydreams. We can pardon fully the incredulity of the far future reader of history when he comes to study the career of this seemingly charmed cruiser (a venture, at that, of an agricultural race against a people cradled on the ocean), and note the result of the Alabama's raid. But again is truth found stranger than fiction. A still more romantic and fuller history might have been hers, had not the Alabama voluntarily sought her doom in the historic English Channel. The grim work was still before her, had the election been to avoid conflict with the *Kearsarge,* and this without a stain clinging to her proud name, overmatched in every particular as she was. Better, however, as it is—her last effort sealing her title to lasting renown.

If one had the proper gift for description, something of great interest might be made of the individualities to be found among the officers and crew of the *Alabama.* In trying to convey any impression of our *personnel,* it is almost indispensable to draw some kind of a pen-picture of the more prominent personages who enter into the narrative. Of these our first "Luff," Mr. Kell, comes upper-most by a head and shoulders. He stands six feet two, and is of stalwart frame, lithe and straight as an Indian, with a fine head, and a mild, benevolent, dark-blue eye, that can flash lightning all the same on occasion. His phenomenal mustache and beard, of auburn color, give him the very presence of an ancient viking. The former will meet behind his head, and the latter flows down to his hips. The second lieutenant, Armstrong, is of more modern type, but also blue-eyed, straight, and fully a six-footer. He has an excitable temperament, is quick of impulse and speech, but always talks and acts to the purpose. He is a born ruler of men. The third lieutenant, Wilson, is shorter by a couple of inches, with dark complexion, eyes, and hair. He is very quick-tempered, and rather vindictive toward his foes, but otherwise a most generous and warm-hearted man. There are two other personages who cannot be omitted from this formal presentment. The first is Evans, our wonderful scout. Though a genuine salt, he, too, is erect on his pins as a drum-major, and quite as sensitive in the matter of personal dignity. I have often thought that Wilson was the most *earnest fighter* I ever saw; but Evans was brave to absolute recklessness. His steel-gray eye is like an eagle's in its concentration of energy. Evans is also a great yarn-spinner, as you shall find when you catch him off duty, and in the mood. His ability to determine the nationality of ships amounts to genius, and upon this point he cannot endure chaffing. Fulham, the prize-master, is a typical Englishman, five feet eight in height, broad-shouldered and muscular, with blue eyes, brown hair, and huge side whiskers. A typical sailor too, big hearted, full of animal spirits and fun. Fulham can spin the toughest yarn of any man on board; and with this quality, joined to his happy and magnetic disposition, he succeeds in keeping chipper even the captains of the prizes he calls upon in the way of duty. Withal, it may as well be said here, Fulham was a most competent officer, and would have graced a lieutenant's commission. At the time of joining us, he was in the English Royal Naval Reserve.

Our crew was in a sense "Hobson's choice," as has been seen. Pretty hard characters, some of them, no doubt; but all the same, a bronzed, stalwart, well-seasoned set of fellows, who now that they have exchanged their nondescript rags for our paymaster's nobby blue-and-white uniforms, look as promising as any set of men that ever went to sea. How this promise was fulfilled is now a matter of history, though we shall have occasion to speak of it as we go.

The writer has frequently been asked if he did not have "a good time" on the *Alabama*. Well, not by any means the sort of a time one usually proposes to himself by way of choice—if he likes comfort and ease. Taking the average, the work of the cruise was done by less than one hundred men: subtract boys and idlers, and the HARD work fell upon a very few. And such work! The captures bear but a trifling proportion to the vessels boarded. With no night, Sunday, or holiday, sea-watches always, at sea or in port. Drill, drill, drill! boarding, boarding, boarding, in all weather! Did men ever go through so much in the two years we were afloat? Talk about army life! why, Jack's synonym for an easy life is "soldiering." The seaman of the present day very little resembles the bronzed, hardened, thoroughly trained salt Jack so fully represented on the *Alabama*. It is certain that no crew able to do the work ours did could be shipped in any port of the world to-day.

The watch-officers of the *Alabama* had all seen service in the United States navy excepting one,—Lieut. John Low (who was an Englishman and trained in the merchant service),—and were thoroughly competent for the exceptional work required of them. The engineers were not only able to handle the engines in all emergencies, but to make the frequent and often difficult repairs that usually are intrusted only to machine-shops. The master's mates were thorough seamen, quite competent to take the deck and manœuvre or navigate the ship. They were invaluable assistants in boarding, and relieving the overworked watch-officers when bad weather made our duties arduous. The midshipmen, as a matter of course, were little experienced except at gun-drill. But they were apt and intelligent, and they had rare opportunities for acquiring seamanship. Before many months they were all able to work the ship, and were handy with sextant and chronometer. We had, as will be guessed, some old man-of-war's men among the crew, competent to take the place of petty officers and to give instruction to the rest, as well as to set an example of submission to man-of-war discipline. This last, by the way, our Jack of the merchant service does not take to quite so naturally as he does to his abundant and well-cooked rations, or his allowance of grog. But with all our advantages, we needed time to organize and drill ere we were fit, not only to fight an enemy's cruiser, but even to capture and board a prize. Our course lay for some days to the N. E. rather out of the track of commerce. Our fires were banked and propeller hoisted, as coal was always to be most carefully economized, and we moved along under easy sail. In this way we burn but one ton of coal per day; and as the boilers are hot, we can always have steam in fifteen minutes when we need it. We are bound for no port, and while coal lasts we are not apt to seek one. The deep will tell no tales as to our whereabouts, and will offer our crew no opportunities for dissipation. The *Alabama* is also nearly as good under sail as steam, and it will be a swift clipper indeed that compels us to resort to the latter in chase, unless we are in a very great hurry. We expect to keep the ocean for many months at a stretch.

We have now been at sea for some days, no sail sighted, nothing to break the monotony but the blue broken clouds above, and the lazy splash of the sea under our forefoot and propeller-well. But the deck is a bee-hive of industry. Here you will see a gun's crew under instruction of the lieutenant and midshipman of the division. At another point boatswain Mecaskey and his mates, marline-spikes in hand, deep in the mystery of a side or train tackle to be altered, and anon growling out an oath or two however the work is going on, a little more emphatic if a lubberly job meets his eye, but a swear or two anyhow, just to let his mates know he is boatswain Mecaskey. Now we have gunner Cuddy with his mates, polish in hand; for you must know that the battery is to be blacked, pumiced, and polished to a degree to put to blush a dude's patent leathers. We doubt not our capable gunner has already loaded his battery with blank cartridge, at least he should have done so; for if the enemy luffs alongside of us in the night it takes less time to return his fire with only shot or shell to be rammed home. But we feel sure that everything is being put shipshape in the ordnance department. Sailmaker Alcott is on the verge of collapse with the importance of his trust; though the first set of sails has just been bent, and from present weather appearances is likely to do many a month's service. Still our "man of canvas" is casting an "eye to windward" for embryo squalls or blows, and putting some spare sails in the locker. Who knows but in him we have a seer, and that is why he is now overhauling the storm maintrysail which is to do such important work on the 16th of October next? Our carpenter, William Robinson, is perhaps the least busy man to be found among our artisans; for unless the first lieutenant has some odd job on hand for him, it is more than likely he will have to "soldier" until some enemy's cruiser has knocked a plank or two off us, or old Boreas has embraced some spar.

Twelve o'clock now. We call it "eight bells." Who watches its advent with more thought and anxiety than Jack? He is impatient for rest and dinner, introduced by a little Jamaica for the thirsty soul. The sailing-master, who, sextant in hand, has been "taking" the sun, touches his hat and reports to the captain standing by his side, "Twelve o'clock, sir—latitude so and so"; the answer comes, "Make it so, sir." The master now reports the time to the officer of the deck, who in turn directs the messenger-boy to strike the bell. As the sounds dies away, the boatswain and his mates pipe to dinner, and a sweeter sound than that from a boatswain's pipe one would not wish to listen to. Jack now files around the grog-tub, and as his name is called, crooks his elbow, throws back his head, and swallows felicity. Forward he rolls, rubbing his paunch and wishing he had it to do over again; and so he would if that vigilant officer had his eye off him for a moment. "Doubling on the grog-tub" is no crime, no, not even a misdemeanor, in Jack's eyes, so watch him well, lieutenant! Let's go forward, even without an invitation, and see these late British subjects at dinner. A stiff "tot" of grog has cheered spirits and loosened tongue; and between chunks of salt horse and hardtack, he is eloquently expatiating on the events of the past few weeks, and giving his opinion of matters general and particular. Jack is never modest in the forecastle, especially if he has doubled the "Horn." But we do not find much of an assortment of silver-ware decorating Jack's table. Seated on the deck, legs doubled under tailor-fashion, with a tablecloth of black painted canvas, and dishes and plates of tinware, sheathknife in hand he cuts a slab of salt beef or pork from the skid, and with a "hardtack" for a plate, makes his attack, alternating with a pull at his coffee or tea dipper. But little time is consumed at the meal, for Jack is a rapid eater—considers time spent in eating almost wasted; pipe and tobacco is the goal of his desire, and he wants all the time possible for the enjoyment of it, and for the inevitable yarn to be spun before the boatswain's whistle calls him to duty again.

We have now been twelve days on our cruise, and constant work getting our ship into fighting and sailing trim has almost banished from our thoughts the prime object of our adventure on the ocean. With constant drilling at great guns, sabre or pistol exercise, repelling boarders with pikes, etc., our crew have at last inspired confidence in their officers and gained it for themselves.

On Sept. 5, after dinner, a sail was made from the masthead, hove-to, with her maintopsail aback. Wind light. We approached her under the United States colors. She did not move tack or sheet. No thought on her part of a Confederate cruiser! A little later the enemy did not tumble into our arms so easily, for ill news travels apace. Still showing United States colors we boarded her. She proved to be the ship *Ocmulgee*. Alongside of her was a large sperm whale, just captured, and being stripped of blubber and bone. A prize-crew was thrown on board of her, her officers and men transferred to the *Alabama,* and we lay all night in sight. We were now on the whaling-ground of the Western Islands; and lest the bonfire should light up the night and stampede the rest of the whaling-fleet, we waited before firing her, in the meantime transferring some provisions and small stores from the prize. Next morning our boarding-officer took his first lesson in the art of firing a ship. Perhaps the reader may imagine there is no art in it. Well, one way to do a thing well, another to bungle, there always seems to be. We have many more to send "where the woodbine twineth"; so listen to the *modus operandi* (though we were not put to the trouble with this whaler—inflammable enough without any preparation). First, you cut up with your broadaxe the cabin and forecastle bunks, generally of white pine lumber. You will find, doubtless, the mattresses stuffed with straw, and in the cabin pantry part at least of a keg of butter and lard. Make a foundation of the splinters and straw, pour on top the lard and butter. One pile in cabin, the other in forecastle. Get your men in the boats, all but the incendiaries, and at the given word—"Fire!" shove off, and take it as truth, that before you have reached your own ship, the blaze is licking the topsails of the doomed ship. We witness to-day for the first time the hauling down of the Stars and Stripes—to those of us who served in the old navy, a humbling of the emblem at our hands, carrying with it many a cruel wrench and sad retrospect. To men who in days gone by had stood on the quarter-deck, with the doff of cap, and amid the glitter of uniforms, presenting of arms, and strains of the national air, and daily witnessed the morning ceremony of hoisting this flag at the peak, it was difficult to disassociate the act with desecration.

The writer can never forget the feelings and impressions of this first capture, and the sight later on of the burning ship brought sorrow to the heart. I may almost say shame; but war! cruel, inhuman war! soon blunts the sentimental impulses, and what seemed at first sheer ruthlessness became in time a matter of course. It must be acknowledged that after a brief space of time the cry, "Sail ho!" from aloft, was received with the heartfelt wish she would prove a prize. The day after the capture of the *Ocmulgee* we made the Island of Flores, and being now on whaling-ground the ship is "hove-to." We can here await the oil-fleet. This is what may be styled "still hunting." Being quite near the land, the boats of the prize, which have been towing astern of us, are hauled alongside, and our prisoners, after being *paroled,* allowed to depart for the shore. They were far from being destitute, having by permission secured full loads of provisions, all their whaling-gear and other odds and ends, and would soon after landing be under the protection of the American consul. The plunder was to them clear gain and pocket-change. We have now been two weeks in commission, having changed colors on Sunday, Aug. 24. Ten o'clock ("four bells") having arrived, we go to muster. Our former vagabonds, arrayed in all the colors of Joseph's coat, would not be recognized just now. Standing in a group on the quarter deck, the commander and his officers abaft of them, the "Articles of War" are read; and as the death penalty is frequently mentioned therein, Jack looks first up, then down, and at his mates most significantly. He is evidently coming to the conclusion there is something serious in this business. This ended, the muster-roll is called; and as his name is reached, each man, now dressed in white frock and pants, pumps and sennet hat in hand, passes around the capstan and forward. "Inspection" is over, and the "pipe down" is "called." It is wonderful what effect even just two weeks of soap and discipline has had on our crew. We had among them a few young boys who had smuggled themselves on board the *Bahama* at Liverpool, and had turned up on deck during our stay at Terceira. Being useful as messenger-boys and "powder monkeys," they were signed and put to duty. Among them was one Egan, and a tougher case Liverpool could not produce. The sailors had brought from port a pet cat; and all who know a sailor will recognize the bond of affection existing between him and his pet, be it what species it may. The cat was missed a few days out of port, and faithful search having been made in vain, Egan was hauled up to the mast charged with knowing the fate or whereabouts of the animal. It seems he was suspected from some known circumstances, together with his reputation for mischief already established. Egan was "spread eagled" in the mizzen rigging barefooted, and was holding out well, denying all knowledge of the whereabouts of puss. In the meantime, a sail was made from aloft, the after pivotgun cleared away for the purpose of heaving-to the vessel. One would suppose Egan to have been a student of Marryatt from his selection of queer pranks when upon taking the tompion from the muzzle of the gun out jumps pussy. Egan soon after confessed judgment, being unable to stand the punishment longer, and upon being interrogated as to why he did it, replied, "Oh, to see what effect the firing would have on the cat!"

Soon after muster we have the cry from aloft, "Sail ho!" The two vessels now approach each other on opposite tacks and with a fresh breeze. The chase of the schooner was most exciting to us, and no doubt her skipper's nerves were on a tension—a touch and go capture, and will be to all time a memorable retrospect to him. The schooner *Starlight* was bound from Fayal to Boston, *via* Flores, to land passengers, and, as we perceived upon getting within two or three miles, had some females on board. She declined showing colors in answer to our English flag flung to the breeze, well knowing her build and cut of sails stamped her American to us, and our blank cartridge significantly hinting our nationality. She had the land about six miles distant, a fresh breeze blowing, the wind abeam, her best point of sailing, and was evidently resolved on reaching the charmed marine league, if possible; before overhauled. The presence of females on her deck precluded our firing a shot, even near her, if avoidable, but the indomitable pluck of her skipper forced the matter. A thirty-two shot was plunged a few feet ahead of her. Still the little captain had no idea of surrender. The breeze was too fresh and land too near. Evidently nothing entered into his calculation but the haven of rest and safety ahead. As usual in such cases, "the bull was taken by the horns," and another shot fired, passing just over his deck, and between the fore and main sails. The jig was up. In a moment the graceful little craft luffed to the strong breeze, jib-sheet to windward. Doubtless but for the lady passengers this typical specimen of a venturesome Yankee would have stood fire and escaped. We could but feel regret at his ill-luck. His pluck deserved success—a brighter fellow under adversity it would be difficult to find. Being now close aboard the Islands, the crew of the prize are landed under parole. We are visited by a number of boats from the shore, and soon the mess caterers are bargaining for fish, turtles, fruit, etc. The governor and staff made us a visit, were entertained, and seemed favorably impressed.

The ship's head is now put off shore under easy sail (generally single reefed topsails), for we are in no hurry—only on a loaf off the group of the Azores. The whaling-fleet are to catch us rather than we them. Each day or so brings along the game; and by the 1st of October we have, in addition to the two captures already mentioned, boarded and burned the following eight vessels—all whalers: *Ocean*

Rover, Alert, Weathergauge, Altamaha, Ben Tucker, Courser, Virginia, and *Elisha Dunbar.*

The capture of the schooner *Courser* was attended with but little excitement, daylight breaking and finding us within a few miles of each other, without previous notice from the night lookouts, so that a simple perfunctory blank cartridge brought her colors to the peak, in answer to our English red, and her jib-sheet to windward, and brail-up of foresail, as soon as our colors were changed for the Confederate flag. We found the *Courser's* skipper quite a young sailor, frank and open under adversity. His cheerful, philosophical mien at once secured our admiration and sympathy. Standing aft on the quarter, Semmes, with the schooner's papers in his hand, informed him his vessel was a prize, and was about to be destroyed, with the addendum to return to his late command, get his men together, with bags and hammocks, and return. His "Aye, aye, sir," spoke volumes of don't-care acquiescence and devil-may-care attention to the order. With a hitch of the trousers, and roll of the shoulders, he was soon in the sternsheets of the boat, our crew pulling for his little craft. We had, towing astern of our vessel, the boats of the whale-vessels *Weathergauge, Altamaha,* and *Benjamin Tucker;* boats able to live in almost any sea or weather. Having the crews of all these vessels on our decks, and now re-enforced by the last capture, nearly equalling in number our own crew, Semmes determined to land them. Giving the prisoners permission to help themselves to whatever pleased the fancy on the doomed *Courser,* the whaleboats are soon laden gunwales down, with a heterogeneous assortment,— salt beef and pork, harpoons, lances, coils of rope, etc., latter articles, perhaps, to "heave-to" the natives with, when on a lark presently. Indeed, a little of everything on board was pitched into their boats. It was a royal present, and profuse were their thanks to Semmes. A sailor and a jackdaw hold equal honors in the art of pillaging.

Our head is now turned toward Flores, some fifty miles off, but dimly in sight. An "offing" of four or five miles secured, we "heave-to," and the long cavalcade of boats, amid thanks, the wave of hats and hands, and let off of a joke or two (so natural to Jack) on the paroled prisoners' part, pull, with stroke in unison, for the shore. The moon is bright, sea smooth, weather balmy, quite a romantic scene, emphasized by the refrain from the boats, borne far over the water by the light air stirring, the long line of procession soon lost in the summer-night haze. Having but one hour's pull we feel assured of their safety. Busy and exciting scenes tonight on Flores; what a swapping of plunder for bed and board! What an excitement attending the trading and bargaining! Many the question to answer. Some future sojourner at Flores could collect material from these scenes to suffice a romance—a hint to the novelist. The prisoners clear of our decks, we stand out to sea again and join the *Courser,* who had stood close in, "hove-to," in charge of an officer, and, clearing her decks of the prize-crew, we put her "in irons," with her canvas beat to quarters, load with fine second shell, and, first at point-blank and after long range, make a target of the little schooner. The first exercise at mimic war we have given our crew. We can simply say of the result it was fair, considering the short time we had been in commission; but not so creditable an exhibition of effective firing as we trust to see some months hence. No material damage done the prize, a boat's-crew fire her, lighting up Flores vividly, and certifying to her late skipper her fate. Like ourselves, the reader must draw on his imagination for conception of the intense excitement on shore now augmented by this brilliant pyrotechnic display, lighting up the sky and sea, and bringing out in bold relief, no doubt, to those on shore, the outlines of the *Alabama,* resting lazily near, watching the result of her grim work.

A small whaling-vessel belonging to the island was cruising in company with the American whale-fleet, and a witness to our work of destruction. We had captured a vessel, and an attempt had been made by our prize-crew to scuttle her, under orders, the idea being to destroy her without having the smoke of a conflagration to warn the enemy of our presence. As the reader can doubtless foresee, it proved a failure from the nature of the cargo, the result being simply that the oil-casks floating to the top forced off the hatches, and the vessel filling with water soon covered the ocean with barrels of oil. Our island whaling-skipper, permission being obtained, soon found himself possessed of a cargo without the risk of hunting. We need not inform you this mode of getting rid of a prize was not repeated. It was evidently conceived and acted on without due thought, and in the excitement and hurry of destruction. No doubt our "Dago" skipper was furnished for all time with a yarn to spin of how he filled up in one day on one of his whaling voyages. Still it was a case of reciprocity, the Portuguese skipper removing so much property that otherwise would most likely have been recovered by the enemy.

The skipper of the *Ocean Rover* brought on board of us an immense fruit-cake put up in tin, the last of four, supplied by the goodwife "to hum" to celebrate the wedding-day—an old custom with the whalers. "Well," remarked the captain, "the wedding-day is not at hand yet, but you had as well enjoy the cake, gentlemen." Little did the thoughtful and provident goodwife imagine under what auspices and surroundings the ceremony of cutting this cake would take place! At the time this labor was undertaken, our land had not even the shadow of the coming eclipse resting over it. All the enjoyment of this rare treat was no doubt on our side, still we could spare our sympathies to the gallant but unfortunate fellow.

It would frequently suggest itself during our cruise in these latitudes why these skippers so readily hove-to at the suggestion of a rifle-shell, and allowed themselves to be boarded, the sea running high at the time, making the casting loose of a gun dangerous in the extreme, and the lowering of a boat hazardous, the boarding of the enemy more so. Nothing was more practical than to refuse our commands, take our desultory and uncertain fire, and await night and fortune, in the way of a friendly rainstorm shutting in, when escape would be certain. Nothing was wanting to make it thoroughly practical and feasible but courage. It must have been ignorance of our comparative helplessness to act in a strong gale that guided these commanders. Surely coolness and courage are qualities not wanting in our average American skipper.

The *Elisha Dunbar* was boarded and fired in a gale of wind, and, had her captain refused our blank cartridge or shot, could easily have made his escape, the gale increasing each moment, and rendering it most dangerous to cast loose a gun, and impossible to do execution with it in so heavy a sea. But her captain seemed to have lost his head, clewing up and heaving-to at the bid of our blank cartridge. The burning ship was a sublime spectacle—the flames leaping in mad play from spar to spar; her sails, unfurled, burning from the yards, and flying in huge fragments to leeward; while the lightning, darting from the angry dark clouds, seemed to mock the doomed ship in her misfortune. Her masts swayed and went by the board, and her hull, rocking on the seas and staggering like a drunken man, finally lurched to leeward and disappeared beneath the wild waves.

We have been but little inconvenienced with the crews of these prizes so far, having the land close aboard all the time, so that we could run in under the lee and land them in their own boats. The pyrotechnic displays must have kept the islanders in constant excitement. For days together the heavens were lit up with these fierce bonfires. The whaler makes a grand blaze. I have no doubt, aside from the captains of the destroyed whalers who in most cases are part owners, the men were well pleased with the adventure. They were given their boats, whaling-gear, provisions, and traps, and indeed were allowed to help themselves to about whatever they fancied. We found no marked cases of excessive modesty on their part. The boats without exception were loaded, gunwales down to the water. These men, having their entire expenses paid by the United States Government to their respective homes, through their consul, were no doubt rather benefited by the introduction to the *Alabama*. We have by this time greatly increased the population of the islands, and to the decided gain of the latter; for unlike the mass of the immigrants to our own land, they have been put on shore with, in the estimation of these islanders, untold wealth. Doubtless a glimpse on shore after the landing of this horde would have furnished an interesting chapter. To this day, that ubiquitous individual, "the oldest inhabitant," causes the eyes of the rising generation to start with wonder as he dilates on the story of the raid of the *Alabama*, the army of people put on shore, and the good bargains had with the strangers. Our prizes had also furnished us with every requisite for the comfort and health of both officers and crew. Whalers are the best provided in all particulars of any class of vessels, their cruises being of long duration, and generally in parts of the world but little frequented. Our paymaster had laid in a carefully selected assortment of clothing, provisions, small stores, etc., and the writer will never forget (being a philosopher of the weed) a large lot of Virginia smoking and chewing tobaccos. The value of this "find" can only be fully appreciated by a fellow who has been without it for a long time. It is an expensive article at best in England, and the war had made it more scarce, hence a very limited supply had been included in our ship-stores at Liverpool. Jack for the rest of the cruise always had his cheek and pipe well filled. The only articles saved from a prize besides those before enumerated, are the flag of the vessel and her chronometers. The flags were consigned to the safe-keeping of the signal quartermaster, though the sailing-master was held officially responsible for them. The chronometers were assigned a place in the cabin, under the immediate eye of the captain, but under the care and in the keeping of the navigating officer. This duty devolved upon the writer; and as it was Semmes's orders they be wound up each day, a process necessary to their good order, it was already quite a task. We had about fifteen of them, requiring half an hour to wind up, with the prospect of a steady all-day job at it in the near future, at the rate we were burning vessels. We had on hand at the end of the cruise, and landed at Cherbourg, seventy-five chronometers; and it need not be added *the winding-up* business soon came to an end, time being too valuable for expenditure on so many recording angels. The reason for saving these instruments was their portability as compared with their value.

It was highly amusing to note the inborn talent and taste of the genuine Downeaster for a smart bargain. No sooner had the captures commenced than our Yankee skippers were concocting schemes to get to windward of Semmes. Without the shadow of a doubt as to the legality of the seizure of the foregoing vessels, some of the captains had the bold assurance to propose bonding their vessels, suggesting as an inducement that the bonded value would no doubt exceed that allowed by the Court of Condemnation. But this proposal did not work. Semmes no doubt considered the "bird in the hand." We have been thirty-seven days in commission, most of the time weather moderate and suitable for the work. The last few days, however, have been ugly, reminding us that the season of storms is about on us. Now we are on our way to the Banks of Newfoundland, having effectually put a quietus on the whaling-fleet. A great change has taken place in the appearance and discipline of our crew—the effects of the last shore debauch having worn out of their systems, replaced by bright eyes and ruddy complexions, the consequence of regular habits, hard work, and substantial rations.

We may safely say now we have a man-of-war under us; the men, from constant practice manoeuvring about prizes, handling their vessel like a toy, and the faithful exercise of the gun-crews at quarters, by the lieutenants and petty officers, has taught them to flirt the battery in and out with most gratifying alacrity. But one chance has been afforded them thus far for exercise at great guns with shot and shell at a prize-vessel, and this was creditable for an introductory. We have also added to our crew somewhat since hunting among the whalers. We have secured fourteen additional men, and have now a crew of ninety-nine men or one hundred and twenty-five officers and men all told. We can meet the enemy now with a fair chance of success. The reader may desire to know something about the *morale* of men so recently recruited from the enemy. Jack is a queer fellow, of a roving, restless disposition, fond of excitement and adventure, and loves the new ship and the new sweetheart best. So seeing this natty, trim, and saucy rover of the seas, apparently having a good time of it, he falls head over heels in love with her, and presenting himself at the capstan, desires through the executive officer, a few words with our skipper. The interview proving mutually satisfactory, our hero signs the articles, and presto! from being a prisoner in the lee scuppers, has the privilege and comfort of sampling the *Alabama's* "Old Jamaica." This is the way the complement of the cruiser was kept up during the cruise, the places of those left behind in port being supplied from fresh captures. We will do our crew the credit to say of them we do not believe they actually deserted, in many cases, but were on shore hid away in some rum-hole or dance-house, stupid from liquor, and in ignorance that their ship was obliged to put to sea upon the expiration of the time allowed her in port. We may further add that Semmes would never ship from the captured vessels any seamen of North American nativity, and was most searching in his inquiries as to their place of birth. Among the prisoners shipping on the *Alabama* during the whaling-raid off the Azores, we will call your attention to little David H. White. He became quite a marked character on our vessel. Dave was a Delaware slave, a boy about seventeen or eighteen years old; and wanting in the ward room mess of our ship an efficient waiter-boy, the lot fell to Dave. He was not only willing but anxious to ship. The natural instincts of the lad told him we would be his friends. He knew Southern gentlemen on sight. Dave became a great favorite with the officers, his willing, obliging manners, cheerful disposition, and untiring attention winning for him the affection of not only the officers, but of the entire ship's company. Poor Dave! he was drowned in the engagement off Cherbourg. It was his privilege to go on shore with the ward-room steward to market; and on all occasions the American consul or his satellites would use all their eloquence to persuade Dave to desert his ship, reminding him of his present condition of slavery and the chance presented of throwing off his shackles, but Dave remained loyal in face of all temptation.

We are on the Banks of Newfoundland, in the Gulf Stream, as indicated by the temperature of the water, and directly in the track of vessels to and from Europe. This was one of the most trying portions of our cruise, dangerous beyond measure, hove-to or under very short sail all the time. We have not only the elements to contend with at this most stormy period of the year, but the hourly danger of being run down by some swift passing steamer or grain-carrier, the nights being unusually dark, and the fogs thick enough to cut with a knife. We have also the danger of swamping when boarding vessels in heavy seas. Some of our officers had already had experience in this line in the last two captures, and did not look forward with a great deal of relish to the prospect ahead. Indeed, the cruise of our ship from this time forward to the day her prow was turned southward, was attended with as much hardship as ever fell to the lot of sailormen. We were constantly boarding vessels, the weather at all times vicious, often unable to remove anything from the prizes but the crews themselves, and this attended with the greatest possible risk of life. Still our captain and executive were incessant in their advice and caution, and through their watchful care we were enabled to finish up this raid on the grain-fleet without the loss of one soul. The plan of boarding vessels was very simple. The Alabama would luff to windward of the prize, allowing the boarding-officer to pull down to her before the wind. After seeing him safe alongside, our vessel would wear ship and take a position to leeward, thus allowing our boat to return in the same way. The cruise in this latitude was one constant succession of storms and boarding of vessels; and, as can well be imagined, both officers and crew were well nigh exhausted after a few weeks of such work.

We are now beginning to realize the hardships of our cruise; and anything but a boon would it be to be able to pierce the future, and contemplate the two years of constant work of this character ahead of us. You have but just left the deck after a four-hour watch in villanous weather, perhaps working ship during the whole of it after some sail, and have begun to appreciate the warmth of your blankets, when the quartermaster flashes a bull's-eye lantern in your face, and you are instanter wide awake, to hear the cheerful intelligence you are wanted on deck at once, to board a vessel just hove-to. You have ample time while bundling into your pea-jacket to anticipate the weather you are to make the trip in, as oftentimes your boots, floating about on the ward-room deck, give the hint that you are not loafing around the tropics at present. If your wishes and inclinations could have full effect, the quartermaster would be in a most unenviable place. A more unwished for visitor, or a more thankless job than his, does not exist on the Alabama. But as Jack says, "We've shipped for it," are "in for it," so must take it fair or foul. One redeeming feature displayed itself in the wind-up; it proved to be healthy. So the end justified the means. We were a lot of lightwood knots at the end of the cruise.

We have reached the 15th of October, and have since the last report captured the following seven vessels: *Brilliant, Wave Crest, Dunkirk, Manchester, Lamplighter, Emily Farnum,* and *Tonawanda.* The last two released on ransom-bond, one protected by neutral cargo, the other as cartel for the large number of prisoners captured on above vessels. On the Dunkirk we found a deserter from the *Sumter,* George Forrest, seaman, who was tried by court-martial, and later on landed in irons and dismissed the service at Blanquilla, an island in the Caribbean Sea (Nov. 26, 1862). The penalty attached to his crime is death, but he had fallen into merciful hands. Lucky fellow! He was tried by a court composed of his old officers of the *Sumter.* Perhaps the recollections of common dangers and vicissitudes softened the hearts of his shipmates. Forrest joined an American fishing-vessel found anchored off the island, and which we could not make a prize of, she being within Venezuelan territory. It is to the credit of Semmes that he was at all times most punctilious in his respect for international law, as witnessed by his numerous decisions growing out of the capture of Northern vessels with quasi-neutral cargoes. Semmes always gave the benefit of the doubt in favor of the cargo, and released the ship under ransom-bond. The reader will notice the large number of vessels thus released by us as bearing out this statement.

The heaving-to of the *Lamplighter* was the most beautiful exhibition of nautical manoeuvre possible. No man-of-war, with her full crew, could have executed the movement better. In a strong breeze, the forerunner of a gale, she downed helm, clewed up all light canvas to topgallant sails at once, then settled her topsails to the cap, and hove aback. It requires the instincts of a sailor to take this situation in fully. This skipper fully appreciated *the* hour had arrived, the doom of his ship sealed, and was determined we should see and feel that he could meet the case becomingly. At the day of which we write no seamen equalled the American of the mercantile marine in handling their vessels.

The skipper of the ship *Brilliant* made a most pathetic appeal to Semmes to spare his vessel. He owned a large share in her, comprising his all, and her destruction meant beggary to himself and family. His pleadings were touching enough to move a heart of stone. He told us that he was a Democrat, with no sympathy with the war-party, looked upon the invasion of the South as an act of ruthlessness; that the war was most unrighteous; his pursuit a peaceful and necessary one for the support of his wife and little ones. I never saw Semmes more moved before, and have never doubted he deeply regretted having to fire this splendid ship. But it was a stern duty to be carried out against all pleadings of his sympathies. The waste is soon after lit up by the fierce flames from the doomed ship; her late captain leaning on our rail, looking on the sublime sight, seeming by his strong gaze of despair to be conjuring up some spirit of the deep to come to his aid. Such is war. But the Geneva award put him all right again.

Chapter IV.

A STERN CHASE; ON NEWFOUNDLAND BANKS; THE CYCLONE; OFF NEW YORK; SOUTHWARD HO! A NEW MAINYARD; MARTINIQUE; ESCAPE FROM THE CRUISER SAN JACINTO; THE RUN TO BLANQUILLA; CRUISING AFTER THE CALIFORNIA TREASURE STEAMER; CAPTURE OF THE ARIEL.

The capture of the brig *Dunkirk* was under beautiful conditions. The moon at near full, the chase a long and exciting one, with a strong breeze, both vessels going free, studdingsails alow and aloft, fairly rushing before the rising gale. The chase was well in view, thanks to the bright night. She proved to be a very fast sailer; but, gaining on her slowly, we felt assured of final success, accident excepted, without use of steam. Towards morning, having the chase well in hand, and wishing to drop the curtain on the scene, berth prisoners, and be ready for morning deck-cleaning, "quarters," and inspection, we sent a "thirty-two persuader" after her. So rapidly did she respond and luff up, foretopsail to the mast, that our rapid headway rushed us far to the leeward of her. The breeze was now a sharp gale, as we hauled on a wind, taking in all sail to topsails, and hove our maintopsail aback. Semmes had been up all night, legs astraddle the hammock-nettings, night-glasses in hand, and nursing his gratification at the business-like way in which the chase carried sail, endangering our spars to follow suit. The officer of the deck and men were worn out with trimming sail to the shifts of breeze.

However, the meeting between the two skippers turned out a pleasant one, the fine sailing qualities displayed by our ship keeping Semmes in a good humor no doubt. He opened the conversation in a facetious vein, recently adopted, and which he seemed to nurse as a pretty good "get off." "Say, Captain, I should judge from the trouble you have put myself and lads to, you must have forgotten (canvas failing) my little 'teakettle' below." The old man rarely displayed temper, except when tangled ownership of cargo cloud ship's papers, and set him over-hauling his law library for "precedents." The skipper might look out for a blast, did Semmes in his search unearth a trick or subterfuge in "certificates." Then, there's many a "d—n your eyes." The weather from the *Dunkirk's* capture onward was unsettled, moderate gales with but little intervening comfort of smooth sea. We had one day some strange visitors—a flock of curlew, blown off from land, settled in our port quarter-boat, wing-weary and starved. We captured them without an effort at escape. So poor in flesh were they as to offer no inducement to our steward. He declined upon inspection converting them into pot-pie. They must have been many days at sea. Our sympathies prompt us rather than our stomachs, the latter cutting no figure in it; so after refreshing them with fresh water and such suitable food as we had to offer, we launched them on the air, to wing their way westward. We cannot say if they were Yankees or Johnny Rebs. Jack was pleased. His superstition as to harming birds is a strong feeling.

We are still on the Banks, the weather for the past few days villanous. If some good bird of that flock said to roost aloft and look out for poor Jack, had by his presence for the past week given us the warning, we undoubtedly should have put up our helm, and under steam dodged the cyclone we are now on the edge of. The barometer has fallen to a point indicating, not simply a severe storm such as heaves up the Atlantic each few days of this season, but a veritable cyclone, that phenomenon of the Western hemisphere all sailors not only dread, but are appalled at. From its fearful vortex, should it be reached, not many vessels escape, and permit the witnesses to picture to owners and friends its awful sublimity. The ship was put under very low sail, close-reefed topsails, forestaysail, and the main storm-trysail gotten up and bent. All light yards were sent on deck, the quarter-boats swung in on their davits and secured, life-lines rove, the hatches battened down. All hands ordered on deck, and all fires put out but the binnacle light. The wind quickly increased to a hurricane. Men had been sent aloft, and the topsails furled and extra gaskets passed around the sails. Delayed until the storm struck, it would have been madness, if not murder, to have ordered the topmen aloft. Still the blast increased, howling as if ten thousand demons had been loosed from Hades. Away goes the mainyard parted in the slings, and in a twinkling the main— and maintopsails fly to leeward, torn from the gaskets and into shreds. In the meantime, the forestaysail has been blown to ribbons, and the ship lies to under only the main storm-trysail, close-reefed, and not much larger than a lady's shawl. It soon went, and we were under bare poles. To convey an idea of the force of the wind would beggar language. Its fury was so great that no sea could get up, the ocean surface having the appearance rather of a mill-stream. The air was white with "spoon-drift," giving the appearance of a heavy snowstorm. The officers and men were cowering under the weather bulwarks, or lashed at important stations. The wheel doubly manned, and in spite of this precaution it at one time, during the violent laboring of the vessel, got away from control, and, with a whirl, threw a man completely over it to leeward. For two hours this mad play of the ocean devils continued. The dark-green clouds nearly met the water, twisting and squirming between each other like snakes or loathsome reptiles as the whirlwinds direct them in their play. In the meantime, our gallant boat was behaving nobly. Though pressed down by the force of the tempest so that her lee guns were quite hid by the water, and the lee quarter-boat twisted from the davits and floating alongside, she lay still and comfortably, but little sea boarding, though the deck was wet by the rain and spray. She was working in her deck seams from the fearful strain, but otherwise demonstrating that we had a gallant seaboat under us. She was making but little water in her hold. One of the curiosities preserved, a souvenir of the cyclone, was the maintopsail-sheet, an iron chain of about two inches diameter, which was blown out to leeward as though a ship's pennant; the force of the wind whipping half-turns in it, and gradually tying it up into a solid mass. It was literally welded to such a degree as to require the use of tools in straightening it out. As stated already, we had now been two hours exposed to the fearful sledge-hammering of the wind, when suddenly, in a twinkling, it died away dead calm. Think not we are to be let off now; it is only a pause—a consultation, as it were, of the elements for our destruction. We are in that dreadful "vortex." Our ship is now exposed to another danger. The removal of the pressure of the wind has allowed the sea to get up, and we are wallowing in it, the water swashing aboard, first in one gangway and then the other. It is all one can do to hold on to the bulwarks. The seas are mounting to appalling heights, and the roll of our ship threatens to jerk the masts out of her; but they are of good Georgia pine, and bend to the strain like willow-branches. The barometer has been noted, and found to be more than one inch higher. Soon we see and hear the dread storm approaching again on the water, sounding in the distance like far-away thunder. The heavens seem, if anything, more threatening than before. Butt-end first it strikes us, screeching and howling as though the air was filled with countless shot and shell in passage. The gallant boat again bows to its command, and with lee guns under water seems to fairly struggle for breath and life, her timbers groaning and creaking as though suffering dying agonies. The clouds are lower than the mastheads, and drawn into narrow ribbons of dark-green color, whose writhing again makes the spectacle appalling. The spoon-drift nearly takes the breath away, the only relief being in burying the head in hands, and turning the back to the blast. Two hours more we hang between life and "Davy Jones's locker," when the storm breaks, though not so suddenly as when we entered the vortex, and once again our ship is staggering among the seas, jolting and butting against each other like sheep driven along a strange road. The barometer is again noted, and found to be rising rapidly. Sail is made to steady ship in the fearful sea, though there is but little wind to fill them. We have got a breathing-spell, and time to look about us. Such a scene of wreck and confusion! We can promise our boatswain, gunner, sailmaker, and carpenter lots of business for some days to come. For a week or so we have dirty, unsettled weather, the effects of the late cyclone; and the ship is kept under close canvas, jogging in towards the enemy's coast. Meantime we capture the *Lafayette, Lauretta, Crenshaw,* and *Baron de Castile,* placing a ransom-bond on the latter, and transferring the crews of the prizes. None of these latter prizes had felt the cyclone, though captured just after it had left us.

We have now nearly completed the second act of the drama, namely, the destruction and demoralization of the "grain-fleet"; for not much of anything but cereals and provisions are seeking the European markets! King cotton is in prison, if we may except the puny efforts of the venturesome English blockade-runners to release him. We have added this grain industry to the North Atlantic whaling-interests, among the things that were, and we shall soon up helm and away to a new field of devastation and destruction. Strange, so far not a protest in the way of a man-of-war has crossed our vision, not so much a wonder just in the latitudes of storm and ugly seas, but that we did not exchange broadsides with our enemy's cruiser off the Western Islands. We had fully looked for it in these calm waters. Still it is not too late, for we are drawing near the enemy's coast for our last raid before leaving for the West Indies. One would suppose the *Alabama* just now to be full of business, being in the track of coastwise trade; but not so. Cause and effect are factors potent at sea as well as on land; trade is prostrated, no customers but the government, and we shall have poor luck boarding many vessels, but all foreign.

How sensitive the pocket nerve! The *Alabama* has been but two months on her mission of destruction, and yet the effects of her exploits are strikingly apparent; for we fail to make a single capture on this coast-raid—the trip is barren of results. We had nursed a fond hope of overhauling a troop-ship bound South, but it was not to be.

We are now near the coast just off New York, and are braced up by some fresh provisions from a bonded vessel, and also have the pleasure of late news from our struggling armies. The New York newspapers of two days previous are before us. All is excitement in Yankee-land over the depredations of the "pirate"; and if threats are to annihilate us, we are doomed. But we have (thanks to our enemy who always posts us) the number and destination of our pursuers. It is time now to make a double (rabbit fashion), for these parts will soon be too hot for comfort. It was a strange thing that the enemy's plan of pursuit was to look for us where last reported instead of studying the future probabilities. We are now bound to the West Indies. It would seem quite natural that the *Alabama* would turn her head in this direction after having stampeded the European grain-fleet, and that we should find the West India Islands swarming with the enemy's gunboats—but we shall see.

Our vessel is once more shipshape, the damage of the late storms repaired, and we are standing south with the weather much improved. We are again rather out of the track of vessels, though we have boarded a number of sail proving to be neutral, and have been rewarded by the capture of the *Levi Starbuck,* whaler, outward bound. She proved a lawful prize, and was fired. Our next prize was the *T. B. Wales,* a splendid India clipper from Calcutta for Boston. This ship proved to be one of the most valuable, besides recruiting our crew to the extent of eleven first-class seamen.

The mainyard of the prize, upon measurement, was found to be of the same dimensions as ours, which was crippled in the cyclone, and which had been "fished" for temporary use. It was brought on board and slung instead of our wounded one. Our young officers have now a lucky chance for improving themselves in one line of their profession. Boatswain Mecaskey and carpenter Robinson are hard at work fitting the new mainyard, and many a revelation in spun yarn and knots will break upon their visions; and the interest in the coming change of spars, the *modus operandi* of sending down the crippled one, and crossing the new one, forms the current topic of conversation at mess-table and on watch; and just now our active boatswain is by all odds the most important character in the ship, not excepting scout Evans. None of these middies have the faintest idea how it is to be done, yet each has a commiserative look on his countenance for his brother middy's nautical ignorance. It was a case where silence is golden with them. But Mecaskey will get it there.

We have now a crew of one hundred and ten men and twenty-six officers, or about fourteen short of a full complement. On the *Wales* we found, as passengers, an ex-United States consul with his wife and family. Among the effects of the consul's good wife were a number of very handsome, elaborately carved, ebony chairs. She was much distressed upon learning they would have to be consigned to the deep, owing to lack of room on a man-of-war. Her lady-like resignation, however, to the inevitable was very sweet. It has always dwelt in the memory of the writer; but such is cruel war—no respecter of persons. I trust she bears us no ill-will. It was the most unpleasant part of our boarding-duty, the transfer of lady passengers to our ship. Not only the danger and discomfort, but the awkward position forced upon them while our guests in the ward room. We always associate timidity with the ladies, but we must say it was not our experience on the *Alabama*. There was never an instance of apparent fear on their part in all our transfers at sea; and frequently the weather was such as to drench them thoroughly in the passage to us, and requiring the use of whip tackle and buckets to sling them over our side. We are now running down for the Island of Martinique, where we expect to meet our transport, the *Agrippina,* which the reader will remember was the custodian of the *Alabama's* armament and stores at Terceira. On the 18th of November we are off the port of Fort de France; and we find the *Agrippina,* laden with coal for us, lying at her anchor. After communicating with the governor and receiving permission, our prisoners of the *T. B. Wales* are landed, and we bid good-by to the consul and his family who had been with us nine days. Our sailor-readers are the ones to fully appreciate the longing that comes over a fellow for fresh grub, after being on "salt horse" for many months. With the exception of one square meal of fresh food, we had been on ship's-rations since leaving Terceira. Our ward-room steward, Parkinson, has *carte blanche* to supply the table. To say we breakfast, dine, and sup does not express it. It is eat all the time, fruits of all kinds between meals not counting. The crew, too, seem to be having a good time generally, but they have somehow managed to smuggle on board quite a lot of the "Oh be joyful." The mainbrace is spliced so often that soon our lads forget who commands the *Alabama.* Matters getting serious, the beat to quarters is given; they recognize the sound, and know they must go there, come what will or whatever their state, and Jack drunk and Jack sober answer to their names. Such the effect of discipline. The more mutinous ones are put in irons, the rest sent to their hammocks to sleep their drunk off. Poor Jack! he is in sense of responsibility a mere child, and with the disadvantage of neglect in early training. The *Agrippina* has been a number of days in port, quite long enough for the enemy, knowing her relations to us, to put in an appearance; so she is ordered at once to the Island of Blanquilla, off the coast of Venezuela, where we can join her and coal ship. The wisdom of this appears the next morning. We are greeted with our first sight of one of the enemy's cruisers. The steam frigate *San Jacinto* lay on and off the mouth of the harbor; and judging from the extensive preparations she was making for battle, she must have had most exaggerated reports of our strength. All day her men were aloft, stoppering sheets, slinging yards, as if expecting a desperate fight. Our coal-ship was off, and well on her way to our rendezvous, and this matter settled we cared nothing for the *San Jacinto. We could steam around her.* At this port we were rather the victims of inordinate curiosity than the recipients of hospitality; for our decks were crowded with a promiscuous and impertinent lot of loungers, and a few officials asking no questions of our officers and crew, but rather disposed to pry out their own conclusions. We were inclined to interpret our lukewarm and rude reception as the reflection of instructions from the French capital. The next night, rain and darkness favoring, we got under way, passed out at the southern channel, and saw nothing of the enemy. We afterwards heard she was at the other channel. There was a crestfallen set on the *San Jacinto* probably, when it was found out at dawn that we had given them the slip.

We are now off, and on our way to Blanquilla to join our old friend Capt. McQueen and his gallant barque. To-day finds the ship's-company busy putting things to rights. Jack moves along with a listless roll; he feels dull, and disinclined for the routine of duty. The brig has been cleared of the delinquents; for Semmes is a kind and merciful superior, understanding the disposition of the sailor thoroughly, and ready to let by-gones be by-gones. And really we have as efficient and happy a crew as could be picked up under most favorable circumstances. They are able, willing, obedient, and cheerful, and attached to their ship by a feeling akin to idolatry. Amusements are allowed and encouraged. When free from duty the evenings are spent on the forward deck; and song and dance, improvised plays, yarn-spinning, etc., have their turn. In this latter accomplishment Jack has no superior, if an equal. You have only to let off your story first, and if he does not land you in the shade—well! you have evolved a pretty tough one. The young officers of the ship, with a view of passing the off hours pleasantly, formed a glee club; and as we had some charming voices among them, it was a real treat to both ward room and forecastle. Weather permitting, and no vessels to be boarded, at the approach of evening the audience gathers; the older officers occupy the "private boxes" (to wit, campstools), the crew, the "gallery" (topgallant-forecastle); and cigars and pipes being lighted by all who list, the programme of the evening is in order. Songs sentimental, songs nautical, and, last but not least, songs national, delight the ears and hearts of all. But it is eight bells (eight P.M.), and we must break up this delightful party. The boatswain's mate has piped "all the starboard watch"; and while the lads of above are to watch and ward over us, the other is to "turn in" to hammocks, and prepare for their turn. The watch is mustered and set, the captain has passed his orders for the night to the officer of the deck, directed what sail to put the ship under, and returned to his cabin, no doubt to hatch out some plan for future tricks on the enemy. The "lookouts" have been stationed, the remainder of the watch, pea-jackets under head, lying down snug under the bulwarks. The quarter-master stands by the wheel "conning" the helmsman. The officer of the deck, stepping up to the wheel, passes the order just received from the captain, "keep her N. N. E.," or "full and by," as the case may be, then stepping to the weather-quarter mounts the "horse-block," trumpet and night-glasses in hand, on the lookout for sails and weather. Now should the wind be light, the silence is deathlike,

"And all the air a solemn stillness holds."

Arriving duly at Blanquilla, we found our transport at anchor, and also the American whaling-schooner *Northern Light* which latter we simply detained until we were ready for sea lest she might report us. There was little of interest, you may imagine, at this point, outside of fishing. This we indulged in to some extent, both with line trolling and the "grains," and turned over a few turtle for the messes. We found men on the island from the mainland of Venezuela, who had cultivated the banana to some extent, it being their principal food, taking the place of bread—and by the way a most excellent substitute. Our men on their pleasure excursions had helped themselves to the fruit rather too bountifully, leaving the natives on rather short rations. Complaining to Semmes, the latter paid the bill with a plentiful supply of ship's-rations, and the swap was most satisfactory to our islanders. We found here in great abundance the iguana, a species of lizard, much esteemed by the South Americans as an article of food; but though we captured quite a number we did not venture to test its toothsomeness, taking the natives' assurance as to its worth as a food product. It was sport to catch them, the modus being to creep up as they lay motionless in the bushes, and lasso them with a long grass with a snood on the end. The reptiles are very watchful and wary. Our young officers are having lots of fun at the expense of our temporary prisoner—the captain of the Yankee schooner. He has become quite sociable since receiving assurance from Semmes that his little property will not be consigned to the flames, and visits our ship daily during spare hours. One fellow will say to him, "Say, Cap, did old Beeswax really tell you he should not burn your schooner?"—"Why, yes; of course he said so."— "It may be all in good faith, Cap," sighs the middy, as he shakes his head, "but it's very like a joke of the old man"; and the skipper is again on the "ragged edge," and the youngster watching the anxious countenance is correspondingly happy.

Having coaled ship, the *Agrippina* is despatched to the Arcas Islands, in the Gulf of Mexico, there to await our arrival, and fill our bunkers with the remainder of her cargo. Bidding Capt. McQueen *bon voyage,* we are now on our way to the east end of Cuba, our object being to intercept the California mail-steamer, and handle a million or so of bright California gold. We coast along the south side of the island of Porto Rico, pass through the Mona passage, and skirt the coast of San Domingo. It is now the 1st of December; and though we have boarded a number of vessels, we have not as yet had occasion to "strike a match," no enemy's vessel interrupting the sight of the horizon. We are beginning to think the *Alabama* has been well advertised in the United States. As we keep our lonely mid-watches in these calm and peaceful seas, our thoughts naturally stray to the past when these latitudes were the haunts of buccaneers, and in fancy picture them bound as we are after rich prizes. Indeed, aside from the legality attending our present mission, there *are* features to suggest a common occupation. There is no gossip or conversation, either forward or aft, that interests but of the California treasure-steamer. Whether convoyed or no; amount of bullion; speed we may expect in her. And every soul on board of us has become a self-appointed lookout. We are having, however, beautiful weather, and enjoying from the deck the exquisite tropical scenery as we lazily creep along the shores of these historic islands.

Meantime, although the *Alabama* has been loafing along lazily, she has kept her eyes about her; and as a result she has captured and burned the barque *Parker Cooke*, provision laden. We had been for some days out of the latitude of a *market-house,* when our thoughtful purveyor put in an appearance. Evans, our factotum, whom we depend on for designating the nationality of a sail, had spent many weary and disappointing days aloft with the spyglass; and though sail after sail would peep up over the horizon, still nothing in the way of legitimate game passed the vision of his glass. So the visit of the *Cooke* was most *apropos.* The wonderful ability of Evans to detect the nationality of a sail made him a very valuable man, aside from his other qualities. He had the eye of Hawk Eye of Cooper fame. It was simply a waste of time and useless labor on the crew working ship in pursuit of a vessel he had pronounced foreign. He could not always locate the stranger as to whether English, French, or what not; but that she was not "Yankee" you could make a book on it at large odds. Having helped ourselves from this prize, secured her chronometer and instruments, the match was applied, and the crew of the *Parker Cooke* accept unsought hospitality. Lucky fellows in that the weather is grand, and sleeping on deck preferable any way to a berth below. We may as well state here that all our prisoners were housed on deck from necessity, the berth-deck being crowded by our own men. But we made them as comfortable as we could under the circumstances, spreading awnings and tarpaulins over them in stormy weather, and in every way possible provided for their comfort. They were allowed full rations (less the spirit part), and their own cooks had the range of the galley in preparing their food to their taste. Indeed, when it is considered that our men had watch to keep and they none, they were better off for comfort than ourselves. We mention these facts as the prisoners, in some cases, reported to the Northern press cruel treatment on our part.

On every boarding occasion it was curious to note the wants that would suggest themselves to those of the officers whose duties never took them on board prizes. The commissions were as numerous as used to bother the head of a family, before railroads came along, going to a market-town. One would want a pocket-knife, another a pipe, some light reading-matter, anything and everything really but bonnets or ribbons. On one occasion a fellow wanted a warming-pan, if the stewardess had such a thing. Sometimes they were made happy, sometimes the reverse. At least it was never the want of money that caused the disappointment, as is so often the case in this cold world of ours. Robinson Crusoe had about as much use for gold as we wanderers just now. Indeed, our sable pedler of the South could ever and anon have lightened our pockets of spare change with his cry of, "Oysters, oysters!" or "Buy a dozen quail, sir!" Beyond this the traps that might be set for our spare cash could never be sprung. We are experiencing the most uneventful period of our cruise, most barren of solid results. We are still out of the track of vessels; and such as we may overhaul are likely to be of light tonnage, and with cargoes of small value. When we consider that the plans cut out for this portion of our cruise, *viz.*, the capture of the California treasure-steamer, and the destruction or scattering of the transport fleet of the Banks expedition to Texas, fail to materialize, we can but suffer some chagrin; still, some good comes out of it, for we are having a rest, and the time thus consumed enables the officers to become thoroughly acquainted with the men, to try them in experimental situations, so that, emergencies arising, each man could be assigned to his best place.

We are out of late newspapers now, and most anxious to learn what is going on in Dixie,—whether Lee has crossed the Potomac, or the enemy is still keeping our armies on the defensive, and eating into our vitals. The capture of a vessel with late papers is an event with us—when it happens. First, they are carried to the cabin; and the skipper, assisted by his intelligent clerk, Mr. W. Breedlove Smith, cons them over carefully. They are looking for movements of the enemy's cruisers, first in importance, next as to how the tide of battle is flowing. This accomplished and noted, the lot is sent to the ward-room mess, thence to the steerage, finally reaching the forecastle. The stay in each department is brief, for the war news is about all we have time for, and Jack likes them to clean brasswork with. Certain sorts of bound literature fares much the same way; and Jack has to appeal to his imagination for the thread of a story, a fragment of which has captivated his interest.

We have entered the month of December, and are stretching over to the east end of Cuba, occasionally boarding a vessel in the night. In the daytime friend Evans saves us the trouble by telling us at once that the ships we sight are neutrals. We take no prizes. On Dec. 5, reaching our cruising-ground, we captured the schooner *Union*, with neutral cargo, and released her on bond, after transferring to her the prisoners of the *Cooke*. The next day was Sunday, and a lovelier day is rarely experienced, even in this delicious climate. And the *Alabama* floats through it like a dandy arrayed for the eye of his best girl. The battery gets the best touches of gunner Cuddy's polish, and shines like patent leather. The decks you might pass your handkerchief over without soil, so perfect has been the work of the holy-stone. The brasswork rivals gold in its brilliancy. The crew are scattered about the spar-deck, their clothes-bags having been ordered up by the boatswain's and mates' pipe to the tune of, "All hands clean yourselves in white frocks and pants." The making of toilets proceeds apace—here a lad performing the tonsorial act on his chum, another elaborating a fancy knot for a messmate's neckwear or his own, with as interested and critical an audience as the same effort would secure among as many girls. Jack has all the instincts of a dude, though he is inclined to be more original in his style of elaborating his inspirations. On a man-of-war these have plenty of encouragement; and it is absolutely required of him that he shall be in a shape to pass the critical inspection of the captain and first "luff" at four bells (ten o'clock) on pain of having his grog stopped.

The crew are at last rigged out duly in their white duck uniforms and sennit hats. But the glory is not to them, nor to the official gray and gold aft. See the older salts eying the messenger boys, who, in ideal creations of nautical skill topped off with silk-embroidered collars and cuffs, strut the decks like young bantams under the proud gaze of their sea-fathers. For time out of mind and in all navies has it been the custom for each youngster to have his proper and responsible relative of this sort, who makes his clothes and duly administers the ship's discipline with a cub of the famous ship's cat on occasion. The master-at-arms, under whose care the boys are supposed to rest, makes no scruple of delegating this duty with the rest; but you may be assured that the "chicken" gets no punishment that he has not well deserved, for no young mother is more jealous of the reputation of her bantling than is Jack.

But now, awaiting the muster-hour, all hands are disposed about topgallant-forecastle and fore-rigging in a very unusual sort of way. We are on watch for the California mail-steamer with its millions of gold. Everybody is sure of being rich before night—not on paper, in promises to pay of the Confederate Congress which may only be redeemed at best in shin-plasters, but in hard, shining, sub-stantial gold! She is due hereabouts to-day, as our invaluable Yankee newspa-pers secured a few days since kindly inform us. But alas! Again is verified the song of the poet,—

"Gold, gold, shining gold,
Hard to get and hard to hold."

In spite of our diligence the mast-head lookout has the best of it as usual, and from thence comes the expected hail, "Sail ho!" We could have forgiven that; but when in answer to the query "Where away?" the answer came, "On the port beam, sir," we understood that it could not be the steamer we were after. Steamer she was though, a big side-wheeler, brig-rigged, and bound South. The treasure-ship would be bound the other way, and should have been sighted on the starboard bow. But she is our meat anyway. All thoughts of Sunday muster are at once abandoned. Taking the deck, the first lieutenant orders the engine fires stirred, has the propeller lowered, clews up and furls all sail, and steaming slowly, places the *Alabama* in a position to have the stranger pass close to us. We know by this time she is not a man-of-war, from showing too much "top-hamper," so there is no necessity for going to quarters. She approaches us very fast, each vessel showing United States colors. We had gotten "athwart her hawse," to convey the idea we wished to communicate; but either we had no signals up to this effect, or she was in a hurry. She sheered, and passed us a biscuit's throw off. Perhaps she suspected us, even under our false colors. However, we had nothing left but to turn in pursuit, and in this manoeuvre some distance was lost. By the time her stern was presented to us she was a quarter of a mile ahead. There being no object in concealment now, our colors were changed. The *Alabama* had not as yet gotten the full benefit of her steam, and it was "nip and tuck" between us, rather, if any difference, in favor of the enemy, who was now, we could see, doing her very best, her paddle-wheels turning with great rapidity, and dense smoke coming from the funnel. We could observe an immense crowd of passengers on her upper deck, principally women, interspersed with wearers of naval and military uniforms. Wishing to cut the matter short, Lieut. Armstrong is ordered to clear away the rifle pivot-gun of his division, and give her a shot above deck, taking care to strike her masts well above the passengers' heads. The *Alabama* is now yawed; and the sea being perfectly smooth, a careful sight is taken, lockstring pulled, and in a moment splinters can be seen flying from the foremast about ten or twelve feet from the deck. Gallant shot! The mast is nearly cut in two, but holds on by the rigging. It was a great relief, you may be sure, to Armstrong that he had taken no life, particularly as the passengers were principally women and children. In a moment the ponderous wheels of the steamer cease to revolve, and she lay motionless on the water, completely at the mercy of the enemy. We came up with the prize fast enough now. Upon being boarded, she proved to be the California mail-boat *Ariel*, Capt. Jones, bound to the *Isthmus*, with a passenger-list of five hundred and thirty-two, mostly women and children, a battalion of United States marines under command of Capt. David Cohen, numbering, rank and file, one hundred and forty-five, and several naval officers, all bound to the Pacific station. Quite an army all told. But it would have been as well had we kept out of her way. No chance now for the capture of a treasure-boat, as the return steamer would not leave the *Isthmus* for New York until after the arrival of the *Ariel*, so the "cat is out of the bag" as to the whereabouts of the *Alabama,* and we are not to have the pleasure of counting eagles and double eagles. Nor does the dilemma end here; we shall have to play nurse to several hundred women and children for some days. The passengers cannot be landed on any neutral territory, international law forbidding our taking the prize into port, nor are we likely, in this part of the world, to capture a vessel of sufficient tonnage to accommodate this army of people.

The boarding-officer having reported considerable consternation among the lady passengers, Lieut. Armstrong and Midshipman Sinclair were sent on board to allay their fears, and assure them of such treatment as Southern gentlemen and officers are accustomed to render to ladies. Arrayed in their bright, new, gray uniforms, swords, and caps, they looked natty indeed. The boat was manned by as handsome a lot of tars as you could wish to see, dressed in their white duck and sennit hats. Freemantle, the coxswain, was justly proud of his boat. We felt sure the appearance of this jaunty combination alongside the prize must dissipate the idea in the ladies' minds that we are ruthless pirates. For some time after boarding the prize, it looked like a hopeless task trying to convince the passengers they would not have to walk the plank. Many of the ladies were in hysterics, fearing the worst. But it did not take our gallants long to secure the confidence of one of the ladies braver than the rest. This accomplished, one by one they came forward, and soon our lucky boarding-officers were enjoying the effect of the reaction. A perfect understanding must have been arrived at between the fair ones and our "rascally" lieutenant and middy, for the latter were soon minus every button from their uniforms, not "for conduct unbecoming an officer and a gentleman," but as mementos of the meeting. We may as well state just here that in no instance during the entire cruise was private property of any description, cash or otherwise, taken from a prisoner. In many instances money in quite large quantities was found on the persons of prisoners, but oath that it was his personal property was all-sufficient with Semmes. Doubtless many a dollar of owners' money was denied our common prize-chest by false swearing, but that remained a matter between the oath-taker and his own conscience. In the case of the *Ariel* a considerable amount of money (greenbacks) was found in the iron safe; but Capt. Jones promptly declared it ship's funds, without the necessity of inquiry. This sum was all that was transferred to our ship from her. The captain and engineers of the prize are removed to our vessel, and a number of our engineers sent on board the *Ariel* in their place, to take charge of her engine. In the meantime Armstrong has had the marine battalion mustered on the quarter-deck of the prize, and proceeds to disarm and parole them. This was met by a vigorous protest on the part of Capt. Cohen commanding, who, upon being ordered to have his men stack arms, hesitated for some time, but finally yielded to the gentle persuasion of the prizemaster, upon having his attention recalled to the frowning ports of the *Alabama* only a few yards removed. Many were the tales these lucky officers of ours had to tell after the bonding of the steamer and their return to their own ship. They had enjoyed a glorious "outing," occupying respectively the head and foot of the dining-table. Champagne having been ordered up from the steward's wineroom, they had the audacity to propose the health of President Davis, which they *requested* should be drunk standing. Their request was complied with amid much merriment. And the saucy girls, not to be outdone, proposed the health of Mr. Lincoln, which was promptly drank amid hurrahs. Strange scene, reader! But we are an odd race—we Americans! *sui generis.* We are now in company with the prize, and for some days steam side and side, our captain hoping to fall in with a vessel to transfer the passengers to, but in this we are doomed to disappointment. No prize comes along, and we are forced to release the *Ariel* under ransom-bond of $160,000. We had found Capt. Jones, who was a guest with us in the ward room, a modest and estimable gentle-man. He had done all he could to save his vessel, and might have succeeded but for the passengers, whose lives he would not have been justified in exposing to our fire. We will do him the credit to relate that he spoke in high terms of the kind treatment received at our hands upon his arrival home. As the two ships parted company the crew of the *Ariel* cheered, and the ladies waved their hand-kerchiefs. We fear our heroes of the boarding-party will take unkindly to "salt horse" and rice, after luxuriating on roast turkey and oysters on the half-shell washed down with champagne—to say nothing of those aching voids in the region of the heart. But a sailor is like the lamp-wicks they make of asbestos,—easily inflamed, never consumed.

We ascertained afterwards that the California home-bound steamer took the Florida passage, convoyed by a man-of-war.

Chapter V.

INTO THE GULF OF MEXICO; AT THE ARCAS ISLANDS; OFF GALVESTON; THE HATTERAS FIGHT.

The excitement of the last capture over, we allow steam to go down, hoist the propeller, and put the ship under sail. We stand along the north side of Jamaica; and after an uneventful run of some ten days without so much as a single prize, though we have passed a few neutrals, we enter the Yucatan passage, and pass into the Gulf of Mexico. The sail through this strait was a reminder to such of our offi-cers as had served on the *Sumter* of their exit here some eighteen months since.

They at that time were fugitives from their homes. They are returning now to have another look at the land they love so well. On the 23d of December, standing in for the Arcas, we made a sail ahead, which proved upon overhauling her to be our coal-transport, the barque *Agrippina*. She had made a tedious voyage from Blanquilla. We anchored together. The Arcas are of coral formation and almost barren, only a few stunted bushes and cactus giving the hint of vegetation. We were anchored in about eight fathoms, yet the water was so transparent the anchor could be plainly seen on the bottom; and about the coral branches, fish of varied hue lazily swam, secure in perpendicular distance from all surface foes. The fish found here are similar to those observed by the writer some years ago in Japan. They are of solid colors, blue, green, purple, red, and others of a combination of two or more colors. We speared numbers of them in the lake in the centre of the largest of the three islands, and we caught many with lines and by trolling. These fish, however, do not compare in flavor to those of the Atlantic coast.

A most amusing episode on one of our fishing expeditions claimed chief engineer Freeman as the hero. The principal island is circular in shape, with a lake in the centre connected with the sea by a narrow channel. At high water the fish would pass into the lake from the sea with ease, but they could not return if they lingered until the last of the ebb tide. There was always, however, plenty of water inside the lake—say two and a half feet. Freeman was bathing, and had waded to the centre of the pond, about a hundred yards from the shore. A number of us were in the dingy spearing fish with the grains, when all at once we discovered a large shark swimming leisurely along, his dorsal fin exposed, and evidently gorged with food, the pond being alive with fish of all sizes. We at once put our worthy engineer on his guard. The shark was between Freeman and the boat; so there was nothing to do on his part but make for the shore—and such fun! I say fun, for the shark had no idea of attacking him. In his mad haste to reach the shore, Freeman first swam, and that not seeming very speedy, he would try wading. This was also found to be slow work, as the water was too deep, and so he alternated between wading and swimming, finding both modes most unsatisfactory under the circumstances. When the beach was gained, for some minutes he lay motionless for lack of breath. In the meantime the peals of laughter from our boats must have reached the ears of those on board ship. It was a side-splitting spectacle. By this time Michael Mars, coxswain of the cutter, had made up his mind to have another sort of fun with the shark. Pushing the boat near, he jumped into the water, and quickly plunged his sheath-knife in the belly of the fish, giving him a fearful rip. The shark raised a terrible commotion, slapping the water with his tail, and bringing his jaws together with a most uncomfortable snap. Mars was peremptorily ordered into the boat; but his Irish blood was up, and the fight was continued until the shark was vanquished. He was towed on shore, and Jack was in high glee. Nothing so much pleases a sailor as despatching a "man-eater."

We coaled from the transport, and giving the captain his instructions to report to Capt. Bullock at Liverpool, saw him off. We shipped from the *Agrippina*, Jan. 4, William Jones, seaman. Our attention is for a few days divided between putting the ship in order and getting all the fun there is to be had. The islands are the resort of innumerable sea-fowl, which come here to lay their eggs and hatch out their young. It is interesting to move up the "streets" between the line of nests, and observe how curiously the mother-bird will look up at you sideways. She will not leave the nest unless forced off with a club. At certain hours the parent-birds, alternating, go to sea for food for self and young. Upon our arrival we first gathered bushels of these eggs from nests, in the absence of the old birds; but finding them stale in most cases, we had to resort to the plan of driving all the birds in a given space from the nests and breaking all the eggs, that on our return again we might find their place supplied with fresh-laid ones. These eggs are not delicate, and some kinds are even rank, yet the men ate and seemed to enjoy them. It was pitiable to see the old mother-birds hover over the heads of the crew, when driven from the nests, uttering their discordant cries of distress. They had no apparent fear of humanity, and would fly so close as to be easily hit with clubs. On one occasion the captain and myself were about to take some "sights" on shore with the artificial horizon to verify the chronometers. Freemantle, the captain's coxswain, was pouring the quicksilver from the jug into the basin, when a sea-gull, unobserved at first, waddled up to us, and after first interviewing us out of the corner of his eye, coolly put his bill into the mercury. Lest he should capsize it, Freemantle pushed him gently away, but to our intense amazement he returned to the charge, and finally we had to handle him quite roughly before he would desist. The time passed rapidly here, one watch at a time at play, the other at work under our industrious and indefatigable executive. Our crew rapidly recuperated from the effects of arduous service and the monotonous sea-diet; for if the islands gave us no vegetables, there was no lack of fish and fowl—the former in great variety and of excellent flavor, and turtle, curlew, plover, and sand-snipe in abundance. We had fine weather, and did not miss the opportunity for cleaning our ship's bottom by careening.

We are shipshape finally, and off for the coast of Texas, looking up Banks and his transport-fleet. But "man proposes, but God disposes." We shall, instead of scattering the Banks transport-fleet, find ourselves in a hornet's nest, and more than lucky to get out of it as well as we do. The fight we got on our hands might have turned out disastrously, for it was a matter of chance that the least powerful of the blockading-fleet came out that night to battle with us.

The run up the Gulf was uneventful, giving all hands ample time for recreation between duties. We have an excellent library of standard works for use of crew as well as officers, and have managed to add considerably to it from prizes. The bustle and constant business of man-of-war life materially interfere with satisfactory reading. The writer, time and weather permitting, preferred to take his book aloft, and straddling the topsail-yard, and making the mast a rest for the back, vary the interest by occasionally casting his eye over the water in the hope of "getting to windward" of the mast-head lookout in making out and reporting a sail to the officer of the deck. In the ward room and steerage, chess, backgammon, and other games are in full blast. Playing cards is positively prohibited. These mess-gatherings are the promoters of much that is entertaining, as also at times instructive, as when some intelligent messmate tells of his travels and observations, or spreads himself in the sciences. At times a group will be all attention to a reading, lecture, or "yarn," when the uncanny wail of a violin in the hands of an amateur, the twang of a guitar, or some other distracting rhythmic monody, proclaims right of free speech. Protests, and even strong language, in this case are often unavailing to support the majority rule. Your musical bore has no conscience, and likes an audience, willing or unwilling, like a youngster in pinafores. A favorite amusement was keeping a set of books containing an account of the owner's share of prize-money. The value of the manifest of each prize was of course carefully recorded, as was the finding of a court composed of a number of the commissioned officers. This record was intended as a memorandum or guide for the Confederate government, which had voted to officers and crew a sum equal to one-half the value of the vessels of the enemy, destroyed or bonded. This division of prize-money was to be made on a sliding scale proportional to rank, and was to the commander and commissioned officers, at the end of the cruise, a large fortune. Hence the deep interest taken in the book. As each vessel would be condemned and burned or bonded, the entry would be copied in the individual ledgers, each officer and man knowing his *pro rata* of the whole. So, as with the people on shore, we have our days of active and also of dull trade. These carefully kept accounts can be bought cheap now, but there is a melancholy satisfaction in feeling that one has once made a fortune. Only one of the *Alabama's* officers ever realized anything. This young gentleman transferred his interest, right, and title to his prize-money to a speculative London Hebrew for about five per cent of its face, just after the sinking of the *Alabama*. This seemed to us a reckless extravagance at the time, but it did not prove so. As the poor fellow was lost at sea soon afterward, leaving no heirs, it is to be hoped the fun he got out of his few thousands left no regrets to be reaped.

Some fine fishing for the past few days, the wind being light and the ship under easy sail. We had good luck with both trolling-lines and grains. The fun was the most of it though, for the Arcas had given us a surfeit of this sort of food. On the afternoon of the eleventh, the mast-head gave us the familiar hail, "Sail ho!" and then promptly following it, "Land ho!" The shore off Galveston is so flat and low that a vessel would be made sooner than the land. In this case the lookout reported a number of ships at anchor, having the appearance of men-of-war, but no transport-fleet. It was soon apparent that the craft were all steamers, and then a shell from one of them was seen to burst over the city. This made the case as plain to us as a Quakeress' bonnet. It seemed to strike all hands at once and in the same way,—Galveston had been retaken by our forces, and the enemy's fleet driven outside the bar. Hence the shelling of the city.

It must not be thought that because the *Alabama* was mainly confined to the high seas by the operation of international law that the world and its doings were entirely shut out from her. The newspapers of the North were allowed an astonishing latitude in dispensing news of the movements of armies and fleets; and the captured vessels frequently supplied us, through copies of these newspapers, with information of the greatest consequence, enabling us to avoid cruisers, and to learn of the movements of armies and transport-ships destined to points of attack on the Southern coast. It was information received in this manner that determined Semmes to attempt the destruction of a transport-fleet destined for the invasion of Texas through the port of Galveston, then in the possession of the United States forces. Gen. Banks fitted out this expedition, and was expected off Galveston about Jan. 10. Semmes, surmising that the expedition would not be convoyed by men-of-war, the South having no navy to attack it, judged that it would be an easy matter for a smart and powerful ship of our class to destroy or disperse it. But it had happened in the meantime that Galveston was recaptured by the river gun-boats supported by the land-forces of the Confederacy; and this had broken into Gen. Banks's plans, turning his fleet by New Orleans and the Red River upon Texas, and the blockade was resumed off the harbor. Of this we had of course no knowledge.

Our situation was critical. Very soon the smoke from the stack of one of the steamers apprised us that she was getting under way, and soon she was bowling along, steering right for us. We had been under sail all the while. At once the fires are stirred, the propeller lowered, and the ship's head put off shore, steaming slowly. Blake signals the admiral as we plainly see; and before the darkness shuts out the view, it is evident that the whole fleet is preparing to get under way. This to us is certainly an ominous sight. We must make a close, quick, yard-arm fight, and if successful, stand not on the order of our going, but GO! For to nautical experience it is well known that the Gulf of Mexico is a dangerous trap, with only two passages for escape. We could not tell what facilities the admiral off Galveston might have for speedily closing these against us.

But it was necessary to get the enemy now approaching as far from the rest of the fleet as possible, and also to allow night to set in before engaging him. We succeed in putting about fifteen miles between us and the fleet, then with canvas furled, steam by this time being sufficient, the engines are stopped, and with officers and men at quarters we await the result. It is now dark, the enemy being but indistinctly seen. Many are the conjectures as to his strength and class, and opinions as to whether the rest of the fleet is on its way out. The concensus of opinion is emphatic that what we do must be done quickly, and that the captain ought to lay us alongside her, if she does not prove too heavy.

The enemy has now come up. We have been standing in shore while awaiting her, but now our head is turned off shore again. Then comes the hail, *"What ship is that?"—"This is her Britannic Majesty's steamer* Petrel,*"* is the reply. The two vessels are now nearly motionless, and both of course at quarters. Our men are wild with excitement and expectation. In the darkness it is impossible to make out her class except that she is a side-wheeler. Our crew have lock-strings in hand, keeping the gun trained on her, and awaiting the command to fire. The two vessels are so near that conversation in ordinary tones can be easily heard from one to the other. For a time the *Hatteras* people seem to be consulting. Finally they hailed again, *"If you please, I'll send a boat on board of you,"* to which our executive officer replied, "Certainly, we shall be pleased to receive your boat." The boat was soon lowered from the davits and began pulling toward us. All occasion for subterfuge being now at an end, word was immediately passed to the divisions that the signal to fire would be "Alabama." When the boat was about half-way between the two vessels, Lieut. Kell hailed, "This is the Confederate States steamer *Alabama!"* The last word had barely passed his lips when sky and water are lighted up by the flash of our broadside, instantly followed as it seemed by that of the enemy. A running fight was now kept up, the *Alabama*-fighting her starboard, and the *Hatteras* her port battery, both vessels gathering headway rapidly. Never did a crew handle a battery more deftly than ours. About six broadsides were fired by us. The enemy replied irregularly, and the action only lasted thirteen minutes. It was evident to us from the trifling nature of the wounds to our hull and rigging that the *Hatteras* was being whipped. A crash amongst her machinery soon settled the business. Then she fired a lee gun, and we heard the quick, sharp hail of surrender, accompanied by the request that our boats be sent to her immediately, as she was sinking. The whole thing had passed so quickly that it seemed to us like a dream. Our battery was hastily secured, and then our boats started for her at lightning speed. The daily practice of our crew in handling boats and boarding vessels now served the enemy in good stead. A few strokes of the oars put us alongside, and none too soon. In two minutes after we cleared her sides only her mast-heads were showing above the water; and in just nineteen minutes from the opening broadside, the officers and crew of the *Hatteras,* wounded included, were on our decks, and the *Alabama* was steaming away at her best speed for the Yucatan passage. This is probably one of the quickest naval duels on record. But it was none too quick for our safety; for as we laid our course their lights were to be plainly seen coming up rapidly in our wake. But there was now no danger, for the *Alabama* was at that time more than a match in speed for any vessel in the admiral's fleet. By the following evening shot-plugs and paint had obliterated nearly all marks of the engagement from the *Alabama*. It is illustrative of the uncertainties attending naval engagements, that the shot of the *Hatteras* should have expended itself so entirely upon the upper works of the *Alabama* where the damage would be but slight, while our shots with depressed guns almost invariably struck her in vital places. The two vessels were so close that frequently their yard-arms could have been locked by a turn of the helm. There was no chance for a shot to miss. The mortality on the *Hatteras* was astonishingly slight in view of the damage inflicted on the vessel. Only two were killed and five wounded. The wounded men subsequently all recovered. And it is scarcely less remarkable that on board the *Alabama,* though her bulwarks were riddled with shot-holes, there was but one casualty, George Addison, carpenter's mate, receiving a slight wound in the cheek from a fragment of a shell. Capt. Blake afterwards said that his purpose had been to run down and board us; but as the *Alabama* had the speed of him his programme could hardly be carried out. It must have been a hot place for the *Hatteras*'s boat, between two fires with only twenty-five or thirty yards intervening. As the boat escaped, the officer in charge of her must have made a sharp move out of the way. Probably the mast-heads of the *Hatteras* sticking up out of the water were discovered by the fleet on their return from the chase, and anticipated the news conveyed by the escaped boat. But it is improbable that the name of the *Hatteras*'s antagonist transpired until the news was received from Kingston.

Chapter VI.

THE HATTERAS PRISONERS ON BOARD; AT KINGSTON,
JAMAICA; TROUBLE WITH JACK; ADIEU TO FORT ROYAL;
FORAGING FOR PROVISIONS; BAFFLING WINDS; A CARGO OF
WINES AND LIQUORS; ENEMIES' SHIPS GETTING SCARCE;
DISPOSING OF PRISONERS AT SEA; IN THE BRAZILIAN HIGH
ROAD; WASHING DAYS FOR JACK.

We are now bowling along, steam and sail, for Kingston, Jamaica, where it is proposed to land the officers and crew of the *Hatteras*. The weather soon after leaving the coast sets in squally with rain, the wind veering ahead. We let steam go down, and battle with it under sail. This is bad, as we have in prisoners a force fully equal to our own, and though on parole, we are anxious to land them as quickly as possible. The strict watch kept over them is very wearing to officers and men, who must sleep at all times on their arms. We were ten days on the passage to Kingston. Capt. Blake was the guest of Semmes, and the remainder of the officers of the *Hatteras* were distributed as to rank in the ward room and two steerages. We found our prisoner officers a rather jolly set; and the time passed very pleasantly, barring the vilianous weather. Porter, the *Hatteras*'s executive officer, seemed to take quite a fancy to me, having known my father intimately. He would keep nearly all my watches with me, pacing the deck and talking of old times. I did everything possible to cheer and reassure him, giving his officers and crew full credit for doing all they could under the circumstances, having to contend against a ship much more powerful than theirs, and from constant practice more efficient in handling her battery. I was amused to observe the blank surprise of Porter when informed that grog was only served to the seamen on our vessel, the officers being positively disallowed it. However, upon being informed that *his* officers were not included in the list, and that our captain had plenty of it for entertaining purposes, he laughingly said, "Well, I suppose we must play the *rôle* of apparent selfishness." Porter greatly admired the speed and seaworthy qualities of our ship, and thought she would cause the ship-owners of the North immense direct as well as indirect loss; and he looked for bitter disappointment, if not censure, from the country, at the result of the late engagement,—the *Hatteras* not even being able to cripple us,—and thought it would be no enviable position to command any vessel sent in pursuit of us. He considered the *Alabama* the most complete ship afloat, all and all, for the purpose in hand. The paymaster of the *Hatteras* was most excellent company. He was my roommate. I remember his first remark as he was ushered into our ward room. "Well," he said, "boys, I'll be d—d if we hadn't a cast-iron atmosphere in our engine-room! I was stationed there, and shell after shell exploded until the air smelt of iron fragments! I don't want any more of it; I'm going home right away, and don't you stop to fight any more cruisers until you land me." Again, pulling some gold pieces from his pocket and shaking them at me, he remarked, "Say, Johnny, ain't there a sight good for any fellow's sore eyes? Don't you want to handle some of them?" But we had the joke on him as he afterwards confessed upon learning that our salaries were paid in "sterling." During the passage we made a sail ahead, and upon overhauling her she showed English colors. We recognized in her our transport, the *Agrippina*. She, like ourselves, had experienced head winds and rough weather.

Of course we kept "mum" as to any previous knowledge of her to our prisoners. One day, the grog being served out, Kell was standing near, and observing an old "barnacle-back" among the prisoners, eying our men as they passed around the grog-tub and brought their inclined plane in contact with the contents of the cup, asked the old fellow if he would like a "tot." Touching his hat quickly with both hands, for he was ironed, the answer came, "Your honor—thanks." Receiving the tin measure from the "captain of the hold" in charge of the grog-tub, he slowly and carefully raised it with his teeth, and at the same time throwing back his head with a dexterous jerk, he emptied it without the spilling of a drop. Soon after many of the prisoners asked permission to ship with us, which was of course refused. The matter was kept from the knowledge of their officers. Such the power of grog over a sailor. These men were not allowed grog in United States service. But we must now get ready to say good-by to our friends of the *Hatteras*. We have made the lighthouse of Fort Royal. The 21st of January we drop anchor. We find several vessels of the British squadron on this station,—flag-ship Jason, also the Challenger and Greyhound, and, as we found it ever after in English colonies, a hearty welcome awaiting us. Civilities are exchanged with the governor of the island and the commanding fleet-officer. Upon being apprised of the recent engagement, and the presence of the prisoners on our ship, the town was of course in a state of excitement beyond description. Everything in the way of a boat that would float was in requisition, and the boatmen probably never in their experience reaped such a harvest of fares. They were many yards deep around our vessel, each struggling to get their passengers to the gangway. At no time during the cruise was our ship in such a state of confusion as during our stay at Kingston. The prisoners were to be landed; and meantime our decks and officers' quarters were besieged with officials and citizens from the shore, besides officers from the fleet and garrison, and these all to be entertained. Ship-coaling, and ship's mechanics engaged in repairing damages of the late fight, stopping shot-holes in the hull, and replacing damaged rigging. Officers with manifold duties suddenly thrust upon them. The most important and onerous service of all was that of a watch to keep, if possible, liquor out of the ship. Having no marine guard to call into service, we could only command the personal services of our lieutenant of marines, Mr. Beckett K. Howell, assisted by the master-at-arms. These officers kept alert, first with an eye on this and now on that bumboat, wherever a suspicious movement on the part of Jack or the bum-boatmen pointed to a mutual understanding. Our ubiquitous first lieutenant, assisted by the officer of the deck and midshipman of the forecastle, also had an eye to the same subject. We miss a marine guard sadly in port; but it must be confessed "a soger" at sea is a fish out of water, in everybody's mess and nobody's watch. However, in spite of the most rigid espionage, some confusion is soon observed, and one by one our fellows begin to be hustled in irons to the "brig." But by this time the prisoners have been landed, and are under the protection of the United States consul, so that half our crew are sent ashore on liberty.

The presence of a large fleet of English men-of-war giving a feeling of perfect security in the event of one or more of the enemy's cruisers putting in an appearance, Semmes, who felt the want of quiet and removal from the scene of confusion and uproar, the unavoidable condition of our present situation, had accepted the invitation of an English gentleman, a merchant of the place, to visit his country-seat in the mountains for a few days. Kell was left in command. His position was surely anything but a bed of roses; but as usual, he managed to fill it with dignity and credit. It was a trying time for us all. Cruising and boarding vessels we had got used to, and we knew pretty well what we could depend on, and what bodily and mental strain we should have to meet; here the unexpected beset us like the troubles of Pandora's box, and there was no such thing as dog-watch or watch below. Every man-Jack of the crew was in for a lark, and discipline had to be relaxed without being quite allowed to "go by the run." We were beset at all hours with visitors of high and low degree, and the courtesies of the ship must not be neglected. Among the officers permission to visit the shore on pleasure was not even thought of.

A serious mortification came to us in the misbehavior of our paymaster, Clarence R. Yonge. Visiting the shore on duty, he was reported to be guilty of traitorous communication with the United States consul, and of drunken consort with paroled seamen of the enemy. Kell at once sent an armed party ashore, arrested him, and kept him under arrest on board until Capt. Semmes's return, when he was at once dismissed the service, and drummed out of the ship. This is the only case of discipline we have to record as regards the officers of the *Alabama,* but one dose of this sort was surely enough. Through this man's influence with our crew, backed by the persuasions of the United States consul, we lost several valuable seamen. He was afterward a secret agent of the enemy's diplomatic corps in London—but that has nothing to do with the present story.

Before leaving Kingston, it was my good fortune to meet Lieut. Cardale of H. B. M. ship *Greyhound,* recently from Norfolk, Va., where he had met and been entertained by members of my family. This brought home news down to within ten days. And only those who have suffered from this banishment—without mails—so rare in modern life, can realize the value of such a happening. In the meantime, Jack is having a good time on shore. Sailor-like he is hobnobbing with the liberty men from the British ships, as well as his late opponents of the *Hatteras,* and supplying funds to the latter, who are "broke." Groups of them may be encountered at every turn of sailor-town, arm in arm, and in every stage of intoxication, from hilarity to fighting humor. When the time arrives to scoop them up, and give the other watch a chance at the sport so-called, officers in uniform with armed boats' crews are scouring the streets and dens. One is reminded of the old problem of ferrying over the river the goose, the fox, and the bag of corn; for no sooner is one lot delivered at the boat and another raid made up-town, than the prisoners break guard somehow and are up-town again. The writer, visiting a dance-hall after dark with a boat's crew, in quest of delinquents, was met at the threshold by a body of men from the English squadron backed by the lady participants in the ball, and good-naturedly but firmly informed that he could not come in, the visit being quite *mal à propos.* One of the ladies remarked, "Say, middy, come some other time. The tickets are limited at this ball; and besides, the company is select!" "Tell old 'Beeswax,'" said another persuasive maiden, "your old piratical skipper, to go to sea, burn some more Yankee ships, and come back. We'll give up the boys then, and you shall have your turn." It took much diplomacy to carry our point; and it was only accomplished by reasoning most earnestly with the soberer of the crew, and a generous amount (on my part) of treating among the fair hosts. Returning with this party to the ship, it was found necessary to put some of the most drunken fellows in irons. And while this was going on, two seamen managed to call alongside a boat in which two negroes were prowling about the harbor. Taking possession of the oars, they put off for shore at a great rate. We started a boat promptly in chase, and were just about to overhaul them when overboard went one of the negroes. Of course we had to stop, and pick the poor fellow up, and this gave the fugitives quite a start. Again, just as we were upon them, they shoved the other negro into the water. However, as they were now out of this sort of amunition, we got them finally before they reached shore. When brought to the mainmast on charge of attempting to desert, they pleaded not guilty. "No idea of deserting, your honor," they declared. "We are part owners of this craft. We only wanted to say good-by to the girls."

We are coaled, the crew has been scraped together as thoroughly as possible, and we are ready for sea, minus seven men. The reader will fail to fully realize the import of the loss. These men have been drilled and educated for the work in hand; and their place must be supplied by volunteers from future prizes, who in turn, however capable as seamen, will require months of drill to bring them up to the standard of the rest of the crew. Besides, we had been all along short of our full complement of men. But for coaling and other unavoidable needs, the voice of our officers would have been never to enter port during the cruise. To us a port was anything but a recreation or pleasure. Our missing men are described on the ship's-books as "deserters." This, however, is a misnomer. Jack has been kept drunk, and hid away in some den until the sailing of his ship. He will wake up, poor deluded child of Poseidon, to find his home swept from him, accumulation of pay sacrificed, and *quasi* friends knowing him no more.

The delinquents are now released from the "brig." We bid adieu to Fort Royal, and are soon outside of the light-ship and on our way to the coast of Brazil. It takes some time to get discipline back to the old high standard, and we are crippled by the loss of our runaways. Time heals all calamities, however. The routine of cruising-life is promptly resumed, working ship after "sails," and the everlasting drill, drill, drill! If the officers find *playing fighting* tedious and monotonous, how must Jack look at it? But it is important, yea, indispensable; and wrestle with it we must. We are running down the coast of Hayti; have made two captures since leaving Fort Royal, the *Golden Rule* and *Chastelaine*, both with food products principally. (A majority of the United States vessels we shall overhaul in these latitudes are provision-laden.) Both of them are fired, after removing such stores and provisions as our ship departments have need of, and transshipping the crews, bags, and hammocks to our decks. The reader by this time must have observed that our prizes furnish all departments of our ship,—canvas and twine for the sailmaker, cordage and naval stores for the boatswain, lumber for the carpenter, with but little, however, for the gunner, unless he comes across a can or two of material for the composition of his gun-polish. Our paymaster, however, is *the grand* freebooter of the ship, taking in provisions, small stores, tobacco, and whatever he lusts after, never crying hold! enough! so long as patience, time, and plunder hold out. The search continues until night, bad weather, or some unlooked for intervention, puts a stop to the raid. But we always manage to find use for everything transferred to our several departments, and then comes the paymaster's chance to return in kind the jokes poked at him by messmates as to his "Mrs. Toodles" proclivities. "There!" will come from "Old Cheese," "didn't I tell you we should find it useful?" We may as well state here for the enlightenment of the reader, that no one, officer or man, was allowed to take from the stores or cargo of a prize for personal use the smallest article, even of the most insignificant value. All articles removed were transferred to the respective departments of our ship, under the care and responsibility of the head of the bureau, and issued only upon requisition, being charged to the account of the officer or man requiring it. A careful account of everything is kept, as representing a part of the prize-money. This rule also had the effect of keeping up discipline, as nothing so demoralizes a crew as being allowed to plunder *ad libitum*. And again, Jack is much like his namesake the jack-daw, with a most decided aptitude for stowing away slyly any and every thing having an unknown value that may come in his way. Indeed, he will hide in the lockers and hammock nettings, old shoes, dilapidated hats, and other rubbish, thinking and hoping the day will arrive when he can produce them for an emergency. It is amusing to observe the old salts on a Sunday morning, watching the first lieutenant in his rounds of the vessel before reporting the ship to the captain as ready for inspection. Old barnacle-back has some treasures, in the above line, stored away, and keeps a keen eye on the officer as he orders some man to throw off the hammock-cloths. He knows well his toys are in danger, and he is all expectation and anxiety. Should the executive trust to the carrying out of his order, and the report "nothing contraband," all serene; but should the distrustful Kell mount a gun-carriage, and glance his own lynx eyes inside, good-by to the traps, and the owner sneaks forward, broken-hearted at the loss of his *penates*—for overboard they go to "Davy Jones's locker." The mortification must be accepted without sign or sorrow; for to acknowledge ownership would not save the trash, but only bring the self-condemned culprit into trouble, or at least stoppage of a day's grog.

We coast along the shores of Hayti, and stand in for the town of St. Domingo. We communicate with the Spanish government, receiving permission to land our prisoners of the *Golden Rule* and *Chastelaine;* and having made as usual some purchases of fruit and fresh provisions, the next day we are under way, and leaving the historic shores of the old town, point eastward. We are in a hurry now, having wasted much time with but little achievement on our western trip, to reach the coast of Brazil, where lots of plunder await us. There is much of interest to be seen and pondered over by a visitor to these shores, but we anticipate seeing little of it but what goes afloat. We coast St. Domingo and enter the Mona Passage, an occasional sail in sight, but all reported neutral by Evans. We are in a comparatively unfrequented latitude for *brisk* trade in our line; still, we make a capture to-day (Feb. 3,'63), the *Palmetto*. Inappropriate name we reflect, for a Yankee vessel. She proves a lawful prize though, and is "looted" of what we require of her stores and cargo, crew transferred, and then burned. We had now been nine days out of port. Three vessels burned, but of insignificant value. We shall not make big hauls until the track of East India bound vessels is reached in Maury's "road of the ocean," a road all vessels *must* follow, cruisers or no cruisers. Navigators have only the choice of some sixty miles of width at one point off the Brazil coast. Neglect warning, stray from the mile-stones, and head or baffling winds and currents will waft you hither and thither, any way but the one wished. So here is the place for us to stand by, and *also* the place for Uncle Sam's cruisers to hold argument with us. It will therefore be understood why anticipation of another fight on our hands off the Brazilian coast makes much of the evening and mess talk. Not that Jack worries about it much. His mourning eye has resumed its dignity, his sore head has healed, and his spirits have their sea-legs on. Song and dance and the glee-club's melodious strains take the deck as of yore; and Semmes himself lights his evening cigar on the bridge, where not only these things may be viewed and listened to, but also the private sentiments of Jack, freely spoken to his messmate in plain English, or in subtlety of yarn or witticism. Semmes understands just how to keep himself near to the hearts and in the confidence of his men, without in the slightest degree descending from his dignity, or permitting direct approach. He does not seem to pay the slightest attention to what is going on below him. But Jack knows well enough that he is taking it all in informally. Individually and collectively Jack has taken soundings of the "old man," and knows pretty well how to steer and where an anchor will hold. The men feel no restraint from his presence—rather they enjoy it. In their way they love him and are proud of him, and he returns the sentiments—in his way.

We have been slowly working along to the eastward, baffled by variable winds and dirty weather for some days. Sight a few sail, but easily make them out to be neutrals. Approaching the last days of February the sky clears up. And then the mast-head hails and hails again, and to the query, "Where away?" reports vessels here, there, and everywhere—all around the compass. As there is but little wind, we have only to pick out our victims. Evans is sent aloft, and soon reports several "Yankees," and says they are changing their courses as if they smelt a rat. This is soon evident enough. They are separating as much as possible, so as to give us a long chase in detail. There is nothing for it but to steam up and make sharp work. We do not make chase with steam except in rare cases. Semmes well knows that he cannot enter port for coal without advertising his whereabouts, and subjecting his crew to the demoralizing effects so lately noted.

The power of our engines soon puts us alongside the first prize; without a moment's delay a prize-crew is thrown on board, under command of Master's-mate Fulham, with orders to follow us as closely as possible, and we are after the next, already well down on the horizon. She also proves to be a lawful prize, barque *Olive Jane* from Bordeaux, bound to New York, with wines, brandies, sardines, olives, etc. In the meantime the prize in charge of Fulham was hull down in the distance, standing towards us as ordered. The character of cargo on board the *Olive Jane,* consisting as it did mostly of liquors, made the "looting" of her, for needed supplies for our vessel, dangerous to the morals of our boarding-crews. The writer, in command of the captain's gig, with faithful Freemantle as coxswain, had charge of the breaking out of the hold of the prize, with strict orders to hurry up the work, and above all things to keep the boat's crew from grog, and see that they did not bring any on board their own vessel. Reader, if you know a sailor, you understand the gravity of the present trust; otherwise you fail to realize the weight of responsibility on the officer's shoulders. Calling Freemantle aside, after taking off the hatches, I explained to him the nature of the cargo, and the strict orders received, at the same time hinting at the utter impossibility of keeping the men from the tempting fluids; and added my determination, arrived at after mature thought, to spread a lunch on the cabin table, furnished from the cargo and ship-stores, of sardines, olives, cheese, etc., flanked by sundry bottles of brandy, burgundy, and claret, that the men would be required while working in breaking out the hold to abstain from opening the casks or cases, but might quench their thirst in an orderly manner from the cabin set-out. The scheme worked to a charm. Jack had no incentive to disobey orders and get into trouble in consequence, and doubtless also felt thrown upon his honor not to get his officer into "hot water." From time to time the cabin was visited for a bite and a nip. And now observe the self-constituted guests at the cabin table of the *Olive Jane,* luxuriating in the comfort of a chair, a snow-white cloth, and verily a four prong fork—the table groaning under the weight of luxuries! Surely Jack could be in no better luck, even as the guest of a Friar Tuck. And you have only to watch narrowly these waifs of the world, and draw for yourself a moral of life. One fellow, but yesterday you noted at his forecastle deck dinner, a hardtack for his plate, a slab of salt pork on it cut with his sheath-knife, handled with greasy fingers to the mouth; the old boyhood training asserts itself, and as he wipes his mustache with his napkin he has given his heart's secret away. A broken-down gentleman with a story! What a store-room of tragedy, comedy, and heartache the forecastle of a man-of-war frequently is! Material for an army of novelists.

Not a bottle of liquor reached our ship; and the boat's crew under my command returned in a *good humor* only, no more. The prize was fired in cabin and forecastle, and made a grand blaze, owing to the highly inflammable character of her cargo. We were not many hundred yards off when the flames could be seen licking the topsails. We secured a quantity of sardines among other delicacies; and if you have never added heretofore to your menu *fried* sardines, reader, do so. We now overhaul the first prize under the charge of Fulham. She proved to be the *Golden Eagle.* It is late when we get alongside of her, the *Olive Jane* having drawn us hull-down away. We find her, upon examination of papers, a lawful prize, and transferring her crew, and adding her chronometers and flag, fire her. Allowing steam to go down, and putting the *Alabama* under short sail, we loaf along. The wind is light; but we are now in "the road," and in no hurry, hence the reduced sail. Single-reefed topsails alone, merely enough to steady the ship. On one beam is the *Olive Jane,* on the other the *Golden Eagle,* both wrapped in flames from spar-deck to mast-head, the sea and heavens glowing in the red glare, the flames varying in brilliancy, as the material for the time being is supplied or denied, suggesting the phenomenon of the aurora borealis. On the rail in groups may be seen the officers and crews of the burning prizes, conversing in subdued whispers,—we cannot flatter ourselves in complimentary terms of us; so, as listeners rarely hear good of themselves, we will not invade the sanctity of their circle. One cannot but admire the nonchalant manner of the American sailor when confronted with danger or disaster, and it makes our hearts go out to him as we mark the cool bearing hiding the avalanche of conflicting emotions. You may not know it, boys, but a sympathy for you dwells in us. We are all of us but the victims of circumstance. But we must smother these feelings—at least for the present. We are here for duty, and must strain our efforts to the utmost, and tread the path resolutely. We should make many captures in this fashionable highway of commerce—at least, we shall have the opportunity to judge the extent of demoralization produced by our past efforts. We are now having a surfeit of chronometers. The winding of them still continues, under orders from Semmes; and a precious lot of time is consumed at it. It was a joyous day to the writer when the time came to rescind the order, and let them take care of themselves till overhauled by a maker. By the way, they supplied the only prize-money ever realized by the custodian. Just before leaving Cherbourg for the fight, the chronometers, some seventy odd in number, were transferred to the British yacht *Hornet,* Capt. Hewitt, and eventually landed at Liverpool. In the year 1867 or 1868 the writer was handed a sterling check by a member of a Baltimore banking-house, as coming from Capt. Semmes, with the remark, "Semmes desires me to say this is your share of the sale of the chronometers abroad, and also requests you to give him the address of Lieuts. Armstrong and Wilson." The request was also made that the transaction be kept shady. The reasons for silence have happily passed away, as also my old friend the banker. Between us we held for many years the secret of this, the only prize-money from the *Alabama.* A small dividend compared to outlay.

We are now in the N. E. "trades," about latitude 20° N., longitude 42° W.— Maury's highway of travel, and in the direct path of commerce to and from Europe and the United States. Two days since we burned the *Olive Jane* and *Golden Eagle,* and since have exchanged colors during daylight with quite a large number of sail, but undeniably neutral. But at night we are quite busy boarding, darkness requiring a visit to ascertain nationality; and the boom of our gun to "heave-to" gives the hint to our enemy, if near, they had better leave the beaten track and be off. In the midwatch we have a sail, suddenly, close aboard of us, on opposite tack, bound north. She flits by like a phantom, or bird on the wing; and soon all is bustle, wearing ship in chase, making and crowding on sail. As she passes, the lookout makes out and reports the stranger a brig. We give her a blank cartridge as we come to the wind on the starboard tack, and the midnight race has begun. As soon as sails are trimmed, a deathlike silence settles on the spar-deck. Nothing to do until the chase is overhauled.

Being near enough for effective fire, and finding she does not down helm, we yaw ship, to bring our guns to bear, and let slip a thirty-two shot, which, while we do not see the effect, we know has passed uncomfortably near her. Still not a budge of tack or sheet. We are at a loss to understand what the fellow means; for we, at least, are in earnest. We are within a few hundred yards of each other, and all as silent as death on board of her. No show of signal-light, no recognition. I cannot remember an incident of the cruise that recalls more intense excitement, or caused more surmise, than this midnight meeting on the ocean. The song of the "Ancient Mariner," as we approached this floating home of silence, suggested itself. We have her so well in hand that a second shot, sent with business intent, would be sheer murder, so hold our fire. We approach close to windward, so close as to becalm and shiver her canvas, and demand her, by trumpet, to "heave-to." She makes the effort; but the seamanship, or rather lack of seamanship, displayed in answering our hail, still more puzzles us. We could by this time interpret great confusion on board,—a multiplicity of tongues, great excitement, and lubberly swinging of yards. Upon boarding she proved the Portuguese brig *Oporto,* from the Brazils to Lisbon. Her ignorant captain and crew have lost sight of the American war evidently, and may be take us for a West India pirate. They were so paralyzed with fear as to lose all presence of mind. It must have taken them some days to get their appetites back. Our boat's crew assisted them to make sail again. That these men are the descendants of ancestors renowned in history for bold adventure by sea seems beyond belief. What effete sons of gallant, pushing fathers!

We had the monotony of every-day life varied to-day. Paymaster's steward Johns hurried to the spar-deck, and whispered to the deck-officer the fact that the spirit-room was on fire next the magazine,—the most dangerous spot possible. In a moment the at-any-time-to-be-expected beat to "quarters" rolled along the spar-deck, and the crew are in a moment standing at quarters. The firebell is rung (a regular feature of quarters' exercise), and in a jiffy the stream of water was about to be directed down the spirit-room hatch to the deck-officer's order, "Fire in the spirit-room." In the meanwhile, "captain of the hold" Higgs had succeeded in smothering the flames. The vapor from the liquor casks had ignited from an open candle used contrary to "regulations." It need scarcely be added the crew at quarters only knew of an actual fire after the "pipe-down." It was a narrow escape from having the tables turned on the *Alabama.*

The next day we have sails in sight constantly, and Evans is kept busy at the mast-head; but he never "squeals" at the duty, indeed, the contrary—he is quite proud of his importance. From time to time he reports neutrals, now English, now Northcountrymen, etc., but none, so far, "contraband," as Ben Butler would have dubbed them. Evans's shipmates are never so pleased as when they can guy him. One middy would say, "Look here, Evans, you are playing the d——l with your reports! This won't do, see? The skipper has turned our head from the chase, and I'd swear she's Yankee!"—"What do you know about the rig of a craft?" growls Evans, his eyes snapping in anger at the insinuation; "I made out vessels in the offing when you were sucking sugar rags." And turning his back in contempt, he mounts the rigging for another scout. The middy signals his chum with a wink of the eye, and rolls forward in imitation of the boatswain's mate. He has had his fun "nagging" Evans. Several days elapse with only neutrals in view. Our past industry is beginning to tell. The enemy's ships are getting scarce. Later in the cruise the reader will witness at times all hands sorely disappointed in their hopes of a prize, though Evans has put his "indorsement" on the back that the sail is "Yank." His judgment is true; but upon being boarded, the vessel, though American-built, is found to be under foreign papers, having been sold and transferred to some other flag. Thus gradually sinks the proud carrying-trade of the North American Republic. We have at last, however, found the Stars and Stripes at the peak of the ship *Washington;* but her cargo (guano) being entirely on neutral account, and not contraband of war, she is bonded and released. The *John A. Parks* next requires our polite attention. Her cargo proving to be enemy's property, her officers and crew are transferred to our ship, the usual removal of nautical instruments made, and the *Parks* is fired. We are experiencing all the same an active, stirring, and exciting life. The ship under close-reefed topsails in the strong "trades," sauntering along in this busy pathway of commerce, the diverging point to the many quarters of the globe, both north and south. The *Alabama,* like a beast of prey crouching on the crossroads, is wide awake and alert. It is a dark night, and the usual "trade" mist spreading out over the water and dimming the sight. The clear, sharp hail comes from a lookout, "Sail ho!" "Close aboard"; and looming up out of the mist a great ship is seen like a ghost rising from a graveyard—a cloud of canvas alow and aloft, bounding by as though perceiving and appreciating the danger. In a twinkling the dead quiet on our deck gives place to bustle and stir. The quick, sharp orders through the deck-officer's trumpet, the shrill pipe of the boatswain's mate's whistle, the rattle of running rigging, the top-men and sail-loosers springing up the ratlines, and in a flash the rover is under a cloud of light-kites and studding-sails, and you realize the magic of the manoeuvre. The wild beast is making his spring. Before the trade-gale the two racers are rushing, feeling "the thrill of life along the keel." Now a flash, lighting up the race-course, a BOOM! and a screech of the rifle-shell; the chase luffs up, and shivers her canvas in the strong breeze—a tremor of surrender and despair. No wonder Jack has become a revelation of quick and methodical motion. Without boast, just now the Alabama's hearties have no equals in ship-manoeuvres. But he is a cheerful fellow under it—indeed, enjoys it to the point of physical exhaustion, as preferable to otherwise languishing under *ennui;* nor does he fail to keep in mind a prospect of fresh grub possibly from the stranger, prize-money, and the inevitable—"All hands splice the main-brace!" Now it is quiet again. The *Alabama* is disrobed to close reefs, the prisoners under guard in the "waist," the burning ship in the distance lighting up the lea and sky, a beacon of warning to the close-hunted foe; the watch again coiled up under the weather bulwarks, snug in their pea-jackets, the insatiate rover stealing along to a next victim. No chance for stagnant blood in this. A wild western hunting-ground offers no more excitement than this promenade of commerce for the next few weeks. The caravans of merchant-traders, passing this narrow belt of ocean travel, bound both north and south, to the United States and Europe, the Pacific, East Indies, China, and Japan, had reason enough for surmise and conjecture in the long line of wreckage encountered day by day—a puzzle doubtless to the mass of them, as there had been no severe weather to propose a solution of the unusual sight. Frequently many hours' labor was required in the effort to reach certain articles of cargo required in one or more departments of our vessel, necessitating the throwing overboard of a heterogeneous mass of boxes, bales, and casks. Could some rascally *North Sea* or *Hatteras* wrecker have these scenes presented to him in a dream, he would awake from a nightmare of grief that such valuable plunder should float so free and far from his rapacious grasp.

A novel but interesting sight it is to watch the curious faces of all hands as the skipper of a detained vessel emerges from the *Alabama*'s cabin. It is the question whether a bonfire or otherwise is the result of the legal examination just completed below. You are not kept long in suspense. Simply note that the skipper, minus his ship's papers, with downcast eyes and lugubrious countenance, saunters aft, and the tale is told. And now our boats leave the side for the work of breaking out cargo, and securing articles manifested on the prize for which requisitions have been filled out. Sometimes, as the boats return after many hours of hard labor, the squeal of pigs and cackle of fowls strike the ear, and the sight of hampers of potatoes and onions the eye; then, not only Jack all smiles, bustles about to "whip" them over the side, but ward room and steerage descend from their dignity, and, with jokes and commendations, reward the returned purveyors. More importance, for the time being, is attached to the improved condition of the commissary than to the prize-money secured by the capture. The one is practical and tangible, the other in the dim future. You may rest assured all thoughts, fore and aft, tend towards the next meal. It would require a phethoric pocketbook to purchase any fellow's seat at table or mess-cloth for the next day or two. We have by this time learned also in what latitudes to look for these windfalls. In cruising off the Brazils an inward or outward bound East Indiaman will never satisfy your cravings for fresh grub. You must find a purveyor from some near port.

We are by this time in the "middle of the road"; and a British vessel passing, bound to London, her captain was induced for a consideration to take our prisoners to port. Paroling them, they were transferred to the barque. Perhaps the reader would like an insight into the *modus operandi* of getting rid of a lot of prisoners, and troubling our English cousins with their care. The inducement is, first ample rations for the prisoners to tide over even an unusually long passage, with the addition of sundry barrels of salt beef and pork, equal perhaps in value to half a year's pay to her captain. Sometimes it takes a chronometer to tempt the skipper's cupidity. This is the bait thrown out; and as it is a personal matter between the two captains, the owners have no cause to protest or claim any share of the reward. You will see that the *Alabama* is equal to any emergency. Being thrown on his own resources, Semmes has often to work "Tom Cox's traverse" in getting rid of his prisoners.

Our vessel is to-day in an uproar of excitement—the capture and burning of a prize is but a calm to it. Johnny Raw happened under the lee of the mainsail, and, being caught in the eddy, was dashed in the sea to leeward. He was a poor sailor at swimming, and was "making bad weather" of it. A request from a boat's crew is complied with, the maintopsail hove to the mast, a boat lowered, and Johnny is brought on board wet, cold, and shivering, and forlorn looking indeed. But we must introduce you to the subject of this stir up. "Johnny Raw" is a bird, raw by name, but not otherwise; he has outlived on board our ship the appropriate cognomen allowed at the time of his first rescue, for his late associations have made him a rascal. Johnny reached our quarter-boat at sea one lucky morning (for him) in an exhausted state, wing-weary and starved, and was taken in and cared for by Jack. The poor orphan soon "came about and got his sea-legs on." A great pet he was, black as a raven, about the size of a field lark, and with a noble carriage. Johnny had a most remarkable gait, hopping, both legs together rapidly, and with giant leaps. He would cover several feet at each hop. When the boatswain and mates piped to dinner he recognized the call, was the first on hand, and moving over the mess-cloths, helped himself to the choice bits, wandering from mess to mess, and disputing with the mess-cooks. He was literally like the marine soger, in "everybody's mess." Johnny soon recovers from the present exciting adventure, and returns to his piratical expeditions to the mess-cloths. To complete his history, now we have been obliged to begin it, he did not survive the cruise, eventually meeting his fate by being blown to leeward in a gale of wind.

We are now jogging along towards the equator—weather good, with a clear horizon, enabling the "mast-head" to see what is to be seen. But strange to say only a few vessels appear. We have boarded one American ship, the *Bethiah Thayer;* but she had to be bonded, her cargo being all neutral and non-contraband. To illustrate the constant danger of being run down by passing vessels, "lying to" as we now are, under only topsails, across the path of travel. Near midnight in the first watch, the writer having the deck, and standing on the horse-block beating the rail with his trumpet for want of something better to do, the outlook sang out, "Sail ho! close aboard!" We were on opposite tacks. As rapidly as thought the sail has passed astern, so near it looked "as though you could throw a biscuit on board." She was under full sail, and bowling along at a lively rate. In a jiffy the reefs are shaken out, helm put up, and soon we are under full sail. The hound is after the fox. As a matter of course the chase is a long one,—all stern chases are,—but the *Alabama* has her seven-league boots on, and time at last is called. Getting within gun range, she answers to the warning of a blank cartridge, gracefully luffing to the breeze, and lays her maintopsail "to the mast." Reader, it is a beautiful sight,—that of a gallant ship, her light-kites spread to the breeze, and careening under the press of canvas, dashing the spray from her cutwater, as a noble steed the foam from his curb. The writer would involuntarily be reminded of the flutter of a bird brought wounded to the ground by the shot of the sportsman, as at the report of our gun the spilt sails flutter in the breeze. She proves upon being boarded the American ship *Punjaub*. Her cargo is neutral (guano). She is released on bond, and the *Alabama* again under low sail saunters along. We have run, you will say, many miles out of our way, and wasted time. But no! any way is our way, so "it's in the road." We are as likely to make a haul here as at the spot left at midnight. We are now in the "doldrums," approaching the equator, light airs and calms, with frequent and heavy tropical showers. The officers and men are paddling about the decks in bare feet, indulging in a fresh water corn-soak, and the stewards and mess-boys filling the officers' wash-tubs preparatory to the luxury of a bath of a sort not to be had every day. Our condenser supplies commonly the fresh water used; but the allowance is just one gallon per day, *per capita,* and deducting the portion needed for the cook's use, but little is left for drinking purposes and ablutions. One reason for this economy of water is the possible danger of accident to the condenser, in which case we should have only enough to last to the nearest port.

During this drift in the light airs and currents, our worthy and thoughtful boatswain has improvised a bathhouse for officers and crew, a safe asylum from that aggressive hunter, the shark. From the lower studding-sailboom, rigged out, Mecaskey has spread a large square sail, sunk some feet under the surface of the water, and kept beneath by solid shot in the centre, the foot, head, and leach of the sail triced up, forming a huge bag. In this contrivance you may sport in comfort and safety, and it is no slight luxury under this scorching tropical sun.

Two vessels of the enemy's fleet have drifted to us, or rather we have drifted together in the light airs,—the ship *Morning Star* and the schooner *Kingfisher*. The first is released on bond, cargo being neutral and non-contraband of war; the latter, a whaling schooner, is condemned and burned. In the meantime we are busy enough boarding vessels, but nearly all neutrals. Evans is constantly aloft, at one moment nearly drowned by a passing torrent of rain, and anon scorched by the blazing sun. And though it is a post of duty which none other of us would like to fill under present conditions, I verily think Evans likes it. It possesses the same excitement that hunting the ostrich on the desert plain does to the African sports-man.

On March 23, about on the "line," we fired the whaling schooner *Kingfisher* at nightfall, an equatorial rain and thunder storm of unusual severity prevailing at the time. The little craft, though oil-soaked, blazed by fits and starts. In the lull of passing rain-squalls, the flames would shoot mast-head high, seeming to play at hide-and-seek with the vivid lightning, anon shrinking beneath a drenching shower, leaving nature to keep up the pyrotechnic display,—a weird-like spectacle. To the returning boarding party, the *Alabama,* hove-to in wait, silhouetted in sharp outline against the horizon, lay pictured, "a painted ship upon a painted ocean." A wilder scene it would be difficult to imagine, and one of the many of our cruise offering a fine chance for the artist's brush. We are constantly, just now, on the *qui vive* for an enemy's cruiser. The belt of ocean travel is very narrow at this latitude; and our beacon fires are daily and nightly lighting up the waste and sky for at least half its width, inviting a clash if we are destined to have one.

The boarding work is quite arduous. Our scout reports many American rigs among the vast fleet drifting lazily in the light variable airs, and the boats are kept constantly at work overhauling and examining. Where transfer papers occur, and they are quite frequent now, the master of the suspect is *requested* (we cannot *order*) to take his papers to the "court-room" (our ship); so far a mere form. They are invariably found to be correct. So Evans is exonerated, and struts to the main-rigging bound aloft for another investigation. We are finding transferred ships plentiful. Rain! rain! rain! We are paddling in it all day, and give us time, we shall become web-footed. However, it is equatorial weather, and, to be frank, we have no good clothes on to spoil in wet; Jack is making himself comfortable in raiment washed in fresh water, free from the sticky and clammy feeling which is the inevitable result of salt water scrubbing. We now approach two ships singled out by Evans as American. We soon come up with them under increased sail. They are the *Charles Hill* and *Nora*. Both proving lawful prizes, their crews are removed, and vessels fired. We received a welcome addition to our crew-list from these latter vessels—nine men.

It is interesting and significant to note the zeal with which our crew enter into the task of gathering recruits from the prisoners. Nor is the motive altogether a patriotic or unselfish one. Our men have realized that a full complement means much less labor to themselves, to say nothing of the security of a full-manned battery. Observe a group of stalwart, lithe, and active North Country and English sailor-prisoners, lounging in the lee-gangway.

Our "hearties," enjoying the after-dinner pipe, have insinuated themselves in their midst. We are still short of men. Semmes and Kell are aft in deep consultation over the group forward, anxious and impatient to have them step to the "mainmast" and request an interview. It would be beneath Semmes's dignity to take the initiative. Casting their eyes forward, they take in the situation. They know our self-constituted shipping-masters are plying all their arts and wiles to secure these halting, hesitating adventurers. Kell telegraphs Semmes a significant look and smile, as much as to say, "Those lads of ours are steering it O. K."; and they part— our captain to his cabin and international law, the first "luff" to his daily round of duties. Now stray forward, and take a stand near the hunters of men and their game. It is easy to guess the line of persuasion and seduction that is employed to secure the services of these picked sailor lads. The items are most alluring,—double pay, *in gold;* generous rations; tobacco *ad libitum;* grog twice a day and in generous quantity; prospective prize-money; and last, but not least, kind and sympathetic officers over them. The bid has been made. Our worthies of the lee-scuppers are lost in revery. They are thinking of the character attached to this lone rover by her enemy (pirate), what might be their fate if captured, and of other consequences of casting off home protection by the act of enlistment. There is an ominous silence on the group for a while. Our men have thoughtfully and judiciously retired to their several tasks, leaving them untrammelled. All at once a concerted move is made for the mainmast, the captain and first "luff" sent for, and shortly the interview is over, and we have secured half a dozen splendid specimens of old Neptune's bantlings. The very danger of the venture has appealed to their instincts; and the romance of the situation, fully as much as other considerations, has captured them, hearts and hands. Jack's very soul loves daring and adventure.

We have for the first time our full complement of men; and take them all round, they are as select and competent a lot as could be picked from the crew of any English man-of-war. Just now some of them need a thorough course of drill at the great guns and at other exercises; but as we shall buckle down to this daily, they will soon be up to the standard. Besides, we usually find in every batch of recruits some who have served in one or the other of the navies, and their former experience at the gunnery-schools enables them to materially assist the officer of division in the training of the "raws."

Our middies are having a circus to-day with their sextants. We happen to be crossing the equator in company with the sun (it is March 29, 1863). It is rather funny to watch them shifting about from point to point, now on the quarter-deck, and then on the forecastle, trying to fathom the unusual behavior of the chariot of Phoebus, which seems for a second time to have fallen into the hands of inexperience (which is in a sense true enough this time). They are in a state of great perplexity, and furtively watch the writer until he turns to the captain at his side with the unusual report, "About twelve o'clock, sir—no latitude—about on the equator, sir." This time there is no calculating to be done, no altitude to calculate from. The young gentlemen avoid each other's eyes as they gravely put up their instruments, and then saunter off to mess-quarters without handing in their reports. Something has dawned upon them, but they are sedulously careful not to invite sympathy.

We are still about helpless, under sail, with the lightest of zephyrs drawing, now from S. E. and anon N. E., then breathless calm with a saturation of solar fervency that is almost intolerable, relieved by a sudden forming of the blackest of clouds, and a down-pour of rain such as the dweller in regions of moderate evaporation has no conception of. A rain that in ten minutes floods the decks so that the swash of the torrent as we roll on the gentle swell would be dangerous to life and limb if the side-ports were not left open to facilitate its escape. In the meantime one is constantly kept in remembrance of Mother Goose's pathetic ballad,—

"The maid was in the garden
Hanging out the clothes,"

for from mast to mast and from all convenient points stretches a web of clothes-lines laden with Jack's *annual* wash. His clothes-bag and his person are for the present, at least, immaculate.

But presently a sail drifts in sight, and Evans, between showers, pronounces her American. A boat is lowered, and an officer sent to board her. She cannot escape, and elbow-grease is cheaper than coal. But could we only have guessed the character of this vessel's cargo, the *Alabama* might very economically have used up her whole remaining stock of fuel to get alongside. She was shortly reported to be the *Louisa Hatch* from Cardiff to the East Indies, and a lawful prize. She had all the coal we needed, and tons to spare; and it was the very quality we preferred, being nearly smokeless, not likely to attract the attention of our prey when out of our sight, and free from the dust and smut which we disliked so much on our decks. We are bound just now to the Island of Fernando de Naronha off the coast of Brazil, where we expect to meet our old transport the *Agrippina*. It will be remembered that we relieved her of her cargo of coals at the Arcas some time since, and sent her back to report to Capt. Bulloch for another load. But we have always felt doubts of Capt. McQueen. He has the Scotch vices, with a very sparing allowance of the Scotch virtues, especially those of loyalty and temperance; and many indications have led us to suspect that honor would not weigh much with him if the interests of McQueen happened to fall into the wrong scale. As he did not keep his engagement with us at Naronha, we were particularly pleased to be rid of him under circumstances so satisfactory. He might have sold us to the enemy's cruisers had the opportunity come in his way. We afterward learned that he sold our coal for his own account on the way to join us. It is therefore hardly needful to add that he took good care to keep out of our possible vicinity during the rest of the cruise.

Necessity very often compelled us to repose confidence where there was considerably less than a perfectly trustful feeling in our own breasts to warrant it. We have as a rule been agreeably disappointed to find so many, not to the manor born, so faithful to their pledges to our struggling young Republic. It is to the credit of human nature that the instances in which we were betrayed were so few; and it is curious, almost to the extent of the marvellous, unless we may say that it was providential, how systematically we were saved from disastrous and even unpleasant consequences as a result of them.

In the "doldrums" we have little trouble in keeping company with the *Hatch*. Her officers and crew are transferred to our decks, and a prize-crew put on board. So for some days we continue boxing about, meeting with no further luck in the way of captures. At last Semmes appears to be tired of it, and as we have "coal to burn," clews up the useless canvas, and puts her for the coast under steam, with the *Hatch* in tow. The run is uneventful. On the 9th of April, 1863, we are at anchor under the lee of the Island of Fernando de Naronha, our prize-transport alongside, and we proceed to open communications with the governor. We have now been just eight months in commission.

Winfield Scott Schley (not to be confused with general-in-chief Winfield Scott, the hero of the War of 1812, Mexican War, and stolid warhorse of the Union forces) had a naval career that literally spanned the entire second half of the nineteenth century, which he detailed in his memoir, Forty-five Years Under the Flag, *published in 1904.*

Like the other naval stars of the Union, he, too, served under Farragut in the Gulf.

Excerpt from
Forty-five Years Under the Flag

BY WINFIELD SCOTT SCHLEY

Chapter II.

The voyage home from Cape Town was begun in March, 1861. The beautiful weather and smooth seas of the trade-wind regions of the southern and northern hemispheres for a vessel of the *Niagara's* size and tonnage were anticipated with pleasure, for under such circumstances a quick trip was possible. We made good headway each day throughout the passage. Approaching our own waters, however, there was a noticeable absence of ships where formerly they were to be met with in great numbers. This occasioned much speculation among officers and men where the cleavage of sentiment was distinct on the issues of those days. But there was no soul on board that great ship whose heart did not devoutly hope that some common ground had been found upon which both sections could and would stand on the paramount issues of those dark days in our history.

Boston was reached in early May, and Cape Cod, as usual, was veiled in fog through which the ship proceeded at slow speed. Our aim had been to reach Boston Bay on Sunday, for the reason that the sailors of that period believed there was generally a southerly wind in Boston Bay on Sunday. With the wearing on of the day the fog lifted, and the welcome sight of a pilot-boat gladdened our hearts. It was not long before the pilot came on board with the pockets of his pea-jacket stuffed with papers. Dolliver was his name. In view of the conversation which followed his arrival on board, neither his name nor the news he brought to our anxious ship's company could ever be forgotten.

As Dolliver approached the ship the officers and men, hungry for news, instinctively moved toward the gangway. There was an impressive silence. As he stepped over the side the captain's anxiety was so great that he, too, was drawn toward this gangway, which was very unusual in those days. His first inquiry was:

"Pilot: what is the news?"

For a moment Dolliver seemed astonished, and certainly looked so. He asked before replying:

"Captain, where have you come from?"

The captain answered, "From Hong Kong."

Dolliver queried again before answering:

"And you ain't heard anything at all?"

"No," said the captain, "not a word, pilot."

Dolliver's answer to this was in terms so memorable and so dramatic that its bluntness in words can be excused. He was telling to us as "news" things that were old to him, when he said:

"Why, captain, the country is all busted to hell!"

It is not easy at this time to describe the emotions of those to whom this portentous news came for the first time. There was hardly a dry eye in that thrilled multitude. Old Glory was flying at the peak, and almost every head was uncovered and bowed in homage to the symbol of our free land and sweet home. Resolves were immediately made by all who had heard Dolliver's thunderbolt. As the ship sped on to Boston the dreadful news of what had taken place at Fort Pickens, at Fort Sumter, at the Norfolk Navy-Yard, the firing on the Sixth Massachusetts in Baltimore, the call for 75,000 men and other exciting incidents had been culled from the papers Dolliver brought.

As is usual in times of great excitement, rumor had preceded the *Niagara's* arrival. It was said and believed that the Southern officers on board intended to seize the vessel and carry her into one of the Southern ports. On shore the excitement was intense, so that it was with some peril that people attempted to ascertain what had happened in the year of absence to those near and dear to them in other parts of our country. Preparations had been made by some irresponsible people looking to the sinking of schooners in the channel near Nix's Mate to prevent supposed threats by Southern officers being carried out. Nobody had once considered how perilous to the city the presence of the *Niagara* in the harbor was, or how readily she could have destroyed Boston had the rumor of the disaffection of her officers been true.

The Government at Washington, however, in order to know who was on its side, had decided as each ship arrived from abroad and was recalled from foreign service, to apply the test of a new oath of allegiance. This was done with the *Niagara's* officers and men in Boston Harbor. Some eight or nine officers and several men refused to renew their fealty to the old flag and were dismissed from the Navy.

The writer was from Maryland. Before subscribing to the paper which was to record anew his fealty to the flag, sufficient time was asked to read the document carefully. This done, there was no hesitation in renewing his adhesion to the old flag. When this decision was announced to Commodore McKean in his cabin, the writer by chance looked up through a windsail hatchway leading to the deck above, and there the folds of Old Glory were seen in the sunlight gracefully unfolding its beauty to a soft and gentle breeze. The writer was standing directly under it, declaring the most sacred decision of his life to his Commander.

The writer did not go on shore for any purpose at Boston, nor did he know until the ship reached New York, a few days afterward, anything of his family. The telegraph lines had been cut south of Philadelphia, the railroad bridges burned and other interruptions to travel and transportation had occurred. As soon as these were repaired and communication was again established, letters came from home and from friends, relatives and sweethearts. One from the writer's dear old father comforted him much, for it counseled him to take the step he had already done, and to devote his life to the country that Washington had given the best years of his life to win and sanctify for his countrymen.

Chapter III.

WITH FARRAGUT IN THE GULF—ORDERED TO VERA CRUZ.

1861–1862

The *Niagara* was ordered to New York, where stores, coal and ammunition were taken to her full capacity and a few needed repairs made to boilers, engines and pumps. The orders received there at first contemplated the defence of the gateway to the capital by placing the *Niagara* off Annapolis. One or two members of the famous Seventh Regiment of New York, left behind when that excellent regiment had gone to the front, came on board for passage. But the necessity of establishing the blockade of Charleston under the President's proclamation being regarded as paramount, the *Niagara* proceeded off Charleston, and on May 12th established the blockade of that port.

In the old days of sail Charleston was a great cotton port, and the offing was filled with vessels bound in and out. Under the law of blockade, the *Niagara's* duty on arriving before the port was to board all vessels bound in and to indorse the fact of the blockade of the port on the ship's papers and to warn them off the coast. A very busy day was spent in doing this duty on arrival, as the *Niagara* was the only ship on the station. The great desire of some of the masters bound inward to communicate by signal their arrival to agents in Charleston emboldened some to attempt to do this after having been boarded and warned off; or, when the *Niagara* had steamed some distance north or south to overhaul others bound in, occasional attempts were made by others to gain entrance, although they had been already warned. A shell across their bows generally reminded such masters that it was dangerous to continue.

One vessel, however, the *General Parkhill,* whose master was a skilful navigator, and a courageous Marylander, persisted, after being warned, in the attempt to run the blockade anyhow, and but for the fact that the wind was light he might have succeeded. One or two shots were fired across his bow and one over his vessel. It was realized that his ship was in great danger, so he concluded to haul his wind and head off shore, but it cost him the capture of his ship. The writer, then a young midshipman, was detailed, with a prize-crew of twelve men, to take the *General Parkhill* to Philadelphia. The master, the first and second mates, as well as the crew, were left on board. After taking charge of the *Parkhill* a thorough search of the ship was made for arms or explosives without result. The first search made had secured everything with which injury might be done to themselves or to others.

The fact was discovered, however, that the vessel was without American colors and that her master had determined to force the blockade if he found that to be possible on reaching the offing of the port. A large Confederate flag, found on board, indicated the master's sympathy with the Confederacy and explained his determined action in attempting to gain the harbor entrance before his vessel should be overtaken.

It was decided from the outset of the voyage to Philadelphia to employ the prize-crew, armed, on deck at the wheel and in handling the rigging and as guards and sentries, and to employ the ship's crew aloft and in handling the sails. This arrangement safeguarded the ship from recapture, which was further provided against by confining the officers to their rooms under armed guard. Against this latter expedient the master protested, though ineffectually, until after the ship had reached Delaware Bay and was taken in tow by the tug *America,* bound for

Philadelphia, where she arrived about the last week in May and dropped anchor off the old Navy-Yard, then commanded by Captain S. F. Dupont, to whom the orders given to the writer had directed him to report.

This vessel was the first square-rigged prize captured during the Civil War. There was, at this early period of operations, some confusion and uncertainty about the forms of law governing prize cases and the legal methods of dealing with vessels so indicted. Feeling ran high with the tap of drums, the tramp of troops moving to the front, and the enthusiasm of loyal attachment to the Union, all of which suggested the thought, at times expressed in the press, that masters and crews of such vessels ought to be classed as pirates. This idea, however, soon vanished as the number of captures increased and the dockets of the courts of admiralty were filled with cases. It caused a number of uncomfortable hours to those whom the laws of war had brought before the courts, and some anxiety to those who had to search the records of our earlier wars for precedents. It ended, however, in releasing the crews after taking their evidence and examining the logbooks or other papers of the ship, and in holding the ship and cargo only under condemnation and sale.

These forms having been observed by Marshal Millward of the District of Pennsylvania, to whom the ship had been delivered in due process of law and precedent, the writer was detached and ordered to the *Keystone State,* Captain Gustavus Scott commanding. Before she could be fitted out orders detaching the writer were received, and a short leave of absence was allowed. This time was passed in Frederick with his family and friends. In July following the writer was promoted to the grade of Acting Master and ordered to the frigate *Potomac* as navigating officer. On August 31, 1861, he was promoted to master in the line of promotion. The *Potomac* was fitting out in New York. The captain was an officer of high character and a valiant Virginian, Levin M. Powell. The needs occasioned by a large increase of ships, officers and men were met by purchasing everything in the open market that could turn a wheel or hoist a sail. The need of officers and men was supplied from the large number of those in the merchant service that were thrown out of employment.

As the white wings of our commerce in those days were seen on every sea, the nation availed itself of this resource from which to draw many skilled officers and men to its service; and it can be said that scores of these good sailors rendered incalculable service to the Navy in its great work for the country during four long, weary years of blockading the coasts and reducing the fortified places on them, from Cape Hatteras to the Rio Grande. The history of this meritorious service, with its experiences, its hardships, its privations and its unceasing perils, will live forever in the song and verse of a grateful people.

A number of these gentlemen were appointed to the *Potomac*. They were good and experienced sailors and ready in learning the drills, discipline and routine of the Navy. They served with merit and distincton until the war ended, when they returned to their former calling in the merchant service.

The *Potomac*, with an excellent crew of officers and men, sailed in August, 1861, bound for the Western Gulf blockading squadron, then commanded by Commodore McKean. Soon after her arrival Flag-Officer D. G. Farragut was assigned to this important command. It was surprising in those days to observe how accurately the men knew and gauged their officers. It often happened in the long hours of a watch that the deck officer would consult with the quartermasters, always old and experienced seamen, about the weather or matters touching the qualities of the ship, etc. In one of these confidences James Barney, an old and competent quartermaster, said that "the men for'd had heard that the commodore (McKean) was ill and had to be sent home." Almost immediately he volunteered the suggestion that if he had anything to do about it, he "would pick out Cap'n Davy Farragut" to take his place. He added that if "Davy Farragut" came down there, "it wouldn't be long till the fur was a-flying." Captain Farragut did come down to relieve Commodore McKean, and Barney's predictions were verified in a short time afterward, for Farragut showed himself, in all that followed, to be one of the greatest and grandest of American captains.

The *Potomac*, on reaching the station, was assigned to the blockade of Pensacola, and was present on the occasion of an attack upon Colonel "Billy Wilson's" regiment in camp outside Fort Pickens by a force of Confederates landed during the night on Santa Rosa Island. A piece of artillery and a company of blue jackets from the *Potomac* were landed, under the writer's command, to the eastward of the Confederates to cut them off. This hastened the abandonment of the island by the Confederates, who had been roughly handled by Fort Pickens and Wilson's regiment combined.

When Flag-Officer Farragut joined his command in the Gulf, the *Potomac* had been attached to the blockade off Mobile. Her position was in the main channel, about four miles from Sand Island Lighthouse, where she lay at anchor for several months. It was wondered often, as she lay helpless in calms, why the Confederate steamers did not venture out for a shot or two with their longer range artillery. It was a fact at that time that the *Potomac's* battery consisted of long 32s and 8-inch smooth-bore shell guns, with two 20-pound Parrott rifles. But as this fact was not known to the Confederates, the *Potomac* lay undisturbed or unchallenged, except by winds and waves, which now and then gave the old ship many an uncomfortable night during this long vigil.

From time to time the monotony of blockade duty was broken by some vessel attempting to elude the squadron's vigilance. The excitement of chasing or that of advancing to attack any unfortunate vessel that had run aground under the guns of Fort Morgan, relieved some of the tedious hours of this wearing duty.

As the war grew apace, vessel after vessel arrived to reinforce those guarding the entrance to Mobile Bay until the fleet contained from twelve to fifteen vessels, the larger proportion being steamers. The custom was to mask all lights at night and to take up the night position after sundown nearer the beach or closer in to the channels, and just before daylight to drop off shore out of range. Many unsuspecting blockade runners ran into the web thus woven.

On the night of December 26, 1861, a schooner bound out before a fine northerly wind was forced ashore under the guns of Fort Morgan and was discovered at daylight. Signal was made at once to the *Water Witch*, Commander A. K. Hughes, commanding, to go in and destroy her, if possible. The writer asked authority to go in the *Water Witch* with two boats for any duty Commander Hughes might require. As the *Water Witch* closed in on this schooner, using her rifled gun, the guns of Fort Morgan took up the gauge and returned the fire with a long range gun, assisted by another gun east of the fort. Though many projectiles struck near the boats and the *Water Witch,* many others passing over and beyond them, neither was struck. When a point had been reached where the shoal water prevented the *Water Witch* from approaching nearer to the schooner, the boats were manned and a dash made for the vessel, but before they could reach her neighborhood her crew set fire to and abandoned her near Fort Morgan. The *Water Witch,* as well as the boats, remained in the neighborhood of the schooner under fire for quite near an hour, until she was completely destroyed. A number of shells landed very near the boats, but none was accurately enough aimed to strike.

The object of the commanding officer having been fully accomplished, the *Water Witch* and boats withdrew. This was the first instance in which the writer had ever been under fire. The sound of projectiles whistling over the vessel or boats was an entirely novel sensation. The jets of water thrown into the air as the shells struck the surface might have been more beautiful under other circumstances, but the greater danger as they came nearer and nearer suggested that the boats turned bows on to the fort presented a smaller target, and thus minimized the chances of hits; and so this experience proved of value then.

In the month of January following (1862), a brig was discovered by the steamer *R. R. Cuyler,* Commander Francis Winslow, near the beach, some twelve miles to the eastward. Not long after the *Cuyler* had reached this brig's locality, heavy firing of guns was heard. The senior officer present in command called the *Huntsville,* within hail, to direct her to proceed to the *Cuyler's* assistance, as that vessel was some miles away and out of signal distance. The writer requested permission to accompany the *Huntsville* with two boats armed for near service. It proved later that these boats were of much service to the *Cuyler's* commander. On nearing the *Cuyler* she was found lying stern to the beach, distant some 250 yards, disabled by the parting of a hawser which her own boats had carried to the brig to pull her off the beach. In parting, the end of the hawser whipped back, was then taken up by her propeller, and a number of turns were taken around its hub, between the propeller and stern-post, completely bringing her engines up. At the same time her two boats were broadside on to the beach in a light surf, with all hands in them wounded save one or two by the rifle fire of the coast guard.

As the assisting boats approached the *Cuyler* to report for orders, her gallant commander hailed the officer in charge, stating that he would not order anyone in under such a fire, as all hands in his own boats were probably killed; but if the boat officer would secure the boats from the surf near the beach he would perform an eminently important public service. A dash was made at once through this fire from the coast guard defending the prize, though not without some loss, a sergeant of marines, the coxswain and one or two men in the assisting boats being wounded. The *Cuyler's* boats were rescued with their dead and wounded, and, though riddled with bullets, were towed back to the *Cuyler,* much to the gratification of her noble commander, who complimented the service highly.

Reaching the deck, Commander Winslow was found on the quarter-deck, and though under heavy musketry fire from the riflemen on the beach, received the report of the rescue of his boats. He remained until the officers of his ship had cleared the propeller by using a cutting spade from a boat under the *Cuyler's* stern, this boat being protected by the boats from the *Potomac* and the battery of the *Huntsville,* Commander Cicero Price. The second hawser from the *Cuyler* was carried to the prize by the *Potomac's* boats, and toward sundown the prize was pulled off the beach and captured. The assisting boats, with the *Cuyler* and *Huntsville,* returned to the blockade off Mobile about 8 P.M., and the wounded men of the *Potomac's* boats were cared for most tenderly. The prize proved to be the brig *Wilder*.

In the decree of the prize court afterward, at New York, through some error made on board the *Potomac* or in transmitting the prize list, the writer's name and those of the assisting crews were omitted, so that although this capture had been made possible by the work of the *Potomac's* boats, they did not participate in the proceeds of the prize.

For some weeks this dreary and wearisome blockade was maintained. The lack of exercise and nutritious food was felt by officer and man, and scurvy, that dreaded pest of ship-life in the olden times, was only avoided by the occasional relief which came to them afterward from the steamers bringing supplies of fresh meats and vegetables in amounts about enough for two or three days. The diet for the rest of the month was composed mainly of salted meats, cheese, hard bread, bad butter, inferior coffee and positively bad tea. It is indeed a wonder that the efficiency of the personnel was maintained at all under such conditions.

In the early part of 1862 news reached the squadrons blockading our coasts that a large fleet, consisting of English, French and Spanish war vessels, with a division of the French army, had descended upon Vera Cruz, Mexico, with the ostensible purpose of collecting debts due to the subjects of each of those countries from Mexican merchants. The *Potomac* was selected to proceed to Vera Cruz to ascertain the purpose of this expedition, as far as that might be possible, on the spot.

On her way to Vera Cruz the *Potomac* looked in at Pass à l'Outre, one of the several mouths of the Mississippi River, to inquire from the *Vincennes* the circumstances of the death of Lieutenant Samuel Marcy, who had recently been transferred from the *Potomac* to the command of the *Vincennes*. Marcy had been killed some days before in a boat attack upon a vessel attempting to force the blockade. After this information had been obtained, the *Potomac* proceeded on to South-West Pass to fill her tanks with water. While doing this, she was attacked by a river steamer, which was driven off after firing about a half-hour.

Vera Cruz was reached early in February. A large fleet of English, French and Spanish war vessels was found anchored in the harbor. Among them were such vessels as the line-of-battle ship *Donegal, Imperieuse, Guerriere,* and many others of smaller class. The combined forces were commanded by such distinguished officers as Commodore Dunlop, Admiral Graviere, Marshal Prim and General Lorenzes. Preliminary to the inquiry into the purposes of such a fleet in adjacent waters, the customary salutes and courtesies were exchanged with the several commanders.

Chapter IV.

MEXICO, MOBILE AND PORT HUDSON.

1862–1863

As Captain Powell's instructions were to ascertain the purposes of such an overwhelming fleet so near our coasts, frequent visits were made by him to the several chiefs in command. At some of these consultations the writer was present, and he recalls distinctly the appearance and bearing of Lorenzes, Graviere, Dunlop, and particularly that of Marshal Prim. Commodore Dunlop and Marshal Prim were frank in assurances of the purposes of their Governments. The latter was explicit in stating that his Government had no intention to occupy the territory of Mexico with any ulterior purpose. He declared, with emphasis, that if his Government had had other purposes it would not have selected him, who was known to be hostile to such occupation from every point of view. These assurances were faithfully and honorably kept, for as soon as the English and Spanish commanders received official assurances that all claims due from Mexico to the subjects of their respective countries would be paid, the forces of these two countries were withdrawn from Mexico.

Commander Dunlop expressed pleasure that the *Potomac* had come to Vera Cruz. He admitted, however, that he had confidently expected, in ten days after his arrival at Vera Cruz, to have had his squadron in operation against ours; but he frankly stated that his Government had no other intention than to enforce the collection of honorable debts in Mexico, and when that had been accomplished the English would withdraw, as they did soon after this assurance was given.

The French officers, however, could give no definite assurances, as they professed to be unfamiliar with the purposes of their Emperor after a satisfactory arrangement of the debt question had been reached. They were invariably courteous at every interview. The ultimate action of the French Government is known, but, as it forms no part of these memoirs, will not be discussed.

During the month of February yellow fever made its appearance at Vera Cruz and among the allied forces, several cases occurring on board their ships. Permission was asked by the allies and granted by the Mexican authorities to move their forces beyond the first line of defence as far as the high land about Orizaba, to avoid the disastrous spread and ravages of this dread disease. Toward the last of February the French forces moved toward Orizaba, and were followed in turn by the English and Spanish. The city of Vera Cruz was then guarded by the sailors from the fleet, although the Mexican flag was hoisted over San Juan d'Ulloa and the city itself.

The history of events subsequently culminating in the establishment of Maximilian as Emperor, his overthrow, capture and execution by the Mexican Government in 1866, closed an incident that had been full of menace to this country and must otherwise have involved it in war beyond all doubt or peradventure sooner or later.

During the month of May the *Potomac* had returned to Pensacola, via Key West. The old ship, after an ordinary lifetime of service on the coasts of most of the countries of the world, had succumbed to the battle of wind and wave. Strain and work in heavy seas, under the weight of heavy batteries, had weakened her fastenings, and she was "laid up" as a store-ship in Pensacola Harbor, which had fallen into our hands a few months before.

The various officers were detached, as well as the greater part of the crew, for service in the different vessels of the West Gulf Squadron, then commanded by the indomitable David Glasgow Farragut, whose name will live in history among the greatest captains.

In July, 1862, the writer was promoted to the grade of lieutenant, and later was detached from the *Potomac* and ordered to the steam gunboat *Winona* as executive officer. Being then in his twenty-third year, the writer was filled with the new responsibilities of this higher position, and they were assumed with much misgiving lest he might fall short of its requirements.

It was not long after reporting on board the *Winona* that official action had to be taken against the commanding officer. It was a most painful experience, but the circumstances were such that it was unavoidable, and all the more disagreeable as it concerned a commanding officer whom he admired and esteemed for his many excellent qualities of heart and mind as well as for his high manhood and courage.

This occurred in the manner to be described. For a week before the new executive officer had joined the *Winona,* her gallant commander had gone in several times and opened fire with her heaviest guns on the sea face of Fort Morgan. After the writer had joined the ship, the same operation being once or twice repeated, a respectful complaint was made to the executive officer by one or two of the other officers, to the effect that while the crew were ready at all times to fight, they did not think their lives ought to be jeopardized when no advantage could accrue therefrom. As the fort was hardly within reach of the *Winona's* guns, while she was well within the range of one or two of the rifle guns of the fort, the position taken appeared reasonable and was referred to the commanding officer only to discover that he was on the verge of delirium. The surgeon of the ship was directed to examine him and report in writing his opinion of his condition. His report confirmed the executive officer's opinion.

For a day or two about this time the weather was boisterous, so that communication between the ships was not possible by boat. On the night of the 23d the heavy sea tested the *Winona* severely. On the 24th the wind and sea abated sufficiently for the executive officer to proceed to the senior officer's ship to report all the facts. Commander Alden relieved the *Winona's* commanding officer in the order which follows:

U.S. STEAMER, *Richmond,*
Off MOBILE, September 24, 1862.

SIR: From your report, as well as that of Asst. Surgeon Mathewson, it is clearly established that your Commanding Officer, Lt. Commander

Thornton, is laboring under a fit of "delirium tremens," and is thereby rendered unfit for duty.

You will, therefore, assume command of the *Winona,* and place him under such restraint as may be necessary to prevent him injuring himself or others.

Respectfully, your obedient servant,

JAMES ALDEN,
Commander and Sen. Officer, Prest.

Lt. W. SCOTT SCHLEY,
Lt. and Executive Officer,
U. S. Gunboat *Winona.*

Oral orders were received at the same time, owing to injuries sustained during the gale, to proceed to Pensacola to report the ship's condition to Admiral Farragut. This incident led to the court-martial of the commanding officer, whom Alden had relieved in the order quoted above, which culminated in dismissing this officer from the squadron. It was a great blow to a gallant fellow, and removed him from opportunities to distinguish himself for a time at least; but, notwithstanding this, before taking his departure from the *Winona* to go north, he was generous enough to tell the writer he had done his whole duty in the matter, and that if he had done less he (the commanding officer) could have had no respect for him.

There was no feeling but of regret and respect in the parting. In the *Kearsarge,* two years later, this splendid officer won imperishable glory for his country and his name. "Peace to his memory" is the tribute of one who honored, respected and admired him, but who pitied the occasional infirmity which brought him a moment of sorrow.

It was believed that service in the Mississippi River, where the *Winona* would not be exposed to the heavy strains of rolling as in blockading outside, would lessen her leak, there being no dock available south of Norfolk for repairs. She was ordered, therefore, into the river for patrol duty between Port Hudson and Donaldsonville, early in December, 1862, where she remained, with varying incidents, for more than a year.

Not long after her arrival on this service rumors reached the admiral that the Confederates were fortifying the heights about Port Hudson with heavy cannon. An expedition to reconnoiter this position, composed of the iron-clad steamer *Essex* and the *Winona,* set out up the river from Baton Rouge in December. It must be borne in mind that the ships were without charts of the river, and had to depend upon Colton's Atlas and the river pilots, whose loyalty at that early day was a debatable question. Running the river, therefore, was limited to daylight, when its bends could be followed and its points avoided. During the night anchorage was sought. The rule generally adopted was to anchor about sundown and, after dark, to shift position some half mile. The vessels were painted an indefinable gray color, the tint being such that it was not easy to distinguish them after nightfall. This had to be done to avoid the harassing fire of riflemen or at times of field guns.

The new commander, who had been ordered to take the place of the old commander, did not observe all these precautions in making a reconnaissance of the fortifications reported to be in course of erection at Port Hudson. In company with the iron-clad steamer *Essex,* the *Winona* came to anchor abreast of the north end of Profit Island, about three miles below Port Hudson, about sundown of December 15th. After dark it was suggested to the commander to shift berth further up the river, but for some reason unknown this precaution was disregarded. The writer, who was executive officer, in turning in for the night, gave orders to be called at the first streak of daylight, and, in undressing, placed his clothes so that, in jumping from his bunk, he would almost literally jump into his clothes.

The Confederates had crossed the river from Port Hudson during the night with a battery of artillery and a supporting company of infantry, and had taken up position behind the levee, out of sight and hearing, abreast of the *Winona*. At the first streak of dawn of the day following, these forces opened a furious fire with artillery and infantry upon the *Winona,* distant about 250 yards from the levee. It was the noise of this firing that awoke the writer, who was on deck in much less time than it takes to narrate the incident. The ship was, customarily, always cleared for action, with guns loaded, cable ready for slipping, steam at sufficient pressure to respond to signals for movement from the officer of the deck, and a watch on deck at the guns. The lapse of time from the first shot from the levee and that from the *Winona's* battery was scarcely to be estimated in seconds, the fire was so rapidly replied to.

In order to be entirely free to choose the most advantageous position to attack these forces, the cable was slipped at once. Apprehending the danger of running aground, the writer jumped to the gangway, got a cast of the lead, and was in the act of getting another when Master's Mate David Vincent approached, saying:

"You have more important work to attend to, and I will take the lead, sir, until the pilot comes on deck."

Scarcely had the writer stepped aside to hand the lead to Mr. Vincent in order to take charge of the deck to direct the fighting, when Mr. Vincent fell at his side, mortally wounded by an artillery shell. Aid was called to carry his body below to the surgeon, and quick directions were given to the helmsman. A few moments afterward the ship touched and hung for some moments upon a bar which, the pilot declared, had formed quite recently off the northwest side of Profit Island.

Unfortunately, in her position only one gun could bear upon the enemy's battery, and for ten or fifteen minutes this disadvantage continued, while a storm of projectiles from artillery and musketry swept the ship. The chief engineer was directed to let steam run up to the highest safe pressure and then to open her engines wide astern. After a few moments the *Winona* glided off into deeper water. She then steamed ahead to straighten up with head to the current. She took her position abreast the battery and for an hour poured her heaviest fire into the enemy's position, driving his forces from the field with considerable loss, notwithstanding they were behind the levee. Several of the larger 11-inch shells pierced the levee a few feet below the top and exploded among the artillery, causing much consternation and loss.

This action continued spirited and fierce for an hour and a half at a range of less than 300 yards. The casualties on our side were few, and when the advantage in the enemy's favor for at least fifteen minutes is considered, this was astonishing. As a rule, the Southern gunners were good shots, and in many instances were trained in the same school and had grown up under the same discipline and fellowship with ourselves in *ante-bellum* days.

The *Winona* was damaged seriously enough, however, to make necessary a trip to New Orleans for repairs. When these were completed she resumed her patrol up the river, where she was almost daily exposed to attack from guerrillas or other irregular bands of soldiers at several points. It was in this river service that the importance of the military top of modern war-ships was first made apparent. During the season of low water it was possible to command a view over the levees only from the top aloft, and to do this a lookout was stationed there to give information of the presence or movement of men behind them. To protect these lookouts from rifle fire at those points of the river where the channel obliged the ships to approach within a hundred feet or so of the bank, resort was had to plates of boiler iron so shaped that the lookout in the top was completely protected. Very often the first intimation the vessels had that danger was near was the bullet sound striking these crude military tops and the lookout's reply from his own rifle, always loaded and ready for such contingencies.

A point of menace was the bend at Manchac, below Baton Rouge, and it was rare to pass it day or night, before the capture of Baton Rouge, without being fired on by what we learned to call the river guerrillas. Another point lower down the river and below Donaldsonville, known to us as Winchester, was the scene of many attacks of greater or less formidability and sometimes of most stubborn attacks from infantry and artillery combined. Indeed there was hardly a day, from the capture of New Orleans to the fall of Port Hudson, on July 9, 1863, when the Mississippi River, from its confluence with the Ohio to the sea, was not the scene at some point of stubborn fights between the various ships in this patrol service and batteries of artillery, with infantry guards, or with both combined, in contesting the right to its sovereignty. At this distance of time it is not easy to recall the indifference which prevailed in the minds of all day after day, as they grew in experience and broadened under danger, when one never knew, from sunrise to sunset, whether his turn might not come to take his place alongside the great hosts who had already fallen that this nation of the free might live; but it was a strain and trial to the young man which was to fit him into the heroic mold of those great captains whose examples were to be imitated in the future struggles of this great Republic.

During the months of January and February of 1863 rumors in one shape or another reached the patrol squadron that Admiral Farragut contemplated a movement against Port Hudson, Louisiana, as the strong fortifications at that place had interrupted access to points beyond as far as Vicksburg. Whatever repairs to engines or boilers or their appurtenances could be effected by the force on board were undertaken, for in those days of war a ship's efficiency for every emergency was determined by the skill of her engine and fire room forces.

So far as spars and sails were concerned, these had been landed before beginning the river campaign, as it was easily recognized then that such things were impedimenta, useful in working a passage to far-off stations when the vessels had to pass through regions where the winds were of regular direction and force, but absolutely useless in war, where the likelihood of injury from shot and shell would make them a positive menace. It was recognized at that time that this necessary expedient in war was only the preliminary step to the mastless and sailless ship of this day. Every precaution then employed to minimize the danger from falling spars or the chances of disabling engines through fouling propellers from rigging shot away in action and trailing astern, was an argument for the supremacy of steam alone in the actions of the future. Out of these conditions grew the battleship and armored cruiser of this day, wherein spars are reduced in size and number and retained only as a means of signaling or for torpedo guns, but stripped of all unnecessary rigging. The close actions of those days emphasized, likewise, the employment of breech-loading guns, and out of this experience the modern high-power breech-loading artillery was evolved, together with the rapid-fire guns of smaller caliber so destructive to the personnel at the superstructure guns.

During the months of January, February and a part of March, 1863, the *Winona* was doing patrol and convoy duty from Donaldsonville to Port Hudson.

Many vessels carrying troops and supplies to various points on the river required the protection of the gunboats against attacks along its banks. A company of our cavalry, about this time, under the intrepid Captain Perkins, operated on both banks of the river, and was a terror to all irregular troops using the levees as protection in their attacks. His movements from side to side were so swift and his crossings being made usually under cover of darkness, the enemy could not know his whereabouts until he was actually upon them. The effect of these operations after a while tended to clear the river banks of danger.

In the early part of March, while lying off Plaquamine making imperative repairs to the condenser, which leaked so badly as to increase the coal consumption greatly as well as to endanger feed pumps and the engines themselves, the fleet, under Admiral Farragut, passed up the river with the purpose of attacking the works at Port Hudson, which at this time had been strongly fortified. Orders, on March 12th, from Admiral Farragut, detaching the writer from the *Winona* to report for further orders, were received on the afternoon of the 14th. The only opportunity to obey these orders occurred on the morning of March 15th, when the coal brig *Horace Boies,* in tow, passed up the river. The squadron was reached off Port Hudson that same afternoon.

The same day the writer was ordered to assume command of the *Monongahela,* as the relief of Captain McKinstry, who had been severely wounded. The same afternoon an attack was made by the *Monongahela* upon the citadel battery at 1,000 yards range for more than an hour with the splendid effect of completely silencing guns and driving gunners from them. But during the night the main work was repaired, and the *Monongahela* was directed to take position once more near this battery. On this occasion her 150-pound Parrott rifles were fired deliberately and with great precision against this fortification until its guns were silenced. A river steamer, lying at the time at a wharf further up in the bend of the river, was driven to shelter out of range behind the point. Many of the enemy's shot and shell passed well over and beyond the ship and many fell short. The accuracy of the *Monongahela's* gunners evidently had disturbed the usual precision of the Confederate guns.

These attacks upon earthworks by ships only proved that it was hardly possible to injure them beyond what could be repaired in a few hours.

Chapter V.

SIEGE AND CAPITULATION OF PORT HUDSON—
FARRAGUT AGAIN.

1863

On March 19th Major-General Banks, commander of the Nineteenth Army Corps, came up the river with a few troops, and with Commander Alden of the *Richmond* went on board the *Monongahela* to reconnoiter the batteries along the river front. On this occasion another river steamer was lying at the wharf in the bend of the river discharging provisions and other supplies, but fled a few moments after the firing began. The *Monongahela* took a position that afforded the best examination of these works, though it was not without challenge from the Confederates. In those days it was the custom, as soon as the ships got within range of their guns, for the batteries to open fire upon them. The accuracy of the gun-fire on both sides was remarkable, but when the shore batteries were on the same level as the ships, or even a little above, the result was almost invariably that the ship's guns drove the shore gunners away from their guns. The level decks of ships favored quicker handling of guns. After this time, supplies were delivered with difficulty to the beleaguered forts by boats on the river, and, if at all, had to be delivered at night, as these river boats would be attacked by day.

After an hour or more of this reconnaissance, the *Monongahela* took a position where General Banks desired, but she was always under the fire of the batteries, to which her guns replied with good effect. When these shore batteries discontinued their practice, the *Monongahela* withdrew and assumed her anchorage below with the other ships of the fleet, just beyond the range of their guns.

On the following day the *Monongahela* and *Genesee*, Commander McComb, again took position at a point from 1,200 to 1,300 yards from the same batteries. Assisted by the iron-clad *Essex*, Commander Caldwell, these three ships maintained for an hour or more a fierce and determined engagement, during which every gun on the river front in range took part, fairly raining projectiles upon the ships. Fortunately, the gun-fire from this combined force of ships was so tremendous as to interfere seriously with the rapidity and accuracy of the guns on shore.

The fleet of mortar schooners, which had done much good work under Admiral D. D. Porter at the attack upon Forts Jackson and St. Philip, in the campaign against New Orleans by Admiral Farragut, were again placed in position on the left bank of the river, and in every attack made from this time until July 9th, when Port Hudson finally capitulated, joined their terrifying fire to that of the other vessels upon the besieged forces within this strongly fortified and gallantly defended post. After General Banks had invested these fortifications on the land side with his splendid corps, the plan adopted by the commanders-in-chief was to harass the enemy day and night.

Faithfully and fully did the forces on the river and those on the land side in the enemy's rear carry this plan into execution. During the day one or two or more vessels were detached to assault the river batteries in front in cooperation with attacks of greater or less fierceness by the army beleaguering the works. The roar of artillery and musketry appeared continuous for well-nigh three months night and day.

Choosing different hours every night of the siege, the mortar fleet, consisting of some eight or ten vessels, were directed to hurl their enormous 13-inch shells for an hour into the enemy's works. The effect of these great shells in curving through the air at high-angle firing, as their burning fuses turned in ever-varying directions, was picturesque and impressive. Through long practice, the officers and men acquired great nicety in cutting and timing their fuses, so that the bursting moment would coincide with that of landing in or about the batteries. These terrific night cannonades were demoralizing features to the enemy in this long siege. The continuous roar and reverberation of discharges were almost deafening, and generally awoke all from sleep below decks, and thus attracted them to the upper or spar deck to watch the whirling shells as they curved upward in their flight and then downward upon the doomed fellows within the enemy's works. By long experience great accuracy of fire was attained and much damage done inside the works. The moral effect of this bombardment nightly was so great that the enemy within the zone of this fire resorted to bomb-proofs, tunneled into the declivities of hills inclined away from the direction of the trajectory of the shells.

After the surrender there were a number of touching incidents related where these great shells had fallen in such proximity to the points of exit of these bomb-proof tunnels that when the explosions occurred these retreats were completely filled with earth, thus suffocating and burying those who had sought safety therein.

On one occasion later, when in temporary command, an attack was made by the writer upon the citadel fortifications. There was almost no breeze beyond an occasional "catspaw," as slight, shimmering streaks of air touching the surface of water are technically known. The signal flags hung listlessly up and down from the flag-ship's mast-heads. The great volume of smoke from our guns, as well as that from the fortifications, settled down upon the river or hung in masses about the ship, increasing the difficulty of distinguishing, much less reading, any signals. In the midst of flying projectiles and smoke, the quartermaster reported a signal flying, but he added that he was unable to read it, as there was not wind enough to blow the flags out so that he could distinguish them.

Directions were given to him to report whenever the signals could be read. As the orders had been to destroy the battery, it was not thought that the signal then flying could refer to us, as our duty under them was specific and distinct. Later, however, it was learned that the signal was intended to withdraw us from action. Not understanding this at the moment, the action was continued until every gun of the enemy had ceased firing. Then the ship lifted her anchor and dropped down with the current to her usual position, where, after anchoring, the customary visit was made to the commander-in-chief to report the result of the combat. Arriving on board, the writer found on the quarter-deck the commander-in-chief, who, after responding to his salute, said:

"Captain, you begin early in your life to disobey orders. Did you not see the signal flying for near an hour to withdraw from action?"

The decided manner and tone in which Admiral Farragut asked this question, taken with the surprising inquiry itself, confused and embarrassed the writer, who felt that the ship's work was creditable rather than censurable. An attempt to explain, somewhat stammeringly made and to the effect that we could not read the signals, which were seen only with difficulty through the smoke, elicited the quick reply from the admiral that he "wanted none of this Nelson business in his squadron about not seeing signals."

The writer succeeded, however, in stating to him that the lack of wind and the smoke of battle enveloping the ship made it impossible to interpret the signal, which, from the nature of his orders to destroy the citadel, could hardly have been supposed to refer to the writer, whose duty in the premises seemed clear—to retire only when that duty was done.

The admiral then invited the writer into his cabin. The moment the door was closed behind him there was an entire change in his tone and manner as he said smilingly, "I have censured you, sir, on the quarter-deck for what appeared to be a disregard of my orders. I desire now to commend you and your officers and men for doing what you believed right under the circumstances. Do it again whenever in your judgment it is necessary to carry out your conception of duty. Will you take a glass of wine, sir!"

The writer, in his career afterward, often recalled this incident in his experience with that great admiral and grand man. He has always believed that the secret of all important success was dependence upon the responsible judgment of an officer on the spot. If circumstances compelled him to disobey his orders to achieve signal success for his country, such constructive disobedience becomes a virtue in much the same sense as the great Jarvis held as a virtue Nelson's unerring judgment in that memorable victory at St. Vincent.

The *Monongahela's* commanding officer, Captain J. P. McKinstry, having been so seriously wounded in the attack by the fleet upon Port Hudson, was sent to the hospital at New Orleans. The steam sloop *Mississippi* having been destroyed in the same action, her commanding officer, Captain Melancthon Smith, and her executive officer, Lieutenant (now admiral) George Dewey, were ordered to the *Monongahela*. The writer was then transferred to the sloop *Richmond* toward the latter part of March.

From this time until Port Hudson surrendered, on July 9th, there occurred twenty or more engagements between the vessels of the fleet and batteries in which the writer participated. The plan decided upon was to harass the enemy day and night. With General Banks's army encircling them on the land side, and with the Navy in possession of the river above and below the forts, the siege was varied by brilliant assaults by both Army and Navy. It became a question of endurance and of supplies for those within the doomed fortifications. Both opponents continued, often with stubborn courage, in the struggles for mastery of the place, and in the years to come the deeds of valor exhibited on both sides around those historic works will thrill the hearts of American readers. It was only when the forces within were decimated and ragged, their ammunition almost exhausted and their rations reduced to mule meat, that the noble fellows surrendered. The courage displayed on both sides should be a priceless heritage of honor to American youth for all time.

On the 27th of May communication was opened with the army on the bluffs below Port Hudson, and the cordon around the fortifications was completed. Almost daily there had been fierce fights, which resulted in driving the enemy inside the battlements built around a ravine back of the port, where the river in some remote time had passed in another channel.

During the first week in June a battery of two 9-inch Dahlgren guns, with their crews and equipments, was landed and placed in position about 300 yards from the right of the enemy's works. These guns, cooperating with the heavy siege artillery of the army, did splendid work under Lieutenant Commanding Edward Terry of the *Richmond,* an officer of rare accomplishments and dashing courage. Some casualties resulted to the crews of these guns from the peerless sharpshooters on the other side, who rarely missed anyone who thoughtlessly exposed himself. Terry's health gave way under the trying exposures on shore with this battery, and it is thought that from this unusually severe ordeal the seeds of that fell disease were laid which carried him off a few years later in the fulness of his young life.

Some time about the latter part of May dispatches from General C. C. Augur related the cheering successes of General Grant's army operating in the rear of Vicksburg. The city of Jackson had been taken. Sherman had routed and almost destroyed the army of General J. E. Johnston. General Banks's army was daily in movement and almost constantly in fights or in the skirmishes tightening the cordon about Port Hudson.

An incident which occurred on the morning of July 4th and astonished everyone was the news of the battle of Gettysburg, communicated by two "contrabands," as the colored man was called in those days. They were taken on board about daylight. When asked their names and what news they brought, one of them replied:

"Massa Lee has struck the Yankees at a place called Guttumburg—I think that's the name. But, oh, Lord! the Yankees done tore 'em all to pieces. The white folks say he done lost some fohty thousand men. Gen'ral Lee had to get away in the night, as the Yankees was all 'round him."

This news was verified a day or two later, as the battle of Gettysburg, with the added intelligence, by steamer down the river, that General Grant had captured Vicksburg, with some forty thousand prisoners, after a series of brilliant and stubborn battles, which will rank with the fiercest ever fought in the world's history. Only a few days later, after this news had been sent in to the gallant General Gardner, the hero of Port Hudson, that stronghold was surrendered and added to the crowning victories of the year 1863. The great river was then in our possession from Cairo to the sea, and never again did it witness any struggle of consequence in disputing free passage to our transports or fleet.

The great dream of Admiral Farragut was realized. The stomach of the Confederacy had been severed from the main body of its force. The fact was made evident that an army could not fight unless it could be fed. The effect upon the waning fortunes of the doomed Confederacy was felt from the Potomac to the Mississippi.

It was during this long siege that the writer first met Major Agnus, who afterward, for gallantry in action, became brigadier-general. He was then a handsome and dashing young officer in the volunteer army, which did such yeoman service for our country and its glories. The rations of those days, while sustaining to life, depended for their nutritive value somewhat upon the additions which foraging parties might make to them from the country where the armies operated. The Navy being in this respect better provided for and more certain to have three good meals a day, because its commissary stores were always carried in the hold of its ships, had advantages which our Army friends from time to time were invited to share. Major Agnus was the writer's guest whenever he came on board, and from this association and companionship grew the friendship and affection which have increased with every year of the forty since it first began. Friendships which spring from associations of exposure to dangers together endure always, and thus was born that feeling which the writer has tried to express in this humble tribute to his lifelong friend and comrade in arms.

During this long and laborious siege there were incidents of heroism on both sides which deserve to be preserved, but none more daring or more original than that of Mr. E. C. Gabaudan, the admiral's secretary. At the time both sides of the river were controlled by Confederate forces, between the *Hartford* and *Albatross* above the forts and the fleet below. The admiral desired to send dispatches to the fleet below the forts of such importance that their capture would have been likely in any attempt to go by the west bank. Gabaudan volunteered to float down the river after dark, supported on one of the many floating logs, or parts of trees, which then dotted the river in the spring flood.

The distance to be covered was several miles. The dangers were in the eddies under the bluffs and the possible lack of endurance on the part of the swimmer for so long a period in rather cold water. Fortunately, the night chosen was very dark, but Gabaudan's mettle had the finest ring. What he may have lacked in physique was more than made up by the "sand" in his splendid determination. He was successful, after a long drift, including a swish now and then in the eddies under the bluffs of Port Hudson, from which he escaped by hanging close to his log and using his unengaged hand to paddle into the current down the river. Favored by the darkness, and with an unusual presence of mind, he escaped discovery by the pickets, who, in one instance, were so near that Gabaudan heard them conversing. He reached the squadron below about 4 A.M., after several hours of exposure. When he was taken from the water and brought on board the senior officer's ship he was much exhausted and greatly fatigued. The doctor, however, took him in charge and in good time restored him. The news of his safe arrival was signaled back across the point from the *Richmond* to the *Hartford* above at daylight.

During the progress of this long and tedious siege the writer saw and was much in the presence of Admiral Farragut. As the admiral in his younger days had known the writer's family, he spoke often of the delightful visits he had made to Middletown and Frederick, and how much he had enjoyed the generous hospitality of the good people there.

The admiral was a man of perhaps five feet seven inches in height. His gait and step were those of a very young man, and in conversation he was an animated and interesting talker. His information and experience were general, and upon almost all subjects—professional, scientific or political—he was interesting and attractive. Like all great men, he was affable and accessible. His manner was one of great mildness and self-poise. His ideas were clear and his methods of doing things were always decided. When he had made up his mind to give battle in a certain way, it was realized that his way was the best. In any of the emergencies of battle his towering genius was readiest and his cool self-possession was an inspiration to everybody.

The wide difference that was apparent between this sprightly, kind, mild and pleasing gentleman, even when under a heavy load of responsibility, and his lion-like character and presence when battle was going on, was the contrast between sunshine and storm. His judgment of men was excellent, as the choice of officers with whom he surrounded himself indicated. The unvarying and complete success he met in everything he undertook in that great war was due largely to his strong personality, unerring purpose and dashing example.

The naval history of the past presents two characters that were much alike in their restless activity, their untiring energy of purpose, their absolute personal intrepidity and self-poise in emergency, and their dogged adherence to the idea that the enemy was to be fought wherever met—Farragut and Nelson. Farragut's private life and high ideals, however, gave him preeminence over his great English compeer.

After the surrender of Port Hudson there was considerable detail of forces to be arranged both on the land and the river. Most of the vessels had been injured so much in service and battle during this period of nearly a year and a half, that orders were given to send the heavier ships North for repairs. In this interval of time the officers and men enjoyed some relief from the strain and exposure to which their long service had subjected them.

The *Richmond* bore quite a large number of honorable scars, the repairing of which could not be deferred longer. The same was true of many others, but as there was lack of facilities at New Orleans and Pensacola for making the extensive overhauling needed, and no docks existed for examining injuries under the water-line, several of the larger ships were sent to New York, where the *Richmond* arrived on the 8th of August, 1863.

Chapter VI.

IN SOUTH AND CENTRAL AMERICA.

1864–1866

On August 18, 1863, while the *Richmond* was in New York, the writer was detached and granted one month's leave of absence. The opportunity afforded by this short respite from duty was improved in order to marry his fiancée, Annie Rebecca Franklin, of Annapolis. This occurred in the midst of war, but as the betrothal had existed a couple of years, both parties had had ample time to test themselves by absence, separation, change of circumstance and a lapse of time which had enabled them to feel certain they had made no mistake. The 10th day of September, 1863, was chosen to begin life together, which, in all the years since, has been one of happiness.

Their older years have been comforted in the three children who were born to them —two sons and one daughter. The oldest son, Thomas Franklin Schley, having chosen the profession of arms, is a captain in the Twenty-third U.S. Infantry and saw service in Manila during the recent war with Spain. The second son, Winfield Scott Schley, is a physician and surgeon, established in New York City. The daughter, Maria Virginia Schley, married the Hon. Ralph Montagu Stuart Wortley, a young English gentleman.

As only a few days of the leave granted remained after the wedding day, a trip to Washington was made, mainly with a view to ascertaining where the next service might be. The chief of ordnance, Captain H. A. Wise, with whom the writer had sailed on board the *Niagara* a couple of years before, was met in the corridor of the old Navy Department building. Captain Wise said it was difficult to get officers for any duty on shore beyond a few months owing to the demands for their services at sea, and that if the writer had no objection he would have him detailed for two or three months at the ordnance factory at the Washington Navy-Yard while his ship was refitting in New York. As the larger vessels of the squadron in which the writer had served were under repairs and there was little chance of further activities for a few months, the offer was accepted, and the orders of September 11th to this temporary duty were placed in his hands.

It was during this visit to the department, the first the writer had ever made, that he had the pleasure of seeing Secretary Welles. In those busy days there was not much time for more than formal politeness. The writer being then only a young lieutenant and sensitive to his own importance, left the Secretary's office under the impression that his reception had been polite, but nothing more. Later on in life, when demands on the Secretary's time and attention were better understood by association, as a bureau chief, the wonder was as great that the Secretary had time to be even polite to anyone during his office hours.

On the 23d of September the new duties at the Navy-Yard were taken up, and as greater familiarity with the work was acquired, greater interest was taken in its details. The natural ambition to lose no opportunity for active service, however, inspired apprehensions that, in the contemplated movements in the Gulf or at Charleston in the fall, by some mischance the writer might be overlooked. But just about the moment when enough courage had been worked up to inquire what the chances might be, and recalling the risk of scant politeness at the department, orders dated December 17, 1863, were received detailing the writer to the double-ender *Wateree,* at Philadelphia, Pa.

After the usual delays, however, the *Wateree,* under command of Commander Francis Key Murray, arrived at Hampton Roads and proceeded thence to Washington. A proclamation had been issued by the President allowing all the old "shell-backs" then serving in the Army to return to the Navy without detriment to their service. The *Wateree's* crew being a number short of her complement, she was delayed until a number of these men could be transferred from the Army. When these old sailors had reached the familiar deck of a man-of-war there was manifest satisfaction. One of these splendid fellows, and a typical seaman, William McGurr, who had served most of his life on board ship, was greatly delighted to get back home again.

When asked why, as an old sailor, he had enlisted in the Army, he replied that he "thought the chance of service on shore would improve his health," but he "had found great trouble in managing a team of mules he had been detailed to drive." The brutes "could not learn his language, and he had discovered he didn't know how to steer anything that had its rudder in front." For this reason he came back to the only service of the two which he knew.

During the month of March, 1864, the *Wateree* dropped down to Hampton Roads to await orders, which soon came, detailing her to service in the Pacific. Her construction was peculiar. She was known at that time as a "double-ender," which, interpreted, meant that her bow and stern were alike, with a rudder at each end. The idea prominent in the construction of this type was service in rivers, where the necessity for turning would be avoided. The draught of water was small and her engines were placed in the middle of the vessel. Her rig was that of a fore-and-aft schooner. The battery was very heavy for her size—about 1,000 tons displacement. Except for passages along the coast in weather that might be chosen, such vessels were in no sense very reliable for service generally. It may have been for this reason that some of these vessels were sent on such experimental voyages as that now directed for the *Wateree.*

Notwithstanding this, the *Wateree* got under way about the third week in March and reached St. Thomas, W. I., after a stormy voyage across the Gulf Stream, during which the high winds and rough seas did much damage to her forward guards, which were repaired in that port after some delay. During the passage it was evident to her commander that she did not possess the highest sea-going qualities of a cruiser. Her rolling was rapid and deep and, with moderate winds or in moderately rough seas, her decks were deluged with water, to the great discomfort of the crew. Her hull being of iron gave her a rigidity of frame that was her salvation in the still more boisterous weather met to the south of the Rio de la Plata and on the east coast of Patagonia, when on the passage to Valparaiso. The small coal-bunker capacity and the uncertain limit of steaming radius, which depended so entirely upon the wind and weather encountered in making a passage of great distance, were matters of continual anxiety to her commander, who realized that if the fuel should give out in traversing unfrequented routes, there would be small hope that her limited sail power could be relied upon to help her into port.

This unfortunate casualty did occur on the voyage of 3,000 miles from Montevideo, Uruguay, begun on May 9th and ending in the latter days of July in Valparaiso, Chile, causing a passage of some sixty-nine days. Notwithstanding a deckload of coal had been taken on board before leaving Montevideo to supplement that in the bunkers, yet the head winds and heavy seas encountered in this winter passage of the southern hemisphere were so frequent, though made through the Straits of Magellan and the inland passage as far as the Gulf of Peñas, that, soon after clearing the Gulf, the coal supply was found to be so short that the ship had to be brought to anchor under one of the wooded islands off the coast, where wood enough was cut to enable the vessel to steam across the open sea for some fifteen miles to reach the inshore passage of the Corcovado Gulf. This wood was so green and full of sap that it merely frittered away, making but little steam.

What has been said of the limited coal-bunker space applied as well to the hold of that vessel for storing provisions. There was a full supply to the hatches on leaving Montevideo, but as the voyage lengthened there was grave solicitude lest it also might fail. Rations were therefore reduced, as some of its elements were exhausted, such as coffee and flour; but as the tide rose and fell some fourteen feet, exposing at the lower level masses of mussels adhering to the rocks, quantities were gathered and steamed for each meal to help out the short rations. Rain and snow were almost constant with the prevailing westerly winds of that region. Naturally there was much discomfort to all hands, but nevertheless there were no complaints heard from anyone. Everyone worked with a will cutting wood to fill the bunkers or in making sails out of the awnings for the improvised yards that were to help on if wind should favor the ship.

A day of sunshine and fair wind came at last when we had finished the sail and filled the bunkers. With these favoring circumstances, the *Wateree* started for Castro, on the island of Chiloa, distant about 250 miles, and with good luck, thanks to the sail, reached an anchorage near that port just as the wind died out and the wood was almost exhausted.

While there was no coal to be had at this point, there was an abundance of dry wood, which the natives cut into cord-wood size, under the direction of an American living among them. There was no end of chickens, eggs, and potatoes, and upon these our men lived bountifully, providing themselves also for the trip to be made beyond.

Taking advantage of favoring circumstances, the *Wateree* got under way for Ancud by the inland passage through the Chacao Narrows, a channel all the more dangerous from the swift tideway and the uncertain surveys of that date. She reached Ancud after a few hours' run in safety. In those far-off days, in those out-of-the-way ports, supplies for ships were not always abundant. There was no coal to be had on shore, but the arrival of a coast steamer a day or two afterward enabled the *Wateree's* commander to borrow some five or six tons which, with the excellent dry wood purchased at Ancud, helped him to reach the port of Valdivia, where a small amount of coal-dust and dirt was secured at an exorbitant figure. With this the port of Lota, or Coronel, was reached. As this port was the center of Chile's coal-mining district, there was no further solicitude about fuel, most of the ports on the station being easily within the steaming radius of the ship.

In making this long voyage in tempestuous weather and rough seas, the severe strains on the great side-wheels of the *Wateree* loosened the radiating arms carrying the paddles so much that, when rolling, the projection of these paddles would strike the guards and shake the vessel from stem to stern. This caused much discomfort to those below decks day and night. It was the cause of serious anxiety to the commanding officer. This was remedied as soon as the facilities of the machine shops of Valparaiso could be employed.

At Valparaiso letters four or five months old were received, giving a *résumé* of all that had occurred since the departure from Hampton Roads. Among other news, the *Kearsarge's* triumph over the *Alabama* off Cherbourg was learned. News, too, that the *Shenandoah*, one of the Confederate privateers, was operating against American merchantmen in China and east of Japan was received.

This news in particular hastened the *Wateree's* repairs, and when these were finished she sailed northward, touching en route at Callao, Panama, San Juan del Sur, Acapulco, San Francisco and Mare Island, where she went into dock and underwent a more general refitting, including calking of decks, the condition of which, from the beginning, had been a source of much discomfort to all on board. After a sojourn of several months at the Yard and in the harbor of San Francisco, the commander-in-chief directed the *Wateree* to proceed to Panama, where there was customarily kept a war vessel to guard the passenger and freight traffic, which in those days before the completion of the transcontinental railways passed mainly by the isthmus route to and from California.

Chronic revolutionary disturbances in the Central American States induced the department to direct a war vessel to the scene of disturbances. The *Wateree*, having been relieved by the old sailing sloop-of-war Cyane, Commander John H. Russell, was soon under way for Punta Arenas, Costa Rica; San Juan del Sur and Realejo, Nicaragua. Realejo was reached in the latter part of April. The news of the assassination of President Lincoln was learned there from the President of Nicaragua, who, without ceremony, came off in person to convey this distressing intelligence to Commander Murray. The national flag was displayed at half-mast and a gun fired every half-hour until sundown as a mark of respect to the memory of this great American, who had perished at the hands of a madman and at a moment when his life and calm council were so much needed by his country.

Rumors of a revolution in San Salvador, soon afterward verified, reached Commander Murray, who proceeded with the *Wateree* to La Union, in the Bay of Fonseca. It was but a short time after her arrival that the revolutionary party was forced back upon La Union. In the custom-house of this port a large quantity of American property was held for shipment. Representations for its protection, made by the U. S. Consular representative to the revolutionary commander, led to the restriction of the consul's liberty to his residence upon certain trumped-up charges of sympathy with the legitimate government and of obstruction to the cause of the revolution.

The writer, with a company of men and a Gatling gun, was sent on shore to protect the consulate against violence, if that should be resorted to, and to require a written guaranty from the authority then in charge of the town that American property and citizens would be respected. Toward sundown fighting between the opposing forces began some distance outside the town and continued until after 9 P.M., when the Government forces, under General La Vega, had driven the revolutionists back to the Plaza, where from barricades they maintained a fierce contest for quite a half-hour, until nearly surrounded by the Government troops, when they fell back, breaking up into fragments in their flight to the water to escape.

Our force of sailors and marines took position in order of battle in front of the custom-house to protect the property therein, should any attempt be made to sack it by the retreating revolutionists or by the soldiers of the successful army, as sometimes happened. As the firing approached the Plaza, which was about two or three blocks distant from the position occupied by the *Wateree's* men, a reconnaissance was made to the nearest point of fighting for observation. As bullets began whizzing about the place selected, it was thought better to fall back upon the main body of the force so as to be ready for defence if the fighting should turn that way.

Fortunately, the captors appeared satisfied with driving the revolutionists from the Plaza, which they afterwards occupied. Their commanding general took measures at once to occupy the city and to maintain order until daylight. One of the important matters first to be attended to was to secure the custom-house, and this brought the general with an escort toward the position held by the *Wateree's* men.

As this motley squad approached it was halted. Demands were made by General La Vega to know whom this force represented and what its purpose was in invading the sovereign state of San Salvador. The writer, being fairly well acquainted with the Spanish idiom, explained that its purpose was to guard all American property in the custom-house and to obtain assurances that it would be protected. When that assurance was given the force would be withdrawn to the ship.

During this colloquy an interesting example of the American seaman's loyalty to his officers occurred. One of the men had moved to the writer's side while the colloquy was going on, with his repeating rifle cocked and ready, supposing the colloquy, which was maintained in elevated tones of voice, meant that the general was abusing the seaman's chief, and as he did so he said, sotto voce, "Just tell me, sir, at the right time, and I'll blow that big hat off him for you." When it was explained that arrangements were being made to take over the custom-house, he replied:

"Oh, I thought he was abusing and cussing you, sir, and I was going to stop that."

The assurance asked for having been accorded, the American force was withdrawn. On the way back to the ship the night was very dark. The water was literally dotted with men from the defeated army, who had waded some distance out to escape from their pursuers. These men begged pitifully to be taken on board ship, while others, more fortunate, had seized boats about the shore and had escaped on board. One of the boats overtaken contained General Dueñas, the revolutionary leader, who had been gravely wounded by several musket balls. He was accompanied by two or three officers, who implored the right of asylum under our flag to save their lives.

Returning on board to report, it was found that a number of women, children and soldiers had fled thither for safety. Some of the little ones were only a few months old. The officers vacated their apartments to the ladies and children.

Promptly on the morning following the ladies and children were landed, because assurance had been given by General La Vega that there would be no danger for them. He insisted, however, that the revolutionary leader, his officers and men, should be surrendered; but ominous reports of musketry firing coming from the shore a little after daylight that morning indicated unerringly that the prisoners taken the night before were being despatched in accordance with the brutal methods of that day. Commander Murray then peremptorily declined to give up the officers, and on the following day weighed anchor and proceeded to Realejo, Nicaragua.

The writer was despatched to Leon, some twenty-five miles in the interior, to arrange for landing the insurgent troops. The trip had to be made on the "hurricane deck of a mule," over a rough road and through some rather dense forest.

Although the start was made about 7 A.M., owing to the heat, the indolence of the guide and the pace of the mule, whose flanks and back were so callous that no amount of urging by spur or whip would hasten his gait out of a slow, shambling walk, Leon was reached about 4 P.M. on the same day. The ride was a hard one for a sailor unused to this sort of navigation, and the writer's condition when Leon was reached was such that a standing attitude for a day or two was much the most comfortable. Then there was that long ride back again to be thought of, and it was not comforting.

Fortunately there was diplomatic delay in the arrangements that gave time to recover from strains, blisters and some loss of epidermis. During this time the society of the American Minister and his family was much enjoyed. In the writer's intercourse with this gentleman, the wonder was that a man of his culture and refinement should have been assigned to a post so little in accord with his tastes and talents. Better acquaintance and a friendlier footing encouraged the writer to ask a question to that effect while waiting for the message which was to be carried back. The explanation has always been interesting, and was as follows:

"Why, it is easily explained. I wrote my friend, Mr. Lincoln, asking him for the position of Marshal of Nebraska, but I wrote such a devilish bad hand that he read it 'Minister to Nicaragua.' So here I am."

The written message was in time handed to the writer at the American Legation. It was sealed and the seal stamped with the great coat of arms of the Republic. In substance, it refused permission to land the officers, but granted the request as to private soldiers, provided they were disarmed and their arms turned over to the custom-house at Realejo.

The return to the ship was in all respects similar to the trip to Leon, but Commander Murray had anticipated the despatch by landing all the privates and handing their arms over to the customs authorities. General Dueñas and the officers were turned over to Captain Dow, who commanded an American steamer, plying on this coast from Panama, and were landed soon afterward at Panama.

The *Wateree's* officers and men, somewhat run down by their service of several months on this unhealthful and hot coast, proceeded southward to Panama, Callao, Chincha Islands and Valparaiso. While at the Chincha Islands, where a large fleet of American vessels were awaiting their turns to take in cargoes of guano, which was shipped in large quantities at this period to ports in Europe and America, a report was brought on board by one of the captains that the *Shenandoah* had been sighted off the island and apparently was coming in.

The squadron had been advised that she was in the Pacific and might make a descent upon the shipping at the Chincha Islands. While lying there, the *Wateree's* steam had been kept in such readiness that her engines could respond to signals in a few minutes. The anchor was weighed at once and Commander Murray proceeded to sea. Turning clear of the North Island, there, sure enough, two or three miles away, was a vessel resembling the *Shenandoah,* but with no colors flying. The *Wateree* was "cleared for action," with her crew at quarters, ready for the combat that all believed would end as gloriously as that of the *Kearsarge* and *Alabama.*

Not wishing to disclose the ship's nationality, Commander Murray delayed showing her colors until a position had been gained about six hundred yards from the supposed enemy. With every gun of the *Wateree's* heavy battery bearing upon her, Murray ran up the colors and gave the preparatory order, "Stand by!" Up went the stranger's colors coincidentally. They were Chilean, the ship being the Chilean corvette *Maipo.* Mutual explanations revealed the fact that the Chilean supposed the *Wateree* to be a vessel from Spain, with whom the country was then at war. The *Wateree's* black hull and straw-colored topsides favored that impression. A single gun fired by mistake at this moment would have resulted in a dreadful catastrophe.

During the night of January 25, 1866, a Peruvian officer came on board to report a formidable insurrection among the Chinese laborers, who had risen and killed the guards on the middle island of the group. The writer was ordered to take a force of seamen and marines to the point of disturbance and to establish order until the Peruvian forces from Pisco could arrive. A landing was effected near midnight on the quay at the north side of the island. Ascent to the top of the cliffs had to be made by a narrow stairway, leading straight up from the quay about one hundred feet to the top of the cliffs, which the Chinese held in force. Stones and other missiles were hurled upon the advancing column as it moved up this narrow stairway, but did not check its progress. Reaching the cliffs above, the American forces were deployed and opened fire upon the rioters, driving them back into a large gowdown, which they surrounded and commanded with their guns. The Chinese leader asked for a parley, which was granted, and resulted in the ultimatum that if any further attempt was made to disturb the peace, fire would be opened upon them. This determination they were obliged to accept, as the menacing attitude of the American forces around them indicated their readiness to carry out their plans.

On the following day a force of Peruvian infantry arrived. The situation was explained to the commander, and the American forces withdrew to their ship. After they had got aboard the ominous crack of musketry from the middle island suggested that summary vengeance was being dispensed to the ringleaders.

The *Wateree* returned to Panama, when the writer was detached and ordered home, where he arrived in the latter part of April, 1866.

Journals, Logs, Letters, Reports, and Articles

James Waddell commanded the commerce raider C.S.S. Shenandoah *(formerly the British vessel* The Sea King*) targeting Union ships primarily along the Pacific coast during the war until August of 1865 (four months after Lee's surrender at Appomattox Courthouse) when a British captain managed to finally convince him that the war was over—at which point he sailed directly to England, surrendering his ship, commission, and "booty" on November 6, 1865.*

His papers were included in The Official Records of the Union and Confederate Navies in the War of Rebellion, *which was published by the Government Printing Office in 1894, part of a massive cataloguing and organization drive commissioned by an act of Congress.*

Extracts from *The Official Records of the Union and Confederate Navies in the War of Rebellion*

ABSTRACT LOG OF C.S.S. *SHENANDOAH,* LIEUTENANT COMMANDING J.I. WADDELL, C.S. NAVY, COMMANDING.

OCTOBER 20, 1864–NOVEMBER 5, 1865.

October 20, 1864.—Having received everything from steamer *Laurel,* put ship in commission as C.S.S. *Shenandoah* and shipped twenty-three men as petty officers, seamen, firemen, etc. Weighed anchor at 2 P.M. and at 6 parted company with the *Laurel;* 6:15, stood under steam to the southwestward.

October 21.—Latitude 31° 17' 40" N., longitude 17° 53' W. From 4 to 8 A.M.: 5:30, got up steam and took in all sail. From 8 to meridian: All hands engaged in putting ship in order.

October 22.—From 8 to meridian: Mounted two 8-inch guns and one rifle, 32-pounder; Palma Islands bore at 3:30 P.M. S. by W. ½ W., 60 miles; mounted two 8-inch guns.

October 28.—At 1 P.M., got up steam and stood in chase of a ship; boarded her at 4. She proved to be an American-built ship, owned by British owners, named *Mogul,* of London.

October 30.—From meridian to 4 P.M.: Latitude 16° 47' N., longitude 26° 43' W.; in chase of a bark which, at 1 P.M., hoisted United States colors, when we hove her to by firing a blank cartridge and sent a boat on board, making a prize of her, she proving to be the bark *Alina,* of Searsport, from Newport (Wales) to Buenos Aires with railroad iron; engaged transferring prisoners, their luggage and stores, from prize remainder of watch. From 4 to 6 P.M.: Having received everything from prize, at 4:15 scuttled her, and at 4:45 she went down; at 5 filled away on our course. From 6 to 8 P.M.: Prisoners were secured in the forecastle; officers of prize, on parole, were put in different messes and allowed their liberty.

October 31.—From 8 to meridian: Shipped five men of the prize bark *Alina*'s crew as seamen and one as coal passer.

November 1.—In chase of a large ship; chase showed British colors, when we let steam go down and wore round to the southward.

November 2.—Estimated value of the bark *Alina* and cargo—vessel $50,000 and cargo $45,000.

November 3.—Released prisoners from irons, as they were paroled.

November 6.—At 5:55 A.M. started fires and stood in chase of a schooner. At 7:45 fired a gun, hove chase to, and sent a boat on board. From 8 to meridian: Chase proved to be the U.S. schooner *Charter Oak,* from Boston to San Francisco with general cargo; made a prize of her and engaged the rest of the watch in sending off her stores, etc., to our ship; received from her as prisoners her captain, two mates, four men, two ladies, and one boy; latitude 7° 35' N., longitude 27° 49' W. At 3 P.M., having finished with prize, set her on fire.

November 7.—From 4 to 8 A.M.: The mates of the two prizes, refusing to do their work, were confined in irons in the topgallant forecastle and their parole withdrawn; transferred other prisoners of war to the berth deck.

November 8.—From 4 to 8 A.M.: Made a sail on lee beam at 7, and made all possible sail in chase. From 8 to meridian: Cut away after part of forward house, rove new main braces, and got one gun run out in position; in chase of a bark. At 2 P.M. started engine and gave chase to a bark. At 2:20 she hoisted the United States flag; fired a blank cartridge, hove her to, and sent a boat on board. From 4 to 6: Chase proved to be the *D. Godfrey,* of and from Boston to Valparaiso, general cargo; made a prize of her; latitude 6° 28' 35" N., longitude 27° 6' W. (at noon). From 6 to 8 P.M.: Having received everything necessary from prize, and her officers and men (ten all told), at 6 set her on fire and went ahead on our course, letting steam go down and making sail to topgallant sails. Shipped five men from *D. Godfrey* as seamen and one as landsman. Shipped one man from *Alina* as landsman.

November 8.—Reeving new braces and getting guns in position.

This log has been kept in sea time; hereafter, by order, it will be kept in civil time.

November 9.—At 5:20 A.M. lowered screw and started engines; stood down toward Danish brig *Anna Jane;* spoke her and put on board the captains, mates, and two men from prize barks *Alina* and *Godfrey.* At 8:15 steamed ahead in chase of ship, which, at 11:30, proved to be the British ship *Royal Saxon,* of Sidney.

November 10.—At 5:30 A.M. set mainsail and came up with the hermaphrodite brig *Susan,* of New York, from Cardiff to Rio Grande. She hoisted the Yankee flag, when we fired two blank cartridges and hove her to; sent a boat on board and made a prize of her. At 7 commenced transferring stores. From 8 to meridian: Having finished taking stores from prize, scuttled her, and at 10:30 A.M. brig sank; received seven persons from prize; two men shipped as seamen and one boy.

November 11.—At 5 P.M. a large ship reported on weather beam; started fires, reduced sail. At 7 lowered screw, took in topsails, and steamed in chase. From 8 to midnight: Under steam in chase; made her out to be a six topsail yard ship and loaded the gun.

November 12.—At 12:15 A.M. fired a gun and hove chase to and boarded her. She proved to be the ship *Kate Prince,* of Portsmouth, N. H., but having a neutral cargo was bonded for $40,000; sent all prisoners on board for passage to Bahia, Brazil; latitude 1° 45' N., longitude 29° 22' W. At 12 P.M. came up with bark ahead, which proved [to be] the *Adelaide,* showing Buenos Aires colors; fired a blank cartridge and hove her to. Meridian to 4 P.M.: Boarded the bark and sent her captain to the *Shenandoah* with his papers. Having no bill of sale on board, condemned her as a prize and commenced to take such articles as we needed. At 3 P.M., having received positive information as to the ownership of vessel and cargo through private letters which were not brought on board by her master, but by an officer, released the vessel and bonded cargo. Ransomed the *Adelaide* in the sum of $24,000; commenced returning articles to her. At 5:30 finished returning effects to the *Adelaide,* and at 6 steamed ahead.

November 13.—At 1:45 P.M. got up steam, lowered screw, and started in chase. At 3:30 came up with her, when she proved to be the American schooner *Lizzie M. Stacey,* of Boston; hove her to by blank cartridge and boarded her. From 4 to 6 P.M.: Condemned schooner as a prize and took off her stores, etc.; at 4:30 hauled fires and hoisted propeller; at 6, having finished transferring stores, scuttled and fired the schooner.

December 4.—From 4 to 8 A.M.: Made sail and came up with and boarded the Sardinian ship *Dea del Mare,* from Genoa to Rangoon; two sails in sight; standing in chase of a bark; at 7:45 hauled off from the chase. At 11 made out the island of Tristan da Cunha. At 4:30 discovered a bark under easy sail on the lee beam;

braced and ran off in chase. At 5:40 came up with the chase and hoisted English colors, to which she replied with American; ran up the Confederate flag, braced the after yards aback, lowered a boat, and sent an officer aboard the bark, which proved to be the *Edward* (whaler), of New Bedford. From 6 to 8: Condemned the bark *Edward* and received all her crew on board; the captain was paroled and the mates and men confined in irons; received a quantity of rope from prize. Messrs. Bulloch and Minor were sent aboard of the prize to take charge of her for the night. Took from the captain £30 ship's money. Latitude 37° 47' S., longitude 12° 30' 30" W. (at noon).

December 5.—From 4 to 8 A.M.: Cleared away the port boat from on the bridge and got it slung to the davits; at 5 a.m. filled away and ran down to the prize; hove to on starboard tack to windward of prize, lowered the port boat, and sent it alongside of the prize in charge of the gunner; wore around to northward, passed close under lee of prize, hove to with maintopsail to the mast, prize on our port quarter. From 8 to meridian: Hove to near prize and received from her a quantity of provisions.

December 6.—Engaged transporting and stowing provisions and other things from prize. At 5:45 P.M. got under way, half speed. At 10:30 burning prize disappeared.

December 7.—Steaming for Tristan da Cunha. At 8 A.M. came up abreast of the settlement and hoisted our ensign; stopped our engine and got three whaleboats alongside to send the prisoners and their luggage on shore; gave the captain of the whaler back his quadrant, spyglass, and epitome; also 60 pounds tobacco, 2 boxes of coffee and 1 of soap. From 8 to meridian: Lying to in Falmouth Bay [island of Tristan da Cunha]. From meridian sent on shore 1,680 pounds of bread for maintenance of prisoners; landed also 4 barrels of pork and other prize provisions given in exchange for fresh provisions. At 3 took departure.

December 29.—From meridian to 4 P.M.: Bark astern of us, coming up on us; showed English colors; she hoisted American ensign; fired a blank cartridge, hove her to, and sent a boat alongside. From 4 to 6: Bark proved to be American vessel *Delphine,* of Bangor, from London to Akyab in ballast; made prize of her; engaged rest of watch receiving stores and her men. From 6 to 8: Received as prisoners of war her captain, two mates, steward, and eleven men; captain's wife, stewardess, and boy were brought on board, making eighteen all told. From 8 to midnight: Hove to near the prize, heading E. by N. to E. S. E.; received her instruments and some cabin stores on board; at 11:25 P.M. set fire to the bark; at 12 boat returned; hoisted her up, ran the gun out, and filled away. Shipped six men of the *Delphine*'s crew for the cruise and confined five of them in single irons; captain and mate signed their parole. Latitude 39° 13' S., longitude 68° 33' E.

January 17, 1865.—At daylight made a sail on the port bow; stood in chase, overhauled and boarded her. She proved to be the five topsail yard American built English ship *Nimrod,* from Plymouth to Port Adelaide [Australia], one hundred and two days out, with a cargo of dials. At the request of the boarding officer the captain of the *Nimrod* came on board with his papers. Having examined the papers, parted company with the ship. Latitude 39° 32' 14" S., longitude 122° 16' 52" E.

January 25.—From 4 to 8 A.M.: Made Cape Otway, Australia, one point on the port bow; at 5 standing along the coast for Port Phillip. At 1:45 steaming up the bay (Hobson's) in charge of a pilot. At 6:45 let go starboard anchor. At 7 Lieutenant Grimball was sent ashore to see the authorities; returned at 10.

January 26–February 17.—Repairing in Hobson's Bay, Australia.

February 18.—From 8 to meridian: Steaming out of Port Phillip Bay. At 1 p.m. discharged pilot. Forty-two men found on board; thirty-six shipped as sailors and six enlisted as marines.

March 24.—Commenced steaming at 4 A.M. At 7:15 made Drummond Island right ahead. At 9:30 stopped the engine. A canoe containing 3 natives came off, from whom we learned that no vessel had visited the island for some time. Latitude 1° 21' S., longitude 174° 22' E.

March 29.—At 4:45 P.M. made a sail on lee beam; stood in chase. 6 P.M.: Hove her to with blank cartridge. Chase proved to be the Honolulu schooner *Pelin,* five months out on a trading voyage.

March 30.—At 2:30 P.M. made Strong Island. From 4 to 6 P.M. stood near enough into Chabrol Harbor to see that no vessels were at anchor there. Latitude 5° 45" N., longitude 163° 46' 30" E.

March 31.—At 9:30 A.M. made McAskill Island N. by W., distant 12 miles. Latitude 6° 6' N., longitude 160° 17' E.

April 1.—At 9:30 A.M. made Ascension Island bearing W. N. W. At 10:30 commenced steaming. Discovered four vessels at anchor close in under the land. At 11:30 took a pilot; steamed inside the reef; came to with both anchors in 15 fathoms. From meridian to 4 P.M.: Fitted out four boats and boarded each vessel; they proved to be the American whalers *Edward Cary,* of San Francisco; the *Hector,* of New Bedford; the *Pearl,* of New London, and the *Harvest,* of Honolulu nominally, but really an American under false colors, having no bill of sale on board, bearing American name, and in the same trade as before; consequently condemned her as prize in connection with the other three. From 4 to 6: Engaged transferring stores, etc., from prizes to our ship; took the captains and mates of each ship on board of us and confined them in irons. From 6 to 8: Confined one of the captains in double irons and gagged him for disrespect; enlisted one man in the marine corps.

April 2.—At 10 A.M. sent an officer on shore with the pilot to invite the chief (Ascension Island) to visit the ship. At 10:30 he came off, accompanied by four attendants and a large number of boats. Sent ashore twenty-two prize muskets and two boxes of tobacco as presents to the chief.

April 3.—From meridian to 4 P.M.: Set fire to the prize bark *Pearl.*

April 4.—From meridian to 4 P.M.: Fired the ships *Hector* and *Edward Cary;* shipped Benedicto Espagnol and Civis de la Costa as landsmen.

April 6.—Shipped George Deas, John Morris, Antonio Delombas (seamen), Joaquin Rodericks (landsman), and Robert Roselle (third-class boy).

April 10.—From 6 to 8 P.M.: Having finished with the bark *Harvest,* cast her off and set her on fire.

April 13.—At 8:30 A.M. unmoored ship. At 7:30 weighed anchor and stood to sea; sent on shore all prisoners. At 8 discharged pilot.

April 28.—At 6 A.M. hoisted the smokestack and started fires. Latitude 26° 45' N., longitude 150° 14' E.

May 21.—At 5 A.M. land bore N. N. W., about 40 miles. Latitude ° 49' 30" N., longitude 155° 9' E. At 12 noon Moukonrushi Island bore W.

May 27.—Meridian to 4 p.m.: Saw large floes of drifting ice to the northward and westward; made a sail on weather bow, standing toward us; came together at 4 and hove to. Latitude 57° 7' N., longitude 153° 1' E. From 4 to 6 P.M.: Hove chase to with a blank cartridge and boarded her; she proved to be the Yankee bark *Abigail,* of New Bedford, on a whaling voyage; made a prize of her and commenced transporting stores, etc., from her to ourselves; paroled the master and mates of prize and released them.

May 28.—From meridian to 4 P.M.: Having received everything necessary from prize, her officers and crew (thirty-five in number) being on board of us, set fire to the prize at 12:10; filled away at 2 P.M.

June 2.—From 8 to meridian: Land, being Lamutki, in Siberia, in sight along port quarter. Latitude 58° 28' N., longitude 151° 25' E. Olskii Island N. W. ¾ N. (true), 35 miles. From 6 to 8 P.M.: Cape Alewin bore N. ½ W., 30 miles distant, about.

June 4.—At 1 a.m. entered a large field of ice and became surrounded by it. Latitude 57° 51' N., longitude 150° 18' E.

June 5.—At 1 A.M. wore ship and got out of the ice. Latitude 58° 5' N., longitude 150° 27' E.

June 6.—At 2 A.M. sighted Cape Alewin, bearing N. by E.; wore ship to the northward and stood in for the land. Latitude 58° 28' N., longitude 150° 49' E.

June 10.—Shipped Thomas S. Manning, seaman, and rated him ship's corporal. Latitude 54° 18' N., longitude 153° 47' E.

June 12.—From 8 to meridian: At 11:30 A.M. made high land on the port beam, bearing E. S. E., distant about 70 miles, being Kamchatka coast. Shipped the following men from the crew of the late bark *Abigail:* Seamen—John Malwa, William Bill, Joseph Long, Alex Givens; landsmen—James French, William Brown, James California, Charles Sailor, John Boy; marines—Maurice Murray and Emmanuel Sylvia. At 4 p.m. Alaid Island Mountain bore E. ½ S. At 9 P.M. Shrinky [Schirinki] Island bore S. S. E., distant 30 miles. Latitude 51° 8' N., longitude 154° 14' E.

June 13.—Moukonrushi Island bore S. W. at 4 A.M. At 5 Shrinky [Schirinki] Island bore N. per standard compass. At 3 P.M. north point of Onekotan Island bore S. W. by W. ½ W. Mount Alaid N. N. W. ½ W. Latitude 49° 50' 45" N., longitude 155° 53' 30" E.

June 16.—At 12 meridian made high land right ahead, supposed to be Copper Island. Shipped Joe Kanaka, landsman; shipped William Burnett, private. Latitude 54° 30' N., longitude 168° E.

June 21.—At 1:30 P.M. made Cape Navarin bearing W. N. W., 15 miles distant. At 3:50 a sail reported to the westward; stood off in chase. From 4 to 6 P.M.: Chase proved to be a rock. Latitude 62° 11' N., longitude 179° 57' E.

June 22.—At 9 A.M. made two sails on port quarter; stood in chase under steam. At 11 hove to and boarded the topsail-yard ship *William Thompson* (whaler), of New Bedford, Mass. Brought on board master and mates and left her in charge of an officer and stood in chase of the other vessel. At 12:05 P.M., latitude 62° 23' N., longitude 179° 46' E., came to near chase and sent a boat on board; she proved to be the ship *Euphrates,* from New Bedford; brought off prisoners with their effects; received a quantity of stores, three chronometers, and one sextant; at 3 P.M. set fire to the prize; the *William Thompson* hove to near us. From 4 to 6 P.M.: Received on board from prize some stores; at 5:45 stood in chase of a sail to the northward and westward; chase proved to be the English whaling bark *Robert Townes,* of Sydney; steamed back to the prize; received from her a quantity of stores.

June 22.—At 3:30 fired prize and at 3:50 A.M. steamed away. From meridian to 4: Captured and bonded for $46,000 the whaling ship *Milo,* of New Bedford, and sent all prisoners on board, ordering her to follow us; fired two shells from port-bow gun and hove to and boarded the whaling ship *Sophia Thornton,* of New Bedford, and gave orders for officer in charge to follow while we steamed in chase of a bark, running to the northward and westward. From 4 to 6 P.M.: In chase of a bark, which we hove to by firing rifle shell from starboard bow at 5:55; chase proved [to be] the whaling bark *Jireh Swift,* of New Bedford, which we burned, taking off her officers and crew. At 9 stopped near prizes *Milo* and *Sophia Thornton;*

a ship and bark to windward working through the ice; a sail just in sight to leeward. Latitude 62° 40' N., longitude 178° 50' W.

June 23.—At 6:30 A.M. saw a sail to the southward and westward; stood in chase. At 7 the *Milo* fired the *S. Thornton.* At 8:10 came up with the chase, which proved to be brigantine *Susan Abigail,* of San Francisco; sent the master and crew of prize to this ship and burned her; estimated value of the brigantine *Susan Abigail* and cargo, $6,500. Latitude 62° 48' N., longitude 179° 4' W.

June 24.—Shipped John Kelley, seaman. At 10:30 P.M. made land on port bow—Lawrence Island. Latitude 63° 26' N., longitude 176° 16' W.

June 25.—At 10 A.M. made two sails. At 11 came up with a bark showing Hawaiian colors; stood in chase of other vessel; chase proving a Frenchman, stood back northward and eastward. At 3 stood in chase of a sail on starboard bow; at 5:10 P.M. came up with chase, which proved to be the ship *General Williams,* of New London; sent an officer on board to burn her and bring off prisoners. From 6 to 8 P.M.: Received thirty-four prisoners, three chronometers, one sextant, and the other nautical instruments, three hogs, $405 from the captain; at 7 set fire to the ship and stood in chase to the northward and westward; paroled the prisoners. Latitude 63° 50' N., longitude 172° 58' W.

June 26.—From midnight to 4 A.M.: Came up with the vessels and took possession of the *Nimrod,* the *Wm. C. Nye,* and *Catharine,* all of New Bedford; received on board their officers and papers; received on board from prizes six chronometers, two sextants; at 4 A.M. burned the three prizes, paroled the master and mates, took the boats in tow with their crews, and stood in chase of five sail in sight to the northward. At 8 came up with the *General Pike,* bark, of New Bedford. From 8 to meridian: Captured the barks *General Pike, Isabella,* and *Gipsey;* bonded the *General Pike* for $———; paroled all of the prisoners and sent them on board the *General Pike* in their boats; burned the *Gipsey;* received on board all of the nautical instruments, etc., from the *Gipsey* and *Isabella;* hauled the *Isabella* alongside and commenced taking on board stores and water from meridian to 4 P.M. From 8 to 12 midnight: Set fire to the prize *Isabella* as soon as she was clear of the ship. Latitude 64° 21' N., longitude 172° 20' W. (at noon).

June 27.—The brig *Susan Abigail* sailed from San Francisco about the 19th of April, bringing dates to the 17th of April. I read from one of the April papers dispatches for [of the] surrender by General Lee to General Grant and an announcement of a proclamation issued by President Davis at Danville to the people of the South, declaring the war would be carried on with renewed vigor.—J. I. WADDELL.

June 28.—At 6:30 Diomede Island bore N. N. E., about 12 miles distant. At 8:15 stood to the southward in chase of a bark; at 10 came up with chase, which proved to be the *Waverly,* of New Bedford; received thirty-three prisoners with their effects and burned the prize. At 1:30 P.M. came up with a fleet of ten sail, many of whom were at anchor; one ship, having been stove by the ice, was being assisted by the others. Took possession of the following vessels: Ships *Hillman, James Maury, Nassau, Brunswick, Isaac Howland,* barks *Martha* (second) and *Congress,* all of New Bedford; barks *Nile,* of New London; *Favorite,* of Fair Haven, Conn., and *Covington,* of Warren, R. I. Bonded the ship *James Maury* for $37,000. Fired the bark *Martha* and ships *Nassau, Hillman,* and *Isaac Howland.* From 4 to 6 P.M.: Bonded the bark *Nile* for $41,600 to take a part of the prisoners to the United States; set fire to the barks *Congress* and *Favorite;* sent all our prisoners to the bonded vessels.

June 29.—At 1 A.M. got through Bering Strait. At 8 A.M. East Cape bore S. ½ W., Diomede Island E. S. E. At 10 A.M. large floes of ice ahead; turned around and stood to the southward. Latitude (noon) 66° 14' N., longitude 169° 6' W. Four to 6 P.M.: Steaming [southward] through Bering Strait. At 9:30 P.M. hove to a ship with blank cartridge from rifle gun; proved to be a Frenchman. At 11:30 spoke the Hawaiian brig *Kohala,* out of Plover Bay.

July 1.—At 1:30 A.M. entered a field of heavy ice; hove everything aback, furled all sail, and got up steam; lowered a boat and ran out lines ahead; made fast to large cakes of ice, and commenced hauling through, turning over engine slowly, breasting off with spars; struck large masses of ice several times, but sustained no material injury. At 4:30 got out of the ice.

July 5.—Steaming through the 172° passage, Aleutian Islands.

August 2.—From meridian to 4 P.M.: Made a sail bearing N. W.; stood in chase; latitude 16° 20' N., longitude 121° 11' W.; at 4:15 stopped the engine; coming up with the chase, lowered a boat and sent alongside the English bark *Barracouta,* from San Francisco to Liverpool, thirteen days out. Having received by the *Barracouta* the sad intelligence of the overthrow of the Confederate government, all attempts to destroy the shipping or property of the United States will cease from this date, in accordance with which the first lieutenant, William C. Whittle, Jr., received the order from the commander to strike below the battery and disarm the ship and crew.

November 5.—Arrived in the Mersey, off Liverpool, and on Monday, the 6th, surrendered the *Shenandoah* to the British nation, by letter to Lord John Russell, premier of Great Britain.

The log is approved.

JAMES I. WADDELL.

Vessels captured, bonded, and destroyed by the C.S.S. *Shenandoah*, from October 30, 1864, to June 28, 1865.

Date	Name of Vessel	Disposition	Value of Vessel	Value of Cargo	Total Value	Appraisers
1864.						
Oct. 30	Bark *Alina*	Scuttled	$50,000	$45,000	$95,000	John Grimball, S. Smith Lee, Jr., I. S. Bulloch.
Nov. 6	Schooner *Charter Oak*	Burned	12,000	3,000	15,000	Do.
Nov. 8	Bark *D. Godfrey*	do.	10,000	26,000	36,000	Do.
Nov. 10	Herma-phrodite brig *Susan*	Scuttled	5,000	436	5,436	F. T. Chew, O. A. Browne.
Nov. 12	Ship *Kate Prince*	Bonded for $40,000.				
Nov. 12	Ship *Adelaide*	Bonded for $24,000				
Nov. 13	Schooner *Lizzie M. Stacey*	Scuttled and burned.	10,000	5,000	15,000	J. Grimball, I. S. Bulloch, O. A. Browne.
Dec. 4	Bark *Edward*	Burned	5,000	15,000	20,000	I. S. Bulloch, J. F. Minor.
Dec. 29	Bark *Delphine*	do.	25,000		25,000	Do.
1865.						
Apr. 1	Ship *Edward Cary*	do.	15,000		15,000	J. Grimball, O. A. Browne.
Apr. 1	Ship *Hector*	do.	35,000	23,000	58,000	S. S. Lee, Jr., J. T. Mason.
Apr. 1	Ship *Pearl*	do.	10,000		10,000	F. T. Chew, J. C. Blacker.
Apr. 1	Bark *Harvest*	do.	10,000	24,759	34,759	D. M. Scales, J. F. Minor.

Date	Name of Vessel	Disposition	Value of Vessel	Value of Cargo	Total Value	Appraisers
1865. (continued)						
May 27	Bark *Abigail*	do.	15,000	1,705	16,705	D. M. Scales, J. F. Minor, J. C. Blacker.
June 22	Ship *William Thompson*	do.	40,925		40,925	J. Grimball, O. A. Browne.
June 22	Ship *Euphrates*	do.	20,000	22,320	42,320	S. S. Lee, Jr., J. T. Mason.
June 22	Ship *Milo*	Bonded for 20,000				
June 22	Ship *Sophia Thornton*	Burned	50,000	20,000	70,000	D. M. Scales, J. F. Minor.
June 22	Bark *Jireh Swift*	do.	35,000	26,960	61,960	S. S. Lee, Jr., J. T. Mason.
June 23	Brig *Susan Abigail*	do.	6,500		6,500	J. F. Minor.
June 25	Ship *General Williams*	do.	20,000	24,740	44,740	S. S. Lee, Jr., J. T. Mason.
June 26	Bark *Nimrod*	do.	15,000	14,260	29,260	Do.
June 26	Bark *Wm. C. Nye*	do.	25,000	6,512	31,512	I. S. Bulloch, Lodge Colton.
June 26	Bark *Catharine*	do.	26,174		26,174	J. Grimball, O. A. Browne.
June 26	Bark *General Pike*	Bonded				
June 26	Bark *Gipsey*	Burned	20,000	14,369	34,369	D. M. Scales, C. E. Hunt.
June 26	Bark *Isabella*	do.	20,000	18,000	38,000	F. T. Chew, J. F. Minor.
June 28	Bark *Waverly*	do.	62,376		62,376	J. Grimball, H. Alcott.
June 28	Ship *Hillman*	do.	25,000	8,000	33,000	S. S. Lee, Jr., J. T. Mason.

DATE	NAME OF VESSEL	DISPOSITION	VALUE OF VESSEL	VALUE OF CARGO	TOTAL VALUE	APPRAISERS
1865. (continued)						
June 28	Ship *James Maury*	Bonded for $37,000				
June 28	Ship *Nassau*	Burned	40,000		40,000	F. T. Chew, C. E. Hunt.
June 28	Ship *Brunswick*	do.	5,000	11,272	16,272	J. C. Blacker.
June 28	Ship *Isaac Howland*	do.	40,000	35,112	75,112	D. M. Scales.
June 28	Bark *Martha*	do.	30,607		30,607	J. Grimball, Henry Alcott.
June 28	Bark *Congress*	do.	30,000	25,300	55,300	S. S. Lee, Jr., J. T. Mason.
June 28	Bark *Nile*	Bonded for $41,600.				
June 28	Bark *Favorite*	Burned	15,000	42,896	57,896	J. F. Minor.
June 28	Bark *Covington*	do.	7,259	22,741	30,000	J. C. Blacker.
			735,841	436,382	1,172,223	

EXTRACTS FROM NOTES ON THE C.S.S. *SHENANDOAH* BY HER COMMANDER, JAMES IREDELL WADDELL, C. S. NAVY.

I was ordered to proceed upon a cruise in the far-distant Pacific, into the seas and among the islands frequented by the great whaling fleet of New England, a source of abundant wealth to our enemies and a nursery for her seamen, and it was hoped that I would be able to greatly damage and disperse that fleet, even if I did not succeed in utterly destroying it. Considering the vast extent of water to be sailed over, the necessarily incomplete equipment of the vessel, and my approaching isolation from the aid and comfort of my countrymen, a letter of specific instructions would have been wholly superfluous. All details regarding the organization of my crew and the necessary alterations required to fit the ship for carrying her battery, preserving the ammunition, the general conduct of the cruise, and my intercourse with neutrals were left to my judgment and discretion, because I would be subjected to constantly varying scenes and incidents, and would doubtless encounter difficulties which could not be foreseen and provided for in advance.

It was believed in moments of doubt, where unlooked-for obstacles and apparent troubles were found in my path, that happy inspiration which rarely fails the conscientious officer who is earnestly intent upon his duty would come to my aid, and that I would intuitively perceive the most judicious course of action. Thus I reflected and pondered over the memorandum of instruction. I did not yet know what officers would accompany me, their experience and ability, which, in the management of a vessel at sea, is more than half the work to be accomplished on such an expedition.

I had the benefit of the counsel, wisdom, and experience of my superior officer in all matters connected with my projected cruise, the probable difficulties in my way, and their solution. The way was paved for my operations so knowingly I had little else to do than follow his advice. The means which were to be placed at my disposal and the arrangement for a proper and safe rendezvous, the process of transferring the armament and stores from the supply vessel to the intended cruiser, and the probable nature of the contract with the seamen to induce them to ship in the Confederate service were matters for reflection, to which must be added the dread of failure in getting the ship to sea without involving a violation of law. The passage to my ultimate cruising ground and the locality in which I would be most likely to find the objects of my search required careful reflection and investigation of charts and reference to the memoirs of the Pacific Ocean and the numerous islands scattered therein.

The ultimate aim of my cruise was the dispersion or destruction of the New England whaling fleet, as pointed out in the memorandum of the honorable secretary of the navy. The ship to be placed under my command had recently returned from her first voyage to Bombay, for which trade she was built, and being designed as a transport for troops, with spacious 'tween decks and large air ports, she was well suited for conversion into a cruising vessel. The log of her voyage out and home showed her to be fast under canvas, and her steam power was more than auxiliary. She had a lifting screw and steamed 9 knots without pressing. She had been docked to insure her commencing the cruise in good and sound condition. Ample stores in every department (except the paymaster's) were provided for a cruise of fifteen months. I left Liverpool, England, in the Confederate supply vessel *Laurel* on Sunday morning, the 9th of October, 1864, for Funchal, island of Madeira, taking with me all the officers but one detailed for my command.

A few picked men selected from the crew of the late C.S.S. *Alabama,* who were specially retained, accompanied me and constituted the nucleus of the new force which I should have to organize at the place of rendezvous. Among the men

was George Harwood, who was chief boatswain's mate of the *Alabama,* a fine seaman, an experienced man-of-war's man, and one calculated to carry weight in
influence with a crew composed exclusively of Englishmen. I gave to him an
appointment of acting boatswain as soon as the supply vessel was beyond English
jurisdiction, and explained to him the intent of my leaving England. I believed he
would assist me materially in persuading the men of the intended cruiser to ship
for the Confederate service.

The supply vessel reached Madeira and was anchored in Funchal Bay on the
night of the 16th of October, 1864, near Loo Rock, in 16 fathoms (93 feet) of
water. On the following day orders were given that there was to be no communication with the shore except that which was necessary for the commander of the
supply vessel in her intercourse with the customs officials and for purchase of coal
for the *Laurel.* A lookout was stationed to report the appearance of all vessels coming in sight off the harbor, and to report such arrivals during the night as well as
during the day, and if any passing vessel hoisted flags or showed lights to inform
the commander of the supply vessel, or, in his absence, to inform me of the character of such vessels and the signals. The supply vessel was quickly coaled and
made ready for sea. Her papers were left at the custom-house.

During the first watch, on a clear, calm, and moonlight night of the 18th of
October, 1864, a ship-rigged vessel came in sight and within a short distance of
the Funchal anchorage, slowly steaming, and showed her signal lights, which is
not an unusual courtesy for vessels passing on or returning from a voyage to
extend to those vessels in harbor; the object of such civility is the announcement of
the vessel's name and tidings of her safety, which would be communicated to
those interested in the progress she was making on her voyage. Marryat's code of
signals furnishes the names of all English and American vessels, and wherever that
book is found, by referring to it, when vessels communicate by signals their names
and character, together with the ports from and where bound, can be known. By
this telegraphic system a communication can be made intelligently. This vessel
excited some suspicions. She soon passed out of sight south of the port, and after
a short lapse of time returned off the port, steaming slowly in the direction from
whence she came; she still burned her signal lights, which the crews of other vessels in port did not seem to notice. It was impossible just then for us to leave port
in order to communicate with the strange steamer, because our commander had
not received his papers from the customs officials the evening before, and while
this intelligence was being communicated to me the black craft disappeared north
of the port and was hidden from our view. Her advent had caused a stir among
those of the supply vessel who found it more agreeable to be on deck at that late
hour engaged in merry chat than below in uncomfortably close apartments, and

when she had again come in view a low suppressed murmur of satisfaction, "That's her," escaped the lips of someone who with others had popped his head over the vessel's rail to watch her movements—pent-up curiosity to discover what I knew had been under tedious suspense for several days, and found relief in the exclamation "That's her."

After the strange black craft had disappeared in the direction she had come from those who had been closely watching her withdrew from the rail of the supply vessel to loafing places about her deck, where each to his confiding shipmate communicated his suspicion of the craft. The intense interest felt for and concerning the vessel was conveyed by the less intelligent ones by a restless demeanor, an enquiring glance at me, much as to ask, "Tell me, Captain, it's all out now," while the more knowing walked to and fro, turning their quids from cheek to cheek, in soft, diligent conversation, giving vent to an occasional chuckle. The excitement somewhat abated and the watchers dropped off one by one to seek repose. They knew we could not leave port until the steamer's papers were returned by the customs official, and that would not be attended to before the next morning, and perhaps not until late in the day. The papers of vessels are always deposited soon after her arrival in port at the custom-house; it is a guaranty of character for customs dues and port regulations.

Daylight came, and the sun rose full of fire; a messenger was dispatched for a customs official to repair on board with the vessel's papers, and while the customs boat was being pulled off to us, accompanied by bumboats and fishing smacks, whose purpose it was to coax in the way of trade the last farthing out of thriftless Jack, that black steamer came in sight again from the north with flags flying from her mastheads which were recognized and answered from our steamer, and the cry arose from the shore boats which surrounded us, *"Otro Alabama,"* i.e., another *Alabama.* The fires had been kindled in our furnaces at daylight, and steam was ready; chain had been hove in to a short stay, and the vessel's quiet swing to a single anchor only increased our restlessness to follow the black steamer, whose symmetrical outlines the bright light played fairly upon and made her appear to be the very object for which we had left Liverpool.

The customs officials being settled with and all strangers seen out of the *Laurel,* her anchor was tripped at 10 A.M. and she stood to sea in chase of the steamer, whose engines were slowed to enable us to come up rapidly. The 19th of October, 1864, was fine; the atmosphere clear and bright, and a wind blew from the southwest. So soon as the *Laurel* had approached sufficiently near the stern of the steamer I saw there three words, in large white letters, and I read through my lorgnette *"Sea King—London."* An idea flashed across my brain—Is she to be a sea king? I ordered the *Sea King* to be telegraphed to follow the *Laurel,* and I sought refuge on the north side of the Deserters [Las Desertas], where I found a smooth sea, no interruptions, and a good but deep anchorage for negotiations and work. The first lieutenant, William C. Whittle, Jr., of Virginia, had taken passage in the *Sea King* from London, as her purser, and joined me at this juncture of affairs.

All acting master's mates were, in the Confederate naval service, first-class petty officers.

The *Shenandoah* was commissioned on the ocean on the 19th day of October, 1864, under the lee and on the north side of the islands known as the Deserters [Las Desertas], only a few miles distant from and in sight of Madeira. She was anchored in 18 fathoms water, and her consort came to and was lashed alongside. The little nook was smooth, the day a bright and lovely one, and I felt a promise of success. In thirteen hours the consort had discharged every conceivable outfit intended for the *Shenandoah,* and was only delayed for such passengers as she was compelled to receive on board. I felt I had a good and fast ship under my feet, but there was a vast deal of work in [side] as well as outside of her to be done, and to accomplish all that a crew was necessary. It became my effort to ship the crew of the late *Sea King,* now the *Shenandoah,* and as many of the crew of the consort as possible and the men were called to the quarter-deck of the *Shenandoah,* when I informed them of the changed character of the *Sea King,* read my commission to them (made my first speech), pictured to them a brilliant, dashing cruise, and asked them to join the service of the Confederate States.

Only twenty-three out of fifty-five men were willing to venture on such service, and a large majority of those shipped for six months only. Those who declined service in the *Shenandoah* were directed to go on board the *Laurel.* My feeble force was then ordered to the break to lift an anchor, which proved too heavy; the officers threw off their jackets and assisted in lifting it to the bow, and the little adventurer entered upon her new career, throwing out to the breeze the flag of the South, and demanded a place upon that vast ocean of water without fear or favor. That flag unfolded itself gracefully to the freshening breeze, and declared the majesty of the country it represented amid the cheers of a handful of brave-hearted men, and she dashed upon her native element as if more than equal to the contest, cheered on by acclamations from the *Laurel,* which was steaming away for the land we love to tell the tale to those who would rejoice that another Confederate cruiser was afloat.

I was truly afloat and, as I had never been before, in command of a vessel constructed for peaceful pursuits, of 1,100 tons English measurement, to be under my directions metamorphosed into not only a cruiser, but an active cruiser, and capable of carrying a battery for which she was not constructed. The deck was to be cleared of the stores thereon before the battery could be mounted on the carriages, and gun ports were to be cut, fighting bolts driven, gun tackles prepared, before the battery could be used. All that service which is done at a navy yard before a vessel is commissioned, with its responsibilities, devolved upon me out in mid-ocean, without even a hope of successful defense if attacked or a friendly port to take shelter in if I should desire protection.

The carpenter of the vessel could find no one who was capable of assisting him in his department; he therefore alone was to make the necessary alterations, and of course the work would progress slowly. Besides the work already mentioned, the bulwarks were discovered too weak for resistance to a shotted gun, and therefore some plan was to be adopted for strengthening them, which being decided upon and arranged, the next work of importance was the selection of a place in the vessel's hold where a powder magazine could be built.

The hold and the berth deck were full of coal, and having no spare space elsewhere, the forehold was selected wherein to build a powder magazine. The powder was placed under tarpaulins in my starboard cabin. There was no other place at that time so safe for the powder as the cabin. There were twenty-four officers, each department having its complement, making all told forty-seven persons.

The novel character of my political position embarrassed me more than the feeble condition of my command, and that was fraught with painful apprehensions enough. I had the compass to guide me as a sailor, but my instructions made me a magistrate in a new field of duty, and where the law was not very clear to lawyers. Managing a vessel in unsettled, stormy weather and exposure to the dangers of the sea was a thing I had studied from my boyhood; fighting was a profession that I had prepared myself for by the study of the best models; but now I was to sail and fight and to decide questions of international law that lawyers had quarreled over with all their books before them. I was in all matters to act promptly and without counsel; but my admirable instructions and the instincts of honor and patriotism that animated every Southern gentleman who bore arms in the South buoyed me up with hope which supported the interior difficulties and the degree of responsibility bearing on me. The public books furnished me, exclusive of works on navigation, were Phillimore's *Laws of Nations.* I had read Wheaton and Vattel on international law, and had also studied the fundamental principles of law found in Blackstone. Most of my leisure hours were devoted to Phillimore, and I found him a good friend, but requiring brown study.

The *Shenandoah* was a composite-built ship—i.e., her frame was of iron and her hull was of teak, 6 inch in thickness. Her lower and topmast, lower topsail yards, and bowsprit were iron, cylindrical. Her horsepower was 180. Under most favorable circumstances she could not steam over 9 knots per hour. Her cylinders were 5 feet and her boilers 18 inches above the water-line. She was capable of condensing 500 gallons of fresh water per day, and consumed from 18 to 22 tons of coal per day. She was very fast under sail, and a pretty vessel. The topsail yards were so heavy [that] if it were not for the winches introduced into the merchant marine for lifting heavy bodies I do not think the crew could have mast-headed there. The power of the entire force was hardly equal to lifting so heavy an iron spar, and yet if that spar had been wooden it would have been heavier. The running gear was generally so damaged it became necessary to reeve anew. A seaman will never neglect his ship because fine weather may be expected. A general overhauling was inaugurated, and everybody had something to do. When the helmsman could be better employed than at the wheel I steered the ship. Of the number of men who shipped, five were found capacitated for the engineer department.

Such disposition of service between the deck hands and the engineer department as would conduce to health and good understanding became a subject for reflection with me, and I determined, as it was all important to run the vessel as speedily as possible away from the rendezvous and to seek lighter winds and a smoother sea for operations, to keep the ship under steam during daylight, and after darkness closed upon us to stop the engines, put the vessel under sail, and change the course for the night. The wind was free; my course was to southward, and as the breeze freshened after night the ship made nearly as much per hour under sail as she did during the day under steam. The crew were seldom disturbed during the night, for the ship was put under short canvas to prevent their being called.

The steamer was supplied with Enfield rifles, cutlasses, and revolvers, and there on the deck in huge boxes lay the guns and carriages. Though impatient to see them mounted and their grim faces projecting beyond our wooden walls, of what great use could they be in defense of so vulnerable a vessel? True, their appearance would go a long way toward reconciling an unarmed foe, but a short scrutiny inboard developed clearly our entire incapacity for contending against a regularly appointed man-of-war.

I concluded to take the offensive immediately. The deck was cleared of such articles as belonged below, the gun boxes lashed to and near the sides where the ports were designed to be cut, and having a partially clear deck, I could, with the aid of an Enfield rifle, investigate a stranger's nationality and, if of the kind I was in search, appropriate her. The crew was not sufficiently numerous to manage the vessel easily, and unless I found the enemy's vessels and succeeded not only in capturing, but in shipping portions at least of their respective crews, my own might grow disheartened and the cruise fail. Work is not congenial to Jack's nature; he is essentially a loafer, and I apprehended that captured men coming on board would judge from them of the ship's condition, and a bad impression might be made which would prove difficult to rectify. I could rely on our men using rough persuasion in the dark with those who were undecided, and I felt sure that each prize would have in its crew one or more adventurous spirits who would gladly embrace the opportunity in hope of prize money and under the assurance of being well cared for by the officers. A sailor appreciates kindness shown him by his officer, but I know of no character so unreliable, and although Jack is charitable when in liquor on shore with his money, he is penurious on shipboard.

On the 22d of October, four days after the vessel had been commissioned, the guns were all on their carriages. The officers, leading the men, had accomplished a vast deal of labor and set so good an example of patriotism and industry that Jack, if flagging a little at times, breathed a new inspiration, and would contend with his leaders for the most difficult job or the heaviest lift. The carpenter had succeeded in discovering a man who could lend him a hand in his department, and two ports were cut on either side of the deck. Other ports were to be cut, and the fighting bolts were first to be found before they could be driven. By some strange accident they escaped the observation of the gunner, and were found a few days afterwards in a beef barrel, stowed with the provisions in the hold. The gun tackles could not be found, and it soon became a matter of certainty they never were put on board. There was a plenty of rope, but no blocks suitable for gun tackles; the absence of them rendered the battery totally useless. I had nothing left me but to look to the enemy to supply the deficiency. I had been directed to live off his supplies, and I suppose inanimate as well as animate objects were embraced in those directions.

The guns were on the carriages, and as the fighting bolts and gun tackles could not then be found, they were secured fore and aft the deck, close to the ship's side, and in the absence of bolts straps were run through scuppers and toggled outside of the vessel, to which the guns were secured. The deck then became more cheerful, and although the work was nearly completed, as far as we then could proceed with it, there was hard work below, for an investigation of what had been put in the vessel before I took charge of her, and of its location, was necessary to our information, and it really seemed as if our labor would never end. The invoices were utterly worthless. Several officers slept on the deck in the absence of berths, and wash-deck buckets were resorted to in the place of basins. The furniture in my cabin consisted of one broken plush-velvet bottomed armchair, no berth, no bureau, no lockers for stowing my clothing in, no washstand, pitcher, or basin. The deck was covered with a half-worn carpet, which smelt of dogs or something worse. It was the most cheerless and offensive spot I had ever occupied. The apartments assigned the commissioned officers were in little better condition, except the room of the executive officer, which was comfortable, and as to the apartment of the steerage officers, it was filled with iron tanks holding bread, and there was no furniture of any kind for it.

Under all those trials our condition created merriment rather than sadness. It seemed to me I was the only anxious person on board. Responsibility weighed upon my mind, and reflection often created an absence of everything in active movement around me. I was often aroused by some cheerful remarks from an officer, whose responsibility was to the extent of four hours' duty each day, about his experience in the steamer, and it was kind of him to divert my attention even for a few moments; but no sooner would the conversation cease than my mind was again occupied with ship thoughts in cases of emergency, and I have no doubt I very often appeared to those with me an unsocial and peculiar man. I think that I never reflected until then, and the subject for reflection was full of interest, because national property and an important cruise were intrusted to me. It was my first command, and upon the accuracy of all the calculations of my judgment in directing a cruise upon so vast a scale depended success or failure. Success would be shared by every individual under my command, but who would share failure with me? The former has friends; what has the latter! Those who knew me in a subordinate capacity elsewhere found me then changed in position, occupying responsibility to a nation which was struggling for their very existence.

On the 25th of October the powder was removed to a small apartment under my cabin, the deck of which was very little below the surface of the ocean, and divided from the steerage deck by a strong, open latticework, which was rendered more secure by heavy canvas tacked to the partition. The powder was in less danger there than where it was previously stowed, but still in a very insecure place; great caution was observed in guarding against accident. It would be too great a labor to enumerate the variety of work which was done, and of that yet to be undertaken and completed, occasioned by the necessary changes and alterations of a thoroughly equipped merchant vessel into a national cruiser, and those who have undertaken the work on a wide and friendless ocean can only appreciate the anxieties accompanying such an expedition. An accident occurred to the machinery, which, added to our perilous condition, did not improve the situation of affairs; the derangement was, however, corrected in a few hours, and the engine in motion again, but it left an unpleasant and questionable impression of its strength and good order on my mind.

By the 26th of October enough coal was removed from the berth deck to fill the side bunkers, from which a supply was drawn for steaming since the 19th instant. The removal of such a quantity of coal developed a large, spacious, and finely ventilated deck, upon which it was designed to berth the crew, and the coal which could not be accommodated in the side bunkers was thrown well aft on that deck. The space occupied by the coal could be spared for athwartships bunker without encroaching upon the quarters required for a full ship's company. I found upon examination of the total length, breadth, and height of the berth deck that there was ample room to berth 200 men, composed of marines, seamen, ordinary seamen, and landsmen. On either side of the deck were metal lattice gratings for ventilations to the hold, and [as] the cool gases escaped thereby, a constant circulation of healthy sea air poured in at the air ports and hatches to the berth deck, keeping up a wholesome circulation. That deck was 7½ feet below the spar deck.

The ship had now reached a low latitude, and was constantly receiving heavy rain and violent squalls of wind, and to our horror the decks were discovered to be leaking like sieves and the seams of the hull were sufficiently open to admit a fine spray as a sea had spent itself on her sides. Lieutenant Chew, an intelligent and promising young officer, erased *Sea King* from the stern of the *Shenandoah*.

On the 27th of October, 1864, the *Shenandoah* took the offensive and entered upon her first chase, and, in compliment to the stranger she was in chase of, crossed for the first time her royal yards. She rapidly overhauled the chase, which proved to be the *Mogul*, of London. Immediately after separating from that vessel she entered upon another chase and overhauled her quickly; she also was British. A seaman is never satisfied as to the sailing capacity of his vessel until in company with other vessels, and the evidence under such circumstances is not to be mistaken. The *Shenandoah* was unquestionably a fast vessel, and I felt assured it would be a difficult matter to find her superior under canvas. The crews of those vessels rushed to their respective rails to look at the little rover, and three times three did the red flag of England dip in salutation to the flag of the South.

The ship had now reached a position where vessels from the westward on an outward voyage would probably be found, and our prospects brightened as she worked her way toward the line through light and variable winds, sunshine, and rain.

The *Mogul*, of London, was an American-built vessel, and, like many other American vessels, she had changed owners in consequence of the war. She may have been sold in good faith; so far as her papers were concerned the sale was in form, but that is not of necessity infallible proof.

On the 30th of October chased, captured, and scuttled American bark *Alina*, of Searsport, bound for Buenos Aires with railroad iron. She was on her first voyage, thoroughly equipped, nicely coppered, and reported by the boarding officer to be beautifully clean. There are no people who understand the equipment of vessels so well as a Yankee shipwright. She was a valuable capture, furnishing the blocks for the gun tackles, a variety of blocks which the steamer needed, and cotton canvas so very suitable for sailmaking. The officers partially fitted themselves out with basins, pitchers, mess crockery, knives, forks, etc. A spring-bottomed mattress fell to my share, and a small supply of provisions were removed to the steamer. The prisoners saved all their luggage, but evidently anticipated something unpleasant in their novel situation. They roamed about the deck like rats in a strange garret, and our men engaged themselves in seductive conversations with the strangers, lighthearted in everything which was passing between them, the prelude only to an enlistment of their sympathy in our cause. Finally five seamen and a coal passer entered their names on the shipping articles, and my crew then numbered twenty-nine. It was fortunate my first capture could be scuttled, for the steamer's position was good and a bonfire would have given alarm to all Yankees within 30 miles, and then, too, a cruiser might have been in the neighborhood, which would have [been] attracted by the red glare of the sky and interfered with our fun. The *Alina* was valued at $95,000—not a bad prize.

The manner of destroying a prize depends on the character of her cargo. If freighted like the *Alina* it was better to scuttle—i.e., knock a hole in her side a few feet below her water-line from inboard—and the vessel sinks rapidly and will finally disappear as a whole, leaving a few pieces of her rifted deck and bulkheads floating over the great abyss which the water had closed upon. It more frequently happens that to destroy a prize fire must be resorted to, and there is no escape from that method, however much it may be condemned. It is better than [to] leave the prize so disabled and injured as to be useless and yet formidable enough to endanger the navigation of the ocean. Fire consumes, and while it burns the wreck serves as a beacon and informs the sailor of danger; it leaves a small portion of the vessel's keel and floor timbers to float, which are formidable enough if a vessel moving rapidly comes in contact with it. We were forced to destroy our prizes because we were not allowed to take them into a neutral port [for] adjudication. To prepare a vessel for destruction by fire it is first necessary to see all living animals, except rats, removed; all useful equipment wanted, and discover what combustibles are in her hold, such as tar, pitch, turpentine, and the removal of gunpowder or its destruction by water. The combustibles are then scattered throughout the vessel, bulkheads torn down and piled up in her cabins and forecastle, all hatches open, all halyards let go that the sails may hang loosely, and the yards counter-braced. Fire is then taken from the galley or cooking stove and deposited in various parts of the hold and about her deck. If she is old she will consume like tinder.

This capture produced a marked difference in the bearing of my crew. The work pressed heavily still upon them, but they were now gathering strength in numbers from the enemy's vessels, and the cry of "Sail ho," was always greeted with manifestations of pleasure. After working hours those who desired playful amusement collected in the gangways and gave themselves up to dancing, jumping, singing, or spinning a shore yarn in which the spinner was the hero. Jack is easily entertained and simple in his credulity.

The course was still southward through the bright rays of a hot sun, popping out from behind a cloud which had just wept itself away, to dry our jackets. Jack says rain water is very wet. This expression is in contradistinction to the effect which salt water produces from bathing in it on shipboard or from a tumble overboard. One never takes cold from exposure in salt water.

On the 5th of November chased, captured, and burned American schooner *Charter Oak*, Gilmer [Samuel J. Gilman] master, of Boston, bound for San Francisco with a mixed cargo. She was supplied with preserved fruits and a few excellent cabin stores, which were appropriated to our use. Two thousand pounds of canned tomatoes were brought on board, and all the delicacies intended for cabin use. Captain Gilmer [Gilman], his wife, her sister (a widow), and her son occupied my starboard cabin. Their personal effects were respected and they messed at the ward room table with myself. I was still without a cabin table, etc. The widow had lost her husband at Harper's Ferry. He had been a sergeant in the Federal Army. The captain said he had only $200 in gold, and I believe him to have told the truth, and when his wife came on board I presented her with the money, in presence of Midshipman Mason, on behalf of the Confederacy, and on condition she would not give any part of it to her husband, to which she agreed; that of course was a mere pretense, for the fact was I felt a compassion for the women, because they would be landed I did not know where, and the thought of inflicting unnecessary severity on a female made my heart shrink within. A statement made by Captain Gilmer [Gilman] in some New York paper acknowledges kindness he received as a prisoner.

The crew of the *Charter Oak* consisted of a mate and three Portuguese, and during the examination of their luggage United States overcoats were discovered; it gradually leaked out they were deserters from the Federal Army, perhaps belonging to that class of enlisted men known as bounty jumpers. A sword found on board of her was the only trophy I preserved, and I will speak hereafter of its fate. The *Shenandoah* received no aid in men from the prize.

I was amused to witness the meeting between the two captive captains. They met for the first time as prisoners under droll circumstances, and their thoughts ran in the same channel. Gilmer [Gilman] said to the Searsport Yankee, "What did he do to you?" (meaning his vessel). "He burnt her," was the reply. There was no consolation to be offered the Searsport Yankee; he had lost money, while the Californian, after a few grimaces, took it to be a good joke. They did not remain good friends long. The Californian found Captain Staples objectionable and not companionable. Gilmer [Gilman] accepted the decision of war like a man, and it was he who told me of the quantity of preserved fruit after this fashion: "For God's sake, bring the preserved fruit on board." He also owned a double-barreled gun which I wanted mightily, but that was confiscated.

The *Charter Oak* was fired late in the afternoon, and to satisfy myself she would be enveloped in flames it became necessary to remain near her after night for a few hours. The wind was light, and the bright flames from her hull taking in succession each sail, following the mast to their very trucks, the red glare could be seen a long way off, and was a signal of accidental fire or the work of a Confederate cruiser, and all vessels on a lookout would suspect something wrong; and if it were a Yankee who was familiar with the bonfires of the matchless *Alabama* he would not venture to ascertain the character of the illumination, but rather move away in an opposite direction. I ran the *Shenandoah* to leeward of the burning wreck sufficiently distant from danger of taking fire. A cruiser, if in that region of sea, would be under sail most likely, and if to leeward could not work up fast enough to investigate the fire; and if under steam, she would run to windward to make her observations, which would give me an advantage of seeing her first, and I could be off. The ports were now all cut, the guns in position, and only required men to work them; there were enough for one gun's crew and the powder division. The *Charter Oak* was valued at $15,000.

On the 8th November chased, captured, and burned the bark *D. Godfrey,* of Boston, bound for Valparaiso with a large cargo of excellent mess beef and pork. I regretted to destroy that cargo, but the steamer was full of provisions and room could not be found for more than 22 barrels of each. She was an old vessel, and fire consumed her rapidly. Six of her complement of men joined the *Shenandoah,* and that increased my number to thirty-five men. The *D. Godfrey* was valued at $36,000. The following day was devoted to chasing and boarding foreign vessels. The engineers engaged making iron plates for strengthening deck in rear of guns, to which iron plates the train tackles of the gun carriages were to be hooked. The deck was of soft pine and only 4 inches thick.

On the 9th of November communicated with the Danish brig *Anna Jane,* and I offered her captain a chronometer, a barrel of beef, and bread to relieve me of certain prisoners, to which he acceded, and I transferred prisoners from my first and third captures to the protection of the Danish flag. The chronometer I gave the Danish captain was taken from the *Alina.* Staples accompanied his chronometer.

Soon after separating from the Danish brig I captured and scuttled the American brig *Susan,* Hanson master, of New York, bound to the Rio Grande with coal. She was a very old vessel, and her cargo assisted in sinking her. She was a long time out from Cardiff, and I am disposed to think her captain was pleased at his good luck in fall-in with the *Shenandoah*. Three of her crew joined us, and we numbered thirty-eight men. The *Susan,* as I have said, was very old and very weak. She leaked badly, and was the dullest sailer I had ever seen; really she moved so slowly that barnacles grew to her bottom, and it was simply impossible for her crew to pump her out as fast as the water made. An ingenious machine, simple, but only useful in a breeze, was devised by someone (the patent should be preserved) to keep her afloat if possible. To the pump was attached a shaft half the beam of the vessel, and to the outer end a paddle-wheel, which made one side look steamerlike. When she was seen the deck officer reported to me she looked like a steamer. It may well be supposed from our condition that the report was received with attention, and to meet such a customer was not my desire. She was closely scrutinized, and to my great relief, I felt a disposition to examine the curious look-ing thing more closely. The immersion of her buckets, like all side-wheel boats, depended upon her draft of water, and the quantity of water discharged from her hold depended upon the velocity of her hull through the water. Her captain was a German Jew to all appearances, the first of the kind I had met with in capacity of sailor, and I am sure the brig *Susan* could have been commanded by no other sort of man, and he was purchasable on the following day in exchange for an acting master's mate's appointment, which I could not confer on him, for, although the rating was first-class petty officer, it was impossible to find ship room for his accommodation.

The sun was going down on the 11th instant when a sail was discovered south and east of the *Shenandoah* on the port tack, standing to the south and west, and I immediately entered the steamer on the chase, calculating that if the stranger was equal in speed to the *Shenandoah* we would be in hailing distance soon after mid-night. That was our first night chase, and few eyes closed, so curious were many to know the character of the stranger, and some persons doubted if we would see her again, while others thought it might be fortunate for the *Shenandoah* if we never did. Croakers are found in all classes of society. A few minutes after midnight, rather earlier than I expected, a lookout cried "Sail ho," and soon a ship was in full view. Her appearance was immediately investigated through glasses, while a boat was being prepared to communicate with her. Now that she was in hail, the first lieutenant demanded her nationality. She proved to be the American clipper ship *Kate Prince,* with a neutral cargo of coal. I ransomed her on bond for $40,000 and sent the lady prisoners on board of her. My starboard cabin was ever afterwards called the ladies' cabin. The boarding officer, Lieutenant Lee, a nephew of Gen-eral R. E. Lee, expressed regret that I found it necessary to ransom her, because all of her crew desired to join the *Shenandoah,* and the wife of her master, who was

Southern, wanted the ship burned because she was slow, and then, too, she wished to sail in the *Shenandoah*. Her crew consisted of twenty-one men, which would have been a great acquisition to the steamer. Late in the afternoon of the same day chased and captured the American bark *Adelaide Pendergrast*, of Baltimore, under Buenos Airean colors. Her captain, Williams, could produce no bill of sale and did not know of an absolute sale; he had been told so; that was all he knew. She was ordered to be prepared for destruction by fire, and the order was partly executed when an officer handed a letter to me directed to her consignee at Rio, which influenced me to countermand my order. She was sailing under an assumed flag, and her owners had done a great wrong to her captain by not informing him of her true nationality, for the concealment exposed him to very grave suspicion. Her destruction was prevented by a sheer accident. She was bonded for the sum of $24,000.

On the 13th of November chased, captured, and burned American schooner *Lizzie M. Stacey*, of Boston, bound around the Cape of Good Hope for Honolulu, island of Oahu, on sale. She was new and fast. Her crew, three in all, joined the steamer, which increased her number to forty-one men. That schooner would have made a capital cruiser, and I would have gladly fitted her for the purpose, but the steamer could not spare ten men.

The *Shenandoah* crossed the line (equator) on the 15th of November, and spyglasses were arranged with a fine thread across the lenses to deceive the greenhorns when they were told the steamer was crossing the line to look through the glasses and see the line. Neptune and his wife and his barber, impersonated by a boatswain's mate, gunner, and gunner's mate, came on board, demanded the name and character of the vessel, and asked for his children. He found most of his victims among the officers. I think Lieutenant Lee was the only lieutenant who had crossed the hue, and he enjoyed the sport in arraigning his messmates before the throne of the god of the sea, in participating in the use of the applications and implements applied to them before admittance to his royal favor. Tar and grease, with a hose throwing from a donkey engine a stream of salt water 2 inches in diameter, was the ordeal through which one passed on his introduction to the line where his majesty is supposed to reside. The officer of the deck, Lieutenant Grimball, felt secure in his position, but an application to me for his release from duty being granted, I assuming the deck duty, his assailants marched him to his stateroom, where he prepared himself for absolution and was duly shaved and baptized. Mr. Alcott, the sailmaker, a singular genius, notwithstanding he had repeatedly crossed the line, was drenched by the way of a little fun. He wanted to fight, and much to the merriment of his assailants.

The course lay south along the coast of Brazil, and with a cracking trade the ship boomed along splendidly. Nothing of interest occurred since crossing the line, except what was gathered from boarding foreign vessels, till the 4th of December, when the American whaleship *Edward,* of and out of New Bedford three months, was captured. This capture took place in latitude 37° 47' S., 50 miles southeast of the island of Tristan da Cunha, which was in sight. The *Edward,* Captain Worth, had taken a right whale and was "cutting out," a technical expression—i.e., cutting the fish up and hoisting the huge pieces on board— when she was captured; her crew was so occupied with the fish that the *Shenandoah* had reached within easy range of her unobserved. Her outfit was of excellent quality, and I lay by her two days supplying the steamer with deficiencies. I think there were removed 100 barrels of beef and as many of pork, besides several thousand pounds of ship's biscuit, the best I had ever seen, put in large whisky-seasoned hogsheads, capable of taking 300 gallons of oil; also a quantity of whale line, cotton canvas, blocks, etc. Two of her boats were new, and took the place of my old and worthless ones.

Two days after her capture she was burned, and I steamed to the settlement on the northwest side of Tristan da Cunha and made arrangements with the chief man, who styled himself governor of the island, to receive the crew of the *Edward,* most of which were Sandwich Islanders, and furnished the captain of the *Edward* with six weeks' rations, which was considered sufficient, for no doubt a vessel would touch there soon after my departure and would give a passage to the unfortunates. A Yankee who had been living there for years, to my surprise, said that the South was right. He was after trade. I stayed only a few hours off the island and then took departure in direction of Australia. I have heard that the Federal gunboat *Dacotah [Iroquois],* Commander Raymond Rodgers, took the released prisoners from Tristan da Cunha and carried them to Cape Town, where he expected to find the *Shenandoah.* The carpenter of the *Edward* joined the *Shenandoah,* and a very excellent man I found him to be. My crew was now forty-two men. Whaleships are only valuable prizes when filled with oil, bone, and furs. The *Edward* was valued at $20,000.

The register and papers accompanying a whale vessel resemble those of ordinary vessels in peaceful pursuit. The strength of vessels which were built forty or fifty years ago illustrates the estimate which American shipwrights placed upon the resistance necessary in constructing vessels to contend successfully against the violence of the tempest and seas of the ocean. The timber then used was double in size that now used, and while perhaps greater strength was secured by the introduction of such unnecessarily large knees, beams, and carlines, space for cargo was sacrificed. The improvements which in the last thirty years have been introduced in shipbuilding have revolutionized former theory and model to so great an extent that those old hulks, as they are familiarly known, were deemed so out of fashion and uncertain in making passages, in consequence of their dull sailing, that it proved more profitable to build on the new model vessels for commerce which required dispatch and turn the old hulks over to the whaling service; and for that purpose they became not only useful but very valuable property, because those vessels are built of very strong, large, and heavy live-oak timber carried from the Southern States of America to New England, which kind of material for shipbuilding is not surpassed by [that of] any other country in the world.

Those whale vessels vary from 90 to 100 feet in length, with great beam, and are more easily turned round titan vessels of greater length; powerfully constructed, dull sailers, and, sheathed for 40 feet from the cutwater, which is generally shod with iron, are calculated to resist contact with ice when met with in navigating the great floes which are found north of the fifty-eighth parallel of north latitude. They are equipped with boats much elevated at either end above the center and strongly buff t. On the sternpost and cutwater are fitted rollers for whale lines to run over when attached to a whale. The line is of white hemp, and from 2 to 2½ inches in circumference, varying from 100 to 250 fathoms (600 to 1,500 feet) in length and coiled in large tubs, a precautionary measure to secure its easy flight, free from danger of entanglement, which might result in the capsizing of the boat by the rapidity with which the whale moves when fleshed by a harpoon. The instruments of destruction used on the whale are the harpoon, the lance, and a 2-inch muzzle blunderbuss, of short barrel, constructed of iron, and weighing, I suppose, 40 pounds. The missile used is an elongated explosive shell of 11 to 13 inches in length. This instrument is used by a powerful man on the first occasion when near to, after the whale is struck; the fuse is short, burns quickly, and explodes the shell inside the animal, causing instantaneous death. The boats attach a line to the head by sharp hooks and tow the fish alongside the vessel and proceed to secure and then cut it. A portion of the midship section of the vessel is converted into and is called the blubber room, in which the flesh is thrown and removed for boiling as quickly as time will allow of. The arrangements for boiling the blubber are found on deck between the fore and main mast, constructed of masonry, braced and backed against heavy weather. In the center of the masonry are one or more large caldrons, into which the blubber is placed, and after the oil is extracted the refuse is used for making fire and generates an intense heat. The hogsheads used for receiving the oil vary in size from 200 to 300 gallons, the very large majority of which are shaken up when delivered to the vessel in port and put together when wanted. Others are used for holding flour in bags, hams, cordage, clothing, ship biscuit, etc., which, when empty, are filled with oil. The odor from a whale vessel is abominable and offensive, although they are not unequaled in that respect by the hide vessels from South America, which may be smelt 50 miles in a favorable wind. The bones of the whale are taken on board and thrown into the whale room, the teeth are barreled up, and the smell of putrefied fish is not a nosegay.

After my departure from Tristan da Cunha for the eastward the steamer was put under canvas and the propeller triced up. While the chief engineer was superintending the securing of the propeller he discovered a crack entirely across the brass band on the coupling of the propeller shaft; that was a sad affair, and further examination satisfied him it was in that condition when the ship came into my hands, but the propeller being then in the water it could not be examined. It must have been known to the former owner before she left the English docks. A temporary arrangement could be made for its use, but no reliance was to [be] placed on it, for the revolving of the shaft might seriously injure the bearings and sternpost. Cape Town was the only place short of Melbourne, Australia, in which such repairs could be made, and after turning the subject over in my mind I decided it best to cross the Indian Ocean under sail, hoping to keep company with good luck, for certainly I had been favored in overcoming difficulties during the seven preceding weeks. The ship was given a more southerly course, that she might be thrown into strong west winds, which belt encircles the earth south of the parallel of 43° with more violence than the corresponding belt north of the same parallel in north latitude.

I crossed the meridian of Greenwich on the 12th of December in a fresh west gale with a high-running sea. The ship rolled very deep, owing to the large quantity of coal in her hold, and steered a little wild, owing to her being by the head; but all sharp and narrow vessels of great length have a tendency to roll deep, while that great length gives stability on a wind. I was instructed to pass the meridian of the Cape of Good Hope by the 1st of January, 1865, and at noon of the 17th of December the *Shenandoah* was east of that meridian with a west wind following fast. The speed of the ship varied with the violence of the wind. When, upon reaching the parallel of 43° 30' S, the wind was ascertained to be a revolving gale, whose path lay southeast, and freshening with increased violence, it was evident that to continue the course would be almost suicidal, and by changing it to north of east the ship would in a short time find better weather. She rolled so heavily that sea after sea tumbled in over her rails and her preparations for freeing herself were so indifferent the water was several inches deep on deck, flooding all the apartments on that deck. A Christmas dinner had been prepared of the supplies taken from destroyed prizes, but it was quite impossible to sit long enough to enjoy it. Most of the dishes left the table for the deck, and notwithstanding the disappointment at the loss of a good dinner, there was still life enough left to enjoy it as an incident of the sea. Should I ever again make a voyage to Australia I should go very little south of the northern margin of the belt of the west winds. The ship ran out of the gale and found a more genial climate north of the parallel of 40° S. The squalls of snow and hail during that gale were frightful.

On the 29th of December the wind moderated as rapidly as it had risen, and was then nearly at south, bringing with it an occasional squall of fine rain and leaving an ugly cross sea that seemed undecided where to expend itself, and the heaviest appeared to break against the sides of the *Shenandoah,* sending fine spray through the open seams of the hull into the berth deck. The decks were then leaking dreadfully, and all the bedding was more or less wet. A wet watch is unpleasant, but to nod in a chair or turn into a damp bed is even more so. While the ship wallowed in that broken sea under short canvas a sail was reported astern, and she could be seen between the fine squalls of rain. It was soon ascertained what canvas she was carrying, and the *Shenandoah* was made to hold her luff to prevent the stranger passing out of gunshot to windward. Everyone having a spyglass or lorgnette watched eagerly the approaching and unsuspecting visitor, whose hull was painted white and green and seemed little like what we wanted. On asking her nationality she hoisted her flag, which was so faded we found it difficult to recognize, but as she was approaching us it was soon made out, which caused a stifled outburst of delight. She continued to approach and raised a blackboard, a familiar way in which one vessel enquires of another her longitude. Finding she could not pass to windward of the *Shenandoah,* she kept away and ran close under her stern, when our flag was hoisted and bang went a gun. She brought by the wind quickly and an officer was dispatched in a boat to communicate with and send her captain to the steamer with his papers. She proved to be the American bark *Delphine,* of Bangor, bound for Akyab after a cargo of rice intended for the Federal armies. When Captain Nichols was informed that his vessel was a prize and would be destroyed, he replied: "It may cause the death of my wife to remove her. The report of the gun has made her very ill." I referred him to the surgeon, upon whose report I would act. The surgeon decided there would be no risk to her health in removal, and a chair was prepared, a whip fitted to the main yard, and very soon two women and a child were safely landed on our deck.

I was in the act of leaving my cabin when they were being conducted to the "ladies' chambers." Mrs. Nichols asked in a stentorian voice if I was captain, and wished to know what I intended doing with them and where they would be landed. "On St. Paul, madam, if you like." "Oh, no; never. I would rather remain with you." I was surprised to see a tall, finely proportioned woman of 26, in robust health, standing before me, evidently possessing a will of her own, and it soon became palpable she would be the one for me to manage, and not the husband. A refractory lady can be controlled by a quiet courtesy, but no flattery. I took only the live stock from the *Delphine,* and burned her. This capture increased the crew of the steamer to forty-seven men, several of whom were Germans, and for whom I felt little sympathy. The *Delphine* had on board machinery for cleaning rice, and it was stated to be the property of a Frenchman. She was put before the wind in flames, but did not run far before her sails were consumed, and her masts fell one after the other over her sides. The *Delphine* was valued at $25,000.

Thirty-first of December closed the year, the third since the war began. And how many of my boon companions are gone to that bourne from whence no traveler returns? They were full of hope, but not without fears, when we last parted. They had fallen in battle in defense of their homes invaded by a barbarous enemy. War, when waged by unprincipled and brutal civilized man, is always more savage and inhuman than when waged by the untutored savage of the woods. The Yankees, in their invasion of the South, came with all the vices and passions of civilized men added to the natural ferocity of the savage. They had no magnanimity or chivalry; they fought on a calculation of profit. This fact never left my mind, and reconciled me to the destruction of property which was captured. I felt I was fighting them more effectually than if I were killing the miserable crowds of European recruits which they filled their armies with. For two years they waged war against the South without attempting to interfere with slavery; it was only when they found the negro could be used for killing the white people of the South and serve as breastworks for Northern white troops that they declared him free; it was a new element introduced into the contest, and a very powerful one. They cared nothing for the unhappy negro; they preferred his destruction to that of their white troops.

The 1st of January, 1865, was a lovely day; the sea was smooth and a fair wind blew us along. The new year was welcomed by the hoisting of a flag which had never before been unfurled to the breeze, and the *Shenandoah* had then been in commission two months and eleven days, and had destroyed or ransomed more property than her original cost. The case is without a parallel. The prisoners were quite accustomed to the situation, and no longer entertained a doubt as to their personal safety. The captain of the late *Delphine* expressed shame for having introduced the condition of Mrs. Nichol's health to save from destruction his vessel, and said enquiringly, "I did not think a lie under the circumstances was wrong." He told me after he sailed on that voyage his little son called his attention to the tenth verse, twenty-seventh chapter of the Acts of the Apostles, Paul's dangerous voyage. The little boy was not over six years.

On the following day saw the island of Amsterdam and hove to off the latter to communicate and explore in search of American whalers; sent an armed boat, in charge of Lieutenant John Grimball, with orders to destroy all property belonging to citizens of the United States which he might find on or about the island. After a close search the boat returned, and Lieutenant Grimball reported having seen two Frenchmen who had been left on St. Paul from a French whale vessel to catch and salt fish while she visited the island of Amsterdam; two small patches of cultivated ground and a temporary shanty improvised from the stern of a vessel which rested high and dry, showing that she had been left there by the receding of the waters. I could learn nothing concerning the vessel's history. I do not think that interesting feature presented itself to the minds of the explorers. The crater of an extinct volcano forms the contracted bay of St. Paul, which was alive with a variety of fish, very gentle and easily taken with the hook. The boat could barely pass the reef. The margin of the crater had gradually given away and so weakened near the surface of the water, when an easterly gale broke through its edges and the water rolling in formed the bay of St. Paul.

The officers brought fish, eggs, a few chickens, and a penguin from the settlement. The penguin was not so large as some I have seen, but in every respect the same species of bird which I have seen on the Falkland Islands. The note is identical with that of the bray of the ass. Covered by gray down, unable to fly, and walked with military erectness. Someone pinned a rag around its neck, resembling a shawl in its folds, which created much merriment, and as the bird walked away Mrs. Nichols exclaimed, "Like an old woman for all the world." She had tamed down somewhat, and I rather admired the discipline she had her husband under. The ship was under steam off the island and after taking departure sail was made and the propeller triced up. The band of the propeller coupling was discovered to be broken again, and [an] additional number of screws were entered to secure it. The course was then shaped for Cape Leeuwin, because vessels often fish off the west coast of Australia, and many captains of vessels prefer the western route to the eastern for America rather than contend with the severe weather to be met with in the passage around Cape Horn. A change of weather prevented the contemplated visit to Cape Leeuwin, and the ship on the 23d of January met an easterly wind, the most unfavorable quarter for us, and with it came a westerly current, throwing the ship away from her course. Working to windward was no easy task against a current, even for so fast a vessel as the *Shenandoah*. It was absolutely necessary that the vessel should be docked, and notwithstanding the injury which may already have been done, or might follow, to the bearings by the use of the propeller, I felt obliged to use steam, because I desired to reach Melbourne in time to communicate with a mail steamer which would leave on the 26th of January, and if I missed her I would not enjoy another opportunity for some time. Cape Otway was made on the morning of the 25th, and soon after the Heads of Port Phillip were visible. A pilot boat came to us, and I received a pilot, Mr. Johnson, who desired to know why I wished the ship taken into Hobson's Bay. I felt irritated, but he said before I made a reply, "My orders are peremptory about Confederate cruisers." I furnished him with a satisfactory reason to his instructions, and the steamer was pointed for the entrance to the port. We were visited at the Heads by a health officer, who was kind and showed interest in the ship. After his return to the shore the character of the vessel was telegraphed to Melbourne, and a little before sunset she dropped her anchors in Hobson's Bay, cheered and surrounded by steamers densely crowded. Newspapers came tumbling from the steamers to our decks. I was prepared for the reception; it was from generous and brave hearts who believed in the righteousness of the Southern cause. The pilot had said, "You have a great many friends in Melbourne." Lieutenant Grimball was sent with the following communication addressed to his Excellency Sir Charles Darling, K. C. B.

On the following morning soon after daylight I was aroused by voices in the adjoining cabin, and I heard Mrs. Nichols say: "If these chronometers and sextants were mine I guess I'd make him give them to me." She had claimed every book which was brought from the *Delphine* and requested their restitution, which was granted. *Uncle Tom's Cabin* Mr. Whittle threw overboard. The early rising was preparatory to desertion. They were getting their things together for an early departure from the steamer. They were told they could go on shore, but they would not be allowed the use of any of the steamer's boats. A shore boat was called and themselves, with their luggage, placed in it and shoved clear from the vessel. Mrs. Nichols's last words were, "I wish that steamer may be burned."

On the 26th a large gang of calkers came on board and commenced calking the vessel inside and outside. Under her quarters calking irons were driven without resistance into the hold of the vessel. This was evidence of the deception practiced in the London docks by [on] the agent who purchased her for our government.

Several of my crew having been induced to desert the steamer through the influence of the American consul and his emissaries, I addressed a note to the chief of police on the subject, and the following is the reply.

I had received several anonymous letters concerning a contemplated destruction of the *Shenandoah* by unknown persons on shore, and on that subject I addressed a note to the superintendent of the water police. Subjoined is Captain Lyttleton's reply:

POLICE DEPARTMENT, *SUPERINTENDENT'S OFFICE,*
Melbourne, February 6, 1865

SIR: I have the honor to acknowledge the receipt of your letter of the 31st ultimo, requesting police protection for the Confederate war steamer *Shenandoah.* I beg to inform you that I have instructed the Williamstown water police to give particular attention to the vessel. I should have replied to your letter before, but that from some cause, which I shall enquire into, it only reached me on the morning of the 4th instant.

I have the honor to be, sir, your most obedient servant,

THOMAS LYTTLETON,
Superintendent.

CAPTAIN WADDELL,
Confederate War Steamer Shenandoah.

The following telegram was sent by the chief of police to Mr. Beaver, assistant superintendent of police, Williamstown.

A large police force surrounded the vessel and took possession of the patent slip. I was in possession of the above telegram when I wrote the following letter. It was secretly conveyed to me by the engineer of the patent slip, who was the most ardent foreign Confederate I had ever seen. On the 14th of February, when the telegram was sent from Melbourne to Mr. Beaver at Williamstown, all the militia at Melbourne were turned out under arms, and artillery companies were sent to the beach to threaten the *Shenandoah,* which was a display [of] intellectual military weakness I was not prepared to witness, for the *Shenandoah* lay in a helpless condition on the slip, where it appears she was decoyed for the purpose of insult. She could not have done more than resist boarding, and so long as the government did not attempt to search the ship nothing could occur to occasion loss of blood or life. The government was informed through rumor that if the ship was not "released within twenty-four hours I would surrender her with officers and crew to Her Majesty's government."

On the 16th of February, 1865, acknowledgment to my letter was given by a clerk in the employ of the attorney-general, and brought to me by a servant of that officer, which was instantly returned to the person who sent it. The information I sought was not furnished by the attorney-general; he could not, perhaps, write intelligently on the subject. I have no record of his name; I think his name is Smeade.

There was a Mr. MacFarlin, a customs official, who did not have the intelligence to draw the distinction between a national and private vessel, who for many days, with his assistants, kept watch over the *Shenandoah.* His visits to the ship were daily, and always very friendly toward us, but that was to cover the indelicacy of his visits. I took occasion to inform him of the character of those visits, and explained to him the difference between a merchant, privateer, and national vessel, which distinction he accepted, and we were not troubled by such visits as much as we had been before. The majority of the governor's council were inimical to the South, many of whom were engaged in trade with the Northern States of America, particularly Mr. Francis, the honorable commissioner of trade and customs, who was part owner in a shop which dealt in Yankee notions. He fraternized with the Yankee consul in business and politics. All the government understrappers manifested a caution in their intercourse with us in ship affairs, but were not backward in asking questions, such as "Where will you go from here?" To which the executive officer gave the laconic reply, "Do you suppose I would be such a —— fool as to tell you if I knew?" The governor, I was told, was our friend.

I now pass from the correspondence to little incidents inaugurated by the hostile shore party to tempt my firmness in observing the laws of neutrality. Every effort was made to entangle me in legal difficulties. In seventeen days I received forty-seven letters, a large majority of which were applications—bogus, of course—for service in the *Shenandoah,* some of which bore signatures or simply initials, asking for paymasters', doctors', clerks', or marine officers' positions, and a few informed me the ship would be destroyed at her anchorage if a constant watch was not kept. I made no reply to any of those communications. I asked protection of the police in reference to the destruction of the vessel. Here is a specimen of the letters asking employment, etc.: An old woman with a lad of twelve years came several times to the ship and represented they were from Mobile; that she was too infirm to support the lad any longer, and asked, as he was born in Mobile, and her grandchild, that I would receive him and ship him in the Confederate service. She was referred to the attorney-general in Melbourne for advice in her case, and directed not to renew the application unless provided with a certificate setting forth her indisputable right to enter the lad in the service of the Confederate States, and accompanying the certificate the attorney-general's consent to such an arrangement. The plot was well laid, but having failed, the old woman and her hireling never returned.

When the superintendent of police, Captain Lyttleton, visited the *Shenandoah* with the search warrant I received him kindly, and he cautiously introduced the subject of his visit, which was that he held a warrant for a certain man (Charlie) who was reported to have joined the *Shenandoah* since the ship anchored in Hobson's Bay, and asked if he introduced witnesses on the deck of the vessel to identify the man if found would they [the witnesses] or any part of them be arrested if it should prove they had deserted from the *Shenandoah*. I replied that the deck of the *Shenandoah* represented Confederate territory, and every violation of the law or the usage of the sea service committed on her deck would be punished by the laws which governed the ship. Therefore if any deserter from the *Shenandoah* appeared on her deck, it mattered not under what circumstances, such arrests would be made. His application to search the vessel was refused, and he was informed, should the Victoria government attempt so great an outrage, the *Shenandoah* would be defended at every risk to life. In consequence of that interview with Captain Lyttleton, Captain Standish, chief of police, was directed by the governor in council to send the telegram to Mr. Beaver, which is embraced in statement made to council, asking opinion as to his excellency's detention of the *Shenandoah* on the slip.

I gave to my crew twenty-four hours' liberty to amuse themselves on shore, and through the agency of the American consul and his emissaries a negro, sixteen Germans, and an Irish-American were induced to desert the steamer. I made application for the issue of arrest warrants for each deserter, and applied to the chief of police for assistance, but each application was denied, a discourtesy which was never extended to any commander of a Federal vessel in a British port.

I was treated rudely by Sir Charles Darling and his council, but the good people of Melbourne were kind and did not forget we were strangers and distinguished from all other visitors on account of our peculiar position politically. The *Shenandoah* left the slip on the afternoon of the 15th of February, 1865, without accident, cheered by a crowd of idle spectators which had collected on the adjacent wharves and saluted by the colonial steamer of war *Victoria*. She was immediately taken to the coal ship *John Fraser*, which vessel had recently arrived from Cardiff with coal and of the kind I wanted, and she was supposed to be my consort, but there was no truth for the suspicion, although the coincidence was singular. She arrived in very excellent time to supply my want, and I purchased of her 250 tons of coal. The afternoon of the 17th of February found the *Shenandoah* at single anchor, under steam, and ready for sea. I was visited after dark on that evening by Mr. ———, with a request from the proprietors of the *Argus* for a copy of the correspondence which passed between the government and myself and expressing their intention to publish it if I would give them copies. The application was gratifying to me, for I desired the Richmond government to know what had transpired, and I also desired the opposition party in Melbourne to be in possession of those letters, which would acquaint it with all the facts connected with the steamer's visit and the action of the Victoria government in the case. The correspondence was published. I had employed a carpenter to make and put up a bureau in my cabin, and while he was engaged about it, fitting it to the side of the vessel, he told me he had heard in a restaurant some Americans discussing the feasibility of smuggling themselves on board, and after the steamer was at sea to capture her. I was in bed during the reception of that *morceau délicieux* of intelligence and replied, "If it is attempted they will fail, and I will hang every mother's son of them."

Repairs and supplies cost the steamer something over £4,000, and my strong box was quite emptied of the £5,000 which was considered amply sufficient by the disbursing agent, Commander James D. Bulloch, for defraying the expenses incident to the cruise which I was ordered to make. When the ship left Melbourne there were not $5,000 on board, nor was I furnished with any letters of credit to fall back upon in case of need. I do not complain of nor do I dwell on this fact, but I state it as a part of the history of the vessel I commanded, and as showing how much or little of the fluids of the Confederate government accumulated in Europe toward the close of the war came into my hands. I feel the more bound to make this statement because my accounts, from the destruction of the Confederate, government, having been subjected to no official inspection, I desire to acknowledge by this public statement my responsibility to the judgment of the people of the South. I was ordered to perform a distant and dangerous service, which excited an anxious solicitude for all concerned, and nothing should have been forgotten, neglected, or denied the steamer which could have been so easily supplied.

The 18th of February, saw the *Shenandoah*'s anchors on her bows, and at 7 o'clock she steamed from the anchorage toward the Heads of Port Phillip, a distance of 30 miles. The pilot, Mr. Johnson, who had brought the steamer in from sea, had since run a vessel on a shoal, which had its bad influences on his professional ability with many ship captains, and a brother called and stated the facts connected with his case to me, adding, "Captain, if you will let him take your steamer to sea he will be again on his feet." The pilot, Mr. Johnson, took the *Shenandoah* to sea. The harbor master, Captain Fergusson, a miserable apology for a man, lent himself in the laudable capacity of spy and fancied himself beyond my discovery. He even directed Mr. Johnson to communicate to him any irregularity which Mr. Johnson might observe during his pilotage of the vessel to sea, and if the steamer received any additional force in men after she left her anchorage. This was all communicated to me by the pilot. All the understrappers of that English nobleman's administration of a colonial government with whom I was brought in contact imbibed that driveling spirit for petty annoyances which characterized the conduct of the overzealous and scrupulous, peddling James G. Francis, commissioner of trade and customs, pressed on by the designs of a less miserable wretch, represented in the official capacity of American consul. I am surprised that even the United States should be so represented. With such characters

English gentlemen have no sympathy, but the very knowledge of their low character, such as Mr. Allen, and the desire to keep them off from any private association,
requires British officials oftentimes, as in this case, to be unusually strict in all official obligations toward them. This attention more frequently is the result of the
contempt in which they are held. Yankee vanity always ascribes it, however, to
admiration for or fear of his country.

Once more on the bright blue sea, standing away from the land, feeling as free
as the ship let loose to the breeze in chase to the westward. The pilot had left us
with his good wishes, but the parting was not accompanied with those home feelings which cluster around the heart when shaking the hand of the man who would
so soon return to our native soil. No letters or words of affectionate recollections
were to be conveyed through him to those we had left behind; a feeling of impa-
tience hurried him over the side, and no regret was entertained for the separation.
The vessels in sight were bound for Port Phillip, when, on their arrival, would be
made known our communication with them and the direction taken by the
Shenandoah. Soon after night closed in the steamer's head was turned toward
Round Island, in Bass Strait. The moon shone beautifully bright, the atmosphere
was clear, cool, and the sky looked more distant than I had ever before observed it,

While the stars that oversprinkle
All the heavens seemed to twinkle
With a crystalline delight.

I had received on the spar deck in bags coal for steaming to the western edge
of the South Pacific. At 1 o'clock of the 20th, during the mid watch of that very
excellent gentleman and gallant officer, Lieutenant John Grimball, land was seen
ahead. It was unexpected, and its appearance showed a powerful local attraction,
which, if the night had been dark, might have resulted in the loss of the ship. At
sunrise we had fairly entered Bass Strait, with the wind at east of north, light and
good for steaming. I continued the vessel under steam until Cape Howe bore per
compass N. N. W., when sail was made and the propeller triced up. The shifts
company was now augmented, receiving in exchange for one Irish-American, sixteen dirty Germans, and a negro, who had deserted in Hobson's Bay under promise of $100 from the American consul (the same was offered a quartermaster by
name of Hall, who informed me), thirty-four young American seamen and eight
others of different nationalities, who had smuggled themselves on board the
steamer the night before she left Hobson's Bay. That increase of men placed on our
deck seventy-two men, equal to any emergency, all quite homeless and accustomed
to a hard life, more in search of adventure and fun than anything else. The execu-

tive officer, Lieutenant William G. Whittle, Jr., who was always active and intelligent in the discharge of his peculiar duties, saw a force assembled and placed under his direction which was nearly sufficient to supply the crews of all divisions. A sergeant, corporal, and three privates formed a nucleus for a marine guard, and their uniforms were to be made cap-a-pie. The sergeant, George P. Canning, represented himself to have been an aide-de-camp to Right Reverend Lieutenant General Leonidas Polk. There were representatives from New England among the crew. (Where is it one does not meet with that class of humanity?) To find a genuine Yankee on the deck of a Confederate war ship, manifesting delight in the destroying of his countrymen's property, was droll indeed. But those men may have been better read in Rawle's *Interpretations of the Constitution of the United States* as enunciated by the founders of that instrument than W. H. Seward and his motley crew.

The wind hung at east of north, forcing the ship sometimes on a course south of east, and then backing in more northerly, she would come up to a course north of east. To the northward were the Middleton, Lord Howe, and Norfolk Islands, which I would like to have visited, but the foul wind prevented, and I could not afford to expend coal in perhaps a fruitless search for whalers. Those islands are claimed by the British government, and lay contiguous to the coast of Australia, and are in easy communication with Sydney. If the ship had been favored with a good wind I would have visited the whaling ground of each of those islands, but to nurture the supply of coal was of the utmost importance. The delay of the steamer at Melbourne had operated against success in the South Pacific. The whaling fleet of that ocean, known as the "South Pacific whaling fleet," had received warning and had suspended its fishing in that region of ocean and had taken shelter in the neighboring ports, or gone to the Arctic Ocean, which was most probable. The presence of the steamer in the South Pacific waters dispersed that whaling fleet altogether. No captures were made there. The number of that fleet is never more than forty. The wind, however, held on at the north and east until the ship had nearly reached the meridian of the Three Kings, situated west of the most northwesterly point of north New Zealand, when a favorable change of wind occurred and the ship made a more northerly course, passing between Fearn and Conway islands, thence along the Fiji, Rotumah, and Ellice Islands, these islands being within the tropics and covered with verdure and undergrowth, temperature varying with the strength of the wind. When to the north of Fearn Island a revolving gale from northeast caught the ship. I had no choice as to what tack to lay the steamer on, for there were too many islands west of her whose exact locality was too indefinitely ascertained to risk the vessel on the starboard tack; nor could she be run for the same reason. Fortunately the gale worked westward, and the ship's head being southeast and easterly, she kept out of its path. I had never [in] twenty-three years' service seen such a succession of violent squalls; she was enveloped in salt mist and tossed about by an angry sea like a plaything. The machinery operated so well and the ship's preparations in port for contesting with adverse weather were so complete in character that wind and wave seemed bent on testing her strength. I have never witnessed a vessel in a gale stand up against her adversary in better style; it was the first occasion of lying to. Her easy motion, stability, and dryness increased my admiration for the little ship. The gale lasted four days, and a calm ensued.

On the 21st of March, in latitude 8° 35' S. and longitude 172° 51' E., failing to pick up the trade winds, and being wearied from excessive heat and a deluge of rain, ordered steam and steered in a northerly direction in search of wind. Sighted Drummond Island and ran sufficiently near to communicate with natives who came out in their canoes to beg and trade a little fruit. They are copper colored, short in stature, and without an article of clothing. A day or two after leaving Drummond Island communicated with a schooner from Honolulu on a trading voyage among the islands in search of tortoise shell, and learned some valuable information about American whale vessels in Lea [Lod ?] Harbor, island of Ascension. Ship under sail again, with a fine trade. The following day made Strong Island and put the steamer under steam. Ran close enough to see into the harbor of Chabrol, which is a place of rendezvous for whale ships. The harbor was empty. Skirted all sides of the island but the north; lifted propeller and made sail for the island of Ascension [Ponapi], one of the Caroline Group.

The ship had now a fine trade wind and was running along smoothly and rapidly toward the island, which came in view during the forenoon of the following day after my visit to Strong Island. A little before midday she was sufficiently near to distinguish four sail at anchor close in with the land, and I began to think if what we believed to be whale ships of New England should prove of other nationality it would be a very good April fool. The Honolulu schooner was the only sail we had seen from the 20th of February to the 1st of April, which was evidence at least that the South Pacific whaling fleet had taken flight. We never on any other occasion were as long without seeing a flag. It was a lonely and solitary feeling that only those in our situation could realize. We were sailing over almost unknown seas, and the monotony in our state of excitement excited an ardent feeling [which] was intolerable.

The ship was under steam, running along the land, when a small boat came in sight from which I received an English pilot (Thomas Harrocke, of Yorkshire, England, was thirteen years on the island), who had been a convict many years before at Sydney, Australia, and who had made his escape therefrom, reaching the island of Ascension, I never learned in what way, and married a native woman. I questioned him about the vessels and the port, found there were American whalers in Lea [Lod?] Harbor, and that there was work enough for the *Shenandoah*. The pilot was directed to anchor the steamer inside the reef, and if he wrecked her I would hold him responsible. The flag was not yet shown, and the pilot was in perfect ignorance as to our nationality, nor did he ask any questions. The preparations for anchoring being made, I accompanied the pilot and kept with him until the steamer was anchored in 15 fathoms water with both anchors down. Three vessels hoisted the American flag; the fourth hoisted the Oahu flag. In that snug little harbor about mid-channel is a rock awash, and the steamer was unavoidably and uncomfortably near to it; she should not swing in its direction too near. To avoid accident it was necessary to run hawsers out from her quarters to stout trees on shore and tie her up. After the steamer was provided against accident four armed boats [four boats were armed], the second and third cutters, port and starboard whaleboats, respectively commanded by Lieutenants Grimball, Chew, Lee, and Scales. These boats varied in dimensions, neither of them being over 32 or under 28 feet in length and less than 6 feet in beam. They were strongly built and carried a prize crew of seven men each. Each lieutenant had one or more subordinate officers under his command and conducted the affairs of his special duty independent of the others, making his report through his subordinate officer to me. The armed boats were dispatched with orders to capture the vessels and to send their officers, ship papers, log books, instruments for navigation, and charts to the *Shenandoah*, and remain in charge of their respective prizes until further orders from me. The charts were all important, because the ship was not furnished with such as whalers use, which show every track and where they have been most successful in taking whales. With such charts in my possession I not only held a key to the navigation of all the Pacific Islands, the Okhotsk and Bering seas, and the Arctic Ocean, but the most probable localities for finding the great Arctic whaling fleet of New England without a tiresome search.

After the boats had left the steamer our flag was hoisted and a gun fired. This signal, announcing the character of the steamer, aroused all the surrounding country; the natives along the shore who were gazing at the vessel sought shelter in the bushes, and the American whalers hauled down their flags. Some officer, directing the pilot's attention to our flag, asked him if he knew it; he said he had never seen it, but as the boats were gone after the Yankees it might be Jeff. Davis's flag, for he had heard of a big war in America, and in all the big battles the South had whipped the Yankees. When I told him of our character he said: "Well, well, I never thought I'd live to see Jeff. Davis's flag." That was President Davis's popular name in Ascension or Pouinipete [Ponapi], which with the natives bore the signification of king. Looking at the flag he said, "It is pretty, and looks like the English white flag." He told me there were five tribes on the island, each having their king, their princes, and chiefs or noblemen; that their currency was the cocoanut, and that metal money was of no value to the natives; that they are fond of finery, tobacco, liquor, powder, and shot; that no principle of honor controlled them in their intercourse, but fear of injury made them respect whatever they solemnly entered upon. They are semibarbarous, have no knowledge of a Creator, or if they have been better informed do not regard it. There is a Yankee missionary on the island, but whatever he may teach in holy things, he has learned them to doubt his contracts with them for tortoise shell. Their king is the object of adoration, and yet I could not observe any great amount of respect paid him. They inhabit an island seven miles in circumference, in constant verdure, covered with fine fruit, their rivers and harbors swarming with food fish. The pilot told me that the king and princes of the tribes had heard of the war through him, and he received his intelligence through newspapers which vessels had left at the island, and that they were great admirers of our chief magistrate. Although the pilot spoke of his Excellency President Davis as Jeff. Davis, he intended to convey no disrespect to that devoted patriot and world-renowned representative of the South. He had heard of the war, and with it he had heard associated the name of the great political chieftain; and with the clash of Southern arms, which electrified the minds of men in the remotest parts of earth, its heroism and dash were "borne upon the wings of the morning" and wafted by the breezes into the very habitations of the isolated barbarians. There in their imaginations stood clothed in brilliancy the peerless son of America, their wonder and admiration. There stood the name of Jefferson Davis in that contracted island, peopled with men little removed by association above the level of brutes, but sufficiently intelligent to appreciate worth and obstinate bravery, for the deeds of brave men were his, and all that arms could win was represented by his name.

The pilot was my interpreter. I sent my gig with a petty officer, accompanied by him, to convey to his majesty the king of the weather tribe (King Ish-y-paw, of Martinile) my earnest solicitation for his health, peace, and prosperity, and a strong desire to have him visit the *Shenandoah*, one of Jeff. Davis's ships. In an hour after the gig had left the steamer she was on her return with the royal party and with several sitters. Seventy war canoes, decorated with faded bunting or colored cotton, pulled at a respectful distance from her. In the gig were seated the king, the hereditary prince, and four chiefs, each with a wreath of flowers encircling the brow, and an apron made of sea grass, which fell from the hips halfway to the knee. Their bodies shone in the sunlight as if covered with oil. I was prepared to receive his majesty and met him at a gangway. He came up the side very cautiously, and, arranging his apron, seated himself between the head-boards of the gangway, smelling furiously of cocoanut oil, a protection against mosquitoes and almost anything else, and blocking the passage to the hereditary prince, who was hanging on outside of the vessel to a manrope. The pilot was still in the gig. It was impossible for me to speak to his majesty. He was therefore very unceremoniously introduced to the deck (by the motions of head and hand), on which he stood perfectly erect, as if expecting a submissive bow from all present; and after his retinue reached the deck and arranged themselves in their respective orders and with respect to their sovereign I was presented to his majesty by the pilot, who simply said with a backward motion of the head, "That's the king, sir." I invited his majesty and suite to my cabin, and the officers were asked to witness the proceedings, for such things are interesting; the absurdity makes it so.

The topic for discussion was postponed till after the introduction of the pipe and Schiedam schnapps, not a bad introduction, as it was a sort of prelude to something else which interested me more, and my august visitor became quite at his ease, although singularly impressed by the objects of capture which were in the cabin, and its general appearance. He said to the interpreter, "I wish to spit, but don't like to spit on the carpet," which had at least a suspicion of gentility, and a spittoon was supplied such as are generally used on shipboard, made of wood and filled with sand. I observed then for the first time that the lobes of the ears were split, and seeing a pipe handle pushed through and suspended in the opening of the lobe, I understood the use made of them. A few glasses of Schiedam drew forth friendly sentiments from his majesty. The officers who had taken charge of the prizes had sent their mates, papers, etc., but the captains were absent on a jollification in one of their boats. An armed boat was kept in readiness to capture the party when it should [make] its appearance in the harbor, which it did about sunset, and was conducted to the *Shenandoah*. The captains of the three Yankee vessels could give no good reason why their vessels should not be confiscated and they held as prisoners, while the captain of the Oahu vessel could not produce a bill of sale and could not swear he was cognizant of the sale of his vessel to a Honolutian of Oahu. She bore the name *Harvest*, of New Bedford; she carried an American register; she was in charge of the same captain who commanded her before the war on former whaling voyages, and her mates were American. I therefore confiscated her and held the captain a prisoner.

The names and value of the vessels were: The *Edward Cary*, of San Francisco, valued at $15,000; the *Hector*, of New Bedford, valued at $35,000; the *Pearl*, of New London, valued at $10,000, and the *Harvest*, valued at $35,000. Taken collectively, their crews numbered 130 men, and were composed of Honolutians, a timid, mongrel race, easily imposed upon and cheated, but suiting the purpose of such men as command whalers. The question of confiscation being settled and the captains being locked up, it became important to sound his majesty on the subject of neutrality, and therefore he made me a special visit with his council to discuss the question. An old axiom is, Politeness and consideration for the acts of others cost nothing and often buy a great deal. One of the captive captains had been engaged in the infamous blocking of the Charleston channel with stone. He was disposed to be impertinent, but a pair of irons cooled him down. Another one of them claimed a Virginia mother; although he was considered a New England man, [he] gave me a good deal of information about the probable places the whaling fleet would be found.

The king is not invested with arbitrary power; is only considered as the first among the citizens. His authority depended more on his personal qualities than on his station. It is easy to imagine that an independent people, so little restrained by law and cultivated by science, would not be very strict in maintaining a regular succession of their princes. Though they paid great regard to the royal family, and ascribed to it an undisputed superiority, they either have no rule or none that is steadily observed in filling the vacant throne; and present convenience in that emergency was more attended to than general principles. The authority of a king must not be considered as altogether elective with the tribes; if any king left a son of an age and capacity fit for government, the young prince naturally stepped on the throne; if he was a minor, his uncle or the next prince of the blood would be promoted to the government. The administration of government, the tacit acquiescence of the people.

On the 3d of April his majesty, accompanied by the hereditary prince and chiefs, came on board and assembled in my cabin. The pipe and schnapps performed their office, and when the king and his court felt themselves comfortably seated the conversation was introduced, through the interpreter, by explaining the position of the ship and the character of the war, which, I said, was so familiar to his majesty it did not need repetition; to which his majesty grunted. I think he questioned his intelligence on that subject. He drank more often than anyone else, and never sipped his liquor—drank bumpers.

I said the vessels in port belong to our enemy, who have been hostile to us for forty years and will be always so until the end of time. "Then," said he, "you don't like one another." "No," said I; "it is incompatible with virtue that the South should ever be reconciled to the North again; blood has been split; life has been taken; our countrywomen have been outraged and the unprotected have been driven into the forest for shelter while their homes are destroyed by fire. I am ordered to capture and destroy their vessels whenever it shall be in my power to do so, and if your majesty's laws of neutrality" (here he looked confused) "would not be violated, I will confiscate the vessels in port; and as there is very little in them which the steamer requires, I propose to present their contents to your majesty, which you can make use of as you may wish, and when your tribe have finished with them I will take them to sea and burn them."

His majesty, after a short conference with his chiefs—the hereditary prince was not consulted—said: "We find nothing conflicting with our laws in what you say; there are shoals in the harbor on which the vessels can be run and there destroyed"; but he desired that I would not fire at them, for the shot would go on shore and hurt some of the tribe. I agreed to all his views, and commenced removing such things to the steamer as were required, and brought the *Harvest* alongside of the *Shenandoah* to receive her fresh water, provisions, and five tons of sperm oil, and directed the officers in charge of the prizes to run the vessels on the shoals and allow the natives to take possession of them until further orders. Among the stores sent to the steamer were seventy down-east muskets, which had been for trade with the islanders, and two dozen infantry pants and coats. The pants would answer for the marine guard which I hoped to be able to recruit for the steamer. I said to his majesty, "My fasts on shore are very insecure; a wicked person could cut them at the very moment when, for the safety of the vessel, they should hold on, and if such an accident should happen to the vessel a flaw of wind might drive her on that rock," pointing to it; several of the men of the prizes were on shore, having deserted their vessels as soon as our flag was hoisted. "Now, I desire your majesty will station one or more of your warriors to guard the fasts, with orders to shoot anyone who should go within prescribed limits." He replied, "I have the warriors, but I have no muskets and ammunition." His majesty was now on such familiar terms with me that I could, without evoking royal displeasure, make suggestions and crack a joke at his expense, and I do not think he considered me undignified, for he frequently addressed me as his dear brother.

I struck a bargain with his majesty by offering him the seventy very dangerous muskets and some ammunition if he would guard the fasts. He accepted the gift and sent his order for guarding the fasts, which was promptly obeyed. No one knew the character of the musket in the hands of the guards, not even themselves; but I would have preferred the muzzle to the chamber as far as danger is concerned. His majesty expressed a desire to examine the steamer with his staff, and when he was informed of the pleasure it would afford me to accompany him, I handed him a sword which I begged his acceptance of, as it might prove of value to him at some future time. That sword was once United States property, and was found on board the schooner *Lizzie M. Stacey* in the North Atlantic. His majesty had never seen a sword and did not exactly understand its use or manufacture. He was induced to belt it to his naked waist, and some one of his chiefs hung it to his right side, which caused me to ask if his majesty was left-handed. His majesty eyed the weapon suspiciously, and his expression of countenance conveyed such an enquiry of doubt as to the propriety of having it so near his royal person that I was quite overcome with laughter, and I endeavored to conceal from his majesty my merriment, when I observed him unbuckling the belt, evidently not well satisfied. I told him it was absolutely necessary he should have the sword during his visit through the ship, and he reluctantly removed his hand from the belt. We had reached the engine-room hatch and were in the act of descending to the engine room when I saw his majesty's legs entangled with the sword and the hereditary prince assisting to disengage it; he could not descend the ladder with the sword to his side, so he removed it and the prince took charge of it. The machinery excited his surprise and amused him, and his expression of wonder was communicated by a cluck of the tongue, which his retinue echoed. He forgot his dignity and rested against a part of the machinery, when he became smeared with a white coating that is used to prevent rust.

His majesty, after his return to the cabin, invited me to pay him a visit at the royal residence, which is only established during prosperous seasons at some locality where the fishing is good. That residence was near the margin of the harbor and built on six piles sufficiently elevated to be above the reach of the flood tide or the overflow of the river "Fresh Water." I have forgotten the native word. The residence was built of cane interlaced with vine and roofed with the broad leaf of the cocoanut, and a pair of rickety wooden steps led to the entrance. A prince met me at the place where I landed with suite and conducted me to the royal residence, but did not go in. There was but one room, six by eight feet, in which the royal family slept, ate, and received their visitors. His majesty's bed was a simple mat, unfolded in a corner to the right of the entrance, and his queen was sitting near him with her hands and chin resting on her knees. He did not rise from his mat when I entered, nor did his queen in any way acknowledge my presence; it would not have been court etiquette for her to do so; but his majesty beckoned me to a seat. The furniture consisted of two wooden chairs, a box, and an old trunk, the latter (being soft on top and empty, I suppose was the seat of honor and used by his majesty on state occasions) was offered to me.

The queen was downright ugly, the first really ugly woman I have ever seen, and his second wife. The king desired to marry her before the death of his first queen, of whom he had grown tired, but the old queen would not consent to the marriage, because she would be put aside to satisfy the law with the tribe that their king can have but one lawful wife. The old queen, however, died suddenly, into which no enquiry was made, and the king married the following day.

The center of the roof was supported by two upright poles and between their heels was an open space devoted to the deposit of fruit and other eatables. The conversation was introduced by the king asking when the steamer would probably sail, and what I intended to do with my prisoners; that he supposed they would all be put to death, for it was right to make such disposition of one's enemies. I told him they would be unharmed, and that in civilized warfare we destroyed only men who were in armed resistance to us, and paroled the unarmed. "But," said his majesty, "war can not be considered civilized, and people who make war on an unoffending people are bad people and do not deserve protection." I consider that pretty good for a savage. He said the above because he feared the prisoners whom I should leave behind.

I told the king I would sail the following day, 13th April, and should convey to our president the kindness which he had shown the *Shenandoah* and the respect he had paid our flag. He said: "[Tell] Jeff. Davis he is my brother and a great warrior, and that I am very poor, and that our tribes are friends, and if he will send your vessel for me I will go to see him in his country. I send these two chickens to Jeff. Davis (they were dead) and some cocoanuts, which he will find very good?" His majesty had no conception of the distance to America, which he took to be an island like his own somewhere, and believed that within a few days the *Shenandoah* would convey safely his royal gifts to Mr. Davis.

The muskets were lying about the yard around the royal residence, and a few natives were oiling them. He seemed to feel perfectly secure from harm now that he was possessed of so many weapons. When I was about to leave he rose from his mat and said he would go with me to the boat, and when I reached her I found the chickens wrapped in cocoanut leaves, and one dozen cocoanuts. The king was always cold and reserved in manner; he was a selfish old beggar until the schnapps and pipe warmed him, and he did not consider it undignified or unselfish to ask for whatever he fancied and show displeasure if refused. He is, however, not unlike his brother sovereigns of this world in that particular, although civilization has caused the powerful to check their wants. Kings are no longer created by wars. He sent on board several times fruit and a few fish, and visited me every day, when he took his schnapps, of which he was too fond. I gave him a silk scarf, which he admired, and he sent me a belt for the waist woven by some one of his people out of fibers of the cocoanut and interwoven with wool, which had been traded for among the whale vessels which touch there to take in yams, water, hogs, and poultry preparatory to a voyage along the line or in the North Pacific. The belt is peculiar, manifesting intelligence in the art of weaving and taste in blending colors. It is preserved as a memento from the only sovereign who had an independence of character and fearlessness of disposition to perform a common duty toward a righteous people and just cause. The prizes were run upon the shoals selected by the king, and the canoes surrounding them were handled more beautifully and skillfuly than I had ever seen man handle boats. Every movable plank, spar, and bulkhead were taken on shore for flooring purposes, and the sails were removed from yards and sail room for tents and to be converted into sails for their canoes, and as the consuming vessels floated higher the canoes approached their sides and peeled the copper from their bottoms. The natives placed a value on that metal, and I was informed some of it would be used for pointing spears and arrows, some would be converted into breastplates and shields, and some traded with the neighboring tribes. I saw a great many of the natives, male and female. They are delicate in form, high cheek bones, flat noses, small feet and hands. The women are decidedly homely, but graceful. His majesty made me a present of the royal princess, which gift I was rude enough to decline; I told him I was married.

Preparatory to leaving Lea [Lod?] Harbor I asked permission of the king to land my prisoners, whom I provided with provisions and two whaleboats. The prisoners preferred to land there than at the island of Guam, and that arrangement suited best. The morning of the 13th of April saw all prisoners clear of the steamer, and at noon she tripped her anchors and stood to sea, leaving to the care of the king and his tribe 130 disappointed whalers, who had been accustomed to illtreat the natives and cheat them, besides introducing loathsome diseases never till then known to the tribes. That harbor will always be one of interest to the Yankee whaler, and tradition will point out the exact shoals on which the prizes were burned, the management of the affair, and where the *Shenandoah* lay calmly at anchor amid that scene of vengeance and destruction.

On leaving Lea [Lod?] Harbor the vessel was continued under steam, passing to the eastward of the island of Ascension until that island bore per compass southwest, and then sail was made to a fine trade wind, and I lifted the propeller. When due east of the island the course was north, leaving to the westward the Ladrone Islands, for it was my intention to keep the ship east of the Los Jardines, Grampus, and Margaret Islands, and passing her to the westward of Camira, Otra, and Marcus Islands.

In all the course of my sea life I never enjoyed more charming weather; the sun shone with splendid brilliancy, and the moon shed her peculiar luster from a dark-blue vaulted sky, while the vast mirror below reflected each heavenly body and flashed with sprightliness as the great ocean plow tore the waters asunder, and for ten consecutive days I would stand for hours on her deck gazing on that wonderful creation, that deep liquid world.

The track of vessels bound from San Francisco and many from the west coast of South America to Hong Kong lay between the parallels in north latitude of 17° and 20°, because the trade wind is better there than a more northerly route would find them, and the track for vessels bound to San Francisco and other ports along the west coast of America from the China coast lay between the parallels of 39° and 45°, because west wind prevails.

I spent several days in cruising along those frequented paths, but did not see a sail; the delay was, however, not without its reward, for the old boatswain had time to see things in his department in good condition for hard knocks. After the vessel had reached the parallel of 43° N. the weather became cold, foggy, and the winds were variable and westerly in direction, but unsteady in force, and that ever-reliable friend of the sailor, the barometer, indicated atmospheric convulsion—change in weather. She was prepared for a change of weather, which was rapidly approaching; the ocean was boiling from agitation, and if the barometer had been silent I would have called the appearance of the surface of the deep a famous tide rip. A black cloud was hurrying toward us from the northeast, and so close did it rest upon the surface of the water that it seemed determined to smother and blot out of existence forever the little vessel; and there came in it a violence of wind that threw the vessel on her side, and she started like the affrighted stag from his lair, bounding off before the awful pressure. Squall after squall struck her, flash after flash surrounded her, and thunder rolled in her wake, while every timber retorted to the shakings of the heavens. It was a typhoon; the ocean was as white as the snowdrift. Such was the violence of the wind that a new maintopsail, close-reefed, was blown into shreds. Æolus soon emptied his wrath upon the bosom of Neptune, and in ten hours the *Shenandoah* was making northing again.

Two days after that fearful typhoon we received another from the same quarter, but it was more civil and lasted a shorter time. The weather continued so threatening I felt as if the uncertainty and violence of the weather, the constant threatening sky, and agitated sea would never allow the vessel to get north of the parallel of 45°. That gale, like its predecessors, had worked to the westward, and the vessel began her northing again. On the 17th of May the ship was north of the parallel of 45°, and the weather, though cold, looked more settled. I think at all seasons bad weather may be expected between the parallels of 40° and 45° N. The week before appears at this time to mete have been more replete with desperate trials of wind and weather for energy and the vessel to overcome than all my former experience or imagination could fortify me to meet. On the 20th of May the Kuril Islands, covered with snow, came in sight, and on the forenoon of the 21st steamed under staysails into the Sea of Okhotsk and ran along the coast of Kamchatka under sail. There is a strong current setting along the Pacific side of the Kuril Islands, which helps to form the Sea of Okhotsk to the northeast.

On the 29th of May captured and burned the whaling bark *Abigail,* of New Bedford. When the *Abigail* was discovered the *Shenandoah* was skirting an extensive field of floe ice, and beyond another she was seen standing toward us; I therefore awaited her arrival, and learned that her captain mistook the steamer for a Russian provision vessel going to the settlement of Okhotsk to supply the Russian officials. A vessel goes there twice a year for that purpose. The *Abigail* was valued at $18,000. Several of the *Abigail*'s crew joined us, and among them a New Bedford man, a genuine downeaster. The captain was frightfully astonished at his situation; could hardly realize his misfortune; he had before fallen into Admiral Semmes's hands, and his vessel was destroyed, and although he had gone almost out of the world to secure a paying voyage he had failed again. He had been away from home for three years when he was captured by me. One of the mates, who was not dissatisfied with the accident to his late captain, said to him: "You are more fortunate in picking up Confederate cruisers than whales. I will never go with you again, for if there is a cruiser out you will find her. You have caught a whaler this time." The captain was heard repeatedly to say: "In New England we can make a substitute for ile" (oil), "but we must 'ave bone" (whalebone).

I continued as far as the mouth of Ghijinsk Bay, but found it so full of ice the steamer could not be entered. Then I stood along the land of eastern Siberia as far as Tausk Bay; then she was forced away by the ice and started for Shantaski Island, but found ice in such quantities before she reached the one hundred and fiftieth meridian of east longitude she was forced to the southward with ice almost in every direction and apparently closing on her. That ice varied from 15 to 30 feet in thickness, and although not very firm, was sufficiently so to seriously injure the vessel if neglected. I desired to reach Shantaski Island (called Green Island), for the fishing is there and in the bays southwest of it.

Within twenty days the ship had run from the tropics into snow and ice, from excessive heat to this excessively cold climate, and yet there was nothing more than catarrhs among the crew, from which they soon recovered. I had been without a stove, and the *Abigail* supplied the requisition. The caution resorted to [to] prevent sickness was an order preventing unnecessary exposure of the crew; consequently the vessel was kept under easy sail. The men were required by the surgeon, Charles E. Lining, an intelligent gentleman and excellent physician, to clothe themselves warmly and keep themselves dry. Extra rations of grog and hot coffee were served at regular hours, and the surgeon's assistant, Dr. Fred J. McNulty, a good fellow, inspected the food for the crew before and after prepared. Indeed, the medical gentlemen can not be complimented too highly for their excellent discretion in preserving the sanitary condition of the vessel.

The gales during the summer months north of the parallel of 40° are frequent, of few hours' duration, and move with excessive velocity, testing the forbearance of every object within its path. The *Shenandoah* experienced several of those gales in the Okhotsk Sea, and the danger of successfully weathering a gale in that sea is a secondary consideration to the heavy ice which a vessel might be forced against and wrecked. She took the first one of those gales to windward of 20 miles of floe ice, and if she had been hove to with the ice under her lee she would probably have been lost and her entire crew. It became imperative to relieve the ship of her perilous situation (she drifted faster than the ice) by finding a more comfortable berth for her elsewhere. She was run a little distance from and along the floe until a passage was seen from aloft through it, and open water beyond. She entered that passage, and in a short time was lying to under close sail, and the floe to windward, which a little time before was our dreaded enemy, was then our best friend, for the fury of the seas was expended on it and not against the sides of the *Shenandoah,* and acted as a breakwater for her. She lay perfectly easy; the water was as smooth as a mill pond, while expended seas on the farther edge of the floe broke furiously, throwing sheets of water 20 feet high. It was a majestic sight, resembling an infuriated ocean wasting itself against an iron-bound coast. The ship being relieved of a threatened danger, the next thought was to prevent her forging into ice during the thick weather which came on with the gale in fine rain and sleet. The wind was bitter cold, turning rain into ice, and forming a crust wherever it fell. The braces, blocks, yards, sails, and all other running rigging was thoroughly coated in ice from a half to 2 inches thick, so that it was impossible to use the braces. She forged easily into a floe which had not been seen, and after entering it a quarter of a mile was completely blocked in on every side. Icicles of great length and size hung from every portion of the vessel and her rigging. The gale lasted nine hours and passed over, and it was calm; the clouds had exhausted themselves and gone. The rosy tints of morn prepared us for a scene of enchantment, and when the sunlight burst upon that fairy ship she sparkled from deck to truck as if a diadem had been thrown about her, awakening exclamations of enthusiastic delight. The crew was ordered aloft with billets of wood to dislodge the ice and free the running gear. The large icicles falling from aloft rendered the deck dangerous to move upon, and it soon became covered with clear, beautiful ice. The water tanks, casks, and every vessel capable of receiving it were filled.

A supply of several hundred gallons of drinking water was not unacceptable, for it saved the consumption of fuel in condensing.

As soon as the rigging was clear of ice, so that the braces would traverse the blocks without danger of chafe, warps and grapnels were run out on the floe and hooked to large blocks of ice, and the ship was gradually worked out of it. Lieutenant Lee, a very excellent seaman, had charge of the deck. She had not been out of that dangerous situation eight hours before she was run again into a detached portion of the same floe and blocked in again. Lieutenant Scales, a gallant young officer, had charge of the deck. She was more quickly relieved by Lieutenant Grimball than in the former case. One gathers experience under certain circumstances and grows reconciled to situations which at first excite anxiety. It was evident from the quantity of drift ice in view that the floe was westward, and to continue the ship in that direction would be useless and dangerous.

She was therefore run to the eastward, and after knocking about till the 14th June, I left the Sea of Okhotsk, entering the North Pacific by the fiftieth parallel passage (or Amphitrite Strait) and steered northeast with a cracking southwester after her. When I gave the course northeast it was to take the ship midway of the most western of the Aleutian and the most eastern of Komandorski Islands, because currents about detached portions of land are irregular in direction and force.

In a few hours after leaving Amphitrite Strait the wind hauled more to the south and then east of south, producing a condensation of atmosphere which terminated in a thick, black fog, shutting the ship in an impenetrable mist to the eyes. I continued to run the ship northeast for the first twenty-four hours, and the wind having hauled still more to the eastward I deemed it prudent to steer E. N. E., because I was without observations and the wind would give the current a set or direction to the northwest, which, if not considered and introduced in my reckoning, would force the ship too much away from a direct course and perhaps uncomfortably near the Komandorski Islands. I therefore allowed two points for drift in a northwest direction. At the end of the next twenty-four hours I was without observations again, and I knew from the dead reckoning that the ship must be near the passage. The wind had drawn more from the land—the east—and the ship was headed more to the north.

During the afternoon the wind fell light from northeast, which change in force of wind was pretty sure evidence of the proximity of land; and immediately with that change of wind the fog lifted a little and the cry of "Land ho!" was made. At intervals it could be seen ahead at a distance of not more than four miles. The shifts deck was in charge of Lieutenant Grimball, who, in obedience to my order, tacked the ship, having just wind enough to turn her around, and it fell calm, leaving a fog denser than ever. That land was Copper Island. It is generally the case that a fog lifts so that objects are visible at distance of five to six miles and that lifting frequently occurs on approaching land, which may be attributed to the rapid absorption of moisture by earth. The ship was thirty-seven miles in error of her reckoning, notwithstanding the allowance made for drift, etc. I ordered steam, furled sails, and entered Bering Sea on the afternoon of the 16th of June, 1865.

The cruising in Bering Sea is not of a very delightful character; changes of weather were more sudden, and although the fogs did not last so many hours as they had done in the Sea of Okhotsk, they were more frequent and lighter in complexion.

I made Cape Navarin on the 21st of June, and, on the 22d, finding a current setting to the northeast, and soon after seeing blubber, I concluded that whalers were cutting out southwest of the *Shenandoah,* and I steamed in that direction. My calculation was well founded, for the steamer had not gone more than an hour in a southwesterly direction when the mast-head lookout cried, "Sail ho!" He reported two sail. The *Shenandoah* was instantly entered on the chase, and soon came up with the ships *William Thompson* and *Euphrates,* both of New Bedford, and before prize crews could be thrown on board of those vessels another sail was reported. A breeze had sprung up, and to work quickly was all important. Seeing the prize officers in charge of the vessels, and their respective captains and crews on board of the *Shenandoah,* I started in chase of and soon overhauled the British bark *Robert L. Townes,* of Sydney. Her captain was anxious to learn the name of the steamer, and I ordered his [her] name to be given the *Petropawlowka.* The *William Thompson* was the largest whaler out of New England, and, after removal of all valuables, set the vessels on fire. The aggregate value of the two vessels was $83,000. Those vessels had on board 800 casks of oil.

The following day [sighted] five vessels near a large body of floe ice, and the steamer stood for them; hoisted the American flag and communicated with the nearest, which proved to be the ship *Milo,* of New Bedford. The *Shenandoah* was run close to her stern and her captain was ordered to come on board with his papers. He complied, and was surprised to learn the character of the steamer; said he had heard of her being in Australia, but did not expect to see her in the Arctic Ocean. I asked for news. He said the war was over. I asked for documentary evidence; he could not supply it; he believed the war ended from what he had heard. I replied that it was not satisfactory, but that if he could produce any reliable evidence I would consider his impressions. He replied he could produce none such. He then said: "I took your command for a telegraph steamer which we have been expecting to lay a cable between Russian America and eastern Siberia." He was informed that I was willing to ransom his vessel if he accepted my conditions. He reflected a little and then said: "I see how it is; I will give bond and receive all prisoners you may put on board." I received his register and bond and directed him to return to his vessel and send all his boats with full crews to the steamer for prisoners and to keep her fore-topsail aback.

The boats came to the *Shenandoah,* and she steamed in pursuit of two vessels which seemed to be in communication. I resorted to the stratagem with the *Milo* of drawing her crew away to prevent her escape, for if I had not removed her crew her captain could have forced me to ransom another vessel, which would have been clever in him. A breeze had sprung up, the vessels had taken alarm, and I knew that the work before me required promptitude and management, or the rascals would have a good joke on me. The captains had communicated and entered their vessels in the floe. The *Shenandoah* ran close to and parallel with the floe and separated the barks, each being distant a mile, and fired at the one farthest in the ice, which made her heave to. Her consort then tacked and stood out of the floe for the Siberian coast with a good wind. I fired a second time at the bark which was hove to, and her captain interpreted it to mean stand out of the floe, and submitted to the prize boat which was in pursuit of her. She proved to be the *Sophia Thornton,* and her captain and officers were received on board the steamer. The officer in charge of the prize (Lieutenant Scales) was ordered to communicate with the *Milo* and order her captain to keep company with the *Sophia Thornton,* which vessel was ordered to follow the *Shenandoah.* The *Milo* would not attempt her escape, because she was without a crew [or] register, and had given a bond for $46,000. There was no inducement to do so, and I have believed that Captain Howe rather enjoyed the sport, for the worst that could happen to him was the loss of his voyage, while his associates lost their vessels and cargoes. The *Jireh Swift* was a fast bark, and had risked her escape to a good breeze, which might run her within a marine league of the Siberian coast. I chased her for three hours before getting near enough to shell her, but Captain Williams, who had made an obstinate effort to save his bark, saw the folly of exposing his crew to a destructive fire and yielded to his misfortune with a manly and becoming dignity. When the boarding officer, Lieutenant Lee, visited the *Jireh Swift* he found her captain and crew with their personal effects packed ready to leave the bark in her boats for the *Shenandoah,* and the bark was in flames twenty minutes afterwards. I think the *Swift* would have escaped if she had continued in the ice, and sharing the danger to which the *Thornton* was exposed would have had a wholesome effect upon the mind of her captain. The prisoners were all transferred to the *Milo,* and she was furnished from the stores of the *Thornton* with supplies, and being given a certificate stating why he was without his register, she was sent to San Francisco that the Richmond government might hear of my whereabouts and of what the steamer was doing. The other two vessels were foreign. Captain Williams stated he did not believe the war was over, but believed the South would yield eventually.

The captains of the three prizes had been visiting a few hours before my arrival, and a difference of opinion upon the subject of the close of the war evidently existed. The *Swift* and *Thornton* had planned their escape in that interview while I was occupied by the *Milo.* Captain Williams said the South had made a mistake in not sending a cruiser to the Arctic Ocean two years before, for the destruction of that whaling fleet, from which New England gathered her wealth, would have more seriously affected the Northern mind than a dozen battles in Virginia.

That remark of Captain Williams indicated a just idea of the Yankee character and its policy in the war; they made money by it, and for this reason they waged it. Politicians fed on fat contracts and immense government expenditures, enriching the agents through whose hands the money passed. A high tariff taxed the people without their seeing it, while the manufacturers realized fortunes. The newspapers of the large cities, filled with the details of battles, greatly increased their circulation, and their proprietors grew correspondingly wealthy. The government stimulated business by issuing paper and creating a debt that is intended the South is eventually to pay. It was thus that the war was waged [and] was continued, and it was only to be stopped on the mercenary principle of showing that it would no longer pay to keep it up. The Yankee captain spoke the genuine philosophy and morality of his countrymen.

The aggregate value of the *Swift* and *Thornton* was $132,000. On the 23d of June captured the brig *Susan Abigail*, of San Francisco and from that city, with California papers containing a number of dispatches, and among them was one that stated the Southern government removed to Danville and the greater part of the army of Virginia had joined General Johnston's army in North Carolina, where an indecisive battle had been fought against General Sherman's army; also that at Danville a proclamation was issued by President Davis, announcing that the war would be carried on with renewed vigor, and exhorting the people of the South to bear up heroically against their adversities. I questioned the captain of the *Susan Abigail* upon the general opinion in San Francisco about the military condition of American affairs, and he said: "Opinion is divided as to the ultimate result of the war; for the present the North has the advantage, but how it will end no one can form a correct opinion; and as to the newspapers, they can not be relied upon." The *Susan Abigail* gave the latest information from America, and she fell into my hands before she had communicated with any vessel; indeed, the *Shenandoah* was the first vessel she had seen since she had left San Francisco. She was burned, and valued at $6,500. Three of the *Susan Abigail*'s crew joined the *Shenandoah*, which was evidence that they did not believe the war ended; and they had been paid their advance, so they had nothing to lose by returning to San Francisco; they were not urged to ship, but rather sought service in the *Shenandoah*. The brig was on a trading voyage after furs, gold quartz, and whalebone, which her captain got of the native Indians in exchange for bright articles of apparel, tobacco, and whisky. The ship had been under steam, but was now under sail and fires banked, and to the northward of the island of St. Lawrence several Eskimo canoes, made of seal skins and other skins, visited the steamer, and the officers traded with them for furs and walrus tusks, in which they took a great interest. Two of the lieutenants, Chew and Scales, had never made a cruise; they had only seen six months' sea service. Such traders were novel sights to those who had never seen anything of the kind before. On the 25th June put the ship under steam in chase of and captured the *General Williams,* of New London; burned her. She was valued at $44,740; her captain was certainly a Jew, and the second of the kind I had seen; he was a dirty old dog. On the 26th of June chased and captured the following six Yankee whale vessels, and burned the whole of them except the *General Pike,* which was ransomed for the sum of $30,000.

Bark *W. C. Nye,* valued at $32,000
Bark *Nimrod,* valued at 30,000
Bark *Catharine,* valued at 26,000
Bark *Isabella,* valued at 38,000
Bark *Gipsey,* valued at 34,000
Aggregate $160,000

It will be observed that within forty-eight hours the *Shenandoah* destroyed and ransomed property to the value of $233,500, more than $200,000 of which was destroyed. The *General Pike* had lost her captain, and the mate was in charge of her, who asked as a special favor of me to ransom the *Pike,* as I should have to ransom one of the vessels. I asked his reason, and he said, "Captain, if you ransom the vessel her owners will think me well to do in getting her out of this scrape, and it will give me a claim on them for the command." I sent all prisoners to the *General Pike* and ordered her to San Francisco. On the 27th June ship under sail with a head wind, and eleven sail in sight, all to windward. I felt no doubt of their nationality, and to attempt the capture of any one of them while the wind blew would be the loss of the greater part of them. Lowered the smokestack and continued in the rear of the whalers, keeping a luff and retarding her progress as much as possible, so as to arouse no suspicions among the Yankee crowd ahead. On the 28th at 10:30 A.M. a calm ensued; the game were collected in East Cape Bay, and the *Shenandoah* came plowing the Arctic waters under the American flag with a fine pressure of steam on. Every vessel hoisted the American flag.

I had heard of the whaleship *James Maury* when at the island of Ascension, and after reaching the Arctic Ocean heard again of her, and also of the death of her captain, whose widow and two little children were on board. While the boats were being armed, preparatory to taking possession of the prizes, a boat from the whaleship *Brunswick* came to the steamer, and the mate in charge of the boat, still ignorant of our nationality, represented that the *Brunswick* a few hours before had struck a piece of ice, which left a hole in her starboard bow 20 inches below the water-line, and asked for assistance, to which application Lieutenant Whittle replied, "We are very busy now, but in a little time we will attend to you." The facetiousness of that reply coaxed a smile from me. The mate thanked Mr. Whittle, and he was asked which of the vessels was the *James Maury;* he pointed to her. The *Brunswick* was lying on her side, her casks of oil floating her well up, and her captain, seeing his vessel a hopeless wreck, had offered (I was told) his oil to any purchaser for 20 cents per gallon. The *Brunswick*'s boat returned. The *Shenandoah,* being in position to command the fleet with her guns, hoisted our flag, and the armed boats were dispatched to take possession of certain vessels (she had only five boats), with orders to send captains with their ship papers to the steamer. Ten American flags were hauled down instantaneously with the hoisting of the flag of the South. The eleventh still hung to the vessel's gaff, and seeing someone on deck with her gun, I sent Mr. Whittle to capture her and to send her captain on board. That bark was the *Favorite,* of Fair Haven, and her captain was unable to take care of himself from drunkenness. His vessel was without a register, liable to seizure in profound peace by the police of the sea. The hurried steps to and fro [on] the decks, the confusion and consternation among the crews in those vessels, the sheeting home of sails in one vessel while chains rattled in another, was a source of amusement to the *Shenandoah.* All the captains and mates were more or less under the influence of liquor, and some of them swore their sympathy for the South, while others spoke incoherently of cruiser, fire, and insurance. A drunken and brutal class of men I found the whaling captains and mates of New England. The boarding officer of the *James Maury,* Lieutenant Chew, sent her mate to me, who represented the widow to be in a very distressed condition with her two little children; that she was very sad, and that the remains of her husband were preserved in a cask of whisky. I sent a message to the unhappy woman to cheer up; that no harm should come to her or the vessel; that I knew she was an owner in the vessel, and that the men of the South never made war on helpless women and children; although an example to the contrary had been set them by their Northern enemy, we preferred the nobler instincts of human nature. The following vessels were captured, and those not ransomed were burned:

Ship *James Maury,* ransomed	$37,000
Ship *Hillman,* burned	33,000
Ship *Nassau,* burned	40,000
Ship *Brunswick,* burned	16,200
Ship *Isaac Howland,* burned	75,000
Bark *Nile,* ransomed	41,000
Bark *Waverly,* burned	62,000
Bark *Martha,* burned	30,600
Bark *Favorite,* burned	58,000

Bark *Covington,* burned 30,000
Bark *Congress,* burned.............................55,300
Aggregate $478,100

Thus, within eleven hours, this unparalleled capture by the *Shenandoah* shows the bonding and destruction of the enemy's property to the sum of $478,000. Within —— hours after those were discovered nine of them were enveloped in flames. The crews of those vessels, taken collectively, amounted to 336 men, and they were equally divided between the cartels. From the fleet I received nine privates, all intelligent soldiers, men who had been educated to use the Enfield rifle and to respect military position. The enlistment of those men in the Confederate service was evidence at least that if they had heard any report of the military failure of the South they considered it so unreliable that it failed to embarrass their judgment in seeking service in the *Shenandoah.* It is not to be supposed that those men would have embarked in a cause which they believed to be lost. No; the failure of the South to establish herself was not known to any person who fell into my hands, or even believed by such persons; for those waters are so far removed from the ordinary channels of commerce that it was simply impossible for authentic tidings of the progress of the American war to reach so remote a part of the world between the time of the actual overthrow of that government and the capture of those vessels. Individuals may lie, but facts can not.

One of the captive captains was a brother of the downeaster who had joined the *Shenandoah* in the Okhotsk Sea. When the brothers met they shook hands, and the captain suddenly showed indignation on learning the position of his brother. In a little while, however, they were in conversation and the captain appeared in a better humor, which was soon explained; he had gone over to the opinion of his brother that it was right to make a living whenever one can do so honestly. That episode of the brothers is Yankee conversion; metallic virtue is the worship of his soul.

The cartels were furnished with certificates stating why they were without the registers; they were furnished with supplies and ordered to depart. An occasional explosion on board of some one of the burning vessels informed me of the presence of gunpowder or other combustibles, and a liquid flame now and then pursued some inflammable substance which had escaped from their sides to the water, and the heavens were illuminated with the red glare, presenting a picture of indescribable grandeur, while the water was covered with black smoke commingling with fiery sparks. Discharges on board often resembled distant artillery, and while that scene of destruction was going on the steamer turned her head northward in search of additional prey. She continued northward and amid snow and iceberg until she reached latitude 66° 40' N., when, in consequence of her great length, the immensity of the icebergs and floes, and the danger of being shut in the Arctic Ocean for several months, I was induced to turn her head southward, and she reached East Cape just in time to slip by the Diomedes when a vast field of floe ice was closing the strait. She was forced to enter the ice, but very slowly, and every caution was observed to save her from injury. For hours she winded her way through that extreme danger, and I hoped it would be the last to encounter, for although we had become familiarized with it, still it was an unpleasant companion and one we desired to avoid. The sun was in his highest northern declination and it was with us perpetual day; when he sank below the northern pole a golden fringe marked his course until his pale and cheerless face rose again from iceberg and snow.

When the *Shenandoah* returned by the island of St. Lawrence there was a fine wind from northwest. I ordered sail to be made and triced up the propeller. While to the westward of that island, and the ship going six knots per hour, a dense fog came on which so perfectly cut off the view of the officer of the deck (Lieutenant Lee) that he found the vessel in pilot ice, which is certain evidence of a large body of ice being near, and before he could shorten sail sufficiently she ran into a large and dangerous floe. She was thrown aback, and she immediately gathered sternboard, and the pressure of her rudder against the ice under her counter parted one of her tiller chains; all sail was taken in as quickly as possible, and while that necessary duty was going on the steamer was in great peril. Sail being taken in, her backward progress was arrested by the ice, and she lay cosily blocked in on all sides by ice twenty to thirty feet in thickness. Warps and grapnels were now run out as on a previous occasion, and her head was gradually swung in the desired direction, and, with strong white rope mats over her cutwater and bows to protect her from bruises and injury, steam was gently applied when her cutwater rested against a large block of ice, which she pushed in front, and like a wedge it opened a track for her; in that way she worked for hours till she gained open water. The tiller chain was easily mended, and I am of opinion that stern impact bent the pintles (gudgeons) to the rudder, for I afterwards observed she had lost most of that thumping which we heard under the counter whenever she was running ten knots and upward per hour. The remedy was severe.

The time had arrived to take the steamer out of those contracted waters into more open seas, because if intelligence had reached any of the enemy's cruisers which were parts of the squadrons of the Pacific or China stations from the cartels which were sent from the Arctic or from other vessels which had received warning of danger from the drift of wrecks or the illumination of the sky by the bonfires, or through the agency of foreign whalers, it would not have been difficult to blockade or force the *Shenandoah* into action, and to avoid such a result was my duty. It would not have been good policy or sensible to risk the steamer in a contest which, even if she had won, taking the most favorable view, would have materially injured and rendered her unfit for service until taken into a port where she could be repaired; and we knew too well what character of neutrality controlled the first naval powers of the earth to suppose that any government bordering on the vast Pacific coasts would endanger their existence by receiving a Confederate cruiser for repairs, and thus incurring the displeasure of the Washington government, while England and France shrunk from such a responsibility. Two days before the steamer left Bering Sea a black fog closed upon us and shut out from our view the sky and all objects fifty yards distant; still she pressed her way toward the Amoukhta [Amukta] Pass, or the one hundred and seventy-second meridional passage of the Aleutian Islands, which are stretched from the Alaska Peninsula, the extreme southern land of Russian America, in a semicircular course toward the coast of Kamchatka, and a cursory glance at a map representing that part of the world shows alternate land and water for a distance of 20° of longitude. When the dead reckoning gave the steamer a position near the Amoukhta [Amukta] Pass, through which I intended she should enter the North Pacific, the fog continued thick and gloomy, but she dashed along on her course trusting to accuracy of judgment and a hope that the fog would lift so that the land could be seen from four to five miles distant should she fail to strike the center of the passage. It would have been a culpable mistake to stop steaming or to run on a circle because the weather was foggy, in a sea and near islands where currents are irregular in direction and force, for the drift of the ship would perhaps prove more fatal than running on a direct course from last observations. I preferred to run the ship for the pass, assuming that three sights taken near noon the previous day, when the fog cleared for a moment, gave an approximate position to the ship which partially corroborated the dead reckoning (although no two of them agreed), and by taking a middle course for the center of the pass that it would be more prudent to go ahead than to wait for clear weather. It only required a little nerve. When I expected the ship to be about the center of the pass, much to my relief land was seen off either beam, and the position of the ship was accurately discovered or ascertained by taking cross bearings. That feeling of security against a danger which is overcome is truly delightful to the senses. It was my first great experience, for it involved the safety of the ship and the lives of all on board. The ship was safe.

Again in the North Pacific Ocean, with fine weather, and the Aleutian Islands astern, I felt an unbounded sensation of freedom on the surface of that vast expanse of water where those who can take care of ships feel at home, and when looking back in that direction where we had seen such hard and dangerous service I involuntarily breathed away dull care; and why not! It was my home for twenty years; my early ideas were associated with the ocean and ships and all that sort of thing; I felt no longer trammeled by iceberg, floe, and land; no longer to hear the mast-head lookout cry "Ice ahead." We had run out of a gloomy vapor into a bright, cheerful, sparkling ocean, and as soon as a hot sun thawed the frosty timbers and rigging of the craft she would be more than a match for anything she might [meet] under canvas.

It was the 5th of July when the Aleutian Islands were lost sight of, and the ship sought the parallel for westerly winds to hasten her over to the coast of Lower California and Mexico to look after the steamers running to and from Panama for San Francisco. She jogged along with light air and dashed before occasional gales until she reached the meridian of 129°W. There she took the north wind which sweeps down the California coast and her course was given parallel with the land, and a sharp lookout was kept, for she was then in waters frequented by the enemy's cruisers, as well as a large merchant marine. The ship had by that time lost that cold, cheerless aspect which circumstances had imposed upon her in higher latitudes; her decks were once more the places of resort where Jack took shelter from a scorching tropical sun under her bulwarks and thirty-seven head of live hogs sunned themselves. The connection is singular, but I have seen Jack use a hog for his pillow, by scratching a hog to sleep in order to use him as a pillow afterwards. A sailor bathes all over every morning, and that is cleanliness; but he is nevertheless a dirty fellow.

On the 2d of August got up steam in chase of a bark, and in a short time came up with and boarded the British bark *Barracouta,* of and bound for Liverpool, thirteen days from San Francisco. The sailing master, Mr. Irvine S. Bulloch, was the boarding officer, and through that officer I received a few papers in which the surrender of the several Southern generals in the field and the capture of President Davis was announced. The following extract is taken from the remarks in the logbook of the lieutenant of the watch under date 2d of August, 1865:

> Having received by the bark *Barracouta* the sad intelligence of the overthrow of the Confederate government, all attempts to destroy the shipping or property of the United States will cease from this date, in accordance with which the first lieutenant, William C. Whittle, Jr., received the order from the commander to strike below the battery and disarm the ship and crew.
>
> D. M. SCALES.

My life had been checkered, and I was tutored to disappointment; the intelligence of the issue of the fearful struggle cast a deep stillness over the ship's company and would have occupied all my reflection had not a responsibility of the highest order rested upon me in the course I should pursue, which involved not only my personal honor, but the honor of that flag intrusted to me, which had been thus far triumphant. I first thought that a port in the South Atlantic would answer all my purposes for taking the ship, but upon reflection I saw the propriety of avoiding those ports, and determined to run the ship for a European port, which involved a distance of 17,000 miles—a long gantlet to run and escape. But why should I not succeed in baffling observation or pursuit! There was everything to gain and only imaginary dangers. The ship had up to that time traversed over 40,000 miles without accident. I felt assured a search would be made for her in the Pacific, and that to run the ship south was of importance to all concerned. Some nervous persons expressed a desire that the steamer should be taken to Australia or New Zealand, or any near port, rather than attempt to reach Europe. I could not see what was to be gained by going in any other direction than to Europe. I considered it due the honor of all concerned that to avoid everything like a show of dread under the severe trial imposed upon me was my duty as a man and an officer in whose hands was placed the honor of my country's flag and the welfare of 132 men. The run down to Cape Horn was expeditious, and before reaching the pitch of the cape, in fine weather, several American vessels passed us going to the westward. One vessel only was standing as we were, to the east, and that English vessel ran away from the *Shenandoah*. I attribute her defeat to the condition of the copper on her bottom, an unpleasant circumstance, for it might require all her fleetness to escape a Federal cruiser.

The wind was northwest on the Pacific side, and for several hours before doubling the cape under topgallant sails the ship ran fifteen knots per hour, and she passed to the eastward of the cape on the 16th September, when she took a gale at N. N. E., which continued unsteady from the northward, forcing the ship to west longitude 24° 40' before she reached the parallel of 40° S. She passed unpleasantly near the Shag Rocks during darkness in boisterous and cold weather. Day after day icebergs and dangerous blocks of ice were near the ship. We were without a moon to shed her cheerful light over our desolate path, and the wind blew so fiercely that the ship's speed could not be reduced below five knots per hour. It was more prudent to go ahead than heave to, for I was without observations for several days and in an easterly current. Some of the icebergs were castellated and good representations of fortifications and sentinels on guard. Although the nights were painfully dark, she escaped injury. Did you ever see darkness so black that it seemed tangible or seemed impenetrable to light? When the senses dwell upon such an envelopment the eye feels oppressed by the black weight, and a feeling of suffocation is produced. These outer struggles of our vessel were in accord with the deep, dark, and gloomy thoughts that now filled our minds; we were without a home or a country; our cruise contrasted sadly with what it had been a few months before; we now avoided instead of seeking vessels. I believe the Divine will directed and protected that ship in all her adventures. The steamer's course was northward, with a good southeast trade wind, and she crossed her outward track on the parallel of 30° S.

The ship had now reached the parallel of Cape Town, and I was favored by the reception of the following official communications. The foregoing communications are a part of the history of the cruise made by the C. S. S. *Shenandoah,* and should therefore be embraced in this narrative. Every officer and man is jealous of his reputation, and therefore it is my duty to respect the feeling of all who were under my command.

The *Shenandoah* crossed the line on the 11th of October, 1865. In latitude 10° N. she took the northeast trade wind. She fell in with a great many sail, but kept at a respectful distance from them, working her way along under sail through the doldrums. On the afternoon of the 25th of October, when she had crossed the trade belt and was running out the northern edge of it in light air, the ship just fanning along, a mast-head lookout cried, "Sail ho!" The cry of "sail ho!" carried apprehension to the hearts of many; the dreaded Federal cruiser might be at hand, and what then? The cry brought many to their feet who were indulging repose, and an enquiring glance conveyed their anxiety of mind; for if a Federal cruiser was to be found anywhere she would be in that region of ocean where most vessels bound to Europe would be intercepted. Glasses swept the northern horizon in search of the stranger, but she was visible from aloft only. I sent a quartermaster aloft with orders to communicate to me only what he could ascertain from the appearance of the sail. He reported her under short sail with her mainsail up or furled, and that from the spread of her masts [seemed] to be a steamer. She was standing a little more to the east of north than the *Shenandoah* was heading. The sun was thirty minutes high and the sky was cloudless. I could make no change in the course of the ship or the quantity of sail she was carrying, because such evolution would have aroused the stranger's suspicion, expose the *Shenandoah* to investigation, and, whatever she might be, she had seen the *Shenandoah* and might be waiting to speak with her. Communication was undesirable to me.

After the sun had gone down, leaving a brilliant western sky and a beautifully defined horizon, I sent that quartermaster again aloft with orders similar to those he had previously received. He reported her to be a cruiser and he believed her awaiting in order to speak. The *Shenandoah* had come up rapidly with the sail and there seemed little chance of escaping communication. A danger was, she would approach too near during light. She could already be seen from deck, and darkness came on more slowly than I had ever before observed it. The situation was one of anxious suspense; our security, if any remained, depended on a strict adherence to the course; deviation would be fatal; boldness must accomplish the deception. Still she forged toward the sail, and it would be madness to stop her. Darkness finally threw her friendly folds around the anxious heart and little ship, and closed the space between the vessels. What a relief! She could not have been four miles off. The *Shenandoah*'s head was turned south and steam ordered. At 9 o'clock the moon rose while our sails were being furled, and the surface of the steamer aloft being greatly reduced by that manoeuver, it would be difficult to ascertain where she lay if looked for. The coal was Cardiff and the smoke was a white vapor which could not be seen two hundred yards, and now that the engine was working and the steamer heading east we had at least all the advantage to be expected. It was the first time she had been under steam since crossing the line on the Pacific side. Indeed the fires were not lighted for a distance [of] over 13,000 miles. The *Shenandoah* was five hundred miles southeast of the Azores, and if there was an American cruiser in that locality on the 25th of October the two ships or cruisers were within five miles of each other. [Latitude (noon) 31° 40' N., longitude 35° 24' W.] The *Shenandoah* was continued on an east course for fifteen miles, and then steered north for one hundred miles, when a strong southeast wind dashed her along up to [within] seven hundred miles of the port of Liverpool. A calm then ensued, leaving us in sight of eleven sail during daylight. The ship was continued under sail until night again took us in its friendly embraces, when, after furling all sails, the vessel was put under steam and pushed her way toward the haven she would be. Discretion is always the better part of valor; I considered it prudent to avail of darkness.

The *Shenandoah* entered St. George's Channel on the morning [of the] 5th of November, just 122 days from the Aleutian Islands, and the acting master, Mr. Irvine S. Bulloch, made an excellent landfall; he had not been able to rate the chronometers since leaving Melbourne, and could only conjecture their accuracy while she was in the Arctic Ocean, for we saw no land after leaving the Aleutian Islands until the beacon in St. George's Channel was seen where it was looked for. We had sailed a distance of 23,000 miles without seeing land. The navigation is very beautiful when that fact is considered. I received a pilot after night, and when he was informed of the character of the steamer, he said: "I was reading but a few days ago of her being in the Arctic Ocean." I asked for American news. He said the war had gone against the South, and I directed him to take the ship into the river Mersey, that I might communicate with Her Majesty's government.

The quiet satisfaction of all countenances for the success in reaching a European port was unmistakable, and I have no doubt a weight was removed from each heart, if I may be permitted to judge others by my own. I felt a great relief, because I felt I had done my duty toward all who were under my command; and after performing my duty toward the power which had placed me in that responsible position, my duty was next to those who had shared the perils and trials and privations of the cruise.

On the morning of the 6th of November, 1865, the *Shenandoah* steamed up the Mersey in a thick fog under the Confederate flag, and the pilot, by my order, anchored her near H. B. M. ship of the line *Donegal,* commanded by Captain Paynter, R. N.

Shortly after the *Shenandoah* anchored a lieutenant of the *Donegal* visited me to ascertain the name of the steamer and give me official intelligence of the termination of the American war. He was very polite toward me, and left me to believe he felt a sympathy for us in our situation. The flag was then hauled down by my order at 10 A.M. of the 6th of November, 1865. I addressed the following communication to Her Britannic Majesty's minister for foreign affairs. It was prepared on the night of the 5th November, after receiving intelligence from the pilot. Of course the subject for such a letter had been pondered over some days before.

The following day a gunboat came alongside of the *Shenandoah* and made fast to her; customs officials took possession of her, and I relieved the officers and crew of all duty. The visit and detention of the gunboat was in consequence of an application from Mr. Adams, or his substitute, that the *Shenandoah* should be secured from getting to sea again. How perfectly absurd that must sound to the reader! It was intended to be an offense offered to a defeated but unconquered enemy; to men who had succeeded in disposing of the *Shenandoah* in a way not congenial to the Yankee nation. The ship and all on board were held by the authorities simply as far as confinement to the vessel; the only person upon whom an absolute restriction was placed was on myself. I was informed that everybody should remain on board, and an order to that effect was given by me; but some officers and several of the crew voluntarily left the vessel with no intention to desert, which was discovered by the lieutenant commanding the gunboat, and he said pleasantly: "I don't care if the lads do take a run on shore after night as long as I do not know it." He then mentioned the officers who had gone on shore, and I informed him I knew nothing of it and regretted to learn that anyone had done so. "Oh," said he, "you won't leave the vessel I know, so it don't matter about the others going on a bit of a lark." I was several times invited to go on board his gunboat, but I invariably refused to leave the vessel; I would leave on only one condition, which was the surrender being received I would be at liberty to go where I pleased; otherwise I must be taken out of her as a prisoner. Captain Paynter visited me sometimes twice a day and expressed his approval of the good conduct exhibited by those who had so recently been under my command under the painful circumstances of our situation. "It is," said he, "the result of discipline and confidence in your rectitude."

On the 8th of November 10 officers, 14 acting appointments, and 109 enlisted men, which constituted the *Shenandoah*'s crew, were unconditionally released. The customs officials inspected our baggage more in hunt of tobacco than treasure, I suppose. My baggage was very closely examined, but that proceeded more from my directions concerning it than any desire on the part of the officials to be impertinently inquisitive. I had neither thoughts nor stores to conceal from anyone. I presented my tumblers, decanters, and bedding, with a few trophies from the islands, to the wife of the lieutenant commanding, in care of whose husband I was left, as a souvenir of our acquaintance. He was a good fellow and was faithful in the discharge of his duty. Before leaving the streamer I transferred all captured money, as will be seen by this copy of the following receipt.

The late officers and men of the steamer were taken to Great George landing, Liverpool, after night at the expense of Her Majesty's government. I thank Captain Paymaster for his kindness to me, and for the interest he showed by his manner in us. During his visits he asked many questions of me for the benefit of the admiralty.

The *Shenandoah* was actually cruising but eight months after the enemy's property, during which time she made thirty-eight captures, an average of a fraction over four per month.

She released six on bond and destroyed thirty-two.

She visited every ocean except the Antarctic Ocean.

She was the only vessel which carried the flag around the world, and she carried it six months after the overthrow of the South.

She was surrendered to the British nation on the 6th November, 1865.

The last gun in defense of the South was fired from her deck on the 22d of June, Arctic Ocean.

She ran a distance of 58,000 statute miles and met with no serious injury during a cruise of thirteen months.

Her anchors were on her bows for eight months.

She never lost a chase, and was second only to the celebrated *Alabama*.

I claim for her officers and men a triumph over their enemies and over every obstacle, and for myself I claim having done my duty.

Admiral David Farragut is probably remembered by most Americans for his bold proclamation at the Battle of Mobile Bay "Damn the torpedoes! Full speed ahead!"

A Southerner by birth, Farragut nonetheless became the Union's greatest naval strategist.

Though he never wrote his own memoir, his son Loyall Farragut pieced one together from bits of his correspondence and journals, connected by bridging text and excerpts from the private papers of his contemporaries. It was published as The Life of David Glasgow Farragut *in 1879.*

What follows are excerpts from this volume, sans the additional materials, to portray this great admiral's experiences in his own words as well as exchanges of letters between himself and General U. S. Grant and Admiral Porter.

Extracts of *The Life of David Glasgow Farragut*

BY LOYALL FARRAGUT

United States Flag-Ship Hartford,
"At anchor off the City of New Orleans,
"May 6, 1862.

"Sir: I have the honor herewith to forward my report, in detail, of the battle of New Orleans. On the 23d of April I made all my arrangements for the attack on, and passage of, Forts Jackson and St. Philip.

"Every vessel was as well prepared as the ingenuity of her commander and officers could suggest, both for the preservation of life and of the vessel, and perhaps there is not on record such a display of ingenuity as has been evinced in this little squadron. The first was by the engineer of the Richmond, Mr. Moore, by suggesting that the sheet cables be stopped up and down on the sides in the line of the engines, which was immediately adopted by all the vessels. Then each commander made his own arrangements for stopping the shot from penetrating the boilers or machinery, that might come in forward or abaft, by hammocks, coal, bags of ashes, bags of sand, clothes-bags, and, in fact, every device imaginable. The bulwarks were lined with hammocks by some, with splinter nettings made of ropes by others. Some rubbed their vessels over with mud, to make their ships less visible, and some whitewashed their decks, to make things more visible by night during the fight, all of which you will find mentioned in the reports of the commanders. In the afternoon I visited each ship, in order to know positively that each commander understood my orders for the attack, and to see that all was in readiness. I had looked to their efficiency before. Every one appeared to understand his orders well, and looked forward to the conflict with firmness, but with anxiety, as it was to be in the night, or at two o'clock A.M.

"I had previously sent Captain Bell, with the petard man, with Lieutenant Commanding Crosby, in the *Pinola,* and Lieutenant Commanding Caldwell, in the *Itasca,* to break the chain which crossed the river and was supported by eight hulks, which were strongly moored. This duty was not thoroughly performed, in consequence of the failure to ignite the petards with the galvanic battery, and the great strength of the current. Still it was a success, and, under the circumstances, a highly meritorious one.

"The vessel boarded by Lieutenant Commanding Caldwell appears to have had her chains so secured that they could be cast loose, which was done by that officer, thereby making an opening sufficiently large for the ships to pass through. It was all done under a heavy fire and at a great hazard to the vessel, for the particulars of which I refer you to Captain Bell's report. Upon the night preceding the attack, however, I dispatched Lieutenant Commanding Caldwell to make an examination, and to see that the passage was still clear, and to make me a signal to that effect, which he did at an early hour. The enemy commenced sending down fire-rafts and lighting their fires on the shore opposite the chain about the same time, which drew their fire on Lieutenant Commanding Caldwell, but without injury. At about five minutes of two o'clock A.M., April 24th, signal was made to get under way (two ordinary red lights, so as not to attract the attention of the enemy), but owing to the great difficulty in purchasing their anchors, the *Pensacola* and some of the other vessels were not under way until half-past three. We then advanced in two columns, Captain Bailey leading the right in the gunboat *Cayuga,* Lieutenant Commanding

Harrison, he having been assigned to the first division of gunboats, which was to attack Fort St. Philip, in conjunction with the second division of ships, and the Hartford the left; Fleet-Captain Bell leading the second division of gunboats in the *Sciota;* Lieutenant Commanding Donaldson to assist the first division of ships to attack Fort Jackson, as will be shown by the general order and diagram sent herewith. The enemy's lights, while they discovered us to them, were, at the same time, guides to us. We soon passed the barrier chains, the right column taking Fort St. Philip, and the left Fort Jackson. The fire became general, the smoke dense, and we had nothing to aim at but the flash of their guns; it was very difficult to distinguish friends from foes. Captain Porter had, by arrangement, moved up to a certain point on the Fort Jackson side with his gunboats, and I had assigned the same post to Captain Swartwout, in the *Portsmouth,* to engage the water batteries to the southward and eastward of Fort Jackson, while his mortar vessels poured a terrific fire of shells into it. I discovered a fire-raft coming down upon us, and in attempting to avoid it ran the ship on shore, and the ram *Manassas,* which I had not seen, lay on the opposite side of it, and pushed it down upon us. Our ship was soon on fire half-way up to her tops, but we backed off, and, through the good organization of our fire department, and the great exertions of Captain Wainwright and his first lieutenant, officers, and crew, the fire was extinguished. In the mean time our battery was never silent, but poured its missiles of death into Fort St. Philip, opposite to which we had got by this time, and it was silenced, with the exception of a gun now and then. By this time the enemy's gunboats, some thirteen in number, besides two iron-clad rams, the *Manassas* and *Louisiana,* had become more visible. We took them in hand, and, in the course of a short time, destroyed eleven of them. We were now fairly past the forts, and the victory was ours, but still here and there a gunboat made resistance. Two of them had attacked the *Varuna,* which vessel, by her greater speed, was much in advance of us; they ran into her and caused her to sink, but not before she had destroyed her adversaries, and their wrecks now lie side by side, a monument to the gallantry of Captain Boggs, his officers, and crew. It was a kind of guerilla; they were fighting in all directions. Captains Bailey and Bell, who were in command of the first and second divisions of gunboats, were as active in rendering assistance in every direction as lay in their power. Just as the scene appeared to be closing, the ram *Manassas* was seen coming up under full speed to attack us. I directed Captain Smith, in the Mississippi, to turn and run her down; the order was instantly obeyed, by the Mississippi turning and going at her at full speed. Just as we expected to see the ram annihilated, when within fifty yards of each other, she put her helm hard aport, dodged the Mississippi, and ran ashore. The Mississippi poured two broadsides into her, and sent her drifting down the river a total wreck. Thus closed our morning's fight.

"The Department will perceive that after the organization and arrangements had been made, and we had fairly entered into the fight, the density of the smoke from guns and fire-rafts, and the scenes passing on board our own ship and around us (for it was as if the artillery of heaven were playing upon the earth), it was impossible for the Flag-Officer to see how each vessel was conducting itself, and can only judge by the final results and their special reports, which are herewith inclosed; but I feel that I can say with truth that it has rarely been the lot of a commander to be supported by officers of more indomitable courage or higher professional merit.

"Captain Bailey, who had preceded me up to the Quarantine station, had captured the Chalmette regiment, Colonel Szymanski; and, not knowing what to do with them, as every moment was a great loss to me, I paroled both officers and men, and took away all their arms, munitions of war, and public property, and ordered them to remain where they were until the next day. I sent some of the gunboats to precede me up the river, to cut the telegraph wires in different places.

"It now became me to look around for my little fleet, and to my regret I found that three were missing—the *Itasca, Winona,* and *Kennebec.* Various were the speculations as to their fate, whether they had been sunk on the passage or had put back. I therefore determined immediately to send Captain Boggs, whose vessel was now sunk, through the Quarantine bayou, around to Commander Porter, telling him of our safe arrival, and to demand the surrender of the forts, and endeavor to get some tidings of the missing vessels. I also sent a dispatch by him to General Butler, informing him that the way was clear for him to land his forces through the Quarantine bayou, in accordance with previous arrangements, and that I should leave gunboats there to protect him against the enemy, who, I now perceived, had three or four gunboats left at the forts—the *Louisiana,* an iron-clad battery of sixteen guns; the *McCrea,* very similar in appearance to one of our gunboats, and armed very much in the same way; the *Defiance,* and a river steamer transport.

"We then proceeded up to New Orleans, leaving the *Wissahickon* and *Kineo* to protect the landing of the General's troops. Owing to the slowness of some of the vessels, and our want of knowledge of the river, we did not reach the English Turn until about 10:30 A.M. on the 25th; but all the morning I had seen abundant evidence of the panic which had seized the people in New Orleans. Cotton-loaded ships on fire came floating down, and working implements of every kind, such as are used in ship-yards. The destruction of property was awful. We soon descried the new earthwork forts on the old lines on both shores. We now formed and advanced in the same order, two lines, each line taking its respective work. Captain Bailey was still far in advance, not having noticed my signal for close order, which was to enable the slow vessels to come up. They opened on him a galling fire, which caused us to run up to his rescue; this gave them the advantage of a raking fire on us for upward of a mile with some twenty guns, while we had but two 9-inch guns on our forecastle to reply to them. It was not long, however, before we were enabled to bear away and give the forts a broadside of shells, shrapnel, and grape, the *Pensacola* at the same time passing up and giving a tremendous broadside of the same kind to the starboard fort; and, by the time we could reload, the *Brooklyn,* Captain Craven, passed handsomely between us and the battery and delivered her broadside, and shut us out. By this time the other vessels had gotten up, and ranged in one after another, delivering their broadsides in spiteful revenge for their ill treatment of the little *Cayuga.* The forts were silenced, and those who could run were running in every direction. We now passed up to the city and anchored immediately in front of it, and I sent Captain Bailey on shore to demand the surrender of it from the authorities, to which the Mayor replied that the city was under martial law, and that he had no authority. General Lovell, who was present, stated that he should deliver up nothing, but in order to free the city from embarrassment he would restore the city authorities, and retire with his troops, which he did. The correspondence with the city authorities and myself is herewith annexed. I then seized all the steamboats and sent them down to Quarantine for General Butler's forces. Among the number of these boats is the famous *Tennessee,* which our blockaders have been so long watching, but which, you will perceive, never got out.

"The levee of New Orleans was one scene of desolation. Ships, steamers, cotton, coal, etc., were all in one common blaze, and our ingenuity was much taxed to avoid the floating conflagration.

"I neglected to mention my having good information respecting the iron-clad rams which they were building. I sent Captain Lee up to seize the principal one, the *Mississippi,* which was to be the terror of these seas, and no doubt would have been to a great extent; but she soon came floating by us all in flames, and passed down the river. Another was sunk immediately in front of the Custom-House; others were building in Algiers, just begun.

"I next went above the city eight miles, to Carrollton, where I learned there were two other forts, but the panic had gone before me. I found the guns spiked, and the gun-carriages in flames. The first work, on the right, reaches from the Mississippi nearly over to Pontchartrain, and has twenty-nine guns; the one on the left had six guns, from which Commander Lee took some fifty barrels of powder, and completed the destruction of the gun-carriages, etc. A mile higher up there were two other earthworks, but not yet armed.

"We discovered here, fastened to the right bank of the river, one of the most herculean labors I have ever seen—a raft and chain to extend across the river to prevent Foote's gunboats from descending. It is formed by placing three immense logs of not less than three or four feet in diameter and some thirty feet long; to the center one a 2-inch chain is attached, running lengthwise the raft, and the three logs and chain are then frapped together by chains from one half to one inch, three or four layers, and there are ninety-six of these lengths composing the raft; it is at least three quarters of a mile long.

"On the evening of the 29th Captain Bailey arrived from below, with the gratifying intelligence that the forts had surrendered to Commander Porter, and had delivered up all public property, and were being paroled, and that the navy had been made to surrender unconditionally, as they had conducted themselves with bad faith, burning and sinking their vessels while a flag of truce was flying and the forts negotiating for their surrender, and the *Louisiana,* their great iron-clad battery, blown up almost alongside of the vessel where they were negotiating; hence their officers were not paroled, but sent home to be treated according to the judgment of the Government.

"General Butler came up the same day, and arrangements were made for bringing up his troops.

"I sent on shore and hoisted the American flag on the Custom-House, and hauled down the Louisiana State flag from the City Hall, as the Mayor had avowed that there was no man in New Orleans who dared to haul it down; and my own convictions are that if such an individual could have been found he would have been assassinated.

"Thus, sir, I have endeavored to give you an account of my attack upon New Orleans, from our first movement to the surrender of the city to General Butler, whose troops are now in full occupation, protected, however, by the *Pensacola, Portsmouth,* and one gunboat, while I have sent a force of seven vessels, under command of Captain Craven, up the river, to keep up the panic as far as possible. The large ships, I fear, will not be able to go higher than Baton Rouge, while I have sent the smaller vessels, under Commander Lee, as high as Vicksburg, in the rear of Jackson, to cut off their supplies from the West.

"I trust, therefore, that it will be found by the Government that I have carried out my instructions to the letter and to the best of my abilities, so far as this city is concerned. All of which is respectfully submitted.

"I am, sir, very respectfully, your obedient servant,

"D. G. Farragut,
"Flag-Officer, Western Gulf Blockading Squadron.
"Hon. Gideon Welles,
"Secretary of the Navy,
"Washington, D.C."

Chapter XX.

FROM NEW ORLEANS TO VICKSBURG— THE GOVERNMENT'S PLAN, AND FARRAGUT'S— PASSAGE OF THE BATTERIES AT VICKSBURG— BRECKINRIDGES'S ATTACK ON BATON ROUGE— DESTRUCTION OF THE RAM ARKANSAS.

April 29th.

"Of course the New Orleans papers abuse me, but I am case-hardened to all that. I don't read the papers, except to gain information about the war. I find all the forts along the coast are surrendering, and we shall have nothing to do but occupy them. I shall be off for Mobile in a few days, and put it to them there. I have done all I promised, and all I was expected to do. So, thanks to God, I hope I have acquitted myself to the satisfaction of my friends as well as my country.

"April 30th.

"We have destroyed, or made the enemy destroy, three of the most formidable rams in the country. Arthur Sinclair declared that the *Mississippi* (ram), which he was to command, was far superior to the *Merrimac*. But we were too quick for them. Her machinery was not in working order, and when I sent after her they set her on fire, and she floated past us, formidable even in her expiring flames. Mitchell commanded the other as flag-officer. Poor Charlie McIntosh was her captain, and is now going on shore in a dreadful condition. It is not thought he will live; but he has a good constitution, and that will do a great deal for him.

"Their fleet has suffered very much in this affair, both in reputation and in vessels. We destroyed them all, some fourteen or fifteen, and many lives were lost.

"One of the city council, in one of our interviews, said to me sadly, when I told him that McIntosh was so badly wounded: 'Well, sir, he knew his task was a difficult one, and said to me before he left, that their work would be no child's play; that he knew his enemy, and that you were as brave as you were skillful.'

"Loyall would have been delighted, as I was, to see the contest between the old *Mississippi* and the *Hollins* ram *Manassas,* after we had passed the forts. I saw the ram coming up. I hailed Melancton Smith, and told him to run her down. Smith turned his ship, head down stream, and they ran at each other. We all looked on with intense anxiety. When within fifty yards, the enemy's heart failed him, and he turned to the right and ran on shore. Smith poured in a broadside, which riddled her. Thus ended the *Hollins* ram. She floated down stream, on fire from her own furnaces; the officers and men making their escape to the shore.

"These rams are formidable things; but, when there is room to manœuvre, the heavy ships will run over them. The difficulty at Hampton Roads was, that the ships were all at anchor and near shoal water.

"I am now going up the river to meet Foote—where, I know not—and then I shall resume my duties on the coast, keep moving, and keep up the stampede I have upon them.

"I have so much to say to my dear wife and boy that it will be the occupation of my declining years, I hope, by the bright fireside of our happy home.

"It is a strange thought, that I am here among my relatives, and yet not one has dared to say 'I am happy to see you.' There is a reign of terror in this doomed city; but, although I am abused as one who wished to kill all the women and children, I still see a feeling of respect for me. The foreign consuls called on me yesterday, and were extremely polite, and appeared anxious for me to aid them in getting provisions for the city. They feared starvation and riots."

UNITED STATES FLAG-SHIP HARTFORD,
Baton Rouge, June 17, 1862.

"SIR: I have to acknowledge the receipt of your communication of the 12th instant, together with its inclosure, in which you are pleased to say that vengeance will be visited upon the women and children of Rodney, if our vessels are fired upon from the town. Although I find no such language contained in the letter of Lieutenant Commanding Nichols, or even any from which such inference might be drawn, still I shall meet your general remark on your own terms. You say you locate your batteries 'at such points on the river as are deemed best suited,' etc., without reference to the people of the town, and claim no immunity for your troops. Now, therefore, the violation is with you. You choose your own time and place for the attack upon our defenseless people, and should, therefore, see that the innocent and defenseless of your own people are out of the way before you make the attack; for rest assured that the fire will be returned, and we will not hold ourselves answerable for the death of the innocent. If we have ever fired upon your 'women and children,' it was done here at Baton Rouge, when an attempt was made to kill one of our officers, landing in a small boat, manned with four boys. They were, when in the act of landing, mostly wounded by the fire of some thirty or forty horsemen, who chivalrously galloped out of the town, leaving the women and children to bear the brunt of our vengeance. At Grand Gulf, also, our transports were fired upon in passing, which caused the place to be shelled, with what effect I know not; but I do know, that the fate of a town is at all times in the hands of the military commandant, who may, at pleasure, draw the enemy's fire upon it, and the community is made to suffer for the act of its military.

"The only instance I have known where the language of your letter could possibly apply, took place at New Orleans on the day we passed up in front of the city, while it was still in your possession, by your soldiers firing on the crowd. I trust, however, that the time is past when women and children will be subjected by their military men to the horrors of war; it is enough for them to be subjected to the incidental inconveniences, privations, and sufferings.

If any such things have occurred as the slaying of women and children, or innocent people, I feel well assured that it was caused by the act of your military, and much against the will of our officers; for, as Lieutenant Commanding Nichols informs the Mayor, we war not against defenseless persons, but against those in open rebellion against our country, and desire to limit our punishment to them, though it may not always be in our power to do so.

"Very respectfully, your obedient servant,

"D. G. FARRAGUT,
"Flag-Officer, Commanding Western Gulf
Blockading Squadron.

"Major-General MANSFIELD LOVELL,
    "Commanding Confederate troops,
        "Jackson, Mississippi."

UNITED STATES FLAG-SHIP HARTFORD,
Off New Orleans, June 3, 1862.

"SIR: I have the honor to acknowledge the receipt of the duplicates of your dispatches of the 16th and 19th ult., as also a dispatch from the Assistant-Secretary, dated the 17th; in all of which I am urged and required by the President of the United States to use my utmost exertions, without more delay, to open the Mississippi River up to Flag-Officer Davis's command. In the dispatch of the 17th it is intimated that I might have forgotten my instructions on that subject, contained in my original orders of the 20th of January.

"Such a thing could scarcely be possible, but the Department seems to have considered my fleet as having escaped all injury, and that when they arrived off New Orleans they were in condition to be pushed up the river. This was not the case; but, the moment the vessels could be gotten ready, the gunboats were all sent up, under command of Commander S. P. Lee, with directions to proceed to Vicksburg, and take that place and cut the railroad. Some time was consumed in trying to procure pilots. I mean, by a pilot, one who has a knowledge of the river, for we were totally ignorant, and from all I could hear it was not considered proper, even with pilots, to risk the ships beyond Natchez.

"As I stated in my last dispatch (No. 100), the dangers and difficulties of the river have proved to us, since we first entered it, much greater impediments to our progress, and more destructive to our vessels, than the enemy's shot. Between getting aground, derangement of the machinery, and want of coal, the delays in getting up the river are great, and in Commander Lee's case there was some misapprehension of orders, by which he says he lost two days in reaching Vicksburg. By the time he arrived there, however, he was satisfied that the force of the enemy was too great for him to venture to take the town, or even to pass it.

"The land in the rear of Vicksburg is about two hundred feet high, on which are placed some 8- and 10-inch columbiads, which are perfectly secure from our fire. Commander Lee made application for more force, and the *Iroquois,* having just arrived from special service, had been sent on by Captain Craven. I directed Captain Palmer to take command at Vicksburg. I also determined to get the ships up there if possible, which I did a day or two after.

"General Williams arrived in the mean time with fifteen hundred men, when I proposed to him, if he could carry the battery on the hill, I would attack the town. He made a careful reconnaissance, and returned to me in the afternoon, when I had all the commanders assembled. He reported that it would be impossible for him to land, and that he saw no chance of doing anything with the place so long as the enemy were in such force, having at their command thirty thousand men within one hour by railroad. A large majority of the commanders concurred with him in the opinion.* I was quite sick at the time, and felt disposed to submit rather to their judgment than my own, and consequently determined to invest it on the lower side with my whole disposable gunboat force, and

---

*Colonel Wickham Hoffman, who was a member of General Williams's staff, tells the story of this interview in his "Camp, Court, and Siege." "Arrived opposite Vicksburg, we boarded the flag-ship to consult for combined operations. We found Farragut holding a council of his captains, considering the feasibility of passing the batteries of Vicksburg as he had passed the forts. We apologized for our intrusion, and were about to withdraw, when he begged us to stay, and, turning to Williams, he said: 'General, my officers oppose my running by Vicksburg as impracticable. Only one supports me. So I must give it up for the present. In ten days they will all be of my opinion, and then the difficulties will be much greater than they are now.' It turned out as he had said. In a few days they were all of his opinion, and he did it."

thereby draw a portion of their forces, guns, etc., from Beauregard's army, which appeared to be the next best thing to be done.

"The army had been sent up with only a few days' rations, and I was compelled to supply them from the squadron, thereby reducing our own supplies, which were barely sufficient to bring the ships back to New Orleans, making allowance for probable delays.

"The river was now beginning to fall, and I apprehended great difficulty in getting down should I delay much longer.

"Captain Morris, in the mean time, had been having coal-vessels towed up the river just above Natchez, which vessels I was obliged to bring down and keep in company with the vessels of war, for fear of their being captured by the guerilla bands which appear to infest almost the entire banks of the river wherever there are rapids and bluffs.

"I had no conception that the Department ever contemplated that the ships of this squadron were to attempt to go to Memphis, nor did I believe it was practicable for them to do so, unless under the most favorable circumstances, in time of peace, when their supplies could be obtained along the river. Our gunboats, although they have heavy batteries, are nearly all so damaged that they are certainly not in a condition to contend with iron-clad rams coming down upon them with the current, as are those of the upper Mississippi, which we built for the purpose, are iron-clad, and are designed to contend with enemy's gunboats coming up against the current. We consider the advantage entirely in favor of the vessel that has the current added to her velocity. . . .

"I arrived at New Orleans with five or six days' provisions and one anchor, and am now trying to procure others. As soon as provisions and anchors are obtained, we will take our departure for up the river, and endeavor to carry out, as far as practicable, the orders conveyed in your different dispatches.

"Very respectfully, your obedient servant,

"D. G. FARRAGUT,
"Flag-Officer, Western Gulf Squadron.

"Hon. GIDEON WELLES,
"Secretary of the Navy."

In a private letter of nearly the same date as the above dispatch, June 2d, he gives free expression to his opinions of the policy of keeping sea-going vessels in a river like the Mississippi:

"They will keep us in this river until the vessels break down, and all the little reputation we have made has evaporated. The Government appear to think that we can do anything. They expect me to navigate the Mississippi nine hundred miles in the face of batteries, iron-clad rams, etc., and yet, with all the iron-clad vessels they have North, they could not get to Norfolk or Richmond. The ironclads, with the exception of the *Monitor,* were all knocked to pieces. Yet I am expected to take New Orleans and go up and release Foote from his perilous situation at Fort Pillow, when he is backed by the army and has iron-clad boats built for the river service, while *our* ships are to be periled by getting aground and remaining there till next year; or, what is more likely, be burned to prevent them falling into the enemy's hands. A beautiful prospect for the 'hero' of New Orleans!

"Well, I will do my duty to the best of my ability, and let the rest take care of itself.

"It was well that the *Merrimac* was blown up, for I never would have had another vessel. Everything was seized for Hampton Roads, to look after the *Merrimac.* Thank God she is gone! I hope now they will send us a monitor. She would keep the river clear and save thousands of lives—as well as the Navy, which the river will use up.

"Senator McDougal, I hear, has asked for a vote of thanks of Congress for me. 'Blessed is he who expecteth nothing, for he shall not be disappointed.' But they can not deprive me and my officers of the historical fact that we took New Orleans. Now they expect impossibilities of me. . . .

"Some will find fault with me for not doing them justice in my report of the passage of the forts; but you can not satisfy all as to the measure of praise, and you know me well enough to know that I will not say what I *don't know;* and as to praising people individually who fought in the dark, for gallant conduct, and whom I did not see, that is out of the question. But I was particular as to all that came under my notice, and sent all the reports of the commanding officers respecting their officers. I regret that Bailey did not get the thanks of Congress as recommended by the President."

"BATON ROUGE, *June 15th.*

"Things appear a little more cheerful to-day, and I have the heart to write. We received letters and papers yesterday, saying that Davis had destroyed the enemy's fleet at Memphis. It was done in handsome style, in presence of all the city, so that now I shall hope to see him down this way soon. Vicksburg will be the half-way house, where the last battle of the Mississippi River will be fought, and then Davis will be left in full possession with his gunboats, which are built and well calculated for the service, while our vessels are too long and draw too much water.

"If I ever go above Vicksburg, as ordered, I do not expect to get down again until spring; for there are places in the river having not half the depth of water drawn by our ships. Still, I could not help hoping something would turn up to help us. Vicksburg is now the only important point on the river in the possession of the enemy, and I hope soon we shall have that.

"I was threatened with an attack of nervous fever on my last visit, owing to loss of rest when my ship was aground. I thought she was gone."

"OFF ELLIS CLIFFS, *June 22d.*

"I just sit down to commune with you, after one of the most trying events. Yesterday, while we were running up the river, everything propitious, the ship ran aground. I never left the deck, except to get a drink of tea, until she was off, this morning at 8:30. Fortunately, General Williams was with me, with eight steamers. They pulled and tugged until they got her off; but I several times made up my mind to spend the summer there—rather, that the ship would. I always feel that I am responsible for the ship that bears my flag; but, thank God! I was patient and did not suffer as I did before, for I knew that I had done all I could to prevent her from being up the river so high, but was commanded to go, and replied that I would go and do the best I could to comply with the wishes of the Department. It is a sad thing to think of leaving your ship on a mud-bank, five hundred miles from the natural element of a sailor.

"At five o'clock we reached this place, where the rebels fired into our transports. Here we met Commander Lee in the *Oneida,* and Nichols in the *Winona.* General Williams landed his soldiers, to stretch their legs and try to catch a few guerillas, but did not succeed.

"We passed Natchez at 8:20 A.M. All the townspeople were on the bluffs to see the fleet go by. It was a pretty sight—sixteen vessels—the *Hartford* like an old hen taking care of her chickens. We saw them all pass ahead safely, and helped them along when required."

On June 26th Farragut writes:

"Here we are once more in front of Vicksburg, by a peremptory order of the Department and the President of the United States, 'to clear the river through.' With God's assistance, I intend to try it as soon as the mortars are ready, which will be in an hour or two. The work is rough. Their batteries are beyond our reach on the heights. It must be done in the daytime, as the river is too difficult to navigate by night. I trust that God will smile upon our efforts, as He has done before. I think more should have been left to my discretion; but I hope for the best, and pray God to protect our poor sailors from harm. If it is His pleasure to take me, may He protect my wife and boy from the rigors of a wicked world."

The general order prescribing the plan of attack was as follows:

"UNITED STATES FLAG-SHIP HARTFORD,
"*Below Vicksburg, June 25, 1862.*

"The mortar-boats and gunboats of the mortar flotilla having been placed by Commander D. D. Porter, according to his judgment, to the best advantage to act upon the batteries on the heights and the fort below the hospital, at 4 A.M. to-morrow they will open fire upon the same and on the city of Vicksburg.

"At the display of the signal for the ships and gunboats to weigh, they will form in a double line of sailing, the *Richmond,* Commander James Alden commanding, leading; the ships *Hartford,* Commander R. Wainwright commanding, next; *Brooklyn,* Captain T. T. Craven, third. The gunboats will form another line, so as to fire between the ships, in the following order: *Iroquois,* Commander James S. Palmer, and *Oneida,* Commander S. Phillips Lee commanding, ahead, but on the port bow of the *Richmond,* so as to fire into the forts at the upper end of the town, without interfering with the fire of the *Richmond;* next in order, the *Wissahickon,* Commander John DeCamp, and the *Sciota,* Lieutenant Commanding Ed. Donaldson, in the line with the *Iroquois* and *Oneida,* but on the port bow of the flag-ship, so as to fire between the *Richmond* and flag-ship; next, the *Winona,* Lieutenant Commanding Ed. T. Nichols, and *Pinola,* Lieutenant Commanding Pierce Crosby, on the port bow of the *Brooklyn.*

The *Hartford* will, as often as occasion offers, fire her bow guns on the forts at the upper end of the town; but the broadside batteries of all the ships will be particularly directed to the guns in the forts below and on the heights. The free use of shrapnel is considered the best projectile, but great care must be taken in cutting the fuses, so as always to be sure that they burst short of their destination. When close enough, give them grape. The inclosed diagram will show the position of the respective vessels in the order of attack.

"When the vessels reach the bend in the river, the *Wissahickon, Sciota, Winona,* and *Pinola* will continue on; but, should the enemy continue the action, the ships and *Iroquois* and *Oneida* will stop their engines and drop down the river again, keeping up their fire until directed otherwise.

"The *Kennebec,* Lieutenant Commanding John Russell, will take position in the rear of, and in a line with, the *Pinola,* so as to fire astern of the *Brooklyn.*

"D. G. FARRAGUT,
"Flag-Officer, Western Gulf Squadron."

"ABOVE VICKSBURG, *June 29th.*

"My last sheet was closed as a letter for my wife and boy, in the event of any accident happening to me in the fight which I knew was to come off in a few hours.

"There were difficulties in the way, and the mortars did not get their fuses right until it was too late for us to move against the town that evening; so I postponed it until the morning of the 27th. We were under way by 2 A.M., and off Vicksburg by daylight. The scene soon became animated, as both parties were doing their best to destroy each other.

"We had no difficulty in driving them from their guns; but the batteries were so elevated that the gunners could lie down until we had poured in a broadside, and then run to their guns and reopen fire as each ship passed. They kept it up pretty well, though we fortunately received little injury. Occasionally a vessel was struck by a large shot. Wainwright's cabin was well cut to pieces, but we lost one man killed and eleven wounded.

"I was in my favorite stand, the mizzen rigging, when all at once the captain of the gun on the poop-deck wished to fire at a battery which would require him to point his gun near me, and requested me to get down, which I did, to avoid the concussion. I was only a moment in doing so, when the whole mizzen rigging was cut away just above my head! Although the shot would not have struck me, I would have tumbled on deck. But, thank God, I escaped with only a touch on the head, which did not break the skin, and has not given me a thought since. This same shot cut the halyards that hoisted my flag, which dropped to half-mast without being perceived by us. This circumstance caused the other vessels to think that I was killed.

"It seems to me that any man of common sense would know that this place can not be taken by ships, when the army in its rear consists of ten thousand or fifteen thousand men, and *they* don't care about sacrificing the city. We did not attempt particularly to destroy the city; it was more important to fire at the batteries. The soldiers have no interest in preserving it, as they know it is only a matter of time for it to fall into our hands. As soon as General Halleck sends the soldiers to occupy it by land, we will drive them out of the forts.

"To-day is Sunday, and we had prayers at eleven o'clock. I signaled the fleet to 'return thanks to Almighty God for His mercies.'

"My report is now bothering me. . . . Such things are painful, but I must tell the truth in my official statements. I do not desire to injure any one. . . .

"I am still well, and so is Bell. All of us are anxious to see an end of this river war. God grant it may be over soon, or we shall have to spend the rest of the year in this hottest of holes."

The following is the detailed official report of the action at Vicksburg:

United States Flag-Ship Hartford,
"*Above Vicksburg, Mississippi, July 2, 1862.*

"Sir: In obedience to the orders of the Department and the command of the President, I proceeded up to Vicksburg with the *Brooklyn, Richmond,* and *Hartford,* with the determination to carry out my instructions to the best of my ability.

"My difficulties and expenses in getting coal and provisions up the river have been very great, and it has only been accomplished by great exertions on the part of Captain H. W. Morris, aided by the army. Captain D. D. Porter's mortar flotilla, which was deemed indispensable to shell out the heights, had also to be towed up. All this caused great delay, but, by the steady exertions of that officer, and the assistance of all in whose power it was to help, we succeeded in getting up sixteen mortar vessels, and arrangements were soon made to bombard the forts on the heights at Vicksburg. Owing, however, to some imperfection in the fuses (which Captain Porter will explain), he was two days getting his ranges. On the evening of the 27th he reported to me that he was ready, and I issued my general order for the attack on the 28th, at 4 A.M.

"At 2 A.M. on the 28th June, the signal was made to weigh, and we proceeded up to the attack in the order of steaming prescribed in the diagram accompanying the general order. At four o'clock precisely, the mortars opened fire, and at almost the same moment the enemy fired his first gun, which was returned by the leading vessels—*Iroquois,* Commander J. S. Palmer; *Oneida,* Commander S. P. Lee; and *Richmond,* Commander James Alden. The other vessels—*Wissahickon,* Commander John DeCamp; *Sciota,* Lieutenant Commanding Edward Donaldson; this ship, Commander R. Wainwright; *Winona,* Lieutenant Commanding E. T. Nichols; and *Pinola,* Lieutenant Commanding Pierce Crosby— next came up, and poured in their fire successively. At almost the same instant, Commander D. D. Porter came up on our starboard quarter with the *Octorara, Westfield, Clifton, Jackson, Harriet Lane,* and *Owasco,* and opened in fine style upon the enemy. The *Hartford* fired slowly and deliberately, and with fine effect—far surpassing my expectations in reaching the summit batteries. The rebels were soon silenced by the combined efforts of the fleet and of the flotilla, and at times did not reply at all for several minutes, and then again at times replied with but a single gun.

"I passed up at the slowest speed (we had but eight pounds of steam), and even stopped once, in order that the *Brooklyn* and sternmost vessels might close up.

"The Hartford received but very little injury from the batteries in or below the town, but several raking shots from the battery above the town did us considerable damage: they were 50-pounder rifle and 8-inch solid shot. The first passed through the shell-room in the starboard forward passage, and lodged in the hold, but did no other harm. The 8-inch struck the break of the poop and passed through the cabin, but hurt no one; the rigging was much cut, and the port maintopsail yard was cut in two.

"If the ships had kept in closer order, in all probability they would have suffered less, as the fire of the whole fleet would have kept the enemy from his guns a longer space of time, and, when at his guns, his fire would have been more distracted.

"When we reached the upper battery we soon silenced it, and it was reported to me that its flag was struck. We therefore gave three cheers; but when we had passed about three quarters of a mile above they reopened fire with two heavy guns. I was unable to reply to this raking fire, being out of range. Although their shots were well directed, they either had too much or too little elevation, and only cut our rigging to pieces, without injuring any one seriously, which was strange, as the *Iroquois*, *Winona*, and *Pinola* were on our quarter.

"At 6 A.M., meeting with Lieutenant-Colonel Ellet, of the ram fleet, who offered to forward my communications to Flag-Officer Davis and General Halleck, at Memphis, I anchored the fleet and went to breakfast, while I prepared my hasty dispatch (No. 120) and telegram for the Department. I also sent across the peninsula to see what was the cause of Captain Craven and the vessels astern of him in the line not passing up. I also desired a list of their casualties, which appear by their letters to have been '*none.*' The casualties in the fleet, as far as heard from, in the passing vessels were seven killed and thirty wounded. Commander Porter reports eight killed and ten or twelve wounded; but that was not his official report, probably, but referred more particularly to the two steamers, *Clifton* and *Jackson,* each of which had an accidental shot—the *Jackson* in the wheel-house, killing the helmsman, and the *Clifton* a shot through her boiler, killing (by scalding) the men in her magazine, six in number, and one man was drowned by jumping overboard. I herewith forward the report of Acting Lieutenant Commanding C. H. Baldwin, of the *Clifton*.

"The Department will perceive, from this (my) report, that the forts can be *passed,* and *we have done it,* and can *do it again as often as may be required* of us. It will not, however, be an easy matter for us to do more than silence the batteries for a time, as long as the enemy has a large force behind the hills to prevent our landing and holding the place.

"General Williams has with him about three thousand men, and, on the occasion of our attack and passing, placed a battery of artillery nearly opposite the upper forts, for the purpose of distracting the raking fire from us while running up; but the fort, having a plunging fire upon them, dismounted one of the guns, and killed a man and a horse.

"It gives me great pleasure to say that General Williams, Colonel Ellet, and the army officers of this division generally, have uniformly shown a great anxiety to do everything in their power to assist us; but their force is too small to attack the town, or for any other purpose than a momentary assault to spike guns, should such an opportunity offer.

"It gives me great pleasure also to report that the officers and men of the ships which accompanied me up the river behaved with the same ability and steadiness on this occasion as in passing Forts Jackson and St. Philip. No one behaved better than Commander J. S. Palmer, of the *Iroquois,* who was not with me on the former occasion. It pains me much to limit my praise, but I can not speak of those who did not come up. It was their duty to have followed me, with or without signal, particularly as it was too early and too smoky to distinguish signals. I inclose their explanations herewith.

"As to Commander R. Wainwright and the officers and crew of this ship, I can not speak too highly of their steadiness and coolness, and the energy with which they performed their duties. This ship was conducted as coolly and quietly as at an ordinary drill at general quarters. There was no confusion of any kind throughout the whole action, and, as far as I could observe the other vessels, the same feeling actuated all the officers and crews engaged.

"The Captain of the fleet, Commander H. H. Bell, was on the poop by my side, and, not being able, as I before stated, to do much in the management of the fleet, owing to the darkness and the smoke, gave his attention to looking up the batteries and pointing them out to the officers in charge of the guns, and assisting them with his judgment on all occasions.

"My secretary, Mr. E. C. Gabaudan, noted the time of passing events, and acted as my aid when required, which duty he performed with coolness and steadiness.

"I must not fail to mention the coolness of our pilot, John J. Lane, who, although this was the first time he had ever been under fire, did not for a moment quit his post, but steadily guided the ship in her course. He is not a *professional* pilot, as *they* can only be obtained by force in New Orleans.

"All of which is respectfully submitted by your obedient servant,

"D. G. Farragut,

"Flag-Officer, Western Gulf Squadron.

"Hon. Gideon Welles,

"Secretary of the Navy."

Chapter XXII.

PASSING THE BATTERIES AT PORT HUDSON.

The following is the Admiral's official report of the action at Port Hudson:

FLAG-SHIP HARTFORD,
"Off Mouth of Red River, March 16, 1863.

"SIR: It becomes my duty again to report disaster to my fleet, although I know neither the extent nor the attendant circumstances; I shall therefore confine my report to those facts which came under my own personal observation.

"On the morning of the 13th instant, off Baton Rouge, I inspected the ships of my command to see that all the proper arrangements had been made for battle, etc., and I am happy to say found everything well arranged, and the ships well prepared in every respect. My General Order had been previously written, and delivered to each commanding officer for his guidance in passing Port Hudson. I had had a consultation with General Banks in the morning, and he informed me that he was ready to move against Port Hudson immediately, and make a diversion in my favor, and attack the place if he found it practicable, etc. At 4 P.M. I signalized to the fleet to get under way, and we proceeded up the river to near Prophet's Island. Early the next morning (14th) we proceeded on up to the head of Prophet's Island, where we found the Essex and the mortar boats all lying ready for their work. I called all the commanders on board of this ship, and consulted Commander Caldwell as to the batteries, his information connected with the place, and the character of the steamers we saw above (they were five in number, two cotton rams for boarding our gunboats, and the others river steamers, transports, etc.). I also directed the mortar boats to commence firing, in order to get their ranges, which they did, but finding the distance too great I directed them to move half a mile nearer. We conversed freely as to the arrangements, and I found that all my instructions were well understood, and, I believe, concurred in by all. The gunboats were assigned to the ships according to their speed, giving the *Richmond*—she being the slowest ship—the *Genesee,* she being the most powerful and fastest gunboat. The stations of the others will be seen in the diagram annexed to my General Order.

"After a free interchange of opinions on the subject, every commander arranged his ship in accordance with his own ideas. I had directed a trumpet fixed from the mizzen-top to the wheel, on board of this ship, as I intended the pilot to take his station in the top so that he might see over the fog or smoke, as the case might be. To this idea, and to the coolness and courage of my pilot, Mr. Carrell, I am indebted for the safe passage of this ship past the forts. At 5 P.M. (14th) I received a dispatch from General Banks, announcing that his command was at the Cross-Roads, and all ready to move upon Port Hudson; in reply I informed him that I hoped to have passed at midnight. At dusk I made signal to the gunboats to take the stations assigned to them. At 9 P.M. I made signal for the fleet 'to weigh,' but from some cause or other the *Mississippi* and *Monongahela* did not come up to their stations, although they answered the signal. At 10 P.M. the tug *Reliance* came alongside, and I sent her to order them to *close up,* and as soon as I could see the vessels in position we went ahead. My instructions to Commander Caldwell were, not to open fire until the enemy opened upon us. I think we took them by surprise somewhat, as they did not open fire upon us until we were abreast of a large light placed on the opposite side to guide their fire there. The lookout threw up rockets, and a battery soon opened upon us, at about 11:20 P.M., but did not answer our broadside. Commander Caldwell, of the *Essex,* now opened in fine style, and the mortar boats did their duty in the most handsome manner, keeping up their fire until two or three o'clock in the morning. This ship moved up the river in good style, Captain Palmer governing, with excellent judgment, her fire according to circumstances, stopping when the smoke became too dense to see, and reopening whenever a fresh battery fired upon us; but we always silenced their battery when we fired. At last the current from around the point took us on the bow and threw us around, almost on shore; but, backing the Albatross, and going ahead strong on this ship, we at length headed her up the river. The upper batteries now opened on us, and we could only reply with the two guns on the poop—a 9-inch and a 30-pounder Parrott rifle—but they both did their duty well.

"When we rounded the bend I saw the *Richmond,* as indeed I had done whenever during the action the smoke was not too dense, and I thought that she was following us in fine style, as I could see the effect of each of her broadsides upon the batteries. Great, however, was my surprise when I found that she did not come up after we had rounded the point, but my fears were not excited until sufficient time had elapsed for the other vessels to join us.

"I soon saw a vessel on fire, and apparently grounded, and I feared she was one of ours. I next saw her drifting down the river, with her guns going off and the shells exploding from the heat. We now arrived at the conclusion that one or more of the vessels had met with disaster, and the rest had dropped down the river again. The firing ceased about this time (2 A.M.), and near 4 A.M. (15th) the burning vessel blew up with a great explosion.

"The nature and details of this disaster will doubtless be communicated to you by the senior surviving officer below Port Hudson, in command of the fleet.

"In conclusion, I can only say that I know not how far I am responsible for this sad affair, but I take it for granted that, as the flag-ship came safely through and saw the others following, the disaster must have been caused by an accidental shot disabling a vessel, and the others stopped to assist her, instead of coming through and letting one of the gunboats take her down; but I have too high an estimation of *each* and *every one* of the officers commanding those vessels to imagine for a single instant that everything in their power was not done to insure success. The only fear I had was, getting ashore in rounding the bend.

"I assigned no gunboat to the *Mississippi,* for two reasons: first, I had but three gunboats; second, she, being a side-wheel steamer, could not take one alongside to advantage, and in fact, with the exception of the assistance they might have rendered the ships if disabled, they were a great disadvantage.

"If, in this effort to come up and cut off the enemy's supplies from Red River and recapture the *Indianola,* misfortune has befallen some of our vessels, I can only plead my zeal to serve my country, and the chances of war; and I felt that my orders of October 2, 1862, fully justified me in doing what I should have done two months ago, but for the disasters at Galveston and Sabine Pass, the strong force of the enemy at Mobile, and the inadequacy of my force to meet all these contingencies.

"I therefore have the satisfaction of knowing that I acted to the best of my judgment, and hence am only answerable for the imperfection of that judgment.

"Concerning the *Hartford,* I can not speak too highly of her captain, officers, and crew. All did their duty as far as came under my observation, and more courage and zeal I have never seen displayed. The officers set a good example to their men, and their greatest difficulty was to make them understand why they could not fire when the smoke was so dense that the pilot could not see to navigate.

"I had two pilots, Mr. Thomas R. Carrell and Mr. J. B. Hamilton; the first-named passed Vicksburg with me, and my main reliance was placed upon him, for I know his great good qualities of courage and skill, and he never disappointed me for a single moment. Mr. Hamilton also conducted himself with great steadiness, and was a valuable aid to Mr. Carrell.

"Captain T. A. Jenkins, captain of the fleet, Mr. E. C. Gabaudan, my secretary, and Mr. Loyall Farragut, who acted as signal officer, assisted by Mr. Palmer, Captain Jenkins's clerk, were all at my side on the poop-deck, and exerted themselves to render every assistance in their power.

"I shall only mention the officers and crew of this ship in general terms, leaving it to Captain Palmer to speak of them more specifically according to their merits. To the good firing of the ships we owe most of our safety, for, according to my theory, the best way to save yourself is to injure your adversary; and although we received some ugly wounds, our casualties were small, as we only lost one man killed and two slightly wounded, and they were both at their guns again in a few minutes, as ready and as willing, if not quite so able as before, to do their duty.

"The *Albatross* being the most vulnerable of the gunboats, and her speed being about equal to that of this ship, was assigned to her; and although it was not in Lieutenant-Commander Hart's power to do much, still he did all that was in his power, and whenever he could bring a gun to bear ahead or astern on the port side it was instantly fired. She suffered to the same extent as this ship, losing one man killed, but none wounded.

"I have the honor to inclose the fleet surgeon's report.

"All of which is respectfully submitted by

"Your obedient servant,

"D. G. FARRAGUT,

"Rear-Admiral, Commanding West Gulf Squadron.

"Hon. GIDEON WELLES

"Secretary of the Navy, Washington, D.C."

Chapter XXIII.

AT VICKSBURG—CORRESPONDENCE WITH GENERAL GRANT AND ADMIRAL PORTER— LOSS OF THE *INDIANOLA* AND *LANCASTER*.

"FLAG-SHIP HARTFORD,
"*Below Vicksburg, March 20, 1863.*

"GENERAL: I herewith transmit to you by the hand of my secretary a dispatch from Major-General N. P. Banks; it was sent up to me the evening I was to pass the batteries at Port Hudson.

"Having learned that the enemy had the Red River trade open to Vicksburg and Port Hudson, and that two of the gunboats of the upper fleet had been captured, I determined to pass up, and, if possible, recapture the boats and stop the Red River trade, and this I can do most effectually, if I can obtain, from Rear-Admiral Porter or yourself, *coal* for my vessel. By my trip up the river I have become perfectly acquainted with the enemy's forces on the banks and his boats in the adjacent waters.

"I shall be most happy to avail myself of the earliest moment to have a consultation, with yourself and Rear-Admiral Porter, as to the assistance I can render you at this place; and if none, then I will return to the mouth of Red River and carry out my original design.

"Very respectfully, your obedient servant,

D. G. FARRAGUT,
"Rear-Admiral.

"Major-General U.S. GRANT."

General Grant wrote:

"*March 21, 1863.*

"ADMIRAL: Hearing nothing from Admiral Porter, I have determined to send you a barge of coal from here. The barge will be cast adrift from the upper end of the canal at ten o'clock to-night. Troops on the opposite side of the point will be on the lookout, and, should the barge run into the eddy, will start it adrift again.

"Admiral Porter is now in Deer Creek, or possibly in the Yazoo, below Yazoo City. I hope to hear from him this evening. As soon as I do, I will prepare dispatches for General Banks, and forward them to you.

"I have sent a force into the Yazoo River, by the way of Yazoo Pass. Hearing of this force at Greenwood, Miss., and learning that the enemy were detaching a large force from Vicksburg to go and meet them, determined Admiral Porter to attempt to get gunboats in the rear of the enemy. I hope to hear of the success of this enterprise soon.

"I am, Admiral, very respectfully, your obedient servant,

"U.S. Grant,

"Major-General.

"Admiral Farragut, U.S. Navy."

To this the Admiral replied:

"Flag-Ship Hartford,
"March 22, 1863.

"General: I am most happy to inform you that the coal barge arrived safely, and we are now coaling from her. She is much larger than our necessities require; but it is a good fault, and we will carry her down with us.

"I see the enemy is building a very formidable casemated work at Warrenton. I fired at it yesterday coming up, but think I did it little or no injury. I see they are at work on it again; and shall interrupt them to-day with an occasional shot or shell, to prevent their annoying me on the way down. But, if you think proper to make a little expedition over that way to destroy it, my two vessels will be at your service so long as I am here. On my way down I shall pass close to it, and do my best to destroy it; but I suppose that will not amount to much, as they will soon be able to repair damages. They do not appear to have any amount of armed force there, but quite an extensive working party, which I have just ordered a gunboat down to break up.

"I shall be happy to receive your dispatches for General Banks.

"There are no batteries between this place and Red River, except Grand Gulf, where they have four 20-pounder Parrotts. There are no steamers on the Mississippi River between here and Red River, or were not when I came up; and, if they have come out since, I shall have them below me when I go down, so that, if Admiral Porter wishes to send down any of his boats, he will know what they will have to contend with. I am greatly obliged to you for your politeness, and remain,

"Your obedient servant,

"D. G. FARRAGUT.

"Major-General U.S. GRANT,
"Commanding U.S. Army at Vicksburg."

General Grant then wrote:

"HEADQUARTERS BEFORE VICKSBURG,
"March 23, 1863.

"ADMIRAL: As you kindly offered me the coöperation of your vessels, and the use of them to transport troops to Warrenton, should I want to send an expedition to destroy their batteries, I have determined to take advantage of the offer.

"I have directed General Steele to select two regiments from his command, and get them to the opposite side of the peninsula to-day, ready to embark as soon as in your judgment you think it should be done. I send no special instructions for this expedition, further than to destroy effectually the batteries at Warrenton, and return to their camp here. They will be glad to receive any suggestion or direction from you.

"This is a bad day for troops to be out, but in that particular may be favorable to us.

"Thanking you, Admiral, for your offer of the services of your vessels, I remain your obedient servant,

"U.S. GRANT,
"Major-General.

"P. S.—Captain Walke, who is the senior naval officer here in the absence of Admiral Porter, asked me yesterday for cotton bales, with which to pack two of the rams for the purpose of sending them to join you. I promised him anything in the world the army has, for the accomplishment of this purpose, and presume the vessels will be sent. I look upon it as of vast importance that we should hold the river securely between Vicksburg and Port Hudson.

"U. S. G.

"To Admiral FARRAGUT,
"Commanding West Gulf Squadron."

In a subsequent letter General Grant wrote:

"With a little lower stage of water, I would endeavor to occupy New Carthage [about thirty miles below Vicksburg, on the Louisiana side]. This occupied, and one gunboat from this fleet below the city, the enemy could be kept out of Warrenton, and also from taking supplies from a rich country that can be reached through bayous with flatboats on this side of the river.

"I see by Southern papers received yesterday, that Vicksburg must depend upon Louisiana, or west of the Mississippi, for supplies. Holding Red River from them is a great step in the direction of preventing this. But it will not entirely accomplish the object. New Carthage should be held, and it seems to me that in addition we should have vessels sufficient below to patrol the whole river from Warrenton to the Red River. I will have a consultation with Admiral Porter on this subject. I am happy to say the Admiral and myself have never yet disagreed upon any policy.

"I am looking for a mail in to-day, and, should one arrive with later dates of papers than you have already been furnished, I will send them over."

"BELOW VICKSBURG.

"It has pleased God to permit me to arrive here in safety, and once more to address you from this ill-fated place. I passed the batteries of Port Hudson with my chicken (the *Albatross*) under my wing. We came through in safety. Your dear boy and myself are well. He was cool under fire, and bore himself well. . . .

"Would to God I only knew that our friends on the other ships were as well as we are! We are all in the same hands, and He disposes of us as He thinks best. The other ships failed to come past the forts, and I fear to hear the news from below. The fight was nothing to us. You know my creed: I never send others in advance when there is a doubt; and, being one on whom the country has bestowed its greatest honors, I thought I ought to take the risks which belong to them. So I took the lead. I knew the enemy would try to destroy the old flag-ship, and I determined that the best way to prevent that result was to try and hurt them the most. It was a grand sight. I did not fear the batteries so much as the sudden turn in the river. The strong current might set us on shore, and we did not miss it much. By hard work and a good pilot, we succeeded in getting round, head up stream. We were hit eight times, losing but one man. God was with us. Poor Smith, I hear through Secessia, has lost his ship, and the other vessels were compelled to drop down the river. I have only this ship and the *Albatross*. I came along up to see what they are doing at Vicksburg, and send you this letter to relieve your anxiety. I trust it may reach you before the news of the affair reaches New York. War has its ups and downs, and we must meet good and bad fortune with becoming fortitude. One of my greatest troubles on earth is the pain and anxiety I inflict upon one of the best of wives. . . .

"D. G. Farragut."

On the 24th he wrote:

"Although the Almighty continues to bless with his protection our dear boy and myself, and in fact my whole ship, considering what we have gone through with, it is marvelous! I dread to hear the particulars of the disaster to the remainder of the fleet. I think so highly of the captains that I feel certain that no slight thing would have stopped them. God grant that my fears may prove untrue! I do not wish you to write me *via* Cairo unless you do so immediately. I shall not be long in this vicinity. General Ellet endeavored to send me down two of his rams to-day. One was destroyed by the enemy, and the other was much injured, but I hope it will soon be repaired. I am in hopes we shall be able to get one or two ironclads from Porter, to keep the river trade shut up.

"I am trying to make up my mind to part with Loyall and let him go home by way of Cairo. I am too devoted a father to have my son with me in troubles of this kind. The anxieties of a father should not be added to those of the commander. . . . God grant that he may be as great a comfort all the days of your life as he has been to me. Much as it will pain me to part with him, I feel that I am making a manly sacrifice for the benefit of my wife and child. May God bless you both!"

"You can not imagine the pleasure I have received to-day by a New Orleans paper which gives an account of the fleet below—to learn that Alden and Smith escaped unhurt. McKinstry, it is said, will lose his leg. I sincerely hope not. Poor Cummings, they say, is mortally wounded; he is a fine fellow and a noble officer. The list of killed and wounded was small, compared to what I imagined. I now give L. money and send him to you."

The following is a letter to Admiral Porter:

"FLAG-SHIP HARTFORD,
"*Below Vicksburg, March 22, 1863.*

"DEAR ADMIRAL: I regret that I did not find you at Vicksburg, and also that my secretary should have deemed it necessary to follow you up the river in your expedition, to bother you when so engaged.

"The General has kindly sent me the coal down, and I am now filled up and all ready to start for the Red River blockade, where I hope to find some one of my unfortunate vessels that failed to get by Port Hudson. I see by the papers that General Ellet is anxious to retake the *Queen of the West,* so that I hope you will be able to let two of the rams and one iron-clad come down and blockade Red River for me. The enemy have only the *Webb* and *Queen of the West,* rams, and another freight-boat protected with cotton, for the purpose of boarding our gunboats, but have no guns on board.

"I felt a delicacy in suggesting anything to General Grant, but my idea is that, if he thinks he can not take Vicksburg, the best thing would be to go down and take Grand Gulf and hold it, and then with 10,000 or 20,000 men go down and attack Port Hudson simultaneously with General Banks from below; and I would aid all I could with this ship and the *Albatross* and any others that might come up to my assistance.

"The Red River trade will be the great blow to their strength. They can get nothing when Red River is well blockaded. The General's coal I shall leave at the bayou below Vicksburg, for any of your vessels that may require it. There is left some four hundred tons, at least.

"Wishing you every success in all your undertakings,

"I remain very truly yours,

"D. G. FARRAGUT.

"D. D. PORTER
  "Acting Rear-Admiral,
    "Commanding Western Flotilla, above Vicksburg."

Under the same date, Admiral Porter wrote:

U.S.S. CINCINNATI,
Deer Creek, Miss., March 22, 1863.

"MY DEAR ADMIRAL: I am too glad to receive a communication from you, for we have heard all kinds of reports. Above all, though, I regret that. . . . the loss of the *Indianola* should have been the cause of your present position. You have had some affairs in your own squadron similar to the *Indianola* affair, causing equally painful results.

"I will do all I can to send you coal, if I can get out of this creek, where I have been fighting for four days without eating or sleeping.

"I sent down a wooden monitor, which destroyed the *Indianola!*—and, could I have done so, would have sent you a messenger. I will float you down coal barges—I did it safely to the *Indianola* and ram *Queen of the West*. It takes a coal barge about three hours to get below Warrenton. When the coal barge leaves, I will fire rockets, and send the coal down on Tuesday and Wednesday nights only. Keep boats out for it.

"I would not attempt to run the batteries at Vicksburg, if I were you; it doesn't pay, and you can be of no service up here at the present moment. Your services at Red River will be a Godsend; it is worth to us the loss of the *Mississippi,* and is at this moment the severest blow that could be struck at the South. They obtain all their supplies and ammunition in that way.

"The *Indianola* is full of coal—if you can get it. I sent a man down to blow her up, which I hope you won't object to, as I hear you think of trying to raise her. You would find it impossible; she is too heavy—though the rebels will get her up, having all the conveniences, and the energy of the devil.

"Do not, for God's sake, let the rebels take you by boarding. They will try it, as sure as you are born. They line their vessels with cotton-bales, which resist shot perfectly. Let me recommend a very hard cotton wad over your shell, thoroughly saturated with turpentine, squeezed nearly dry. I set fire to the City of Vicksburg in that way.

"And now, my dear Admiral, I am so worn out that I must stop writing, without saying half that I wish to. The sharpshooters are plugging away at us, and I have to sit down in a hot corner. General Sherman is driving the rebels before him, and I hope to-night to have a good sleep.

"Yours very truly,

"DAVID D. PORTER,
"Acting Rear-Admiral,
"Commanding Mississippi Squadron.

"Rear-Admiral D. G. Farragut,
"Commanding Western Gulf Squadron."

Four days later Admiral Porter wrote:

"U.S. Mississippi Squadron,
"*March 26, 1863.*

"My dear Admiral: I send down to-night a barge with the provisions required for the Hartford and the other steamers. It will leave here as the moon goes down, and no doubt will go safe. If it does not, and the rebels get it, they will have a jollification. They have not seen a piece of salt pork for months.

"I intended to get over to see you, but General Grant says that it is a very long walk. I have been so much confined to the ship, since I have been here, that I have almost lost the use of my legs. All my time is spent at my desk, and I get no exercise; which does not agree with me. My trip up the river has been of great service to me, and I feel like a new man. I wish we had the opportunity to move about more; but the rebels are up to all our dodges; they are a wide-awake set of fellows. That man Acklin says that the rebels have the guns of the *Indianola* mounted at Red River. Can not you ascertain whether this is so or not? She had two 11-inch guns in her casemate, and two 9-inch aft. They could easily be recovered, if they are still on board. Your ship could hoist out the 9-inch, and, by blowing up the casemate, drag out the 11-inch. If left there, they will have them certainly. I have a diver here, who will find out all about it, if you like. Mr. Krœhl is not ready to blow up the *Indianola;* he wanted so many things to do it with, that I told him to let it alone. Please remember me to Jenkins and Palmer. When you come up again, I have room for all hands to come and stay a day or two, and enjoy the good things of life, of which I keep a stock on hand. I hope they will be serviceable.

"Your son got over here safe, and I took him in. I expect he will give you an amusing account of my ménage. The first evening he came, we had eight dogs in the cabin. I have to resort to all kinds of things for amusement. Loyall was quite at home on mush and cream and fresh butter, all of which we have in abundance.

"Kind regards to all friends, and believe me

"Yours truly and sincerely,

"DAVID D. PORTER.

"I have written to the Honorable Secretary, explaining how it was that the ram *Lancaster* was lost. She was a miserable concern, and would not have been of the slightest use to you—all worn out."

Farragut had written to Porter:

Flag-Ship Hartford,
"Below Vicksburg, March 26, 1863.

"Dear Admiral: I find myself in a most awkward predicament, being here with only my ship and the little *Albatross* as a tender, unable to do anything but go up and down the river, or, what is of much more importance, blockade the mouth of Red River for a limited period. I have expressed the desire to you to have an ironclad, one at least, and two rams, to assist me in this matter, and I now repeat it, so that, when it becomes absolutely necessary for me to go down the river to replenish my provisions and resume my duties in command of the blockading squadron, I may do so without reopening the Red River trade. There is nothing below or in Red River that could successfully compete with an ironclad and two rams.

"General Ellet called on me, to know if I desired two of his rams. I replied that I needed such vessels, and would be very much gratified to have them, but 'would not interfere with Admiral Porter'; that I understood his boats to be a component part of your fleet. He said all he desired to know was, 'whether I considered it to the benefit of the country and the cause to have them below Vicksburg,' to which I replied, 'certainly.' And he said that was all he desired to know, and that he should run down in the night. I told him that, although I was very anxious for the force I had asked of you, and was ignorant of your relative positions, I feared he was wrong in doing so; although it might be done in safety during the darkness of the night, which he said he could avail himself of.

"I had made an arrangement with General Grant, and more particularly with Colonel Wood, of the 76th Ohio Volunteers, to convoy a party to Warrenton and cover the attack at that place, for the purpose of breaking up a casemated battery. General Ellet proposed that his two rams should carry over the party, while we attacked the batteries when they should arrive below. All these arrangements were made, the troops ready for embarkation, the night serene and beautiful—so much so that I sincerely hoped the General would not think of sending his vessels down. And just as I had to come to that conclusion, between half-past five and six o'clock in the morning, I heard the batteries open. I felt that all was lost, unless by the merest accident. My fears were realized. The *Lancaster* was totally destroyed. The *Switzerland* had two shots in her boilers—otherwise not materially injured.

"I write this letter for two purposes: first, to exonerate myself from any charge of a disposition to interfere with your command; and secondly, with a hope to excuse General Ellet from any feeling to do that which he thought disagreeable to you. On the contrary, all who surrounded him at the time thought, and so expressed themselves, that it would be in accordance with your wishes, were you present.

"In conclusion, I beg to state that I shall now return to the mouth of the Red River, which I consider the limit of my jurisdiction under my old orders, but which will be curtailed to below Port Hudson, once I pass that place, until it is captured by our own forces.

"On my arrival below, I shall endeavor to communicate with General Banks across the isthmus opposite Port Hudson, when he will have a full understanding of General Grant's views as to an attack on that place above and below.

"Very truly yours,

"D. G. FARRAGUT.

"D. D. PORTER,

"Acting Rear-Admiral,

"Commanding Mississippi Squadron."

To which Porter replied:

"U.S. Mississippi Squadron,
"Yazoo River, March 26, 1863.

"My Dear Admiral: Yours of 26th, at Biggs's Plantation, has been received. I should have made an effort to get down to see you (and hope to do so still), but I thought that you had dropped below Warrenton. I came back and found a great many things to do—many letters from the Secretary requiring immediate answers. General Ellet, with his new brigade, also belongs to my command, and I have been occupied all the morning with him.

"In relation to the *Switzerland,* keep her with you, but please make the commander understand that she is under *your* command, or he will go off on a cruise somewhere before you know it, and then get the ship into trouble. She is a very formidable ship as a ram, but I would never expect to see her again if she got out of your sight. With her and the *Albatross* you can defy all the vessels the rebels have.

"The great object is to cut off supplies. For that reason I sent down the *Queen of the West* and *Indianola.* I got them past the batteries without a hurt, as I would have done with the *Lancaster* and *Switzerland,* had I been here.

"I would with great pleasure give you one or two ironclads, but I have none that are fit for service just now, and the fight at Haines's Bluff must come off soon. The *Queen of the West* or the *Webb* would walk right through these ironclads, while a ram would keep them in check. They say the rebels have the *Indianola's* guns. Can you ascertain if such is the fact? At low water the whole thing will be exposed. It will be an object for you to remain at Red River as long as possible, and I hope you will do so. It is death to these people; they get all their grub from there.

"Very respectfully, your obedient servant,

"DAVID D. PORTER,
Acting Rear-Admiral,
"Commanding Mississippi Squadron.

"Rear-Admiral D. G. Farragut,
"Commanding Western Gulf Blockading Squadron."

Farragut had also written:

"FLAG-SHIP HARTFORD,
"*Below Vicksburg, March 25, 1863.*

"DEAR ADMIRAL: Since my last letter, I have received your last letter by my secretary, Mr. Gabaudan. I am delighted to find that our ideas agree so well on the subject of the blockade of Red River; but you say nothing of the ironclads and rams to assist me in that operation when I shall be compelled to leave there and make my way down to New Orleans. I was in hopes you would have never been here in time and sent me an iron-clad to assist in demolishing this casemated battery at Warrenton—unless a force is landed and captures it—a thing I think easily accomplished at present, as the town is surrounded by water, and assistance, except by infantry, is not easily obtained.

"My isolated position requires that I should be more careful of my ship than I would be if I had my fleet with me. I can not get to a machine-shop, or obtain the most ordinary appliances for repairs without fighting my way to them. I deeply regret the rashness of General Ellet in sending his boats past the batteries in broad daylight. You say truly that I have had some disasters in my own fleet similar to that of the *Indianola.* I consider the Galveston affair the greatest blow that the Navy has sustained during the war. It has emboldened our enemies to undertake anything, and in many cases demoralized our own people.

"We are pretty well prepared for boarding. Wishing you every success in your different undertakings, I am

"Yours truly,

"D. G. FARRAGUT."

"U. S. MISSISSIPPI SQUADRON,
"*Yazoo River, March 28, 1863.*

"MY DEAR ADMIRAL: You misunderstood the purport of my letter. I never supposed for a moment that you wanted the ironclads for your own security, for the *Hartford* could whip all the rebel navy in these waters. I only spoke of the greater efficiency of the *Switzerland.* I have here only five ironclads that can stem the current—not mentioning the *Lafayette,* which I had brought down here to have her completed. She will not be fit for service for a time to come.

"If you could see the five ironclads that have just returned from the most remarkable expedition vessels ever started on, you would not think them very suitable for running any distance. They are almost to pieces—rudders gone, pipes down, every boat smashed, decks swept, and wheels broken.

" 'The play was worth the candle,' and, had we got through and formed a junction with the expedition that got through Yazoo Pass, it would have settled Vicksburg. But I could not afford to run any risks, and, our army being far behind for want of transportation, I gave it up (as I since found out) very wisely, as the enemy sent 6,000 men up there with heavy guns. So we had all our knocking to pieces for nothing. That I don't mind, as long as I lose none of the vessels; for our people at the North howl so over the loss of an old rat-trap that it makes me cautious. My idea is, 'nothing venture, nothing gain.'

"I thought you wanted the ironclads right off, which could not very well be done; but I shall have no difficulty in getting a force to Red River before you leave. We are going to work our way down the Bayou Macon, and some morning you will see us coming out of the mouth of the Red River. Please don't send a broadside into us.

"The route I speak of is very practicable, and is now open. There will be some fighting to do, but that we get paid for.

"I hope you received your provisions. I heard a gun fire about the time the barge arrived opposite the town, which I presume was an alarm given, caused by the smell of pork, which the nostrils of the rebels are not used to. Could they have captured that barge, they would have saluted with two hundred guns.

"I don't know yet how our expedition down the Yazoo Pass gets along. They waited one week longer than they should have done—for some soldiers; when their orders were to push on and wait for nothing. They gave the enemy just time to erect a fort of six heavy guns, which our fellows have been fighting ever since, with a loss of thirty-six killed and wounded.

"When I get all my chickens together, we will commence the descent of the Bayou Macon into Red River. If the rebels have not recovered those 9-inch guns, we can clean out that country in a short time. If they have got them, they can give us trouble, in a narrow river where only two vessels can fight abreast.

"Your son went up last night. I sent him in one of our vessels.

"I was sorry not to see you before you went, but I was so worn out after the late expedition that I was not fit to attempt the walk. I have been suffering lately with dysentery, and am not strong. Remember me to Palmer and Jenkins, and, when you meet my old friend Alden, say a thousand kind things for me. I hope it is not true that Cummings is killed. He was a gallant officer, and too good a man to lose.

"With my best wishes for your success and safe arrival below,

"I remain truly and sincerely yours,

"DAVID D. PORTER,

"Acting Rear-Admiral.

"Rear-Admiral D. G. FARRAGUT,

"Commanding Western Gulf Blockading Squadron."

The following letter was written by Farragut just before leaving the vicinity of Vicksburg:

"BELOW VICKSBURG, *March 27, 1863.*

"MY DEAR BOY: I was gratified to hear that Colonel Abbot treated you so kindly, and that you got up to Porter's fleet with so much ease. I trust in God for your safe arrival home to the embrace of your dear mother, whose sufferings must have been great to have a husband and son in such constant danger. But she knows that our lives are always in the hands of the Supreme Ruler. I trust you will make up for the lost time you have sustained by the temporary sojourn with me. I hope it is not time wasted. You have seen much in a short time, and know what your father's sufferings have been for the honors he has gained; that his life has not been spent on a bed of roses. But, my son, follow your father's rules to the best of your ability. Do as little wrong as the weakness of your nature will permit, and as much good as you can. Pray to God to give you good understanding, and keep you from evil and protect you from harm. I know you will always be affectionate to your mother, and make amends for your father's absence and take care of her when he is gone. You know we must all fade away by turns. God grant that you may both enjoy a long and happy life, and be free from this terrible affliction, civil war, which miserable demagogues have brought upon our once happy country. May God bless and preserve you, my devoted son.

"Your affectionate father,

"D. G. FARRAGUT."

Chapter XXIV.

DETAILED REPORT OF THE MOBILE BATTLE.

"United States Flag-Ship Hartford,
"*Mobile Bay, August 12, 1864.*

"Sir: I had the honor to forward to the Department, on the evening of the 5th instant, a report of my *entrée* into Mobile Bay, on the morning of that day, which, though brief, contained all the principal facts of the attack.

"Notwithstanding the loss of life, particularly on this ship, and the terrible disaster to the *Tecumseh,* the result of the fight was a glorious victory, and I have reason to feel proud of the officers, seamen, and marines of the squadron under my command, for it has never fallen to the lot of an officer to be thus situated and thus sustained.

"Regular discipline will bring men to any amount of endurance, but there is a natural fear of hidden dangers, particularly when so awfully destructive of human life as the torpedo, which requires more than discipline to overcome.

"Preliminary to a report of the action of the 5th, I desire to call the attention of the Department to the previous steps taken in consultation with Generals Canby and Granger. On the 8th of July I had an interview with these officers on board the *Hartford,* on the subject of an attack upon Forts Morgan and Gaines, at which it was agreed that General Canby would send all the troops he could spare to coöperate with the fleet. Circumstances soon obliged General Canby to inform me that he could not dispatch a sufficient number to invest both forts; and, in reply, I suggested that Gaines should be first invested, engaging to have a force in the Sound ready to protect the landing of the army on Dauphin Island, in the rear of that fort, and I assigned Lieutenant-Commander De Krafft, of the *Conemaugh,* to that duty.

"On the 1st instant General Granger visited me again on the Hartford. In the mean time the *Tecumseh* had arrived at Pensacola, and Captain Craven had informed me that he would be ready in four days for any service. We therefore fixed upon the 4th of August as the day for the landing of the troops and my entrance into the bay; but, owing to delays mentioned in Captain Jenkins's communication to me, the *Tecumseh* was not ready. General Granger, however, to my mortification, was up to time, and the troops actually landed on Dauphin Island.

"As subsequent events proved, the delay turned to our advantage, as the rebels were busily engaged during the 4th in throwing troops and supplies into Fort Gaines, all of which were captured a few days afterward.

"The *Tecumseh* arrived on the evening of the 4th, and, everything being propitious, I proceeded to the attack on the following morning.

"As mentioned in my previous dispatch, the vessels outside the bar, which were designed to participate in the engagement, were all under way by forty minutes past five in the morning, in the following order, two abreast, and lashed together: *Brooklyn,* Captain James Alden, with the *Octorora,* Lieutenant-Commander C. H. Green, on the port side; *Hartford,* Captain Percival Drayton, with the *Metacomet,* Lieutenant-Commander J. E. Jouett; *Richmond,* Captain T. A. Jenkins, with the *Port Royal,* Lieutenant-Commander B. Gherardi; *Lackawanna,* Captain J. B. Marchand, with the *Seminole,* Commander E. Donaldson; *Monongahela,* Commander J. H. Strong, with the *Kennebec,* Lieutenant-Commander W. P. McCann; *Ossipee,* Commander W. E. Le Roy, with the *Itasca,* Lieutenant-Commander George Brown; *Oneida,* Commander J. R. M. Mullany, with the *Galena,* Lieutenant-Commander C. H. Wells. The ironclads—*Tecumseh,* Commander T. A. M. Craven; *Manhattan,* Commander J. W. A. Nicholson; *Winnebago,* Commander T. H. Stevens; and *Chickasaw,* Lieutenant-Commander G. H. Perkins—were already inside the bar, and had been ordered to take up their positions on the starboard side of the wooden ships, or between them and Fort Morgan, for the purpose of keeping down the fire from the water battery and the parapet guns of the fort, as well as to attack the ram Tennessee as soon as the fort was passed.

"It was only at the urgent request of the captains and commanding officers that I yielded to the *Brooklyn's* being the leading ship of the line, as she had four chase-guns and an ingenious arrangement for picking up torpedoes, and because, in their judgment, the flag-ship ought not to be too much exposed. This I believe to be an error; for, apart from the fact that exposure is one of the penalties of rank in the Navy, it will always be the aim of the enemy to destroy the flag-ship, and, as will appear in the sequel, such attempt was very persistently made, but Providence did not permit it to be successful.

"The attacking fleet steamed steadily up the main ship-channel, the

Tecumseh firing the first shot at forty-seven minutes past six o'clock. At six minutes past seven the fort opened upon us, and was replied to by a gun from the *Brooklyn,* and immediately after the action became general.

"It was soon apparent that there was some difficulty ahead. The *Brooklyn,* for some cause which I did not then clearly understand, but which has since been explained by Captain Alden in his report, arrested the advance of the whole fleet, while, at the same time, the guns of the fort were playing with great effect upon that vessel and the *Hartford.* A moment after I saw the *Tecumseh,* struck by a torpedo, disappear almost instantaneously beneath the waves, carrying with her her gallant commander and nearly all her crew. I determined at once, as I had originally intended, to take the lead; and, after ordering the *Metacomet* to send a boat to save, if possible, any of the perishing crew, I dashed ahead with the *Hartford,* and the ships followed on, their officers believing that they were going to a noble death with their commander-in-chief.

"I steamed through between the buoys, where the torpedoes were supposed to have been sunk. These buoys had been previously examined by my flag-lieutenant, J. Crittenden Watson, in several nightly reconnoissances. Though he had not been able to discover the sunken torpedoes, yet we had been assured, by refugees, deserters, and others, of their existence; but, believing that, from their having been some time in the water, they were probably innocuous, I determined to take the chance of their explosion.

"From the moment I turned northward, to clear the Middle Ground, we were enabled to keep such a broadside fire upon the batteries of Fort Morgan, that their guns did us comparatively little injury.

"Just after we passed the fort, which was about ten minutes before eight o'clock, the ram Tennessee dashed out at this ship, as had been expected, and in anticipation of which I had ordered the monitors on our starboard side. I took no further notice of her than to return her fire.

"The rebel gunboats *Morgan, Gaines,* and *Selma* were ahead; and the latter particularly annoyed us with a raking fire, which our guns could not return. At two minutes after eight o'clock I ordered the *Metacomet* to cast off and go in pursuit of the *Selma.* Captain Jouett was after her in a moment, and in an hour's time he had her as a prize. She was commanded by P. V. Murphy, formerly of the United States Navy. He was wounded in the wrist, his executive officer, Lieutenant Comstock, and eight of the crew killed, and seven or eight wounded. Lieutenant-Commander Jouett's conduct during the whole affair commands my warmest commendations.

The *Morgan* and *Gaines* succeeded in escaping under the protection of the guns of Fort Morgan, which would have been prevented had the other gunboats been as prompt in their movements as the *Metacomet;* the want of pilots, however, I believe, was the principal difficulty. The *Gaines* was so injured by our fire that she had to be run ashore, where she was subsequently destroyed; but the *Morgan* escaped to Mobile during the night, though she was chased and fired upon by our cruisers.

"Having passed the forts and dispersed the enemy's gunboats, I had ordered most of the vessels to anchor, when I perceived the ram *Tennessee* standing up for this ship. This was at forty-five minutes past eight. I was not long in comprehending Buchanan's intentions to be the destruction of the flag-ship. The monitors, and such of the wooden vessels as I thought best adapted for the purpose, were immediately ordered to attack the ram, not only with their guns, but bows on at full speed; and then began one of the fiercest naval combats on record.

"The *Monongahela*, Commander Strong, was the first vessel that struck her, and in doing so carried away her own iron prow, together with the cutwater, without apparently doing her adversary much injury. The *Lackawanna*, Captain Marchand, was the next vessel to strike her, which she did at full speed; but though her stern was cut and crushed to the plank-ends for the distance of three feet above the water's edge to five feet below, the only perceptible effect on the ram was to give her a heavy list.

"The *Hartford* was the third vessel which struck her, but, as the *Tennessee* quickly shifted her helm, the blow was a glancing one, and, as she rasped along our side, we poured our whole port broadside of 9-inch solid shot within ten feet of her casemate.

"The monitors worked slowly, but delivered their fire as opportunity offered. The *Chickasaw* succeeded in getting under her stern, and a 15-inch shot from the *Manhattan* broke through her iron plating and heavy wooden backing, though the missile itself did not enter the vessel.

"Immediately after the collision with the flag-ship, I directed Captain Drayton to bear down for the ram again. He was doing so at full speed, when, unfortunately, the *Lackawanna* ran into the Hartford just forward of the mizzen-mast, cutting her down to within two feet of the water's edge. We soon got clear again, however, and were fast approaching our adversary, when she struck her colors and ran up the white flag.

"She was at this time sore beset; the *Chickasaw* was pounding away at her stern, the *Ossipee* was approaching her at full speed, and the *Monongahela, Lackawanna,* and this ship were bearing down upon her, determined upon her destruction. Her smokestack had been shot away, her steering-chains were gone, compelling a resort to her relieving tackles, and several of her port-shutters were jammed. Indeed, from the time the *Hartford* struck her until her surrender, she never fired a gun. As the *Ossipee,* Commander Le Roy, was about to strike her, she hoisted the white flag, and that vessel immediately stopped her engine, though not in time to avoid a glancing blow.

"During this contest with the rebel gunboats and the ram *Tennessee,* which terminated in her surrender at ten o'clock, we lost many more men than from the fire of the batteries of Fort Morgan.

"Admiral Buchanan was wounded in the leg; two or three of his men were killed, and five or six wounded. Commander Johnston, formerly of the United States Navy, was in command of the *Tennessee,* and came on board the flag-ship to surrender his sword, and that of Admiral Buchanan. The surgeon, Dr. Conrad, came with him, stated the condition of the Admiral, and wished to know what was to be done with him. Fleet-Surgeon Palmer, who was on board the *Hartford* during the action, commiserating the sufferings of the wounded, suggested that those of both sides be sent to Pensacola, where they could be properly cared for. I therefore addressed a note to Brigadier-General R. L. Page, commanding Fort Morgan, informing him that Admiral Buchanan and others of the *Tennessee* had been wounded, and desiring to know whether he would permit one of our vessels, under a flag of truce, to convey them, with or without our wounded, to Pensacola, on the understanding that the vessel should take out none but the wounded, and bring nothing back that she did not take out. This was acceded to by General Page, and the *Metacomet* proceeded on this mission of humanity.

"I inclose herewith the correspondence with that officer. I forward also the reports of the commanding officers of the vessels that participated in the action, who will no doubt call attention to the conduct of such individuals as most distinguished themselves.

"As I had an elevated position in the main rigging near the top, I was able to overlook not only the deck of the *Hartford,* but the other vessels of the fleet. I witnessed the terrible effects of the enemy's shot, and the good conduct of the men at their guns, and although no doubt their hearts sickened, as mine did, when their shipmates were struck down beside them, yet there was not a moment's hesitation to lay their comrades aside, and spring again to their deadly work.

"Our little consort, the *Metacomet,* was also under my immediate eye during the whole action up to the moment I ordered her to cast off in pursuit of the Selma. The coolness and promptness of Lieutenant-Commander Jouett throughout merit high praise; his whole conduct was worthy of his reputation.

"In this connection I must not omit to call the attention of the Department to the conduct of Acting Ensign Henry C. Neilds, of the *Metacomet,* who had charge of the boat sent from that vessel when the *Tecumseh* sank. He took her in under one of the most galling fires I ever saw, and succeeded in rescuing from death ten of the crew, within six hundred yards of the fort. I would respectfully recommend his advancement.

"The commanding officers of all the vessels that took part in the action deserve my warmest commendations, not only for the untiring zeal with which they had prepared their ships for the contest, but for their skill and daring in carrying out my orders during the engagement. With the exception of the momentary arrest of the fleet when the *Hartford* passed ahead, to which I have already adverted, the order of battle was preserved, and the ships followed each other in close order past the batteries of Fort Morgan, and in comparative safety too, with the exception of the *Oneida.* Her boilers were penetrated by a shot from the fort, which completely disabled her; but her consort, the *Galena,* firmly fastened to her side, brought her safely through, showing clearly the wisdom of the precaution of carrying the vessels in two abreast. Commander Mullany, who had solicited eagerly to take part in the action, was severely wounded, losing his left arm.

"In the encounter with the ram the commanding officers obeyed with alacrity the order to run her down, and without hesitation exposed their ships to destruction, to destroy the enemy.

"Our ironclads, from their slow speed and bad steering, had some difficulty in getting into and maintaining their position in line as we passed the fort, and, in the subsequent encounter with the *Tennessee,* from the same causes were not as effective as could have been desired; but I can not give too much praise to Lieutenant-Commander Perkins, who, though he had orders from the Department to return North, volunteered to take command of the *Chickasaw,* and did his duty nobly.

"The *Winnebago* was commanded by Commander T. H. Stevens, who volunteered for that position. His vessel steers very badly, and neither of his turrets will work, which compelled him to turn his vessel every time to get a shot, so that he could not fire very often, but he did the best he could under the circumstances.

"The *Manhattan* appeared to work well, though she moved slowly. Commander Nicholson delivered his fire deliberately, and, as before stated, with one of his 15-inch shot broke through the armor of the *Tennessee,* with its wooden backing, though the shot itself did not enter the vessel. No other shot broke through the armor, though many of her plates were started, and several of her port-shutters jammed, by the fire from the different ships.

"The *Hartford,* my flag-ship, was commanded by Captain Percival Drayton, who exhibited throughout that coolness and ability for which he has been long known to his brother officers. But I must speak of that officer in a double capacity. He is the fleet-captain of my squadron, and one of more determined energy, untiring devotion to duty, and zeal for the service, tempered by great calmness, I do not think adorns any navy. I desire to call your attention to this officer, though well aware that, in thus speaking of his high qualities, I am only communicating officially to the Department that which it knew full well before. To him, and to my staff in their respective positions, I am indebted for the detail of my fleet.

"Lieutenant J. Crittenden Watson, my flag-lieutenant, has been brought to your notice in former dispatches. During the action he was on the poop, attending to the signals, and performed his duties, as might be expected, thoroughly. He is a scion worthy the noble stock he sprang from, and I commend him to your attention.

"My secretary, Mr. McKinley, and Acting Ensign H. H. Brownell, were also on the poop, the latter taking notes of the action, a duty which he performed with coolness and accuracy.

"Two other acting ensigns of my staff, Mr. Bogart and Mr. Heginbotham, were on duty in the powder division, and, as the reports will show, exhibited zeal and ability. The latter, I regret to add, was severely wounded by a raking shot from the *Tennessee* when we collided with that vessel, and died a few hours after. Mr. Heginbotham was a young married man, and has left a widow and one child, whom I commend to the kindness of the Department.

"Lieutenant A. R. Yates, of the *Augusta,* acted as an additional aid to me on board the *Hartford,* and was very efficient in the transmission of orders. I have given him the command temporarily of the captured steamer *Selma.*

"The last of my staff to whom I would call the attention of the Department is not the least in importance. I mean Pilot Martin Freeman. He has been my great reliance in all difficulties in his line of duty. During the action he was in the main-top, piloting the ships into the bay. He was cool and brave throughout, never losing his self-possession. This man was captured early in the war in a fine fishing-smack which he owned, and though he protested that he had no interest in the war, and only asked for the privilege of fishing for the fleet, yet his services were too valuable to the captors as a pilot not to be secured. He was appointed a first-class pilot, and has served us with zeal and fidelity, and has lost his vessel, which went to pieces on Ship Island. I commend him to the Department.

"It gives me pleasure to refer to several officers who volunteered to take any situation where they might be useful, some of whom were on their way North, either by orders of the Department or condemned by medical survey. The reports of the different commanders will show how they conducted themselves. I have already mentioned Lieutenant-Commander Perkins, of the *Chickasaw*, and Lieutenant Yates, of the *Augusta*. Acting volunteer Lieutenant William Hamilton, late command-ing officer of the *Augusta Dinsmore*, had been invalided by medical sur-vey, but he eagerly offered his services on board the iron-clad *Chickasaw*, having had much experience in our monitors. Acting volunteer Lieu-tenant P. Giraud, another experienced officer in ironclads, asked to go in on one of these vessels; but, as they were all well supplied with officers, I permitted him to go in on the *Ossipee*, under Commander Le Roy. After the action he was given temporary charge of the ram *Tennessee*.

"Before closing this report, there is one other officer of my squadron of whom I feel bound to speak—Captain T. A. Jenkins, of the *Richmond*, who was formerly my chief of staff: not because of his having held that position, but because he never forgets to do his duty to the Government, and takes now the same interest in the fleet as when he stood in that rela-tion to me. He is also the commanding officer of the second division of my squadron, and, as such, has shown ability and the most untiring zeal. He carries out the spirit of one of Lord Collingwood's best sayings: 'Not to be afraid of doing too much; those who are, seldom do as much as they ought.' When in Pensacola, he spent days on the bar, placing the buoys in the best position, was always looking after the interests of the service, and keeping the vessels from being detained one moment longer in port than was necessary. The gallant Craven told me, only the night before the action in which he lost his life: 'I regret, Admiral, that I have detained you; but, had it not been for Captain Jenkins, God knows when I should have been here. When your order came, I had not received an ounce of coal.' I feel I should not be doing my duty did I not call the attention of the Department to an officer who has performed all his various duties with so much zeal and fidelity.

"Very respectfully, your obedient servant,

"D. G. FARRAGUT,
"Commanding W. G. Blockading Squadron.

"Hon. GIDEON WELLES,
"Secretary of the Navy."

The Monitor

Sometimes it is not the commanders who claim the fame, but rather the ships themselves.

Such is the case with the legendary ironclad the Monitor.

More than just a warship, it was, at the time, a technological marvel, but unfortunately, like many commanders, it, too, did not survive the war, and went down off Cape Hatteras in 1862.

In the place of an autobiographical memoir, the following is an assembly of documents related to the most famous of the ironclads, as well as an article from Century *magazine.*

Captain Eggleston's Narrative of the Battle of the *Merrimac*

BY JOHN R. EGGLESTON

Being one of the lieutenants of the *Virginia (Merrimac)* during the whole of her career under the Confederate flag, I give the following account from my own knowledge of what took place in that famous naval battle of the Confederacy, for it is as fresh in my mind as if it happened yesterday.

When the Federals evacuated the Norfolk Navy-Yard immediately after the passage by Virginia of the ordinance of secession, they set fire to the public property there. This included the largest battleship then in the world, viz: the *Pennsylvania*, of 120 guns, used as a receiving ship, and several valuable vessels lying in ordinary—that is, stripped of their rigging and spars and roofed over and put in charge of caretakers. Among these was the frigate *United States,* which, under command of Decatur, had captured the British frigate *Guerriere,* and the then modern steam frigate *Merrimac.* For some reasons the Federals did not set fire to the old frigate, and when the Confederates afterward tried to sink her as an obstruction in the channel below Norfolk, it was found impossible to cut through her hard live oak timbers. I shall tell later what use we made of her.

from The Southern Historical Society Papers, v. 41 (1916).

The *Merrimac,* with her sister ships, the *Minnesota,* the *Colorado,* the *Roanoke* and the *Wabash,* represented the highest type of naval architecture reached at that time. She was a full rigged sailing vessel and steamer combined, of about three thousand tons displacement, and carried a battery of forty nine-inch Dahlgren guns.

Before she had been completely destroyed by the fire lit by the retreating Federals, the Confederates succeeded in sinking her in order to save what was left. Subsequently the hull was raised and converted into the formidable ironclad destined to revolutionize naval architecture and tactics. The following description of the completed ironclad is from the pen of her executive officer, Lieutenant Catesby Jones:

"The hull was 275 feet long. About 160 feet of the central portion was covered by a roof of wood and iron, inclining about 36 degrees. The wood was two feet thick. It consisted of oak plank four inches by twelve laid up and down next to the iron, and two courses of pine, one longitudinal of eight-inch thickness, the other twelve inches thick. The intervening space on top was closed by permanent gratings of two-inch-square iron, two and one-half inches apart, leaving openings for four hatches, one near each end and one forward and one aft the smokestack. The roof did not project beyond the hull.

"The armor, consisting of two courses of two-inch solid iron plates, was bolted to the wooden backing, the inner course longitudinally, the outside course up and down, making the thickness of armor four inches. The hull, extending two feet beyond the roof, was plated with one-inch iron.

"The prow was of cast iron, wedge-shaped, and weighted fifteen hundred pounds. It was about two feet under water, and projected about two feet from the stem. It was not well fastened. The rudder and propeller were unprotected.

"The battery consisted of ten guns, four single-barreled Brooks rifles and six nine-inch Dahlgren shell guns. Two of the rifles, bow and stern pivots, were seven-inch, the other two, on the broadside, 6-4-inch guns, one on each side, near the furnaces, were fitted for firing hot shot. The only solid shot used in the fight were those that had been cast for this special purpose.

"The engines were radically defective, and had been condemned as such by the United States government a few months before."

"The crew, numbering 320 men, had been hard to obtain. They were made up mostly of volunteers from the various regiments stationed about Norfolk at the time. I think the Georgians among them were in the majority. There was a sprinkling of old man-of-war's men, whose value at the time could not be overestimated.

"Leaving these latter out of the reckoning, we had a crew that had never even seen a great gun like these they were soon to handle in a battle against the greatest of odds ever before successfully encountered."

We drilled this crew at the guns of the old frigate *United States* every day for about two weeks, while the *Merrimac* was undergoing her remodeling. The first and only practice of these men behind the guns of the Merrimac herself was in actual battle.

We had all been brought up in the United States Navy, and had recently resigned it. Captain Franklin Buchanan, of Maryland, had stood second to none among the officers of the old navy. Here for the information of laymen, I will say that a captain in the navy ranks with a colonel in the army; a lieutenant in the navy with a captain in the army, etc.

Buchanan was a typical product of the old-time quarter-deck, as indomitably courageous as Nelson, and as arbitrary. I don't think the junior officer or sailor ever lived with nerve sufficient to disobey an order given by the old man in person. On the Japan expedition, under Commodore Perry, Buchanan commanded the steam frigate *Mississippi*. While going up the Canton River in charge of a Chinese pilot the vessel struck the ground, Buchanan, who was standing by the pilot, turned on him so fiercely that the Chinaman jumped overboard.

Lieutenant Catesby Jones bore a high reputation in the old navy as an ordnance officer. The selection of the battery and equipment generally of the marines had been left entirely to him.

All the other commissioned officers had borne good reputations in the navy.

When the *Merrimac* was put in commission she was rechristened the *Virginia*. Shortly after Captain Buchanan came down to Norfolk and assumed command of the *Virginia* and the several small vessels in the water about Norfolk.

At 11 A.M. on Saturday, March 8, we started on our trial trip down the Elizabeth River, which lies between Norfolk and Portsmouth. The population of both cities seemed to have massed along the wharves on both sides, bidding us godspeed with others, and waving handkerchiefs. But all the people were not there. The churches were thronged with women and children, many belonging to those who were going into battle. They were praying for our success and the preservation of their loved ones.

Leaving the *Virginia* for a moment let us glance at the force that "our friends, the enemy," had at their disposal for our reception. Off Newport News, blocking the mouth of the James River, were the frigate *Congress,* of 450 men and fifty guns; the *Cumberland,* 360 men and twenty-two guns of much heavier caliber than those of the *Congress;* one small gunboat and formidable land batteries within point-blank range of the vessels we were about to attack.

A few miles distant, and in full view of Old Point Comfort, lay the steam frigates *Minnesota* and *Roanoke,* each with 550 men and forty guns, and the sailing frigate *St. Lawrence,* with 450 men and fifty guns, making in the aggregate about 3,000 men and 230 guns.

Accompanying the *Virginia* as tenders were two tugboats, each mounting one 32-pounder on the bow. They were the *Beaufort,* Lieutenant Parker, and the *Raleigh,* Lieutenant Alexander. Blockaded up the James River were three Confederate vessels, viz: the *Patrick Henry,* with six guns, commander, John R. Tucker; the *Jamestown,* two guns, Lieutenant Barney, and the tugboat *TenzerE1,* one gun, Lieutenant Webb. The first two vessels named were walking-beam bay boats, with boilers above the water-line.

Let us return to the *Virginia* as she is threading her way through the channel leading into Hampton Roads. Dead ahead is Fortress Monroe and the Rip Raps guarding the channel that leads past the mouth of Chesapeake Bay into the Atlantic Ocean. Off about two points on the port bow the two Federal vessels, *Congress* and *Cumberland,* are quietly laying out their anchors.

Saturday is the day in which the sailors of a man-of-war wash their clothes in the morning watch, and the washed clothes of the *Congress* are now stretched upon horizontal lines between the main and mizzen rigging—the clothes of over four hundred men—the white clothes on the starboard side, the blue on the port, according to naval custom.

Many a poor fellow who scrubbed his shirt or his trousers, spread on the white deck this morning, shall have no more use for them after their day's work shall have been done.

I had served on both ships as midshipman. The *Cumberland* had been altered beyond recognition from a fifty-gun fighter to a sloop of war, but the *Congress* looked as she did when she was my floating home for nearly three years. Little did I think then that I should ever lift a hand for her destruction.

Only the commander and the executive officer knew the point of attack that had been decided upon, but all at once the ship is headed for the two vessels off

Newport News, and the drum and fife are sounding the call to quarters. We see the washed clothes of the *Congress* lowered to her deck and hear over the water her drum and fife in the identical notes as our own calling her crew to quarters.

We go quietly to our stations, cast loose the guns, and stand ready for the next act in the drama.

I commanded the two hot-shot guns directly under the main hatch, and just over the furnace. All great guns then were muzzle-loaders. The hot shot was hoisted from below in an iron bucket, placed by means of tugs in the muzzle of the gun, slightly elevated and allowed to roll against the well-soaked wad that rested against the powder. Another soaked wad kept the shot in place.

The view from my station was restricted to the gun port, some three by four feet. For a time only the wide waters of the bay and the distant shores were visible, till suddenly the port became the frame of the picture of a great ship.

It was the *Congress* only about a hundred yards distant. But for an instant was she visible, for suddenly there leaped from her sides the flash of thirty-five guns, and as many shot and shell were hurled against our armor only to be thrown from it high into the air. As by a miracle, no projectile entered into the wide-open ports. But some time during the action, the muzzle of two of our guns were shot away, resulting in the loss of two men killed and twelve wounded.

Lieutenant Davidson, in direct command of the disabled guns, continued to fight with what was left of them while the battle lasted.

We had returned with four guns the broadside from the *Congress*, and scarcely had the smoke cleared away when I felt a jar as if the ship had struck ground. A few seconds later Flag Lieutenant Bob Minor passed rapidly along deck waving his cap, calling out: "We've sunk the *Cumberland*."

The *Cumberland* lay higher up the river than her consort, and, while carrying fewer guns than the latter, was really the more formidable vessel of the two. We particularly dreaded her two eleven-inch guns on pivot at bow and stern. It is for that reason Buchanan selected the *Cumberland* for the first victim. The blow was preceded by a shot fired with his own hands by Lieutenant Simmons from the seven-inch rifle in the bow. It was said that this shot almost annihilated the crew of the *Cumberland*'s eleven-inch pivot gun.

She sank rapidly after she had been struck, dragging with her the great iron prow from our bow. I have often thought since that if the prow had been held fast we would have gone to the bottom with our victim.

There is another afterthought that I wish to record. While I am sure that the officers and crew of the *Cumberland* were as gallant a set of men as ever lived, it is not certain that they merit the compliment paid them, even by Buchanan, of "going down with flying colors." It is more reasonable to suppose that on a rapidly sinking ship no one in the rush to save his life paused long enough to perform the quite unnecessary task of pulling down a flag upon which no enemy was firing.

After disposing of the *Cumberland,* we ascended the river for some distance, in order to find a place wide enough to turn. In doing so we exchanged shots, going and coming, with the shore batteries. Past their very batteries, the Confederate vessels I have alluded to as being blockaded in the James boldly dashed at the first sound of our guns, and threw themselves into the midst of the fray. A shot striking the exposed boiler of the *Patrick Henry* had killed and wounded a dozen men.

We were afterward told by the prisoners that when the *Congress* people saw us again up the river they gave three cheers, under the belief that we were running away. But when we made directly for her, the *Congress* slipped her cables and tried to escape under sail. She ran aground in the attempt. We then took position under her stern, and a few raking shots brought down her flag.

The surrendered frigate was now lying under our guns, protected by three white flags from her peak and masts. Buchanan had ascended to the upper deck. Parker, in the *Beaufort,* had by order gone alongside the prize to take off the prisoners, preparatory to setting the vessel on fire. Sharpshooters on shore opened fire on him, killing several of their own men, prisoners on the *Beaufort,* and Parker was forced to draw off.

Flag Lieutenant Minor then volunteered to board the *Congress* in one of the ship's boats. He had reached a point a little over one hundred yards from the *Congress,* his boat also bearing a white flag, when suddenly Buchanan, in a ringing voice I can never forget, called down the hatchway under which I was standing:

"Destroy that —— ship! She's firing on our white flag!"

It was even so, incredible as it may seem. Minor was shot through the stomach, and one of his men had an eye shot out.

Soon after Buchanan himself was shot in the thigh from the same treacherous source. We had thought that this last shot had been fired by a sharpshooter on shore, but a few years ago I received a letter from an ex-Federal officer in Boston, saying that a man there, a former marine in the *Congress,* boasted of having shot Buchanan, while himself protected by a white flag.

Dearly did they pay for their unparalleled treachery. We raked her fore and aft with hot shot and shell, till out of pity we stopped without waiting for orders.

The loss of the *Congress* in killed and wounded was 121—more than 25 percent.

With us of the navy it was real civil war. On both sides we were fighting men with whom we had lately intimately associated in a common profession. We all knew one another personally or by reputation. When Parker stepped on the deck of the *Congress* he saw there the dead body of her commanding officer, Lieutenant Joe Smith. The two men had been classmates at Annapolis, and intimate friends and messmates for more than one long cruise at sea.

On our way back across the bay that night we gathered about the stateroom in which our wounded commander was lying. In a voice filled with emotion, he said: "My brother, Paymaster Buchanan, was on board the *Congress.*" In the border States families were often divided.

After the fight was over, Catesby Jones, who had succeeded to the command, passed my station while on his rounds about the ship. "A pretty good day's work," I said to him.

"Yes," was his answer, "but it is not over. The *Minnesota,* the *Roanoke* and the *St. Lawrence* are on the way up to engage us."

But when these great ships saw what had happened to their consorts, they had no stomach for the fight, but as we pressed them at long range, on our way over to our batteries at Sewell's Point, they shook the heavens and the earth with the thunders of their broadsides. The *St. Lawrence* fired seventy-two shots, and her commander reports and says that one of our shells passed through the starboard quarter of his ship, doing considerable damage.

Arriving off Sewell's Point, we sent our dead and wounded on shore. Our little wooden vessels had anchored near us, and an impromptu reunion was held on board the *Virginia* by the officers of the several vessels. I noticed that the uniform of Webb, of the *TenzenE1,* was riddled by minie balls.

That night, as officer of the deck, I had the middle watch from 12 to 4.

At about two bells (1 o'clock), there was a sudden lighting up the sky, followd by a heavy explosion in the direction of Newport News. The fire had reached the magazine of the *Congress.*

With the first light of the morning of Sunday, March 9, 1862, we looked eagerly out over the bay. There was the *Minnesota* lying aground where she had struck the evening before, and near her was the strangest looking craft we had ever seen before. A cheese on a raft, as she was designated by a correspondent, James Barron Hope.

We "piped" to early breakfast, and when it was over we weighed anchor and steamed toward the *Minnesota* to renew the battle. The *Monitor* came boldly out to meet us, and then began the first battle between ironclads.

In the narrow channel the *Monitor* had every advantage, for she drew only ten feet of water, and the *Virginia* twenty-three feet. Her two eleven-inch guns, thoroughly protected, were really more formidable than our ten guns of from six- to nine-inch caliber, and pointing through open ports. We never got sight of her guns except when they were about to fire into us. Then the turret slowly turned, presenting to us its solid side, and enabled the gunners to load without danger.

The first shots exchanged were at long range, but the vessels soon came to close quarters, as near at times as fifty yards. The *Monitor* circled around and around us, receiving our fire as she went, and delivering her own. We saw our shells burst into fragments against her turret.

Once I called Jones's attention to my men standing at rest. "It is a waste of ammunition," I said, "to fire at her."

"Never mind," he said, as he passed on, "we are getting ready to ram her."

We did ram her, but whether because our prow was gone or because we eased up too soon, we did not do her any apparent injury. However, about that time the *Monitor* gave up the fight and retreated out of our range into shoal water, where she was safe from our pursuit. She was not only whipped, but she stayed whipped, as will be shown in the sequel.

The *Virginia,* in undisputed possession of the ground, after the flight of the *Monitor,* turned her undivided attention to the *Minnesota,* still hard aground, about a mile away, and out of range of the direct fire of our smooth-bore guns.

I was firing mine at ricochet—that is, with the gun level—so that the shot would skip along the surface like pebbles the boys "skell" along a pond. But Davidson, with his rifle guns, just forward of me was actually "plumping" the target by direct fire, as we learned later by the enemy's official report. At the time, we could not see that we were inflicting any serious damage on her.

The *Monitor* had fought us gallantly for over three hours, and we had continued our attack on the *Minnesota* for nearly another hour, when Jones, pausing at each division as he passed along the deck, held an informal council of war with his lieutenants. This is what he said to me in effect:

"The *Monitor* has given up the fight and run into shoal water; the pilots cannot take us any nearer to the *Minnesota;* this ship is leaking from the loss of her prow; the men are exhausted by being so long at their guns; the tide is ebbing, so that we shall have to remain here all night unless we leave at once. I propose to return to Norfolk for repairs. What is your opinion?"

I answered: "If things are as you say, I agree with you." So did the other lieutenants, with the exception of Lieutenant John Taylor Wood. He stepped over from his gun to mine for a moment, and said, "I proposed to Jones to run down to Fortress Monroe and clean up the Yankee ships there or run them out to sea."

This alternative course suggested by Wood shows that the *Monitor* was no longer a factor in the situation. As for the proposition on its merits, to attack a vastly superior naval force, protected by the guns of one of the greatest fortresses in the world, was too hazardous to be considered by a cool-headed commander like Jones, with all the responsibility on his shoulders.

While writing at the age of seventy-five, necessarily with a flying pen, this, my last article on this subject, let me pay one passing tribute to the memory of my gallant old friend, my classmate at Annapolis, my messmate on the *Virginia,* the late Commander John Taylor Wood, C. S. A., a grandson of General Zachary Taylor. He had inherited the indomitable pluck of that old hero. During the fight with the *Monitor* he had called for volunteers to go with him to board that vessel from an open boat, and try to wedge her turret to prevent her from turning it. The withdrawal of the *Monitor* frustrated the attempt.

Subsequently during the war Commander Wood received the joint thanks of the Confederate Congress for capturing at different times and places, by boarding them, sword in hand, eight vessels belonging to the Federal navy.

That to the dead; this is to the living: To my former messmate and senior on the *Virginia,* the gallant Hunter Davidson, commander C. S. A., now living in Paraguay, at an age exceeding eighty, the world owes to the Confederate States the use of the torpedo in war, and the Confederate States owe it to Davidson. He received the thanks of the Confederate States of America Congress for attacking the *Minnesota* with a torpedo carried at the end of a pole in an open boat.

The main object of this article is to fix in the minds of the younger generation the fact that the *Virginia (Merrimac)* defeated the *Monitor* in her encounter with that vessel, instead of being defeated by the *Monitor,* as is falsely stated by Northern writers. I will conclude this article by heaping "Pelion on Ossa" in the shape of proofs. The two opposing armies on each side of the bay say the *Monitor* ran away. I have before me the written words of three eye-witnesses of her fight, via: my brother officers Jones, Simms and Davidson. I, myself, saw her run twice.

On the 8th of May, 1862, we were lying anchored off Norfolk when we heard a terrific bombardment going on down the bay. We ran down at full speed and discovered that a squadron of Federal vessels, led by the *Monitor,* was encircling around in front of Sewell's Point and throwing their broadsides into our works there as they passed. We heard later that it was a show for the benefit of Mr. Lincoln, who was on a visit to Fortress Monroe. At our approach they fled ignominiously and huddled for safety under the guns of Fortress Monroe. The *Jamestown* went in and cut out transport vessels almost under their guns, and they pocketed the insult. The British ship of war *Rinaldo* was lying in the Roads, and as we passed her on our return, her crew mounted the riggings and gave us three cheers.

The career of the famous ship was now drawing to a close.

She had never been the effective fighting machine that the hopes of her friends and the fears of her enemies had made her. I am sure she could not have repeated her exploit during her fights of two days with as little injury as she actually received. She never was more than a floating battery, forming part and parcel of the fortifications of Norfolk. She was utterly unseaworthy, and could not ascend the James River without first lightening her so that with the exposure of her wooden hull she would no longer be an ironclad.

Notes on the
Monitor-Merrimac Fight.

BY DINWIDDIE B. PHILLIPS,

SURGEON OF THE *MERRIMAC*

The *Virginia* (or *Merrimac*), with which I was connected during her entire career, bore some resemblance to a huge terrapin with a large round chimney about the middle of its back. She was so built as not to suit high winds and heavy seas, and therefore could not operate outside the capes of Virginia. In fact she was designed from the first as a defence for the harbor of Norfolk, and for that alone. In addition to our guns, we were armed with an iron ram or prow. The prow, not being well put on, was twisted off and lost in our first encounter with the *Cumberland*. I am also satisfied that had not our prow been lost, we should have sunk the *Monitor* when we rammed her on the 9th of March, 1862. Admiral Worden is of contrary opinion. In a private letter to me, dated March 13th, 1882, he says:

"If the prow of the *Merrimac* had been intact at the time she struck the *Monitor,* she could not have damaged her a practice more by the blow with in that she did in hitting her with her stem; and for the following reasons: The hull of the *Monitor* was in breadth, at her midships section, 34 feet, and the armored raft which was placed on the hull was, at the same point, 41 feet 4 inches in breadth, so that the raft extended on either side 3 feet 8 inches beyond the hull. The raft was 5 feet deep and was immersed in the water 3½ feet. The *Merrimac*'s prow, according to Jones, therefore, if on, would have struck the armored hull 1½ feet above its lowest part, and could not have damaged it. Further, the prow extended 2 feet forward from the stem, and had it been low enough to reach below the armored raft, it could not have reached the hull by 1 foot 8 inches."

We left the Norfolk Navy-Yard about 11 A.M. of that day. As our engines were very weak and defective, leaving been condemned just before the war as worthless, we were fortunate in having favorable weather for our purpose. The day was unusually mild and calm for the season, and the water was smooth and glassy; and, except for the unusually large number of persons upon the shores watching our motions, there was nothing to indicate a serious movement on our part. Our vessel never having been tested before, and her model being new and unheard of, many of those who watched us predicted failure, and others suggested that the *Virginia* was an enormous metallic burial case and that we were conducting our own funeral. Though we withdrew on the first day of the battle, at 7 P.M., and went to our anchorage at Sewell's Point, our duties kept us so constantly engaged that it was near midnight before we got our supper, the only meal we had taken since 8 A.M. Afterward the attractiveness of the burning *Congress* was such that we watched her till nearly 1 A.M., when she blew up, before we went to our rest, so that when we were aroused to resume the fight on Sunday morning, it seemed as though we had scarcely been asleep. After a hurried breakfast, and while the crew were getting up the anchor, I landed Captain Buchanan, Lieutenant Minor, and the seriously wounded men at Sewell's Point, for transmission to the naval hospital at Norfolk. Returning, I pulled around the ship before boarding her, to see how she had stood the bombardment of Saturday and to what extent she had been damaged. I found all her stanchions, iron railings, and light work of every description swept away, her smokestack cut to pieces, two guns without muzzles, and ninety-eight indentations on her plating, showing where heavy solid shot had struck, but had glanced off without doing any injury. As soon as I had got on deck (about 6:25 A.M.), we started again for Hampton Roads.

On our way to the *Minnesota,* and while we were still too far off to do her much damage, the *Monitor* came out to meet us. For some length of time we devoted our attention to her, but having no solid shot, and finding that our light shell were making but little impression upon her turret, Jones ordered the pilot to disregard the *Monitor* altogether, and carry out his first instructions by placing the *Virginia* as near to the *Minnesota* as possible. Instead, however, of taking us within a half mile of that ship, as we afterward learned he could have done, he purposely ran us aground nearly two miles off. This he did through fear of passing under the *Minnesota*'s terrible broadside, as he confessed subsequently to Captain A. B. Fairfax, Confederate States Navy, from whose lips I received it. After fifteen or twenty minutes we were afloat again. We sheered off from the *Monitor* in order to get a chance to turn and ram her. This was the time when Captain Van Brunt was under the impression we were in retreat and "the little battery chasing us." As soon as the move could be effected, we turned and ran into the *Monitor,* and at the same time gave her a shot from our bow pivot-gun. Had our iron prow been intact, as I have already said, we would have sunk her. As it was, she staggered awhile under the shock, and, sheering off from us was for a time inactive. The battle was renewed, but shortly after noon the *Monitor* again withdrew.

We continued our fire upon the *Minnesota*, at long range, for about half an hour longer, when we took advantage of the flood-tide and returned slowly to Norfolk. That we did not destroy the *Minnesota* was due solely to the fact that our pilot assured us we could get no nearer to her than we then were without grounding again.

In the *Monitor* Turret

BY COMMANDER S. D. GREENE

The keel of the most famous vessel of modern times was laid in the shipyard of Thomas F. Rowland, at Greenpoint, Brooklyn, in October 1861, and on the 30th of January, 1862, the novel craft was launched. On the 25th of February she was commissioned and turned over to the government, and nine days later left New York for Hampton Roads, where, on the 9th of March, occurred the memorable contest with the *Virginia*. On her next venture on the open sea she foundered off Cape Hatteras in a gale of wind (December 29). During her career of less than a year, she had no fewer than five different commanders; but it was the fortune of the writer to serve as her only executive officer, standing upon her deck when she was launched, and leaving it but a few minutes before she sank.

So hurried was the preparation of the *Monitor* that the mechanics worked upon her night and day up to the hour of her departure, and little opportunity was offered to drill the crew at the guns, to work the turret, and to become familiar with the other unusual features of the vessel. The crew was, in fact, composed of volunteers. Lieutenant Worden, having been authorized by the Navy Department to select his men from any ship-of-war in New York harbor, addressed the crews of the *North Carolina* and *Sabine* stating fully to them the probable dangers of the passage to Hampton Roads and the certainty of having important service to perform after arriving. The sailors responded enthusiastically, many more volunteering

From *The Century* magazine, Vol. XXIX, March, 1885

than were required. Of the crew selected, Captain Worden said, in his official report of the engagement, "A better one no naval commander ever had the honor to command."

We left New York in tow of the tugboat *Seth Low* at 11 A.M. of Thursday, the 6th of March. On the following day a moderate breeze was encountered, and it was at once evident that the *Monitor* was unfit for a sea-going craft. Nothing but the subsidence of the wind prevented her from being shipwrecked before she reached Hampton Roads. The berth-deck hatch leaked in spite of all we could do, and the water came down under the turret like a waterfall. It would strike the pilot-house and go over the turret in beautiful curves, and it came through the narrow eye-holes in the pilot-house with such force as to knock the helmsman completely round from the wheel. The waves also broke over the blower-pipes, and the water came down through them in such quantities that the belts of the blower-engines slipped, and the engines consequently stopped for lack of artificial draught, without which, in such a confined place, the fires could not get air for combustion. Newton and Stimers, followed by the engineer's force, gallantly rushed into the engine-room and fireroom to remedy the evil, but they were unable to check the inflowing water, and were nearly suffocated with escaping gas. They were dragged out more dead than alive, and carried to the top of the turret, where the fresh air gradually revived them. The water continued to pour through the hawser-hole, and over and down the smokestacks and blowerpipes, in such quantities that there was imminent danger that the ship would founder. The steam-pumps could not be operated because the fires had been nearly extinguished, and the engine-room was uninhabitable on account of the suffocating gas with which it was filled. The hand-pumps were then rigged and worked, but they had not enough force to throw the water out through the top of the turret—the only opening—and it was useless to bail, as we had to pass the buckets up through the turret, which made it a very long operation.

Fortunately, towards evening the wind and sea subsided, and, being again in smooth water, the engine was put in operation. But at midnight, in passing over a shoal, rough water was again encountered, and our troubles were renewed, complicated this time with the jamming of the wheel-ropes, so that the safety of the ship depended entirely on the strength of the hawser which connected her with the tugboat. The hawser, being new, held fast; but during the greater part of the night we were constantly engaged in fighting the leaks, until we reached smooth water again, just before daylight.

It was at the close of this dispiriting trial trip, in which all hands had been exhausted in their efforts to keep the novel craft afloat, that the *Monitor* passed Cape Henry at 4 P.M. on Saturday, March 8th. At this point was heard the distant booming of heavy guns, which our captain rightly judged to be an engagement with the *Merrimac,* twenty miles away. He at once ordered the vessel stripped of her sea-rig, the turret keyed up, and every preparation made for battle. As we approached Hampton Roads we could see the fine old *Congress* burning brightly, and soon a pilot came on board and told of the arrival of the *Merrimac,* the disaster to the *Cumberland* and the *Congress,* and the dismay of the Union forces. The *Monitor* was pushed with all haste, and reached the *Roanoke* (Captain Marston), anchored in the Roads, at 9 A.M. Worden immediately reported his arrival to Captain Marston, who suggested that he should go to the assistance of the *Minnesota,* then aground off Newport News. As no pilot was available, Captain Worden accepted the volunteer services of Acting Master Samuel Howard, who earnestly sought the duty. An atmosphere of gloom pervaded the fleet, and the pygmy aspect of the new-comer did not inspire confidence among those who had witnessed the destruction of the day before. Skillfully piloted by Howard, we proceeded on our way, our path illuminated by the blaze of the *Congress.* Reaching the *Minnesota,* hard and fast aground, near midnight, we anchored, and Worden reported to Captain Van Brunt. Between 1 and 2 A.M. the *Congress* blew up, not instantaneously, but successively; her powder-tanks seemed to explode, each shower of sparks rivaling the other in its height, until they appeared to reach the zenith—a grand but mournful sight. Near us, too, lay the *Cumberland,* at the bottom of the river, with her silent crew of brave men, who died while fighting their guns to the water's edge, and whose colors were still flying at the peak.

The dreary night dragged slowly on; the officers and crew were up and alert, to be ready for any emergency. At daylight on Sunday the *Merrimac* and her consorts were discovered at anchor near Sewell's Point. At about half past seven o'clock the enemy's vessels got under way and steered in the direction of the *Minnesota.*

At the same time the *Monitor* got under way, and her officers and crew took their stations for battle. Captain Van Brunt officially reports, "I made signal to the *Monitor* to attack the enemy," but the signal was not seen by us; other work was in hand, and Worden required no signal.

The pilot-house of the *Monitor* was situated well forward, near the bow; it was a wrought iron structure, built of logs of iron nine inches thick, bolted through the corners, and covered with an iron plate two inches thick, which was not fastened down, but was kept in place merely by its weight. The sight-holes or slits were made by inserting quarter-inch plates at the corners between the upper set of logs and the next below. The structure projected four feet above the deck, and was barely large enough inside to hold three men standing. It presented a flat surface on all sides and on top. The steering-wheel was secured to one of the logs on the front side. The position and shape of this structure should be carefully borne in mind.

Worden took his station in the pilot-house, and by his side were Howard, the pilot, and Peter Williams, quartermaster, who steered the vessel throughout the engagement. My place was in the turret, to work and fight the guns; with me were Stodder and Stimers and sixteen brawny men, eight to each gun. John Stocking, boatswain's mate, and Thomas Lochrane, seaman, were gun-captains. Newton and his assistants were in the engine and firerooms, to manipulate the boilers and engines, and most admirably did they perform this important service from the beginning to the close of the action. Webber had charge of the powder division on the berth-deck, and Joseph Crown, gunner's mate, rendered valuable service in connection with this duty.

The physical condition of the officers and men of the two ships at this time was in striking contrast. The *Merrimac* had passed the night quietly near Sewell's Point, her people enjoying rest and sleep, elated by thoughts of the victory they had achieved that day, and cheered by the prospects of another easy victory on the morrow. The *Monitor* had barely escaped shipwreck twice within the last thirty-six hours, and since Friday morning, forty-eight hours before, few if any of those on board had closed their eyes in sleep or had anything to eat but hard bread, as cooking was impossible; she was surrounded by wrecks and disaster, and her efficiency in action had yet to be proved.

Worden lost no time in bringing it to test. Getting his ship under way, he steered direct for the enemy's vessels, in order to meet and engage them as far as possible from the *Minnesota*. As he approached, the wooden vessels quickly turned and left. Our captain, to the "astonishment" of Captain Van Brunt (as he states in his official report), made straight for the *Merrimac,* which had already commenced firing; and when he came within short range, he changed his course so as to come alongside of her, stopped the engine, and gave the order, "Commence firing!" I triced up the port, ran out the gun, and, taking deliberate aim, pulled the lockstring. The *Merrimac* was quick to reply, returning a rattling broadside (for she had ten guns to our two), and the battle fairly began. The turret and other parts of the ship were heavily struck, but the shots did not penetrate; the tower was intact, and it continued to revolve. A look of confidence passed over the men's faces, and we believed the *Merrimac* would not repeat the work she had accomplished the day before.

The fight continued with the exchange of broadsides as fast as the guns could be swerved and at very short range, the distance between the vessels frequently being not more than a few yards. Worden skillfully manoeuvred his quick-turning vessel, trying to find some vulnerable point in his adversary. Once he made a dash at her stern, hoping to disable her screw, which he thinks he missed by not more than two feet. Our shots ripped the iron of the *Merrimac,* while the reverberation of her shots against the tower caused anything but a pleasant sensation. While Stodder, who was stationed at the machine which controlled the revolving motion of the turret, was incautiously leaning against the side of the tower, a large shot struck in the vicinity and disabled him. He left the turret and went below, and Stimers, who had assisted him, continued to do the work.

As the engagement continued, the working of the turret was not altogether satisfactory. It was difficult to start it revolving, or, when once started, to stop it, on account of the imperfections of the novel machinery, which was now undergoing its first trial. Stimers was an active, muscular man, and did his utmost to control the motion of the turret; but, in spite of his efforts, it was difficult if not impossible to secure accurate firing. The conditions were very different from those of an ordinary broadside gun, under which we had been trained on wooden ships. My only view of the world outside of the tower was over the muzzles of the guns, which cleared the ports by a few inches only. When the guns were run in, the portholes were covered by heavy iron pendulums, pierced with small holes to allow the iron rammer and sponge handles to protrude while they were in use. To hoist these pendulums required the entire gun's crew and vastly increased the work inside the turret.

The effect upon one shut up in a revolving drum is perplexing, and it is not a simple matter to keep the bearings. White marks had been placed upon the stationary deck immediately below the turret to indicate the direction of the starboard and port sides, and the bow and stern; but these marks were obliterated early in the action. I would continually ask the captain, "How does the *Merrimac* bear?" He replied, "On the starboard-beam," or "On the port-quarter," as the case might be. Then the difficulty was to determine the direction of the starboard-beam, or port-quarter, or any other bearing. It finally resulted, that when a gun was ready for firing, the turret would be started on its revolving journey in search of the target, and when found it was taken "on the fly," because the turret could not be accurately controlled. Once the *Merrimac* tried to ram us; but Worden avoided the direct impact by the skillful use of the helm, and she struck a glancing blow, which did no damage.

At the instant of collision I planted a solid one-hundred-and-eighty-pound shot fair and square upon the forward part of her casemate. Had the gun been loaded with thirty pounds of powder, which was the charge subsequently used with similar guns, it is probable that this shot would have penetrated her armor; but the charge being limited to fifteen pounds, in accordance with peremptory orders to that effect from the Navy Department, the shot rebounded without doing any more damage than possibly to start some of the beams of her armor-backing.

It is stated by Colonel Wood, of the *Merrimac*, that when that vessel rammed the *Cumberland* her iron ram, or beak, was broken off and left in that vessel. In a letter to me, about two years since, he described this ram as "of cast iron, wedge-shaped, about fifteen hundred pounds in weight, two feet under water, and projecting two and a half feet from the stem." A ram of this description, had it been intact, would have struck the *Merrimac* at that part of the upper hull where the armor and backing were thickest. It is very doubtful if, under any headway that the *Merrimac* could have acquired at such short range, this ram could have done any injury to this part of the vessel. That it could by no possibility have reached the thin lower hull is evident from a glance at the drawing of the *Monitor*, the overhang or upper hull being constructed for the express purpose of protecting the vital part of the vessel.

The battle continued at close quarters without apparent damage to either side. After a time, the supply of shot in the turret being exhausted, Worden hauled off for about fifteen minutes to replenish. The serving of the cartridges, weighing but fifteen pounds, was a matter of no difficulty; but the hoisting of the heavy shot was a slow and tedious operation, it being necessary that the turret should remain stationary, in order that the two scuttles, one in the deck and the other in the floor of the turret, should be in line. Worden took advantage of the lull, and passed through the port-hole upon the deck outside to get a better view of the situation. He soon renewed the attack, and the contest continued as before.

Two important points were constantly kept in mind: first, to prevent the enemy's projectiles from entering the turret through the portholes—for the explosion of a shell inside, by disabling the men at the guns, would have ended the fight, there being no relief gun's crews on board; second, not to fire into our own pilot-house. A careless or impatient hand, during the confusion arising from the whirligig motion of the tower, might let slip one of our big shot against the pilot-house. For this and other reasons I fired every gun while I remained in the turret.

Soon after noon a shell from the enemy's gun, the muzzle not ten yards distant, struck the forward side of the pilot-house directly in the sight-hole, or slit, and exploded, cracking the second iron log and partly lifting the top, leaving an opening. Worden was standing immediately behind this spot, and received in his face the force of the blow, which partly stunned him, and, filling his eyes with powder, utterly blinded him. The injury was known only to those in the pilot-house and its immediate vicinity. The flood of light rushing through the top of the pilot-house, now partly open, caused Worden, blind as he was, to believe that the pilot-house was seriously injured, if not destroyed; he therefore gave orders to put the helm to starboard and "sheer off." Thus the *Monitor* retired temporarily from the action, in order to ascertain the extent of the injuries she had received. At the same time Worden sent for me, and leaving Stimers the only officer in the turret, I went forward at once, and found him standing at the foot of the ladder leading to the pilot-house.

He was a ghastly sight, with his eyes closed and the blood apparently rushing from every pore in the upper part of his face. He told me that he was seriously wounded, and directed me to take command. I assisted in leading him to a sofa in his cabin, where he was tenderly cared for by Doctor Logue, and then I assumed command. Blind and suffering as he was, Worden's fortitude never forsook him; he frequently asked from his bed of pain of the progress of affairs, and when told that the *Minnesota* was saved, he said, "Then I can die happy."

When I reached my station in the pilot-house, I found that the iron log was fractured and the top partly open; but the steering-gear was still intact, and the pilot-house was not totally destroyed, as had been feared. In the confusion of the moment resulting from so serious an injury to the commanding officer, the *Monitor* had been moving without direction. Exactly how much time elapsed from the moment that Worden was wounded until I had reached the pilot-house and completed the examination of the injury at that point, and determined what course to pursue in the damaged condition of the vessel, it is impossible to state; but it could hardly have exceeded twenty minutes at the utmost. During this time the *Merrimac,* which was leaking badly, had started in the direction of the Elizabeth River; and, on taking my station in the pilot-house and turning the vessel's head in the direction of the *Merrimac,* I saw that she was already in retreat. A few shots were fired at the retiring vessel, and she continued on to Norfolk. I returned with the *Monitor* to the side of the *Minnesota,* where preparations were being made to abandon the ship, which was still aground. Shortly afterward Worden was transferred to a tug, and that night he was carried to Washington.

The fight was over. We of the *Monitor* thought, and still think, that we had gained a great victory. This the Confederates have denied. But it has never been denied that the object of the *Merrimac* on the 9th of March was to complete the destruction of the Union fleet in Hampton Roads, and that in this she was completely foiled and driven off by the *Monitor* nor has it been denied that at the close of the engagement the *Merrimac* retreated to Norfolk, leaving the *Monitor* in possession of the field.

In this engagement Captain Worden displayed the highest qualities as an officer and man. He was in his prime (forty-four years old), and carried with him the ripe experience of twenty-eight years in the naval service. He joined the ship a sick man, having but recently left a prison in the South. He was nominated for the command by the late Admiral Joseph Smith, and the result proved the wisdom of the choice. Having accepted his orders against the protests of his physicians and the entreaties of his family, nothing would deter him from the enterprise.

He arrived on the battle-ground amidst the disaster and gloom, almost despair, of the Union people, who had little faith that he could beat back the powerful *Merrimac,* after her experience with the *Cumberland* and *Congress.* Without encouragement, single-handed, and without specific orders from any source, he rose above the atmosphere of doubt and depression which surrounded him, and with unflinching nerve and undaunted courage he hurled his little untried vessel against his huge, well-proved antagonist, and won the battle. He was victor in the first iron-clad battle of the world's history.

The subsequent career of the *Monitor* needs but a few words.

On the day after the fight I received the following letter from Mr. Fox, assistant secretary of the navy:

"U. S. STEAMER ROANOKE, OLD POINT
"March 10, 1862

"My Dear Mr. Greene:
"Under the extraordinary circumstances of the contest of yesterday, and the responsibilities devolving upon me, and your extreme youth, [Ed. Note: I was twenty-two years of age, and previous to joining the *Monitor* had seen less than three years of active service, with the rank of midshipman.—S.D.G.] I have suggested to Captain Marston to send on board the *Monitor,* as temporary commanding, Lieutenant Selfridge, until the arrival of Commodore Goldsborough, which will be in a few days. I appreciate your position, and you must appreciate mine, and serve with the same zeal and fidelity.

"With the kindest wishes for you all, most truly;

"G. V. FOX."

For the next two months we lay at Hampton Roads. Twice the *Merrimac* came out of the Elizabeth River, but did not attack. We, on our side, had received positive orders not to attack in the comparatively shoal waters above Hampton Roads, where the Union fleet could not manoeuvre. The *Merrimac* protected the James River, and the *Monitor* protected the Chesapeake. Neither side had an iron-clad in reserve, and neither wished to bring on an engagement which might disable its only armored naval defense in those waters.

With the evacuation of Norfolk and the destruction of the *Merrimac,* the *Mon-*

itor moved up the James River with the squadron under the command of Commander John Rodgers, in connection with McClellan's advance upon Richmond by the Peninsula.

We were engaged for four hours at Fort Darling, but were unable to silence the guns or destroy the earthworks.

Probably no ship was ever devised which was so uncomfortable for her crew, and certainly no sailor ever led a more disagreeable life than we did on the James River, suffocated with heat and bad air if we remained below, and a target for sharpshooters if we came on deck.

SINKING OF THE *MONITOR*, DECEMBER 29, 1862

With the withdrawal of McClellan's army, we returned to Hampton Roads, and in the autumn were ordered to Washington, where the vessel was repaired. We returned to Hampton Roads in November, and sailed thence (December 29) in tow of the steamer *Rhode Island,* bound for Beaufort, N. C. Between 11 P.M. and midnight on the following night the *Monitor* went down in a gale, a few miles south of Cape Hatteras. Four officers and twelve men were drowned, forty-nine people being saved by the boats of the steamer. It was impossible to keep the vessel free of water, and we presumed that the upper and lower hulls thumped themselves apart.

No ship in the world's history has a more imperishable place in naval annals than the *Monitor.* Not only by her providential arrival at the right moment did she secure the safety of Hampton Roads and all that depended on it but the ideas which she embodied revolutionized the system of naval warfare which had existed from the earliest recorded history. The name of the *Monitor* became generic, representing a new type; and, crude and defective as was her construction in some of its details, she yet contained the idea of the turret, which is today the central idea of the most powerful vessels.

S. D. GREENE
Commander U. S. Navy

The Hunley

The Union had the revolutionary marvel of the Monitor.

The Confederacy had its own marvel as well—the Hunley.

Though the Hunley *was not the first navigable submarine, it was the first to sink an enemy warship in battle, and like its Union marvel counterpart, it, too, did not survive the war.*

Its official records do speak for themselves.

Official Documents
Relating to the Sinking of the
USS *Housatonic* by the CSS *Hunley*

Order of Rear Admiral Dahlgren, U.S. Navy, commanding South Atlantic Blockading Squadron, ordering defensive measures against Confederate torpedo boats.

FLAG-STEAMER *PHILADELPHIA,*
Off Morris Island, South Carolina, January 7, 1864.

I have reliable information that the rebels have two torpedo boats ready for service, which may be expected on the first night when the water is suitable for their movement. One of these is the *David,* which attacked the *Ironsides* in October; the other is similar to it.

There is also one of another kind [H. L. *Hunley*], which is nearly submerged and can be entirely so. It is intended to go under the bottoms of vessels and there operate.

This is believed by my informant to be sure of well working, though from bad management it has hitherto met with accidents, and was lying off Mount Pleasant two nights since.

There being every reason to expect a visit from some or all of these torpedoes, the greatest vigilance will be needed to guard against them. The ironclads must have their fenders rigged out and their own boats in motion about them. A netting must also be dropped overboard from the ends of the fenders, kept down with shot, and extending along the whole length of the sides; howitzers loaded with canister on the decks and a calcium [light] for each monitor. The tugs and picket boats must be incessantly upon the lookout, when the water is not rough, whether the weather be clear or rainy.

I observe the ironclads are not anchored so as to be entirely clear of each other's fire if opened suddenly in the dark. This must be corrected, and Captain Rowan will assign the monitors suitable positions for this purpose, particularly with reference to his own vessel.

It is also advisable not to anchor in the deepest part of the channel, for by not leaving much space between the bottom of the vessel and the bottom of the channel it will be impossible for the diving torpedo to operate except on the sides, and there will be less difficulty in raising a vessel if sunk.

JOHN A. DAHLGREN,
Rear-Admiral, Comdg. South Atlantic Blockading Squadron.

INFORMATION ON THE *HUNLEY* OBTAINED
BY THE U.S. NAVY FROM THE INTERROGATION
OF CONFEDERATE DESERTERS.

JANUARY 7, 1864.

The *American Diver,* [H. L. *Hunley*] was built at Mobile and was brought on two platform cars from Mobile to Charleston; saw her in all stages of construction at Mobile. Sometimes worked near her in the same shop. Thinks she is about 35 feet long; height about same as *David* (5½ feet); has propellers at the end; she is not driven by steam, but her propeller is turned by hand. Has two manholes on the upper side, about 12 to 14 feet apart. The entrance into her is through these manholes, the covers being turned back. They are all used to look out of. (Will give a sketch and description of her.) She has had bad accidents hitherto, but was owing to those in her not understanding her. Thinks that she can be worked perfectly safe by persons who understand her. Can be driven 5 knots an hour without exertion to the men working her. Manholes are about 16 inches high and are just above water when trimmed. Believe she was brought here about 1st September; has seen her working in the water afloat; passed her in the gigshe being [sic] the last time before his arrival. Has drowned three crews, one at Mobile and two here, 17 men in all. When she went down the last time, was on the bottom two weeks before she was raised. Saw her when she was raised the last time. They then hoisted her out of the water, refitted her, and got another crew. Saw her after that submerged. Saw her go under the *Indian Chief*, and then saw her go back under again. She made about one-half mile in the dives. Saw her dive under the *Charleston;* went under about 250 feet from her, and came up about 300 feet beyond her. Was about twenty minutes under the water when she went under the *Indian Chief.* Her keel is of cast iron, in sections, which can be cast loose when she wishes to rise to the surface of the water. Believes she is at Mount Pleasant. One of her crew, who belongs to this vessel, came back for his clothes, and said she was going down there as a station, where they would watch her time for operations.

U.S. NAVY INTERROGATION OF GEORGE L. SHIPP, CONFEDERATE DESERTER, REGARDING THE HUNLEY.

JANUARY 8, 1864

Believes that the *American Diver* [H. L. *Hunley*] is at Mount Pleasant; saw her when they were getting the drowned men out of her. She was pulled upon the wharf at the time. He was about 30 yards from her. There were seven men drowned in her. Was looking at her when she went down 60 yards from the receiving ship. She went down several times but came up again. She would stay under water ten minutes each time, and would come up 75 to 80 yards from where she went down. At last she went down and would not come up again. She remained down nine days before she was raised. This was about two months ago. She was then taken to the wharf and hauled up. They launched her again in about a week, but nothing was done with her until lately, when they fitted her up again and sent her down to Mount Pleasant, where she now is. Does not know that she has dived since. It was promised to the men that went in her that she would not dive again. When she does not dive, she only shows two heads above the water about the size of a man's head. He thinks she is about 20 feet long and the manholes are about 8 feet apart. She is made of iron.

REPORT OF REAR-ADMIRAL DAHLGREN, U.S. NAVY, REGARDING THE CONFEDERATE *DAVIDS* AND THE *DIVER* (H.L. *HUNLEY*).

FLAG—STEAMER *PHILADELPHIA,*
Off Morris Island, January 13, 1864.

SIR:

I have the honor to acknowledge having received your letter of the 5th instant, enclosing one from Mr. Haynes.

The information therein contained is, I doubt not, substantially correct in general.

One week ago, however, two deserters made known to me the whole project more in detail, confirming much that I had previously suspected.

It seems there are ten *Davids* building in Charleston, similar to that which torpedoed the *Ironsides.* Of these, one is completed and ready for service; the others are in different stages from the mere keel to a more advanced stage.

The *Diver,*[H. L. *Hunley*] as she is now called, is also ready, and with the original *David* is now at Mount Pleasant, [S.C.], on the lookout for a chance.

The action of the *Davids* has been, of course, pretty well exemplified on the *Ironsides;* that of the *Diver* is different, as it is intended to submerge completely, get under the bottom, attach the torpedo, haul off and pull trigger. So far the trials have been unlucky, having drowned three crews of 17 men in all. Still she does dive, as one of the deserters saw her pass twice under the bottom of the vessel he was in and once under the *Charleston.* The *Diver* can also be used as a *David,* so that there are really three of these machines ready to operate.

On receiving this intelligence I caused additional means of prevention to be used, as will be seen by copies of enclosed orders, and the Department may be assured that if any of our monitors are injured it will not be for lack of the utmost vigilance.

It is only in smooth water, and when the tide is slack, that any danger is imminent. As my flag-ship is disabled in the rudder, and has therefore to remain in the inlet, I leave her at night, go aboard of some steamer in the roads, and pass the night near the ironclads, giving my own personal attention to their condition. Last night I went up to the advanced monitor about nine o'clock. It was an ugly, rainy night, but I found all on the alert. It is indeed dangerous to approach an ironclad, as they fire on the instant. Besides their outriggers and submerged nettings, the water in advanced and around is patrolled by several steam tugs and a number of cutters, while the scout boats are thrown out far ahead.

If those who so ignorantly or basely endeavor to persuade the public that the monitors here are idle could witness one night of such vigils, they would feel disgraced at having so wantonly traduced the officers and men, who give themselves to such incessant and hard service; a battle would be far preferable.

There is, no doubt, much to be apprehended from these torpedoes, and I have already suggested to the Department an extensive use of similar means. I again respectfully urge on your consideration the most prompt resort thereto; nothing better could be devised for the security of our own vessels or for an examination of the enemy's position.

The length of these torpedo boats might be about 40 feet, and 5 to 6 feet in diameter, with a high-pressure engine that will drive them 5 knots. It is not necessary to expend much finish on them.

With the ample mechanical means of the North it seems that in one month five or six could be gotten into service.

The deserters say that the rebels believe that their batteries will do us much damage if we attack, but rely chiefly on the torpedoes for defense, and apply them in a variety of ways, at the bows of their ironclads, upon their *Davids*, upon rafts, which carry six of the 60-pounders in a line, and even their small boats are equipped to receive a torpedo.

I regret to find that the strike among the mechanics (referred to by the Department December 3) has delayed the completion of the monitors *Onondaga, Tecumseh,* and *Canonicus* even beyond the date (January 1) anticipated by the Department (December 3).

They will be very welcome when they do come.

The *Nantucket* and *Montauk* are the only monitors here in the hands of the mechanics. The latter requires some attention to her boilers, which are rather tender, and a new gun; the *Nantucket* requires the additions, repairs, etc.

I shall be ready, however, when the *Onondaga, Canonicus, Tecumseh,* and *Sangamon* arrive.

Yesterday I had an interview with the agent for raising the *Weehauken.* He informs me that he is proceeding as rapidly as possible with the work, and proposes to construct a wooden coffer, so as to pump the water from above the vessel as well as out of her.

The following statement by one of the deserters is of interest: He is a mechanic from Michigan, and some for years since crossed into Kentucky, pursuing his vocation. Moving about, he at last found himself in Alabama, driving an engine on the railroad from Montgomery to Mobile. Forced by the conscription to bear arms, he chose the navy as affording better chance to leave, and was sent to Charleston, where he was put into a boat. He, with two others, watched their chance for two months. It is evident that when the rebels are compelled to use such men as engineers and mechanics to pull a bow oar, they are consuming their own vitals.

I have the honor to be, very respectfully, your obedient servant,

JNO. A. DAHLGREN,
Rear-Admiral,
Comdg. South Atlantic Blockading Squadron.

Hon. GIDEON WELLES,
Secretary of the Navy, Washington, D.C.

REPORT OF CAPTAIN GREEN, U.S. NAVY, COMMANDING USS *CANANDAIGUA*, ON THE SINKING OF THE *HOUSATONIC*.

U.S.S. *CANANDAIGUA*,
Off Charleston, S.C., February 18, 1864.

SIR:

I have respectfully to report that a boat belonging to the *Housatonic* reached this ship last night at about 9:20, giving me information that that vessel had been sunk at 8:45 P.M., by a rebel torpedo craft.

I immediately slipped our cable and started for her anchorage, and on arriving near it, at 9:35, discovered her sunk with her hammock nettings under water; dispatched all boats and rescued from the wreck 21 officers and 129 men.

There are missing, and supposed to be drowned, the following-named officers and men:

Ensign Edward C. Hazeltine, Captain's Clerk Charles O. Muzzey, Quartermaster John Williams, Second-Class Fireman John Walsh, Landsman Theodore Parker.

Captain Pickering is very much, but not dangerously, bruised, and one man is slightly bruised.

I have transferred to the *Wabash* 8 of her officers and 49 men, on the account of the limited accommodations on board of this vessel.

Very respectfully, your obedient servant,

J. F. GREEN,
Captain.

Commodore S. C. ROWAN
Commanding Officer off Charleston, S.C.

REPORT OF LIEUTENANT HIGGINSON, U.S. NAVY, EXECUTIVE
OFFICER OF THE USS *HOUSATONIC.*

U.S.S. *CANANDAIGUA,*
Off Charleston, S.C., February 18, 1864.

SIR: I have the honor to make the following report of the sinking of the U.S.S. *Housatonic,* by a rebel torpedo off Charleston, S.C., on the evening of the 17th instant.

About 8:45 P.M. the officer of the deck, Acting Master J. K. Crosby, discovered something in the water about 100 yards from and moving toward the ship. It had the appearance of a plank moving in the water. It came directly toward the ship, the time from when it was first seen till it was close alongside being about two minutes.

During this time the chain was slipped, engine backed, and all hands called to quarters.

The torpedo struck the ship forward of the mizzenmast, on the starboard side, in a line with the magazine. Having the after pivot gun pivoted to port we were unable to bring a gun to bear upon her.

About one minute after she was close alongside the explosion took place, the ship sinking stern first and heeling to port as she sank.

Most of the crew saved themselves by going into the rigging, while a boat was dispatched to the *Canandaigua.* This vessel came gallantly to our assistance and succeeded in rescuing all but the following-named officers and men, viz, Ensign E. C. Hazeltine, Captain's Clerk C. O. Muzzey, Quartermaster John Williams, Landsman Theodore Parker, Second-Class Fireman John Walsh.

The above officers and men are missing and are supposed to have been drowned.

Captain Pickering was seriously bruised by the explosion and is at present unable to make a report of the disaster.

Very respectfully, your obedient servant,

F.J. HIGGINSON,
Lieutenant.

Rear-Admiral JOHN A. DAHLGREN,
Commanding South Atlantic Blockading Squadron.

FLAG-STEAMER *PHILADeLPHIA,*
Port Royal Harbor, SC. February 19, 1864.

SIR: I much regret to inform the Department that the U. S. S. *Housatonic,* on the blockade off Charleston, S. C., was torpedoed by a rebel "David" and sunk on the night of the 17th February about nine o'clock.

From the time the *David* was seen until the vessel was on the bottom a very brief period must have elapsed; so far as the executive officer (Lieutenant Higginson) can judge, and he is the only officer of the *Housatonic* whom I have seen, it did not exceed five or seven minutes.

The officer of the deck perceived a moving object on the water quite near and ordered the chain to be slipped; the captain and executive officer went on deck, saw the object, and each fired at it with a small arm. In an instant the ship was struck on the starboard side, between the main and mizzen masts; those on deck near were stunned, the vessel begun to sink, and went down almost immediately. Happily the loss of life was small: Ensign E. C. Hazeltine, Captain's Clerk C. O. Muzzey, and three of the crew, Quartermaster John Williams, Second-Class Fireman John Walsh, and Landsman Theodore Parker.

Two boats of the *Housatonic* were lowered and received all they could hold; the *Canandaigua,* which knew nothing of the catastrophe, sent her boats immediately on hearing of it, and took off the crew, who had ascended into the rigging.

The enclosed printed orders will show the precautions which have been directed from time to time to guard the ironclads that lay inside the bar, and would naturally be the objects of attack from their importance and proximity, and I also transmit copy of a communication (January 15) to the senior officer outside on the same subject.

In addition I have been in the habit of giving personal attention to the inside blockade, sometimes visiting the picket monitors several hours after dark.

Being notified on the 5th of February by General Gillmore that he was about to throw a force into Florida, and would need naval assistance, I left promptly for the *St. John's*, in order to be sure that no aid should be wanted that was possible, leaving Commodore Rowan, an experienced officer, commanding the *Ironsides*, in charge of the blockade of Charleston.

On my return I touched here to examine into the condition of our depots, and particularly in regard to the repairs on the monitors, intending also to visit the blockade of Savannah River.

The Department will readily perceive the consequences likely to result from this event; the whole line of blockade will be infested with these cheap, convenient, and formidable defenses, and we must guard every point. The measures for prevention, may not be so obvious.

I am inclined to the belief that in addition to the various devices for keeping the torpedoes from the vessels, an effectual preventive may be found in the use of similar contrivances.

I would therefore request that a number of torpedo boats be made and sent here with dispatch; length about 40 feet, diameter amidships 5 to 6 feet, and tapering to a point at each end; small engine and propeller, an opening of about 15 feet above with a hatch coaming, to float not more than 18 inches above water, somewhat as thus sketched.

I have already submitted a requisition on the Bureau of Construction (January 16) for some craft of this kind, copy enclosed, which, with the great mechanical facilities of the North, should be very quickly supplied.

I have also ordered a quantity of floating torpedoes, which I saw tried here and thought promised to be useful. Meanwhile I hope the expected monitors may soon arrive, when an attack on the defenses of the lower harbor may be made.

I have attached more importance to the use of torpedoes than others have done, and believe them to constitute the most formidable of the difficulties in the way to Charleston. Their effect on the *Ironsides*, in October, and now on the *Housatonic*, sustains me in this idea.

The Department will perceive from the printed injunctions issued that I have been solicitous for some time in regard to these mischievous devices, though it may not be aware of the personal attention which I have also given to the security of the ironclads; I naturally feel disappointed that the rebels should have been able to achieve a single success, mingled with no little concern, lest, in spite of every precaution, they may occasionally give us trouble. But it will create no dismay nor relax any effort; on the contrary, the usual enquiry will be ordered, though the whole story is no doubt fully known.

I desire to suggest to the Department the policy of offering a large reward of prize money for the capture or destruction of a *David;* I should say not less than $20,000 or $30,000 for each. They are worth more than that to us.

I have the honor to be, very respectfully, your obedient servant,

JNO. A. DAHLGREN,

Real Admiral, Comdg. South Atlantic Blockdg. Squadron.

Hon. GIDEON WELLES,

Secretary of the Navy, Washington, D.C.

ORDER OF REAR ADMIRAL DAHLGREN, U. S. NAVY,

FLAG-STEAMER *PHILADELPHIA,*

Port Royal Harbor, S.C., February 19, 1864.

The *Housatonic* has just been torpedoed by a rebel *David,* and sunk almost instantly.

It was at night and the water smooth.

The success of this undertaking will, no doubt, lead to similar attempts along the whole line of blockade.

If vessels on blockade are at anchor they are not safe, particularly in smooth water, without outriggers and hawsers stretched around with rope netting dropped in the water.

Vessels on inside blockade had better take post outside at night and keep underway, until these preparations are completed.

All the boats must be on the patrol when the vessel is not in movement.

The commanders of vessels are required to use their utmost vigilance—nothing less will serve.

I intend to recommend to the Navy Department the assignment of a large reward as prize money to crews of boats or vessels who shall capture, or beyond doubt destroy, one of these torpedoes.

JOHN A. DAHLGREN,

Real Admiral, Comdg. South Atlantic Blockading Squadron.

REPORT OF CAPTAIN GREEN, U.S. NAVY, REGARDING AN EXAMINATION OF THE WRECK OF THE SUNKEN VESSEL.

U.S.S. *CANADAIGUA,*
Off Charleston, S.C., February 20, 1864.

SIR: I have examined the wreck of the *Housatonic* this morning and find her spar deck about 15 feet below the surface of the water. The after part of her spar deck appears to have been entirely blown off.

Her guns, etc., on the spar deck, and probably a good many articles below deck, can, in my opinion, be recovered by the employment for the purpose of the derrick boat and divers.

Very respectfully, your obedient servant,

J. F. GREEN,
Captain.

Commodore S. C. ROWAN,
Commanding Officer Present off Charleston, S. C.

ORDER OF REAR ADMIRAL DAHLGREN, U. S. NAVY, TO A BOARD OF OFFICERS COMPRISING A COURT OF ENQUIRY.

FLAG-STEAMER *PHILADELPHIA,*
Port Royal Harbor, S.C., February 22, 1864.

GENTLEMEN: You are constituted a court of enquiry to ascertain the facts of the recent disaster that befell the U. S. S. *Housatonic* through the agency of a rebel torpedo.

Which you will state, with your opinion thereon. Second Lieutenant Young, of marines, will act as judge-advocate.

Please to signify to me, as soon as possible, what officers and men may be required for evidence, so that they may not be sent away when needed.

Very respectfully, your obedient servant,

J. A. DAHLGREN,
Rear Admiral, Comdg. South Atlantic Blockading Squadron.
CAPTAIN J. F. GREEN,
U. S. S. *Canandaigua.*
CAPTAIN J. DE CAMP,
U.S.S. *Wabash.*

Lieutenant Commander WILLIAMSON,
U.S. Flag.

BALTIMORE, *March 2, 1864.*

The torpedo boat *David,* that sunk the *Housatonic,* undoubtedly sank at the time of the concussion, with all hands. How the *Housatonic* was sunk was not known at Charleston until the 27th, when the prisoners, captured in a picket boat, divulged them the facts.

C. C. FULTON.

Hon. G. V. FOX,
Navy Department.

ABSTRACT LOG OF THE U.S.S. *CANANDAIGUA*, CAPTAIN GREEN, U. S. NAVY, COMMANDING.

February 17, 1864.—Bearings of vessels at sundown: *Wabash*, S. E.; *Mary Sanford*, N. N. E.; *Housatonic*, N. N. E. ¾ E.; *Paul Jones*, N. N. E. At 9:20 P.M. discovered a boat pulling toward us. Hailed her and found her to be from the *Housatonic*. She reported the *Housatonic* sunk by a torpedo. Immediately slipped our chain and started for the scene of danger, with the *Housatonic*'s boat in tow. At the same time sent up three rockets and burned Coston signals No. 82 and soon after burned 82 again. At 9:30 P.M. picked up another boat from the *Housatonic*, with Captain Pickering on board. At 9:35 arrived at the *Housatonic* and found her sunk. Lowered all boats, sent them alongside, and rescued the officers and crew, clinging to the rigging. At 10:30 all were brought from the wreck. Brought on board of this ship, belonging to the *Housatonic*, 21 officers and 137 men. At 11:30 stood toward the *Wabash*, to the southward and westward. Made signal to the *Mary Sanford*. The tug *Daffodil*, from inside the bar, communicated with us, Lieutenant Commander Belknap on board. At 12 communicated with the *Wabash* and sent on board of her 8 officers and 49 men belonging to the *Housatonic*.

February 18.—At 12:40 A.M. Lieutenant Commander Belknap left the ship and went inside the bar in the tug *Daffodil*. Clear and moonlight till 3:30 A.M., when the moon went down. At 6 A.M. picked up one of the *Housatonic*'s launches, sent it inside the bar in tow of the tug. At 7:45 steamed by the *Housatonic* and at 8 A.M. let go our anchor near our old station in 5 fathoms water, Sumter bearing N. W. W. and Breach Inlet N. N. W.

February 20.—At 8:15 A.M. came to with the port anchor near the *Housatonic*'s wreck, in 5 fathoms. Sent boats to the *Housatonic* to wreck her.

February 22.—At 1 P.M. sent on board the tug *Jonquil* to take to the *John Adams* 40 men lately belonging to the *Housatonic*.

PROCEEDINGS OF A COURT OF ENQUIRY CONVENED ON BOARD THE U. S. S. *WABASH*, FEBRUARY 26, 1864.

U.S. STEAM FRIGATE *WABASH, March 7, 1864.*

The testimony having been closed, the court was cleared for deliberation, and after maturely considering the evidence adduced, find the following facts established:

First. That the U. S. S. *Housatonic* was blown up and sunk by a rebel torpedo craft on the night of February 17 last, about nine o'clock P.M., while lying at an anchor in 27 feet of water off Charleston, S.C., bearing E. S. E., and distant from Fort Sumter about 5½ miles. The weather at the time of the occurrence was clear, the night bright and moonlit, wind moderate from the northward and westward, sea smooth and tide half ebb, the ship's head about W. N. W.

Second. That between 8:45 and nine o'clock P.M. on said night an object in the water was discovered almost simultaneously by the officer of the deck and the lookout stationed at the starboard cathead, on the starboard bow of the ship, about 75 or 100 yards distant, having the appearance of a log. That on further and closer observation it presented a suspicious appearance, moved apparently with a speed of 3 or 4 knots in the direction of the starboard quarter of the ship, exhibiting two protuberances above and making a slight ripple in the water.

Third. That the strange object approached the ship with a rapidity precluding a gun of the battery being brought to bear upon it, and finally came in contact with the ship on her starboard quarter.

Fourth. That about one and a half minutes after the first discovery of the strange object the crew were called to quarters, the cable slipped, and the engine backed.

Fifth. That an explosion occurred about three minutes after the first discovery of the object, which blew up the after part of the ship, causing her to sink immediately after to the bottom, with her spar deck submerged.

Sixth. That several shots from small arms were fired at the object while it was alongside or near the ship before the explosion occurred.

Seventh. That the watch on deck, ship, and ship's battery were in all respects prepared for a sudden offensive or defensive movement; that lookouts were properly stationed and vigilance observed, and that officers and crew promptly assembled at their quarters.

Eighth. That order was preserved on board, and orders promptly obeyed by officers and crew up to the time of the sinking of the ship.

In view of the above facts the court have to express the opinion that no further military proceedings are necessary.

J. F. GREEN,
Captain and President.

JAS. B. YOUNG,
Second Lieutenant, U. S Marines, Judge-Advocate.

Forwarded for the information of the Navy Department by,
Very respectfully, your obedient servant,

S. C. ROWAN,
Captain, Commanding South Atlantic Blockading Squadron.

REPORT OF REAR ADMIRAL DAHLGREN, U. S. NAVY, TRANSMITTING REPORT REGARDING THE CONDITION OF THE WRECKS.

FLAG-STEAMER *PHILADELPHIA*,
Port Royal Harbor, November 28, 1864.

SIR: I transmit herewith a report of the squadron diver in relation to the wrecks of the *Housatonic* and some blockade runners which were driven ashore at different times by the vessels of the blockade.

It is to be presumed that all perishable articles are now valueless; the metallic parts will be recovered whenever the services of the divers can be spared from the vessels in service.

I have the honor to be, very respectfully, your obedient servant,

J. A. DAHLGREN,
Rear Admiral, Comdg. South Atlantic Blockading Squadron.

Hon. GIDEON WELLES,
Secretary of the Navy.

U. S. SCHOONER *G. W. BLUNT,*
PORT ROYAL HARBOR, S.C., NOVEMBER 27, 1864.

SIR: After a careful examination of the wrecks of the sunken blockade runners and *Housatonic,* I have the honor to make the following report:

I find that the wrecks of the blockade runners are so badly broken up as to be worthless. The *Housatonic* is very much worm-eaten, as I find from pieces which have been brought up. She is in an upright position; has settled in the sand about 5 feet, forming a bank of mud and sand around her bed; the mud has collected in her in small quantities. The cabin is completely demolished, as are also all the bulkheads abaft the mainmast; the coal is scattered about her lower decks in heaps, as well as muskets, small arms, and quantities of rubbish.

I tried to find the magazine, but the weather has been so unfavorable and the swell so great that it was not safe to keep a diver in the wreck. I took advantage of all the good weather that I had, and examined as much as was possible.

The propeller is in an upright position; the shaft appears to be broken. The rudderpost and rudder have been partly blown off; the upper parts of both are in their proper places, while the lower parts have been forced aft. The stern frame rests upon the rudderpost and propeller; any part of it can be easily slung with chain slings, and a powerful steamer can detach each part.

I have also caused the bottom to be dragged for an area of 500 yards around the wreck, finding nothing of the torpedo boat. On the 24th the drag ropes caught something heavy (as I reported). On sending a diver down to examine it, proved to be a quantity of rubbish. The examination being completed, I could accomplish nothing further, unless it is the intention to raise the wreck or propeller, in which case it will be necessary to have more machinery.

Very respectfully, your obedient servant,

W. L. CHURCHILL,
Acting Volunteer Lieutenant, Commanding.

Rear Admiral J. A. DAHLGREN,
Commanding South Atlantic Blockading Squadron.

NOTES FROM PAPERS OF
FIRST ASSISTANT ENGINEER TOMB, C. S. NAVY,
REGARDING THE SUBMARINE TORPEDO BOAT.

CHARLESTON, S. C., *January, 1864[5]*.

There was a submarine torpedo boat, not under the orders of the navy, and I was ordered to tow her down the harbor three or four times by Flag-Officer Tucker, who also gave me orders to report as to her efficiency as well as safety. In my report to him I stated, "The only way to use a torpedo was on the same plan as the *David*—that is, a spar torpedo—and to strike with his boat on the surface, the torpedo being lowered to 8 feet." Should she attempt to use a torpedo as Lieutenant Dixon intended, by submerging the boat and striking from below, the level of the torpedo would be above his own boat, and as she had little buoyancy and no power, the chances were the suction caused by the water passing into the sinking ship would prevent her rising to the surface, besides the possibility of his own boat being disabled. Lieutenant Dixon was a very brave and cool-headed man, and had every confidence in his boat, but had great trouble when under the water from lack of air and light. At the time she made the attempt to dive under the receiving ship in Charleston Harbor, Lieutenant Dixon, James A. Eason, and myself stood on the wharf as she passed out and saw her dive, but she did not rise again, and after a week's effort she was brought to the surface and the crew of 7 men were found in a bunch near the manhole. Lieutenant Dixon said they had failed to close the after valve.

The last night the *David* towed him down the harbor his torpedo got foul of us and came near blowing up both boats before we got it clear of the bottom, where it had drifted. I let him go after passing Fort Sumter, and on my making report of this, Flag-Officer Tucker refused to have the *David* tow him again. The power for driving this boat came from 7 or 8 men turning cranks attached to the propeller shaft, and when working at their best would make about 3 knots. She was very slow in turning, but would sink at a moment's notice and at times without it. The understanding was that from the time of her construction at Mobile up to the time when she struck *Housatonic* not less than 33 men had lost their lives in her. She was a veritable coffin to this brave officer and his men.

J. H. TOMB.

REPORT OF LIEUTENANT COLONEL DANTZLER, C. S. ARMY.

HEADQUARTERS BATTERY MARSHALL,
Sullivan's Island, February 19, 1864.

LIEUTENANT: I have the honor to report that the torpedo boat stationed at this post went out on the night of the 17th instant (Wednesday) and has not yet returned. The signals agreed upon to be given in case the boat wished a light to be exposed at this post as a guide for its return were observed and answered. An earlier report would have been made of this matter, but the officer of the day for yesterday was under the impression that the boat had returned, and so informed me. As soon as I became apprised of the fact I sent a telegram to Captain Nance, assistant adjutant-general, notifying him of it.

Very respectfully,

O. M. DANTZLER,
Lieutenant Colonel.

Lieutenant JOHN A. WILSON,
Acting Assistant Adjutant-General.

FEBRUARY 20, *1864.*

As soon as its fate shall have been ascertained, pay a proper tribute to the gallantry and patriotism of its crew and officers.

G. T. BEAUREGARD,
General, Commanding.

CHARLESTON, S.C., *February 21, 1864.*

GENERAL: A gunboat sunken off Battery Marshall. Supposed to have been done by Mobile torpedo boat, under Lieutenant George E. Dixon, Company E, Twenty-first Alabama Volunteers, which went out for that purpose, and which I regret to say has not been heard of since.

G. T. BEAUREGARD.

CHARLESTON, S.C., *February 27, 1864.*

Prisoners report that it was the U. S. ship of war *Housatonic,* 12 guns, which was sunk on night 17th instant by the submarine torpedo boat, Lieutenant Dixon, of Alabama, commanding. There is little hope of safety of that brave man and his associates, however, as they were not captured.

G. T. BEAUREGARD,

General, Commanding.

General S. COOPER,

Adjutant and Inspector-General, U. S. Army, Richmond, Va.

EXTRACT FROM CHARLESTON DAILY COURIER, FEBRUARY 29, 1864.

On Friday night about half past nine o'clock one of our naval picket boats, under command of Boatswain J. M. Smith, captured a Yankee picket boat off Fort Sumter containing 1 commissioned officer and 5 men. A large barge, which was in company with the captured boat, managed to escape. The officer taken prisoner is Midshipman William H. Kitching, acting master's mate of the United States blockading steamer *Nipsic.* The rest of the prisoners are landsmen.

By the prisoners we learn that the blockader sunk by our torpedo boat on the night of the 17th instant was the United States steam sloop of war *Housatonic,* carrying 12 guns and a crew of 300 men. They state that the torpedo boat, cigar shape, was first seen approaching by the watch on board the *Housatonic.* The alarm was given, and immediately all hands beat to quarters. A rapid musketry fire was opened upon the boat, but without effect. Being unable to depress their guns, the order was given to slip the cable. In doing this, the *Housatonic* backed some distance and came in collision with the cigar boat. The torpedo exploded almost immediately, carrying away the whole stern of the vessel. The steamer sunk in three minutes' time, the officers and crew barely escaping to the rigging. Everything else on board—guns, stores, ammunition, etc., together with the small boats—went down with her. The explosion made no noise and the affair was not known among the fleet until daybreak, when the crew was discovered and released from their uneasy positions. They had remained there all night. Two officers and three men are reported missing and supposed to be drowned. The loss of the

Housatonic caused great consternation in the fleet. All the wooden vessels are ordered to keep up steam and go out to sea every night, not being allowed to anchor inside. The picket boats have been doubled and the force in each boat, increased.

This glorious success of our little torpedo boat, under the command of Lieutenant Dixon, of Mobile, has raised the hopes of our people, and the most sanguine expectations are now entertained of our being able to raise the siege in a way little dreamed of by the enemy. The capture of the picket boat reflects great credit on the gallant boatswain in charge of our barge, as well as on the unceasing vigilance and energy of Lieutenant J. H. Rochelle, commanding the naval picket detachment on board the *Indian Chief*. He has watched the operations of these picket intruders for some time past, and planned the movements for taking some of them in out of the wet.

LETTER FROM GENERAL BEAUREGARD, C.S. ARMY, TO MR. LEARY, ANNOUNCING THE PROBABLE LOSS OF THE TORPEDO BOAT *H. L. HUNLEY* AND HER COMMANDING OFFICER.

HEADQUARTERS, *ETC., March 10, 1864.*

SIR: I am directed by the commanding general to inform you that it was the torpedo boat *H. L. Hunley* that destroyed the Federal man-of-war *Housatonic,* and that Lieutenant Dixon commanded the expedition, but I regret to say that nothing since has been heard either of Lieutenant Dixon or the torpedo boat. It is therefore feared that that gallant officer and his brave companions have perished.

Respectfully, your obedient servant,

H. W. FELDEN,
Captain and Assistant Adjutant-General.

H. J. LEARY, *Esq.,*
Marietta, Ga.

LETTER FROM CAPTAIN GRAY, C.S. ARMY, TO MAJOR GENERAL MAURY, C.S. ARMY, REGARDING THE LOSS OF THE *H. L. HUNLEY* AND HER CREW.

OFFICE SUBMARINE DEFENSES,
Charleston, S.C., April 29, 1864.

GENERAL: In answer to a communication of yours, received through headquarters, relative to Lieutenant Dixon and crew, I beg leave to state that I was not informed as to the service in which Lieutenant Dixon was engaged or under what orders he was acting. I am informed that he requested Commodore Tucker to furnish him some men, which he did. Their names are as follows, viz: Arnold Becker, C. Simkins, James A. Wicks, F. Collins, and —— Ridgeway, all of the navy, and Corporal C. F. Carlsen, of Captain Wagener's company of artillery.

The United States sloop of war was attacked and destroyed on the night of the 17th of February. Since that time no information has been received of either the boat or crew. I am of the opinion that, the torpedoes being placed at the bow of the boat, she went into the hole made in the *Housatonic* by explosion of torpedoes and did not have sufficient power to back out, consequently sunk with her.

I have the honor to be, general, very respectfully, your obedient servant,

M. M. GRAY,
Captain in Charge of Torpedoes.

Major General DABNEY H. MAURY,
Mobile, Ala.

ORDER OF REAR ADMIRAL DAHLGREN, U.S. NAVY, TO CAPTAIN ROWAN, U.S. NAVY, REGARDING MEASURES OF PRECAUTION AGAINST INJURIES FROM TORPEDOES IN CHARLESTON HARBOR.

FLAG-STEAMER *PHILADELPHIA*,
Port Royal Harbor, S.C., February 19, 1864.

SIR: The *Paul Jones* is just in, with the unpleasant news of the disaster to the *Housatonic*.

I shall leave here for Charleston as soon as one of the steamers can be made ready. The *Nipsic* and *Paul Jones* both need coal and some slight but necessary repairs.

The success of this attempt will no doubt cause a resort to the torpedoes along the whole line of blockade, and it behooves the commanding officer to resort to every precaution to avert a series of disasters.

As the torpedo boat passed by the ironclads within the bar, I think the inference is fair that the means used to protect them have been tried by the *Davids*, perhaps, unknown to us, and found sufficient.

All vessels at anchor, inside or outside, are therefore to use outriggers and hawsers with netting, or, if outside, are to keep underway.

You will take any further measures that you may deem necessary to keep off these torpedoes.

You will at once clear the inner harbor of all vessels not required for the blockading vessels. Some can leave for this place or Stono, and those which remain inside must anchor in the least water, with outriggers, etc.

The *Wabash* may leave for this port, as she is not capable of much movement, and is too valuable a mark for the torpedoes.

Respectfully, your obedient servant,

J. A. DAHLGREN,

Rear Admiral, Comdg. South Atlantic Blockading Squadron.

Captain S. C. ROWAN,

Comdg. U.S.S. *Ironsides,* Senior Officer off Charleston.

ORDER OF REAR ADMIRAL DAHLGREN, U.S. NAVY, TO ACTING MASTER CHILDS, U.S. NAVY, COMMANDING U.S.S. ACACIA, TO PROCEED TO DUTY ON THE CHARLESTON BLOCKADE.

FLAG-STEAMER *PHILADELPHIA,*
Port Royal Harbor, S.C., February 20, 1864.

SIR: Upon being relieved by the U.S.S. *Water Witch,* you will proceed with the *Acacia* under your command to Port Royal, and there take in coal and supplies, using all possible dispatch.

You will then proceed to Charleston, S.C., and report to the commanding officer there for blockade duty.

Respectfully, your obedient servant,

J. A. DAHLGREN,
Rear Admiral, Comdg. South Atlantic Blockading Squadron.

Acting Master J. D. CHILDS,
Commanding U.S.S. Acacia.

ORDER OF COMMANDER REYNOLDS, U.S. NAVY, TO ACTING ENSIGN FROST, U.S. NAVY, TO ASSUME TEMPORARY COMMAND OF THE U.S.S. OLEANDER.

NAVAL DEPOT,
PORT ROYAL, S.C., February 22, 1864.

SIR: Upon the departure of Acting Master John S. Dennis, you will assume temporarily the command of the *Oleander* until the receipt of further orders.

Respectfully,

WILLIAM REYNOLDS,
Commander.

Acting Ensign JOS. FROST,
Oleander.

ORDER OF COMMANDER REYNOLDS, U.S. NAVY, TO ACTING
MASTER POTTER, U.S. NAVY, COMMANDING U.S. SCHOONER
RACHEL SEAMAN, TO PROCEED TO NEW YORK.

U.S. SHIP *VERMONT*,
PORT ROYAL HARBOR, S.C., February 23, 1864.

SIR: Having discharged your freight and taken in ballast and completed
the transfer of such of your crew as was authorized by Rear Admiral
Dahlgren, receiving in their place men whose times have expired, you
will proceed to sea and make the best of your way to New York, and
report on arrival to Rear Admiral H. Paulding, commandant Brooklyn
Navy Yard.

Respectfully, your obedient servant,

WILLIAM REYNOLDS,
Commander, Commanding Naval Depot, Port Royal, S.C.

Acting Master CHARLES POTTER,
Commanding U.S. Schooner *Rachel Seaman*.

REPORT OF REAR ADMIRAL DAHLGREN, U.S. NAVY,
REGARDING THE ARRIVAL OF THE U.S.S. WINONA IN A
DISABLED CONDITION.

FLAG-STEAMER *PHILADELPHIA*,
Charleston Roads, February 23, 1864.

SIR: The *Winona* arrived this morning from Hampton Roads, and I was
congratulating myself on the use of another steamer, when the commander handed me a report from his engineer, stating various defects of
bearings, crossheads, etc., and asking for twenty-one days to repair at
Port Royal; some of this is attributed to a gale off Hatteras.

I have the honor to be, very respectfully, your obedient servant,

J. A. DAHLGREN,
REAR ADMIRAL, COMDG. SOUTH ATLANTIC BLOCKDG. SQUADRON.

Hon. GIDEON WELLES,
Secretary of the Navy, Washington, D.C.

REPORT OF ACTING MASTER COLLINS, U.S. NAVY, REGARDING
EXPEDITION FOR THE DESTRUCTION OF MACHINERY FROM
STRANDED BLOCKADE RUNNER.

U.S. SCHOONER *GEORGE MANGHAM,*
Off Murrell's Inlet, February 25, 1864.

SIR: I have the honor to report to you that I received information from
Captain Parker that the rebels were taking the machinery out of the
blockade-running steamer on the beach near my station to put into a
steamer that they are building at Georgetown, S.C. He gave me orders to
destroy all that I could of it. I proceeded toward the steamer. On
approaching I saw a number of men at work on her. I opened fire on
them, which made them run for the woods for shelter. I fired three shells
at them and called away the first cutter, manned with 14 men, well armed.
It being high water at the time, I found it smooth inside the steamer's
stern and it gave us a safe landing. I went on board the steamer and found
that they had some of the machinery out of her, and a number of pieces
were lying on the steamer ready to go on shore. They left all their tools on
the beach, consisting of mauls, axes, augers, saws, crowbars, wrenches,
and a cutter fall and blocks for hoisting it out with. I commenced with my
men to destroy all the machinery I could find, and a large cargo winch,
which they had to hoist with. The steamer was full of water at the time,
and I could not get at what was left in her, and at low water it was too
rough to land. I took all the tools with me on board and made sail for my
station. I had not sailed far when the rebels came back to the steamer,
took a hasty survey, and then left in haste. I think they will have to wait
some time for machinery for their steamer, as I think it will puzzle them to
put it together again. I shall give them another call as soon as it is smooth
enough to land on the beach. I think the tools belonged to the steamer,
and it will be some time before they can get more to work with.

I am, sir, very respectfully, your obedient servant,

JOHN COLLINS, JR.,
Acting Master, Commanding.

Rear Admiral JOHN A. DAHLGREN,
Comdg. South Atlantic Blockdg. Squadron, of Charleston.

INSTRUCTIONS OF REAR ADMIRAL DAHLGREN, U.S. NAVY, TO CAPTAIN ROWAN, U.S. NAVY, IN PREPARATION FOR DEPARTURE OF THE FORMER FOR PORT ROYAL, S.C.

FLAG-STEAMER *PHILADELPHIA,*
Off Morris Island, February 25, 1864.

SIR: I am about to leave for Port Royal. You will therefore be in command of the naval forces at this anchorage, inside and outside the bar.

The outer blockade is, of course, under the direction of Captain Green, but he also will be under your direction as senior officer.

As you have been present and have personal cognizance of the duties to be performed within the bar, I need hardly go into more detail than is indicated by my orders of December 3, January 7 and 12.

The disaster to the *Housatonic* will, no doubt, be sufficient to avert anything of the kind from other vessels of the outer blockade; after dark it will no doubt be best to keep underway when the sea is smooth, and not run too close in.

Inside, the security of the monitors is the first consideration; the vigilance practiced and the measures indicated by previous orders will, I hope, render them safe. Patrols of tugs and boats, scout beats, etc.

I refer you to my letter of the 5th for whatever may be omitted here.

Outside, Captain Green must watch the *Rattlesnake* closely.

You will keep me advised of the state of affairs.

You will make whatever disposition your judgment indicates to be best for the forces here.

Respectfully, your obedient servant,

J. A. DAHLGREN,
Rear Admiral, Comdg. South Atlantic Blockading Squadron.
Captain S. C. ROWAN,
Commanding U.S.S. *New Ironsides.*

Published Source Materials

Dewey, George. *The Autobiography of George Dewey, Admiral of the Navy.*
Farragut, Loyall. *The Life of David Glasgow Farragut.*
Morgan, James Morris. *Recollections of a Rebel Reefer.*
Porter, David Dixon. *Incidents and Anecdotes of the Civil War.*
Schley, Walter Scott. *Forty-five Years Under the Flag.*
Sinclair, Arthur. *Two Years on the* Alabama.